THE REFORM MOVEMENT
IN JUDAISM

THE
REFORM MOVEMENT
IN JUDAISM

BY

DAVID PHILIPSON, D.D.

AUTHOR OF "THE JEW IN ENGLISH FICTION,"
"OLD EUROPEAN JEWRIES," ETC., ETC.

A reissue of the
NEW AND REVISED EDITION
with an Introduction
by
SOLOMON B. FREEHOF

KTAV PUBLISHING HOUSE, INC.

Manufactured in the United States of America
Library of Congress Catalog Card No. 67-11906

PREFACE TO THE NEW EDITION

DURING the twenty-three years which have elapsed since this book was first published, the liberal movement in Judaism whose story it unfolds has marched steadily on. The later developments especially in the United States, England, Germany and France are detailed in the closing chapter of this new edition.

Perhaps the most striking feature in the changing panorama of Jewish religious endeavor, notably in the United States, is the coming of what is now called conservative Judaism upon the scene. Although its spokesmen are unsympathetic with and even opposed to Reform Judaism, as is evidenced by their occasional public utterances, still, paradoxical as it may sound, this neo-conservatism is intimately related to the reform or liberal movement. The same causes that led to the arising of the reform movement, *cæteris paribus,* have also brought forth this latest departure from the orthodox Judaism of rabbinical tradition. It is largely a question of more or less.

Noteworthy in the story as given in this volume is the newest off-shoot of the liberal spirit, namely the recently formed World Union for Progressive Judaism. The liberal forces are combining in a world movement which, though still of small beginnings, has undreamed-of possibilities.

It has been thought advisable to print the great mass of footnotes at the end of the volume instead of at the bottom of the pages as was the case in the first edition.

The issuing of this new edition has been mainly in response to the request of men and women in this country and abroad who urged that this only English history of the reform movement in Judaism should be made available anew to a later generation.

May this second edition meet with as generous a reception as did the original which has been out of print for some years.

D. P.

Cincinnati, Ohio
October, 1930

PREFACE TO THE FIRST EDITION

In October, 1897, I published in the *Jewish Quarterly Review* an article entitled "The Progress of the Jewish Reform Movement in the United States." This article was the beginning of a series of further studies on the reform movement in Judaism. These studies, which form the chapters of this book, aim to present a connected story of the progressive movement in Judaism, the most striking Jewish religious phenomenon of modern times.

It has been possible in this survey to take account only of the corporate activities which translated the theories of the reformers into practice. Many statements of individual scholars and writers, however interesting as contributions to the store of liberal Jewish thought, could not be included, since this is not a history of the literary output, but of the practical achievements of reform. This point can be well illustrated by adverting to the case of Russia. There a number of prominent writers have pleaded strongly for reforms in religious practice and belief, but no public official steps have been taken toward carrying out these reforms. The reform movement has found no lodgment in the corporate and congregational Jewish life of Russia, hence no chapter is devoted to Russia in this work, however illuminating might be the statements that can be culled from the writings of Russian Jewish authors.

It has been my aim to present as objectively as possible the purposes and accomplishments of the reform movement. We are still too near the beginning of the movement to take account of ultimate effects and results. I have therefore refrained from all theorizing upon this aspect of the subject, but have permitted the facts to speak for themselves.

My thanks are due Mr. Claude G. Montefiore, editor of the *Jewish Quarterly Review,* for the permission to include within this volume a number of studies which have appeared in the pages of that magazine.

DAVID PHILIPSON.

Cincinnati, Ohio, 1907.

CONTENTS

Introduction

When civilization is in a period of stability the generations
follow each other in friendly succession but when the world
changes rapidly, each young generation feels that the adult
generation represents a dying past, while it itself represents
the future. Our world in the last two centuries has undergone drastic changes in technology, in the relationship between the classes, in the organization of governments and in
the mood and mind of men. Thus there has hardly been a
generation in the last two hundred years which did not feel
itself sharply at variance with the generation which was its
parent. Sometimes this tension is merely the frustration but
when the changes are rapid the tension between the generations becomes actual hostility. Nowadays we might paraphrase Ecclesiastes' statement and say, "A new generation
cometh. It opposes the generation that goeth, for the world
no longer remains the same."

This increase of tension between the generations in a
rapidly changing world is, of course, a visible phenomenon
to varying degrees in every family, in all our colleges, and
also in historic religious institutions. Yet these new opinions
are not neccessarily better or more correct than the old which
they hope to supplant. Nevertheless they are indispensable
because the world *is* different and the new ideas are meant to
be more expressive of the new moods and more practical in
meeting new needs. But because the new ideas of the new generation are tied up with a struggle for personal independence, they have always a strong infusion of emotion and are
therefore being part of a rebellion, consequently unlikely to
do justice to the worth of the older opinions which they seek
to supplant. To us in our youth the past which we oppose is

always "the dead past" or the past which ought to be dead. We can hardly be expected to appreciate the fact that the older generation was at one time a young generation and its ideas were also a sort of rebellion and a new truth. To attain a balanced appreciation of history it is necessary for the generation that "cometh" to learn to understand sympathetically the ideas advocated by the generation that "goeth," for each set of ideas may be the true idealistic faith of its time.

This reissue of Dr. David Philipson's *Reform Movement in Judaism* gives us an opportunity to understand the earlier and the creative mood of a new world of idealism which the generation to which Dr. Philipson belonged represented and which, indeed, may seem partly outdated in the era of the writer of the present preface. When I came to the Hebrew Union College fifty-five years ago, Dr. Philipson had already ceased to be a regular member of the faculty of the College. He was still active and influential on its Board of Governors. He was the Rabbi of the Rockdale Avenue Temple which, being situated in the Cincinnati suburb in which all the students lived, was the Temple whose services we students regularly attended. We heard him preach every Sabbath and already then, half a century or more ago, we sensed that although he must still have been in the prime of life, he lived in a world which to us seemed somewhat passe.

The autobiography which David Philipson wrote near the end of his career *(My Life as an American Jew)* reveals at once the wide difference in mood and philosophy between our two generations. To us the Hebrew Union College (with its renowned faculty including Dr. Gotthard Deutsch the historian, David Neumark the philosopher, Moses Buttenweiser the Bible critic, and presided over by Kaufmann Kohler, a veritable apostle of Reform Judaism and a pupil of one of its founding fathers, Abraham Geiger) seemed an historic and strong institution which, as far as we were concerned, was and would remain permanent in Jewish life. But David Philipson lived during its uncertain and unpredictable beginnings. He was a member of its first class which entered in the year 1875. He knew and associated with the first Reformers in America. His whole life was tied up with its growth, and his career developed as the Reform movement developed. He and the movement went on step by step, from strength to strength.

Furthermore, when our generation came to the Hebrew Union College there were many types of academic careers open to American Jewish young men. If we had not chosen to come to the Hebrew Union College and pursue a rabbinical career, we could have gone to any one of a number of other schools, Jewish or secular, and chosen to enter upon any one of a number of professions. But when David Philipson was a boy in Columbus, Ohio, it was very rare for any one to receive more than a grammar school education. All boys went into some sort of business immediately after grade school. Very few had a high school education. David Philipson entering the Hebrew Union College was thus enabled to go to high school and then to university. His whole personal culture and career were made possible by the nascent institution in whose very first class he enrolled as a student. The deep sense of gratitude and devotion which he felt for the institution of Reform Judaism in which he became both pioneer and beneficiary could not possibly be equalled by our generation which had a choice of many other opportunities for growth and advancement. We grew to love our College and to appreciate the opportunities it gave us but we could never attain the grateful devotion which he felt all through his life.

This devotion of his went beyond the sense of personal obligation. It translated itself into a complete absorption into the ideas of the early founders of Reform. These ideas which to us seemed to need considerable modification because of changing times became for him fixed and sacred principles from which he never deviated. One may appreciate, even when disagreeing with some of those ideas, what gratitude and adoration created David Philipson's unswerving loyalty to the ideas and moods out of which Reform Judaism originally sprang.

David Philipson was born in Wabash, Indiana, in 1862. Isaac M. Wise, who was Rabbi in Cincinnati, traveled all over the Middle West helping to found congregations, to dedicate new synagogue buildings, and had become acquainted with the scattered Jewish families throughout the Middle West. He knew David Philipson's father who had been a Hebrew teacher in Sandusky, Ohio, and then in search of a livelihood moved to Wabash, Indiana, and then to Columbus, Ohio, where he was a mail carrier. Dr. Wise knew that Philipson had a young son David who was about to be Bar Mitzvah. He asked whether David could not be sent to Cincinnati to become a student in the new rabbinical college which was to be opened the following autumn. This meant a new world of culture for young David. It meant the high school and college education which, if it had not been for this invitation from Isaac M. Wise, he certainly never would have had. He was Bar Mitzvah in Columbus, then came to Cincinnati, entered Hughes High School that autumn of 1875 and was in the first class of the Hebrew Union College which met in the basement of one of the synagogues. He was therefore in the first graduating class in 1883. His first congregation was Har Sinai in Baltimore which had been led in the past by David Einhorn, the German Reformer who represented undeviating doctrinal Reform as opposed to Isaac M. Wise's practical, compromising and accommodating Reform. After a few years in Baltimore he returned to Cincinnati to head the Rockdale Avenue Temple and to teach at the Hebrew Union College. Then when Dr. Wise founded the Central Conference of American Rabbis, David Philipson assisted him in this work. During all of his long career he was a man of influence and authority in American Reform Judaism. Always a conscientious student, he wrote a number of books, *The Jew in English Fiction, Old European Ghettos,* and a biography of his famous predecessor in the Rockdale Temple, Max Lilienthal. He also edited the selected writings of Isaac M. Wise and contributed papers and essays to the publications of the American Jewish Historical Society. *The Reform Movement in Judaism* here being reissued was his magnum opus.

This book had its origin in a number of essays on the history of Reform Judaism which he contributed to the *Jewish Quarterly Review,* the magazine founded in England by Claude Montefiore and Israel Abrahams which lasted through twenty volumes in England and then was moved to the United States, published by the Dropsie College and is now in its fifty-sixth volume. While the book is as complete a history of the beginnings of the Reform movement as one would have the right to expect, nevertheless the author has purposely omitted certain interesting material that another author with another point of view might well have included. David Philipson was completely an "organization man." He participated in the beginning of many of the characteristic institutions of Reform Judaism and was a leader in them through an active lifetime. He was therefore interested in personalities and opinions, primarily insofar as they embodied themselves into the organized institutions of Reform. But there were many other manifestations of the urge to Reform Judaism which never achieved any tangible organizational results. For example, there was the strong advocacy of reforms in Jewish observance and in Jewish education voiced in the writings of the East European Maskilim. But all these aspirations for the reform of Jewish religious life were thwarted by later historical events and other movements supplanting the modernizing Haskala arose in eastern Jewry, nationalist, socialist, etc., which wiped out the older ideas of East European Reform and left it only as a curiosity of past Jewish literary history.

In Western Europe, however, in Germany, first of all, then in England and in the United States, the aspiration for Reform succeeded in changing the nature of numerous congregations and had founded new congregations and organizations of congregations and rabbinical seminaries. The ideas of Reform in Western Europe and in America created enduring institutions and so they outlived the early period when they were merely aspirations and ideas. Since, therefore, David Philipson was a builder and a developer of such institutions in America, he was not especially interested in those ideas which "died a-borning." He was concerned only with those which had a traceable and objective influence on Jewish history. He therefore pays little attention to the thwarted ideas of Reform in Eastern Europe but, with remarkable competence, tells the story of those ideas which eventuated in institutions. A study of this book will therefore present the reader with a picture of those ideas which swept through Jewry at the beginning of the modern age, but particularly those of the ideas which were advocated with such earnestness and devotion as to have changed the socio-religious configuration of Jewish life. Since the opportunity for such change was more available and successful in Western Europe and in America than in Eastern Europe, that became the setting for this work.

The reader, therefore, will be translated from the realm of ideas to the arena of action. He will notice the first attempt to initiate changes in the prayerbook in certain communities, the modernization of the style of preaching, of the music, of the very architecture of the synagogue building. He will learn of the bitter controversies which these proposed changes engendered, of the founding of new synagogues when the old one could not be modernized, of the struggle with autocratic governmental authorities who tended to consider all reform in any field as potentially revolutionary and, therefore, dangerous to the stability of the state. The book describes the first gathering of like-minded liberal rabbis, then the synods in which congregations and rabbis united in the effort to achieve an orderly and a legal Reform. The book is a classic of meticulous recording and clear visu-

alization of events and for a whole generation it stood alone
in the field.

While the book is clearly written and the subsidiary material which might impede the flow of the thought is properly
relegated to the notes, nevertheless its point of view will
present a difficulty to the modern reader. He will find it
strange that certain ideas appealed so strongly to intelligent
men when these ideas now seem to be vague and almost unreal. He will also find it hard to understand why there was
such vehement debate about small matters of changing a
word or two or omitting a paragraph or two from the prayer-
book. The whole mood of our life has changed and it will take
a definite act of intention to appreciate the generation which
was so different from ours. A number of generations have
gone by since the beginnings of Reform Judaism and the
world has changed a number of times. It is important therefore to try sympathetically to read ourselves back into the
minds of those who thought differently and felt differently
from us.

The historical epoch in which Reform was founded was
the period following the French Revolution when the death
knell was sounded for the medieval age. The great hope of
mankind then was political, not economic as it became in a
later generation. Freedom from the tyranny of autocratic
government was the dream of enlightened men. If only political freedom could be achieved, mankind could attain happiness. This indeed was the mood of the American Revolution
and of the French, and it was this atmosphere of the hope for
political liberation when Man, the subject, will become Man,
the citizen, which was breathed by the pioneers of the Reform
movement.

This hunger for political liberation had an especial meaning for the Jews of Europe. They were not only oppressed
as all the subjects of tyranny were oppressed, they also had
the additional disability which was placed upon them as
Jews. They were kept apart from the life of Europe, confined
in ghettos. Therefore in the longings for liberty, emancipation, there was the special hope that Jewry should become an
integral part of the world that was advancing toward freedom. Jews dreamed not only of liberty but of fraternity, not
only of emancipation but of comradeship with fellow citizens. Soon, they hoped, the time would come when the Jews
of Europe would not only be liberated but respected and
accepted as brothers. For this reason, in the name of the new
hope for comradeship, the Reformers were often scornful of

such Jewish observances as tended to separate the Jews from other people. They considered that many Jewish customs, their food habits and their special speech, intensified their isolation.

Whether this judgment was right or not is perhaps besides the question. When Franz Josef in Austria wanted to open all modern education to the Jews of his vast empire, many of the Hungarian rabbis bitterly opposed it. They considered that it would take away the distinctiveness of Jewish life and that when Jews would mingle in schools, etc., with others, it would destroy or weaken Jewish existence. To Reform pioneers were at the other extreme in this argument. They declared that Judaism was a universal religion, that it had something to say to all human beings. The radical Reformer Samuel Holdheim advocated the abolishment of a vast number of Jewish observances on the ground that they were merely national and belonged properly in ancient Palestine when the Jews existed as a separate state. So the desire of the Reformers to modernize the service with modern music, modern translations, was more than the desire to make the prayers meaningful to the Jews and the whole service suited to their changing taste; it was concerned also with Judaism as well as with the Jews, and its aim was that Judaism should become a living, universal force in an era that was surely moving toward liberty and comradeship.

Spurred by these high hopes Reform Judaism developed a definite program. The first was the struggle for political rights. The various tyrannical governments continuing the disabilties against the Jews inherited from the past had to be resisted and efforts made to achieve equality. While this seemed to be primarily a political struggle, it was fought on the field of culture because of the great faith in the transforming power of education. It was, after all, still before the age of psychology in which we have learned to look upon the prejudices as rooted in the personal needs and inadequacies of the prejudiced. This was still the age of rationalism in which it was believed that if people are prejudiced it is only because of their ignorance. True knowledge would conquer all error. This, in fact, was one of the great motives behind the new scientific study of Jewish history and literature, namely, to dispel the ignorance about Jews and Judaism. As one rereads the introduction of Zunz's great work on preaching in the synagogue, he will find this motive abundantly clear. Zunz began his public life as a reformer of Judaism. His pioneer work on *Preaching in the Synagogue*

(Gottesdienstliche Vortraege) was motivated by a clear purpose. He indicates in his introduction that Jewish disabilities will tend then to vanish before the growing respect which the cultured world will have attained toward the historical Jewish past.

In this liberating process of enlightenment the Reformers felt that the Jews must play their part. In Germany the inherited jargon must give way to modern German, and the old medieval garb and custom and those ceremonials which isolate have to be abandoned. Thus the first changes in the synagogue service were in the direction of modern aesthetic taste. It was all part of the general hope to bring about an overcoming of medievalism with its isolation and prejudice and thus hasten the coming of equality and justice.

This attitude of the Reformers born of the high hopes of the libertarian period was harshly misunderstood by their opponents. It was described as assimilation, a desire to "water down" Judaism, to bring it nearer to Christianity, and in the controversial statements of some of the opposing rabbis was described as a conscious step toward the conversion of the Jews to Christianity and to the destruction of Judaism. It was the reverse: These men wanted Judaism to grow stronger. They wanted it influential. If they modernized it, it was because they wanted to become more able to exert a great influence in a modern world. The "world mission of Israel" was an inspiring idea to them.

Of course, times changed and the new era of history came to mock the roseate dreams of the Reformers. The pogroms in Russia revealed a degree of bloody hatred which shocked the cultured world, which nevertheless held on to its faith in the blessings of culture by saying that such bloodthirsty hate could only occur in Russia which was still a barbaric state. But then anti-Semitism grew in Austria and in Germany, revealing that even the most thoroughly modernized of nations can be moved by ancient hates. In fact science itself with its technology became an instrument for such systematic murder which shocked even the disillusioned mind of modern man.

Simultaneosuly with this revival of ancient hatreds there developed a mutual contempt among the nations. The old concept of a universal, brotherly world united by common culture was supplanted by an ever-increasing national self-worship. The world in which Reform Judaism began, the world of hope, of brotherhood and culture had disappeared.

It would be narrow and harsh to mock the radiant dreams

of the early Reformers. They could not possibly have predicted the ever-increasing national bitterness, the revival of
ancient hatreds, the use of scientific technology through
clever propaganda to intensify those hatreds, and the tech-
nological improvements which allowed certain nations to
dream of increasing power and even of world dominance.
We know now how they were deluded but our knowledge is
ex post facto. We are wiser then they, yet surely sadder and
wiser.

We wish that it were not so, but it *is* so that the world
atmosphere in which Reform was born belongs to a vanished
past. It is comparatively easy for our generation to see that
fact, to acknowledge it, and change our life methods accordingly. But a change of this kind was virtually impossible for
a man like David Philipson who grew up in the period when
these ideas were still tenable, and who in addition was an
American, a citizen of the land of broad horizons, of bound-
less confidence, a land whose laws "gave to bigotry no sanction and to persecution no assistance." How proudly and how
often did Philipson quote that grand sentence from the letter
of George Washington to the Jewish congregation in New-
port, Rhode Island! In his heart and in his mind Philipson
rejected all the increasing particularisms of the modern
world. Above all it was impossible for him to accept the
growing concept of Jewish nationalism. To him nationalism
was a denial of the role of Judaism as an ethical and cultural
influence in the world. It was a new isolationism. The only
citizenship which had any meaning for him was his American citizenship ("Washington is our Zion"). He was proud
of the fact that as a young rabbi in Baltimore he was called
to the Pittsburgh Conference in 1885, at which the clear
statement was made that we are no longer a nation. So he
remained an unyielding anti-Zionist to the end of his life.
Of course as all members of the Reform movement, he supported Jewish settlements in Palestine, but the concept of a
revived Jewish nationalism was to him a betrayal of all the
dreams of the past.

Philipson had no doubt that he was right, but in the
Reform movement in general there was a great struggle lasting over decades over nationalism and Zionism. Perhaps the
struggle was greater than in any other section of Jewry for
Reform Judaism was institutionally strong. It had hundreds
of congregations organized in a powerful union of congregations. It had a well established rabbinical college spreading
out into many branches. It had a strong, independent-minded

conference of rabbis. All these institutions perpetuated in
their past resolutions and in the minds of their veteran leaders the older views of the world. Had Reform Judaism not
developed into permanent and growing institutions, the old
ideas of the Enlightenment might have just quietly faded
away, but here they remained and were perforce brought
into contact and conflict with the newer nationalism and
Zionism. Finally a balance was achieved. The Conference
passed resolutions in favor of cooperation with the Jewish
State. A small group which could not be reconciled to the
new ideas formed a separate organization without, however,
leaving their historic affiliation. For the bulk of the movement the controversy was over.

As for the other ideas which prevailed in the earlier days
of the movement, it would perhaps be difficult to gauge exactly how they stand. Which of the old beliefs that created
the movement are still operative in it? Is there still a conviction that mankind moves inevitably toward unity and
equality? In this age in which psychology reveals the jungle
in the souls of men is it still believed that the intellect and
enlightenment will banish misunderstanding and hatred?
Does Reform still believe that Judaism is or potentially may
become a world force in influencing mankind in the direction
of brotherhood and enlightened faith? Does it still believe
that modernizing, beautifying the services will call Jews
back to synagogue worship? It is hard to say exactly how
much of the old doctrines still have meaning, but it seems
clear that they still are operative in spite of modern disillusion and bitterness. As, for example, in the relationship
between the old universalism and modern nationalism, it
would seem that Reform Jewry had struck its own balance.
It believes that the Jews have the right to become a nation
and the Jewish nation in Israel has been and will continue to
be a blessing to world Jewry. But it does not and apparently
will not accept that complete national doctrine which declares that Jews everywhere are members of that nation and
are exiles until they become its citizens. Reform Jews still
believe that Jewry is a world influence and that part of its
world influence comes from Israel.

Related to this new hospitality to the once-scorned idea of
nationalism are certain changes of worship in the Reform
synagogue. Whereas in the past certain Jewish ritual observances were deprecated on the ground of being separatist
or outworn, and Reform Judaism had moved more and more
towards an intellectual non-ceremonial expression of an

ethical philosophy, now there is a growing increase of interest in older ceremonial observances. Bar Mitzvah was almost non-existent in Reform Temples in America, having been supplanted by Confirmation. It has now been reinstituted in almost every Reform congregation in the land. Some have special Havdala services. Many have a ceremonial lighting of the candles in the synagogue. Whereas fifty years ago there were very few cantors, now most Reform congregations have cantors and the Hebrew Union College-Jewish Institute of Religion has a special school for the training of them. There is a strong tide towards ceremonialism. Judaism has been embellished by Jewishness.

This change is due to a number of causes. First of all the new emphasis on Jewish nationalism meant a new interest in such things as are distinctly Jewish. A Jewish ceremonial besides pictorializing an idea is also a product of Jewish history. Moreover, the interest in ceremonial is the result of the shift in intellectual interest from philosophy to the modern interest in psychology. Whereas earlier Reformers would have asked about a certain ceremony, "What is its meaning, what does it teach," the modern Reform rabbi will ask, "What feeling does it engender? What mood does it create?"

These changes in increased ceremonial observance have not nullified the basic Reform principle that ideals and ethical devotion are the essential and that ceremonials are only auxiliary. Just as certain ceremonies have been adopted for their mood, so they can very well be rejected again if they cease to be helpful in promoting basic ideas and attitudes. If, for example, Bar Mitzvah which has been almost universally adopted in Reform synagogues in recent years proves for various reasons to be a drawback to spiritual progress, it may very well be widely rejected as it was once widely reintroduced. Reform still holds firm to the basic principle made clear in Dr. Philipson's book that only the ideals and the spiritual faith are the essentials and such observances as the various ceremonials are incidental and dispensable.

The fact that the Reform movement considers itself free to accept or reject historic Jewish ceremonies reveals its basic attitude toward the Jewish legal system. As is abundantly clear in the various debates described in Dr. Philipson's book, Reform began as a revolt against the Jewish legal codes. A study of the collection of rabbinic opinions gathered by the rabbinate of Hamburg in 1818 against the new Reform Temple established there reveals clearly (see especially the opinions of Moses Sofer) that every single word in the prayerbook must be deemed a valid expression of God's law and that we may not make even the slightest change in our inherited tradition. If, therefore, the early Reformers had bowed to the principle of the God-given authority of the entire rabbinic legal system, they could not even have gotten started. Reform therefore was compelled to break away from the inherited law and deny its authority. In the place of the Talmud and the Shulchan Aruch, Reform in its early years returned to Scripture, especially to the Prophets and more especially to the universalistic vision of world peace in the prophecies of Isaiah. It would be almost correct to say that the early Reform was primarily Isaianic or in general prophetic. One of its favorite self-descriptions was Prophetic Judaism. Isaac M. Wise also held firmly the validity of the direct Biblical revelation at Sinai.

This exclusive emphasis on the Prophets and Scripture has somewhat weakened and there is an increasing appreciation of the post-Biblical rabbinic literature. Besides the general tendency to the increase of Jewishness owing to the historic trends mentioned above, there is the feeling that the verbal revelation of Scripture itself has been shaken by modern Biblical criticism and that therefore it need not be in essence different in status from the post-Biblical literature. If we take the Bible to mean man's discovery of God, then we can well say that the Bible, especially the prophetic part of it, is man's discovery of God through conscience and the Talmudic literature is man's discovery of God through intelligence. At all events, the rabbinic literature has risen in status in the Reform movement. That does not, of course, mean that it has risen to the status where it is deemed to be a Divine-given mandate. It is respected as the manifestation of the people of Israel seeking to define and to clarify the will of God.

Hence there is an increase of questions and responsa in the realm of Jewish law. If a certain commandment in Jewish law is directly contrary to our conscience as, for example, a law based upon the inferior legal status of women, this law would not be deemed to have authority. But wherever the law is not contrary to our conscience, which happens perhaps in the majority of the questions asked, Reform rabbis much prefer to follow it. The newer attitude to the law in the Reform movement may be defined in the phrase that the Halacha is not our governance but our guidance.

All these changes are the result of a change in world atmosphere. The cooperation with the national State of Israel is the outcome of the disillusion with the immediate possibility of world comradeship. The greater interest in ceremonialism is largely due to the modern emphasis on psychology rather than on philosophy, and the greater willingness to be guided by the Halacha is due to the fact that Reform has established its independence and no longer needs to be revolutionary. Thus one generation has gone and another generation has come and the world does not seem to be the same. But after all what Ecclesiastes meant was that in spite of the fact that one generation goes and a different generation comes, the world still stands and its basic ideals continue. Reform was the child of a hopeful, idealistic, intellectual era. It has lived into a more realistic emotional era but its essential doctrine, namely, the right to change externals for the sake of maintaining the essence still stands firm.

As for David Philipson, his work is no longer unique. Other histories have been written. First there was Simon Bernfeld's *Toldot Ha-Reformazion Ha-Datit* (Warsaw, 1908). Then Caesar Seligmann in 1922 published his *Geschichte der Judaschen Reformbewegung* and in 1963, Gunther Plaut wrote his fine source book, *The Rise of Reform Judaism*. But David Philipson's book remains the classic description of those struggles and debates which led to the organizations, most of which still endure. It is the pioneer history of Reform and still breathes the original idealism of its founders. This perhaps is its chief historical interest, precisely because we have grown away from many of its attitudes. But above all, the book will always have a unique quality because David Philipson, who entered in 1875 at the age of thirteen in the first class of the Hebrew Union College and worked with all the builders of the foundations, was in himself part of the movement which later generations inherited. Only of Philipson as historian can it be said as Tennyson said of Ulysses:

"I am part of all that I have met,
Much have I seen and known—Of men,
    councils, governments,
Myself not least but honored of them all."

SOLOMON B. FREEHOF

CHAPTER I

THE BEGINNINGS OF THE REFORM MOVEMENT IN JUDAISM

THE Jew has always been susceptible to the influences at work in the environment in which he has chanced to be. His mind is singularly open to the thought-waves that permeate his intellectual surroundings. The keen inquirer can learn often the leading cultural *motifs* of the various civilizations in whose midst the Jew has dwelt by familiarizing himself with the remains of Jewish literary achievement. From early times this has been the case.[1] The Bible indicates in many a passage the proneness of the Israelites to adopt the customs of the surrounding peoples and to accept their viewpoints of religion and life.[2] That the Babylonian civilization with which the Jews came into contact during the exile and after, left more than a passing effect there can be little doubt;[3] the feast of Purim may be instanced as a striking proof of this; Babylonian in origin, it was given a Jewish dress and became incorporated into the system of Jewish observance.[4] Thus, too, the Persian environment in which the Jews found themselves after the passing of the Babylonian empire into the power of Cyrus and his successors left its mark;[5] to mention but one result of the contact with Zoroastrian beliefs, it is necessary only to refer to the influence of the Persian system of angelology and demonology on Jewish thought;[6] the so-called Hellenistic movement among the Jews of the two pre-Christian centuries is indication sufficient of the hospitality afforded to Greek thought;[7] the writings of Philo testify to the welcome which was accorded the Alexandrinian Neo-Platonic philosophy; in the Talmud[8] there are indications that Jews were influenced by customs and thoughts that prevailed among their neighbors; traces of Neo-Persian influence are not wanting;[9] the Arabic philosophical movement is reflected in the pages of Saadia's *Faith and Knowledge,* and the Aristotelian revival in Europe through the Christian scholiasts finds its Jewish counterpart in the Judeo-

1

Spanish medieval philosophers; so noticeable, in fact, was the mirroring of the life and thought of the surrounding Christian world in Jewry that it passed into a popular proverb in the form *"wie es sich christelt, jüdelt es sich"*; the reciprocal influences of Christian and Jewish life [10] were so pronounced that more than one church council issued edicts prohibiting this. All this free interplay ceased as a matter of course when the ghetto became an established official institution throughout Europe; [11] the Jew, shut up within the ghetto walls and barred from all contact with the outside world by the ghetto gates, gradually became also intellectually ostracized from the thought-currents in the world without. The visible material ghetto had as its concomitant the imperceptible intellectual ghetto. The period from the sixteenth to the eighteenth century, the era of official ghettoism, is coincident with the exclusion of the Jew from all sympathetic concern with the culture of the world. His intellectual outlook was bounded by the Talmud and its dependent disciplines. His *Weltanschauung* was restricted by the narrowing influence of the *Shulchan Aruk* [12] and all that this implies. The constant restriction of the Jewish mind to the study of the Talmud and the casuists resulted in the fantastic ingenuities of pilpulism, and the rigid observance of the enactments codified in the *Shulchan Aruk* made of the religion a legalistic system. Pilpulism and *Shulchan Arukism* were the logical accompaniments of ghettoism. The jargon language went hand in hand with these phenomena. The degradation of the Jewish communities of Europe was almost complete by the middle of the eighteenth century. The Jews were cramped intellectually; they were social pariahs; politically they were non-existent; they spoke a language which was a strange conglomerate of Hebrew and German, with a sprinkling of terms and phrases from the other languages of Europe. The systematic exclusion of centuries had done its work. But this could not last for ever. It was unnatural. The Jew must once again come into contact with the larger world, and when this would prove to be the case, he would follow the example of former generations, as just recounted, would emerge from the intellectual prison-house in which he had been confined during the ghetto centuries and participate in the highest cultural aspirations of his time; the form which the public expression of his religion had assumed, and the interpretation which the religion had received during these dark ages, would be subjected to searching examination in the light of the broader culture. Intellectual and religious emancipation usually advance *pari passu;* it is the story of religious reform resulting from the acquisition of secular education and civil emancipation among the Jews that it is the purpose of these pages to unfold.

At the very outset it may be well to indicate briefly a few distinguishing marks of this movement which is so radical a departure from the rabbinical traditions. Apart from the purely external reforms that aimed at beautifying, making intelligible and bringing order and decorum into the public service, the gradual introduction whereof will appear in the course of the unfolding of this history, there must be borne in mind chiefly and above all the principles which mark the reform movement.

In the first place, in the view of rabbinical Judaism every command of the written law in the Pentateuch (*Torah sh'bik-thab*), and of the oral law (*Torah sh'b'al peh*), as codified in the *Shulchan Aruk,* is equally binding. The ceremonial law has equal potency with the religious and moral commands. Reform Judaism, on the other hand, claims that a distinction must be made between the universal precepts of religion and morality and the enactments arising from the circumstances and conditions of special times and places. Customs and ceremonies must change with the varying needs of different generations. Successive ages have their individual requirements for the satisfaction of the religious nature. No ceremonial law can be eternally binding. No one generation can legislate for all future ages. Mankind grows. The Biblical books and the Talmudical collections, when approached in this spirit, yield wonderful results. The stream of change and development is perceptible throughout.

Some striking instances may be cited to prove that, although the movement for religious reform as a distinct, concerted movement is a modern phenomenon, yet the reinterpretation and revaluation of religious teachings and the accommodation of religious institutions to meet changed situations and conditions which are the *motifs* of the reform movement, appear in Jewish experiences from very early days. The feast of Passover was ordained to be celebrated by the people on the fourteenth day of the first month. Provision, however, was made for such as because of hindering circumstances could not observe the feast on that day; they were allowed to observe the feast one month later.[13] Even so fundamental a ceremony as circumcision was intermitted because of unfavorable circumstances.[14] Because the brazen serpent which Moses had set up became conducive to idolatry, King Hezekiah broke it in pieces, even though it dated back to the great lawgiver.[15] Originally, it was ordained that every first born should be consecrated to serve in the tabernacle;[16] when this was found to be impracticable, the ceremony of the redemption of the first born, known as *Pidyon ha-ben,* was instituted and the tribe of Levi took the place of the first born for service in the tabernacle.[17] Ezra is reported to have laid down ten injunctions, among them the ordinance that readings from the Torah should take place on Mondays and Thursdays, in all likelihood because, on these days, the people came into Jerusalem and advantage was to be taken of their presence and the Torah to be read, even though it was not the Sabbath.[18] In Talmudical days, great rabbinical authorities set up hermeneutic rules whereby Biblical laws were occasionally interpreted in a spirit of accommodation to changed needs and circumstances.[19] A classical instance of early reform is the Prozbul which Hillel instituted to ameliorate the hardships caused by the observance of the Sabbath year as laid down in the Mosaic Law.[20] This institution practically abrogated the Mosaic ordinance; the reason given for this Hillelian reform is "the need of society."[21] When after the fall of Jerusalem in 70, Jamnia became the center of Jewish life, Johanan ben Zakkai ordained that certain privileges peculiar to Jerusalem should be transferred to Jamnia;[22] Joshua ben Chananyah laid down the dictum "do not impose on the people any demand by which the majority cannot abide";[23] the rigor of the laws of Sabbath observance was ameliorated by the legal fictions of *erube techumin* and *erube hazerot.* Great rabbinical authorities of later days likewise accommodated the laws to the changed needs of the time.[24] The universal commands implanted in the heart of man, and dependent on neither time nor place, are the essentials which never change, as Abraham Ibn Ezra puts it; the special laws, however, which arise from temporary and local conditions, are not written indelibly in the eternal scheme of things. This test Reform Judaism applies to the traditions, and in all its development this has been the guiding principle.[25] Not that Reform Judaism repudiates tradition or has broken with Jewish development as is often charged erroneously; it lays as great stress upon the *principle* of tradition as does rabbinical Judaism, but it discriminates between separate traditions as these have become actualized in forms, ceremonies, customs, and beliefs, accepting or rejecting them in accordance with the modern religious need and outlook, while rabbinical Judaism makes no such discrimination. In a word, Reform Judaism differentiates between *tradition* and *the traditions;* it considers itself, too, a link in the chain of Jewish tradition, the product of this modern age as Talmudism was of its age.

Rabbinical Judaism, teaching as it does, the eternal validity of all the laws and ceremonies, whether prescribed in the Pentateuch or developed by tradition, takes a peculiar stand in reference to such laws whose fulfillment is dependent upon residence in the land of Palestine. These laws, it claims, are suspended for a time owing to the dispersion; they are not abrogated, but only suspended, and will be again binding when the Jews will be restored to their ancient land. This brings us to a second point of difference. The burden of the thought of rabbinical Judaism is national. The hope expressed in the traditional prayers is that the Jews will return to Palestine, again become a nation under the rule of a scion of the house of David, reinstitute the sacrifices under the ministration of the descendants of Aaron, and worship in the temple rebuilt on the ruins of the temple of old. The Jews, in their dispersion among the nations, are in a state of exile; their century-long sufferings are a punishment for the sins committed by the fathers while living in Palestine; when the measure of the expiation will be full, the restoration will take place. This doctrine Reform Judaism rejects.[26] It contends that the national existence of the Jews ceased when the Romans set the temple aflame and destroyed Jerusalem. The career in Palestine was but a preparation for Israel's work in all portions of the world. As the early home of the faith, as the land where the prophets uttered their world-subduing thoughts and the psalmists sang their world-enchanting hymns, Palestine is a precious memory of the past, but it is not a hope of the future. With the dispersion of the Jews all over the world, the universal mission of Judaism began. The Jews are citizens and faithful sons of the lands of their birth or adoption. They are a religious community, not a nation.[27]

Connected with this change of the conception of Judaism from a national to a universal faith is the difference in the attitude on the Messianic question. Rabbinical Judaism posits the coming of a personal Messiah; Reform Judaism, rejecting this, teaches the coming of the Messianic age of universal peace and good will among men. In the wake of the thought of the great unknown prophet of the captivity, commonly known as the second Isaiah, Reform Judaism applies the idea of Messianic leadership to the people of Israel, not to any one individual.[28] As in the theology of Reform Judaism the thought of the priesthood of the whole people of Israel has been substituted for the priesthood of the families of Aaron, so also has the belief in the Messiahship of the people displaced the traditional faith in the advent of the individual, personal Messianic king.

Although the movement which has given practical expression to these doctrines is primarily of a religious nature, yet can it not be adequately understood unless viewed in connection with other phenomena in the life of the Jews, for it involved not only a change in the religious outlook, but also a new interpretation of the educational, literary, cultural, and political aspirations of the Jewish communities.

No religious movement of this kind is isolated.[29] It is the outcome of preceding causes. The immediate causes in this case were three; first, the new intellectual movement inaugurated among the Jews along lines different from the old methods;[30] secondly, the linguistic emancipation—if I may so term the acquisition by the Jews of a pure language—through the medium of Mendelssohn's *Torah* translation; this pure language displaced the jargon, and enabled the Jews to participate in the remarkable literary awakening that took place in Germany in the closing quarter of the eighteenth century and to acquire the culture of the time;[31] and, thirdly, the civil emancipation which began with the act of September 27, 1791, of the National Assembly of France, that declared the Jews to be citizens of the country, and the similar enactment of the Batavian Republic in 1795. A complete revolution in Jewry resulted. The Jews were being brought once again into touch with the life and culture of the world. The old order was changing. New hopes and ideals stirred hundreds among this people. In all the larger Jewish communities of Germany men who had acquired the new learning began to appear. Although comparatively few in number at first, their influence was none the less telling, chiefly because of their attainments. A sign of the times was the publication of the Jewish magazine, *Ham-meassef,* in Königsberg in 1783; the band of men who wrote for its pages, mostly friends or disciples of Mendelssohn and known as the *Meass'-fim,* did much toward spreading the new culture among their coreligionists.[32] These phenomena caused unwonted disquiet in the Jewish communities, and rabbis of the old school felt correctly that the new education was dealing a deathblow to the old era;[33] hence their anathema against Mendelssohn's translation of the Pentateuch and Hartwig Wessely's open letter to his coreligionists, which advised them to educate their children along the lines laid down in the Toleration Edict of the Emperor Joseph II of Austria in 1782, viz., in secular branches and in the German language. But anathemas cannot stay the progress of events. They are usually the last resort of the entrenched authorities who feel their power waning. An interesting side light is thrown on the conditions at this critical juncture, when the old Judaism was struggling to retain its hold and the new had not yet made its appearance, by the document addressed by one of the foremost rabbis of the time to his congregation. I refer to the letter of farewell written by Rabbi Hirschl Levin, the aged chief rabbi of the Berlin community. He was not a fanatic. He did not join with other rabbis in their denunciation of Mendelssohn and Wessely. On the contrary he was an admirer of Mendelssohn. This rabbinical chief was greatly distressed at the disquieting conditions prevalent in Germany's chief Jewish congregation toward the close of the eighteenth century. He recognized that changes were impending, but he could not comprehend what it all meant. Judaism seemed to him to be threatened with some great danger and to be near dissolution. Because of this sad situation he states that he desires to resign his office and go to Jerusalem to end his days in the Holy Land, for he cannot bear to witness any longer the decay of the religious life among his people.[34] From such expressions the inference is drawn readily that the rabbinical interpretation of Judaism had ceased to appeal to a large section of the community. There was a conflict between the demands made by the traditional religion and the life the people were leading. Further, such as had acquired the philosophical and literary culture of the time, could find no religious satisfaction in the observance of forms, customs, and ceremonies that had been unhesitatingly and unquestioningly accepted by the fathers as constituting an essential element of the faith. No wonder that the old rabbi felt that the ground was slipping from beneath his feet. He, and such as he, knew but one rule for the Jew, and that was the faithful performance of every jot and tittle of religious observance as codified in the *Shulchan Aruk*. Here,

however, were hundreds [35] upon whom this obligation sat
lightly, aye, who disregarded utterly many an injunction that
he considered of supreme importance. But although the impending change was in the air, the eighteenth century witnessed but
one practical demonstration of the working of the new spirit.
This, too, not in Germany but in Holland. In 1796 a congregation was organized in Amsterdam under the name and title
Adath Jeshurun, whose avowed purpose was to introduce some
reforms, but these were so insignificant that although the formation of the congregation was the outcome of great agitation,[36] the results were painfully inadequate. These results
were merely the abolition of some *piyyutim* [37] or liturgical
pieces wherewith the synagogal service had become over-
burdened, and the use of the vernacular in public addresses.[38]

Before passing to the story of the reform movement and
detailing its significance and its progress, the attitude in this
matter of Moses Mendelssohn, the foremost Jew of the eighteenth century and of one other prominent figure in eighteenth-
century Jewry who made a peculiar attempt toward solving the
religious problem involved in the transition from the old life of
the ghetto to the new life of the latter days in which he lived
must be considered briefly. Mendelssohn is frequently spoken
of as the originator of the reform movement in Judaism. This
rests upon a misconception. True, Mendelssohn made the reform
movement possible by giving the impulse to modern education
among the Jews. But a religious reformer he was not.[39] Quite
the contrary. He conformed strictly to every requirement and
demand of rabbinical Judaism. His conception of Judaism
was that it is divine legislation; [40] that since the ceremonial
law was revealed by God, it has potency and must be observed
until it shall be repealed distinctly by another revelation. But
Holdheim pointed out in a number of passages [41] how poorly
taken Mendelssohn's position was in this matter. The Pentateuch as well as the prophets teaches positive religious doctrines; therefore Judaism demands belief as well as practice.
As for the contention that another revelation is necessary to
repeal the ceremonial laws, Holdheim gave utterance to the
striking thought that the spirit of the age is also a revelation of
God, and that this commanded the abolition of many observances that had religious sanction at one time; besides, many of
the ceremonies considered obligatory by the rabbinical Jew are
the products of the Talmudic age; were these also revealed?

Mendelssohn's position was altogether inconsistent. He would not grant that religious beliefs and practices are subject to the same laws of change and progress as obtain in other provinces of human thought and activity. For him Judaism was a closed chapter. The contention of Reform Judaism is the very opposite. For Mendelssohn every ceremony was of eternal validity; for the Jewish reformers ceremonies were transitory expressions of the religious spirit and had to be accommodated to the changing needs of successive ages. But Mendelssohn did not live to see this thought become dominant. In his own life he succeeded in avoiding the conflict between the old Judaism and the new culture; how artificial his position was grows clear from the religious experiences of his own offspring; being children of the era of enlightenment and having received an intellectual training in accordance with the spirit of the time, they could find no satisfaction in the ceremonial observance that passed for Judaism, and hence they abandoned the ancestral faith. There were hundreds in a similar plight; the reform movement was the outcome of the clear thought that distinguished the permanent from the transitory in religion. Mendelssohn, interpreting Judaism to be mere legislation, could not have formulated such a program. He was as little a religious reformer as was Ezekiel Landau of Prague, one of the hyperorthodox rabbis who pronounced the ban upon his German translation of the Pentateuch.[42]

A peculiar attempt at the solution of the religious difficulties in Judaism at the close of the eighteenth century was made by David Friedländer, the best known of the disciples of Mendelssohn. Friedländer was a man of broad culture and was keenly interested in the forward movements among his coreligionists. He was one of the leading spirits in the foundation of the first school that taught secular branches to Jewish children. This was the Jewish Free School of Berlin, founded in 1778. He was also active in a literary way, and published among other things a translation of the Hebrew Prayer-Book (Berlin, 1786). This translation met with opposition on the part of the rabbis of the old school similar to that aroused by Mendelssohn's Pentateuch translation. Eleazer Fleckeles of Prague denounced it vehemently in his *Olath Zibbur,* and declared the translation of the Hebrew prayers into German to be one of the greatest of sins. Friedländer answered him in an "Epistle to the German Jews,"[43] in which he set forth the necessity of

the people understanding the prayers, and denounced the obscurantism that finds in the mere use of the Hebrew some saving
power, even though what is prayed in that language be unintelligible."⁴

The distressing condition of affairs among the Jews of
Berlin toward the close of the eighteenth century, religiously
speaking, led Friedländer to take a fantastic step. As said
above, rabbinical Judaism which had degenerated into a casuistical system of legalistic intricacies had lost its hold upon
many; the service in the synagogue, with its sale of the *mitzwot,*
its disorder, its interminable length, was undignified, and
repelled rather than attracted them. Added to this was the fact
that these men found the doors leading to the professions or
official careers closed to them because they were Jews. All these
circumstances led to an extensive abandonment of Judaism.
Conversions to Christianity were numerous. This appalling
state of affairs induced Friedländer to write in 1799 his
notorious "Epistle of Several Jewish Fathers to Councillor
Teller." ⁴⁵ In this communication Friedländer declared himself and his sympathizers ready to accept Christianity, on the
condition that they might dispense with the distinctive Christian
doctrines such as the trinity, the divinity of Jesus, and the
observance of the Christian festivals. He declared further that
Judaism in its essentiality requires belief in but three doctrines,
the unity of God, the immortality of the soul, and the mission
to reach out toward moral perfection. Teller's answer was discouraging, as was to be expected from an orthodox Christian;
for even though the writers of the Epistle had expressed their
willingness to call themselves Christians, what they proposed
was far from a declaration of Christianity; it was the play of
Hamlet without Hamlet. From the Jewish standpoint, too,
Friedländer made a serious mistake. In truth he evidenced by
this Epistle that he did not understand Judaism. The past
development of Judaism cannot be thrown overboard lightly as
he purposed to do. Judaism represents a growth, as the Jewish
reformers taught constantly. True, their opponents contended
unceasingly that the reform movement implied a complete break
with the past: but the scholars and thinkers who are the
founders of reform in Judaism justified their standpoint by
the fact that their researches had convinced them that in Judaism there was a constant development; that the past furnished
ample indications that the stream of thought was ever flowing;

that forms, prayers, and ceremonies were the products of different times.

> Every era in the history of Judaism is of importance; the present can break with the past as little as any separate limb can dissociate itself from the body without suffering serious injury. Such a connection with the past means not the dominance of dead custom, but the persistence of the living idea which permeates all ages with its vigor, and if it leads to different developments this does not justify a disregard of its origins. If anywhere it is in the religious province that reform alone brings blessing.

Thus wrote Geiger,[16] and his position was shared by all who understood the true inwardness of the reform movement.[17] In truth, it was the investigations of scholars into the past productions of the Jewish mind and spirit that laid the foundations for the true reform movement. Friedländer therefore was most superficial in his sensational letter to Teller. If, as has been stated by an apologist for Friedländer,[18] this letter was a counsel of despair because of the wholesale defections from Judaism, the proposed remedy was equivalent to killing the patient.[19] This incident illustrates how deeply the waters of Jewish life were stirred in the years immediately preceding the birth of the reform movement; the ship of Judaism had been loosened from the old moorings and was floundering in strange waters; many had deserted the ship; far-seeing ones among the faithful discerned that the ship required a new anchor; this they found in the movement that reconciled the teachings and practices of Judaism with the culture, the needs and the spirit of the time.

Schools. Israel Jacobson

The road to the reform movement lay really through the schools of modern tendency that began to be founded among the Jews in the closing decades of the eighteenth century.[50] True, from time immemorial there had been provision for the education of the young. But this education had come to be restricted to purely Hebrew instruction. In Germany the Jewish schools had fallen to a sorry state. The schoolmasters, called *melammedim*, were for the most part uncouth Poles, devoid of all pedagogical ability. The *cheder*, as the Jewish school was called, was synonymous with disorder; the instruction was hap-

hazard and the influence of the teachers was not for the best.
A thoroughgoing reform of the school system was necessary
if the Jews were once again to participate in the life of the
world, as seemed likely from the signs of the times. This was
accomplished by the establishment of schools in various places
where training in the Hebrew branches was supplemented by
instruction in secular studies; a decree providing for the establishment of one of these schools declared that

> A regular school should be founded in which the chil-
> dren, besides receiving instruction in the religious branches,
> should be taught pure morality, love for humanity, their
> duties as subjects, as well as writing, reckoning, language,
> geography, history, and natural science, in order that the
> rising generation may be educated to become useful citizens
> of the State.[1]

Children reared in such a school could not help but become
disaffected with the views and conditions that had been accepted
by their parents as a matter of course. The first of these schools
in order of time was the Jewish Free School of Berlin, adverted
to above as having been founded in 1778 by David Friedländer and his brother-in-law Isaac Daniel Itzig. This school
was superintended for a time by that remarkable thinker,
Lazarus Bendavid, a Kantian and a fine spirit. Bendavid was
one of the foremost figures among the Jews of the "enlightenment" period; he had been ordered to leave Vienna by the police
on the charge of being an "innovator," because in a pamphlet,
"The Characteristics of the Jews," called forth by the Toleration Edict of Joseph II, he had given expression to several
very liberal ideas on ceremonialism and religion: the statement
which gave the greatest offense was the assertion that the faults
of the Jews arose from the oppression to which they had been
subjected; this was construed as an attack on Christianity. Coming to Berlin he lived the quiet life of the thinker, supported
himself by grinding lenses after the manner of Spinoza, and
lent what influence he possessed to the forward movement
among his coreligionists. In 1791 the Wilhelmsschule was instituted in Breslau in accordance with the decree mentioned above;
similar schools were founded in Dessau (Herzogliche Franz-
schule, 1799), in Seesen by Israel Jacobson (Jacobsonschule,
1801), in Frankfort-on-the-Main (the Philanthropin, 1804),
in Wolfenbüttel (Samsonschule, 1807), in Cassel (1809). It

was through the influence exerted by the instruction given in such schools that the first reform of the ritual and the public worship became actualized; in these schools a service was instituted for the pupils in which reforms were introduced that would not have been tolerated in the synagogue; thus the children became accustomed to innovations, and when they grew to maturity often enlisted in the cause of reform; [52] frequently when the reformers did not venture to introduce sermons and songs in the vernacular into the service in the synagogue, this was done in the schools, and these school services were attended by many adults who would have felt compunction in encouraging by their presence a similar service in the house of worship proper. [53]

The name of Israel Jacobson has been mentioned in connection with the foundation of the school at Seesen. He was the man of action who instituted the first reforms in the Jewish service. Born in Halberstadt in 1768, he married at the age of nineteen the daughter of Herz Samson, the wealthy *Hofjude* of Brunswick. Through his business connections he traveled extensively and noted the peculiar conditions existing among the Jews. Deeply attached to his people and his faith, he could not but view with concern the indifference of the cultured Jews of the period, notably in Berlin, to their religion; the rupture between this cultured class and the mass of the people was becoming more and more pronounced; the Judaism of the synagogue had degenerated into a lifeless formalism; the forms, customs, and ceremonies had usurped the place of the essentials; the public service consisted of an endless recitation of frequently unintelligible liturgical pieces, and was marked by such noise and indecorum as consorted ill with the spirit of devotion; there was nothing to attract one to whom religion meant something more than the slavish observance of traditional forms which however religiously significant they may once have been, had lost much of their former power to impress. He felt that there must be some middle way between the contemptuous attitude of the so-called enlightened class toward Judaism and the official expression of the faith from which the living breath had departed, leaving only the dry bones. This middle way spelt reform; Jacobson became convinced that reforms of some kind must be inaugurated; he himself was not capable of introducing a thoroughgoing reform based upon an intimate acquaintance with the sources of Judaism and its development; he had neither the knowledge nor the grasp to accomplish this. He was neither a scholar nor a philosopher. He was a practical man of great intelligence and some learning who understood the needs of the people. He had the inclination and the means to work in the cause of religious progress. He proceeded cautiously and began his activity by founding the school at Seesen. Through his generosity, his wealth, and the prominence of his family connections he acquired an influential position. His influence grew from year to year because of his untiring activity. The French occupation of western Germany afforded him his long-desired opportunity. The kingdom of Westphalia was formed by Napoleon for the purpose of giving his brother Jerome a throne; the code of France became the law of the land; the Jews were benefited by the change; they received the full rights of citizenship, and by a decree of March 31, 1808, there was established, after the French model, a Jewish consistory with its seat in Cassel that was to direct and regulate all Jewish affairs. Jacobson was named president of the consistory. The other members of the consistory were three rabbis and two laymen. The manner in which the consistory was to proceed was a matter of great concern to Jacobson; he consulted with three of the foremost Jews of the generation as to the best course to pursue, viz., David Friedländer of Berlin, Aaron Wolfsohn of Breslau, and David Fränkel, director of the Francis School of Dessau and an editor of the newly established magazine *Sulamith,* the first Jewish periodical edited in the German language. Friedländer was particularly insistent that the consistory should blaze a new path. But the officers of the consistory, although giving him a respectful hearing, determined not to antagonize rabbinical Judaism. Jacobson directed the activity of the consistory along the lines he had laid down at Seesen. A school was established at Cassel in which instruction was given in elementary branches. Divine service was held every Saturday in the chapel of the school; the prayers were partly in Hebrew, partly in German; a member of the consistory, frequently the president, delivered an address in the vernacular; German hymns were sung. These slight innovations were the beginning of the reform movement as a practical achievement. The rabbis who were members of the consistory took pains to show that these apparent innovations did not transgress any prescribed rabbinical enactments. The school service met with such favor that Jacobson determined upon a bolder step. He built a temple at Seesen at his own expense, placed an organ in it, and formed a choir from among the pupils of the school. This temple was dedicated with great *éclat* on July 17, 1810. The event was described as the Festival of the Jewish Reformation. Professors, Christian clergymen, and governmental officials were present. Jacobson was enthusiastically praised in more than one literary effusion inspired by the occasion. The dedication of this temple was considered the beginning of a new era for the Jewish people. From this temple a new spirit was to go forth that would revolutionize Jewry. The Jewish people would now emerge from the isolation of centuries. Many of these expressions were bombastic and extravagant. Jacobson, however, seems to have taken them quite seriously. He really thought that the religious difficulties that were corroding the very vitals of his people were now solved. But the evil lay deeper than he had the power to fathom. The reforms with which his name is associated were purely external. He did all he could according to his light. But he did not, because he could not, penetrate to the heart of the distemper that was playing such havoc with the inherited traditions. He failed to recognize that there was an essential conflict between the viewpoint of rabbinical Judaism and that of the new era which was dawning for the Jews. His was not the philosophical insight to determine and to designate the essentials of the religion, to show how these had been overshadowed by non-essentials and to define the real significance of the ceremonial law and its proper place in the outworking of religious development; his was not the scholarly acumen to set forth clearly the theses that would prove the new movement to be a necessity if Judaism was to continue to influence as a religious force those born within the pale, and if there was not to be a complete break between religion and life. The superficial ills only were evident to him. He had noted the estrangement of many from the faith. He had observed also that many a custom had crept into the public service which was unæsthetic, that the manner of conducting the service offended good taste, and that many of the prayers were unintelligible. He thought that these things alone were the causes of the alienation of Jews, especially in the larger cities, from the synagogue. Hence his whole aim was to æstheticize the service; German sermons, German hymns, some German prayers—these he considered the means of making the religion a living entity to his generation as it had been to the fathers. But these few

external reforms did not meet the case. They simply touched
the rim of the problem. But with all his limitations his fame is
secure as the pioneer who led the way in taking active steps
toward the reform of the service.[54]

The German sermon as a regular feature of the service was
considered a marked innovation and aroused the opposition of
the rabbis of the traditional school. They were accustomed to
preach but twice a year, on the Sabbath preceding Passover
and on the Sabbath of the penitential season between New
Year's Day and the Day of Atonement. In these sermons, or
rather expositions, they explained the laws to be observed in
connection with the festivals. They spoke either in Hebrew or
in the German-Jewish jargon. To preach in pure German was
therefore denounced as an unjustifiable innovation, for no other
reason than that it had not been done in the past. True, the
dedication of the Jacobson temple was not the first occasion on
which a German sermon had been preached in a synagogue,
but it gave prominence to the practice and assured it an accredited place in the service as a regular feature. The earliest record
we have of such a sermon is connected with the name of Moses
Mendelssohn. He wrote three sermons, which were preached
in the synagogue of Berlin by the chief rabbi David Hirschel
Fränkel, in celebration of the victories of Frederick the Great
at Rossbach and Leuthen and of the conclusion of the treaty of
peace at Hubertusberg.[55] These were, however, exceptional
utterances. The first preacher who made a practice of delivering
sermons in German was Joseph Wolf, coeditor with David
Fränkel of the magazine *Sulamith*. Wolf delivered his first
German sermon in Dessau in 1805.[56] Although preaching in
the vernacular was considered one of the chief reforms, still
was it in reality merely a return to a practice that was quite
prevalent in a much earlier day. It is true that such preaching
had been unknown among the Jews for some time past. But
this was due to untoward circumstances. Such as did not know
the development of Jewish homiletic effort imagined that there
was some inherent objection to it. Here was an instance in
which scholarship became the handmaid of reform. In his
epoch-making book, *Die gottesdienstlichen Vorträge der Juden*
(Berlin, 1832), Leopold Zunz proved beyond the possibility of
a doubt that preaching in the vernacular had obtained among
the Jews in many lands in earlier times, and that therefore the
outcry against sermons in German as being in violation of

Jewish tradition was due to ignorance of that tradition. Jacobson had the correct intuition that preaching in the vernacular might attract to the synagogue some who had become estranged. The rabbis of the old school were living practically in an age that was past; their generation had outgrown them; they were unable to meet the religious requirements of the people; they could not preach; what they called preaching was an explanation of rabbinic observance or a fantastic explanation of Biblical passages which in many instances they did not understand, owing to their ignorance of Hebrew grammar; [57] nor could they be expected to preach in a manner edifying to men and women whose outlook upon life and whose interpretation of religion was so much broader than theirs. [58]

As long as rabbinism was the acceptable interpretation of Judaism the spoken word was not missed by the people; the rabbis explained the laws of religious practice which were the be-all of the religious life; the rabbi was not expected to be a preacher, but an adept in casuistical interpretation, with its thousand-branched tree growing from the roots of Talmudical dialectics. But when life began to mean something more than rabbinism could explain satisfactorily, when the two civilizations came into conflict, the old represented by rabbinism and suited only to ghetto-conditions, that is, an existence self-centered and isolated, and the new adopted by the people of the contemporaneous age who had emerged from the exclusion of the ghetto and were sharing in the larger life of their new possibilities, it was inevitable that the old had to give way if the children of the latter days were to be retained within the fold. Their religion would have to be expounded in an intelligible and acceptable manner; hence the necessity, among other things, of the sermon in the vernacular.

To sum up then, we may say that Jacobson's place as the pioneer of the reform movement in Judaism is based upon his effort and his success in making the service attractive to many of his contemporaries. The true significance of this earliest effort in behalf of reform lies in the attention it aroused to the possibility of giving Judaism a public expression sympathetic to the living generation. It also stresses the fact that the reform movement in Judaism emanated from the people and not from the theologians. The new ghetto-liberated life which the Jewish people were leading in a new time brought forth the liberal movement. Although great rabbis like Geiger, Hold-

heim, and others gave the movement later direction yet it was
in its inception a people's movement.[58] The Jacobson movement
as such did not spread beyond Westphalia, and even there did
not continue long, for with the downfall of Napoleon the Westphalian kingdom ceased to be a French possession, and the
French institutions, among them the Jewish consistory, were
abolished. This, however, did not end Jacobson's activity in
behalf of the reform of the ritual. We shall meet him again as
a prominent figure in the early attempts at reform in the
Prussian capital, whither he removed after the collapse of the
consistory at Cassel.[59]

The French Synhedrin

We must interrupt the thread of the narrative of the development of the reform movement in Germany for a brief space, in
order to cast a glance upon Jewish conditions in the neighboring country of France. The Jews of that land had obtained civil
emancipation by the act of the Assembly of September 27, 1791.
The political events in France were of so absorbing a nature
during the next fifteen years that everything else sank into insig-
nificance. There were, it is true, no inner agitations within the
Jewish communities to compare with the stir among the Jews
of Germany. The new learning which was the immediate cause
of the dissatisfaction with rabbinism among the German Jews
had not asserted itself among their French brethren. Although
civilly emancipated and to all intents and purposes citizens of
France, medieval conditions, religiously and intellectually speaking, continued among them. The emancipation of the Jews, too,
had not been accepted with equanimity by all classes. There
were constant complaints against the unfitness of the Jews for
citizenship as being not only distinct in their religion but a
strange people within the state.[61] Notably from Alsace did
these charges emanate, especial stress being laid upon the usuri-
ous practices of the Jews, and the consequent helplessness of
the peasants who may have fallen into their clutches: the further charge was made that the Jews had no sense of patriotism
or civic honor. Napoleon, who from the beginning of his
career had been quite favorably disposed toward the Jews, had
changed his attitude after the battle of Austerlitz.[62] The affairs
of the Jews were discussed at length in several meetings of the
council of state in the year 1806. Napoleon, speaking through
his mouthpiece Molé, was for curtailing the rights of the

Jews.⁶³ This met with determined opposition on the part of several members of the council. It was thereupon determined to call a convention of Jewish notables, through whom the affairs of the Jews were to be regulated. In a decree issued May 30, 1806, the Emperor commanded the attendance at Paris in July of that year of the foremost men among the Jews (*"une synagogue générale des Juifs"*), who were to voice the sentiments of the Jews and to make such suggestions as should induce their brethren to exchange the degrading occupations that they were engaged in for honorable trades. The call aroused great enthusiasm among Jews of foreign lands,⁶⁴ who knew nothing of the immediate cause of the Emperor's action or of his own feelings toward his Jewish subjects, which were anything but friendly.⁶⁵ The assembly opened on July 26, 1806, in the Hôtel de Ville. There were one hundred and ten notables present, who had been elected by the prefects of the various departments of France, of the German provinces that had come under French rule, and of Italy which was likewise under French suzerainty. Abraham Furtado of Bordeaux was elected presiding officer. The most distinguished man of the assembly was David Sinzheim, rabbi in Strassburg.⁶⁶ The Emperor submitted to the second meeting, on July 29, twelve questions for discussion and decision. These questions were:

1. Are Jews permitted to marry several wives?

2. Does the Jewish law permit divorce? Is such divorce valid without the sanction of the civil court or if obtained by laws which are in opposition to the French code?

3. May a Jewess marry a Christian or a Jew a Christian woman? or does the Jewish law permit marriages between Jews only?

4. Do the Jews consider the French their brethren, or do they look upon them as aliens?

5. In either case, what duties does their law prescribe for the Jews toward Frenchmen of other faiths?

6. Do the Jews who are natives of France and are treated as French citizens by the law look upon France as their fatherland? Do they consider themselves in duty bound to defend it? Are they obliged to obey the laws and to satisfy all the demands of the civil code?

7. Who appoints the rabbis?

8. What magisterial power do the rabbis exercise

over the Jews and what judicial authority do they possess?

9. Does their authority rest upon written laws or upon tradition?

10. Are there trades which are forbidden the Jew by his religion?

11. Does their law forbid the Jews to exact usury from their coreligionists?

12. Does it forbid or permit them to exact usury from their non-Jewish fellow citizens?

It was notably the third question which aroused the most active and heated discussion. It was in this debate that the statement was made for the first time in a public assembly that Judaism had been distorted frequently by rabbinical enactments in the course of the centuries,[87] and that it was necessary to return to the Bible as the source and basis of religious practice. Such an utterance indicated clearly that a new era had dawned, and that the people were growing restive under the yoke of rabbinism. The question was answered evasively to the effect that marriage between Israelites and Christians contracted according to the laws of the "Code Civil" are from a civil standpoint binding and valid, and although such marriages cannot be invested with the religious forms, they shall not entail disciplinary punishment (anathema [88]). The other questions were readily and satisfactorily answered. The replies of the assembly showed clearly that the Jews were not a "nation within the nation," [89] that their non-participation in the past in the interests of the nation was not their own fault, but was due to the repressive legislation to which they had been subjected, that they were distinct from their compatriots in their religion only. The answers were satisfactory to the Emperor. Desiring to give them the force of law and yet not wishing to issue a special decree for that purpose, he determined to attain this end through the agency of a Jewish legislative body to be known as the Great Synhedrin. In a letter dated August 23, 1806, he wrote to his minister De Champagny that it is his purpose "to constitute the Assembly actually gathered in Paris into a Great Synhedrin, whose acts shall be placed beside those of the Talmud as articles of faith and principles of religious legislation." This body was to consist of seventy-one members, like the great Synhedrin of old in the land of Palestine. The assembly of

notables was directed to make all preparations for the session
of the Synhedrin. On October 6, 1806, Napoleon issued a decree
in Hebrew, French, and Italian, convening the Great Synhedrin. The sessions of the Synhedrin opened on February 9,
1807; its organization was on the lines of the ancient Synhedrin, the presiding officers being called *nassi, ab beth din,* and
chakam. Its meetings continued through one month, final
adjournment taking place on March 9. It accomplished little
beyond placing the seal of its approval upon the answers of the
assembly of notables. It was undoubtedly Napoleon's love for
the sensational and the spectacular that prompted him to
attempt this revival of the old Jewish legislative body on
French soil. The French Synhedrin requires mention in the
history of the reform movement because, even if its members
did not declare in so many words the repudiation of the traditional belief in the return to Palestine and all the doctrines
dependent upon this, yet their answer to the fourth and sixth
questions, to the effect that they looked upon Frenchmen as
their brethren and France as their native country, implied this,
and the answer to the eighth question indicated that they considered rabbinical jurisdiction in civil and judicial matters a
thing of the past. Still, in spite of this approach to the spirit
of the reform movement, this latter made but little headway
among the French communities beyond some æsthetic improvements in the service here and there; even these external reforms
were slow in being adopted, for as late as 1839, Oryl Terquem,
the author of the famous Tsarphati letters, declared, "If reforms
are not introduced the Jews will either become absolutely indifferent or enter the Christian Church." [70] Rabbinical Judaism
continued to be officially recognized; the reform movement did
not make great progress there, and the result was much as
Terquem predicted.

Early Reforms in Berlin. The Science of Judaism

The famous edict of March 11, 1812, issued by the King of
Prussia, Frederick William III, at the initiative of his noble
and liberal-minded prime minister Hardenberg, was interpreted
by the Jews of that country, and notably by those living in the
city of Berlin, as the beginning of a new period of light and
freedom. And in truth they were justified in entertaining this
feeling. In unmistakable terms this emancipatory edict removed
from the Jewish inhabitants of the Prussian state the restric-

tions and wrongs of centuries. It declared them to be natives, and raised them to the rank of Prussian citizenship on the condition that they took family names and employed the German or any other living language in place of the jargon in their daily lives and transactions. It gave them permission to settle anywhere in the land and to acquire real estate; it made them eligible for teachers' positions and for communal offices; all restrictive trade conditions were abolished, as well as all special taxes which they had been compelled to pay as Jews. In return they had to assume all the obligations of citizenship, such as taxes and military service. Rabbinical jurisdiction was to cease. There were a number of inhibitory paragraphs also, but the general tendency of the edict was such as made for freedom in so marked a degree, that it is not surprising that the Jews of Berlin looked upon it almost in the light of their *magna charta;* the elders of the Jewish community, David Hirsch, Bendix, Friedländer, and Gumpertz, addressed a letter of thankful appreciation to the king.[71] True, the edict did not touch the religious affairs of the Jews further than to demand that rabbinical jurisdiction cease; it left expressly for future consideration the ecclesiastical conditions and the education of the Jews, for the regulation of which "men of the Jewish faith who enjoy the public confidence because of their attainments and uprightness"[72] were to be drawn into consultation. Here again, as in Westphalia, we find that the acquisition of civil emancipation was the beginning of active efforts for religious emancipation. Shortly after the promulgation of this edict David Friedländer wrote a pamphlet, entitled "On the Changes in the Service in the Synagogues made necessary by the new Organization of the Jewish Schools in the Prussian States."[73] In this pamphlet he indicated the lines along which the religious and educational affairs of the Jews ought to be directed. He dwelt particularly on the necessity of a reorganization of the schools and a reform of the service; the chief features of the latter were to be the abolition of all prayers having a national Jewish coloring and the introduction of the German as the language of the service. This publication met with decided disapproval on the part of the rabbinical Jews, who were opposed to any and every change in the ritual or the customs; the king to whom Friedländer had submitted a copy of the pamphlet intended to answer the author to the effect that he would give his recommendations consideration on the condition that they involved no innovations. Frederick William was essentially a reactionary; he was prevented from answering in this wise by Hardenberg, who showed him the meritorious points in Friedländer's program. Hence the prohibition against making any reforms or innovations was not issued; still it was only delayed; after Hardenberg's death it appeared.

The first active step toward reform in Berlin was taken in 1815. In the Prussian capital, as in Westphalia, the reform movement was inaugurated by public-spirited, practical men. Here, too, as there, the movement arose from the desire to make the public services decorous and intelligible. Israel Jacobson, who had removed from Cassel to Berlin, established such a service in his own home on the Feast of Weeks in the year 1815 on the occasion of the confirmation of his son; this service was accompanied by organ music, singing by a choir, a German sermon, and prayers in the vernacular.[74] The room in Jacobson's house being too small to accommodate all who wished to attend, Jacob Herz Beer, a wealthy banker, father of the celebrated composer Meyerbeer, instituted a similar service in his home.[75] The sermons were delivered by talented young men. Isaac Auerbach, Eduard Kley, Leopold Zunz, Isaac Noa Mannheimer, and C. S. Günsburg,[76] three of whom became commanding figures in later years, Kley as one of the founders and preachers of the reform congregation of Hamburg, whose story will be recounted shortly, Zunz as a master of Jewish scientific research and one of the greatest of scholars, and Mannheimer as the famed preacher of the Viennese congregation. The services were attended by hundreds from among the cultured classes of Berlin Jewry. The government, however, was not in favor of innovations of any kind or anywhere. Notably was the dissatisfaction of cultured Jews with their inherited faith agreeable to the king, for this led frequently to an abandonment of Judaism and the adoption of Christianity. Further, the rabbis of the old school and their followers were but too ready to appeal to the government against the reformers. These latter had not formed a new organization. They simply conducted these private services in private homes, which any one was welcome to attend. But they were not left unmolested long. In 1817 the government ordered all private synagogues to be closed. This was the first definite victory of the adherents of rabbinical Judaism. The order was directed against the two private temples, Jacobson's and Beer's. This is the earliest

instance of that disastrous policy of calling in the aid of the
government to suppress the reformers which was the cause of
so many scandals during the next three decades. When the
orthodox leaders saw that the reformers were likely to succeed, or in fact had succeeded, in establishing a foothold, they
preferred charges with the government against the reformers
as being fomenters of disturbances by the introduction of innovations. Reference need be made only to the Geiger-Tiktin
affair at Breslau,[77] the *cause célèbre* of Löwi, the reform rabbi
of Fürth in Bavaria,[78] the attitude of Bernays, the orthodox
rabbinical chief of Hamburg, toward the reform congregation
of that city,[79] and the disgraceful proceeding of some Jews of
orthodox proclivities against Leopold Löw when rabbi of Papa,
in Hungary.[80] But it was not only the orthodox party that
sinned in this respect; the reformers too were guilty occasionally of compassing their object by the help of the civil
power; fairness, however, demands the statement that the
orthodox party was given to this course far more than the
reformers. But to return to the case in hand. Beer's private
temple evaded the immediate consequences of the decree of
1817 by the peculiar circumstance that, owing to the fact that
repairs were being made in the chief synagogue, this private
temple was used as the temporary communal house of worship.
The struggle was now on between the old and the new. The
service in the temple met with great favor on the part of many,
notably the young. However, the orthodox party would have
none of it. The rabbinate of Berlin, chief of which was Meyer
Simon Weyl, was unalterably opposed to any reform; they
would not even sanction the appointment of German teachers
(as contradistinguished from the rabbis), whose sole duty was
to be the preaching of sermons, while the rabbis were to continue to perform the same functions and wield the same
authority as of old. A commission was appointed by the Minister of Public Worship to suggest a possible solution of the
difficulty. A number of compromises were suggested, such as
to make the synagogue which was now undergoing repair large
enough to accommodate all the Jews of all tendencies of religious thought; and thus to have practically two synagogues
under one roof, one orthodox and the other reform; another
suggestion was to have two services on Sabbath and holidays;
first a service along traditional lines, and after that another
service with German prayers and a German sermon. This latter

suggestion met with the approval of the Minister of Public Worship. The orthodox party, sure of the sympathy of the king, appealed to him; they found a ready hearing, and the monarch issued a decree (*Cabinetsordre*) on December 9, 1823, commanding "that the divine services of the Jews must be conducted in accordance with the traditional ritual and without the slightest innovation in language, ceremonies, prayers, or songs." [11] A decided reaction had set in in all respects. The high hopes that had been aroused by the edict of 1812 in Prussia and by similar emancipatory decrees in other German states had been shattered by the events that had taken place after the downfall of Napoleon and the meeting of the Congress of Vienna. In several parts of Germany the Jews had been subjected to outrages reminiscent of medieval days; the *hep hep* cry resounded in the streets of cities like Frankfort and Würzburg. This reactionary spirit made itself felt also in the movement for religious reform. The year 1823 is marked by a number of restrictive edicts besides the one just mentioned; a rescript of March 11 of that year declared that "the Jewish religion was only tolerated, and that its confessors have no ecclesiastical officials," and similarly the general legislation for Prussia promulgated for that same year stated that "Jewish rabbis are not instructors of youth, and cannot be looked upon as religious teachers in the same sense as Christian clergymen, because they have no ecclesiastical standing such as the Christian clergy have." All this meant the absolute triumph of the orthodox party; the private temples were closed; every innovation in the service and preaching in the vernacular was [12] forbidden: efforts in the cause of reform in the chief city of Prussia were intermitted for a number of years. The orthodox element was too short-sighted to see that they were playing directly into the hands of the orthodox Christian king; he had forbidden innovations in the Jewish service on the ground that with the rise of Christianity Judaism had ceased to be a living religion, that it had persisted through the centuries as a dead stock and only as such must it continue; that to permit the introduction of reforms and innovations would be equivalent to granting that there was still some life in the religion. The victory of the orthodox party was costly indeed; it was during the years immediately succeeding that the conversions of Jews to Christianity took place in great numbers; this would certainly have been prevented in part had the reform movement not been stifled in the bud.[83] The cultured Jew found the synagogue unattractive and its services unsympathetic; rabbinism belonged to a past age; he became lost to Judaism altogether either by absolute indifference or by being converted to Christianity. On the other hand, opponents and critics of the reform movement have asserted occasionally that Reform Judaism is a bridge leading to conversion to Christianity.[84]

This condition of affairs was made possible further by the fact that the Jews had little or no knowledge of their own past and of the lofty achievements of the Jewish spirit in the ages agone. For the great mass of even the so-called cultural Jews Judaism spelt merely a barren legalism; it was simply the repository of some worn-out customs that were no longer harmonious with the new spirit that had breathed upon the world; even the reformers had been impelled to their acts, not by the thought of Jewish development, but by the artificial motive of making the external expression of the faith respond to an æsthetic longing. That Judaism had an intellectual development and that even during the Christian centuries, the Jewish spirit had brought forth many remarkable products were facts unknown not only to the government (which, upon the information by a Jewish Philistine, had branded the rabbis contemptuously as "Kauscherwächter," as though the inspection of meats were all of Judaism, and it was therefore unworthy of a place among the religions recognized by the state), not only to the Christian populace that viewed the Jews and Judaism only through the glass of prejudice, but also to the great body of the Jews themselves. The governmental interference with internal Jewish affairs for the stifling of the reform movement and the reactionary events of 1817 and the following years but accentuated this. Then it was that a number of young men conceived the correct idea that salvation would come only from within, that the Jews and the non-Jews must be made acquainted with what Judaism, its history and its literature, really were, and that only if the science of Judaism (die Wissenschaft des Judenthums) were made the basis of reform would the new movement have stability. These young men, some fifty in number, under the guidance of Leopold Zunz, Moses Moser, and Eduard Gans, founded in 1819 in Berlin "The Society for the Advancement of the Science of Judaism" (Verein für Cultur und die Wissenschaft des Judenthums [85]).

Although this society was able to carry out but a fraction of its ambitious program, which included the foundation of a Jewish institute of learning, the building up of a great Jewish library, the establishment of a magazine embodying the results of the research into Jewish history and literature; [86] although, further, the high hopes of the founders ended in disappointment and temporary despair with the dissolution of the society in 1824, yet had they struck the true note, and its watchword, "The Science of Judaism," was to become the motto of the second movement for reform in Judaism in Germany under the leadership of Geiger, Holdheim, Einhorn, Philippson, Stein, Hirsch, and the other scholarly guides among the second generation of reformers. Zunz, who had begun life as a preacher in the private reform temple of Jacob Herz Beer, applied all his great powers to the field of research after this temple had been closed by the government. [87] His first great literary work was really the outcome of this incident; the reason given for this action was that Judaism, being only a lifeless survival since the rise of Christianity, it could put forth no such new shoots as preaching [88] and prayers in the vernacular or any other innovations that involved a departure from traditional custom and usage. Zunz undertook the task of proving in his work, *The Homilies of the Jews; Historically Developed,* [89] the falsity of this claim; the theses he set out to establish were that homiletic exercises, such as interpretation of Scripture and preaching in the vernacular, had been customary among the Jews in many localities at different times, that the literary spirit had been constantly active, and that Judaism, far from being a lifeless survival, had put forth new shoots in age upon age, and hence inferentially there was no reason why it should not do so now. [90] In this book [91] Zunz proved that no one has the right

> to prohibit the introduction of new prayers; from the time of the Great Synod to the present day the Jewish liturgy has been constantly enriched by Soferim, synhedrial authorities, teachers of the Mishnah, Emoras, Gaonim, Paitanim, and rabbis, by poets, cantors, congregational leaders, cabbalists. [92] . . . Prayer in the vernacular was permitted by all authorities, yea, even commanded in certain instances. [93] . . . The most important part of these improvements in the service consists in the return from

abuse to normality, from the dead to the living form.
Hence resistance to reforms in this field is to be looked
for from prejudice and ignorance rather than from true
insight."

The conclusion at which he arrives as the result of his
researches is that reform is the mission of the present generation, whose work it must be to discover the real needs of the
present and assert their dominance in the political situation of
the Jews, in the field of learning and in the religious province,
and, further, to embody these progressive ideas in institutions."
The closing paragraph of this book discloses its purpose most
clearly, and may be quoted as a classical expression of the hopes
and expectations of the early reformers:

> The closest attention in the movement for improvements
> in the service of the synagogue should be given to the
> removal of faults and abuses, and to the reintroduction of
> regular sermons. Let the speaker be called what he will,
> preacher or rabbi, teacher or orator, so long as he under-
> stands how to expound the word of God from the Bible
> and the Hagadah, to extract the pure gold from old and
> new fields, to teach the present generation its true work
> and to reach all hearts by skillful speech. Then the divine
> spirit will return to thy temples, O daughter of Zion, and
> will become manifest in deeds flowing from words of
> enthusiasm. The rekindled spark will never be quenched
> again; persecutions will only cause it to flame the more
> brightly, for reform and the triumph of speech propound-
> ing reform are irrevocable as are the victories of freedom
> and civilization, the civil emancipation of the Jews and
> their scientific culture."

Zunz performed a great service to the reform cause by this
book: he gave the movement a scientific basis, and pointed the
way for future workers." Although modern Jewish research
had produced some results before the appearance of this book,"
yet will it be considered always the first great achievement of
the Jewish literary renaissance of the nineteenth century.
Clearly as the book proved the fact of a constant development
in Judaism, yet were its effects further reaching than the triumphant establishment of its thesis that this inner development
in Judaism demanded and justified sermons in the vernacular,

necessary changes in the liturgy, and corresponding reforms. The scientific spirit was revived, and through the influence and devotion of Zunz and such other kindred spirits as Rapoport, Luzzatto, Geiger, Krochmal, Reggio, and many others, Judaism celebrated a literary rebirth; these investigators into the products of the Jewish spirit achieved the purpose set forth in the program of the *"Verein für Cultur und die Wissenschaft des Judenthums,"* viz., "to bring the Jews into harmony with the age and the countries in which they live by means of a development proceeding from within." [99]

The Hamburg Temple

The earliest attempt at reform in Berlin ended, as we have seen, in failure. The orthodox party had succeeded in suppressing completely the efforts of the innovators with the aid of the government. It was a Pyrrhic victory, however. As a result, Judaism suffered great defections from its ranks. Reform was an absolute need, but the rabbis of the traditional school were blind to the need. Their signal defeat seemed to lame the energies of the progressivists, and it was years before another active effort was made in the Prussian capital to organize a second movement along similar lines. But the ideas that swayed the Berlin reformers were not confined to any one place. They were in the air, as it were; the necessity was being felt generally for an intelligent expression of the underlying principles of the faith in accordance with the culture of the time. Thus, for example, although preaching in German had been forbidden in Berlin, it continued at Dessau; and it was not long ere the practice became quite general in southern Germany; as early as 1814 the confirmation ceremony [100] had been introduced by the Jewish congregations of Denmark at the command of the government; in Austria the candidates for the rabbinical office were required to have a university education by a decree issued in the year 1820, and furthermore the use of the vernacular was commanded; sporadic though these phenomena were, yet were they all indicative of the general unrest that was agitating Jewry and the desire for liturgical reforms of some kind.

Of all the early attempts that of the so-called Hamburg Temple congregation aroused the most widespread attention; several of the most important contests between the old and the new school were waged about this as the storm center. In 1817

Eduard Kley, who had been one of the preachers of the private
reform temple of Jacob Herz Beer in Berlin, had removed from
that city to Hamburg to accept the post of director of the Jewish
free school in the Hanseatic city. He began to agitate for a
reformed service almost immediately, and finding a number of
sympathizers, organized together with these a reform society;
they at once took active steps for the erection of a house of
worship, and on October 18, 1818, dedicated the building that
became famous as the Hamburg Temple. The bitterest opposition was engendered. The three rabbis of Hamburg set all
things in motion to suppress the new movement. The Hamburg
reform movement is of especial importance, because it was
the occasion of the first definite official clash between the two
tendencies in Judaism. The issue was not so clear-cut as it
might have been because the reformers hedged considerably;
although ostensibly a protest against rabbinism, yet when the
test came they sought to justify their reforms from the rabbinical standpoint instead of standing fully and uncompromisingly upon the right of instituting such changes of custom and
interpretation as the modified requirements of their day
demanded.[101] The Talmud was the norm of authority for rabbinism; for centuries Judaism had been held to be synonymous
with Talmudism; it excites little wonder therefore that the early
reformers sought to find Talmudical and rabbinical support for
their innovations; it was an artificial attempt;[102] the spirit of
the new time was opposed to the spirit of rabbinism, and the
religious viewpoint of the Jew, the emancipated citizen of the
state, was altogether different from that of his forefather, the
excluded pariah of the ghetto. Like all compromises, this too
was unsatisfactory, but it was not recognized as such till a later
day. The introduction of the first reforms really sounded the
death knell of the authority of the Talmud as the absolute rule
for Jewish practice; years before the reform movement took
shape life had decided the question; to all intents and purposes
the Talmud, or rather its codification, the *Shulchan Aruk,* had
lost its hold as the authority for many Jews; officially, it is
true, it was still recognized, and the struggle promised to be
long and bitter ere its authority should be definitely renounced
by any representative body.[103] From our present point of vantage we see that the issue between the party of tradition and
the party of reform was clear and decided; they represented two
incompatible tendencies; the former held that every jot and

tittle of past custom and practice had eternal validity and could not be changed; the latter declared that the dead hand of the past must not be permitted to rest upon the present, and that, unless the expression of the religion conformed with the requirements of living men, these would drift away from its influence altogether. The one party defended the principle of stability and immutableness in religious practice, the other that of progress and change. But in the formative years this difference was not consistently adhered to. As just said, the reformers attempted to base the validity of their reforms on the authority of the Talmud, thus showing that they themselves were not thoroughly cognizant of the real significance of the movement they were sponsoring. They were really struggling in the dark. There was no definite program founded upon clearly enunciated principles. Reform in its first stadium then was an inadequate though honest effort to meet the almost revolutionary changes that had taken place in Jewry consequent upon the civil, social, and intellectual emancipation which had thrown them from the isolation of the ghetto into the life of the world. The truth must be confessed that the men who fathered the reform movement were not equal to the task. They had not the philosophical breadth to comprehend the real significance of the conditions they were attempting to meet. This grows very apparent from the Hamburg movement. There is no thoroughgoing definiteness.[104] The distinctive features that marked the Temple as a departure from traditional lines were for the most part opportunistic. These features were—some changes in the liturgy, notably in the prayers for the coming of the personal Messiah; the introduction of German prayers; [105] and the use of the organ; they adopted the so-called Portuguese pronunciation of the Hebrew and abolished the traditional cantillation employed in the reading from the Pentateuch at the public services. Here again we note the same fact as we did in connection with the initial steps toward reform taken by Jacobson at Seesen. The æstheticization of the service was the seeming be-all and end-all of the work of the reformers. True, the partial omission and partial modification of the traditional prayers for the coming of the personal Messiah and the omission of such liturgical portions as stated unequivocally that the Jews regarded themselves as foreigners in the lands of their sojourn are indications that there was some consciousness of the deeper significance of the changed phase whereon Judaism had entered. But even here there was not entire consistency. Some prayers for the restoration of Zion and the coming of a deliverer in the person of a Messiah were retained. In his masterly critique of the inconsistencies in the Hamburg Temple Prayer-Book Geiger says that the position taken on this point "looks entirely too much like a compromise; there is apparent the desire not to surrender the old view but to evade its injurious effects;" [106] and with deep insight he sums up in a sentence the merits and the defects of this first reform prayer-book when he declares that the principle which guided those who arranged and edited this new order of prayers was "to reestablish the external conditions of devotion without clashing too much with the current views on prayer, and to remove such passages as were in conflict with the civil position of the Jews"; there was but little attempt at a thorough reform of the service by which alone the demands of the devout disposition could be satisfied. [107]

The time was out of joint as far as the religious situation among the Jews was concerned, and commendable as were the unselfish efforts of Kley and his associates, L. J. Riesser, M. I. Bresselau, S. Fränkel, and others, still did they have no full grasp of the principles involved. [108] Yet have the formation of this Hamburg reform congregation and the dedication of its first temple become historic in Jewish annals because of the consequences. The three rabbis of Hamburg, Baruch ben Meir Oser, Moses Jacob Jaffe, and Jechiel Michael Speyer, issued a proclamation denouncing the heresies of the new movement. Feeling ran very high. L. J. Riesser, the son-in-law of Raphael Kohn, rabbi of Altona, and father of the great advocate, the central figure in the stirring history of Jewish emancipation in Germany, Gabriel Riesser, issued an address to his coreligionists in Hamburg, counseling peace and calling attention to the fact that the need for reform was undeniable. [109] His words fell upon deaf ears. The orthodox party now took the reprehensible step of attempting to induce the Senate of Hamburg to close the new house of worship. This caused the reformers to bestir themselves; the officers of the new congregation requested rabbinical authorities for an expression of opinion on the validity of the reforms they had introduced. This resulted in the publication of a volume, [110] under the editorship of Eliezer Lieberman, containing a number of opinions favorable to the new departure. The most noteworthy deliverance in this controversy is that of Aaron Chorin, [111] rabbi of Arad in Hungary, one of the most interesting figures of the early years of the reform movement. Chorin defends all the reforms introduced at Hamburg by citations from rabbinical authorities; he recommends these reforms as necessary, and condemns without stint the abuses which the reformers had taken steps to remove; he speaks a word of encouragement to the members of the new congregation, and urges them to continue in the work upon which they had entered.[112] The rabbis of Hamburg also appealed to their colleagues for support in the stand they had taken; they received twenty-two responses.[113] These all seconded the position taken by the rabbis of Hamburg, and denounced violently the reforms. They condemned *ex cathedra*. Some of their expressions are characteristic and well worth citing, as indicative of the feelings entertained generally by the opponents of reforms in Judaism. Rabbi Moses Sofer,[114] the celebrated chief of the Jewish community of Pressburg, Hungary, calls the reformers "infidels," "foxes which destroy the vineyards." He objects to the placing of an organ in the synagogue or the use of any musical instrument in the service on the ground that the Jews are in exile and mourning because of the destruction of Jerusalem, and therefore all music as expressive of joy and pleasure must be excluded from the service. Mordecai Benet, chief rabbi of Moravia, declared that the Hamburg reformers were "neither Jews nor Christians, but people without faith"; that "their prayers were sinful and their only purpose in introducing reforms was to curry favor with the Christians." These condemnatory responses [115] had no practical result. The orthodox party did not succeed in having the temple closed by the government as they had hoped to be able to do. The reform congregation continued to flourish. Shortly after the dedication in October, 1818, Gotthold Salomon was called from Dessau to fill the post of preacher in connection with Eduard Kley. Still, in spite of the fame of its preachers and their splendid activity, the practical activity of the congregation remained local, except for one achievement, viz., the establishment of a branch reform synagogue at Leipzig during the great yearly fairs or *Messen*. Merchants from all over Europe gathered at Leipzig during these fairs, and the institution of a reform service in the year 1820 was missionary work for the new cause. The ideas expressed in the sermons preached here were taken home by the hundreds of strangers who heard them, and became frequently the incentives toward work along the

lines of reform in their home communities.[116] J. L. Auerbach
of Berlin was the preacher of this cosmopolitan congregation.
The congregations at Hamburg and Leipzig were the salvage
rescued from the wreck of the ship of reform on the shoals of
reaction. These two congregations, and notably that of Hamburg, existed on as the visible symbol of reform. The mere
fact of this continuance was a great service to the cause.[117]
During the years intervening between the triumph of the orthodox party in Berlin in 1823 and the beginning of Geiger's
activity in 1835 the Hamburg Temple was the one congregation in Germany that represented the reform principle, in spite
of the inconsistencies whereof it was guilty in its attempts at
compromise. "Is the rabbi consistent who germanizes and
deorientalizes his sermons and his theological disquisitions so
far as language, form, and style are concerned, and at the same
time worships with covered head and has his children do likewise? is he consistent if he recites the prayer *hanoten t'shua*[118]
composed for some Asiatic despot or Italian condottiere, and
immediately thereafter speaks of civic conditions in the light
and spirit of our century? is he consistent when he strains every
nerve to have order and decorum in the synagogue on the ninth
of Ab and then permits torn clothes and unshaven faces on
occasions of private mourning? is he consistent when he
preaches conciliation and tolerance toward all and then does not
dare abolish the prayer *welamalshinim*?"[119] These words,
which a critic of the Hamburg Temple wrote[120] in denunciation of the inconsistencies in its ritual and its service, showing
that it had not gone the whole length of reform by any manner of means, may not obscure the great service performed by
this congregation during the years mentioned; for "it cannot be
gainsaid that it contributed greatly by its mere existence to the
rejuvenation of the service in places far and near, and exerted
a great influence upon the renewed discussion and treatment of
this question."[121] Before proceeding to the account of this
period of "renewed discussion and treatment," the time of the
second generation of reformers, some finishing touches to the
account of the beginnings of the reform movement, may be
given. An edict regulating the affairs of the Jews in the Duchy
of Saxe-Weimar was promulgated by the Grand Duke Carl
Friedrich on June 10, 1823. It consisted of thirty-four paragraphs, whereof the following are concerned with the subject in
hand; the whole service was to be in German, with the excep-

tion of the readings from the Torah and the Haftarah, which
were to be in Hebrew, to be accompanied, however, by a translation into the vernacular; the benediction preceding the reading
from the Torah, the benediction accompanying the blowing of
the Shofar, and the priestly benediction were to be recited in
Hebrew. A number of the paragraphs of the edict aimed at
overcoming the disorder in the house of worship; thus the
"Haman beating" on Purim as well as the beating of the breast
during the confession of sins on the Day of Atonement was
forbidden, likewise the selling of "mitzwot"; the frequent opening and closing of the ark on New Year's Day and the Day of
Atonement were to cease; the prayers *adonai elohe yisrael,
shomre yisrael,* and *kol nidre* were abolished; the Kaddish
prayer was to be spoken by the reader in German and repeated
quietly by the mourners.[122] The district rabbi of Saxe-Weimar was Dr. Mendel Hess, one of the most ardent, yes, one
of the most fanatical of the early reformers; it was undoubtedly due to him that these drastic provisions were included in
this "Judenordnung"; all opposition to this decree was crushed
by governmental aid; but the resentment aroused by the
attempt to enforce its enactment was so great among the Jewish congregations that it was not carried into effect till 1837.[123]
Hess was guilty of the same unpardonable offense as the orthodox party in Berlin, viz., the invoking of the police power of
the government in private religious concerns; he made the same
mistake as did so many reformers of this first generation;
instead of educating the people up to their ideas and founding
reform upon a philosophical basis, they aimed merely to establish certain improvements in the service; reform in this light
dealt merely with externals, while in reality it was a new interpretation of ceremonial Judaism.

In 1833 Joseph Abraham Friedländer, the chief rabbi of the
Duchy of Westphalia and the barony of Wittgenstein, introduced into the synagogue a number of reforms. The orthodox party preferred charges against him to the government on
the ground that he had tampered with the traditional ritual;
the accusation contained seventeen counts; this proceeding
gives an excellent idea of the status of affairs in those days
when such insignificant reforms as these were considered so
great breaches in the wall of tradition. The offenses of Friedländer as enumerated by his accusers were these: the singing
of the introductory Sabbath hymn, *lecho dodi,*[124] by the choir;

the responsive reading of the introductory Sabbath psalm, *mizmor shir l'yom hashabboth;* [126] the singing of *sh'ma yisrael* by the choir; the abolition of the section *bameh madliqin,* [126] and *ezehu m'qoman,* [127] the placing of a pulpit in the synagogue; the responsive reading of the *p'suqe d'zimrah;* [128] the singing of German hymns before and after the sermon; the abolition of the *n'ginah;* [129] the reading of the *haftarah* by the cantor instead of by some member of the congregation; the responsive reading of the *ub'nuchoh yomar* [130] and of the *Hallel;* [131] the choral-like singing of the *yigdal;* [132] the prohibition to remove the shoes and sit on the floor on *tish'a b'ab;* [133] the confirmation service. The government declined to entertain the charges on the ground that such points of internal administration were without its province and belonged to the jurisdiction of the congregation. The reforms continued to be observed.

This Joseph Abraham Friedländer is an interesting figure; he was one of the few older rabbis who espoused the reform cause, the reason for which action he gave in these words in 1842 when he was eighty-six years old:

> Thought cannot be checked. It progresses. Those who advocate the principle of progress in all other directions cannot possibly expect that in religious matters alone antiquated notions should rule. If we refuse to reform our faith in accordance with the culture of the time we will force an ever greater number of the present generation, yes, I may say, the majority of them, either to become hypocrites or to find their faith uncongenial. [134]

During these years of the interregnum, if I may so term it, between the activity of the first and second generation of reformers, *i.e.* between the collapse of the first reform movement in Berlin and the appearance on the scene of Geiger and his contemporaries, a period of some twelve years, although there was no agitation on a large scale and apathy seemed to have succeeded the strenuous labors of the earliest reformers, still was this only as a calm preceding the great struggles of the fifth decade of the nineteenth century that culminated in the rabbinical conferences of Brunswick, Frankfort, and Breslau in 1844, 1845, and 1846 and the formation of the Berlin reform congregation in 1845. True, various reforms had been introduced in a number of congregations in Germany, Austria, and France; but in most places the party of tradition held the official reins and the cleft between life and Judaism was growing wider and wider.

> The number of those who withdraw themselves completely from all participation in the religious services grows considerably from year to year, not because they do not experience the need of true religious edification, but because the services in the synagogue, as conducted at present, are not such as to meet this need.

Thus wrote an intelligent observer in Frankfort-on-the-Main in 1837.[135] This expressed the state of affairs throughout Germany, notably in the larger centers of population.

However, it was not alone the dissatisfaction with the service in the synagogue that gave evidence of the religious unrest among the Jews, but the entire attitude toward the state, toward life, toward the future, was different from what it had been in the days when the *Shulchan Aruk* was the *vade mecum* of the Jew. An indication of the usual condition of Jewish religious affairs at this time is presented in a document of the year 1835, an edict of the Bavarian government calling for assemblies of Jewish representatives, rabbis, teachers, and laymen in the various districts of the land to deliberate and arrive at decisions upon doctrinal, educational, and administrative matters; one of the reasons mentioned for issuing the edict is that there is no unanimity nor certainty among Jewish congregations as to what are the articles of faith; "there are differences as to the number and content of the fundamental principles; these differences exert a marked influence on the question of the civil position of the Jews." [136] This statement points undoubtedly to the difference in the attitude of the parties of tradition and reform on the question of the return to Palestine, since this involved the fundamental consideration as to whether the Jews still looked upon themselves as a nation or merely as a religious community whose members had no national hopes and aspirations other than those of their fellow citizens of other faiths. Such and similar basic differences were involved in the changed interpretation of which the reform movement was the expression.[137] The spirit of change was at work in many quarters, and this survey of the beginnings of the reform movement in Judaism can be closed no more effectively than by quoting an outburst occasioned by the dedication of a new temple in the city of Prague; this temple was dedicated on April 3, 1837, with choir, organ, German sermon, and the abolition of the *piyyutim*,[138] the *beth din*, consisting of the rabbis of the city, was present at the dedication; the editor of the *Allgemeine Zeitung des Judenthums*, the leading, in fact the only, Jewish newspaper of the time, was moved to supplement the report of this event with these words:

> Oh, the change! In the year 1819 the rabbinate of Prague anathematized every such innovation in the well-known book *Ele dibre habb'rith:*[139] thus mightily works the spirit of the age.[140]

CHAPTER II

THE condition of religious affairs in German Jewry in the fourth decade of the nineteenth century was far from encouraging; it must be confessed that the high hopes entertained by the founders of the reform movement that this would prove the panacea for all the ills from which Judaism was suffering had not been realized; the problem had not been solved; the conflict between traditional Judaism and modernism was as pronounced as ever. The Jews were divided into various parties which were characterized as follows in the year 1835 by one of the keenest observers:

> The one party wishes everything to remain as it is . . . ; no one shall presume to deprive them of anything which they have considered holy at any time; they mock at history, and all progress is monstrous in their eyes; they mock also at the true spirit which animates the synagogue, but they do not know this nor yet believe it, for proofs carry no weight with such. Then there is the other extreme. Because Judaism as constituted at present suffers from defects, therefore (think they) it should not exist at all; they would have it extirpated, and in its place would put an insignificant little tree which does not take root, nor blossom nor bear fruit. . . . And can you imagine even for a moment that such an unstable reed can take the place of the deeply rooted tree of the synagogue which furnished cooling shade and produced refreshing fruit for so many centuries? This tree has grown too rank, and possibly crooked, but prop it up, prune it, and it will do better. Has not the present age, which has caused you to adopt views so radically different from those of your fathers, also the power to make you conscious of the good in the past so that you destroy this not willfully? [1]

Between these two extremes there were many varying shades of opinion inclining more or less to the one or the other. The

waters were deeply troubled. The reformers had not grasped
the situation in its totality. They thought that a few synagogal
reforms were all that was necessary to solve the conflict between
rabbinical Judaism and the modern spirit, but they overlooked
the all-important fact that the public worship in the synagogue
has never been all of Judaism; they were influenced too much
by their Christian environment in this matter; in Protestantism,
and still more in Catholicism, the church service is the pivot on
which the whole system revolves; all religious acts are connected in one way or another with the ecclesiastical cult; important as the place of the synagogue and its services in Jewish life
had always been, yet did they not loom so large upon the
horizon of Judaism as did the church and its services upon the
horizon of Christianity; there were many religious acts and
customs which had no necessary connection with the synagogue
service, but were performed in the home, under the blue of
heaven, on a journey, or where not? Judaism is not so much a
churchgoing institution as a view of life: its teachings are concerned with the whole tangled web of existence; therefore by
laying all the stress of their activity upon the improvement of
the public worship the early reformers, notably of Westphalia,
Berlin, and Hamburg, betrayed their incompetency to deal with
the problem; the trouble lay too deep to be removed by the
introduction of a few liturgical changes and improvements;
the real task consisted in the adaptation of the ideas and ideals
of Judaism to the new circumstances wherein the people found
themselves in their new environment. The rising generation
was drifting further and further away. Religious affairs were
in a chaotic condition in many places: a number of congregations had no rabbi; since the death of Hirschl Levin in 1800
the congregation of Berlin, for example, had no rabbinical
chief; a rabbi of the old school was not appointed to the position because he did not understand the new situation, nor was
a younger man, graduated with the degree of doctor of philosophy from one of the universities, appointed, because many
feared that such were not imbued sufficiently with the traditional spirit. Yet, although the reform movement had not
brought thus far the healing to distracted Jewry that its advocates had expected confidently, still did this not minimize by
one jot the necessity for reform.[3] The first generation of
reformers had diagnosed the disease correctly, but they had not
found the proper remedy. The time had come for a more

thorough consideration of the problem. If those first reformers had not mastered the task they had undertaken, they had pointed the way at least. They were succeeded by a number of remarkable men, whose activity in the cause of reform began in the latter half of the fourth decade of the nineteenth century, and whom we distinguish as the second generation of reformers. These men, chief among whom were Abraham Geiger, Samuel Holdheim, David Einhorn, Ludwig Philippson, Leopold Stein, Samuel Hirsch, Abraham and Samuel Adler, Joseph Aub, and others, placed the reform movement on the sound basis of scholarly investigation, philosophical reasoning, and latter-day justification. The program of this second generation, under whose guidance and activity the reform movement entered upon a new phase, was well expressed by the greatest of their number, when he wrote:

> We are beyond the point of considering the salvation of Judaism dependent upon external embellishments (of the service) and of paying no attention whatsoever to the religious view-point and the religious life as a whole, on the plea that the entire religious life is a matter of private concern and touches the individual conscience; no, the question of the hour is this,—to determine what are the spirit and the teaching, the doctrines and the duties of life peculiar to Judaism and inherent in it.[3]

This was the new note struck by this new generation. Although they recognized the necessity of external reforms in the service, and advocated them, yet they gazed more deeply into the heart of the situation; for them this was only an incident, not the essence of reform; their purpose was to get at the root of the matter by research and investigation, to set forth the principles of Judaism, to establish the eternal validity of those principles, to express them in a manner consonant with the outlook of their generation, to distinguish between the permanent and the transitory elements, to bring Judaism into harmony with the changed conditions in which the people were placed in the new time—in a word to clothe the spirit of Judaism with a new form.

Active with tongue and pen, adept in ancient lore and modern learning, they grappled earnestly with the problem that confronted them. However, before giving a more or less detailed account of their thought and work, it is fitting to let them express themselves on the general aspect of the subject, with which their names will be identified for all times in the annals of Judaism:

> Reform means for us, changed, new appearance; a rejuvenated life, forms permeated and saturated with the spirit. The difficult and the easy, the whole and the part, are to receive meaning and significance, to uplift the spirit, and kindle the heart, in order that the religion may influence the entire view and course of life.[4]

>   .   .   .   .   .   .

> We wish to be, we should be children of our time, and as children of this age we must strive to realize for our contemporaries the true standpoint of Judaism, which has never been content to be a faith divorced from life or a practice at variance with belief.[5]

Thus wrote Geiger, and Holdheim expressed himself similarly:

> I shall attempt to answer the question why our time is so completely different in all its elements and requirements from those of rabbinical Judaism; but one of two alternatives is possible for the Jew, either to be a rabbinical Jew and live aloof from the age, or to live in the age and cease being a rabbinical Jew. The spirit of rabbinical Judaism is diametrically opposed to the spirit of our time. Rabbinical Judaism has converted into religious ideas and tendencies all the exclusive national ideas and tendencies of the Bible which were intended for entirely different conditions and circumstances, and has thereby given them eternal validity. The rabbis have perpetuated as religion the temporary part of Mosaism, the symbolism and particularism of the theocracy, and, on the other hand, they misconceived and neglected its eternal element, the ideal of universalism, which was in truth the real purpose of the theocracy. Hence the irreconcilable conflict between rabbinical Judaism and the spirit of the modern age.[6]

The matter was never put more clearly than in the response of David Einhorn to a Christian, who had written to him for information as to the meaning and purpose of the new movement in Judaism:

A thorough reform of Judaism based upon the immovable foundation stones of Mosaism, viz., monotheism and revealed religion, certainly finds full sanction within the bounds of Jewish ecclesiastical history. Nearly all modern Jewish theologians have made such a reform their program, and at the very outset have postulated by silent agreement the following two principles of procedure as demanded by the necessities of the case: first to unchain by the breath of the living spirit the forms that had become rigid and to make them fluid, and secondly to sift these forms according to their antiquity and essentiality, and in accordance with the results of such sifting to reduce their great number, beneath whose burden Judaism, without a doubt, is sighing and panting. The solution of the latter half of this program is dependent palpably upon that of the first half. First of all, the principle of sincerity as opposed to empty formalism had to be re-established on the basis of prophetical teaching, the religion had to be restored to its original purity, and the relation of doctrine to legislation had to be determined hereby, in order that it would be possible to distinguish the human, political, and temporal elements in Judaism from the divine, essential, and permanent.[7]

And as one further statement of the situation the words of the foremost organizing genius of the group of reformers, the editor of the *Allgemeine Zeitung des Judenthums,* may be reproduced:

We have devoted ourselves to and have acquired the culture which mankind has developed during the course of thousands of years; but Judaism has preserved its eternal divine content in forms, the most of which were the outcome of temporal conditions; they have therefore lived their day. This exterior must be re-fashioned, this form must be changed if Judaism is to continue to influence the lives of its followers in accordance with its purpose and its power, and if it is to persist among the world forces in a manner worthy of its high destiny.[8]

As is apparent from these utterances the situation was grasped clearly, but how was it to be met successfully? Here the second generation of reformers profited by the shortcomings of their

predecessors. Instead of directing all their energy to the introduction of external liturgical reforms, they determined to begin
at the foundation and work upward; their program was, to
establish reform on a scientific basis, to set forth clearly the
essential truths of Judaism, to let the light of investigation play
upon its principles, to investigate the validity of every doctrine
and every form, to determine which religious institutions had
outlived their usefulness, and were hindering rather than helping the religious life, which conduced to the furtherance of the
Jewish ideals, and which were in conflict with the modern spirit
and modern needs; [9] and then when scholarship had thus established the foundation and had separated the permanent from
the passing, the essential from the formal, the work of practical reform was to begin. It is apparent that here was a new
departure; there was to be no break between past and present;
the reform movement was shown to be justified, because there
had always been development in Judaism; investigation proved
that different forms arose in different ages, that Judaism in
separate lands adapted itself to conditions, that authorities of
aforetimes did not scruple to meet extraordinary situations by
extraordinary enactments, that the whole body of Jewish
observance is a product of the ages, that the liturgy of the
synagogue, its prayers, its benedictions, were the growth of
centuries. All this being established by a study of the sources
and by the insight into the conditions of the past, the logical
conclusion was that the present requirements could be satisfied
by such measures as the situation required, for life spelt
progressive development and standstill meant decay and death.[10]

The man who more than any other directed the reform movement into this channel was Abraham Geiger, born at Frankfort-
on-the-Main, May 24, 1810. Geiger possessed all the necessary
qualifications for such a task. He combined a thorough mastery
of the Jewish sources with a modern university education. His
erudition was profound, and his insight keen. When he was but
twenty-three years of age he published his doctor's dissertation,
What did Mohammed take from Judaism? [11]—a study which
evinced a splendid grasp of both Mohammedan and Jewish
sources, a study, too, whose value the lapse of time has not
diminished, for a new edition was issued almost seventy years
after the original publication (in 1902). In addition to his
special Jewish activities he found time to carry on investigations in the broader field of general Semitic learning, for con-

tributions from his pen appeared in learned periodicals, notably in the foremost Oriental publication of his day, the magazine of the German Oriental Society (*Zeitschrift der deutschen Morgenländischen Gesellschaft*). In him were joined great scholarship and practical activity, for he was preacher and student, reformer and scientific investigator, fighter for his political rights before the government, and keen solver of difficult literary problems. He was most ingenuous in his interpretation of difficult points of Biblical exegesis and of Jewish literature and history, as his *Urschrift der Bibel* and the many studies in the two magazines [12] he established, amply prove. His three series of lectures on Judaism and its history [13] show a fine philosophical grasp of the intent of Judaism from Biblical times; his epoch-making essay on the Pharisees and Sadducees [14] revolutionized the thought of the learned world on the significance of these two parties in Jewish antiquity. [15] The current ideas about these parties were founded particularly upon the notices in Josephus and the New Testament: the Pharisees were looked upon as the reactionary party among the Jews, the formalists, the religious hypocrites, slaves of the letter, enemies of the spirit; Geiger's researches into Jewish literature convinced him that quite the contrary was the case, that the Pharisees were the party of progress and the Pharisaic leaders or, in other words, the great rabbis and teachers from the second pre-Christian century onward, interpreting the law in a spirit required by the necessities of the people, protested against the assumptions of the Sadducees, the conservative party of the priestly and aristocratic classes.

Speaking broadly, it may be said that he viewed the whole story of Judaism from its very beginnings as an evolution; he claimed that the rabbinical party, who made the Talmud the final court of appeal in religious belief and practice misinterpreted Judaism, and he used the significant term, "*Talmud-Karaites*," when writing of them. The Talmudic period was only a phase in the development of Judaism; to base all doctrine and practice upon the Talmud through the *Shulchan Aruk* and to claim that this was the norm of authority for all future generations, was in its way Karaism as rank as any that the sect founded by Anan was guilty of. The term, however, was in reality a retort upon the rabbinical party, one of whose favorite charges against the reform movement, was that it was simply Karaism over again, that is, a renouncing of all tradition, and an acceptance of nothing as authoritative except the letter of the Bible. To Geiger and his coworkers, however, this did not apply; for them Judaism was an ever-developing faith; they accepted and even insisted upon the *principle of tradition,* but they refused to accede to the rabbinical claim that *all tradition was in the Talmud;* neither Bible nor Talmud, neither casuistics nor philosophy, neither commentaries nor codes, are the whole of Judaism, but are links in the century-long chain; they are aspects of Judaism, and the time had come for the age-old religion to assume a new aspect; life demanded it, the changed circumstances required it. Geiger presented this thesis in a hundred different ways. For him the reform movement was a necessary incident in the history of Judaism.

True, he was not altogether original in his claim that a study of the sources would prove that there had always been a living stream of thought-development in Judaism. As has been shown this had been the program of the short-lived "Society for the Science of Judaism" (*Verein für die Wissenschaft des Judenthums*),[16] as it had likewise been the thesis which Zunz had undertaken to prove in his *Gottesdienstliche Vorträge der Juden.*[17] But Geiger brought this theoretical program into conscious connection with practical effort, and thus made it a living issue; it became the starting point of the second chapter in the history of reform in Germany. Geiger was convinced firmly that by this procedure only would reform be able to take the place it should as the necessary and logical interpretation of Judaism in the changed conditions wherein the lives of its confessors were passed at this time.

> Judaism must receive its scientific foundation [he once wrote]; its truths must be clearly expressed, its principles must be probed, purified, established, even though they be not finally defined; the investigation into the justification and the authority of its sources and the knowledge of these are the constant object of study. Dependent upon this theoretical work is the practical purpose which keeps in view the needs of the community, at least of the German-Jewish community; from this union of the theoretical and the practical will flow the insight into what rules of life are necessary, and which institutions and religious practices will serve indeed to improve the religious life, which are moribund, and which are in such contradiction with

our needs and conditions as to preclude any further helpful influence from them, but the obstinate adherence to
which will lame strong and active purposes. This knowledge of the true significance of Jewish doctrine and of the
present must arouse to united effort all such as are sincerely interested, so that a transformation of Jewish religious practices in harmony with the changed point of view
of our time may result, and awaken true inner conviction
and noble religious activity.[18]

Imbued with these thoughts Geiger began his active work in
the cause of reform by establishing in 1835 the critical magazine already mentioned, his *Wissenschaftliche Zeitschrift für
jüdische Theologie;* this was to be the organ for the expression
of such views and for the publication of studies on Jewish
theology, history, and literature. The opening article from the
pen of the youthful editor (he was twenty-five years of age at
the time) is in a manner the declaration of the aim and purpose
of the magazine; it is entitled "The Judaism of our Time and
its Aims." Two brief extracts will set forth the trend of the
writer's thought.

Salvation lies not in the violent and reckless excision of
everything which has descended to us from the past, but in
the careful search into its deeper meaning, and in the aim
to continue to develop historically that which has grown
historically now that we have become organs of history,
checking here, helping forward there, following the wheel
of time here, forcibly putting our hand to its transformation there, and constantly furthering its development with
steadfast purpose.[19]

and a little further along he writes:

We need men who show that Judaism has become what
it is gradually, and who will not hesitate to demonstrate
by valid proofs against such as are biased in their views,
that much which is now believed and observed is not tradition, and cannot be established by a correct exegesis, but is
a product of a certain age, and can therefore be removed
by time.[20]

Geiger was rabbi in Wiesbaden at this time; he had already
taken his place as a leader, despite his youth; in him many

recognized the coming man who was to reconcile Judaism with the new life. It is interesting to note that just at the time that Geiger was beginning his work, which was to become devoted to the reform cause more and more pronouncedly with the passing of the years, another youthful savant made his appearance in the world of letters with a publication that denounced the reform movement and espoused the cause of rabbinical Judaism with positiveness and decision. Samson Raphael Hirsch, the rabbi of Oldenburg, published anonymously in 1836 his *Nineteen Letters of Ben Uziel,* in which he attempted to establish the thesis that every jot and tittle of the written and the oral law are of eternal validity. The letters were written ostensibly in answer to the questions and doubts of an inquirer, whose inherited traditional beliefs had been disturbed sadly by the spirit of the new age. The letters were regarded as a polemical utterance against the reform tendencies of the time, and aroused much attention and discussion. Rabbinism, as well as reform, had found its champion in a scholar, who combined modern learning with a thorough knowledge of Hebrew lore. Abraham Geiger and Samson Raphael Hirsch are the foremost names in the theological history of modern Judaism, as representing the two opposing streams of thought. Not even his bitterest opponents denied Hirsch's sincerity and the intense warmth of his religious nature; but in order to explain and to justify the ceremonies he resorted to a forced symbolism. He had no sympathy with the cry that there was a conflict between rabbinico-ceremonial Judaism and the life in the modern world; if there was such a conflict, life had to be conformed to traditional practice; [11] Hirsch's Judaism spelt antiquarianism and romanticism; in his opinion, the ceremonial and not the universal prophetic element was the main consideration; he stated his position broadly thus: "Every distinction between eternal and temporary, absolute and relative in religious affairs, is both false and conducive to falsehood." This statement expresses the irreconcilable conflict between rabbinism and reform, and basing upon utterances like this the reformer is unassailable in his contention that the rabbinical party must either observe every enactment and injunction contained in the rabbinical codes or else in honesty concede the correctness of the reform position. If the progress of time and the needs of life in these latter days have made impossible the observance of even one Talmudical or rabbinical enactment of unquestioned validity in the heyday of rabbinical Judaism, then the reform standpoint is justified. It is not a matter of quantity, but of universality in observance. Either the fourfold code has authority, or it has not. If it has, who shall distinguish between its ordinances as of greater or less validity? The reformer declares openly that the *Shulchan Aruk* has no binding authority; the rabbinist presumably accepts the code's authority and yet disregards many of its injunctions, as indeed he must, or life would be impossible in the modern environment.

The ceremonialism and legalism of rabbinical Judaism were an esoteric product. As long as Jewry was a close community without connection with the world this esoteric product might well pass muster as a satisfactory expression of the religious consciousness. But when Jewry put out feelers and began to share in the larger interests of the world, when the badge of exclusion was exchanged for the insignia of citizenship, when Judaism had to strive with the world's materialistic forces for the upper hand in shaping the life and thought of its followers, then truly rabbinism no longer proved a competent expression of the religious spirit; it did not maintain a harmony in the life of the Jew within and without the synagogue, nor did it satisfy the intellectual and spiritual aspiration of thousands. Reform sought to remedy this, and in the thought of Geiger, Holdheim, their contemporaries, and successors, it is more than a matter of disregarding rabbinical enactments, more than a system of pale negations. It represents a positive standpoint. If rabbinism stands for the esoteric system of custom and practice developed in Judaism while this was separated from the surrounding world, then reform is expressive of the broader development of the universal religious element in Judaism. The absolute conflict between rabbinism and the larger life, which the Jew entered after the dawn of the era of emancipation, bred that indifference to the religion which marked so many. Judaism had ceased to mean anything for them. In its rabbinical guise it was merely an echo of a past age. The point at issue was, are life and religion things apart? Judaism had always answered this question in the negative. Its guiding spirits had attempted always to establish a connection between the religion and every act of life; this in truth had been the purpose of that phase of the religion which we designate by the term rabbinism. But when the life of the Jews began to assume the larger sweep, rabbinism, as it had found definite expression in the fourfold code, was not equal to the task of religious guidance. It could not and would not burst its legalistic shell, and hence life and the religion drifted further and further apart in the new time, and thus there was violated the vital principle of their necessary and intimate connection; this principle it was the purpose and desire of reform to confirm in a changed environment, by interpreting the eternal verities of the religion in a manner that should appeal to a state of mind, thought, and belief as distant from the outlook of Jewish medievalism as is pole from pole. The reform movement then is not a religious freak, nor was it correctly described when its purpose was declared by its doughty antagonist to be "to take a standpoint outside of Judaism, to accept a conception derived from strangers of the purposes of human life and the object of liberty, and then in correspondence with this borrowed notion to cut, curtail, and obliterate the tenets and ordinances of Judaism." [22] It has its proper place in the development of Judaism as a religion, the prime article of whose practical endeavor has been from the very beginning to inform all of life with the religious spirit; it is in this sense that this movement is to be interpreted, viz., as the earnest effort to reconcile the life of the modern Jews with the religion, and to make the religion the living expression of latter-day aspirations. The fourth and fifth decades of the nineteenth century witnessed many practical efforts to give these ideas shape; it was a time of great religious activity, notably in Germany; the hosts of rabbinism and reform were pitted against each other as never before. The leading German-Jewish communities, such as Berlin, Breslau, Frankfort-on-the-Main, and Hamburg, were the scenes of notable conflicts between the parties; three rabbinical conferences gathered together the leading exponents of the teachings that passed under the name of reform: the agitation spread also to other lands, such as Hungary and England. The most notable of these episodes in the history of the reform movement must be detailed in order to give as complete a picture as may be of religious conditions in that "fermentation period" of Jewish life.

CHAPTER III

THE all-absorbing episode in German Jewish religious life
at the close of the fourth decade of the nineteenth century was
the strife engendered in the congregation of Breslau by the
election of Abraham Geiger as rabbinical colleague to S. A.
Tiktin, who had served in the capacity of rabbinical chief of
that community since the year 1821. Tiktin was a typical representative of the old school of rabbis. He interpreted his duties
to consist chiefly in the answering of ritual questions and in
the presiding over the rabbinical court (*Beth Din*), which still
had jurisdiction in such matters affecting Jewish life as the
granting of divorce, the giving of *Chalitzah*,[1] etc. He was
totally deaf to the voices of his generation. He was a survival
from a past age, and could not adapt himself to the new surroundings. The Jewish community of Breslau, like other congregations in the large cities of Germany, was no longer satisfied with the old condition of affairs. The desire was abroad
for a preacher, who, a child of the new age, would be able
to set forth the truths of the religion in the vernacular, to guide
and teach the young, many of whom were being repelled by
religious methods that were unintelligible and incomprehensible
to them, and to win back to the fold scores who had drifted
away, because the religious attitude of such leaders as Tiktin
was uncongenial to them. The latter-day generation was out
of sympathy with the official interpretation of Judaism, and
something had to be done to stem the tide of dissatisfaction
and indifferentism. The officials of the community therefore
determined to secure the services of some one of the new
school of rabbis, a man cognizant of the needs of his generation, in sympathy with the religious spirit of the time, capable
of preaching in the vernacular, able to superintend the religious
education of the young by methods in consonance with the
standards obtaining in the new world wherein the Jews were
now living, and at the same time an adept in rabbinical lore

and thoroughly familiar with the traditional duties of the rabbinical office. In a word, official demand was made by a large
Jewish congregation in Germany for a rabbi who was to combine a modern scientific university training and pulpit eloquence
with Jewish learning and rabbinical knowledge.* A number of
names were considered, but the choice fell upon Geiger. His
views were well known; he had declared his religious standpoint clearly, viz., that the requirements of the age had to be
met, that the Talmud was not an infallible authority, that the
rites and ceremonies of the religion had to be subjected to
research, and if found to be subversive of the spirit of true religion rather than helpful, to be changed or discarded; ceremonies
that furthered the religious life in one generation might be a
drawback to another; he even quoted the Talmud in support
of this, adducing the Talmudical dicta that only such religious
enactments are valid as are adopted by all Israel or as are recon-
cilable with the demands of life;* he did not then object to
ceremonies as such, but to the abuse of ceremonialism; he had
given public expression to these thoughts frequently. However,
he felt that though the individual might entertain these ideas,
yet as a member of the House of Israel he must observe what
had traditional sanction until an authorized body had declared
its validity at an end; therefore, while still at Wiesbaden, he
had issued a call for a rabbinical conference (the first call of
its kind) for the consideration of the problems that were vexing
the Jewish communities, and for the adoption of such practical
measures, and bringing into being such practical institutions,
as might meet the necessities of modern Jewry. This conference
will be discussed in its proper place. He was thus thoroughly
alive to the situation. After six years of service in Wiesbaden
he found himself cramped in his activity and unable to influence the communities of Nassau, the country whereof Wiesbaden was the capital, as he wished; he therefore determined to
resign and return to his birthplace, Frankfort-on-the-Main;
shortly after this the announcement of the Breslau congregation calling for applications for the rabbinical post appeared;
he was induced to preach there on July 21, 1838; five days
thereafter he was elected to fill the position.

A wretched campaign of petty personalities and worse began
to be waged against him at once. One of the most distressing
features in this Geiger-Tiktin affair, as in all similar controversies between the rabbinical and the reform parties at this

time, was the introduction of personalities and the employment
of any measures whatsoever to discredit the opposition. In the
controversy in question it was the Tiktin party that was guilty
of these tactics. They called into play every imaginable device
to fortify their own position and to prevent the accession of
Geiger to his new office. The first gun in the campaign was fired
from Wiesbaden. A communication dated from that place
appeared in the columns of the *Allgemeine Zeitung des Judenthums,* which stated that Geiger had been forced to leave Wiesbaden because of certain religious irregularities, such as the
desecration of the Sabbath and the like. I mention this dis-
agreeable incident in order to give a place to the wise words
uttered in connection therewith by the famous champion of
Jewish emancipation in Germany, Dr. Gabriel Riesser. In addition to a communication from the officers of the congregation
of Wiesbaden contradicting the calumnious report, a letter was
written by Riesser in defense of Geiger. In this letter the great
Jewish statesman gave utterance to some general statements
that throw light upon the situation. He wrote:

> May those who represent advanced views bear in mind
> that true wisdom is always joined with mildness, that
> malice never converts the erring but strengthens him in his
> attitude, and that it is very unfitting to combat error (so
> long as this does not assume the aspect of injustice) with
> the weapons of hatred. But may those others who do
> battle for traditional opinions recognize that personal per-
> secution, intrigue, and calumny have as their own result
> the dishonoring and shaming of the cause they mean to
> serve.*

The second step was taken by the Breslau opposition; before
Geiger could assume the position to which he had been elected
it was necessary for him to receive his naturalization papers
as a citizen of Prussia. Four members of the congregation
petitioned the government to refuse this; they charged that the
election was not regular; the government sustained the officials
of the congregation who had elected the candidate by a vote of
fifty-six to one; the opposition thereupon accused Geiger of
being an innovator, and quoted the various governmental edicts
of former years forbidding innovations in the Jewish service;
in vain: the government seemed to have passed beyond the
stage of petty interference with the private affairs of Jewish

congregations, as was apparent from the answer to the final great effort of the opposition. They memorialized the government in a detailed statement in which Geiger was charged with holding views completely and thoroughly opposed to the rabbinical standpoint. Politics, whether civic or religious, make strange bedfellows. The protagonists of the orthodox rabbinical party of Breslau besought the aid of a notoriously lax Jew, Joel Jacobi (who, in fact, was converted to Catholicism shortly thereafter), in the preparation of the document which they desired to present to the government. The Minister of Public Worship submitted portions of this document to Geiger, who had settled in Berlin while these negotiations were pending, for answer. His answer was so satisfactory that the government declared the election valid, and granted him his naturalization papers on December 6, 1839, fifteen months after his opponents had inaugurated the campaign against him. His persistence had won the victory; during his residence in Berlin he left no stone unturned; he kept the matter constantly before the government officials, and was justified of his course in the end.[5]

His political status assured, he returned to Breslau and delivered his inaugural sermon on January 4, 1840, in which he sounded the keynote of his thought in these words:

> Judaism is not a finished tale; there is much in its present form that must be changed or abolished; it can assume a better and higher position in the world only if it will rejuvenate itself; all should unite in this work.[6]

He gave practical earnest of his thought by untiring activity in the cause; he preached in the vernacular, instituted classes for the instruction of the young, delivered lectures on Jewish history and literature, and continued his literary work. All this, too, in spite of the fact that the opposition toiled unremittingly to undermine his position. Tiktin, as a matter of course, refused to recognize him as a colleague. The old rabbi was fully consistent in this; for him Judaism meant the unquestioning observance of every Talmudical injunction no matter how absurd or impossible; for him, too, the time element in religious development did not exist; whatever was prescribed was sacred; to remove one stone from the Talmudical foundation whereon rabbinical Judaism rested meant for him the endangering of the safety of the whole edifice. Hence anyone who denied the validity of each and any Talmudical enactment, stood without the pale of Judaism. His standpoint and that of Geiger who denied such inviolability to Talmudical legislation was irreconcilable. The two interpretations of Judaism were thus brought face to face in practical life as they had never been before. The vital question embodied in the conflict attracted the attention of all Jewry; the agitation in the Breslau congregation assumed far more than local importance; a great principle was at stake; stripped of all side issues the situation narrowed itself down to the one all-important and significant point as to whether a man who examined the institutions of Judaism critically, and announced his honest conclusions as to their development and their present validity could hold the rabbinical office; in other words, whether freedom of thought and research could go hand in hand with the exercise of rabbinical functions. Tiktin and his sympathizers maintained that the whole system of rabbinical tradition was sacred and not to be desecrated by the profane touch of investigation; what the former generations had prescribed was of eternal sanction and authority; as he put it tersely, "Whoever disregards any command or prohibition of the Talmud must be considered an unbeliever and as standing without the pale of Judaism, and is therefore an untrustworthy witness." [7] Hence the occupant of the rabbinical office must suppress all desire for historical, critical, and scientific study of the rabbinical literature; [8] he must approach it not as an investigator but as a blind partisan; this was the sheerest obscurantism; the last refuge of intrenched authority is to deny the right of inquiry into the sources of such authority; the doctrine of infallibility is the logical outcome of this obscurantism, but, much as the Tiktins, the Egers, the Bernays, and their fellows declared for Talmudic and rabbinic infallibility they were bound to come to grief, for they were in conflict with the spirit of Judaism which had always permitted the widest freedom of thought.

The situation in the congregation was becoming intolerable. Rabbinical jurisdiction was suspended practically because of Tiktin's persistent refusal to bow to the will of the congregation. Geiger continued in the even tenor of his way; his opponents gave vent to their spite in a number of unseemly acts, undignified incidents in the controversy which are best passed over in silence. [9] The officers of the congregation, in their desire to relieve the situation, suggested that Geiger be merely the preacher and not the rabbi of the congregation. This

separation of the office into two parts as a solution of the difficulty was resorted to by a number of congregations in those
days, as Vienna, Prague, and somewhat later, Berlin. It implied
the recognition of an old and a new Judaism, the old represented
by the rabbi, a strict rabbinist of the Tiktin type and the new
by a young man of modern education. The rabbinical and the
homiletic functions were thus kept absolutely distinct. The
rabbi presided over the *Beth Din,* and was supreme in all
matters of ritual; the preacher delivered sermons in the vernacular and conducted the educational activities of the congregation. Geiger refused to be a party to any such compromise.
He claimed that the division of Judaism into two parts, the
one quick and the other dead, which this arrangement presupposed, harmed the religion incalculably in the estimation of
its own followers. It made the formation of two parties
inevitable, the one, following the leadership of the rabbi, must
look upon the preacher as an unbeliever, while the other, adher-
ing to the preacher, would consider the rabbi an ignorant
obscurantist; such states of mind must lead without fail to a
schism in fact as well as in thought, and Judaism would be in a
sorrier condition in the end than it had been at the beginning.
No, the spiritual guide of the congregation must combine within
himself both functions; in him past and present must meet;
such an artificial distinction was purely opportunistic; if such a
division of functions were sanctioned how could the continuity
of historical Judaism ever be impressed upon the present generation? [10] Geiger was undoubtedly right in this position, and
he contributed greatly toward a correct appreciation of the
situation by his firm and immovable stand. If the new conditions in Jewry, arising from the civil and educational emancipation, demanded a readjustment all along the line of Jewish
life and thought, then the real leaders would be men, who, thoroughly versed in the lore of the past, were at the same time of
the present; the breach between the traditionalists and the
moderns could be healed only if the people had ocular evidence
of the fact of the continuity of Judaism in the attainments and
activity of the rabbi-preacher, the meeting-point of the two
streams, tradition and modern culture, that would have to
coalesce were Judaism to be a living force in the modern time
and under the new conditions. Only a keen mind like Geiger's
could pierce to the heart of this matter which involved really
the whole question as to whether Judaism was a religion that

could adapt itself to the changing needs of successive generations or a closed system without capability of development.
If the former, then the separation of the functions of the office
was justified, and the rabbi, the representative of the principle
of fixedness, was the true leader, while the preacher was simply
the representative of a latter-day fad superimposed upon Judaism. If the latter, then such a separation was invalid, for the
functions of the preacher were simply the modern expression
of the rabbi's duties.[11] Hence, although in the Jewish annals
of the time some men are designated rabbi and others preacher,
showing that this artificial distinction was sanctioned and
officially recognized in some places, we cannot but feel that
Geiger was correct in his attitude and had the true conception.

Here then was an *impasse*. Tiktin would not consent to serve
with his newly elected colleague, and Geiger would not agree
to the separation of the functions. The relations became so
strained that the governing body of the congregation was
forced to suspend Tiktin from office. In order to fortify himself in the position he had taken, Tiktin had addressed various
rabbis of Upper Silesia for an expression of opinion. He
obtained responses from the rabbis (all of the olden school)
of Posen, Lissa, Beuthen, Lubinitz, Nicolai, Ratibor, Myslovitz,
Rybnick, Guttentag, Rosenberg, and Landsberg, all of whom,
as was to be expected, upheld him in the stand he had taken;
nine of their number addressed the administrative body of the
congregation directly. In June, 1842, Tiktin published a
pamphlet entitled *Darstellung des Sachverhältnisses in seiner
hiesigen Rabbinatsangelegenheit* wherein he presented his side
of the case; he included in this the response of Solomon Eger,
rabbi of Posen, the response of the rabbinate of Lissa, and the
address of the nine rabbis. This was an appeal to the larger
Jewish world, and the controversy passed beyond the local
stage. Tiktin and his colleagues stated their position clearly and
unmistakably. They read Geiger and all who thought as he did
out of Judaism. They declared the plenary inspiration of the
Talmud a dogma of Judaism. They denied the right of freedom of thought and investigation as far as any traditional
form, custom, or ceremony that was observed in Israel was
concerned. Never before had these things been so apodictically
stated. The issue was now clear. According to these rabbis
Judaism was a fixed and immutable system. Every minor law
codified in the *Shulchan Aruk* was of equal validity with any

religious command of the Bible; such a law as ordered a married woman to conceal her natural hair beneath a wig had equal sanction with the Ten Commandments. Absurd as this seems when thus baldly stated, it is really the standpoint of rabbinical Judaism as appears from the statements of Geiger's opponents. The chief rabbi of Posen, Solomon Eger, declared that:

> Only he can be considered a conforming Jew who believes that the divine law book, the Torah, together with all the interpretations and explanations found in the Talmud, was given by God himself to Moses on Mt. Sinai to be delivered to the Jews and to be observed by them for ever; further, Moses delivered the oral and written law revealed to him to his successor Joshua, Joshua to the so-called *Zekenim* (elders), these to the prophets, and the prophets to the men of the Great Assembly. These oral divine traditions are the very same as, collected in the Talmud, we are commanded to obey. He, however, who departs from these paths, who believes in the authenticity of the written law alone as divinely given, but considers the interpretation of this written law as Talmudically ordained and prescribed a purely human work, subject to changes, is not to be considered an Israelite, but belongs to the sect of Karaites, who separated themselves from the Jewish as well as the Christian religion.[12]

This dogma was stated even more explicitly by the rabbinate of Lissa:

> All commandments and prohibitions contained in the books of Moses, and that, too, in the form that they have received by Talmudical interpretation, are of divine origin, binding for all time upon the Jews, and not one of these commandments or prohibitions, be its character what it may, can ever be abolished or modified by any human authority.[13]

These statements represent the standpoint of Tiktin and his confreres, and basing upon this interpretation of what is authoritative in Judaism, Tiktin accused the governing board of the congregation of having

> selected a *dayan* in disregard of and opposition to the religious convictions of well-nigh the entire congregation as

well as of the traditional Judaism of a thousand years'
standing; a *dayan* who in spoken and written discourse
denies unreservedly the authoritative validity of this traditional Judaism and whose call and mission appear to be
to extirpate it root and branch for all time!

The position could be stated no more strongly and definitely
than thus. These men acted and wrote according to their light.
Holding the convictions that he did Tiktin could not have done
otherwise, and although the petty persecution and the childish
petulance which he and his party indulged in are inexcusable, yet
he can not but be respected for the firm stand which he took
in support of his beliefs. However narrow, bigoted, and fanatic
he and his partisans may be considered to have been, it may not
be forgotten that he and they believed sincerely that Geiger
and the reformers were undermining Judaism. The fact of the
matter was, however, that Geiger was misrepresented somewhat in the statement of Tiktin which has been quoted above.
He had declared openly and clearly that the same man could
and should separate his rabbinical from his literary activity,
i.e. a rabbi might as a critical student declare against the propriety and validity of some or many practices in Judaism, and
yet he must observe them in his practical activity as rabbi until
they be changed or abolished by the concerted opinion or action
of competent leaders and authorities. Thus the rabbi as student
in his investigations into the origin and significance of the
Mosaic institution of *chalitzah* (release from levirate marriage), might be persuaded that this act is out of place under
modern conditions, and yet in his official capacity he must countenance it until the religious authorities of the generation
declare that the act is to be no longer performed among Jews.
The individual rabbi might hold and promulgate the most
advanced and radical views on the significance of traditional
doctrines and practices, but in the conduct of his office he must
conform to tradition so long as a competent and recognized
authoritative body had not legislated otherwise. In other words,
liberality of thought and investigation and orthodoxy in practice could be combined in one and the same person. The truth
of the matter is, however, that the spirit of the age worked
silently, and many a rabbinical enactment and many a practice
of aforetimes went by the board simply because they had
become impossible under the changed circumstances in which

the people lived. Therefore hundreds of the injunctions which constituted the body of rabbinical observance up to the nineteenth century passed out of Jewish life without special enactment by any authority, for the simple reason that they had lost all meaning. Life legislated them out of existence. The spirit of the age was indeed the new revelation.

But to return to our narrative. The governing board of the Breslau congregation was put on the defensive by the manifesto issued by Tiktin and his party; they were accused of having subverted the traditions of Judaism by their act of electing a rabbi whose explanation of the religion was different from the orthodox interpretation. There was, however, a much farther-reaching point involved. The rabbis of Posen, Lissa, and Upper Silesia had declared that the whole body of Talmudical and rabbinical legislation was inviolable; to doubt its eternal validity was heresy; they had read out of Judaism any one who denied the dogma of Talmudical infallibility; hence they practically denied freedom of thought. This was vital. Were free thinking and free investigation compatible with the rabbinical office or no? was the rabbi simply an interpreter of what the past had handed down, or was he permitted to flood each and any institution and doctrine with the light of investigation? was it true that Judaism had ever denied freedom of thought? The officials of the congregation determined to submit these all-important questions to recognized leaders of thought in Jewry. They stated the point at issue well and clearly in the address which they presented to these leaders. They wrote thus:

> The question to be decided is whether progress is possible in Judaism or whether strict fixedness is commanded; whether the great number of our co-religionists, who entertain opinions about the value and validity of Talmudical enactments different from those held in former centuries, may still claim the name Jew or are to be considered unbelievers; whether Jewish theology can endure scientific treatment and free investigation or whether the traditional views which are at variance with all culture may not be touched, nay, not even examined; and whether a man who champions openly and strives eagerly to spread a free, scientific, Jewish-theological conviction is entitled to occupy the rabbinical office or is unfitted for it. Tiktin has empha-

sized these points with unmistakable clearness, and has declared most positively the non-permissibility of any progress; the impossibility of even the slightest change; Eger (of Posen) has even stated that any one who deviates from the Talmudical interpretation of Biblical commands must be considered an unbeliever and a renegade from the House of Israel.

Such being the state of affairs, they felt themselves called upon to obtain expressions of opinion on these points from men of standing and authority. They received a number of important responses which they published as a reply to Tiktin's *Darstellung* in two volumes in September, 1842, and March, 1843, under the title *Rabbinical Responses on the Compatibility of Free Investigation with the Exercise of Rabbinical Functions.*[14] The first volume contained the responses of the Rabbis Joseph Abraham Friedländer of Brilon, Aaron Chorin of Arad, Samuel Holdheim of Schwerin, B. Wechsler of Oldenburg, Abraham Kohn of Hohenems, S. Herxheimer of Bernburg, David Einhorn of Hoppstädten, M. Hess of Stadt Lengsfeld, M. Gutmann of Redwitz, and M. Wassermann of Mühringen; the second volume included the responses of the Rabbis B. Levi of Giessen, Joseph Aub of Baireuth, Joseph Kahn of Trier, Joseph Maier of Stuttgart, L. Adler of Kissinben, Leopold Stein of Burgkunstadt, and E. Grünebaum of Landau.[15] This was the most important publication that had yet appeared in this agitated religious period, more important indeed than a similar collection of responses published a short time previously by the officers of the Hamburg congregation on the subject of the new edition of their prayer-book,[16] for these responses called forth by the Geiger-Tiktin affair really covered the whole field of the justification of reforms in Judaism. Because of this it is necessary and profitable to quote characteristic and telling paragraphs from these responses, for they express well the tendencies of the religious thought of the time.

Joseph Abraham Friedländer, rabbi of Westphalia, one of the few older rabbis who appreciated that a new era had arisen for Israel and that a reformation was imperative if Judaism was to be something more than a lifeless survival from a past age,[17] wrote:

Mishnah and Talmud were not delivered to Moses on Sinai, but are a collection of interpretations of the law

dating from a later age. They have no eternal obligatory
authority. The ancient sages and interpreters did not
desire to prevent later generations from modifying their
decisions in accordance with the changed needs and circumstances of their age, nor even from adding to or subtract-
ing from them; on the contrary, they laid down the most
widely differing subjective interpretations in order that
every one might be able to choose whatever view appealed
most to him.[18]

The reason for obeying the commands and ceremonies
is always given (Exod. xii. 17; Lev. xxvi. 43). The
teachers of all ages have done likewise; they investigated
thoroughly the reasons for all enactments. And for this
reason, the Israelites of aforetimes reformed the ritual as
often as they considered it necessary, and changed conditions have not diminished in the least this right to reform
for modern Jews.[19]

The rabbis followed to the utmost consequences the principle
הוראת שעה היתה "it was a need of the hour." Thus we read
in the Talmud that a certain man who rode an ass on the
Sabbath was condemned to death by a *Beth Din*. The court
was reminded that such a penalty was not prescribed in the Law
for this offense. The court answered, "the time demands it,
for there are too many violators of the Sabbath." [20]

Aaron Chorin, the aged rabbi of Arad in Hungary, who at
this time was seventy-six years of age, was the most celebrated
of the older rabbis among the progressists.[21] He had suffered
persecution for his reform tendencies and activities. He urged
particularly the convening of a synod which should decree the
necessary reforms and place the stamp of authority upon them.
He had broken many a lance in the cause of progress in a number of well-known writings.[22] He cited in his response many
instances from the Talmud and the rabbinical writings in support of his position. He stated as a general principle the
following:

It must be confessed that customs, laws, and ceremonies
are so absolutely necessary for every religious community
that its existence is almost unthinkable without them. But,
on the other hand, it is not only repellent to human nature,
but inconsistent with the dignity and sublimity of the
divine will, that any ceremonies connected with the reli-

gious services, ritual observances, or ascetic institutions should be considered binding and unchangeable for all times and places under all changing conditions and circumstances.[23]

He exclaims impatiently in a note:

I do not know whether I ought to consider the statement of the rabbis (quoted by Tiktin in his *Darstellung*) to the effect that any divergence from a Talmudical opinion is absolutely forbidden as involuntary delusion or intentional blindness. Why, the greater part of the Talmud is merely an aggregate of contradictory and conflicting opinions; and we are to consider all this as divine revelation, dispassionate criticism of which lays one open to excommunication![24]

It is a principle of Jewish tradition that every sanhedrin has the duty to uphold the religion (לחזק הדת) for its day and generation, and in order to further the welfare of the community (מפני תקון העולם) it shall not only simply cling to the dry letter of the law, but be guided by its spirit, and bind and loosen according to the needs of the age, even as Maimonides says (*Mamrim*, II, 4), "every *Beth Din*, even though it fall behind its predecessor in knowledge and in numbers, is warranted to abrogate for an indefinite time the ordinances of that preceding *Beth Din*; for the ordinances of a *Beth Din* cannot possibly be of greater authority than those of the Torah, which also are suspended indefinitely, because this is necessary for the maintenance of our faith."[25]

And he declares, in direct reference to the case at issue:

It is absolutely against the spirit of our holy religion to either condemn or excommunicate a rabbi because of individual views or opinions concerning the temporary forms of our faith. In as far as his activity furthers that higher religious and moral tendency, which is the chief object of our faith, he is deserving of that appreciation and respect which ought never to be withheld from him who strives to be true to the duties of the holiest vocation, and who perseveres courageously despite all the obstacles placed in his path.[26]

Samuel Holdheim, second in importance only to Geiger in the history of the movement for reform in Judaism, wrote a lengthy response, in which he discussed thoroughly the true significance of tradition in Judaism. Because of Holdheim's great importance as a leader in the reform movement, space must be given here to a brief characterization of his life and thought. He represents the interesting evolution from extreme orthodoxy to radical reform. Born in Kempen in the province of Posen in 1806, he received a thorough Talmudical education, and became an adept in Talmudical dialectics. His great Talmudical attainments were supplemented by modern philosophical and literary culture acquired in the universities of Prague and Berlin. He was appointed rabbi of the congregation of Frankfort on the Oder in 1836, and almost at once became a leading figure in the Jewish religious world. He espoused the cause of reform in sermon and pamphlet, pointing out the distinction between the temporary and the eternal in religion, between the "perishable shell" and the "everlasting kernel" of divine truth. He became chief rabbi of Mecklenburg-Schwerin in 1840. In an answer to an anonymous assailant who had attacked the new edition of the Hamburg Prayer-Book issued in 1841, he made his position on the significance of tradition and the Talmud very clear. He believed with Geiger in the principle of tradition but not in the infallibility of the Talmud as an authority; the Talmud is the product of many centuries and of many minds, and the most divergent opinions are to be found in it; he claimed that to demand unquestioned acceptance of every expression of every rabbi was to confuse things human and divine. His chief contribution toward a solution of the vexing problems of his day was his book published in 1843, *Autonomy of the Rabbis and the Principle of the Jewish Marriage Laws.*[27] The direct cause for the writing of this book lay in the peculiar state of affairs in Mecklenburg touching marriage and inheritance among the Jews; these were regulated according to Talmudical legislation, and there were frequent difficulties. Holdheim advanced the thesis that the laws of the state and not Talmudic legislation should regulate these things. An additional incentive to action on his part at this time arose from the circumstance that the Prussian government was contemplating an Act of Incorporation for its Jewish subjects; by this Act the Jews were to be incorporated into separate communities of their own, apart from their fellow citizens. Hold-

heim contended against this with all his might. He urged that
the Jews were no longer aliens but natives, and did not desire
a separate incorporation. The contemplated legislation would
be a decided step backward from the law of 1812, which had
declared the Jews to be distinct in their religion only.[28] The
modern life of the Jew demanded three things: first, that the
autonomy of the rabbis must cease; secondly, that religious
affairs must be separated from civil and political issues; and
thirdly, that marriage is a civil act according to the teachings of
Judaism. In other words, he insisted that Jewish nationality
had come to an end long ago, and that the Jews are as all other
citizens in all national and civic functions, and are distinct only
in their purely religious concerns.

As time went on Holdheim grew more and more radical in
his views. He was elected rabbi of the newly organized reform
congregation of Berlin in 1846; in his book, *The Principles of
Reformed Judaism*, published in 1847, he develops at length
the thought of the permanent elements in Judaism as contrasted
with the transitory. His radicalism of thought found practical
expression in such extreme steps as declaring valid marriages
between Jews and such as hold the monotheistic belief, and the
introduction of services on Sunday. The barest outline of his
thought has been sketched here because his views on the many
subjects involved in the religious controversies of the period
will be given throughout these pages.[29] He went to much
greater lengths in the practical application of his ideas than did
Geiger, who, radical as he was in thought, remained more conservative in practice than did his great contemporary. Holdheim discarded altogether in his practice as in his thought the
particularistic features that characterized traditional Judaism;
his purpose was to teach the universal in religion as it had
found expression in Jewish thought; in his campaign against
the excesses of Talmudic formalism, he made the serious error
of quite underestimating the place of ceremony in the religious
life. However, the service that he performed in setting forth
clearly and unequivocally the philosophy of the reform movement is invaluable; his pamphlets, books, and sermons are a
treasure trove of high thoughts on the eternal realities and permanent verities of the Jewish faith. In his response on the
Geiger-Tiktin affair he treated particularly the question of the
place of tradition in Judaism. He contended that the duty of
the Jew in this matter was to believe in the principle of tradi-

tion as exemplified in the Talmud, but not in the Talmud as such nor in the utterances of the rabbis of ancient times as such. He speaks of this principle of tradition as "the principle of eternal youth, the principle of continuity, constant development and growth out of the primitive germs which God himself placed in Scripture." After adducing many instances showing that even in times agone the great lights of Jewish learning had laid no claim to authority for their decisions without giving Scriptural warrant for them, and that they therefore never arrogated to themselves more than human power, he continues:

> If then the rabbis never assumed a higher authority than they had a right to as men, and took no step without giving the reasons which justified them in taking this step, a later generation can certainly not be prevented from examining by earnest investigation the validity of this justification, in order to learn whether their authority, which was rightfully respected at one time, has not ceased, and whether a later age has not an equal right to determine what is absolutely necessary for its welfare and to satisfy its religious needs in a suitable manner. . . . The spirit remains the same although the times change. The genius that moved and enlivened the old world of the rabbis moves and enlivens us also. It is the same striving to develop our ancient faith continually and to rescue it from destruction.[30]

> Had the rabbis lived in our times [he says further on] and become imbued with their tendencies in an equal degree, as they did with the tendencies of their own age, they would have explained the Bible in a different manner. Their interpretation, then, is naught else but a product of the religious point of view of their time.[31]

B. Wechsler, rabbi in Oldenburg, whose name figures frequently in Jewish publications of this period, and who played a prominent part in the religious activities connected with the forward movement, put this pertinent query:

> Who would deny to Judaism the capacity for development which is in truth its by nature, because, forsooth, our coreligionists sought their salvation in the ages of oppression and persecution by holding fast anxiously to past tradition, especially since even in those troublous times the need of the age sometimes forced them to take a pro-

gressive step, as witness the pronouncements of Rabbenu Gershom [32] against polygamy and the levirate marriage, etc.[33]

On the point at issue as to the compatibility of freedom of investigation with the exercise of the rabbinical office, he says clearly:

> Jewish theology not only sanctions scientific method and free research, it even insists on them; they are indispensable. If light is to break in upon the chaotic confusion of opinions and views, if proper limits are to be set to the caprice of subjective interpretation and explanation in the religious province as well as to the useless reference to ambiguous authorities—scientific method alone will accomplish this. But all minor considerations and circumstances aside, that system of theology is not deserving the name . . . which answers the thinker with edicts of excommunication and with persecution instead of with reasons; in pursuing such a course our religion would depart from the way of intelligence and enter the desert of witless sanctity founded upon works, whereas Moses and the prophets insist continually on an intelligent grasp and recognition of those things that constitute Judaism.[34]

Abraham Kohn,[35] rabbi of Hoherems in Tirol, summed up his thoughts in a number of paragraphs, in the first of which he contended that the institutions of the Jewish faith are not unchangeable, and illustrated this statement by pointing out the various stages that the public worship had passed through. He then continued:

> The statutes of rabbinical Judaism, despite their manifoldness and their particularity, were never applied so strictly as to overlook the demands of life (in its broader scope); in truth one of its main principles is "that man may live through them (Lev. xviii. 5) and not die through them." From this we learn, says Maimonides (*Hil. Sab.*, II, 3), that the commandments of the Torah were intended to bring into the world not revenge (inconsiderate severity), but mercy, consideration, and peace; and Scripture says of such heretics as declare an act done to save a human life to be a desecration of the Sabbath: "I gave them also

statutes which were not good and judgments whereby they should not live" (Ezek. xx. 25). Now, the Jews of our century in Europe find themselves living under entirely new conditions, such as could not be imagined in a former day, and for which no provision could be made; analogies must be sought, and, in accordance with them, such alleviations as were granted in exceptional cases must be permitted, not in order that we may make our life more convenient, but in order that we may fulfill our duties to ourselves and our new surroundings the better without breaking with our religion.[36]

He diagnosed the religious situation thus:

There is a fatal split among Jews, first, because religious tenets and institutions have been kept forcibly on the level of a vanished era, and not permeated with the divine breath of refreshing life, while life itself hurried forward stormily; and, secondly, because the religious leaders, lacking all knowledge of the world and of men, dreamed of other times and conditions, and held themselves aloof from the life of the new generation—hence resulted a superficial rationalism, inimical to all positive and historical faith, side by side with a rigid, unreasoning formalism. On the other hand, only good can follow from the recent endeavors to rejuvenate the religious forms and to re-establish the requisite harmony between life and the faith; the formation of a new sect [37] is to be feared all the less since appreciable differences in the ritual as well as in religious customs have always existed side by side in rabbinical Judaism.[38]

Solomon Herxheimer, rabbi in Bernburg for over fifty years,[39] and known particularly for his translation of the Bible into German and for his splendid work in the cause of the religious education of the young, declared without circumlocution that

the same need and the same justification which led the teachers of the synagogue of former days to make changes exist in a greater degree than ever to-day; if our modern rabbis do not, like those of former times, make the changes required by European conditions, our co-religionists will take the initiative themselves and, even as daily experience shows, will renounce one rabbinical and Mosaic command after another, and pass gradually into indifference and unbelief;[40]

and he locks horns with the rabbinate of Lissa in no unmistakable manner, by stating

that they prove their assertions by no manner of means.

On the other hand, in rebuttal of their position, he refers to the dictum of Maimonides (*Hil. Mamrin,* II), that every *Beth Din* must abrogate even Mosaic commands if this be necessary for the preservation of the religion in the light of the needs of the time. אפילו דברי תורה יש לכל בית דין לעקרו הוראת שעה Even the ultra-conservative Isserles says in his response (תשובות רמ"א כ"א) :

But if anything arise that the former teachers knew not or were not called upon to decide, then surely a change is as necessary as any alteration mentioned in the Talmud; for the reason that the former authorities had not the present condition in mind when they introduced the custom.

Many examples may be cited to prove that Biblical or Talmudical statutes have been modified or abrogated at various times, *e.g.* the abrogation of the levirate marriage, the modification of the Mosaic law commanding the cancellation of debts in the Sabbatical year (פרוזבול),[41] the permission to use oil purchased from a heathen, etc.[42]

David Einhorn, one of the finest thinkers among the Jewish leaders, was just beginning a career that was characterized by fervid enthusiasm in the cause of reform. Both in Germany and America he did yeoman's work for the furtherance of the movement he had so much at heart. A clear writer and a great preacher, he stands easily among the foremost. The correct attitude toward the Talmud has probably never been stated better than in the few words which he wrote in his response:

Such an infallibility, such an apotheosis (as Tiktin and his supporters claim) we cannot and we may not grant to the Talmud; however strong our belief in its veracity may be, we must refuse and reject such deification; we address the Talmud in these words, "Israel believes thee, but not in thee; thou art a medium through which the divine may be reached, but thou art not divine." [48]

And in reference to the abolition of the ceremonies, which was after all the great issue between the two parties in Judaism, he says:

> The departure from ceremonial laws, which is the result neither of caprice nor frivolity but the outcome of the honest conviction that such departure is in keeping with the spirit of Judaism and is a pressing demand of its natural development, does not unfit a man for holding the rabbinical office. Naturally such departure may not be merely a matter of fashion or convenience, and may have nothing in common with the forcible introduction of un-Jewish points of view into the province of Judaism, nor with mere subjectivity, nor, in short, with a sort of antipathy to inherited conditions; it must be, however, the product of a deep, honest, unprejudiced investigation into the sacred sources, of a pious earnestness, a glowing enthusiasm, and finally of a ripe conclusion arrived at after weighing all causes and effects in company with other competent men, zealous for God and religion. Then will such a departure be not a condemnable but a highly commendable act, the like of which took place frequently in Talmudical and post-Talmudical times (see Talm. Bab. *Jeb.* 39b, 90b; *Sotah,* 48 a, etc.). [44]

Moses Gutmann, rabbi in Redwitz, analyzed the situation very clearly when he wrote:

> If ever the Talmudical application of the Biblical sentence עת לעשות ליי הפרו תורתך (Ps. cxix. 126) "it is time to work for the Lord, they disregard thy law," seemed necessary, this is the case in our days. One must either close one's eyes intentionally in order not to see, or must transport himself into the dark days of the past when stupor and death lamed every aspiration among the Jews, and thus be out of all touch with the life and activity of the present, if one fails to recognize the great changes which have been taking place for more than a generation in the religious convictions of our co-religionists, and which are growing day by day. . . . The number of those who

cannot acknowledge as divine commands the innumerable laws which have been deduced by the rabbis of later centuries is increasing constantly. In addition, life and the state make far different demands upon the Jew to-day than was the case formerly. . . . Sufficient to say, a conflict exists between the traditional interpretation of the faith, and the life and convictions of a great number of Jews, and a remedy is immediately and absolutely necessary, if the breach is not to grow and in the end become incurable.[45]

Joseph Aub, rabbi in Baireuth at this time but later in Berlin, called attention to the inevitable result of the practical acceptance of the thesis of the opponents of Geiger:

The consecrated and the consecrating spirit, not the dead and killing letter, is to be preserved. Karaism holds fast to the letter of the Torah. Will it prove less injurious to hold fast to the letter of the Talmud than to that of Sacred Writ? Hence one is almost tempted to cast the reproach of Karaism upon those who charge with it such of their colleagues as do not shun scientific investigation. Let them do away with the weapons of damning and heresy-hunting which are foreign to Judaism, and pursue the method of peaceful refutation and explanation. No sensible persons can be frightened, nor any intelligent court be deceived by the cries of deism or atheism which the obscurantists raise at every deliverance of science. It is possible to stand firmly on the basis of positive Judaism without swearing unswerving allegiance to Talmudism.[46]

In the same vein Joseph Maier, ecclesiastical counselor (Kirchenrath) and rabbi in Stuttgart, expressed himself:

As far as I am concerned personally, I state openly and above board that I consider the subordination of the reason to the authority of any person to be idolatry as pronounced as that of blind heathenism. For where lies the difference if I bow the knee before a lifeless image of wood or stone or worship as divine the dead letter of a Rabbi Aqiba, a Rabbi Tarfon, etc.? Yet up to the time of the rabbinate of Lissa no teacher in Israel demanded such blind subjection to the pronouncements of the Talmudists; in truth, the foremost teachers of the synagogue recognize the right of the reason to investigate the whole content of religion; yea, they deem it to be the duty of the Israelites to make the teachings and truths of religion a matter of conviction by means of thought and research (see Bachya, Introduction to *Chobot hal-l'babot,* Saadia in his *Emunot wedeot,* Elia del Medigo in his *Bechinat ha-Dat,* etc.).[47]

As the closing extract from this important collection the words of Leopold Stein, rabbi in Burgkunstadt, Bavaria, later in Frankfort-on-the-Main, who became one of the striking personalities in Jewish life in the nineteenth century, may be quoted.

We feel [he wrote] that Israel also is likely to suffer from the throes of the present age, and from the pangs of mankind struggling for better things; and just as little as we doubt the success of the latter, even so do we trust with unshakable confidence in God that lasting peace will ensue from the contests now being waged in Israel, and that our holy faith will issue from the struggle purified and clarified. Our hope lies in the future, our zealous striving in the present. This zeal, however, must go hand in hand with rational insight and calm weighing of conditions. The friends of progress, in whose ranks I gladly enroll myself, may not forget, in their eagerness to reach the goal, to tread the path of moderation, which alone can lead to success. They must consider constantly whether they do not harm their cause more than they benefit it by their words and deeds, and they may never leave out of account the great number of their co-religionists who think differently, and to instruct whom must be one of their prime objects. The conservatives, on the other hand, against whom are arrayed all the signs of an agitated, progressive age, must beware especially of blind fanaticism and harsh condemnation of such of their co-religionists as think differently from them, lest they alienate these still more, and our religious community, which in fundamentals is one as yet, be divided into irreconcilable factions by mischievous and irremediable methods.[48]

The decisive answer of so many respected Jewish leaders, to the effect that freedom of thought and investigation was compatible with the occupancy of the rabbinical office, and that Judaism had never sanctioned the fettering of the intellect, as Tiktin and his sympathizers demanded, was indeed a conspicuous signpost in the march of religious progress. The governing board of the Breslau congregation felt itself justified in the steps it had taken. In August, 1842, the members of the congregation presented an address to Geiger, in which they denounced the tactics of his opponents, and expressed their appreciation of his work as a teacher of real Judaism (*echtes Judenthum*).[49] He was confirmed in his position from many sides. Still the bitterness of the opposition was not assuaged. The death of Tiktin, in March, 1843, might have put an end to the unfortunate state of affairs, had not a governmental decision, delivered a short time before, declared his suspension by the officers of the congregation invalid. This inspired his party with new hope, inasmuch as they counted now on the support of the government. The certainty that Geiger would be elected chief rabbi, the position that Tiktin had filled, caused the opposition to take the decided step of withdrawing from the congregation and resolving to form a new congregation. The government was appealed to by the officers of the congregation, and, although unwilling at first to meddle any further in the affairs of the Jewish community, still it was forced to take a hand, as the only effective way of settling the dispute, which waxed more unpleasant from day to day. On October 26, 1844, the government issued a rescript, in which it declared that Geiger was the chief rabbi, that a second rabbi was to be elected, and that there should be no split in the congregation; the rescript continued:

> We serve notice that the Government cannot interfere in the controversies of the Jews concerning their ritual; it is incumbent upon them to come to some agreement as to what they consider necessary and proper for the furtherance of the spirit of their religious affairs.[50]

The opposition protested, it is true; they had elected Tiktin's son as rabbi in his place, but they had to submit at last to the government's decision. Twenty-one years previously the Prussian government had stopped all changes in the ritual by declaring that no innovation of any kind was permitted; now, by stating that the Jewish congregations themselves had to regulate their own internal affairs, it implied the right of the congregations to govern themselves as they would, and hence to make whatever internal changes they considered necessary. The outcome of the Geiger-Tiktin controversy was a decided gain for the cause of progress; it resulted in the open discomfiture of the party of obscurantism, and in a triumphant vindication of the essentially Jewish doctrine of liberty of thought and research.

CHAPTER IV

THE HAMBURG TEMPLE PRAYER-BOOK CONTROVERSY

WHILE the Geiger-Tiktin affair was at its height another struggle between the two wings of Jewish thought was waged in a locality that had been a field of battle in this conflict some years previously. In the year 1841 the Hamburg Temple became a storm center once again. In the twenty-three years that had elapsed since its organization this congregation had maintained itself as a distinct association. After the exciting incidents attending its formation [1] the congregation had been left in comparative peace and had been less in the public gaze. In November, 1841, however, a keen and competent observer, Dr. Samuel Holdheim, who had attended the services at the Temple, published an account of his impressions. [2] He declared unreservedly that "the temple is undeniably the most important incident in the history of culture in Judaism," and stated that it stood for the purely religious idea as opposed to the nationalistic and that its great service consisted in giving practical demonstration of the fact that Judaism is capable of progress and development. A number of events conspired together just about this time to direct pronounced attention, once again, to this pioneer reform congregation. It had grown greatly in membership so that it was found necessary to enlarge its place of worship. The two decades which had passed from the time it had been called into being had witnessed a development of thought among the reformers, and therefore it was found expedient to revise the prayer-book used by the congregation and to issue it in a new edition. As in 1818 the prayer-book of the congregation had aroused the opposition of the rabbis of the old school and had caused the first decided clash between the rabbinical and the reform parties, so in 1841 it was again the prayer-book in its revised form which became the bone of contention. Before entering into a detailed account of this, however, it is necessary to indicate briefly the changes wrought in various localities during the years bounded by the two occurrences wherein this congregation occupied the center of the stage of Jewish attention. In 1818 when the Hamburg congregation was formed, not one established congregation in Europe had been touched by the modern spirit; in 1841 when the new edition of its prayer-book appeared, this modern spirit had made its influence felt in many quarters with more or less pronounced results. There can, in truth, be no doubt that the spirit of progress which was embodied in the Hamburg congregation was at work in many places, and although no other congregation had labeled itself "reformed," still was the influence of the new learning and culture thrown into the scale for religious reforms of some sort. The program adopted by the Vienna congregation in 1826 became the model for many other congregations; this program included German sermons, music by selected choir, decorum in the service; the Viennese congregation owed its great influence to the two men who stood at its head, Isaac Noa Mannheimer, the illustrious preacher, and Solomon Sulzer, the celebrated cantor. Although not a reform congregation in any sense when judged by changes in doctrine or in the content of the prayers, yet its program seemed to satisfy the religious needs of such as desired to see the body of tradition clothed in a garb acceptable to the modern age.[3] This Vienna program was adopted by congregations in Bohemia,[4] Hungary,[5] Wurtemberg,[6] the Palatinate;[7] also by the congregations of Amsterdam,[8] Copenhagen,[9] Munich,[10] Mayence,[11] Bernburg,[12] Karlsruhe,[13] Bingen,[14] and other places.

Governmental edicts touching this matter of Jewish customs and services also indicate the tendencies of the period; in 1835 Alexius Frederick Christian, the Duke of Anhalt, issued a set of instructions to the chief rabbi of the duchy, in which this official was bidden take steps to "remove all abuses which had crept into the synagogue and all non-essentials which, on the one hand, obscure the true Mosaic religion and morality, and, on the other, lead to contentions in the house of worship and in the congregation."[15] The thirty-second article of the decree of 1837, regulating the affairs of the Jews of the kingdom of Hanover, ordered that "a sermon in German be delivered on every Sabbath and holiday by the rabbi or such other functionary as may be at the head of synagogal affairs."[16] In Baden a decree of 1838 demanded the introduction of chorals into the service of the synagogues;[17] this had been commanded as early as 1824 [18] but had not been respected; the reiterated decree was obeyed. The shifting attitude of the Bavarian government in this matter of Jewish reforms is interesting; in 1834 some Jews of Baireuth lodged complaint with the government against the rabbis who had eliminated from the liturgy certain prayers, which according to their opinion expressed no longer the true aspirations of the modern worshiper. The government sided with the rabbis, but decreed at the same time that such individuals as desired to pray these prayers at home privately could do so; [19] in 1835, in the month of November, the government issued a decree calling for assemblies of Jewish representatives in all the districts of the country to discuss and to determine upon all points of belief and practice concerning which there were decided differences of opinion among Jews. In accordance with this decree a number of these district synods were held, one of which declared that the belief in the coming of the Messiah is to be taken in the spiritual, not the political sense, that the Jews do not expect a return to Palestine nor the reëstablishment of the Jewish state; the synod, therefore, resolved to remove from the prayer-book all passages petitioning for the coming of the Messiah and the return to Palestine; [20] this decree of 1835 seemed to be animated by the liberal spirit, as was also the governmental edict of 1838, issued to the congregations of Middle Franconia; [21] however, an edict of October 23, 1838 (repeated December 31, 1839), indicates that the orthodox party had gained the ear of the government, for this edict declares that the king desires the appointment of rabbis who are thoroughly cultured but who are at the same time strict adherents "of all genuine Mosaic doctrines and ceremonies, and who discountenance all destructive neology." [22] This same reactionary attitude on the part of the government appears in a decree of July 22, 1840, which forbids the continued observance of the ceremony of confirmation which had been introduced by Dr. Löwi, the rabbi of Fuerth. [23]

A decree promulgated in the Duchy of Saxe-Meiningen, in December, 1839, comprising instructions to the district rabbis is interesting; it commands these rabbis to conduct the services in accordance with the essentials of the Mosaic religion and the needs of the time, to remove from the public services and the religious instruction everything which is unessential and objectionable. The fifth paragraph orders that a German sermon be

delivered every two weeks, and the eighth paragraph instructs
the rabbi to promote the improvement of the services in all the
congregations of his district, to remove abuses, to have more
and more of the prayers read in German, to establish choirs, to
have the prayers and the Pentateuchal readings pronounced in
a dignified manner in place of the traditional sing-song, and to
abolish the selling of the *mitzwot*. The decree also commanded
the conducting of the confirmation ceremony yearly.[24] On the
other hand Prussia had reënforced the decree of 1823, forbidding any changes or innovations in the Jewish service, by
two subsequent decrees of May 25, 1829, and October 25, 1836.

Thus the currents moved to and fro. The Jewish communities were being constantly stirred by the agitations. A
striking instance of how widespread the movements against the
old order were is offered by a remarkable address issued by
fifty-four Jews of Wilna in September, 1840, to their coreligionists in Russian Poland; this document urged improvements
in the religious condition of the Jews and declared that the evils
were superinduced by three causes; first, the incompetency of
the rabbis and teachers who were for the most part ignorant,
"understood no intelligible language, possessed no scientific
training, were absolutely inexperienced in worldly matters . . .
made no efforts to improve manners and morals, to spread true
enlightenment, to incline their people to participate in the general welfare of the community or to impress upon them the
necessity for the pursuit of industrial and agricultural pursuits"; secondly, the neglect of the instruction of the young,
and thirdly, the superstitions and the divisions caused by the
Sabbatian and Chassidaic movements. These evils, they
declared, could be remedied only by the foundation of a rabbinical seminary where rabbis would receive a scientific Jewish
education combined with secular learning;[25] in the meantime
"let German rabbis who are versed in the Talmud and in
branches of secular knowledge be elected as district rabbis and
teach the religion in its purity . . . ; let these rabbis form a
consistory with its seat in the place where the seminary is
located, this consistory to conduct all religious and congregational affairs, regulate the public worship,"[26] etc. Although
religious reform as such is not mentioned in this address yet
it testifies to the longing for changes and improvements even in
such communities as have been supposed by many not to have
been affected in any way by the modern spirit.

Two remarkable contemporaneous individual utterances are indicative of the character of the period under consideration. In a *lettre pastorale*,[27] addressed in 1835 to the rabbis and the faithful in his district, Arnaud Aron, the newly elected *grand rabbin* of the Strassburg consistory, used the following language after speaking of such as contemn and disregard their ancestral faith:

> Avoid the course of those other Israelites whose blind faith poisons the present generation with another serious evil no less disastrous in its results. Refusing for themselves all higher culture, at whose door they lay all blame for the ills of unbelief, they remain sunk in the lethargy of moral disintegration. Deaf to the cry of the progressive enlightenment of humanity they never cease to bow their head beneath the yoke of abasement, clinging obstinately, at the same time, to the prejudices which, in their eyes, are the only stay of the religion of their fathers.[28]

And the author of the famous Tsarphati letters [28] wrote in 1836:

> Let us observe the Sabbath, the feast of the creation, but let us change the day; let us keep the divine covenant, let us change the manner; let us emancipate woman, she is part of human kind. Let us preserve our collections of prayers, the magnificent songs of the Psalmist, but let us change the idiom; let us introduce successively Protestant preaching, the Catholic organ, the harmonies of the Meyerbeers, the Halevis.[29]

After this somewhat hurried survey of the changes effected in Jewish religious practice and thought during the interim of twenty-three years between the publication of the first and second edition of the Hamburg Prayer-Book, we return to the interrupted narrative. The passing of the years had made it evident that the first edition of the book could not be considered final; when this first edition was well-nigh exhausted, the directory of the Temple appointed a commission, in April, 1839, consisting of the two rabbis, Drs. Gotthold Salomon and Eduard Kley, and three members of the congregation, Dr. M. Fränkel, M. I. Bresselau and M. Wolfson, to revise the prayer-book in view of the new edition which was to be issued, it being provided that "the principle of revision shall conform to that spirit of contemporary progress which has ruled in our house of worship up to this time." The resignation of Dr. Kley as rabbi of the Temple caused his withdrawal from the commission and the appointment of his successor, Dr. Naphtali Frankfurter, in his stead and the vacancy caused by the death of M. I. Bresselau, the secretary of the congregation, was filled by his successor, M. M. Haarbleicher. The commission was instructed to revise the prayer-book but not to prepare an entirely new ritual. The commission was guided by the following four principles:

1. The prayer-book, which aims to be the expression of a religious community that rests on a positive historical foundation, must not only uplift and edify the spirit of the worshiper, as does every prayer-book, but it must indicate that positive foundation in its peculiarity as it appears in doctrine and history.

2. Spirit and heart must be addressed in a manner as compatible as possible with the modern status of European culture and views of life.

3. The existing and traditionally received material is to be retained preferentially, as long as it does not controvert the requirements indicated above.

4. The entire content of the prayer-book, as well as of the whole service, must be permeated with the pure teaching of our ancestral religion; whatsoever opposes this must be removed.[30]

The commission was guided too much by the spirit of compromise; as was the case with the first edition of the prayer-book, so also in the revision there were no fixed guiding principles; in defense of their course the commission claimed that "had they been truly and fully consistent they would have had a book true to principle, but they would have had no congregation; even in the most favorable case their congregation would have become entirely isolated from the rest of the Jewish community"; therefore they took the middle course and avoided extremes.

Still, despite this, their expectation was not fulfilled. The book appeared about the same time that the Temple, owing to the growth of the membership, was enlarged. For twenty years the congregation had grown and prospered and comparative peace had reigned between it and the orthodox community. These two events, however, the new addition to the Temple and the new edition of the prayer-book, stirred the latent opposition into flame, and were the signals for the new agitation which caused this congregation to occupy the central place in the religious life of German Jewry a second time and stamped it as the particular representative of the reform cause. The ecclesiastical chief of the orthodox community, the so-called *Chakam,* Isaac Bernays, issued a public notice (מודעה) warning all Israelites not to use this book and declaring that anyone who did so did not perform his duty as a Jew. This document appeared on October 16, 1841, two months after the publication of the prayer-book. It was promulgated far and wide and the Temple authorities found it necessary to answer it; on October 21 they published the following declaration, which was signed by J. Warendorff, temporary president, Dr. G. Riesser,[31] Dr. M. Fränkel, and E. J. Jonas:

> Since Mr. Isaac Bernays has deemed it proper to declare in the local synagogues that our prayer-book violates the fundamental principles of the Jewish religion, the directorate of the new temple association, after due consultation with its preachers, considers it incumbent upon itself to declare, both to the members of our association and to all who attend our services:
> 1. Mr. Isaac Bernays has no authority, as far as our organization is concerned, to condemn us publicly as he has; hence this condemnation is to be spurned as unseemly.
> 2. A malicious, intentional disregard of the contents of the prayer-book is apparent in the judgment given; the accusations moreover evince the densest ignorance of all theologico-liturgical knowledge.
> 3. Therefore such a proceeding can affect in nowise the members of the Temple Society who recognize in it only the expression of powerless partisanship; they regret it, because the seed of discord has been sown in the congregation in so wanton a manner and because the cloak of religion has been used to cover such a course.

Still this statement did not end the controversy; indeed it proved only the beginning. True, by an order of the Senate of Hamburg, of January 12, 1842, Bernays' מודעה was removed from the synagogues; the Temple authorities had removed their counter-declaration some time before. In place of the מודעה the Chakam substituted a Caution (אזהרה) : "it is forbidden to pray the obligatory prayers and benedictions from the book which appeared here during the past year entitled 'Prayers for Israelites.' " The public notice and the Caution of Chakam Bernays attracted such widespread attention that the directorate of the Temple considered it necessary to obtain the opinions of recognized Jewish theological authorities on the question as to whether the prayer-book justified the condemnation of the Chakam as being a non-Jewish prayer-book, implied in his statement that any one using it did not perform his duty as an Israelite; they obtained responses from twelve well-known rabbis: J. Aub of Baireuth, J. L. Auerbach of Leipzig, A. Chorin of Arad, J. A. Friedländer of Brilon, Abraham Geiger of Breslau, M. Gutmann of Redwitz, S. Holdheim of Mecklenburg-Schwerin, A. Kohn of Hohenems, J. Maier of Stuttgart, I. N. Mannheimer of Vienna, L. Philippson of Magdeburg, and L. Stein of Burgkunstadt. The two rabbis of the Temple, Drs. G. Salomon[32] and N. Frankfurter,[33] had expressed their views in separate publications shortly before. In the preface to the volume containing these responses, the directorate, through their spokesman, Dr. M. Fränkel, stated:

> Twelve theological opinions are more than sufficient to outweigh two ungrounded declarations and to prove their instability. Time has passed judgment on the rabbis of 1819. Had we desired we could have increased the number, if we had wished to address all Jewish theologians who combine piety with a free scientific spirit. The directorate of the temple wished to exclude no worthy rabbi; they addressed a certain number of theologians known to them with the hope that others would voluntarily join the number.

The twelve opinions were preceded by an introduction in two parts written by Dr. Fränkel; the first part giving the history of the controversy and the second being a disquisition on the Temple Society, its reason for existence, its place in the religious life of the day and its relation to Judaism at large.[34]

One of the chief charges advanced against the prayer-book was that it denied leading Jewish doctrines, notably the doctrines of the Messiah, the bodily resurrection and the eventual redemption of Israel by the restoration to the land of Palestine.

Dr. Salomon, the rabbi of the Temple, at once published an essay, "The New Prayer-Book and its Persecution," wherein he defended the orthodoxy of the book and cited accredited authorities with whose opinions the book was in perfect accord. On one point, however, he was forced to acknowledge the correctness of the charges, and that was in reference to the Messianic belief. The traditional belief was in the coming of the personal Messiah; the view expressed in the prayer-book was the hope for the coming of the Messianic time without any reference to Palestine and without the reinstitution of the sacrificial cult; this change of view necessitated certain alterations in the traditional form of the prayers; these alterations consisted for the most part in the elimination of those expressions which indicated these beliefs and hopes. However, even here vacillation was apparent; some prayers were retained which should have been struck out had the compilers of the book been truly consistent. Thus, on the one hand, they omitted such supplications as the following in the Mussaf of the holidays: "Gather together our dispersed from the four corners of the earth and assemble our exiled from the uttermost parts thereof and restore us with exultation to thy city Zion and to Jerusalem thy holy house, with everlasting joy," etc.; also this, "Build thy house as aforetimes and establish thy temple firmly and let us see its erection and gladden us with its restoration and bring back the priests to their ministrations, the Levites to their songs, the Israelites to their homes; thither will we pilgrim and appear before thee and prostrate ourselves on the three high feasts." The omission of such supplications seemed to indicate clearly the position of the congregation on this question of the return to Palestine, the reinstitution of the sacrifices, the rebuilding of the Temple, and the restoration of the Jewish state. They seemed to declare that they had repudiated Israel's nationalistic hopes and had given a purely spiritual interpretation to the Messianic idea, taking it in its universal meaning as the Messianic era of peace and justice. On the other hand, however, a number of the nationalistic prayers which supplicated for the coming of a personal Messiah and the rebuilding of the Temple of Jerusalem were retained; for example, "let our eyes see thy return to Zion in mercy," and the prayer "that God take pity on his sanctuary, rebuild it speedily and increase its glory." Here was a manifest inconsistency; it looked like an attempt at compromise; on the one hand, the desire of the Jews to be considered citizens of the land in which they dwelt necessitated the repudiation of the belief in Palestine as their homeland; on the other, the anxiety to remain in good repute as part and parcel of the whole community of Israel caused them to retain certain prayers which petitioned for the return of God to Zion. The compilers of the book felt this to be inconsistent, and Dr. Salomon in his defense attempted to explain it away by declaring that the Temple congregation did believe in the restoration, but "it does not believe that the restoration is conditioned by the bodily personal presence of each and every Israelite in the land of Palestine. We can desire with all our hearts the reëstablishment of an unfortunate fatherland, can even make supplication to God for this, and become enthusiastic for the idea; and together with this we can remain in the land wherein Divine Providence has placed us, continue to live there and obey, serve, and give allegiance to its ruling powers." He instances the fact that many Jews remained in Babylon at the time of the return from the Babylonian exile. This explanation does not explain; it is a begging of the question. But one of two positions is possible in this matter, either the belief that the Jews everywhere are in a state of exile and will remain in this state until God in his own time will put an end to the exile and restore them to Palestine under the leadership of a personal Messiah, or the belief that the dispersion of the Jews over the world is providential, that nationally they are not distinct and have no national hopes other than those of their fellow citizens of other faiths, that the future of Judaism is to find its consummation not in the reëstablishment of the Jewish state but in the fulfillment of the prophetic visions of universal peace and the universal acceptance of the unity of God. The one conception considers the repossession of Palestine the crowning of Israel's career, the other claims that Israel's early life in Palestine was for the preparation for its larger work in all parts of the world during the dispersion.

In his statement concerning the preparation of the prayerbook Dr. Fränkel, one of the compilers, pleaded guilty to the charge of inconsistency, but excused the commission on the ground that thoroughgoing consistency would have involved complete severance from the Jewish community at large; this they desired to avoid and therefore they sailed the middle course; the result proved disappointing; the orthodox chiefs condemned the book for its changes and emendations and declared it heretical, while, on the other hand, the congregation lost the opportunity of standing as a true leader, championing those new ideas for a bold and uncompromising declaration of which thousands were waiting. Instead of trying to justify their position as reformers the Temple authorities were anxious to prove the acceptability of the prayer-book even from the traditional standpoint. The Hamburg congregation indicated the possibilities of a strong concerted movement, but it did not become what it might have been, the leader of such a mighty forward work. It obtained the opinions declaring the validity of its prayer-book even from the traditional Jewish standpoint, and continued a single, isolated, separatist congregation. It never advanced beyond the standpoint it took at the start; it had great possibilities but did not realize them; the formation of the congregation was a great achievement, its members were content to rest on these laurels; the birth-throes seemed to have exhausted their energies.[35]

All the opinions published in the collection *Theological Opinions on the Prayer-Book of the New Israelitish Temple Society in Hamburg* [36] condemned Bernays' attitude toward the prayer-book without reservation. They all declared in different ways that the prayer-book conformed completely with the spirit of Judaism, and that anyone who prayed from it performed his full duty as an Israelite. It is not necesary to quote these opinions at length or even in an abbreviated form, although they present an interesting array of facts and opinions on the very important question of the liturgy. It will be sufficient to reproduce here two of these opinions representative of the radical and conservative wings of Jewish thought, viz., the opinions of Samuel Holdheim, the radical, and Isaac Noa Mannheimer, the conservative.

Immediately upon the appearance of the prayer-book Holdheim had published a review of it in pamphlet form, with the title *The Prayer-Book of the New Israelitish Temple in Hamburg.* [37] In this he declared that the prayer-book was entirely satisfactory and could be used in any Jewish congregation because it disparaged no historical truth, no essential doctrine of Judaism, no tradition of the synagogue, no universally acknowledged rabbinical nor any positive Biblical law. It steered the middle course and satisfied the progressive as well as the conservative party. Somewhat later he felt called upon to write a second pamphlet in defense of the Temple and its prayer-book, entitled, *Heresy Hunting and Liberty of Conscience. A Second Vote* [38] in answer to a violent anonymous attack *Jew and non-Jew. An answer to the Writings of the Triple Alliance.* [39] The triple alliance referred to was Holdheim and the two preachers of the Temple, Salomon and Frankfurter, all three of whom had issued publications in defense of the prayer-book. [40]

In his opinion, published in the collection, [41] Holdheim averred that the book contained no changes from the traditional ritual that are subversive of the spirit of Judaism; the changes are only such as are necessitated by the development of the universal conception of Judaism out of the national; this change was given point to even in ancient times by the establishment of the synagogues as houses of prayer to take the place of the Temple at Jerusalem, the national religious center. As for the spiritual interpretation which the authors of the prayer-book give to the Messianic belief, as contrasted with the personal and as affecting all mankind and not Israel alone, they deserve our thanks. They have accentuated the prophetic interpretation of the doctrine; they have succeeded in combining the traditional Jewish spirit with the universal teaching which is the finest flower of prophetic Judaism, and they have done well in eliminating from the prayer-book all those elements which are incompatible with the pristine teaching of the synagogue and with the spirit of modern culture.

Mannheimer, [42] the celebrated Viennese preacher, a man of a decidedly conservative bent, declared that the permission to use the vernacular in place of the Hebrew as the language of prayer was indisputable even from the Talmudico-rabbinical standpoint. The excision, changing, or recasting of the *piyyutim* and *selichot,* is the prerogative of every congregation. It can be proven easily that the inclusion of the *piyyutim* in the ritual was disputed with much greater justice than is their exclusion to-day.

A number of prayers were simply the individual expressions of their authors and were never intended to have lasting validity and authority. Such are the late והוא רחום, the penitential prayer for Mondays and Thursdays, the so-called יהי רצון, the long drawn out confession of sins (על חטא) in the ritual of the Day of Atonement; such and others like them can be either

abbreviated or abolished without sinning against the rules of
the ritual.

He goes on to say:

> Although I usually plead for historical continuity and
> tradition yet I cannot but agree with the stand taken by
> the authors of the book in the matter of the omission of
> the prayers for the reinstitution of the sacrifices; they have
> merely expressed what all modern enlightened theologians
> think, even such as cling with all their heart to the inher-
> ited traditions and forms; I am one of those who do not
> rationalize the Messianic belief; I believe in and defend
> the national interpretation of this dogma and hope for a
> national restoration, yet I am free to confess openly that
> the reinstitution of the bloody sacrificial ritual does not
> form part and parcel of these hopes and promises; see the
> many expressions of the prophets, the sages, and notably
> Maimonides, who declares that the sacrifices were intended
> only for the child-period of Israel's development. . . .
>
> If Bernays had contented himself with warning his own
> followers and all such as cling to the traditional ritual
> against the use of this prayer-book no one could have
> objected. But decided protest must be entered against the
> animus wherewith he attacks an honorable congregation
> that has pursued the highest ideals for the past twenty-two
> years; such bigotry and one-sidedness cannot be con-
> demned too strongly; the less that the rabbis of the school
> of Bernays have taken to heart the need of remodeling
> the service, and the more that they have viewed with indif-
> ference the estrangement of thousands from the house of
> God, the less right have they to pretend to be zealous in
> the cause of God as over against such as have taken active
> steps to stem the tide of indifference and reclaim those
> who have drifted away.

One other opinion must be mentioned although it did not
appear in the collection published by the Temple authorities,
namely that [43] of Zacharias Frankel, chief rabbi of Dresden.
Frankel, one of the foremost Jewish scholars and rabbis of the
time, became known as the leading exponent of what he termed
"positive historical Judaism"; he claimed to occupy the middle
position between the reformers and the party of strict tradition.

He condemned the action of Bernays, as he would any presumptuous attempt on the part of constituted authority to interfere with the spirit of progress. To his mind the prayer-book was open to criticism because the compilers had not been guided by any strict principle of procedure; they had exercised an unauthorized eclecticism in the omission and retention of prayers. He breaks a lance with the "templeites" on the Messianic question; here he is altogether at variance with them; he claims that the hope of the return to Palestine still had power to arouse the enthusiasm of the Jew and that a future independent existence was the true consummation of Israel's Messianic hopes. Still, in spite of his objections to the book, Frankel was frank to acknowledge that the intention and aim of the Hamburg congregation were honest, but he feared that its mode of procedure was schismatic.

Salomon answered this criticism in a caustic and ironical rejoinder,[44] in which he repeated his views on the Messianic idea. Frankel replied, and set forth his thoughts on the question a second time and at great length.[45] This then was really the pivot on which the reform movement was to revolve; if Judaism was a universal religion as the reformers claimed, then all things connected with the religion, as ceremonies, doctrines, and laws, must be interpreted in this light; the dead hand of the past must be removed and the present be given due and proper consideration as a vital factor in the development of the faith; if, however, Judaism was a national religion, then had the prophets dreamed vain things and uttered foolish babblings; the issue was becoming well defined; "either a common country or a common idea";[46] either Judaism had the power and potency of a world religion and could satisfy the spiritual aspirations of mankind, or it was fitted to be only the religious experience of a single race; the outlook of the reformers was the world, that of their opponents a corner of western Asia.

The practical result of all this agitation, as far as the Hamburg Temple congregation was concerned, was that it became more assured in its position as an independent congregation, and was permitted to pursue its course peaceably and quietly; on December 7, 1845, a commission was appointed by the congregation, consisting of the two rabbis, one member of the directorate, and four members of the congregation, to which were to be referred all matters pertaining to the public service and such private domestic functions as were of a religious nature;" this commission was to bear in mind always the purpose of the Temple organization, viz., "the combining of the spirit of the religious consciousness of the age with the historical spirit of Judaism."

CHAPTER V

OUR story of the movement for religious reform in Judaism has been confined thus far almost exclusively to Germany, but the movement spread beyond the borders of that country, and toward the close of the fourth and in the beginning of the fifth decade of the nineteenth century a stirring episode in the conflict between the old and new tendencies in Judaism was enacted in the British metropolis. Before giving a detailed account of this it will be necessary to indicate briefly the religious conditions in London at the time when the first official effort toward reform was made, viz., in the year 1836. As throughout Europe, the bulk of the Jews in London had, up to the nineteenth century, acquired but little if any education in secular branches of knowledge. They were cut off almost absolutely from all contact with the outer world, except in business relations involved in transactions on the Stock Exchange. The education of the great majority of the children was received in schools that were scarcely worthy the name. The Spanish and Portuguese congregation conducted a day school called *Shaare Ticvah* (Gates of Hope), in which according to the statement of a prominent member of the congregation, the boys "were taught little Hebrew and less English. For aught they knew Julius Cæsar was a Lord Mayor of London some fifty years ago, the equator may be the name of a strange animal, and Alps and Pyrenees are, perhaps, two kinds of foreign fruit. And in this state of mind they leave the school where they are supposed to have been instructed for years, and enter the world, throwing upon the establishment and upon the authorities who look after them the greatest disgrace." [1] The Talmud Torah, the day school conducted by the German Polish congregation, was no better, being presided over by a *melammed,* himself frequently ignorant and uncouth, who confined his teaching to Hebrew and the translation of the Bible into Yiddish. English was never heard in the schoolroom. Matters improved considerably with the organization of the Jews' Free School as a primary school in which secular branches also were taught. This was the beginning of the educational emancipation of the Jews of London from the régime of the *cheder* and the *melammed,* and all that these two institutions implied.

Religiously speaking, the Jews of London were divided into two communities, the Sephardi or Spanish-Portugese and the Ashkenazi or German-Polish; the affairs of the Sephardi community, with its historic synagogue in Bevis Marks, were regulated by the *Mahamad,* or governing board, consisting of four wardens and the treasurer. The rule of the *Mahamad* was wellnigh despotic; it was almost an oligarchy.

The *Ascamoth,* or rules of the Spanish-Portuguese congregation, prescribed the course of life of the members not only within the synagogue but also without.[2] For example, no member of the congregation was permitted to bring any suit against another member in any court of law, civil or criminal, without first giving notice thereof to the *Mahamad;* failure to comply with this regulation involved the payment of a fine of five pounds. The only exception to this was a suit in which "delay might prove prejudicial," or one arising from failure to meet a Bill of Exchange. Further, the members were forbidden to publish any book treating of religion or politics in any language without the permission of the *Mahamad;* they were also forbidden to join any party "which any of the people may form against the government or ministry or judicial administration of the kingdom."[3]

These rules, as a matter of course, date back to the time when the Jews were a tolerated alien community, and great care had to be exercised lest any suspicion of any kind attach to any one of their number as being opposed to the powers that were, or sympathizing with any sentiment or movement against them. The rules of the German synagogue did not attempt to interfere with the political opinions or activity of the members, but disputes between members of the synagogue were brought frequently before the governing board and settled without recourse to the courts of the land.

Such rules and regulations were possible of enactment and enforcement because the Jews were to all intents and purposes a separate community [4]—or really two separate communities —and could continue in force only so long as this remained the case; this jurisdiction of the synagogue over the public

activities of its members had to cease with the letting down of
the barriers that excluded the Jews from participation in the
civil and political activities of the country. At the time whereof
I am writing the agitation for the civil emancipation of the
Jews had been renewed. In 1753 a bill for the emancipation
of the Jews had passed both Houses of Parliament, but had
been repealed at the instance of the populace; since then the
bill had been introduced into the Lower House several times,
but in 1831 most determined steps were taken by Robert Grant,
Lord Macaulay, and other famous members of Parliament; the
bill had passed in the Commons but was defeated in the House
of Lords; the friends of the measure never ceased agitating
for it from that time onward until it was finally passed in
the House of Lords in 1858, and thus became a law of the
land.

All these movements for educational and civil emancipation
worked together just as was the case in Germany, and there
can be no doubt but that the spirit of freedom which called
these activities into play made itself felt also in the religious
life, and gave a great impetus to the sentiment of dissatisfaction with the conditions in the synagogue which had received
occasional expression even before the organization of the
reform congregation.

Furthermore, the influence of the movement for reform in
Germany must be taken into account. That this influence was
of moment in the agitation for religious reform in England
may be gathered from the first official mention we have of the
movement in that country among the members of the Spanish
and Portuguese congregation. A petition was presented to the
Mahamad on December 4, 1836, by a number of the members,
asking for the introduction into the service of "such alterations
and modifications as were in the line of the changes introduced
in the reform synagogue in Hamburg and other places." [5] Some
time before this, however, in the year 1812, a member of this
congregation, J. King by name, had addressed the wardens,
calling attention to the indecorum during the services and
claiming that as matters stood the synagogue "was not a place
of devotion and prayers could be better said in the closet." He
called upon the officers to introduce reforms, but his suggestions received scant consideration, as did also subsequent communications which he addressed to them on the same subject. [6]
Sixteen years later, on December 4, 1828, a committee for the

Promotion of Religious Worship was appointed to inquire into
and recommend the best means of raising the tone of the public service and infusing therein greater decorum and devotion;
the committee suggested a number of measures to this end;
they recommended that the *Mahamad* take steps to shorten the
service as far as practicable, but the most interesting portion
of their report is that in which they declared that moral and
religious discourses were essential, and therefore they urged
that an English sermon be delivered every Saturday afternoon
and its text be taken from Scripture; this suggestion was acted
upon and such sermons were delivered for some years, beginning in 1831, the preacher being the Reverend David de Aaron
de Sola, but after a brief period this practice was discontinued
until a later day.[7]

In May, 1823, a number of prominent members of the chief
Ashkenazi synagogue, surnamed the Great, called the attention
of the officers of the congregation to the indecorum that prevailed during the public worship; they claimed that this was
caused in great part by the prolonged *Misheberak* (benedictions
for money offerings), and petitioned that this portion of the
service be shortened, for, wrote they, "it is pitiful to behold
how indecently our solemn services are hurried on, particularly
during the sacred holidays, in order to allow time for a system
of finance, which, however beneficial in its operation, is certainly inconsistent with decorum and public order." In 1824
a committee of the vestry of this same synagogue recommended
some improvements in the mode of reading the service; although the recommendations were acted on, the evils com-
plained of did not abate. In 1832 the Hambro synagogue
abolished the sale of the *mitzwot,* but the hope of such as
desired to see the *Misheberak* abrogated was not fulfilled except
in the case of the reform synagogue which was founded in
1841, as shall be set forth shortly.

There had been agitations for reforms in Manchester which
led to the introduction of preaching in the vernacular in this
congregation in 1838.[8]

This desire for reform in England was due to the fact that
Judaism here, as elsewhere, had fallen out of touch with many,
to whom the services in the synagogue seemed disorderly and
unedifying. At this time the Spanish and Portuguese congregation had no *Haham,* as the spiritual chief of this community
was designated; no successor had been elected to H. H. Meldola,

who had died in 1828; his son, David Meldola, was appointed chief of the *Beth Din;* the chief rabbi of the German community was Solomon Hirschel, a typical rabbi of the old school. He had occupied the position since 1802.⁹ He preached twice a year in Yiddish, on the Sabbath before the Feast of Passover and on the Sabbath of the Penitential season, expounding the laws for the holidays. Both these men did all in their power to prevent the successful outcome of the active efforts for reform which, beginning with the petition of December 4, 1836, resulted in the formation of the reform congregation. This petition called forth a counter-petition from forty-five *Yehidim*, as the members of the congregation are termed technically, on December 13, protesting against any reforms. The elders, and in fact the majority of the congregation, being in sympathy with the framers of the counter-petition, the memorial of the members who advocated the alterations met with little sympathy, although the elders in the resolution which they passed discountenancing reform, credited them with purity of motive and intention. The same cry as is always raised in similar circumstances was emitted also here; it was urged that such changes would split Judaism into sects; this argument carried especial weight in England, for there, as everywhere, the Jews are affected by their surroundings, and the doctrine of conformity to an established church which represents the prevailing religious attitude in England reacted and reacts without a doubt upon the Jews, and for that reason it proved so difficult for reform to gain a foothold in Anglo-Judaism. The petition of the reformers, however, had the effect of causing the elders to take steps to introduce better order into the services.¹⁰

But the wheels of progress could not be stopped by such obstacles nor were the reformers to be satisfied with such slight measures. Even the advocates of the established order understood this, and the next step in the campaign was taken by some very orthodox members who, in order to meet any further agitation for reform, organized a society which they called *"Shomere Mishmeret Akodesh,"* and defined as a "society for supporting and upholding the Jewish religion as handed down to us by our revered ancestors and to prevent innovations or changes in any of its recognized forms and customs, unless sanctioned by the recognized authorities."¹¹ The elders of the synagogue evinced their impartiality by urging that this society be dissolved, on the ground that it was unnecsary and would only tend to promote disunion.

The reformers petitioned the elders again in 1839; as before they set forth the necessity for changes in the service and urged their claim for consideration. The points on which they laid particular stress were, the diminution of the prayers, a more convenient hour of service on Sabbaths and holidays, English sermons, a choir, and the abolition of the observance of the second day of the holidays. This petition met the same fate as its predecessors; it was disregarded. The reformers now took a more decided step. Not wishing to secede from the congregation they requested the elders to grant them permission to erect a branch synagogue in the West End of London in the vicinity of their homes, in which they might introduce the desired changes while the mother synagogue continued along traditional lines. This well-intentioned plan, whereby an absolute break might have been avoided, was rejected by the elders, because it involved an infraction of the first *ascamah* or rule of the congregation, which forbade, under pain of excommunication, the establishing of any house of prayer, or the holding of any divine service, not of a domestic nature, within a radius of four miles of the synagogue.[12] Nothing remained now for those desiring reforms but to organize a new congregation, which they did, in connection with some members of the German community who sympathized with their views. At a meeting held on April 15, 1840, by twenty-four gentlemen, eighteen of whom were Sephardim and six Ashkenazim, a reform congregation was organized. The reasons for doing so were set forth by the founders in the following declaration:

We, the undersigned, regarding public worship as highly conducive to the interests of religion, consider it a matter of deep regret that it is not more frequently attended by members of our religious persuasion. We are perfectly sure that this circumstance is not owing to any want of conviction of the fundamental truths of our religion, but ascribe it to the distance of the existing synagogues from our place of residence, to the length and imperfections of the order of service,[13] to the inconvenient hours at which it is appointed, and to the absence of religious instruction in our synagogue. To these evils we believe that a remedy may be applied by the establishment of a synagogue at the western part of the metropolis, where a revised service may be performed at hours more suited to our habits and in a manner more calculated to inspire feelings of devotion, where religious instruction may be afforded by competent persons, and where, to effect these purposes, Jews generally may form a united congregation under the denomination of British Jews.

To give the movement definite shape, the following resolutions were adopted:

That it is expedient to establish a synagogue in the western part of the metropolis and that it be designated the West London Synagogue of British Jews.

That a revised service be there performed in the Hebrew language in conformity with the principles of the Jewish religion, and in a manner best calculated to excite feelings of devotion, and that religious discourses be delivered in the English language.

In the Introduction [14] to the prayer-book, adopted somewhat later by the newly formed congregation, the following interesting statement is made in reference to the designation "British Jews" used in the address and resolution just quoted and in the title adopted by the congregation, namely, "The West London Synagogue of British Jews":

The differences which formerly existed between the Portuguese and German Jewish congregations, and which caused them to consider each other as half aliens in religious matters, have happily, by the progress of liberal sentiments, been removed, in as far as they obstructed that brotherly feeling which the unity of our religious system requires; and the efforts of our newly-established congregation have been directed, we hope successfully, to the obliteration of every vestige of that useless and hurtful separation. We have discarded the names indicating a connection between us, natives of Great Britain professing the Jewish religion, and the countries from which our ancestors immigrated, and we have adopted for our place of worship the sufficiently explicit designation of "West London Synagogue of British Jews." In making this statement, it is expedient to notice that the term "British Jews" has been chosen with a view only to efface the distinction now existing between the German and Portuguese Jews, and not in any way to constitute a new distinction, in a religious point of view, between the Jews of Great Britain and those of any other country.

The inclusion of the abolition of the second day of the holidays among the desired reforms indicates that one of the primary causes of reform in Judaism was life itself. The life of the Jews in the new time when they were participating in the activities of the world was altogether different from what it had been when they were a ghetto-community. The orthodox element who were arrayed against this reform had no other argument to offer than that it was handed down by tradition; they refused to recognize the fact that originally only one day had been observed, and that the keeping of the second day as a sacred day was in itself an innovation of a later time; the reformers, on the other hand, claimed that the exigencies of life in the modern time demanded the abolition of the second day, that there was no warrant or sufficient reason for continuing its observance, that if the requirement of one age justified its institution, the necessities of the present justified no less its abrogation. Religious institutions must shape themselves according to the needs of the age, if they are to continue as living forces and not as dead letters.

The movement to form the new congregation agitated the community greatly. While it was taking shape the chief rabbi of the German community, Solomon Hirschel, and David Meldola, chief of the *Beth Din* of the Spanish and Portuguese congregation, addressed a lengthy communication to the London Committee of Deputies of British Jews and to the various congregations, calling their attention to the reports that such a congregation was being formed, and urging them to use all their influence to prevent it. They contended that this movement, if successful, would disturb the peace of the community and introduce the evil of schism; they pleaded for the observance of the law which had been the main bulwark and protection of Israel during twenty centuries: "Let us hesitate a long while ere we sanction any innovation, ere we tear down rashly any portion of the 'fence of the law' which is sanctified by the reverence of centuries and still more by the authority of those who created it." Sincere the two ecclesiastical chiefs undoubtedly were, but they closed their eyes to the fact that the *people* had begun to disregard the law, that the *people* had broken down "the fence" whereof they wrote so earnestly and pathetically. And when the people have taken such a step, when life has begun to make inroads, no legal or ecclesiastical provision, prohibition, or fiat will prove of much avail. The constituted authorities of the synagogue in England, as had been the case in Germany, were blind to the signs of the times. The onrushing waves of the ocean of life swept away many of the pickets of the fence of the law; this they would not or could not see; they attributed the reforms to willful presumption, whereas they were really the result of the new currents of life that were flowing through the Jewish community.

The rabbinical address was received sympathetically by the existing congregations with the exception of the Western Synagogue [15] which refused to receive the communication; one of them, for example, the New Synagogue, passed a resolution declaring any member of a "place of worship which does not conform in religious matters to the ecclesiastical authorities (agreeably with Law 1 and 2 of the Deputies) is not eligible to the office of deputy of this synagogue.[16]

The Bevis Marks congregation put forth a final attempt to stop the reformers from carrying out their plan by the suggestion that a branch synagogue be erected in the West End of the city where most of the reformers lived, but that the service in this branch synagogue be exactly like that in the mother synagogue. Naturally, this did not meet the requirements of the case, and the proposal was not urged. The reformers remained insistent and continued perfecting their plans for the new congregation. Many meetings were held by both sides. Partisan passions were aroused and bitter feelings engendered. On June 2, 1841, the Bevis Marks congregation called upon the other congregations of the city to join with them in the effort to prevent such a flagrant violation of the traditional rules and laws of the faith as the program of the new congregation intended.[17] Even this did not deter the founders of the new congregation from continuing in the work which they had undertaken. On August 24 they addressed a communication to the elders of the Bevis Marks synagogue, wherein they announced the fact that they intended to open a new place of worship and to introduce innovations and changes in the ritual;

they enumerated these as follows: [18] the service was not to exceed two hours and a half; to make this possible the prayers had to be abridged; they had therefore revised the prayers; there was to be preaching in the vernacular; the offerings were to be abolished except on the three high festivals when voluntary offerings [19] could be made upon the return of the scroll of the law to the ark; the second days of the holidays were to be abolished for "it is not the intention of the body of which we form a part to recognize as sacred days those which are not ordained as such in Scripture; and consequently they have appointed the service for Holy Convocations to be read on days only thus designated." [20] They disclaimed, however, all desire to produce a schism in the community and declared their willingness and their purpose to advance the interests of the mother congregation as they had hitherto. It was in a truly religious spirit that they wrote that these views have been carried into effect, not with any desire to separate "but through a sincere conviction that substantial improvements in the public worship are essential to the weal of our sacred religion, and that they will be the means of handing down to our children and our children's children our holy faith in all its purity and integrity. Indeed, we are firmly convinced that their tendency will be to arrest and prevent secession from Judaism, an overwhelming evil which has at various times spread among many of the most respectable families of our community. Most fervently do we cherish the hope that the effect of these improvements will be to inspire a deeper interest in and a stronger feeling toward our holy religion, and that their influence on the minds of the youth of either sex will be calculated to restrain them from wavering in their faith or contemplating for a moment the fearful step of forsaking their religion, so that henceforth no Israelite born may cease to exclaim, 'Hear, O Israel, the Lord is our God, the Lord is One.' We contemplate encountering considerable difference of opinion, and even a strong prejudice against our proceedings, but we venture to hope that on further consideration, our motives and intentions will be duly appreciated and that those kindly feelings, which ought to exist between every community of Jews, will be maintained between the congregation which you represent and the small body whose views we have endeavored to explain."

The Elders made no acknowledgment of this communication, but adopted a resolution denouncing the movement to open a

new synagogue, and declaring the action of the promoters of
the plan schismatic; but matters had gone too far and the
denunciation proved futile. Unfortunately, the affair did not
stop with verbal denunciation and recrimination. As at Hamburg the ecclesiastical heads of the existing congregations
issued a Caution [21] against the new congregation and its
prayer-book, dated the ninth of Marheshvan, 5602 (October
24, 1841), in which they said:

> When we saw this great evil we arose and supplicated
> the help of God to remove this stumbling-block from the
> path of our people, our brethren of the House of Israel
> . . . we hereby admonish every person professing the
> faith of Israel and having the fear of God in his heart
> that he do not use or in any manner recognize the said
> book of prayer because it is not in accordance with our
> Holy Law and whoever will use it for the purpose of
> prayer will be accounted sinful.

This Caution was sent to all the congregations in England;
the congregations of Liverpool and Manchester disapproved of
it and returned it, while the Plymouth congregation burnt it. [22]
Evidently the terrors of ecclesiastical excommunication had
become a thing of the past. In truth there were but few changes
in essential teachings if any in the prayer-book which the new
congregation issued in August with the title "Forms of Prayer
used in the West London Synagogue of British Jews," and
which was prepared by a committee consisting of Reverend
D. W. Marks, Francis H. Goldsmid, Abraham Mocatta, and
Moses Mocatta. In the introduction to the book the editors,
referring to the recent studies of Jewish scholars, explained
that the ritual of the synagogue represents a growth and drew
from this fact the conclusion of the right and the necessity of
producing a book of prayers that would appeal to their generation or as they put it:

> It being thus evident that time has exerted its influence
> on these prayers, it is but meet that the exigencies of the
> time should again be consulted, when we have arrived at
> the conviction that the house of prayer does not exercise
> the salutary influence over the minds and hearts of the
> congregants which it is intended and capable to exert. His-

tory bears us out in the assumption, that it becomes a congregation of Israelites to adapt the ritual to the wants of
its members; and it must be universally admitted that the
present mode of worship fails to call forth the devotion,
so essential to the religious improvement of the people.

The changes consisted mostly in abbreviation and elimina-
tions whereby the service was shortened; such sections as the
במה מדליקין, איזהו מקומן, יקום פורקן, etc., were omitted; the
Amidah of the *Mussaf* service was shortened and contained
only the מעין הברכות, the epitome of the benedictions. The
most significant change possibly was the rendering of the Aramaic portions notably the *Kaddish* prayer into Hebrew. A few
original prayers for special occasions were included. Petitions
for the restoration of the sacrificial cult in the Temple of Jerusalem were eliminated although the prayers for the return to
Zion and the coming of the Messiah were retained. The editors
of the book were quite right when they asserted that the service they had adopted was altogether based on the existing ritual
with the exception of the few slight changes mentioned, and
the edict of excommunication of the ecclesiastical authorities
was therefore an extreme step even from the standpoint of
tradition.

The new congregation dedicated its synagogue in Burton
Street, on January 27, 1842. David W. Marks, who had been
elected secretary of the congregation, delivered the sermon;
Mr. Marks had been secretary and Reader of the Law of the
congregation in Liverpool. In looking about for a leader the
founders of the reform congregation decided upon Mr. Marks,
who had acquired a reputation as an able and eloquent preacher.
The choice was fortunate indeed, as his distinguished career
proved. In his dedicatory sermon Mr. Marks defended the
right of the congregation to introduce reforms, and defined
the position of the congregation toward the Talmud, denying
the authority of the oral Law and accepting the Bible only as
authoritative;[23] he declared that it was not the purpose of the
congregation to weaken their inherited faith; but to strengthen
those great principles of the Law that their forefathers had
heard at Sinai; they did not intend to abolish the old simply
because it was old, nor yet to introduce the new merely because
it was new; their only guide was to be the call of truth and

the service of God in a manner that would satisfy the needs of their generation."

Even before the Caution against the prayer-book was published, a meeting had been held on September 9, 1841, at the residence of the Chief Rabbi Solomon Hirschel, which was attended by the wardens and honorary officers of the different synagogues and by the members of the London Committee of Deputies of British Jews; at this meeting a declaration was read and approved as follows:

> Information having reached me from which it appears that certain persons calling themselves British Jews, publicly and in their published Book of Prayer, reject the Oral Law, I deem it my duty to declare that, according to the Laws and Statutes held sacred by the whole House of Israel, any person or persons publicly declaring that he or they reject and do not believe in the authority of the Oral Law cannot be permitted to have any communion with us Israelites in any religious rite or sacred act; I therefore earnestly entreat and exhort all God-fearing Jews, especially parents, to caution and instruct all persons belonging to our Faith that they be careful to attend to this Declaration and that they be not induced to depart from our Holy Laws.

This was signed by S. Hirschel, Chief Rabbi, and was accompanied by the indorsement of the ministers of the Portuguese congregation in these words:

> We, the undersigned, fully concurring in the foregoing Doctrines, as set forth by the Reverend Solomon Hirschel, certify such our concurrence under our hands this Twenty-Fourth of Elul, 5601 A.M.
>
> David Meldola,[25]
A. Haliva,
J. Levy,
A. Levy,
A. L. Barnet.

Although written in Elul (September) this document was not promulgated till the following January, the reason being given in these further words accompanying it, "The promulgation of the above Declaration has been delayed in the hope [26] that there would have been no necessity to give it publicity;

circumstances, however, now require that it should no longer be withheld from the community"; dated the 9th of Sebat, 5602 (January 22, 1842). The circumstances referred to were the forthcoming dedication of the synagogue of the reform congregation and its outspoken attitude on the question of authority as given voice to a few days later in the inaugural sermon of its minister.

On January 19, 1842, the members of the new congregation addressed a letter to the Spanish and Portuguese congregation asking that their names be stricken from the list of members of the old congregation;[27] they had delayed taking this step in the hope that some method of reconciliation would be found and that in time reforms would be introduced in the mother congregation. The break was now complete. Brother was arrayed against brother, whilom friend against friend. The traditionalists believed that the strength and salvation of Judaism depended on strict conformity in practice and belief to what had been handed down from the past, the reformers believed no less strongly in the right of private judgment in religious as in all other matters; each party held to its conviction with the tenacity typical of the English character.

The letter of January 19 resulted in drastic action on the part of the old congregation. The matter was considered at several meetings and finally it was resolved that the signers of that letter "had forfeited all claims to the rights and immunities which they enjoyed as members of our community, that the grants made to them of seats in our synagogue are rescinded and annulled. They are also declared ineligible to act in any religious office or to perform a *Mitzvah* of any kind in the congregation.[28] Neither shall any gift or offering be accepted from them, or in respect of them, in any way or under any form whatever, during the time they remain in contumacy; they shall not be allowed burial in the *carriera* of our *Beth Haim* nor receive any of the religious rites and ceremonies paid to departed members of our communion."[29] Thus was the *Herem* or edict of excommunication formally and solemnly pronounced against the reformers. On December 14, 1845, a committee was appointed to consult with the ecclesiastical authorities upon the validity of this edict of excommunication; for the friends and relatives of the excommunicated, who had remained faithful members of the mother congregation were disquieted because of the religious disabilities under which the seceders were laboring; besides, the passing of time had somewhat softened the bitter feelings aroused at the time of the incident. After lengthy deliberations and protracted consideration the ecclesiastical authorities lifted the ban from the reformers on March 9, 1849.[30]

The organization of the new congregation led to other serious practical consequences. On February 2, 1842, the reform congregation, through a committee named for that purpose, and consisting of Francis H. Goldsmid, Moses Mocatta, and John Simon,[31] sent official notice to the Board of Deputies of British Jews, the president of which was Sir Moses Montefiore (the most prominent Jew in England and famous particularly because of his great services in connection with the notorious Damascus affair of 1840), of the existence of the congregation and requested them to certify that Mr. Marks was secretary of the synagogue. This was especially important in order to give validity and legality to the marriages performed by the minister of the congregation or, as he was officially called, the secretary. Every marriage had to be registered and naturally only marriages registered by one who was certified to be the secretary of a synagogue would have legal recognition and sanction. Sir Moses refused the request in a reply dated February 8, in which he stated that he had referred the matter to the ecclesiastical authorities of the Board of Deputies; on the following day he declared that he did not recognize the new organization as a Jewish congregation. The West London Synagogue, in its answer, dated February 14, called attention to the facts that the Board of Deputies counted no ecclesiastical authorities among its number and that every synagogue *de facto* has the right of existence in England without further ado or authority; hence they asked a second time to have Mr. Marks registered as secretary of a synagogue and therefore empowered to perform all the acts of an accredited head of a congregation. Sir Moses persisted in his former declaration and maintained the position he had assumed. The committee of the West London Synagogue in its reply deplored the fact that a man of Sir Moses' distinguished services should so use his position as to cause internal strife in the community; for if the attitude of the president of the Board of Deputies should be upheld it could result in but one of two things, a contest before a court of law or in Parliament. They would not, however, resort to these extreme measures for the present because they wished to avoid the notoriety that would result from the public airing of the internal strife in the Jewish community; still they would not hesitate to take one of these steps should any difficulty be encountered in the registration of marriages performed by their minister. Sir Moses answered this pronouncement by making public the resolutions adopted by the committee of the Board of Deputies on February 7, which declared that all religious matters were to be referred to the ecclesiastical chiefs as heretofore; this was accompanied by the declaration of the ecclesiastical authorities quoted above to the effect that the new organization was not to be recognized as a Jewish congregation, and also by the resolution adopted by the whole Board of Deputies on February 14, in which they declared their entire approval of Sir Moses' course. Such couples as desired to be married by Mr. Marks had to be married first by the registrar to legalize the marriage which was thereupon solemnized by the minister according to the rites of the religion.[32] In 1845 the West London Synagogue appealed to the government which on its part referred the matter to the then Chief Rabbi, Dr. Nathan Marcus Adler, the successor of Solomon Hirschel who had died while the controversy between the two factions was still raging.[33] How high the feeling ran even at this time may be learned from a remarkable action of Chief Rabbi Adler which was the occasion of the issuing of an address by the West London Synagogue on March 3, 1846, detailing the course of events since the congregation had come into existence;[34] the action referred to was the refusal of the Chief Rabbi to permit the solemnization of a marriage between a member of the orthodox community and a girl whose father was affiliated with the reform congregation, and who herself had attended services there, unless the latter would promise to live in accordance with orthodox practice and never set foot in the reform synagogue.[35]

In 1846 Parliament passed the Religious Opinions Relief Bill whose purpose it was to grant property and other rights to dissenters; the supporters of the West London Synagogue claimed that the effect of the bill was to legalize marriages in their place of worship by its registration in the same manner as dissenting chapels were heretofore registered.[36] The incident was closed by the passing of an Act of Parliament, on July 29, 1856, entitled "An Act to Amend the Provision of the Marriage and Registration Acts," the twenty-second section of which makes special mention of the West London Synagogue

of British Jews, and empowers its certified secretary to register
marriage ceremonies; the Bill also empowered the secretary of
this synagogue to certify to the secretaries of other synagogues
who would adopt the same ritual.[87]

Thus the congregation reached the haven of peace after years
of trial and struggle. Since then it has continued along the
lines first laid down, but has not made much further headway
in this direction; in fact, it has become quite as wedded to its
traditions as are the orthodox congregations to theirs. The
confirmation ceremony was introduced at the very beginning,[88]
and on September 26, 1859, an organ was placed in the second
house of worship of the congregation in Margaret Street, which
had been dedicated in 1849. Reform has made comparatively
little progress in the United Synagogue, although preaching in
the vernacular and the choir have been generally introduced;
greater decorum, too, marks the services of the constituent congregations of the United Synagogue than was the case in the
days when the reform congregation was organized.[89] In only
three other cities have reform congregations been established,
namely in Manchester, Bradford, and Liverpool.[40] On February 22, 1890, the Reverend Morris Joseph inaugurated the
Hampstead Sabbath afternoon services, which were of a reform
tendency. They continued for three years. An agitation somewhat similar to that attending the formation of the reform congregation was witnessed in 1902 when the Jewish Religious
Union was launched in London. The story of this most recent
forward step for religious reform by a body of English Jews
will be recounted in the proper place.

CHAPTER VI

THE Jewish community of Frankfort-on-the-Main had been for centuries one of the foremost in Germany; it was distinguished for the learned men who had filled the rabbinical position there, for the stirring scenes that had been enacted in its famed "Gasse" [2] and for the prominence and wealth of a number of its families. While the city was an imperial fief its Jewish community had been ruled by special legislation (*Judenordnungen*) which the emperors issued from time to time; when the sway of the emperors came to an end in 1806, Frankfort passed under the rule of the Prince Primate of the Rhenish Confederation, Karl von Dahlberg. This ruler published a new order for the government and protection of the Jews which was not much of an improvement on the old *Judenordnungen,* for it withheld from them expressly the right of citizenship. When the Duchy of Frankfort with its own constitution was formed, upon the dissolution of the Rhenish Confederation, the representatives of the Jews induced the Archduke Dahlberg to promulgate a special law in consideration of a great sum of money; this law declared that the Jews of Frankfort "with their children and descendants should enjoy civil rights and privileges equally with other citizens." The Jews took the oath of citizenship and it seemed indeed as though the long night of medievalism had passed away and the morn of freedom had dawned. But it was a deceptive hope. After the fall of Napoleon a reactionary period set in, the evil effects of which were felt for the time being by the Jews throughout Germany.

The Congress of Vienna, which was convened in 1814 for the purpose of regulating the affairs of the European states after the fall of Napoleon, and which was participated in by the great statesmen of the allied countries, gave some consideration also to the Jewish question; the fourteenth Article of the first draft of the Acts of the Congress, as agreed upon by the representatives of Austria, Prussia, and Hanover, had declared that

Jews who performed all the duties of citizens should be accorded all the rights of citizenship, and that wherever the existing laws of a state presented obstacles to the consummation of this program, those obstacles should be removed as soon as possible. A number of the representatives of the smaller German states protested against this paragraph, but the two great Powers, Austria and Prussia, insisted upon its retention. The free cities, among them Frankfort, which had obtained its autonomy in the meantime, objected particularly to the term "rights of citizenship" (*Bürgerrechte*) and demanded the substitution of the phrase "civil rights" (*Bürgerliche Rechte*). This alteration was made, and in its final form the Article included the further provision that until such a change became an accomplished fact the Jews of the separate states should continue to be governed by the special legislation in force at the time. This action of the Congress gave ground for the hope that the spirit of medievalism that still obtained in the conduct of the affairs of the Jews would soon disappear. A violent anti-Jewish literary campaign ensued, however, in various cities of Germany, which culminated in the turbulent and disgraceful hep-hep outbreaks of the year 1819 in Frankfort and elsewhere.[3] A bitter struggle waged between the Senate of Frankfort and the Jews for eight years (1816 to 1824), in which latter year the Jews succeeded in obtaining certain rights. The movement for Jewish civil emancipation went bravely forward until it was crowned with success in the revolutionary year 1848 in most of the German states, although it was not until 1864 that the last vestige of civil discrimination against the Jews of Frankfort disappeared.

But the agitation for change was not confined to the political and civil disabilities under which the Jews rested; the dissatisfaction with the *status quo* had invaded the religious province also. In former chapters the earliest efforts toward religious reform in Berlin, Hamburg, Breslau, and London, in which cities sharp contests had been waged between the traditionalists and the reformers have been traced. An encounter between traditionalists and reformers similar to those already described took place in the community of Frankfort-on-the-Main, which has an interest all its own because other aspects of the struggle were brought prominently to the fore.

In Frankfort, possibly more than anywhere else, the intimate connection between the newer educational movement among the

Jews and religious reform is apparent. Frankfort was noted among the Jewish communities of Germany for its excellent school, the *Philanthropin,* where modern methods of education had superseded the *Cheder* altogether. The children who attended this school received instruction in all branches of knowledge commonly taught in secular educational institutes; instruction in Jewish subjects only, as was the case in the *Cheder,* had given way to a more extended curriculum; life necessarily had a larger outlook for the pupil who attended such a school than it had for the child whose education was restricted to Jewish subjects. The spirit of the new time ruled in the one place while the spirit of the ghetto still brooded over the other. It is in the *Philanthropin* that the first faint traces of the reform agitation in Frankfort are discernible. Devotional exercises for the pupils were introduced in the year 1813; religious instruction had been imparted regularly since the organization of the school in 1804, but the need for a service that should edify the pupils was felt more and more strongly. In the synagogue of the general community, as a matter of course, there was no sign of change; the rabbi, Solomon Abraham Trier, was one of the most uncompromising opponents to any innovation whatsoever, as shall appear later on; the rising generation was repelled rather than attracted by the public worship; the service instituted on Sabbath and holidays in the *Philanthropin* was of a character to stimulate devotion and intensify the religious spirit of the young people within its walls; it was conducted partly in the vernacular and an address was delivered in German weekly, either by the headmaster, Dr. M. Hess, or the teacher, J. Johlson.[4] Thus the German sermon was introduced into this community without any struggle, whereas had the attempt been made at this early day to have such sermons delivered in the communal synagogue it would have entailed a bitter struggle with the adherents of the old order, as had been the case in Berlin.[5] As the children who attended this school grew into manhood and womanhood they leaned naturally toward reform; nay more, the services conducted in the school began to attract adults in the course of time.

In 1825 Dr. Michael Creizenach was called from Mayence to teach in the school. Creizenach was a man of great ability and of marked personality; he was an earnest advocate of the reform cause, although he wavered between decisive outspokenness and the desire to conciliate the orthodox party;[6] like so

many writers of that time he aimed to prove the justification for
reform in Judaism from the Talmud; he hoped thus to bridge
over the differences between the traditionalists and the
reformers, and to reconcile the former to the changes which
were taking place in the interpretation of Judaism and which
he felt were absolutely necessary. But in this he could not succeed, eloquently and learnedly as he defended his thesis in a
number of his earlier writings.[7] For the thesis rested upon a
fallacy.[8] True, passages can be cited from the Talmud in support of the contention that authorities of former times sanctioned departures from established law and custom because of
changed conditions;[9] but these were isolated instances; the body
of authority remained the same. The new movement in Judaism, however, meant something altogether different; the Jews
were facing a state of affairs as subversive of their past as was
the case when the temple of Jerusalem was destroyed and they
exchanged their national existence for a world mission. Circumstances had compelled the postponement of the active carrying out of this prophetic world mission; for eighteen hundred
years they were forced into isolation by the inhuman policy of
both church and state, and as a defense against their hostile
onslaughts "the fence of the law" was built up, and surrounded
the religion in its every activity; this was the religious counterpart to their political state; now another crisis was at hand; the
ghetto isolation was apparently drawing to a close, as eighteen
hundred years before the national existence had ceased. The
Talmudical legislation no longer fitted conditions and the spirit
of the Talmudical legislation could not be invoked to summon
forth the light which was to distinguish between chaos and
order, between past repression and prospective freedom.[10] The
fortunes of Jewry were undergoing a revolution; the Talmudical legislation in its details could not be accommodated to the
changes superinduced by this revolution; there must be a new
adjustment of the standards even though this involved a new
interpretation of the principles of tradition; the purpose of God
was as apparent in the present changes as it had been in any
past events, and since God had brought this to pass it was as
truly a divine revelation as any recorded of former times:[11]
hence it might be necessary to disregard the form that the
faith assumed under the Talmudical guise and clothe it in garments altogether different. The Talmudical legislation could
not be expected to meet so radical a change as the new time

involved, hence the failure of such as attempted to sail the craft of Judaism through the agitated waters of the sea that had been unknown to the Talmudical mariners, by the compass and chart fashioned by them. Creizenach himself recognized this [12] before his death, which occurred in 1842, a short time before there took place the sharp and definite clash between the opposing parties in Judaism in the city of his adoption, which crisis he, possibly more than any single individual, helped to precipitate.

His appointment as teacher in the *Philanthropin* proved to be of far-reaching effect not only in the educational but also in the religious life of the scholars of the institution; nay more, his influence extended beyond the walls of the school into the community at large. On the one hand he preached definitely and positively against the indifference of such as, having ceased to be strict observers of traditional law, form and custom, had swung to the opposite extreme of aloofness from the religious life altogether, and on the other hand he denounced the formalism into which rabbinical Judaism had degenerated, and which, being the recognized official expression of the faith, was the primary cause of the alienation of those who looked to religion to be a living reality, and not merely the observance of a mass of forms, the most of which had ceased to have any significance whatsoever for that generation. Creizenach gave utterance to these ideas not only in his publications but still more effectively in the sermons preached at the weekly services in the school. Through these sermons, the services attracted many adults and the number of participants grew to such an extent that a special chapel known as the *Andachtssaal* was erected in 1828. The confirmation service for boys and girls was introduced. Similar services were conducted in another educational establishment, the Weil Institute.[13] The most noteworthy effect of these services and sermons in the vernacular was that they paved the way for reform.[14] However, the traditionalists were not blind to what was going on; they denounced the influence of the teachers of the *Philanthropin* as disintegrating and demoralizing, and blamed the instruction in secular branches as being responsible for the breaking away from the traditions. Hence they concluded that the situation could be saved only by the reëstablishment of an old-time school wherein Hebrew branches alone should be taught. It became apparent before long that such a school was doomed to failure; in order to ensure its success they determined to introduce secular studies into the curriculum, these to be secondary, however, to the Hebrew instruction. Even with this concession the school did not flourish and had to be closed. This failure did not discourage the advocates and upholders of the traditional system of Jewish education. They sought to establish a higher institute for the exclusive study of the Talmud and the allied disciplines. A long and heated controversy on the Talmud and rabbinism ensued; voices were heard pro and con, but the Talmudical party were championing in this instance, as it proved, a hopeless cause. They received no encouragement at the hands of the Senate of the city in their plea for the establishment of this special Talmudical academy, and the attempt was abandoned.[15] The cause of reform was winning its way quietly not only through the educational work within the community, but it was furthered also by the attitude of non-interference on the part of the lawmaking body of the city. As has been already mentioned, ever since the Jews had been permitted to dwell in Frankfort they had been governed by special legislative acts. After Frankfort had become a free city, and notably after the passing of the sway of Napoleon and the meeting of the Congress of Vienna, the Jews petitioned for the rights of citizenship. The sixteenth article of the proceedings of the Congress, as adopted finally, gave rise to prolonged discussions in the Senate, which resulted in the passing of the law of September 1, 1824, defining the restrictions and rights of the Jews. This law declared that the Jews could regulate their own religious affairs and were exempt from all interference by the state or the Christian community in their internal religious organization.

The agitations in the community, growing out of the differences between progressivists and reactionaries, in the fourth decade of the nineteenth century were converging gradually to the point of gaining a majority representation on the governing board of the community. This promised to be of far-reaching importance because of the fact that the old age of the rabbi made the election of an associate imperative. The progressive party naturally wished to secure the appointment of one of the new school of rabbis to the post; the traditionalists were just as desirous of electing a rabbi of the old school, to whom Talmud and *Shulchan Aruk* were oracle and authority. This contingency, together with other difficulties arising out of questions which touched the administration of all the affairs of the community, induced the Directory of the same to request the Senate to pass a general act on the organization, the duties and the mode of procedure of the governing board of the Israelitish community. This petition aroused intense excitement, and an address signed by 212 members of the community was presented to the Senate, in which the request was preferred that all the religious and ecclesiastical affairs of the community should be taken out of the hands of the Directory, who should thereafter concern themselves only with the political, civil, social, and other non-religious concerns of the community, and that the religious affairs be made the care of a special committee as suggested in the address. This called forth a counter-address, signed by 272 names, denouncing the unwarranted procedure of the signers of the first address. The result of all this agitation was the passing of an Act by the Senate on February 16, 1839, for the regulation of the affairs of the Israelitish community; the communication of the Act to the Directory was accompanied by an extract from the proceedings of the Senate which contained these striking words:

> The Senate will be ready always to oppose every- and anything that may wound the conscientious scruples of believing Israelites or may disturb or place obstacles in the way of their traditional worship, but on the other hand it will encourage and support such institutions as the progressive needs of the age make necessary for the true and essential demands of religion.

Cognizance is taken here of the differing wings of religious thought in Judaism. The fourth paragraph of this Act of 1839 is of particular interest and import in the story of Jewish reform, notably in the light of later events. This paragraph was concerned with the question of the qualification of the future rabbis of the congregation; it required that the candidates for the position "be German by birth, that they must have graduated from a German gymnasium and have taken courses in Oriental languages, in historical and philosophical branches in a German university." [16] This implied, as a matter of course, that the day of the rabbi trained and educated in the *yeshibah* only was past, and served notice that the aspirants to the rabbinical position in this community must be men of modern education and modern training. In so far, the progressive party had gained a victory, and the old rabbi who, as was mentioned

specifically in the Act, was to remain undisturbed in his position could not but be troubled by the evident signs of the
impending introduction of a new order of things in the religious
guidance of the community.

These signs had been apparent for a number of years past
in private circles within the Jewry of Frankfort to a much
greater degree than appears from the official history of the
community as embodied in Acts and regulations. Since the
breaking up of medieval conditions there had been in Frankfort, as in Berlin and other German cities, a coterie of Jewish
laymen, who, educated in the gymnasia and the universities,
were dissatisfied with traditional Judaism, and formed a nucleus
for the dissemination of ideas advocating the reform cause.
Individually, these men were at variance with the official representatives of Judaism; they were out of sympathy with the
existing conditions in the synagogue; when Geiger established
his *Wissenschaftliche Zeitschrift für Jüdische Theologie* they
hailed this as the dawning of a new day; here was a platform
for the discussion of the new wants and a forum for the scientific exposition of the principles and the literature of Judaism.
The gradual appearance on the scene of German Jewish life of
a new school of rabbis, men graduated from the universities, a
number of whom contributed to this magazine, encouraged
them in the hope that definite steps would be taken toward an
official adjustment of Judaism to life; but the rabbis advanced
too slowly for them; with very few exceptions these rabbis considered it advisable to proceed very cautiously, and to reconcile
the old with the new rather than discard the old in the interest
of the new; in theory many of the rabbis quite agreed with the
most pronounced opinions concerning the inadequacy and the
unsuitedness of the Talmudical legislation to modern needs and
the modern spirit, but in practice they continued to conduct their
office along the traditional lines; they declared their sympathy
with religious progress by enlisting under the banner of what
they called progressive rabbinism (*der fortschreitende Rabbinismus*); the laymen just spoken of had no patience with this
Fabian attitude; they wanted an outspoken declaration expressive of the change that had come over Judaism; they began to
accuse the rabbis of cowardice and to take matters into their
own hands; they wrote slightingly and bitingly of the lack of
courage displayed by the rabbis in not rising to the occasion,
and coined the phrase "creeping rabbinism" (*der fortkriechende*

Rabbinismus) as a substitute for the rabbis' own designation "progressive rabbinism."

A company of such laymen was much in evidence in Frankfort in the fourth and fifth decades of the nineteenth century; they had formed a society significantly entitled "The Society of the Dawn" (*Die Lesegesellschaft zur aufgehenden Morgenröthe*), the members of which were described by one of their number in 1841, as "not subscribing to Talmudical ceremonialism which separates the Israelites from their fellow-citizens," after a rhetorical outburst in the following strain: "How long will the Talmud-devotees confound the pure religion of an Isaiah, a Jeremiah, a Micah with the ceremonial religion of the Pharisees? . . . How long will they continue to oppose the progress of civilization and the civic life?" [17] The first of these questions shows how little men of this stamp comprehended the true inwardness of the reform movement in its attitude toward the Talmud and how superficial was their understanding of the true development of Judaism.

An anonymous article which appeared in Geiger's *Wissenschaftliche Zeitschrift* in 1837, [18] and which was written supposedly by one of these Jewish laymen of Frankfort, [19] describes their attitude so fully and so clearly that it may be considered almost in the light of a preliminary notice of the formation of the Society of the Friends of Reform, the subject of this chapter. The article is entitled "Jews and Judaism," and has the subheading "Reflections of a Layman." After setting forth the progress of the Jews in various branches of learning in the new era, their strides in the struggle for civil emancipation and their growing participation in the life and endeavor of society, he declares broadly that although "the Jews have progressed, Judaism has stood still." There may be some, he continues, who have a correct understanding of what Judaism really is, but as long as there is no clear, unmistakable declaration of what is to be considered pure Judaism and what only temporary form, so long will the religion continue in its present distortion; "as yet Judaism is supposed to include every jot of the traditional rabbinical interpretation; the *Shulchan Aruk* with its insatiable commentaries and super-commentaries is still recognized as the authoritative code, a deviation from which is considered equivalent to a deviation from the religion itself." He declares that the prime need is a sifting of the mass of accretions that have attached themselves to Judaism, and the separation of the pure metal from the dross; the rabbis should do this; he recognizes, however, that the rabbis, ministering as they do to congregations composed of many elements, are placed in a difficult position, and in their longing to have the confidence of all are fearful of taking decisive steps forward even if they would. Be this therefore as it may; be the rabbis chargeable with neglect in a fearless expression of their religious convictions or no, "it becomes the duty of us non-theologians, if we have the welfare of Judaism, truth, and progress at heart, to make solemn declaration of our views in order to remove from ourselves the reproach—first, of indifference, and secondly, of a contradiction between our thoughts and acts on the one hand and our religious profession on the other, as well as to encourage by this sign of earnest participation such rabbis as are perhaps ready and anxious to take decisive steps forward." He recognizes that non-theologians have neither the requisite knowledge nor authority, but this declaration of theirs is to be only a general statement of their convictions, and is to be rather in the nature of an address to the rabbis of Germany calling upon them to state whether the declaration is a truthful presentation or no. But of all things it was necessary to publish such a declaration; all else was detail that could be worked out later; this declaration should make known that the signers "do not feel in conscience bound to invest the prescriptions of the Talmud, to say nothing of those of the later rabbis, in as far as these cannot be proven by scientific exegesis to have been derived directly from the Bible or to have been handed down by Moses, with any greater authority than is accorded all other temporary religious institutions whose reasonableness and whose agreement with the spirit of Judaism must first be established." He concludes by saying that in whatever community a sufficient number of intelligent laymen may be found they must unite in a declaration of this kind. The cleft between practice and profession must be removed. . . . The differences in Judaism exist; better that the sympathizers range themselves together than that they act single-handedly; better that a clear understanding be arrived at than that compromises be resorted to; better, in short, that the present state of affairs be made the starting point of true progress than that, through willful blindness, it lead to complete disintegration.

Without doubt, such were the sentiments that prevailed with

a large number of Jews throughout Germany; these sentiments crystallized into definite form in Frankfort, where in November, 1842, a number of Jews formed themselves into a society which they called "The Society of the Friends of Reform" (*Verein der Reformfreunde*). They were all laymen; it was distinctly a lay movement; the absence of all theologians from the membership of the society was so noticeable a feature that it could not but arouse comment, especially as the purpose of the society was preëminently religious. The charge was preferred against its promoters that the exclusion of theologians was intentional; Dr. M. A. Stern of Göttingen, famed as a mathematician and undoubtedly a man of exceptional intellectual powers, wrote a series of open letters.[20] in answer to attacks upon the society. I shall have occasion to refer to these letters frequently, as they are the *apologia* for the society. In one place he meets the charge of exclusion of rabbis from the society by claiming that there is no longer any priestly caste in Judaism; there is no distinction between rabbis and laymen on the score of sacerdotalism; the only recognized distinction in Judaism is between those who know and those who do not know the law. Herein lies a great principle of religious freedom, and the fact that the society is composed altogether of so-called laymen is equivalent to a rebuke to the assumptions of the occupants of the rabbinical office who would bring into Judaism this distinction between rabbi and laymen, a distinction thoroughly foreign to the genius of the faith;[21] he refers to the article published some years previously in Geiger's theological magazine, which urged the formation of societies of laymen for the very purpose for which the Frankfort Society was founded.[22] Still, despite this explanation which contains a great and salient truth, there seems to be little doubt that the real reason for the exclusion of rabbis was a certain contempt which the "intellectual" among the laity felt for the occupants of the rabbinical position. The rabbis had not grappled with the religious problem as vigorously as these laymen thought they should have done; they themselves would therefore take the matter in their own hands and lead the way.[23] Geiger, the foremost figure in the Jewish theological world, was a close friend of Stern's; letters passed between them in one of which Geiger speaks of "your contempt for the theologians—which you deny, it is true, but which is only too apparent."[24] This sharp differentiation was unfortunate inasmuch as it accentuated the very distinction that Stern claimed the society desired to eradicate, and arrayed all the rabbis, with one exception,[25] against the movement.

The brief career of the Frankfort Reform Society was one of the most striking episodes of the drama of Jewish religious development that is being unfolded in these pages. The men who formed the society were actuated by the conviction that there must be many Jews throughout Germany who were ripe for a new expression of the principles of Judaism, since the changed political and social status, the acquisition of secular knowledge; in short, the complete break between their external fortunes and the conditions of the life of their ancestors must make them feel the impossibility of fitting the rabbinical interpretation of the religion to the modern Jewish environment. It was also felt that if they would make a short, sharp, and definite declaration of what they considered the essential principles of the faith, this would encourage all who entertained like sentiments to do the same, and the concerted movement away from rabbinical Judaism (many of whose enactments were disregarded by a multitude of contemporaneous Jews) and toward a modern Judaism would be begun.

The members of the society met privately for deliberation and discussion. They formulated five principles as their declaration of faith, viz.: (1) that they consider the Mosaic religion capable of continuous development; (2) that they do not consider binding the various ritual, dietary, and other laws concerned with bodily practices that emanated from the ancient polity; (3) that they do not consider circumcision binding either as a religious act or a symbol; (4) that they do not recognize the Talmud as authoritative; and (5) that they do not expect or long for a Messiah who will lead the Jews back to Palestine, but regard the country to which they belong either by birth or citizenship as their only fatherland. This original declaration of principles was altered at a subsequent meeting, when it was determined to omit paragraphs 2 and 3 and cast the other three paragraphs into another form; this was done and the revised draft, which will be cited presently, was adopted and promulgated as the creed of the society. The omission of the two paragraphs was due to the argument which was advanced successfully that such a declaration should be general in character and not touch special points about which there were still such decided differences of opinion, even among many who might confidently be expected to sympathize with a forward movement.

They did not make their deliberations nor this declaration public at once, for they felt that the time was not yet ripe; they desired to secure first the coöperation of sympathizers throughout Germany. The declaration of principles, together with a prefatory address setting forth the objects and aims of the society, was sent privately to prominent men in various localities to obtain their signatures; this delayed the work greatly as it took weeks at times to secure one signature; as a result, only some fifty signatures had been obtained by the beginning of August, 1843.[26] The most celebrated of the men whom they addressed were Gabriel Riesser, of Hamburg, the dauntless champion of Jewish political emancipation in the German states, who had expressed frequently his sympathy with the movement for religious reform,[27] and Dr. M. A. Stern, of Göttingen, who had been present at some of the preliminary meetings. Letters were exchanged whose purpose was the free and unhampered expression of opinions; these letters were of a confidential nature, but some of those that passed between Riesser and Stern were given out for publication by an adherent of the orthodox party into whose hands they had fallen,[28] together with excerpts from the proceedings of the society which had been altogether private; these extracts were garbled and edited in a manner to discredit the society, which in self-defense was now forced to give to the public prints the address and declaration mentioned above. This was in August, 1843.

These official documents of the society were three in number marked *A, B,* and *C. A* was a circular letter accompanying the documents; *B* was the address which explained the reasons and aims of the movement, and was entitled "Program of a Declaration of German Israelites. Presented for Consideration to friends of religious reform in Judaism, 1843"[29] and *C* was the declaration proper.[30] The letter, which was signed by Simon Maas, Dr. jur., in the name of the Jewish Friends of Reform, requested the coöperation of the addressee in the undertaking with which a number of reputable Israelites had declared themselves in sympathy, and for the furtherance of which many highly respected men in Germany were ready. The founders of the society requested the signatures of all "who do not expect a Messiah to lead them back to Palestine; all who do not accord any authority or obligatory power to the confused and frequently meaningless rabbinical interpretations and injunctions; all who strive for a form of faith whose enlivening principle is pure Mosaism." The letter asserted further that reform in Judaism existed in reality, and that all that was necessary was an open declaration; as a result of this the reform movement would be sure to receive fitting recognition and become a working force in Jewish life.

The so-called program opens with a eulogy of Moses and the religion he established; this religion is capable of unceasing development; however, many of the institutions of Mosaism were of a national character and dependent upon the possession of a particular land. When in the course of time the land was lost and the nationality came to an end, many of the Mosaic ordinances ceased to exercise any binding force, *e.g.* the laws regulating the ownership of land, the prerogatives of the priests and Levites, the sacrificial ritual and the criminal code. Their place was taken, however, by a mass of ritual and ceremonial laws to which in time the greatest importance came to be attached, and Judaism became a system of observances whereby the spiritual content and import of the religion were dimmed. This externalism assumed ever greater prominence during the ages of exclusion and oppression; the Jew clung to every observance, custom, and ceremony that had developed in the course of the ages. When, however, the era of freedom dawned, men arose who realized with dismay how far Judaism had traveled along this path and how pronounced was the difference between the inner purity and dignity of the divine truth of the religion and the external form that it had assumed. The new opportunities had been grasped by such as these, and they had acquired the culture of the people among whom they lived. They sought to extricate the jewel of Judaism from the dross with which it had become encrusted; they found their inspiration in the prophets of the Old Testament who had proclaimed that the spirit of the religion was independent of the blood of bullocks. . . . Yet attempts at reform up to this time consisted merely in liturgical imitations of other religions or in compromises with the followers of rabbinism. Rarely did any one think of emphasizing *the capacity of Mosaism for unending development*. In so far the charge is true that no decisive step has been taken by the Jews to conform their religious practice to the higher culture to which they owe their intellectual progress. Civilization has freed them from rabbinical jurisdiction; it must be our task to purify the religion of all antiquated disfigurements and present it in a worthy form.

In our day the difference between the inner truth of Judaism and its external form has become especially acute. Nurtured by the intellectual culture of the age many of those who are accounted members of the Mosaic religious community have arrived at the conviction that most of the practical commands, the observance of which constitutes the bulk of present-day Judaism, rest on human and temporary premises. They claim rightfully that this external form is for the most part without significance—yes, even unworthy of pure religion—and they draw the inner content of divine truth, which an earlier generation found in the Law, from those treasures of wisdom alone which have won over to the truth so many great spirits of all nations. Thus thousands have renounced allegiance to Talmudic rabbinical Judaism, and are connected outwardly with the Mosaic religious community only by habit or by the control of the state or by family ties. This condition of affairs is destructive and immoral; for as long as a man lives in a community he should not pass as something altogether different externally from what he is in thought and inner conviction. The Jew who has grown indifferent to his religion on this account must decide whether he will continue to be known merely as a Jew by birth, thus sacrificing free-will to habit, and being deprived of all outward religious association that is expressive of his inner conviction or—whether, longing for some tangible form, he will join some other religious association. . . . But those who cannot content themselves with either of these alternatives will pin their faith to the belief in the capacity of Judaism for development, and instead of continuing in a state of indolent lethargy will aim to harmonize their spiritual convictions with their professions. . . . Moved by these considerations, a number of German Israelites have determined to give expression to their opinions of the present conditions in Judaism through a public declaration, and to renounce formally their allegiance to all objectionable commands, and to all antiquated customs, which to all intents and purposes they have rejected long ago.

They disclaimed any purpose of desiring to obtain through this declaration more political rights than were accorded to the strict observers of the rabbinical code; neither did they intend to formulate any dogmas or create a sect or a schism; all that they aimed at was an open, honest statement of facts and beliefs as had obtained in Jewish life for a number of years past; and particularly did they desire to convince competent religious teachers that truth has a home in Israel, and to encourage such to support with all the weight of their learning the religious standpoint of truth-loving laymen. The address concludes with the words:

> Least of all is it our desire to hurt the susceptibilities of the strict adherents of rabbinical Judaism. Let us hope that success will crown this our honest endeavor, not only to give our religion a worthier form, but also to expound the pure content of Judaism, and to remove from it everything which has degraded and dishonored it in the eyes of thinking men. Every participant in this movement feels already great inner satisfaction in that he has chosen his standpoint in reference to the highest spiritual interests, and has paid allegiance to the truth. Let us begin bravely, then, a task not only necessary from the civic standpoint and intellectually justified but also highly moral and, in all truth, pleasing to God.

Hereupon followed the famous Declaration; it consisted of three paragraphs as follows:

> 1. We recognize the possibility of unlimited development in the Mosaic religion.
> 2. The collection of controversies, dissertations, and prescriptions commonly designated by the name Talmud possesses for us no authority either from the dogmatic or the practical standpoint.
> 3. A Messiah who is to lead back the Israelites to the land of Palestine is neither expected nor desired by us; we know no fatherland except that to which we belong by birth or citizenship.

As already mentioned, the publication of these documents was premature, and had been forced by the excitement aroused by the reports circulated by the enemies of the society in the public prints; it had been the intention of the founders of the

society to refrain from all public activity and agitation until so
many signatures had been obtained from all sections of Germany as to prove that this was a great popular movement; they
had not had time to accomplish this purpose, if in truth it could
ever have been accomplished with the program they had formulated. This, of course, must remain conjecture for all time; the
facts in the case are that the publication of the documents of
the society called forth a storm of opposition and denunciation
that was in truth overwhelming; orthodox, conservatives, moderates, reformers, all joined in reprehending the presumption
of this handful of men whose address and declaration showed
how illy prepared they were for the task they had undertaken,
and how inadequately they understood the true import of
Jewish development. The thunders of the opposition sounded
from all quarters; the rabbis—from Holdheim,[31] Geiger, and
Einhorn, the reformers, to Trier and Ettlinger, the uncompromisingly orthodox—wrote in criticism and disparagement; the
society found but one sympathizer and defender among the
rabbis, M. Hess of Saxe-Weimar. But not only among the
rabbis was this resistance met with; the most prominent layman in all Germany was Gabriel Riesser; as soon as he became
acquainted with the three points of the declaration he announced
his unalterable opposition in a letter to Stern; although an active
and enthusiastic advocate of religious reform, he declared the
Frankfort movement a step backward rather than a step forward. He feared also the impression that the paragraphs of
the declaration would make upon the general public; the first he
considered a mere phrase; the second and third were simple
retorts upon the watchwords of Judæophobia. He despised
this tendency "for it does not serve the truth; its only purpose
is the effect it may produce upon the civic authorities."[32] Stern
answered him at length, but I pass this answer by for the present since I shall give at length his elaborate defense of the
society which appeared some time later;[33] Riesser found no
time to reply to Stern, but that he had not been convinced
appears from the fact that when the affairs of the society
became a matter of newspaper comment in the summer of 1843,
and Stern and Riesser were named as its chief sponsors, Riesser
denied this statement publicly and declared his opposition to
the society.[34] The most striking attacks upon the organization
were made by Leopold Stein, rabbi in Burgkunstadt, Bavaria,
and elected rabbi of Frankfort in March, 1844,[35] M. Gutmann,

rabbi in Redwitz,[36] S. D. Luzzatto,[37] David Einhorn,[38] Michael
Sachs,[39] Zacharias Frankel,[40] and by many others whose
opinions were published in the collection of responses gathered
by the aged rabbi of Frankfort, Solomon Abraham Trier, and
which will receive extended notice in the course of this chapter,
when the attitude of the society on the circumcision question
will be considered. The most notable defense was that of M. A.
Stern in answer to the attacks of Stein, Gutmann, Einhorn,
Hirsch, and Mannheimer; the society was also defended by
M. Hess in five leading articles in his newspaper.[41] In these
articles he applauds the act of the founders of the society; he
states that the Jews have advanced, but not Judaism, and that
official Judaism is at fault, that life calls for reforms, and that
this declaration is the first evidence that enlightened Jews have
given of a clear understanding of the situation. He defends the
society from the chief charges that had been made against it;
these charges were that the three paragraphs of the Declaration
are not far-reaching enough; that they are only negative (thus
Frankel called them "articles of unbelief," and Einhorn "a confession of unbelief"); that they were indefinite; that the third
paragraph discredits the patriotism of Jews who still believe in
the personal Messiah and the return to Palestine; and lastly,
that it was fathered altogether by laymen and non-theologians,
while theologians alone could and should inaugurate such a
movement. I cannot stop to give Hess' reply to these charges
and criticisms, notably as I feel that space should be
given primarily to the defense of M. A. Stern which also
answered these points. The open letters of Stern written in
answer to the attacks upon the society by Rabbis Stein and
Gutmann are the most remarkable literary product of the agitation called forth by the formation of the Reform Society.[42]
He takes up the criticisms of Stein and Gutmann point for
point and answers them without reserve, often sharply, sarcastically, and caustically. A brief *résumé* of his argument
makes unnecessary the separate quoting of the objections of
Stein and Gutmann, as these are indicated sufficiently in the
reply. The first letters are addressed to Stein. The reason for
laymen taking the initiative was that rabbis had not done so,
although they had bewailed frequently the sorry condition of
affairs in Judaism and had declared reform absolutely necessary.[43] The Reform Society, inspired by these statements, had
taken the bold plunge, but had indicated in its declaration only

the absolutely necessary doctrines that would appeal to the contemporary generation as expressing the idea of development in Judaism.[44] In answer to Stein's designation of them as reformers he says, "We are not reformers; we could not and would not be. We are merely reformed; the age, advanced intelligence, possibly also progressive rabbinism, are the reformers. We desire to make no proselytes; we wish to induce no one, who is not of a like opinion with us, to join us; we have merely called upon such who think as we do to combine with us. Therefore the 'Declaration' is drawn up in such a way as to express our individual view." [45] As for the third paragraph concerning the Messiah, rabbis had said the same thing time and time again, and Stein does not even advert to this paragraph in his criticism, hence he must agree with it.[46]

"As to the second declaration Stein does not argue; he simply accuses us of not knowing the Talmud"; Stern answers sarcastically, and enters a flat denial claiming that they do know the Talmud; this, however, is not to the point; the point is the authority of the Talmud. "The Talmud shall receive acknowledgment for all that is of value in it. We have denied only its authority, not its historical value." [47] It is the first paragraph of the Declaration, however, that has been made to bear the brunt of the hostile attacks; and yet, what does it say?— That the members of the society recognize in Mosaism the possibility of unlimited development; what does this imply but the principle of reform? something which progressive rabbinism, the religious standpoint of Stein, has declared time and again.[48]

Stern then discusses the permanent element in Judaism; this is certainly not the ceremonies as progressive rabbinism has stated often, certainly not the belief in miracles, certainly not metaphysical truths which are rare in the Bible. "What then is the permanent element in Judaism? Nothing else is unchangeably permanent except the glorious idea of its world-embracing destiny to which its whole history bears witness, nothing else but its divine mission to develop within itself the belief in God and to spread this over the whole earth. Therefore, too, it must be able to appreciate the ideas of all ages and the conditions of all places; therefore it must not be limited by any temporal institution. . . . It must eliminate all institutions that have outlived their usefulness, and must bear within itself the possibility of unlimited development." The Reform Society considered it a bounden duty to give expression to this thought;

it is a jewel which has been recovered out of stunted rabbinical Judaism."[49]

The purpose of the Reform Society was simply to make this general declaration, not to carry it out in practical reforms as applicable to special Mosaic laws; this is to be the work of the rabbis. Some of the members of the society, the writer among them, wished to go farther and specify certain Mosaic institutions that have outlived their original significance, but the majority decided otherwise on the ground that their chief purpose was to gain the adherence of all who believe in the principle that Mosaism is capable of unlimited development.[50]

In answer to Stein's question in what the society was specifically Jewish, and whether the most orthodox Christian or Moslem could not become a member, he says that the first paragraph shows that this is impossible, because neither Christian nor Moslem believes in the possibility of the unlimited development of Mosaism, holding as they do that a new revelation was necessary for the salvation of mankind.[51]

He denies the statement made frequently at that time that Bruno Bauer's essay on the Jewish question[52] was the direct cause of the formation of that society. The deliberations looking to its formation began in September, 1842; in the beginning of November the writer had communicated with Dr. Riesser on the subject, and Bauer's essay did not appear till several weeks later.[53]

He meets Stein's charge that the doings of the society retarded the civil emancipation of the orthodox Jews, by saying: "if you demand that we shall not retard your civil emancipation we may demand certainly with equal justice that you should not interfere with our spiritual emancipation, for what is sauce for the goose is sauce for the gander. We are not enacting a farce, nor is our society a mere matter of convenience that we will abandon at your desire; we have a sacred duty to fulfill which is nothing less than to extricate ourselves from a thoroughly false religious situation."[54]

Stein had averred that the paragraphs of the Declaration were purely negative; Stern retorts by calling upon him to show the way and to give them something positive, fortified with "reasons taken not from policy, but from Jewish theology, with reasons that do not presuppose the authority of the Talmud, and which would therefore not satisfy us."[55] He denies that he is the author of the official documents of the society, and claims that he saw them only after they were published; [54] he closes with accusing the progressive rabbis, among whom Stein classed himself, of cowardice and with wishing to conciliate both parties, and hence with having no definite principles. "You and all who share your opinions are greatly mistaken," thus he addresses Stein in taking leave of the subject, "you will never succeed in conciliating the orthodox party; they will use you against progress so long as you permit yourselves to be used; but the moment you presume to act against their will you will be damned. The orthodox know full well that they cannot surrender one iota without endangering their whole position. You will alienate more and more the cultured and progressive elements because you refuse to satisfy the demands of culture, inasmuch as your practical reforms restrict themselves to a few changes in the service. . . . What is the gain of such a scarcely perceptible advance? Is this the only factor, the only institution in which salvation is to be found, or is it not rather in the purified religious consciousness for whose edification the external institutions will adapt themselves of necessity? . . . If you are not possessed of courage, then be content to lose yourselves among the crowd, and do not aspire to leadership; least of all should you glorify your faint-heartedness as the correct policy and call the courageous foolhardy. Let him who is cowardly and faint-hearted turn back and go to his home. Judaism will fulfill its mission without you and in spite of you; help and salvation will come from another place." [57]

In his open letter to Gutmann, Stern discusses first the Messianic question, and shows how the hope for the coming of the Messiah has developed in Judaism; he challenges Gutmann's statement that this hope runs like a red thread through the Bible; the Pentateuch says nothing concerning it, nor do many of the prophets; it is a late growth on the stem of Jewish thought, and thousands of the present generation have repudiated it; this being the case, how can they utter the prayers supplicating for the coming of a Messiah and the rebuilding of Jerusalem; such prayer is really blasphemy, for it is equivalent to uttering a falsehood; "if we make supplication to God for something the direct opposite of which we wish for in our hearts, what is this but a mockery? does it not change prayer, the purest relation of man to God, into shocking blasphemy?" [58] He therefore declares that he will cease to attend the synagogue as long as these conditions exist unless forced to do so by law,

a possible contingency in view of certain proposed strange legislation. It is absolutely necessary for the Reform Society to
institute a service which will express the honest convictions of
the Jew of to-day. He calls upon the rabbis to revise the prayer-
book as proposed by the rabbinical conference just held at
Brunswick,[59] and to eliminate altogether those prayers which
are at variance with the people's belief; "the attempt has been
made, it is true, to eliminate some of these prayers, but is a
lie less a lie because it is uttered once instead of ten times?"[60]

Since the authority of the Talmud was repudiated, the Bible
was accepted naturally as the all-important authority; but the
letter of the Bible is dead like every letter, and becomes living
only if it receives the breath of the spirit; it requires human
interpretation.[61] The meaning of the first paragraph of the
Declaration is this: "the progressive development of mankind is
unlimited; if Judaism is to keep pace with this, if it is to share
in the shaping of the future of mankind, if it is not to pass
away, it must contain within itself the possibility of unlimited
development. This is the plain meaning of the first paragraph
of our Declaration."[62]

There must be development in religion; the divine is perfect,
it is true, but it must accommodate itself to human imperfection; hence a command suitable for one age may be outgrown
by a subsequent age; thus, blood-revenge is sanctioned in the
Bible; but this does not mean that all future ages must regard
this primitive institution as sacred. "Mankind outgrows laws
which were formulated for earlier imperfect stages of civilization as a child outgrows its clothes; the law ceases to be operative of itself as soon as the conditions that gave it birth cease.
Hence if we do not wish to surrender the sublime conception
of the continual progress of mankind, we will have to concede
that religion, the expression of the human cognition of God,
must keep pace with this progressive development."[63] He proceeds to explain the purpose of the Reform Society: "Away
with all explanations that simply introduce new shackles of the
law in place of the old ones; let us thank God that Judaism has
no dogmas; away with attempts at compromise in this our time,
in which scarcely any two persons think alike in religious matters. What we can and should do is to clear away that which is
dead; for this we should unite in active endeavor,—this is the
purpose of the Reform Society."[64] Gutmann had charged that
the Reform Society denied divine revelation; Stern replies with

a definition of revelation as the progressive advance of the spirit of man; belief in the literal revelation as described in the Bible, Exod. xix-xxi, is not defended by any but the most orthodox; the least rationalizing of this passage would lay any one open to the charge directed against the Reform Society, and surely Gutmann would not defend the literal acceptance of this passage which states that God descended upon Mount Sinai, that he spoke, that the elders saw God, that Moses approached God, etc., and continues, "It must be proved whether the positive element of Judaism consists of stories or of its history (*in Geschichten oder in seiner Geschichte*) of the manner in which it grew, or of that which it became"; [65] he demands from Gutmann a statement as to whether he accepts this passage of Exodus literally; if he does not he occupies the same platform as the Reform Society.

Despite this spirited and full defense the society, one might almost say, "died a-borning." Yet although it proved so flat and well-nigh complete a failure as a practical organization, and although its founders did not grasp or comprehend the true significance of the development of Judaism, one point cannot be denied, nor may it be overlooked, and that is that the Frankfort Reform Society was an honest attempt to make open declaration of the sentiments that were entertained by a large section of Jews. Reform was an accomplished fact in the lives and thoughts of thousands; the commands of traditional Judaism were not observed by them; Judaism had entered upon a new stage; the Reform Society was a sign of the times; its promoters wished to square profession with practice. That their Declaration was inadequate and their method ill chosen, that their procedure was violent instead of ordered, that they simply negatived instead of building up from a sure and positive foundation, that they represented revolution rather than reform, [66] schism rather than continuous development, may not blind our eyes to the all-important merits of honesty of intention and recognition of the true state of affairs in Jewry. [67] But their action was little more than a spasmodic outburst; the three articles of their creed evince all the limitation of their thought, and their failure to grasp the true idea of development in Judaism, which is the keystone in the arch of reform. This appears clearly and unmistakably from the first two paragraphs of the Declaration, viz. the cry "back to Mosaism," and the repudiation of the Talmud. It was fashionable in those days for

anti-rabbinical and anti-Talmudical Jews to affect the style and
title of professors of the Mosaic Faith (*Bekenner des mosaischen Glaubens*), indicating thus their hostile attitude toward the
Talmud; [68] this earned for them the soubriquèts of Mosaites
and Protestant Jews, for it was claimed that theirs was an attitude similar to that taken by the Protestants of the Reformation period in the history of Christianity; viz. the acceptance of
the Bible and the repudiation of all subsequent tradition. Now
the true knowledge of Judaism makes it clear that the Books of
Moses and the remaining writings preserved in the Bible represent stages in the development of Judaism, as do the literary
remains of every succeeding era; the Bible made Judaism as
little as did the Talmud; Judaism brought forth the books of
the Bible as well as the Talmud, and all other products of the
Jewish spirit. Hence it is an utter misunderstanding of Judaism to disregard any phase of its development; each age had its
needs and met them as well as it could; the Talmud and the
codes served their purpose in the outworking of the faith, as
well as did the Biblical books; what is true in any is eternal;
what was temporary in any was for special times and circumstances, but from all as from every expression of the spirit of
Judaism true reform draws its inspiration. It is folly to limit
the possibilities of Judaism to the content of Mosaism; it is
folly no less to attempt to erase from the record the centuries
marked by the rise and rule of Talmudism; every mode of
expression that Judaism has assumed, Mosaism, prophetism,
Talmudism, rabbinism, even cabbalism, contributes its quota to
the understanding of the essentials; each represents the fitting
of the eternal elements of the faith to particular circumstances;
this is the principle at the root of the reform movement, and
therefore those who interpreted it correctly defined it as a new
phase in the age-long development, a new aspect produced by
the new revelation of God in the unfolding of the ages. [69] This
the Frankfort reformers failed utterly to grasp. The third paragraph of their Declaration repudiating the belief in the personal
Messiah and the return to Palestine, was correct in itself as a
tenet of the reform movement, but should have been merely one
of a number of statements instead of being posited as the only
special declaration, the other two paragraphs being of a general character.

The almost unanimous disapproval of the society was justified by the facts in the case, and it takes its place in the history

of the reform movement, not for any full and rounded interpretation it gave of the purpose of this movement, but as one of
the significant births of that period of travail, the fifth decade
of the nineteenth century. Still it is quite possible that this
Reform Society would not have been the storm center of so
fierce a tempest had it confined itself to the theoretical statements comprised in its program, and not become identified with
the agitation that shook the Frankfort community from center
to circumference in connection with the circumcision question.
This it was which really roused its opponents. As mentioned
above, the first draft of the Declaration contained five paragraphs, the third of which asserted that the members of the
society do not consider circumcision binding, either as a religious act or symbol. Although this paragraph was eliminated
from the final draft, it expressed the convictions of a majority
of the members of the society, and when an instance really
occurred of a father neglecting to have his child circumcised,[70]
the excitement aroused in the community knew no bounds.[71]

The attention of the sanitary bureau of Frankfort had been
called to the fatal outcome of a number of cases of circumcision; in order to prevent such mishaps in the future this
bureau promulgated a measure placing the circumcision of
Jewish children under the direct supervision of the sanitary
office; the third paragraph of this measure ordered that "Israelitish citizens and inhabitants, is as far as they desire to have
their children circumcised (*sofern sie ihre Kinder beschneiden
lassen wollen*), may employ only persons especially appointed
to perform the rite of circumcision." Members of the Reform
Society and others who sympathized with them interpreted these
words to mean that the rite of circumcision was to be performed or omitted at the desire of the father. It was not long
before the actual occurrence took place that made the matter
a living issue. The question as to whether circumcision was a
conditio sine qua non of entrance into Judaism had been discussed at the meetings of the Reform Society. Although it is
true that at the time the agitation broke forth the society
had not made any public official declaration pro or con the sentiments of its members were well known, and it became identified
in the public mind with the anti-circumcision agitation. The
aged rabbi of Frankfort, Solomon Abraham Trier, believing
that one of the very fundamentals of Judaism had been
wantonly disregarded by the individuals who had neglected to

have their children circumcised, addressed the Senate on February 26, 1843, calling the attention of the lawmaking body to the importance of circumcision from the religious standpoint, and pointing out the dangers that would threaten the integrity of the Jewish community were the performance or omission of this rite to be left to the caprice of the individual father; he therefore requested the Senate to issue a definite declaration that should counteract the effect of that phrase in the regulation of the sanitary bureau, which had been seized upon by the opponents of circumcision, as a justification of their position, the phrase, namely, "in as far as they desire to have their children circumcised." The Senate answered him on March 10 by saying that it was not the intention of the regulation in question to abolish a religious ordinance of the Jews. This, however, was not definite enough, and the agitation continued unabated. The danger of calling in the aid of the State to decide upon the private concerns of a religious community, was pointed out by clear thinkers, but the old rabbi and his party felt that the very existence of Judaism was imperiled, and hence considered any and every step justified, even the employment of force through the legislative arm. On August 4, Trier again appealed to the Senate, requesting that it declare that no child of Jewish parents could be received into the congregation as a coreligionist unless he had been circumcised; he made similar representations on September 15 and October 31; the Senate took action in the matter on February 13, 1844, by expressing its regret that certain members of the Jewish community gave cause for complaint to their coreligionists, and by stating its inability to take the step suggested by Trier.[72]

This was a distinct defeat for the rabbinical party, and its ill advised move to secure the support of the civil power against the nonconformists. It has been shown above[73] how frequently this was done in those days; certainly nothing is more harmful to the true interests of religion than the use of force through the instrumentality of the government, to ensure the fulfillment of its behests and commands.[74]

Trier did not confine his activity to these attempts to secure governmental interference. He addressed also a communication to the rabbis of Europe asking for their opinions upon the Reform Society, and upon the significance of circumcision. His communication appeared as the introduction to the volume, *Rabbinical Responses on Circumcision.*[75] He speaks of the

Reform Society as schismatic, and as masquerading under the deceptive guise of reform, but as being in reality the opponent of positive Judaism; he denounces it as a new sect [76] standing outside the pale of Judaism; [77] he pleads for the preservation of positive Judaism which is exposed to the devastating hurricane of a misunderstood spirit of the age; [78] he asks for an opinion on the new sect, and invites suggestions as to what measures should be taken against such as refuse to have their sons circumcised through frivolity and unbelief. The communication was sent to eighty rabbis; forty-one responses were received, and twenty-eight were printed in the volume designated; these were from the rabbis Samson Raphael Hirsch of Emden, Nathan Marcus Adler of Hanover, Felsenstein of Hanau, Lazar Horwitz of Vienna, Jacob Aaron Ettlinger of Altona, S. Ullmann of Crefeld, M. Wetzlar of Gudensberg, Adler of Oberndorf, Samuel Hirsch of Luxembourg, Seligmann Bär Bamberger of Würzburg, A. Wechsler of Schwabach, H. Aub of Munich, S. D. Luzzatto of Padua, I. N. Mannheimer of Vienna, L. Adler of Kissingen, S. L. Rapoport of Prague, A. A. Wolff of Copenhagen, B. H. Auerbach of Darmstadt, B. Levi of Giessen, J. Bamberger of Worms, A. Sutro of Münster, J. Löwenstein of Gailingen, S. Fürst of Heidelberg, H. Traub of Mannheim, Wassermann of Mühringen, L. Schott of Randegg, J. Mecklenburg of Königsberg, and H. Schwarz of Hürben. All of these responses took strong ground in favor of circumcision; in fact it was stated that all the responses which had been received were uncompromisingly and unreservedly opposed to the Reform Society and its position. This was not quite in accordance with the facts in the case, for the response of Rabbi Elias Grünebaum was suppressed because of the difference of his views from those of the rabbi of Frankfort. [79] Zunz also wrote a response which was, however, not included in the volume, but was published separately. [80] In this the great scholar took positive ground against the abolition of the rite; he warns against heresy trials and ecclesiastical penalties; he urges that the father, who fails to have his son circumcised, continue to be recognized as a Jew; he would not have the synagogue closed to him nor give him pain, although he give pain to others. But circumcision is of the very essence of Judaism. It is not a ceremony, but an institution; not the act of circumcising but the being circumcised is the kernel of the command. Other acts take place frequently in life; if neglected they can be atoned for and performed. In this case, however, a single omission is decisive, and the son who has not been circumcised by his father because of principle, will scarcely remain within Judaism for principle's sake. It is not necessary to quote very extensively from the opinions contained in the volume published by Trier. Men of all shades of thought are represented in the volume; Samuel Hirsch the reformer, Isaac Noa Mannheimer the conservative, and Jacob Aaron Ettlinger the ultra-orthodox clasp hands in agreement upon the question at issue, although their reasons may not be the same. The twenty-eight responses present a practical unanimity of opinion to the effect that an Israelite who denies the obligatory character of the command to circumcise, and neglects to have his son circumcised on the ground that he does not consider it essential to Judaism, is to be considered a denier of the divine law, and a destroyer of the eternal covenant. S. R. Hirsch stated that by such declarations and acts, they (the members of the Reform Society) have cut themselves loose from Judaism, and the rabbi of the community to which they belong must treat them as no longer members of his community; they are apostates (*mumrim*).[81]

The response of N. M. Adler, rabbi in Hanover, is of interest because of his election shortly thereafter as chief rabbi of Great Britain. Adler considers the question from three standpoints—the Biblical, the historical, and the religio-philosophical; he shows that although commentators and philosophers may have differed widely as to the significance of circumcision, this one explaining it as a symbol of purification, that one as a sign of priestly selection, this one giving it a social, that one an ethical, and a third sanitary interpretation, yet all agreed as to its being an absolute requirement for the Jew; he therefore concludes that the one who disregards the command is an apostate, and incurs all the sad consequences which the law ordains in the case of apostates; all association with him must cease;[82] he must be looked upon as excluded from the congregation of Israel.[83]

The renowned scholar, S. D. Luzzatto of Padua, declared that the members of the society are heretics and deniers of the Mosaic Law, and that according to their own confession they stand without the pale of the Jewish religion. His response, however, evinces a beautiful spirit; although positive in his attitude of unfailing opposition to the Reform Society, and although he opines that no congregational office or honor should be bestowed on its members, or any gift or offering be received from them, yet he recommends leniency, and counsels that words of truth and peace be addressed to them; possibly thereby they will be induced to renounce their error and return to the right path.[84]

The Viennese preacher, I. N. Mannheimer, disputes the right of the few to break away from the great community; Judaism is a historical system; it rests not on philosophy; it is life, it is experience; it is made up of a thousand forces, and any violent action such as this of the Reform Society is treason to the spirit of Judaism. He apostrophizes the Reform Society thus:

> Cut yourselves loose from us! you have nothing in common with us! You speak of the force which we apply to you and to your conscience; and do you expect us to submit humbly to your capricious procedure; do you expect for one instant that we shall or can permit that each and every one shall obey or disregard the commands of our religion according to individual whim or caprice, that any and every insignificant or irresponsible person shall rise and contemptuously disregard Talmud and commentators to-day, and Moses and the prophets to-morrow?[85]

Further along he asserts that the refusal to have a child circumcised is equivalent to a renunciation of the covenant of God;[86] he declares also that should such a case occur in his congregation, he would not admit the boy to any Jewish function, would not register him as a Jew, would not confirm nor marry him, nor permit him to be buried in a Jewish cemetery; in Austria no Jewish child is registered unless circumcised.[87]

Finally the opinion of S. L. Rapoport, the celebrated scholar and rabbi of Prague, may be cited; he presents the argument from history, saying that from the time of Abraham none have questioned the fact that circumcision is a necessary condition for entrance into Judaism; he indulges in the strongest terms of condemnation of the members of the Reform Society, speaking of them as "that frivolous company, which denies the fundamental principles of our religion, and confesses publicly that it does not accept our traditions";[88] "those reformers have no definite standpoint in Judaism; their only purpose is to break down all the preventive measures which the divine law has set up against human passions";[89] "we must exercise the greatest care and warn our co-religionists most earnestly to have no association of any kind with the members of this Reform Society, particularly not to form any matrimonial alliances with them." [90] I refrain from quoting any further from these opinions, since the extracts which have been given indicate the sentiment that runs throughout the volume; as already mentioned, each and every one represented in this collection argued strongly and often passionately in favor of circumcision as an absolute requirement for the Jew; it is but just, however, that the other side also be given a hearing, and I therefore feel it necessary to introduce the opinions of the two leading reformers of the time, Geiger and Holdheim. Although Geiger was quite as opposed to the course pursued by the Reform Society, as were the strict traditionalists, [91] still he sympathized with them in their opposition to circumcision; in a letter to Zunz, written March 19, 1845, he says in discussing Zunz's [92] opinion on circumcision:

> I was not in sympathy with the Reform Society; it had no clear idea of what it was striving for, neither was it honest enough in its utterances; instead of proceeding calmly and sanely, it aroused the greatest antagonism by attacking at once the rite of circumcision, which was considered a very fundamental of Judaism. . . . As for myself, I must confess that I cannot comprehend the necessity of working up a spirit of enthusiasm for the ceremony merely on the ground that it is held in general esteem. It remains a barbarous bloody act . . . ; the sacrificial idea which invested the act with sanctity in former days has no significance for us. However tenaciously religious sentiment may have clung to it formerly, at present its only supports are habit and fear, to which we certainly do not wish to erect any shrines. [93]

Geiger, however, did not express himself publicly in this wise; this was written in a private communication. Holdheim, on the other hand, issued a pamphlet entitled *Circumcision, Viewed Religiously and Dogmatically;* [94] he considers the subject at length from three points: (1) is circumcision so important a condition in Judaism that the uncircumcised individual who has been born of Jewish parents is not to be considered a Jew? (2) is the father who neglects to have his son circumcised still to be considered a Jew? (3) what is to be the attitude of the

Jewish religious authoritative body if circumcision is neglected? may it resort to force—in such cases as it has the power to do so —to compel a father to have the ceremony performed, or in case it has not the power, may it call in the aid of the civil authorities? [95] The third question he answered with a decisive negative; the individual's freedom of conscience may not be tampered with by the application of force; the religious leaders in Judaism may exercise only the task and the right to teach. In regard to the first two points he contended that circumcision was a sign and condition of the theocratic-national, but not of the religio-universalistic covenant in Judaism; not circumcision then makes the Jew, but birth; circumcision is not an all-essential requirement in Judaism, therefore both the father who neglected to circumcise his son, and the son who was not circumcised, are to be considered Jews. [96]

The result of all this agitation was to leave the question, as to the necessity of circumcision as a *conditio sine qua non* [97] of Judaism, much the same as it had been before. With the fewest exceptions, the authoritative voices had expressed themselves strongly in the affirmative. Holdheim and Hess stood alone among the theologians in their radical views on the subject; Geiger apparently agreed with them, but he did not give utterance to his views otherwise than in private correspondence. [98] Practically the ceremony continued to be, and still is, almost universally observed; the rabbinical conference that met in Breslau in 1846 made a number of declarations of a practical bearing, but uttered no decisive opinion on the cardinal point of the essentiality or non-essentiality of the ceremony; at the meeting of the Central Conference of American Rabbis held in the city of New York in 1892, the majority of the members present voted that circumcision was not necessary in the case of proselytes to Judaism.

All things considered, the outcome of this whole agitation was a gain for the progressive movement. Although the extremists who had called the Reform Society into being did not meet with much sympathy, yet on the other hand it had become apparent that the days of usefulness of extremists at the other end of the scale, like Trier, were over, and that the community of Frankfort required a rabbi of the new school. Events had been moving toward this end for some years, but it was not till 1844 that it was consummated. In March of that year Leopold Stein, rabbi of Burgkunstadt in Bavaria, was

elected as associate rabbi to Trier. This choice of the directorate was extremely displeasing to the old rabbi, and, had the
circumstances and the year been the same, there would have
been undoubtedly a repetition of the Geiger-Tiktin affair; but
even during the short space of six years great changes had taken
place in the religious atmosphere enveloping Jewry, and the
strenuous experience of Geiger was not repeated. Still Trier
did not accept the inevitable without a struggle; a few weeks
after the election of Stein he refused to deliver his semi-annual
derashah on the Great Sabbath; he had protested to the Senate
of the city against the election of Stein; the Senate referred
him to the directorate of the congregation as having jurisdiction
in the premises. Trier resigned as rabbi in May.

Stein, who styled himself an adherent of the progressive rabbinical party, at once began reforming the service; as early as
July, 1844, he introduced sixteen liturgical reforms. Among
them may be mentioned the change of the benediction שלא עשני
גוי [99] to שעשני ישראל;[100] the elimination of the benediction
שלא עשני אשה;[101] the substitution of an appropriate German
prayer for the יקום פורקן [102] and the מי שברך;[103] and the substitution of German songs for the לכה דודי [104] and the לכו
נרננה;[105] the introduction of the German sermon; and the singing of German hymns before and after the sermon.

The activity of Stein in the reform cause, although by no
means satisfactory to the members of, and sympathizers with
the Reform Society, for whom he did not go far enough, still
had the effect of blunting the edge of their weapons. The communal congregation having placed at its head a rabbi of the
new school, it was felt generally that there was no need for a
special reform society or congregation. In truth the Reform
Society as an organization disappeared from the public communal life; it was heard from but twice again; once when it
declared that the time had come for Sunday services to be introduced and appointed a committee of five to look for a suitable
preacher, and to request the congregation to grant the use of
the *Andachtssaal* for this purpose,[106] and again when, in June,
1845, it issued a circular letter, in which it expresses gratification at the progress of reform ideas, after calling attention to
what was done at the Brunswick Rabbinical Conference,[107] it
calls upon every Israelite to support the rabbis who are leading
the hosts onward. It welcomes the formation of the Reform
Association of Berlin.[108] It suggests a meeting of reformers

from all over Germany in the fall of 1845, for the discussion of ways and means of uniting the various reform tendencies among German Jews. The letter ends with the words "let us remain united, firm and loyal, and the success of our efforts will discomfit the false zealots, will put to shame the selfish indifferentists, and Judaism will become the bond that unites us without separating us from our century, our fatherland and mankind." [109] These words may be considered the valedictory of the Frankfort Society; considering that it had never in reality passed beyond the formative stage, the prominent rôle that it played during two eventful years is remarkable; that it gave a great impulse to the progressive movement, not only in Frankfort, but throughout Germany, cannot be gainsaid; nor can it be denied, on the other hand, that its members, pursuing the method they did, showed that they did not have the correct understanding of the development of Judaism. The extreme individualism and the animus against the theologians and rabbis, at once stamped the society as partisan beyond measure, but more than all else the absolute inadequacy of its platform proved that its founders were not competent leaders in that stormy period of Jewish life. It represents, however, a groping for the light, and although it failed signally in the work it set out to do, still will it remain in Jewish annals as one of the most interesting episodes of a most stirring epoch. It had panegyrists and detractors; [110] it aroused bitter passions. These things have passed. Looking back from the vantage ground of eighty years after, we recognize that the Reform Society of Frankfort represented the extreme left of the hosts marching under the reform banner; in some respects it had separated from the main army, but with it all, its members desired to remain within Judaism, and we may write as its eptitaph the closing words of its last public utterance, that its aim was to make "Judaism the bond which unites us without separating us from our century, our fatherland, and mankind."

CHAPTER VII

THE RABBINICAL CONFERENCES, 1844-6

As early as 1837 Abraham Geiger is on record as advocating a conference of like-thinking, progressive rabbis for the discussion of the essentials of Judaism and the consideration of the practical religious problems that were demanding solution. Individuals had given expression to the necessity of freeing the religion of the accumulated mass of outgrown forms wherewith it was burdened; they had likewise called attention to the facts that in the changed conditions of their life thousands of Jews were disregarding the commands of rabbinical Judaism, and that the cleft between what passed as the authoritative official expression of the faith and the practice of the people was growing wider and wider. Geiger, therefore, felt that the needs for a gathering of religious leaders was imperative in order that some conclusion as to how the difficult situation was to be met might be arrived at; his ideas of the purpose of such a conference are set forth in an open letter written on May 10, 1837, while he was still rabbi in Wiesbaden, and entitled "The Rabbinical Assembly; Epistle to a Friend in the Jewish Ministry." [1] In this communication he says that the conference is not "to formulate a new Judaism nor to assume synodal authority; it is to afford honest men the opportunity of discussing the best methods of conducting their office, and is to be a beginning toward a resuscitation of the well-nigh vanished spirit of Judaism." [2] He shows how this form is being disregarded here and that precept there, how one coreligionist believes that the service of God demands the punctilious observance of every iota of the traditional ritual, while another entertains altogether different views, and believes that the salvation of the faith depends upon its being delivered from the rigidity of formalism (*Formenstarrheit*) : all this was giving rise to unutterable confusion, and the people were drifting along helplessly, and each one was like to become a law to himself: "If, however, a number of rabbis make unanimous declaration as to the non-essentiality of this or that observance the bonds of formalism will be loosened." [3] Hence, even though such a conference were only deliberative and not authoritative, it would nevertheless give a mighty impetus to the progressive movement; the people would go forward with greater confidence if they knew that their leaders had agreed upon a standpoint that expressed a conception of Judaism based upon the spirit and not merely upon the observance of unnumbered forms, many of which were no longer religiously significant.

I confess [he concludes] that I cannot conceive how we can hold up our heads if we will not stand courageously for our innermost convictions; I cannot rest satisfied to continue to wear a mask any longer, politic as such a course would be undoubtedly. I leave it to your own conscience to decide how friends of truth and integrity will judge us, and by what name posterity will stigmatize us if we continue to speak high-sounding phrases but to enact weak deeds. [4]

Here Geiger was a pioneer; this was the first call for a rabbinical conference to consider the present condition of Judaism; [5] the gathering took place at Wiesbaden in August, 1837, and was attended by Geiger, J. Aub of Baireuth, M. Bloch of Buchau, J. A. Friedländer of Brilon, E. Grünebaum of Landau, M. Gutmann of Redwitz, S. Herxheimer of Bernburg, A. Kohn of Hohenems, I. Löwi of Furth, J. Maier of Stuttgart, L. Stein of Burgkunstadt, H. Wagner of Mannheim, M. Wassermann of Mühringen, and B. Wechsler; M. Hess of Eisenach arrived too late. True, the conference accomplished little, much less than Geiger expected. The only practical results of the meeting consisted, first, in the adoption of a resolution that studies on subjects of practical import should be published in Geiger's theological magazine, and that thereupon all the rabbis who were in attendance should give expression to their opinions on these subjects through the same medium; and, secondly, in the appointment of a commission, consisting of Löwi, Maier, and Stein, to prepare a manual for domestic devotion. [6] Still, even though the results were so meager, it was an achievement to have brought together a number of Jewish leaders. [7] Geiger recognized clearly that one of the greatest needs of this disturbed time in Jewry was that the guides of the congregations should arrive at some agreement on the subjects of practical moment that were agitating individuals and communities. Although the Wiesbaden Conference exerted scarcely any influence, still was the idea of its originator to be vindicated brilliantly some time later in the assembling of the famous rabbinical conferences of Brunswick, Frankfort, and Breslau in the years 1844, 1845, and 1846, which form the subject of the present chapter.

Each day well-nigh in that stormy time brought evidence from here, there, and everywhere in Germany of the difficulties encountered by Jews of living the new life in the world into which emancipation had thrown them, and carrying out faithfully the commands of rabbinical Judaism.[8] Many had cut the Gordian knot by simply disregarding the legislation of the codes, but there were thousands who were troubled honestly and sincerely, and who were looking anxiously for a way out of this *cul-de-sac*: the conflict between religion and life had to cease; the problem cried for solution: who so qualified to solve it, if indeed solved it could be, as the religious and theological experts? The seven years succeeding Geiger's initial effort disclosed the necessity for the gathering of these experts more and more clearly; the ranks of those who could not fulfill conscientiously every jot and tittle of the rabbinical codes were swelling day by day,[9] many had ceased to be affiliated with the synagogue, and were Jews in name only; the demand was imperious for the reconciliation of the life of Jew with his religious confessions. Hence when, in the beginning of the year 1844, Ludwig Philippson, the editor of the most widely circulated Jewish publication of the time, issued a call for a rabbinical conference, his words met with an instant and sympathetic response; the time seemed to be ripe now. In this call Philippson wrote as follows:

Let us speak plainly. The issue is no longer the permissibility or non-permissibility of this or that synagogal institution, of this or that alleviation for civil and social life; the issue before us is concerned with the entire content of our religion, which we must present and strengthen in its purity and divinity in order to rescue it from deadening rigidity on the one hand and from benumbing unbelief on the other. Judaism is weakening in its hold upon its followers day by day, and every layman is asking us, What

are you doing? The objects of the conference shall be—
(1) to bring the rabbis into closer relation and acquaintanceship; (2) to promote unanimity in the conduct of the
rabbinical office; (3) to further the founding of communal
institutions; and (4) to take counsel together on all Jewish
affairs.[10]

The readiness wherewith a large number of rabbis declared
themselves to be in sympathy with the object of this call showed
their eagerness to contribute toward solving what was becoming an intolerable condition of affairs for those who felt that
many Jewish institutions did not comport with the religious
conceptions of the generation, and that these institutions
demanded a thoroughgoing and comprehensive reform. It must
never be forgotten that the conferences were intended to be
erected upon the broad foundation of fitting the essentials of
Judaism to the practical requirements of the new life whereupon the Jews had entered, and which was as different from the
existence of the ghetto centuries as the cramped life of these
centuries had been from the freedom of the Palestinian commonwealth of old. Short as the conferences came of fulfilling
this great expectation, yet this was undoubtedly the hope of the
great majority of the men who were instrumental in calling
them into being.

(a) The Brunswick Conference

It was determined to hold the first conference at Brunswick.
The meeting took place there, June 12-19, 1844. The conference was attended by the following rabbis: A. Adler of Worms,
S. Adler of Alzey, Adler of Minden, Ben Israel of Coblentz,
L. Bodenheimer of Hildesheim, S. Formstecher of Offenbach,
N. Frankfurter of Hamburg, A. Geiger of Breslau, Goldman
of Eschwege, P. Heidenheim of Sonderhausen, L. Herzfeld
of Brunswick, S. Herxheimer of Bernburg, M. Hess of Stadt
Lengsfeld, S. Hirsch of Luxembourg, Hoffmann of Meiningen, S. Holdheim of Mecklenburg-Schwerin, J. Jolowicz of
Marienwerder, J. Kahn of Treves, J. Klein of Stolp, J. Maier
of Stuttgart, L. Philippson of Magdeburg, G. Salomon of
Hamburg, L. Schott of Randegg, L. Sobernheim of Bingen,
and B. Wechsler of Oldenburg.

Geiger, who was prevented from being present at the opening session of the conference, addressed a letter to the members, in which he urged that this first conference be merely preparatory and not resolutatory—that it concern itself with practical issues, and not with theoretical discussions, and that it avoid laying down any hard-and-fast rules.[11]

J. Maier of Stuttgart, was elected president of the conference. In his address of acceptance he recommended, as had Geiger in his letter, that the conference bear in mind constantly the practical requirements of the day, and confine its attention to solving as far as it could the vexing problems that were agitating Jewish life. The rabbinical conference was expected to become a permanent institution; hence it was necessary to declare at the very outset what its purpose was to be; the first paragraph of the rules governing the conference defines this as follows: "The rabbinical conferences have as their purpose that the members shall take counsel together in order to determine by what means the preservation and development of Judaism and the enlivening of the religious consciousness can be accomplished." [12] The discussion of this paragraph touched the all-important question of the authoritative character of the conference. Was the conference simply to discuss and deliberate upon questions of importance, or was it also to pass resolutions and render decisive opinions? If the latter, in how far could these be considered binding on the congregations? Would the congregation accept the decisions of the rabbis? In a word, was the conference to become a new body of authority for Judaism, or were its deliberations to be purely academic and without practical import? Some very interesting opinions were enunciated during the lengthy discussion: the general feeling seemed to be that the conference had not a synodal character, that its resolutions could not be enforced, and that at best any rabbi present who voted with the majority on any question was bound morally to carry out such resolution in the practical administration of his office;[13] on the other hand, it was held that the very fact that certain resolutions had been adopted by the conference would give strong support to any rabbi who might need such support, and that after all the chief thing was the confidence of the people; if the people had confidence in them their work would prove to be of a lasting character, and would receive an authoritative stamp; if not, all their efforts were in vain. This was expressed excellently by Holdheim, who said:

The purpose of our gathering is to work for the preservation and development of our holy religion; all our deliberations are concerned herewith, and we pass resolutions as to how this is to be accomplished. Have we any synodal justification? No; we as little as the rabbis of former times. What gave them their power was the confidence of the congregations, and this confidence was reposed in them because they were scholars and adepts in the law. The same holds with us.[14]

In a later discussion he expressed himself again on this question of authority:

All the talk about a Talmudical Judaism is an illusion. Science has decided that the Talmud has no authority dogmatically or practically. Even those who will not acknowledge this go beyond the Talmud. The question is, Who gives us the right to change the liturgy? This question requires an unequivocal answer. The אנשי כנסת הגדולה (The Men of the Great Assembly) have authority only for their age; what they ordained was timely, and on this the sanction of their ordinances rested. We have the same authority for our age if we give utterance to the consciousness of our age,[15] [but] even though the Talmud is not authoritative for us we do not wish to disregard the intellectual activity of two thousand years. We say merely this: Anything which upon unbiased, careful criticism contradicts the religious consciousness of the present age has no authority for us.[16]

As to the real significance of the decision of the majority for the individual rabbi, Samuel Hirsch said well:

Our conference must have a moral consciousness and must state that it has this, so that a rabbi who has voted with the majority can refer to the resolutions of this assembly. He must be empowered to say: "Although this or that may be in opposition to a paragraph of the *Shulchan Aruk*, I teach or do it, and thus many rabbis have voted with me, to whom I can refer."[17]

The whole discussion, as in fact did all the discussions, showed in what an unsettled state Jewish opinion and practice were; with scarcely an exception the men who had assembled at Brunswick desired reform; the question was merely how much? Broadly speaking, the rabbis present might have been classed in three divisions—first, representatives of what might be called the orthodox-reform party, if so paradoxical a term is permissible, *i.e.* such as demanded that if any changes were made this must be done consistently with the Talmudic-rabbinical standpoint; they were not opposed to slight changes, but these must not affect the existing structure of Judaism as based on Talmud and *Shulchan Aruk*. This party was represented but slightly, by three advocates at the most. Secondly, there was the reform element, which was in a great majority; for them Talmud and *Shulchan Aruk* were authoritative no longer; they claimed that Judaism, as legalistic rabbinism, had lost its power over the present generation, and that the spirit of the religion must be emphasized as over against the formalism into which it had degenerated; they held that Judaism in its fundamental concept as ethical monotheism was what it had always been at bottom; this fundamental concept had been obscured by accretions of forms; these had to be cleared away to such an extent as they no longer fed the religious nature, and their place had to be taken by such religious forms, ceremonies, and institutions as were in accord with the religious outlook of the modern Jew; such traditional ceremonies and institutions as still possessed vitality were, as a matter of course, to be retained, and if necessary to be interpreted accordingly. Thirdly, there was what might be termed the party of compromise, who desired to march under both banners; they wished to make haste very slowly, to preserve the traditions, and yet satisfy the needs of the new time which they could not help but recognize; such were opposed to any declaration of principles or to any positive expression that might indicate a break in any way with the consensus of Jewish tradition.

The character of the conference as a reform gathering, however, appeared constantly during the discussions. Thus, when Schott, a representative of the rabbinical party, denounced the tendency to abrogate existing customs, and asked, "Shall we negate always?" Holdheim answered him by saying that what Schott called negation was really affirmation in the light of the declared purpose of the conference, viz. "the preservation of Judaism." "The preservation of the essential," he claimed, "is conditioned by the excision of the non-essential. The healthy portion can be saved only by the removal of the diseased part." [18] Hess stated that until the conference would declare boldly that the Talmud had no significance dogmatically they would have no basis for their resolutions. As to Schott's claim about their negative attitude, he would say that the reproach of being destroyers is more applicable to the rigid rabbinites,[19] since they deny that the consciousness of the age is a moving force with many Jews of the present day; they were responsible that so many had become alienated, as for example in Frankfort. In the discussion on the liturgy, Samuel Adler used the following strong words:

> What right we have to reform! the traditional right to modify the Biblical ceremonial according to temporal and local conditions. The question was asked often whence we obtained that right. From the people. The free will of the people recognized the Talmudists, the free will of the people will recognize us also. We too are Talmudists. Hence we can insist on this same right.

And during the discussion on the Sabbath, Gotthold Salomon declared that they must seek to save the Sabbath as soon as possible, and strive to harmonize the Sabbath laws with life and the age; for "life must be regulated by and permeated with religion. The age is also a Bible through which God speaks to Israel." [20] These expressions illustrate in the main the spirit of the conference; it was emphatically of a reform tendency; the orthodox and the conservatives were in such a minority that they were almost a negligible quantity.

This being the first large gathering of Jewish theologians since the inception of the reform movement, it was but natural that voices should make themselves heard demanding that the conference state what the fundamental principles of Judaism are; for it was felt by these that such a declaration of principles was necessary in order to give the conference the proper foundation whereon to build. It was the same sentiment as had actuated the members of the Society of the Friends of Reform in Frankfort [21] when they contended that, in order to clear the controversial atmosphere in which Judaism was enveloped at that time, it was requisite to formulate in as brief a space as possible the essential fundamentals in which all Jews of modern views could agree. True, the question of formulating a declaration of principles was not one of the set subjects of discussion at the conference; still it was referred to a number of times in the course of the various debates. In the discussion on the prayer-book Bodenheimer, who was of a markedly conservative tendency, contended that before any intelligent action could be taken on the subject of determining what prayers are expressive of the religious convictions of the people to-day the question as to what the Jewish articles of belief are had to be settled. He claimed that the greatest confusion existed here, that even Maimonides contradicted himself, that Chasdai differed from him, and that Abarbanel in his turn differed with Chasdai.[22] He suggested, therefore, that a commission be appointed to formulate a statement of the fundamental articles of Jewish belief. In this he received the endorsement of Hess the radical, who advocated likewise the appointment of a commission for the drafting of a confession of belief which should state what the conference considers the essence of Judaism, and in what it conceives the relation of the moral to the ceremonial law to consist.[23] The rabbi of Luxembourg, Samuel Hirsch, expressed himself in a manner diametrically opposed to this; he too was a radical in many of his opinions, and the wide difference between him and Hess on this vital subject is most suggestive of the character of the conference and the difficulty of reconciling the many individual views represented; he declared that he was opposed to the proposition to appoint such a commission, because "we have no articles of belief in the commonly accepted interpretation of the term, viz., that we should or must believe what cannot be known or comprehended."[24] Holdheim too took strong ground against the formulation of any creed: "Every Jew is obligated by his birth; Judaism is inalienable, and does not depend on the acceptance of any dogma according to this or that interpretation."[25] Formstecher[26] sided with Bodenheimer and Hess; he averred that in all things there must be a principle from which to proceed: else there can be no results. "We require a principle in our relations with our congregations: else our work will be open to suspicion always, and some passages from some Hebrew book will always be able to be cited against us. . . . I do not demand a creed, as Hirsch maintains against me, but we must have a principle, a rule of procedure, by which we must be guided."[27] In more or less direct wise the debatable subject of creed and dogma was touched upon in these various utterances: Are there dogmas in Judaism or no? is still a favorite theme of discussion. Is a set creed compatible

with or foreign to the spirit of Judaism? remains to this day
an unsettled point of debate;[28] there can be no doubt that a set
creed is a great obstacle in the path of the progressive development of a religion, and that therefore reform Judaism must
always be impatient of a set creed;[29] still Formstecher was correct in the main when he urged that the conference should
formulate a declaration of principles. Such a declaration was
necessary, particularly in view of the decided differences
between the traditionalists and the reformers on a number of
controverted points. Such a declaration need not nor should
it have been regarded as of a fixed character; any future conference should have been considered at liberty to modify it as
soon as the opinion of an age concerning any article of such
a declaration should have undergone a change. A creed is fixed
and binding, a declaration of principles is fluid; possibly, however, the reformers as a body had not yet reached that unanimity of opinion which would have made such a declaration
possible. Twenty-five years later the idea to which Formstecher
had given expression at Brunswick was carried into practical
effect when the conference of rabbis at Philadelphia adopted
as the working basis of the conference a statement of principles.[30] This was not a new formulation of a creed, for most
of the men present at that conference were reformers of an
advanced type, and would, therefore, not have given their suf-
frages to the manufacture of any creed; that they adopted a
declaration of principles is indication sufficient of the essential
difference between this and a statement of creed binding upon
the individual as a necessary condition of salvation.[31] Although
the Brunswick Conference adopted no declaration of principles,
still there was an approach to this in the action touching the
answers given by the French Synhedrin to the questions of
Napoleon in 1807.[32] Philippson had moved at the afternoon
session of June 14 that the conference approve the attitude
taken by the Synhedrin for two reasons; first, to give assurance to the various governments of the patriotic attachment
of the Jews, and to show that there is nothing in Judaism at
variance with the best and highest interests of the state;[33]
and, secondly, to evince by this approval that the conference
was the successor in spirit of that notable assembly. By basing
upon the French Synhedrin, the first gathering of Jewish representatives resulting from the changes superinduced by the
political emancipation of the Jews which was one of the fore-

runners of the religious emancipation, viz. the reform movement, the conference, whether consciously or unconsciously,
declared itself the official voice of the modern spirit. Philippson's motion was referred to a commission consisting of Holdheim, Salomon, and Frankfurter, who reported at the session
of June 18. The conference indorsed the answers of the Synhedrin, making slight changes and additions here and there.
The consideration of the question as to whether the intermarriage of Jew and Christian was permitted caused a stormy
debate. The French Synhedrin had declared that a marriage
between a Jew and a Christian which had been solemnized by
a civil officer must be considered valid; the commission of the
conference reported thus: "Marriages between Jews and Christians, marriages between monotheists generally, are not forbidden." Hess desired the insertion of the additional words, "and
the rabbi is permitted to solemnize them"; however, he received
no support in this extreme attitude. S. Adler declared himself
as opposed to the adoption of this paragraph because it did
not fall within the scope of a rabbinical conference: "How
will the permission of intermarriage aid towards the reawakening of the religious spirit?" he asked pointedly. However, he
went on to say: "If they were to make a declaration on the
subject, their approval of intermarriage must be coupled with
the demand that the children born of such marriages must be
reared in the Jewish faith." This was the sense of the majority, and the report of the commission was amended to read:
"The marriage of a Jew with a Christian, marriage with adherents of montheistic faiths in general, is not forbidden, if the
laws of the state permit the parents to rear the children of such
a union also in the Jewish faith." [84]
    The answer to the question concerning the sentiment enter-
tained by the Jews toward the land of their birth or adoption
expresses excellently the political creed of the modern Jew:
"The Jew is bound to consider the land to which he belongs
by birth and civic conditions as his fatherland, to protect it,
and to obey all its laws." [85] That the members of the conference would take this stand was foreshadowed at a previous
session during the discussion of a proposition submitted by
Dr. Mayer of Hechingen on "Efforts towards the Emancipation of the Jewish Church." In this discussion the opinions of
the rabbis present on the religious and political elements, as
far as they touched Jewish thought and practice, were given

expression to. Holdheim declared that the religious principle must be kept clearly distinct from the political. "It is difficult," said he, "to keep the two separate, because they have been connected closely for so long a time. For this very reason it is important that two things which have been joined so improperly should be sundered finally. When and how shall this separation take place? That we cannot determine here and now, but it is the task of the present age. We do not grant that there is such a thing as a 'Christian state,' and certainly we should not speak of a 'Jewish state,' or of the overlapping of the religious and the political in Judaism. . . . Let the Jewish clergyman concern himself with religious instruction; that is plain! only let there be clearness, clearness in our religious conceptions." [36] Holdheim expressed here the thought that he gave voice to in many different forms in his published writings, both before and after this conference; [37] the separation of the religious and political elements became in time one of the marked features of the reform movement, which, therefore, is incompatible with a movement like political Zionism. So also Frankfurter declared that nothing was of greater importance than that they keep the religious and the political clearly distinct; "religiously speaking, we form a closely joined community, not over against the state, but within the state; but in all broadly human and political activities we consider ourselves subjects and members of the state on each and every count." [38] The special subject under discussion was the supervision of Jewish schools. Dr. Mayer of Hechingen had proposed that the governments should be petitioned to place the Jewish day schools under the supervision of the rabbi instead of a non-Jewish official, as was the case in many instances; the conference negatived this by a large majority, the sentiment being that such a demand would assume the appearance of political separatism.

The most important and lengthiest debate during the sessions of the conference was on the question of the reform of the liturgy. The debate was occasioned by the motion of Dr. Joseph Maier of Stuttgart, the president of the conference, that a commission be appointed to report to the next conference on the following six points: (1) Whether and in how far the Hebrew language was necessary for the public religious services, and, even if not necessary, whether its retention appeared advisable for the present among the Jewish congregations of the German fatherland? (2) In how far the dogma of the Messiah and all kindred doctrines must receive recognition in the prayers? (3) Whether the repetition of the שמנה עשרה (the eighteen benedictions) was necessary, and whether the *Mussafim* must be retained? (4) In what manner the קריאת התורה and ז" קראים (the reading from the Law and the calling up to the Law) could be arranged so as to cause less disturbance than at present, and to further congregational devotion and edification? (5) What steps could be taken to make the תקיעת שופר and נטילת לולב (the blowing of the ram's horn on the New Year's Day, and the shaking of the palm branches on the Feast of Tabernacles) less objectionable to the æsthetic sense? (6) Whether the organ is permissible in the synagogue?

These questions involved so many points which were the subjects of heated controversy that it cannot excite wonder that the discussion that ensued upon their presentation to the conference touched most of the subjects that emphasized the differences between traditionalists and reformers. The public service is the official expression of the religious convictions of the community, therefore it is almost as a matter of course the first point to which the attention of reformers is directed. As has been shown,[39] the earliest efforts of the new movement in Judaism had been directed toward a reform of the public services; the main attention, however, had been paid to æstheticizing the service, of making it decorous where it had been disorderly, of excising *piyyutim*, and thus shortening it, of introducing choral music and the German sermon; but less thought had been given to the matter of making the prayers express the principles of the reform movement. So much was involved in this reform of the ritual, so many points of detail, that it is not surprising that the men of that time who were in the very thick of the controversy could not see the forest because of the trees. The six questions upon which the discussion in the Brunswick Conference was based indicated excellently the difficulties which a comprehensive reform of the liturgy was compelled to encounter. Inasmuch, however, as the motion was simply to refer these questions to a commission to report to the next conference, and the discussion on this report will have to receive detailed consideration in its proper place, it is unnecessary to reproduce here the opinions expressed at this conference on the points at issue. Sufficient to say that the recommendation to elect such a commission was acted upon favorably, and the following rabbis were constituted members thereof—Joseph Maier, Levi Herzfeld, Levi Bodenheimer, Samuel Holdheim, and Gotthold Salomon.

Another subject that aroused prolonged discussion was the so-called oath *more Judaico.*[10] Whenever a Jew appeared as a witness before a court, and the oath was administered to him, the whole proceeding was extremely humiliating to the self-respect of the Jewish witness; he had to go to the synagogue accompanied by the judge, the rabbi, and ten Jews above the age of thirteen, and, decked with the *tallith*[11] and the *tefillin,*[12] had to take the scroll of the law upon his arm; the rabbi had to impress upon him the solemnity of the oath; the witness then spoke a set formula and had to give assurance that he would not attempt to have the oath abrogated by a Jewish ecclesiastical court, and that he would not consider it annulled by the *Kol Nidre* prayer spoken on the eve of the Day of Atonement; that he did not consider the Christian an idolater, etc. Much was written at this time by Jewish scholars on this subject,[13] and attempts were made to have this barbarous medieval proceeding abolished; possibly the most famous case was that tried in Saverne in which Cremieux, the future senator of France, defended M. Lazare Isidor, at the time rabbi of Pfalzburg, and later chief rabbi of France. Isidor had refused to permit the administration of the oath *more Judaico,* had locked the door of the synagogue, and had declared that he would never permit such a profanation of God's name.[14] This case aroused so much attention that it was the beginning of the final abolition of the oath *more Judaico* in France. The Brunswick Conference took a firm stand on this subject, and declared that "the oath of a Jew in the name of God is binding without further ceremony."[15] The conference declared further that the *Kol Nidre* prayer was unessential, and the members present promised to use every effort to eliminate it from their services on the coming Day of Atonement.[16]

While the Jews were separate alien communities with no political rights or affiliations, they had their own jurisdiction, and were governed in many vital relations of life, as marriage, divorce, and the like, by their own laws. When they were striving for civil emancipation and were being incorporated in the body politic in various states, it was found that their traditional laws came into conflict frequently with the laws of the land. Reforms were necessary. It was for this reason that Jolowicz presented a resolution calling for a revision of the Jewish marriage laws. Holdheim moved that a commission be appointed to report to the next conference a plan for the reform of the marriage law, this being demanded urgently by the conditions and circumstances of the time. This was agreed to, and Holdheim, Herzfeld, Maier, Bodenheimer, and Geiger were elected members of this commission.

Shortly before the convening of this conference the Jewish world had been agitated by the circumcision controversy.[47] An echo of this agitation sounded in the conference hall when Hess introduced the following resolution:

> Be it resolved by this conference that, although it has learned with pain that some co-religionists observe no longer a command so universally considered sacred as circumcision, yet it declares against all external coercion and exclusion as has been demanded by a number of rabbis, and expresses the opinion that those who do not observe the command of circumcision are to be considered members of the Jewish religious community despite this, and as admissible to the taking of the oath, the giving of testimony, and the contracting of marriage with a Jewess.

The resolution was disposed of by the indorsement of the suggestion of the president to the effect that since this matter was the subject of such bitter discussion in Jewry just at this time it be passed over, it being inadvisable to give occasion to the play of passion on the floor of the conference.

At the closing session of the conference Samuel Hirsch proposed that the conference take steps to reconcile the differences between Jewish doctrine and practice by the abrogation or the amelioration of a number of Sabbath and dietary laws. He stated that the matter would not be so grave were the Sabbath laws disregarded only in the household economy, but that the public desecration of the Sabbath demanded that something be done to save the situation. If the members of the conference would address themselves to this subject in full earnestness they would give evidence to the world that they are not negativists and destroyers, but conservers and builders.[48] Schott, the ultra-conservative, held that no action was necessary on their part, "since the Sabbath laws do not conflict with their duties as men and citizens, rabbinism having permitted certain necessary ameliorations." A. Adler, after declaring that the modern point of view is altogether different from that of the Talmud, proceeded to say that "there is a cleft between life and the traditional Sabbath observance. We must reconcile this difference, not continue it." [49] Herxheimer called attention to the difficulties which were confronting the rabbi constantly because of the inconsistency between his preaching and teaching and the practice of his people. This would continue until life and profession would be reconciled. [50]

Holdheim declared flatly: "We cannot adopt the rabbinical conception of the Sabbath. We must ask our conscience what is the intent of Sabbath observance. Perhaps we can preserve Sabbath observance without Sabbath rest"; and Salomon exclaimed: "We must attempt to save the Sabbath as soon as possible, and to reconcile the Sabbath laws with life and with our age. For after all the object of religion must be to regulate and permeate life." [51]

So important a question, possibly, the most important among the practical problems in Jewish life, demanded the most thorough discussion and consideration; this it could not receive in the closing hours of a conference. A Sabbath commission was therefore elected to report on the subject at the coming conference; the commission consisted of Geiger, A. Adler, S. Adler, Wechsler, and Kahn.

The conference adjourned on Wednesday, June 19, after determining to meet at Frankfort-on-the-Main on July 15 of the following year. No event in that agitated period stirred the Jewish communities more than did this conference. Denunciations fierce and invectives severe were hurled at the rabbis who had met at Brunswick. The conference was assailed as negative and destructive. Attacks by opponents called forth defenses by friends; articles in newspapers, essays in magazines, pamphlets appeared in rapid succession; scathing criticism [52] on the one hand and admiring laudation [53] on the other characterized the temper of the writers; the orthodox accused the conference of having undermined the very foundations of Judaism, the reformers acclaimed it for having given voice bravely to the true spirit of Judaism. Only the more important of these controversial publications can be referred to.

Most unexpected was the criticism of the conference by Ludwig Philippson, who had been mainly instrumental in calling it into being; the conference had traveled a path far different from that which he had expected and hoped that it would take.

In discussing its work, he wrote that it was unfortunate that the conference had developed a critical tendency instead of devoting itself to the task of reviving and creating; it criticized existing institutions, but paid no attention to organizing other institutions which the practical needs of the people required; had the conference been a scientific congress, learned criticism would have been in place, but the conference was intended to contribute primarily toward awakening and strengthening the religious consciousness of the people, and in this province the critical spirit can accomplish nothing.[54] He regretted beyond measure that the principle of compromise (*Prinzip der Vermittelung*) did not guide the deliberations of the conference; this represented his standpoint; those who were guided by this principle wished to build on historical foundations, recognizing the needs of the present and having an eye to the future, but they would not abrogate existing customs and ceremonies until they had something positive to take their place; the misfortune was that the conference was dominated by such as had an abstract ideal of positive religion, which they pursued without regard for the past, and for whom nothing had any value except that which comported with the demands of cold reason and the critical faculty.[55] Philippson was of a decidedly practical bent; he felt that reform must move slowly and accommodate itself to existing conditions; it was his firm conviction that if the conference would call into being practical institutions like a rabbinical seminary, a publication society and the like, it would do much more for the religious advancement of the people than by the discussion of abstract religious ideas. The philosophical principles of the reform movement received but little consideration in his writings; he praised the conference for not having formulated a declaration of principles, and stated that in future conferences the conservative element must be strengthened, for this alone would ensure their efficacy, authority, and beneficial influence.

The individual criticism of the conference which aroused the greatest attention was that of Zacharias Frankel.[56] He claimed that the members of the conference were not impressed sufficiently with the significance and gravity of their task, that they were not careful enough in their utterances and proposals, and that they did not keep in view the religious state of the people. He held that a rabbinical conference cannot pass resolutions, only a synod can do this, a conference can only discuss and deliberate. The Brunswick Conference discussed the weightiest matters; in a number of instances the members showed their unpreparedness and incapacity. Thus in the discussion on the mixed marriage question the attitude of the French Synhedrin had been misrepresented; the Synhedrin had not declared that "the marriage of a Jew with a Christian is not forbidden," as the conference had reported, but that "the marriages between Jews and Christians which had been performed in accordance with the laws of the civil code are binding civilly, and although they cannot be solemnized religiously, they are not anathema." He also blamed the conference for applying the scalpel of criticism to customs and ceremonies close and dear to the heart of the people; what the people consider edifying and binding must be respected; the conference had made the mistake of keeping in view only the "age," and not the "faith"; the members had spoken constantly of the spirit of the age, but did not bear in mind the warm religious sentiment of the people who still clung to many a form and custom in which the religious philosopher, standing on the advanced intellectual outposts of the time, recognizes only a meaningless survival of the past, but which may yet have power to move and edify. Frankel's attack called forth many answers, notably from Holdheim,[57] Maier,[58] the president of the conference, and Samuel Hirsch,[59] all of whom defended the conference warmly. The first named took pains to show how fallacious was Frankel's argument that the members of the conference should not have criticized such religious forms and beliefs as were close to the heart of the people, and still had power to move them; superstitions often have this power, shall superstitions never be attacked for this reason? who are the better judges of what is the truth of religion, the people or the religious guides? the timeserver has his hand on the people's pulse, the true leader, worthy of the name, will not be deterred in his course, no matter what the people may believe or think. Even Frankel stated in another connection that everything is not as it should be in Jewry, and advocated reforms because of the conflict between life and the faith;[60] but there is no such conflict, Holdheim goes on to say; the conflict is between life and the Talmudical interpretation of the faith, between life and rabbinical formalism and ceremonialism, and not between life and Judaism; there must be a thorough reform of traditional rabbinical Judaism and the conflict will disappear from the life of the modern Jew. Frankel himself is not clear;

now he advocates reform, and again he decries it; let him be honest and not attempt to attain to a supreme position in the estimation of the common people by such palaver to the effect that what still appeals to the bulk of the people has religious validity; the majority rule is not the gauge by which the truth is to be measured.

Dr. Maier, the president of the conference, in his defense touches the same point; he says that if Frankel's contention be true that the popular sanction of religious forms and institutions must guide their observance or discontinuance, the function of religious leaders would be that of gravediggers who have only to bury decently what has disappeared from the life of the people; he puts this apt query to Frankel:

> Suppose that it had so chanced that instead of becoming chief rabbi of Dresden you had become chief rabbi of Moldavia or Wallachia, where Chassidism which finds religious edification and satisfaction in the observance of senseless cabbalistical customs is rampant—Chassidism which considers holy and God-pleasing many acts that true piety is backward in even mentioning—would you hesitate for one moment in attacking and removing these customs, even though, to use your own phrase, "They had received popular sanction and acknowledgment"? The revealed will of God is the incontestable standard for reforms, not the will of a party, even though that party form for the nonce an overwhelming majority.

Every command, every institution whose retention can only harm the essence of religion, and which has either no foundation in Scripture or was ordained for a certain time that is past, or a certain political phase that has ceased, must be surrendered or changed, even though Talmud and *Shulchan Aruk* declare it to be Mosaic and of external validity; on the other hand, every command, every institution which strengthens the true content of religion must be retained, even though it emanate from the latest teachers of the people. The acceptance of such recommendations and proposals made by the religious leaders depends not on them. They cannot force this acceptance, for they have no police power, nor have they the slightest wish to exercise such power. Theirs it is only to fulfill the duties of their office and to show the people the way. This, continues the president, was the standpoint of the conference.[61] A number of men had

gathered "to take counsel together as to what must be done for
the preservation of the religion, and they had paid especial
attention to those religious institutions and customs, the reform
of which was necessary and urgent." After reviewing and
rebutting Frankel's criticisms of the specific points in the proceedings of the conference, Maier closes his defense thus
strongly:

> As a matter of fact the rabbis of the old thoroughly
> orthodox school were far more careful, honest, and honor-
> able than those of the chiaroscuro type of to-day. The
> former declared art and science, in short all culture except
> that of a purely religious character, as absolutely incom-
> patible with Judaism, and characterized every Jew who
> read a German book as a heretic פושע באלהי ישראל; this
> attitude was consistent and intelligible; the latter, however,
> advise that modern schools be attended by Jews, and the
> arts and sciences be cultivated by them, but denounce all
> such as advocate a reform of the ritual and the cult,
> because these do not harmonize with modern culture—this
> attitude is inconsistent and unintelligible. But history
> adjusts every inconsistency, and we may be sure that the
> present inconsistency in Judaism will be adjusted, even
> though dozens of Frankels strive against it with might
> and main. As for you, my friends and brothers, who are
> not concerned for your own aggrandizement, but for the
> weal of our co-religionists: not for the realization of selfish
> plans and opinions, but for the preservation of our reli-
> gion: be you not misled by appearances like this which I
> have just discussed. The struggle of light with darkness is
> still on, but victory must follow as surely as does the day
> the dawn.

Much as some other writings that the conference called forth
deserve detailed mention, notably the answer of Samuel Hirsch
to Frankel, mentioned above, and the pamphlet of Gotthold
Salomon,[62] they must be passed by with a mere reference in
order that space may be given to the most famous of all the
publications resulting from the deliberations and recommendations of the conference. The protest of seventy-seven orthodox
rabbis of Germany, France, and Hungary aroused as great com-
motion at the time as did the conference itself. The protest was
in the form of an address to the faithful in Israel שלומי אמוני

ישראל, and the words of the prophet Ezekiel, xxxiii, 6-7, were placed at the head of the document as the motto. It was in the main a fierce denunciation of the conference and its members. Some of its salient sentences read, "Judaism is slandered by men who call themselves its protectors and its teachers." "No authority is respected, not even that of the two-thousand-year-old Great Synod, among whose members even the last of the prophets were numbered. The barriers of truth are battered down; the Talmud with all the traditional divine laws contained in it is vilified in the most unsparing manner, and its fall is gloated over." The protest speaks of the members of the conference as desiring to erect in the place of the hegemony of the Talmud "the throne of Karaism or possibly the rule of the idol of convenience and sensuality." The protest proper is worded thus:

> After carefully conducted written negotiation and conscientious probing of all the proceedings of said conference, we, the undersigned, have united to inform you, the faithful in Israel, that all the resolutions of the so-called Brunswick rabbinical conference—with the sole exception of the one that defines the political attitude of the Israelites towards the state, in which is to be included also the resolution declaring for the sacred inviolability of the oath—are opposed to true Judaism, and are therefore false and condemnable for the believing Israelite; that a destructive spirit of revolution and sectarianism breathes through the proceedings; that the work which has been projected for a future conference is of the same condemnable character; and that we regard it therefore as the duty of every truly believing Israelite not only not to take part in such proceedings, but also to oppose such novelty-seeking efforts by every legally permitted means.

The signers of the document (which reached later the number of one hundred and sixteen) acknowledge the growing indifference in Israel, and declare it to be the duty of the religious leaders to do all they can to stem it, but they denounce the method of the reformers as false; instead of invoking the divine aid to save the ship of Judaism which is tossing about in agitated waters, they think to ensure its safety by throwing overboard one divine law after the other. "O the fatuity of those blinded leaders in Israel! . . . Neither we nor any person

have the power to abrogate even the least of the religious laws."
They then call attention to such incidents in the past as the
idolatry of the people during the first commonwealth, the
apostasy preceding the Maccabean uprising, the formation of
the Sadducean and Karaite sects; all these have passed away
with the exception of a few thousand Karaites while the
observers of the Law still exist and flourish.

> Therefore, ye faithful in Israel! [the protest concludes]
> do not permit yourselves, because of the scarecrow of reli-
> gious decay which has been set up, to be misled to sanction-
> ing reforms and innovations which result only in increas-
> ing this decay. Turn hopefully with us to Him who desires
> the well-being of all his children on earth, praying that He
> may heal soon the sickness of our age which is suffering
> from materialism, and that He may bring back to the true
> faith the erring in Israel.[63] . . . Until then let us guard
> our very ancient religious fortress faithfully, and protect
> it against those who approach it in the guise of friends in
> order to undermine its foundations undisturbed.[64]

The protest was signed among others by such paladins of
orthodoxy as N. M. Adler of Hanover, B. Auerbach of Darmstadt, Jacob Bamberger of Worms, Seligman Bär Bamberger
of Würzburg, Jacob Aaron Ettlinger of Altona, Samuel Freund
of Prague, Samson Raphael Hirsch of Emden, E. L. Teweles
of Prague, G. Tiktin of Breslau, and S. A. Trier of Frankfort.
This protest may be considered an official document of the
party of tradition. "Neither we nor any person have the power
to abrogate the least of the religious laws"; this sentence sums
up their position. In their eyes the Brunswick reformers were
traitors and worse to the cause of Judaism. Their cry was the
same as that of the rabbis who over half a century previously
had denounced Mendelssohn's German translation of the Pentateuch and Wessely's plea for secular education, and later the
Hamburg Prayer-Book and Geiger's attitude. For them Judaism was a closed chapter; at any rate they were consistent; they
considered modern influences of whatever kind as inimical to
Judaism; their opposition to the Brunswick Conference was
justified from their standpoint, and one can understand and
even sympathize with this opposition if that standpoint is borne
in mind. But they were enlisted in a lost cause, the day of
rabbinism and *Shulchan-Arukism* was past for the Jew living in

modern surroundings. Judaism was demanding a new reading, and even though the Brunswick conferees did not render that new reading completely, still were they nearer the true understanding of the underlying principles of the faith than were their bitter though sincere opponents; the Brunswick conferees lived in the present, and appreciated the changes that had come upon Jewry, the signers of the protest lived in the past and could not, I will not say would not, see those changes.

The protest called forth many counter-replies; from Mannheim,[65] Giessen,[66] Karlsruhe,[67] Worms,[68] Heidelberg, and other communities came addresses signed by many names upholding the conference, and denouncing the attitude of the seventy-seven; a brief extract from one of these addresses will serve to indicate the spirit that pervaded all of them:

> In the present critical phase of Judaism we await only beneficial results from the efforts of the rabbinical conference; its published proceedings enlist our full sympathy, and we look forward with the greatest confidence to its future transactions which we expect will free our sublime religion from the excrescences of past ages, and set forth its truths in a manner suited to the time wherein we are now living.[69]

Thus the Brunswick Conference, as could not fail to be the case, was condemned bitterly in some quarters and commended strongly in others; the published proceedings offer but a faint reflex of the spirit which animated the conference; many who attended did so at great sacrifices, being impelled by the longing to contribute toward a solution of the difficulties that were besetting Judaism. This conference did pioneer work; it grappled with vital problems; the members were sincere in their presentation and discussion of these problems; the solution was not to be expected in a week, many of the problems there touched upon have not been settled to this day; the question of Hebrew in the service, and the Sabbath question, are still the fruitful subjects of debate. In truth, the members of this conference could do no more than indicate a program for future conferences, and this they did by appointing commissions to report on vital subjects at coming meetings. One of two courses was open to them, either the theoretical or the practical; had the conference resolved itself into a committee of the whole to consider and perfect plans for the founding and maintenance of practical institutions like a rabbinical seminary, a publication society and the like, as Philippson and also Geiger desired, it would have aroused less opposition and have set in motion useful and needed agencies. But under the circumstances this could have been but one phase of its activity at best. It is difficult to see how, in that period of storm and stress, any gathering of rabbis could have avoided the consideration of those burning questions in Jewish life that the Brunswick Conference discussed; for even though the discussions were theoretical and academic they had also a distinct practical bearing. Principle is all important; the Jewish communities required a clear understanding of the principles of Judaism as they found expression in the liturgy and the public institutions of the faith, and who was to discuss and determine upon these principles if not the religious leaders? This the rabbis assembled at Brunswick did, and for that reason this conference is so important an incident in the history of the reform movement.[70]

(b) The Frankfort Conference

The second meeting of the "Conference of the Rabbis of Germany"[71] took place at Frankfort-on-the-Main, July 15-28, 1845; those present were A. Adler, of Worms; S. Adler, of Alzey; J. Auerbach, of Frankfort; Ben Israel, of Coblentz; David Einhorn, of Birkenfeld; S. Formstecher, of Offenbach; Z. Frankel, of Dresden; A. Geiger, of Breslau;[72] J. Gosen, of Marburg; Güldenstein, of Buchau; S. Herxheimer, of Bernburg; L. Herzfeld, of Brunswick; M. Hess, of Stadt-Lengsfeld; S. Holdheim, of Schwerin; S. Hirsch, of Luxembourg; Hoffman, of Waldorf; J. Jolowicz, of Kulm; I. M. Jost, of Frankfort; J. Kahn, of Trier; J. Maier, of Stuttgart; L. Philippson, of Magdeburg; M. Reiss, of Altbreisach; G. Salomon, of Hamburg; L. Schott, of Randegg; L. Sobernheim, of Bingen; L. Stein, of Frankfort; S. Süsskind, of Wiesbaden; A. Treuenfels, of Weilburg; H. Wagner, of Mannheim; and B. Wechsler, of Oldenburg. L. Stein, the recently appointed rabbi of the Frankfort congregation was elected president; A. Geiger, vice-president, and I. M. Jost and S. Hirsch secretaries.

The Frankfort Conference is notable because of the full and thorough discussion that the report of the Commission on Liturgy received at the hands of the rabbis present. This commission appointed at Brunswick reported through its chairman, J. Maier, of Stuttgart. The discussion of this report occupied the greater portion of the session. For nine days (July 15-24) the members of the conference debated the various recommendations of the report; the discussion was conducted on a very lofty and scholarly plane, and in the course thereof many striking things were said. Although most of the rabbis present leaned decidedly toward reform, still the conservative side was represented, and, as will be seen, the recommendations were by no means radical in character, although of a reforming tendency throughout. The men gathered at Frankfort were for the most part open-minded and clear-sighted; they combined a thorough knowledge of Hebrew lore with a keen appreciation of the religious conditions in the Jewish communities, and fearlessly yet reverentially gave themselves to the task of casting their Jewish inheritance into a modern mold.[73] The discussions on the liturgy are indicative of the spirit that permeated the conference and must therefore be given at some length, notably as the points debated are of significance still to-day, eighty years later.

The Hebrew Language in the Service

The commission reported, in answer to the question whether and in how far the Hebrew language was necessary for the public religious services and if not necessary whether its retention was advisable for the present,[74] that there is no objective necessity for Hebrew throughout the service, and that not even Talmudic authority can be cited for this, barring few exceptions. But since a subjective necessity for the Hebrew possibly exists among a great portion of German Jewry at present, the commission deems it advisable to retain the Hebrew in the typical parts of the liturgy, viz.: ברכו with its sections, the פרשת שמע, the first and last three benedictions of the תפלה and the קריאת התורה; the remainder of the service to be in German.[75]

Zacharias Frankel, who had criticized the Brunswick Conference so caustically,[76] and who had appeared at this conference with the purpose of directing the discussions into a more conservative channel, took occasion at the very outset of the meeting to define his religious standpoint and his attitude toward reform. He used here the famous phrase "positive historical Judaism" as expressive of his position. He discussed not so much the point at issue, viz. Hebrew in the service, as the whole question of reform. It is necessary, first of all, said he, to lay down the principles that guide us. "Lack of principle (*Prinzipienlosigkeit*) is the greatest enemy of the faith and must be combated from all sides." He declared his platform to be positive historical Judaism. True, we cannot return to the letter of the Bible and take this as our guide, but shall we be guided, on the other hand, by the spirit of the age? The spirit of the age is as changeable as time itself. Further, it is cold; it may appear reasonable, but it will never be able to satisfy the heart, to comfort, soothe and edify; Judaism, however, is always inspiring and edifying. The reform of Judaism is not a reform of the faith, but of legal acts. These still exercise a living and definite influence on the people. It should not be our purpose to weaken, but to strengthen, this influence. We should not pay any heed to individuals who do not carry out the customs; we are not a party, but must have a care for the whole community. The need of the hour is to prevent each and every division in Israel; not to call new parties into existence, but to reconcile with one another those already existing. Another principle must guide us, viz. the science of Judaism; this must be the foundation whereon every reform must build. There are great scholars who are not rabbis in active service, and who are therefore excluded from our meetings; they should have a voice in such matters as require a scientific exposition of the thought and development of Judaism; it would be well, therefore, to secure their opinions, which could be done if all important resolutions were printed and spread abroad before a vote is taken here upon them." He concluded by stating that he considered the rabbinical conference an excellent institution, but that he could sanction its gatherings only if they would have in mind constantly the entire body of positive Judaism. He would therefore implore and adjure the assembly to declare its principles first of all, and to permit no discussion whose only purpose was the expression of private opinions and views.

The President replied to Frankel, and declared that they were quite at one in their views.

After this introductory digression, the debate on the subject in hand proceeded, the main features of which are reproduced here. Frankel opened the discussion proper by saying that the Hebrew language is interwoven with the very life of Judaism, and that for him it is the holy language. The Hebrew name of God, *Adonai*, means much more to the Jew than the German expression *Gott*. The retention of the Hebrew is necessary for the preservation of a knowledge of Holy Writ. Without this all true understanding of the Bible would be entirely neglected among the Jews.

Geiger asserted that all authorities agree that prayer may be spoken in any language. The question whether Hebrew is objectively necessary in prayer must be understood as meaning whether it is legally necessary. At all events, there is no prohibition anywhere to use other languages. This suffices.[78]

Salomon claimed that not one of the recognized legal codes obliges us to pray in Hebrew. Mishnah and Talmud say distinctly שמע בכל לשון and תפלה בכל לשון (the *sh'ma* and the eighteen benedictions may be spoken in any language); so also we read in the *Shulchan Aruk* יכל להתפלל בכל לשון אשר ירצה (*Or. Ch. Hil. Tef.* 101.4), "Man can pray in any language that he desires," and in the Book of the Pious (ספר חסידים, par. 588 and 785) it is said expressly that the chief prayers should be uttered in the language which is understood and that it is better "not to pray at all than to pray in a language that one does not understand." Hence there is no religious obligation to pray in Hebrew.[79]

A. Adler averred that the designation of Hebrew as the holy tongue is no evidence for the necessity of its use as the language of the divine service; this name indicates only that it is the language of sacred Scripture whose sanctity depends not on the verbal expression, but on the thought expressed. He objected to the distinction made by the commission as between the objective and the subjective necessity for the use of Hebrew in the service; this was of no importance. The vital question was whether the liturgy should be fixed for present needs or for always.

Reiss dissented from report by claiming that the precept אסור לשנות ממטבע שטבעו חכמים בברכות (it is forbidden to change the form into which the wise men have cast the benedictions)[80] involves a prohibition to eliminate Hebrew, and particularly the forms of the benedictions which can be reproduced exactly in no other language. Further, a distinction must be made between the private prayer of an individual and the public service in the synagogue; only in the former case is German permissible as the language of prayer.

Einhorn stated unequivocally that no possible doubt can be entertained as to the legal permissibility of any language for prayer.

Nay, I go further, and state that the introduction of the vernacular into the service is necessary. Hebrew is the language of the study of the Law, but it is not the organ wherewith to express the feelings of the people. Afore-times prayer was only a cry of pain; a scarcely intelligible expression sufficed for this; but now people need a prayer that shall express thoughts, feelings and sentiments; this is possible only through the mother tongue.

Samuel Adler agreed that the Maimonidean precept quoted by Reiss is of weight. But on what does this pronouncement rest? There is no reason given for it because it is axiomatic. The wise men in Israel worked for the people; set prayers were necessary in order that prayer might not become merely a mat-ter of caprice; the people, being incapable of giving a worthy form of expression to prayer, require that prayer be cast into set formulæ. Hence that precept of Maimonides was meant for the people only, not for the teachers. It is reported of Jizchaq Saggi Nahor that he was dissatisfied with many of the bene-dictions; thus for example he substituted כונן כסא דוד ובונה ירושלים (who establisheth the throne of David and buildeth Jerusalem) for בונה ירושלים (who buildeth Jerusalem). All *chakamim* (wise men, teachers) had the same privilege and the rabbis of the present day are subject to the same sacred duty of providing for the people according to the needs of the present.

Stein called attention to the fact that prayers like *Yekum Purkan* and *Kaddish* were spoken in Aramaic and not in Hebrew, because the former was the popular tongue at the time they were introduced into the service.

Upon the taking of the vote on the question as to whether it is objectively legally necessary (*objektiv gesetzlich noth-wendig*) to retain the Hebrew as the language of the service, all voted in the negative except four, who refrained from voting, viz. Frankel, Formstecher, Schott, and Philippson. On the following day three of these declared their position defi-nitely; Frankel voted with the majority, and stated that there was no law demanding the use of the Hebrew, except in a few instances, such as the priestly benediction; Schott, referring to the decision of Maimonides that had been quoted during the discussion, voted that Hebrew was legally necessary; Philipp-son declared that he withdrew his objection, which referred only to the form in which the question was put, and voted also with those who answered the question in the negative; hence, all present, with the exception of Schott and Formstecher, placed themselves on record to the effect that objectively considered it was not legally necessary to retain Hebrew as the language of the service.

But this was only the first portion of the question under debate; the conference proceeded to discuss the latter half, viz. "Is the retention of the Hebrew in the public service objectively necessary on other than legal grounds?"

Hirsch opened the discussion by stating that he considered the exclusion of Hebrew from the synagogue unwarranted. True, Hebrew had become unfamiliar to the people, and this was one of those instances of a collision between life and profession the reconciling of which was their especial task. They should aim to solve the question as to how Hebrew could be taught in the schools without encroaching too much upon the time necessary for proper instruction in other branches. The chief reason why Hebrew should not be excluded from the service was that in such case the gulf between the theologians, who alone would understand it, and the non-theologians would become wider and wider, and as a result the distinction between clergy and laity, which is foreign to Judaism, would creep in.

Holdheim claimed that a weakening of the religious spirit would not result from the removal of Hebrew from the synagogue, for this does not depend on any language, but on its inherent strength. The use of the vernacular in the service wherever it was found necessary would contribute very much toward clarifying the religious conceptions, and far from harming Judaism, would make for a strengthening of the religious consciousness among the Jews and secure recognition of the mission of the religion in the outside world.[81]

Herzfeld gave voice to the vague sentimentalism of the romanticist when he claimed that the Hebrew should be retained because there was something mystical in it; "even though some things be not clearly understood, this does no harm."

Geiger held that it was desirable that the service be conducted in the mother tongue, because this is the language of the heart (*Gemüth*). "All our deepest feelings and sentiments, all our highest thoughts, receive their expression through it." He felt constrained to confess that a German prayer aroused in him deeper devotion than did a Hebrew prayer, even though Hebrew was his second mother tongue; nay, he might say his

first, since he had learned it first. Hebrew lives no longer
among the people; it is not difficult to perceive that even the
reading from the Law wearies the greater portion of the congregation. It had been claimed, continued he, that if the Hebrew
were to be eliminated from the service the very foundations of
Judaism would be shattered; he, for his part, considered it a
most serious reflection on Judaism if it be held that it required
the prop of a language to endure. Further, if the Hebrew is
looked upon as an essential in Judaism, this would stamp the
religion as a national religion, since a peculiar language is the
mark of an isolated national existence; and certainly no one
present would assert that Judaism is necessarily dependent upon
a separate nationality.[82]

Frankel contended that religion as something abstract
required outer symbols which remind us of God. This was the
purpose of such commands as enjoined the use of מזוזה, תפלין,
etc., etc.; this also is the purpose of Hebrew as the language
of prayer. So much that is characteristic of Judaism has been
surrendered already that it is time to call a halt. True, a portion
of the service should be in German, but the Hebrew must be
the preponderating element. The ancient teachers who had permitted the use of other language in prayer had in mind only the
weak, who would not have found solace in a non-Hebrew
prayer without such permission. These teachers never thought
of eliminating Hebrew from the service.

Maier challenged the claim that the Hebrew was the Jews'
mother tongue; this has not been the case for centuries; it may
edify some few, but the congregation does not entertain such
a sentiment. This was recognized aforetimes so clearly that
special books of devotion for women (תחנות) were composed in
German; these aroused the women to greater devotion than
did Hebrew the men. The only point that appears worthy of
notice is the national significance of the language as a sign of
the common bond among Jews; but a minimum of Hebrew is
sufficient for this, e.g. the retention of שמע and קדושה, the
priestly blessing and the reading from the Torah.

Philippson urged that all extremes be avoided; it is apparent
from what has been said that no one desires to eliminate the
Hebrew altogether, and that no one, on the other hand, objects
to the introduction of German; it is only a question of how
much. The German and Hebrew elements must be combined
organically. The Hebrew is indispensable as the point of union

among Jews. German Jews are German; they think and feel
as Germans and desire to live and be active patriotically. But
Judaism is not German, it is universal; the dispersion of the
Jews is not the dispersion of Judaism. The confession of Judaism represents this in content, the Hebrew language in form.[83]

Abraham Adler held that they must bear in mind but one
object, viz. the search for truth; all sentimentalism is to be
avoided. It may pain us to relinquish some things, and yet it
may have to be done if necessity demands. It has been claimed
that Hebrew is sacred; not at all; the language which expresses
sacred things is sacred; if I speak truth in German, then the
German word is sacred; if I lie in Hebrew, then the Hebrew
word is unholy. Not the letter nor the sound makes the Bible
holy, but the content. It is claimed, further, that the Bible will
lose its influence if we dispense with Hebrew as the language of
prayer. Not at all. Philo has been cited as the horrible example
of the effect of the ignorance of Hebrew (in one place he
mistranslates a Hebrew phrase, rendering ותקבר בשיבה טובה
"thou shalt be supported" instead of "thou shalt be buried in a
good old age"). Even though he knew the Bible from a Greek
translation only, his works are more truly religious than many
passages in the Talmud. . . . The eternal creations of the mind
preserve a language; sacred Scripture is immortal through
itself and requires no props. Again, it has been asserted that
the Hebrew supplies the mystical element to the service which
is a necessity; I grant that there is truth in genuine mysticism,
which is frequently the subtlest comprehension of the truth; but
the unintelligible is not mysticism, and truth is not revealed in
the irrational.[84]

Auerbach injected a new element into the discussion; much
has been said on the score of sentiment as an argument for
retaining the Hebrew, he remarked; but sentiment is an unsafe
guide unless linked with principle. The chief factor in the pending discussion has not been mentioned, viz. the historical. The
most important issue of the day in Judaism is involved here,
i.e. the relation of the national to the religious element. If these
are to be separated, no one is justified in accusing us of surrendering our national position for the sake of civic advantages
in the countries wherein we are living. Whoever would charge
us with this would misunderstand the issue altogether; the issue
is not what we wish to do to solve our mission, but what we
must do. History has decided. Centuries lie between the

national and the purely religious. Yet, despite this, the attachment to the Hebrew is not mere sentimentalism. The national was not really divorced from the religious in Judaism, but the latter is rather a development out of the former; the purely religious element is the flower of Jewish nationalism. We must hold fast the thread of this development if we would not surrender the principle of Judaism. Judaism is essentially history; the history of Judaism is at the same time religion. The Book of Books holds the balance between the national and the religious elements. The chief significance of this for us lies in the fact that Israel, whose name is found on every page of the Bible, still exists. Judaism is not merely a religious confession; it differs from other religions in the relation of Israel to the holy books. Therefore we must continue to foster an intimate knowledge of Sacred Scripture and that, too, through the medium of the original tongue, whose higher significance for us must be acknowledged also in our time and the study of which must be encouraged and furthered in our schools. As for Hebrew in the service, we must bear in mind always that we should have in the service a fixed and a variable portion; the Hebrew portion is the fixed element; this fixed part has not the devotional purpose in view, but forms the background for the service.

Einhorn began by confessing that he was not learned enough to surrender healthy common sense. The prime consideration is that the service should be understood, and therefore the mother tongue is the only admissible language. Even though the theologians were the only ones to possess a knowledge of Hebrew, this would not constitute them into a hierarchy, as had been argued. A hierarchy is founded upon privileges, not upon learning. Sentiment is praiseworthy, but not that sickly sentimentalism which lames—nay, kills—all spiritual life. We cannot strike the rock of a dead language and expect the living waters which will quench the thirst of the people to issue from it.

Herzheimer asserted it to be nonsense to address God in a language one does not understand. The sermon in the vernacular became necessary because the דרשות (rabbinical homilies) had become unintelligible; likewise the German prayer has become necessary because the Hebrew is no longer understood.

Stein pleaded for the retention of the Hebrew as a bond of union among Jews. We are brethren, descendants of one father; argue against it as one will, the national element will never be entirely eliminated from Judaism. We are no longer a nation, it is true, but a great religious community scattered all over the earth; the Hebrew, then, is the bond of union of the widely scattered sections of our great family.

The vote on the question as to whether the retention of the Hebrew in the service is objectively necessary for other reasons than the legal resulted in a division, thirteen voting in the affirmative and fifteen in the negative.

The third question was now broached, viz. whether it appeared advisable, *i.e.* subjectively necessary, to retain the Hebrew in part in the public service. This was not debated at length, and the vote showed that the members of the conference answered the question unanimously in the affirmative.

This point having been disposed of, the question arose as to how much Hebrew there should be in the service. The commission had reported that the following portions should be in Hebrew: ברכו with its sections, שמע to the close of the first section; the first three and the last three benedictions of the תפלה; and the reading from the Torah.

Maier, the chairman of the commission, impressed upon the conference that they must keep in mind, not the adherents of the *Shulchan Aruk,* nor the irreligious element who have turned their back on Judaism, but those who desire to pray to the God of their fathers in the spirit and whom the traditional prayers no longer satisfy either in form or content. The best rule to follow is to return to the pristine simplicity of the ritual as recovered by the investigations of scholars (especially Zunz). Hence we should retain in Hebrew those sections which express most clearly our common faith, our common descent, and our common hope. The portions designated by the commission do this. The remainder of the service should be in German.

The debate on this point elicited some interesting remarks on the Reading of the Law.

Wechsler expressed himself as opposed altogether to the commission on this point. The chief reason for the reading from the law was that the people learn its contents; the reading was not intended to be an exercise to show familiarity with the language nor yet a demonstration (Deut. xxxi, 11), But in our day the קריאת התורה (Reading of the Law) is not instructive; it has neither rhyme nor reason. The people do not understand it. If it be our desire to carry out the original object of the institution, viz. that the people learn the contents of the law, then it should be read in the language the people understand. Let such portions as cannot be read in German because of their content be read in Hebrew.

Herzfeld declared flatly that the Reading of the Law must be in Hebrew. There is a mystical element in this that seems to me important. Were we to relinquish the קריאת התורה this would entail the entire removal of the ספרי תורה (Scrolls of the Law) from the synagogue, and such a proceeding would call forth a universal cry of horror.

Salomon suggested that the Torah be finished in a triennial cycle instead of annually. Following the hints in the Talmud that certain passages of the Bible were partly not read and partly not interpreted, we too may assume the right to omit such portions of the Pentateuch as no longer suit our time. The reading should be in Hebrew without translation, because the sermon is based on the portion read, and through the sermon the congregation learns the contents of the Torah section. Besides the translation would lengthen the service needlessly. Hirsch held that the Torah section should be read in Hebrew in abbreviated form, while Jolowicz argued that the reading should be in German, and proceeded to say that no passage is objectionable to him who comes into the house of God with a pure heart.

Holdheim maintained that the Torah should be read in Hebrew. Our children must learn the Pentateuch in the original tongue. In addition to the Pentateuchal section portions should be read from other books of the Bible in the vernacular for the benefit of the women.[85]

The recommendations of the commission as to the Hebrew portions of the service were adopted by a vote of eighteen to twelve.

The Messianic Question—The Jewish State

The all-important question of the present attitude of Jewish thought on the Messianic hope occupied the attention of the conference in the discussion of the next point in the report of the commission. This involved such allied matters as the particularistic or the universalistic interpretation of Judaism, the return to Palestine and the restoration of the ancient polity. The issue was clear between the reformers who interpreted the Messianic doctrine in its universal world-wide significance as the hope for the coming of the Messianic age and the traditionalists, for whom it implied a personal Messiah and a restored Jewish state, as clear as it is at this day between political Zionism with its national program and reform Judaism with its universalistic outlook.

Before the debate opened Geiger, who presided, called attention to the fact that the point at issue was not the framing of a distinct doctrine on the Messianic question, but merely how existing prayers were to be judged, and if necessary changed, in the light of present thought on the question. Undoubtedly there was the widest divergence of opinion on the Messianic question, but it should be stated at the very outset that the loyalty to the state of even such as hold the traditional view on the Messiah in its strictest form is not to be questioned for a moment.[86] The only object the conference had in view was to satisfy the demand that nothing be uttered in the prayers which contradicts present Jewish conviction.

The report of the commission read: "The Messianic idea is to occupy a prominent place in the liturgy also in the future, but all politico-national elements are to be eliminated."

Einhorn, who throughout his career was a true prophet of universalistic Judaism, said that the idea of the Messiah is most closely connected with the whole ceremonial law; after the disappearance of priest and sacrifice, the Jew thought salvation possible only through the restoration of the state, the return of the people to Palestine, and the reinstitution of the sacrifices; hence, so many lamentations over the destruction of the temple. Wonderful indeed was the conviction and the courage that could indulge in hope in spite of ghetto and persecution. Now, however, our views have changed; formerly the people believed that God's protection rested particularly on the holy land and the holy people; they believed that He took pleasure in sacrifices and that the priesthood was a necessary institution for the remission of sin. The prophets preached against this narrow view. The loss of political independence was bewailed formerly as a misfortune, but in reality this loss was really progress and entailed not a cramping, but an expansion, of the religious spirit. Israel approached nearer the fulfillment of its mission. Devotion took the place of sacrifice. From Israel's midst God's word was to be carried to all portions of the earth. Only the Talmud moves in a circle; we, however, favor progress.

Formerly I looked upon the Messianic idea as a surrogate of the idea of immortality, but I do so no longer; I see in it the hope of both earthly and heavenly salvation. There is nothing objectionable in the idea. Also the belief in the election of Israel contains nothing that is repugnant; nay, we must retain it as the consciousness of an undeniable advantage, for it creates a beneficial self-consciousness over against the ruling church. I vote for the elimination of all petitions for the restoration of bloody sacrifices and political independence; on the other hand, I wish that the Messianic prayers be framed in such a manner as to express the hope for the spiritual re-birth and the union of all men in faith and in love through the agency of Israel.[87]

Hess asserted that the belief in a personal, *i.e.* a political Messiah, had disappeared from among German Jewry; it should therefore be eliminated from the liturgy, for we should not petition God for that in which we no longer believe.

Holdheim called attention to two points requiring correction. (1) It is held, on the one hand, that the hope for a political restoration is in conflict with the feelings of patriotism for the fatherland; while it is asserted, on the other hand, that these are not in conflict. (2) We have been warned not to accentuate the national element because of possible misinterpretation. As against this it has been correctly stated that we are not to pay any attention to misinterpretations. The petition for a return to Palestine to establish a political state for those who still suffer oppression is superfluous, on the one hand, because both those who are oppressed, as well as the rest of us, would be helped only by the removal of oppression; hence, we should petition for this; on the other hand, it is inadmissible because it makes of the Messianic expectation, not a religious, but a purely material hope, which is cheerfully surrendered wherever the political status is satisfactory. But the Messianic hope truly understood is indeed religious. It expresses either the wish for redemption and liberation from spiritual evil, and the realization of the Kingdom of God on earth or for the political restoration of the Mosaic theocracy which alone makes it possible for the Jew to fulfill the whole Mosaic Law. This latter religious wish can be surrendered only by those who have a higher conception of Judaism, who do not believe the fulfillment of its mission to be dependent on the existence of a Jewish state, and who are convinced that the ceasing of the separate political existence of Jewry was necessary for the highest interests of Judaism and commanded by the religion. Only a clarified religious point of view can displace an obscure one. But those who consider a political restoration necessary in the interest of the religion may not surrender this, however prosperous they may be, since religion, as they view it, demands categorically the fulfillment of this expectation. The rigidly orthodox, as well as the reformers, stand on religious ground; the difference between them is that the former desire the restoration of the old political status in the interest of the religion, while the latter posit the closest adherence to the politico-national conditions of the present as the demand of religion.[88]

Hirsch declared that the Messianic doctrine is the center of Judaism. . . . The perfectibility of mankind on this earth is the characteristic mark of Judaism whereby it is distinguished from all other religions. All the prophets agree in this. If they were able to picture the Messianic time only in terms of a prosperous Jewish state, this was due to their human limitations. The prophets revealed the future only to improve their own age; therefore, they did not stand above their age and had to teach the truth in the terms of their age. In the Talmudic era, the time of oppression, the Messianic doctrine had to shape itself accordingly. Everywhere the Jewish doctrine of the Messiah is fulfilling itself rapidly. Everywhere the emancipation of mankind is being striven for so that a morally pure and holy life may be possible of being lived by man on this earth.[89]

Salomon contrasted the heathen poets who sang of a golden age in dim antiquity with the Jewish prophets who proclaimed the golden age in the far future, the time of light, truth, harmony and peace. This is the Biblical idea of redemption. . . . If we consider that the intelligent section of Jewry to-day repudiates the belief in a personal, political Messiah, that even a great number of the so-called "pious ones" restrict the belief in a personal Messiah to the prayers in the synagogue, while in their life there is not a trace of their acceptance of this belief, it is absolutely necessary, unless we would make a sport of religion, to frame the expression of the Messianic doctrine in such a manner as to make it purely spiritual, particularly as our ancient teachers were unanimous in the belief that our redemption would take place, not through human agency, but would be accomplished by God himself.

Maier stated that the hope for a political restoration has been repudiated by the majority of the Jews in Germany, and if we do not wish that the attendants at our services should be guilty of mental reservations when the petition for the restoration of a Jewish state is uttered, we shall have to remove it from the liturgy and give expression only to the universal and spiritual interpretation of the Messianic doctrine.

A. Adler criticized the statement frequently made to the effect that the monotheistic belief is the only thing that differentiates Judaism from other religions. This statement he contended, confounds principle with content. Monotheism is indeed the principle of Judaism, but it does not constitute its chief content. There are other religionists who believe in the unity of God and still are not Jews. The belief in a future Messiah is peculiar to Judaism and differentiates it from other religions more than does monotheism. This belief gives us the assurance:

1. That goodness, virtue and holiness will issue as victors from the contest with evil, vice and sin.

2. That the history of the world does not move in a circle, but will finally reach a goal, viz., the highest development of mankind.

3. That mankind is not doomed forever to darkness, but will be reconciled with God in the end.

It contains implicitly the belief in the ideal resurrection of the nations and assures therewith the immortality of individual man. We will prove our true religiosity when, instead of declaring what the Messianic belief is not, we will state how it is to be conceived in its very truth. By negating we merely take away and contribute nothing, by positing we contribute something important and take away nothing. Therefore we must substitute in our prayers the true idea of the Messiah for the personal representation and give this adequate expression.

Auerbach held that the Messianic idea is the soul of positive Judaism and its development lies in the transformation of the national into the purely religious. In the Talmud the national ideals are uppermost; the whole Talmudic system was in opposition to such individual utterances as expressed other interpretations of the Messianic idea. At that time the national expectation could not be surrendered. In our days, however, the ideals of justice and the brotherhood of men have been so strengthened through the laws and institutions of modern states, that they can never again be shattered; we are witnessing an ever nearer approach of the establishment of the Kingdom of God on earth through the strivings of mankind.

Herzfeld: Whatever is false must be excised. No empty phrases! Everything must be clear and definite. The conference must declare what it means by redemption; yes, it should state that we are now entering upon the period of redemption. Freedom and virtue are spreading, the world is growing better.

Herxheimer emphasized the thoughts that the Messianic idea seems to express discontent with present conditions, trust in the goodness of Providence and hope for a happier future. In times of misfortune the people recalled the better past and associated this with David and his time. The best course to pursue in this matter is to retain all general expressions of these hopes and to eliminate every utterance which was called forth by the oppressions of the Middle Ages.

Wagner claimed that the Messianic belief is a fundamental doctrine of Judaism and as old as this itself. It must have always a prominent place in the liturgy, because it is a characteristic mark of Judaism, includes definitely the idea of the election of Israel, and voices our hopes that the fundamental truths of Judaism may become the common possession of all peoples. Let the rebuilding of Jerusalem and Zion be mentioned in our prayers as a tribute of piety to the holy city and the seat of holiness. The petitions for a return to Palestine and the restoration of the sacrificial cult must be stricken out.

Kahn averred that the Bible does not require us to believe in a personal Messiah. The prophets are not soothsayers, but truthsayers (*nicht Wahrsager sondern Weissager*). Not all of them prophesy the coming of a personal Messiah, but all agree in picturing an ideal Messianic era. So do we also expect the coming of a Messianic era, but not of a personal Messiah with accompanying political changes. The prayer אתה בחרתנו (expressing the doctrine of the election of Israel) may be retained as historically significant, but not such passages as emphasize a still existing difference between Israel and other nations (המבדיל בין ישראל לעמים).

Stein in opposition to most of the members pleaded for the retention of the prayers for the coming of the personal Messiah.

Although our hopes are for the coming of the Messianic era of peace and good will, still we may surely leave to God the manner of the fulfillment; all great events in the world's history have been accomplished by great personalities; may we not then confidently expect that this greatest and highest consummation of all, the ushering in of religious harmony, peace and brotherhood will be accomplished through one sent of God? [90]

He also pleaded for the retention of the prayers for the rebuilding of Jerusalem and the temple and continued: [91] The followers of all the religions founded upon the Bible look to Jerusalem as the holy city and I believe that when the Kingdom of God will be established on earth and all men will be united in the belief in the One God and in brotherly love the holy city will arise from its desolation and a magnificent temple where all peoples will worship together will be built there as the visible symbol of that spiritual brotherhood and union.

On the other hand, the petition for a return to Palestine must be excised, for this does not come from our hearts and is therefore untrue. We know but one fatherland, that in which we live; we cannot pray "mayst thou take us back in joy to *our* land," as though our present home were strange to us and our true home lay a thousand miles distant.

There is another reason for this. Our fathers, oppressed and trampled to the earth, had to consider the dispersion as a curse perforce, and therefore they prayed, ומפני חטאינו גלינו מארצנו ("because of our sins we were exiled from our land"). Quite a contrary conception is ours. We have begun to recognize that the dispersion was a blessing, that God has scattered us over the earth as "the seed of truth," so that there might be worshipers of the one only and true God everywhere. (Is. lxi, 9. Zach. viii, 13, 23.)

Formstecher remarked that scientific theology must recognize the Messianic idea as the red thread which runs through all the stadia in the development of Judaism, but where lies the necessity of incorporating a formulated Messianic doctrine into the liturgy? We have the Messianic doctrine in the Bible. Any concrete form into which we would cast it would constitute it a dogma and Judaism desires no dogmas. Therefore this whole Messianic matter should be excluded from the liturgy and its place be taken by readings from the prophets on the subject to be supplemented by the sermon.

Philippson said epigrammatically that revelation is the foundation, and the Messianic idea the roof of Judaism. Judaism, however, includes no political striving for a realm of its own, even though the term nation must be retained because of the fact of descent. All political features must be discarded.

The resolution on this subject as adopted finally by the majority reads:

> The Messianic idea should receive prominent mention in the prayers, but all petitions for our return to the land of our fathers and for the restoration of a Jewish state should be eliminated from the prayers.

The Mussaf Prayer for the Restoration of the Sacrifices

The whole commission agreed on reporting that a repetition of the תפלה (the eighteen benedictions) was unnecessary, and the majority of the commission held that the whole *Mussaf* (additional) service was inadmissible because the sacrificial cult was outgrown and no longer expressed the religious *status quo*.

This report also called forth a lengthy debate, a few expressions from which follow:

Salomon: With our conception of the Messianic idea the *Mussaf*, which is primarily a petition for the sacrifices, is a *contradictio in adjecto*.

Formstecher: Basing as we do on the positive historical standpoint, we should mention the sacrifices in our prayers as a historical reminiscence, not in the way of petition for their reinstitution, but in the way of thanks that we have substituted prayer for sacrifice in accordance with the utterances of the prophets.

Holdheim: According to the legal interpretation of Judaism sacrifice is expiation; repentance alone does not bring forgiveness, altar and priest are necessary. This idea was combated by the prophets, but it persisted among the people, and the Talmud adheres to this external justification; therefore prayer is conceived in it as only taking the place of sacrifice in the interim until this shall be restored. We, however, occupy an altogether different position in this matter and cannot possibly petition for the sacrificial cult. However, the entire elimination of the *Mussaf* service would meet with general disapprobation. Let us retain the form, but substitute for the traditional prayers such others as express our religious standpoint in the matter.

The vote on the question—"Shall the petitions for the

restoration of the sacrificial cult be removed from the prayers?" was unanimously in the affirmative.

"Shall the sections of the Torah which command the offering of sacrifices continue to be read?" Majority in the affirmative if the text be read in Hebrew.

"Shall reminiscences of the sacrifices find a place in the liturgy?" Majority in the affirmative.

Cycle of Torah Readings

The commission recommended the triennial cycle, and the abolition of the *Aufrufen* (calling up of seven men during the reading from the Torah); the referee Maier, however, declared for the retention of *Aufrufen*.

The triennial cycle received all the votes but five.

All voted for the translation of the Pentateuchal section in order to make the people again familiar with the Torah as has been the purpose of the Targum of old; the only difference of opinion arose from the consideration of the best manner of carrying this out; many felt that this translation or explanation should take place only when there was no sermon.

The decision in favor of the triennial cycle brought up the question of the celebration of שמחת תורה (the Feast of Rejoicing in the Law).[92] Should this feast be celebrated annually or triennially and should the Pentateuchal sections זאת הברכה[93] and בראשית[94] be read annually or triennially?

During the debate on these questions, Maier contended that שמחת תורה is only the second day of שמיני עצרת; therefore he was opposed to the annual reading of זאת הברכה.

Philippson expressed himself similarly because we have in שבועות (the Feast of Weeks) a feast of rejoicing in the Law. Holdheim asserted that the significance of the holiday as שמחת תורה is of late origin; in the original prayers for the Feast of Tabernacles no mention is made of it; it is thus designated only in the *Piyyutim*. The vote showed the majority to be in favor of the triennial celebration of the holiday.

Aufrufen (Calling to the Law)

The commission, with the exception of Maier, reported in favor of its abolition.

Gosen, one of the ultra conservatives, made the surprising statement that he wished the *Aufrufen* retained because the Jew looks upon it as a kind of confession of faith, as a personal acceptance of the Law, almost as the Christian does the Eucharist.

Holdheim called the correctness of this statement into question; but, said he, if this is the case, it is a reprehensible error, for the removal of which it were desirable to so arrange the Torah reading that the people would consider it an exercise for instruction; but it may never become the occasion of introducing a sacrament into Judaism, which has no sacraments in the Christian interpretation of the term. Therefore he favored the abolition of *Aufrufen* if for no other reason than to prevent the error that the Jew considers it equivalent to a confession of faith.

A. Adler favored its abolition because the *Aufrufen* accentuates the distinction between the sexes in religious functions, men alone being called to the Torah, while we must insist upon equality of men and women in religious functions. Further, the whole congregation would take more interest in the reading were there no *Aufrufen,* since many look upon the reading as especially for those who are called.

In spite of these spirited expressions the great majority voted for the retention of the *Aufrufen,* but against the repetition of the מפטיר. (The closing section of the weekly portion.)

The Organ [95]

The question, Is the organ permitted in the synagogue? was decided in the affirmative by a unanimous vote without debate.

A further question was "May and should the organ be played by Jews on Sabbath?" This occasioned a debate whereof a few expressions follow:

Löwengard: Yes, the expression אין שבות במקדש (rabbinical legislation for the Sabbath is not considered binding in the performance of any service in the temple) must be applied also to the synagogue, since we no longer pray for the restoration of the Temple of Jerusalem.

Einhorn: If the Talmudists make a distinction between temple and synagogue, the reason is that they consider the offering of sacrifices necessary for full divine service. We, however, consider the abolition of sacrifice as a step in advance and therefore אין שבות במקדש is also applicable to the snyagogue.

Holdheim: We have almost unanimously resolved to eliminate from our prayers the petition for the return to Jerusalem and the reinstitution of the sacrificial service, and have declared clearly that our houses of worship are on an equal footing with the Temple of Jerusalem, that our service, with its devotional inwardness is of a higher character than the sacrificial service, displaces it for the whole future and makes it dispensable. If, then, the sacrificial service in itself involves no desecration of the Sabbath, if the instrumental music accompanying it gave a higher consecration, why should this be less the case with our service that is of a loftier character according to our conviction?

The question was decided unanimously in the affirmative. This closed the consideration of the report of the commission on the liturgy.

Circumcision

A communication was addressed by Dr. Fr. Th. Baltz to the conference on the subject of circumcision. He wrote that circumcision has evil results, giving rise to sexual diseases and sometimes to impotence. He proposed that, if it cannot be abolished altogether, it should be performed in such a manner as to preclude danger and evil results. The conference answered by stating that it recognized gratefully the good intentions of the writer; as for the supposed evil results of circumcision that he mentions, it must be said that there are other medical authorities who claim just the opposite; Jewish marriages are very fruitful, as is well known. At any rate, the matter is of the highest importance and for that very reason is not ripe for consideration. As for the manner of performing the operation, most of the German governments had passed laws on the subject and put it under the supervision of the sanitary police. The conference would undoubtedly take up the subject at some future time and would then take into consideration the communication of the writer.

The Status of Woman

During the debates on the report of the Commission on Liturgy, the necessity of declaring the equality of woman with man in the performance of public religious functions was mentioned by several speakers. One of the marked achievements of the reform movement has been the change in the religious status of woman. According to the Talmud and the rabbinical codes woman can take no part in public religious functions; the question was brought formally before the conference by

Samuel Adler in the resolution which, after reciting the traditional view, goes on to say that the conference declares that "she has the same obligation as man to participate from youth up in the instruction in Judaism and in the public services and that the custom not to include women in the number of individuals necessary for the conducting of a public service is only a custom and has no religious basis."

The subject was not debated at length and was referred to a commission consisting of S. Adler, Einhorn, and A. Adler for report at the next conference.

The Sabbath Question

A commission, consisting of Geiger, A. Adler, Wechsler, S. Adler, and Kahn, had been appointed at the Brunswick Conference on the motion of Hirsch to report on the question, "If there were any means, and if so, what, to reconcile Jewish doctrines and the demands of modern life in reference to the Sabbath." [96] President Stein suggested that owing to lack of time the consideration of the report of the commission be postponed until the next conference. Since the whole report was constructed upon one leading idea as its basis, said he, it would not be fair to dismember the report by taking up some points and neglecting others. The report should be considered as a whole. He suggested that the report be printed and distributed to the members of the conference who would then have time to study it and come prepared for a full and free discussion next year. However, he did not wish to dictate to the conference and he would put the question whether the members wished to enter into a discussion of the whole report. This was negatived.

The question was then put whether special points in the report should be taken up.

Geiger, the chairman of the commission, desired special points in the report to be discussed: they are of such importance and are so constantly brought to the attention of all rabbis that they must have been thought upon earnestly by all, and therefore all must be ready to discuss them. The difficulties presented by the question of Sabbath observance are among the most serious confronting us. It is not a question of theory, but of practice. The demands of life require action on our part. Even though we may not all agree on principles, still we may be able to agree on results.

However, the conference decided to postpone the consideration of the separate points also till the next conference when the Sabbath question was to be first order of business. It was also decided to print the report of the commission.

The commission was directed to consider also all questions connected with the observance of the holidays and fast days, and incorporate this in their report.

Revision of Marriage Laws

Time not permitting the extended consideration necessary for so important a subject, the Commission on the Revision of the Marriage Laws appointed at the Brunswick Conference was ordered to publish their report, which would be taken up at the next conference.

Jewish Theological Faculty

Philippson offered the following resolution:

> The rabbinical conference declares that it considers the foundation of one or more Jewish theological faculties in Germany a worthy and high endeavor and that it will coöperate earnestly with such work.
>
> Resolved, that a commission be appointed whose aim it shall be to interest the public in this noble cause and to work for its consummation in connection with representative and discerning men in all walks of life.

The commission named consisted of Geiger, Philippson, Stein, Holdheim and Salomon.

Name

The President suggested the advisability of changing the name of the conference from "Conference of the Rabbis of Germany" to "German Rabbinical Conference." The former name, said he, confines the conference within too narrow bounds, since it excludes all foreigners. There is no German Judaism. Judaism is universal. Thus he knew of a Hungarian and a French rabbi who wished to attend. The majority agreed with him, and it was resolved to call the society "The Conference of German Rabbis."

It was resolved to issue an address to the congregations summarizing the work of the conference. This was referred to the editorial commission, which consisted of Stein, Jost, Auerbach and Formstecher.

A commission consisting of Philippson, Stein and Formstecher was appointed to prepare a manual for domestic devotion.

The commission for further consideration of the prayerbook was named, viz. Stein, Salomon, Geiger, Maier, Herzfeld.

The election of the executive committee for the next conference resulted in the choice of Geiger, Philippson, Holdheim, and Herxheimer.

Addresses to the Conference

One of the most striking features of the Frankfort Conference is the evidence that has been preserved of the keen interest it aroused throughout Germany. Numerous congregations and societies sent addresses of confidence and sympathy; these addresses came from Bingen, Darmstadt, Alzey, Alsfeld, Mayence, Ekenkoben, Frankenthal, Grünstadt, Musbach in the Palatinate, Breslau, Mannheim, Obermoshel, Schwitzingen, Neustadt in Upper Silesia, Münster, Worms, Giessen, and Frankfort-on-the-Main.

The most significant of these addresses were the memorial from the recently formed Reform Association of Berlin and the address signed by one hundred and sixty-eight Jews of Breslau. These ought not to be dismissed with a mere mention. The Berlin society in its famous "Appeal" had declared for the convening of a synod that was to be the authoritative Jewish body and was to decide upon moot questions. When the necessity of instituting a public service became plain, the question arose whether steps toward this should be taken before or after calling the synod. The "synodists" held that no prayerbook could be written unless there was a definite declaration of faith whereon it would be based, and hence the synod must be convened first to formulate this creed; however, the need for a service was so great that steps were taken to institute it at once. Yet the sentiment for the indorsement of an authorized gathering was so strong that it was determined to send a deputation to the rabbinical conference, which, though not of a definitely authoritative nature, had something of this character. To enter into relationship with the conference partook of the nature of listening to authoritative voices without sacrificing autonomy. The object of the address to the conference was to pave the way for the synod; the Berlin congregation represented the laity, the conference represented the rabbinate; these two were the component parts of the future synod. Dr. S. Stern, the most prominent member of the Berlin congregation, had said, in urging the address to the conference, "If we recognize the necessity of the coöperation of both elements for reform in Judaism and desire that both join in the future synod, a preliminary agreement must take place now." [97]

It was decided to send a deputation consisting of Stern, Rebenstein and Simion, who were to read the address to the conference, but this was to be understood to be merely an act of courtesy and nothing more.

At the first session of the conference this deputation appeared and presented the memorial from the congregation. This memorial is of importance because it marks the first public activity of the Berlin society since its definite organization two months previously in the month of May. The memorialists set forth the purpose of their society thus:

> We have undertaken the great task of breaking through the standstill which has barred the development of Judaism for centuries and has required of us the unchanged retention of forms which conflicted more and more with our thoughts and sentiments, and with the needs of our advanced life. We have united for the carrying out of the following purpose: to redeem Judaism, our most precious heritage, from all antiquated forms, not only for the benefit of ourselves or of special classes, but of all its confessors, and to preserve its eternal truth in and through a form suited to our age in order that it may once again permeate our life with the power of its divine essence. We have not failed to recognize the difficulty of this great undertaking, but that which forces and necessitates us to awaken ourselves and our co-religionists out of the state of comfortable ease and to enter upon the severe struggle with indifference on the one hand and millennium-old prejudice on the other, is the consciousness that we should publicly confess that which we have recognized as the true and the right, and that not only for our own sake, but in the name of Judaism, we must make possible for it that development which has been denied to it for so long a time.

We are encouraged to undertake this difficult task because we are convinced that the old vital force has not died out of nor been weakened in Judaism, and that the need we feel is not an isolated phenomenon, but will come to the fore with equal force among thousands of our cultured and advanced co-religionists as soon as the initiative is taken. But we are encouraged most of all by our faith in the progressive consciousness of the age—which urges us on to freedom of thought and lends the strongest support to all efforts which are directed towards bringing pristine and pure truth to light even though this is obscured by dense millennium-old fogs.

The memorial lays stress upon the necessity for rabbis and laymen to work together in the cause; theirs is a lay movement, it has gone forth from the people; the conference is a rabbinical movement; neither alone is representative, however; people and rabbis must join to form an authoritative body, viz. a synod.

The memorial concludes by expressing the hope that the conference will give expression to its official recognition of the work and purpose of the Reform Association, which aims, not at the destruction of Judaism, but its strengthening and preservation.

The conference answered by declaring that its members recognize that the Reform Association owes its existence to the religious need to reconcile modern life with Judaism, and that it was gratifying to know that this conviction of the need of reform in Judaism was felt in the congregations as well as by the rabbis. Gladly would they work hand in hand with the Reform Association if the latter were guided by the same principles as were considered necessary by the conference for true reform in Judaism. They would watch with interest the steps taken by the Reform Association toward the formation of a synod.

The address issued to the conference from Breslau contained a strong presentation of the religious state of many Jews, and of the confusions arising from the conflicts between the demands of life and the observance of the traditional laws; particular attention is called to the need of a reform of the liturgy and to the necessity of a solution of the difficulties connected with Sabbath observance.

The great majority of the Jews, even those who pose as the zealous watchmen of orthodoxy, have really no holidays. The children attend school on the Sabbath, the apprentice must work on this day as on every other at his trade or in business, and when the young man has finally become his own master, he will scarcely be inclined to observe a day which he has not been accustomed to observe from childhood, even though able to do so; but how few are there in our time who can observe this day without great danger of ruin!

Attention was called also to the need of a reform of the dietary laws. The writers proceeded to say that they had called the attention of the conference to these things because they felt that the leaders of the people should know the state of affairs among the people; it were cowardice to conceal it, and they hoped that the rabbis would deal courageously with these pressing questions of the time and find the means of so interpreting Judaism as to enable the Jew to live fully and freely the life in the world without becoming false or untrue to his faith.

The conference answered by saying that it appreciated the service rendered by the writers of the address in stating thus clearly the conflicts between official Judaism and practical life; but the conference must move slowly, and could not solve all the great questions of the time in a trice. This conference had taken up the liturgy and considered it thoroughly; future conferences would undoubtedly give earnest attention to the other great questions which the writers touched.

There is apparent in the answers of the conference to the various addresses the same broad spirit and wise counsel as characterized the discussions and deliberations. The men who participated in this conference were imbued thoroughly with the serious responsibility of the Jewish religious leader in that era of upheaval. With but two or three exceptions they were not drastic in their suggestions and methods, but desirous of reforming gradually. The discussions evince a full knowledge of the past development of Judaism and a thorough grasp of present conditions. Opinions differed, it is true, as to the length that the reforms should go, but the spirit that ruled the conference was that reform must proceed along the lines of past endeavor; for every reform that was suggested some warrant was sought from Talmudic authority. The sensational withdrawal of Zacharias Frankel from the conference after the third day's session was absolutely inexcusable therefore, even from his standpoint. Frankel's action was the focus of the opposition to this conference, as the protest of the one hundred and sixteen rabbis had been to the Brunswick Conference. As stated above [98] Frankel had criticized the Brunswick Conference very sharply and severely, and therefore his appearance at the Frankfort Conference was gladly welcomed, for he had been the only rabbi of note with reform leanings who had denounced so unsparingly the first conference. At the very outset he had taken pains to define his position as being that of adherence to positive historical Judaism; this phrase was grasped at eagerly by the opponents of the reformers as the club wherewith to belabor them, notably later by the Breslau school; but, as Stein, the president of the conference, said in his reply to Frankel's opening speech, this phrase defined exactly the reform position; the reformers, too, built on positive historical Judaism; it was not their purpose to break with the Judaism of the past, but to develop it further. Frankel gave as his excuse for withdrawing that the conference should not have voted that it was "advisable" (*rathsam*) to retain the Hebrew in the service but absolutely essential. This resolution had been passed on the afternoon of July 17, which was the last meeting that Frankel attended; in the issue of the *Oberpostamtszeitung* [99] of July 18 he published a statement explanatory of his withdrawal from the conference. At the morning session of July 20 the President called the official attention of the conference to this article of Frankel's, and read also an answer [100] which had been written and which he submitted for the approval of the members. After citing the resolution of the conference that the retention of the Hebrew was only advisable and interpreting this action of the conference to mean that it was the duty of the rabbis to abolish it gradually, Frankel goes on to say:

> I dissent from such a resolution, not only because of a difference of view, but also because of a difference of tendency. This spirit which leaves unnoticed so many weighty elements and supplants that which is of weight and power in every confession, viz., the historical element, makes, in my opinion, not for the preservation, but the destruction of positive historical Judaism, which I had

explained clearly to the conference as representing my position. This spirit must invalidate the future resolutions of the conference for all such as stand on the platform of positive historical Judaism, because, as I explained also to the conference, it depends not only on the number of votes cast, but on the motive for voting, and only he who has come to a decision himself and seeks only a formal endorsement can find an apparent comfort in a general vote.

For this reason he must not only protest against the conference, but feels it necessary to declare that his standpoint is altogether different from that of the conference; he regrets that the conference, instead of keeping in mind the high aim of securing universal confidence and thus bringing about a compromise between opposing elements, had again by this act alienated thousands. He had come to the conference with the purpose of reaching an understanding with opposing opinions, and with the hope of making the conference the reconciling influence and establishing it as the representative Jewish body, but this action of the conference had demonstrated to him the vanity of this hope, and therefore he felt compelled to withdraw, no matter though his action be misinterpreted.

The conference answered this declaration by calling attention to the fact that the vote on the resolution in question showed that thirteen held the same views as Frankel, while the majority vote was only fifteen, and three had abstained from voting; hence Frankel stood by no means alone, and if he was sincere in his declaration it was surely his duty to continue in the conference. The conference resents the implication that by this majority vote it abandoned the standpoint of positive historical Judaism, which it had declared with loud acclaim the day before to be its standpoint no less than it was that of Dr. Frankel. The vote on the advisability of the retention of the Hebrew was concerned with the question of opinions, not of tendencies.

The positive historical standpoint demands development out of present conditions, not a haphazard creation without definite preëxisting material, and thus our prayers should attach themselves to the existing liturgy, and be developed in form and content wherever possible from that which we have received from the past. The conference can grant as little that prayer in a non-Hebrew language implies a denial of the historical element as Dr. Frankel on his part will admit that the Talmudists attacked positive historical Judaism when they permitted the holiest of our prayers to be uttered in Aramaic; yes, when they allowed the whole service, with the exception of a few passages, to be performed in a non-Hebrew language, as Dr. Frankel admitted this when he voted that there was no legal necessity for the employment of Hebrew as the language of prayer. The conference believes therefore that Dr. Frankel, by making this issue the cause of his breaking with the conference, has abandoned not so much the conference as himself and the consequences of his own position.

Some members of the conference desired a clause to be inserted to the effect that Frankel mistook the tendency of the conference, while Geiger held that the only way to meet such arrogance was to pass it by in silence; he begged the conference to avoid all polemical utterances against Frankel, who, being absent, was unable to defend himself.

Frankel answered this reply of the conference in a letter dated Mayence, July 22;[101] he reiterated his former statements, but did not succeed in defending his position strongly.

To offset, in all likelihood, the two addresses of commendation sent to the conference from Breslau, the one by the officials of the congregation [102] and the other by one hundred and sixty-eight private individuals, sympathizers with Frankel sent him an address applauding his action; Graetz, later the historian of the Jews, but at that time a rabbinical candidate, was particularly active in the matter;[103] this demonstration on the part of the orthodox element in Breslau was inspired by opposition to Geiger. The orthodox party of Stettin and Frankfort also memorialized Frankel for his stand in the matter.[104]

L. Schott, rabbi of Randegg, followed the lead of Frankel and withdrew from the conference. Frankel became from now on the recognized leader of the conservatives whose motto was *sauve qui peut;* not principle but accommodation guided this party; the Breslau rabbinical seminary founded in 1854, of which Frankel became the head, supplied the leaders for this party.[105]

The Frankfort Conference will always be notable in the

annals of Reform Judaism for the remarkable discussions on
the liturgy; the intent and purpose of reform were grasped
firmly by the leaders assembled there and the universal elements in Judaism received expression in lofty strains time and
again; the members of the conference did not attempt the
impossible; they had practical problems to solve and did so
with the needs of their generation constantly in view;[106] they
were thoroughly awake to the situation, and were justified in
hoping that, as the president stated in his closing remarks, "a
new era of active participation in our ancestral faith here and
elsewhere would date from the second rabbinical conference
held at Frankfort."[107]

(c) The Breslau Conference

The third rabbinical conference met at Breslau, July 13-24,
1846. The very fact that it was convened in this East-Prussian
city near the Silesian border was equivalent to throwing down
the gauntlet to the opposition to the conferences, much of which
had emanated from that section. This opposition was now
clearly defined. There was in the first place, as was natural,
the rigidly orthodox party whose opposition had not lessened
since the days of the famous protest of the one hundred and
sixteen rabbis against the Brunswick Conference; then there
was the so-called positive historical school, led by Frankel,
whose sensational exit from the Frankfort Conference had
aroused such notice the preceding year; and thirdly, the radicals who were dissatisfied because the Frankfort Conference
had not declared against and abolished the whole ceremonial
and traditional system.[108]

This combined opposition may have been the reason why a
smaller number assembled at Breslau than at Frankfort. In
order to cripple the conference, too, Frankel had issued a call
for an assembly of theologians to be held at Dresden, October
20, 1846, which meeting, however, never took place.

All this opposition, however, merely served to direct even
more attention to this third conference than to its two predecessors, if such a thing were possible, notably as it was known
that the deliberations were to be devoted primarily and chiefly
to the all-absorbing Sabbath question. There were present at
this conference: A. Adler, Worms; S. Adler, Alzey; J. Auerbach, Frankfort-on-the-Main; Ben Israel, Coblentz; D. Einhorn, Birkenfeld; S. Formstecher, Offenbach; A. Geiger, Bres-

lau; Goldstein, Waren; J. Gosen, Marburg; L. Güldenstein, Buchau; L. Herzfeld, Brunswick; S. Herxheimer, Bernburg; M. Hess, Stadt-Lengsfeld; S. Holdheim, Schwerin; J. Jolowicz, Coslin; J. Kahn, Trier; M. Levy, Breslau; L. Lövy, Münsterberg; J. Löwengard, Lehren-Steinfels; Pick, Teplitz; L. Philippson, Magdeburg; G. Salomon, Hamburg; L. Sobernheim, Bingen; L. Stein, Frankfort-on-the-Main; H. Wagner, Mannheim; B. Wechsler, Oldenburg.

Geiger was elected president; Stein, vice president; and A. Adler and J. Auerbach, secretaries.

In his opening address as chairman of the executive committee Geiger referred to the increasing agitations in the Jewish communities since last they met, the many signs of reawakened life on the one hand and the disturbances of the peace on the other; therefore, many a rabbi had been undoubtedly tempted to withdraw from active participation in the conflicts of the time lest he be misunderstood and antagonized. However, they who had assembled again spurned such cowardly retreat and felt in duty bound to search out the remedies for the religious distemper in Jewry. He defined the purpose of the conference —yes, of true reform—finely when he said:

> The conditions are difficult, and confusion in religious affairs appears to be on the increase; despite this you are in this conference again making the courageous attempt to place the pure eternal content of Judaism in a form suited to the present and thus to breathe into it a new and powerful spirit. You wish to convince, to lead to the truth, not to forge bonds and fetters; you know full well that you do not appear here as guardians of consciences, that you have no sovereign power over the inalienable religious freedom of congregations and individuals; nay, you would repudiate such power were it to be offered you, for true religion can prosper and grow only in the atmosphere of freedom of conviction. Not, then, as spiritual despots are we assembled, but as men, who, familiar with the sources and history of Judaism, and anxious for its living preservation, both by our inner as well as our outer calling, are fitted by constant attention to passing occurrences and by experiences in office, to become acquainted with the needs and to propose remedies to the congregations with whom lies the final decision. Not the cleric stands

over against the layman (a distinction foreign to Judaism), but the knower of Judaism, the man who has made it his task to follow up the movements of history and to foster the religious life; such a one seeks to exchange opinions and experiences with his colleagues and thereupon to recommend to his congregation the results of such deliberation and consultation. Our mission is to strengthen the hold of truth and piety, and in such instances where these have become stunted we must seek to burst the crust which has formed about them. This is a סתירה על מנת לבנות, a tearing down in order to plant; we shall foster the living and the virile; may the creeper which sucks sap and strength from the tree be uprooted.

The chief interest in the Breslau Conference centers about the Sabbath discussions. Possibly nowhere was the conflict between the commands of rabbinical Judaism and the demands of life so apparent as in the matter of Sabbath observance. The casuistry of Talmudical dialectics ran riot in this field. Thirty-nine chief categories (ל"ט אבות) were enumerated in the Mishnah, i.e. important labors that were forbidden and from these were derived the innumerable תולדות or minor tasks that were prohibited likewise. Then there were the many סייגים (fences) מנהגים (customs) and תקנות (enactments) which the Talmudists framed in their anxiety to guard the completeness of the Sabbath rest. The fiction of the עירוב demonstrated most forcibly the lengths to which casuistry was driven to maintain a forced system and the refinement of dialectic speculation has surely never gone further than in the matter of שבות. As long as the Jews lived in isolated communities such an observance of the Sabbath was quite possible, but when they began to participate in the life of the larger world, the collisions between that life with its changed industrial, economic and social conditions and the hundred and one prohibitions wherewith the Talmud had hedged about the observance of the Sabbath were constant. It was not long before the question of Sabbath observance became a burning issue in Jewish life; the inadequacy of Talmudism and rabbinism to cope with the situation was more painfully apparent here than anywhere else. To observe the Sabbath as the Talmud and the codes demanded was simply out of the question. Many without scruple disregarded all the traditional enactments touching Sabbath observance, but there were thousands who were troubled sincerely; The Sabbath had always been one of the basic institutions of Judaism; they desired to observe it; but life was pressing on every side; strict Sabbath observance as required by the code, and life's demands were apparently incompatible. Was there any method of reconciliation? could the Sabbath be preserved and the demands of life be satisfied at the same time? Here, if anywhere, the people looked for help and guidance to their religious leaders.

These leaders appreciated the seriousness of the problem which soon assumed a leading place among the practical difficulties that assailed Judaism in the new era, and because the most of them were unable to find any effective solution they hesitated to grapple with it. However, it was too insistent and too important to be disregarded [109] and notably at gatherings where vital questions of Jewish thought and practice were the topics of the hour. Hence, Samuel Hirsch proposed at the first conference that the collision between life and doctrine be removed by the abolition or alleviation of numerous Sabbath and dietary laws.[110] This was at the closing session of the conference, but the subject was too difficult and of too great moment to be taken up at so late an hour. It was therefore resolved to refer it to a commission to report at the following conference. This commission consisting of Geiger, A. Adler, S. Adler, Wechsler, and Kahn reported at the Frankfort Conference, but so much of the time of that conference had been devoted to the discussion of the report of the Commission on the Liturgy that it was considered advisable to postpone the consideration of the report of the Sabbath commission till the next conference, when it was to be made the first order of business. The report of the commission was not unanimous; a majority—Geiger, A. Adler, and Wechsler—signed the report but the two other members, S. Adler and Kahn, dissented. The majority report was ordered to be printed and distributed to the members of the conference so as to give them ample time to study it during the intervening year. The majority report [111] opened with a brief statement of what constituted the essentiality of the Sabbath idea; in the opinion of the majority of the commission "the Biblical idea of the Sabbath is the celebration of the day; it is a שבת, a cessation from the work which marks the other days of the week, different however from the rest which is equivalent to complete idleness.

The celebration is a consecration of the day (ויקדשהו, לקדשו, ענג) and this consecration implies an abstention from the daily professional and business pursuits. While the prophets place the consecration (*Weihe*) of the day in the foreground, the legislative portion of the Bible lays stress on the prohibition against work (מלאכה) and names it שבת rest, the interruption of the daily toil." In the Bible, rest from work was commanded in order to make possible the consecration of the self on that day. In the later outworking of the Sabbath conception in Mishnah and Talmud the greatest stress was laid on the necessity of rest. Complete absolute rest was taken to be the essential point in Sabbath observance; hence the scrupulosity of Talmudic legislation on this point and the prohibition of numberless activities on the ground that, although harmless in themselves, they might lead to an infraction of the commands touching the Sabbath.[112]

The report then proceeds to lay down the general principle which the signers say they believe guided the conference in its deliberations, viz. that they must adopt the Biblical point of view and that individual instances of Biblical legislation may be modified only in case circumstances that gave rise to them have been changed, but that Talmudism is only a stadium in the historical development of Judaism, and that therefore the Talmudical interpretation can lay claim to consideration only when harmonizing with the demands of life.

> Applying this principle to the case in hand, we must return to the Biblical idea of the Sabbath, which, as is the case with divine truth in general, has eternal validity, while the Talmudic conception whenever it is not the development of the Biblical idea, but contradicts it as well as our own religious consciousness, can lay no claim to consideration. We must then reëmphasize the Biblical idea that the Sabbath is a day of consecration which is sanctified through our sanctifying ourselves; a day the distinctiveness of which is to be brought forcibly home to us by our ceasing from our daily toil and our special tasks, and giving ourselves to contemplation of the divine purpose of our existence as indicated by Jewish teaching. Hence, no task should be forbidden which conduces towards recreation and spiritual elevation and which serves to lift us out of our circumscribed environment and to arouse in us thoughts of a higher nature. The detailed enumeration of

prohibited tasks in the Talmud is characteristic rather of juridical method than of true religious striving. The all-important consideration in this matter of prohibited activity is whether such activity interferes with or furthers Sabbath consecration.

Since, then, rest is not an end in itself, but only a means towards a higher end, viz., the consecration of the day, and since in our time that consecration expresses itself through divine service, all such activities as are necessary for the furtherance of that service must be permitted.

The commission recommended the following definite program:

1. That the conference declare that the members consider it one of their most important duties to work towards the restoration of a worthy observance of the Sabbath.

2. That the conference declare that all such activity as is part and parcel of the daily business or professional vocation is forbidden, while any activity that makes for recreation or spiritual elevation, particularly if it tends to arouse a religious mood, not only does not harm Sabbath observance, but furthers it.

3. That the conference declare that any task which conduces towards a dignified and uplifting public divine service, or which makes it possible for the individual to participate in an edifying service, may be performed also by a Jew. Of such is particularly the performance of music on the Sabbath both at home and in the synagogue; walking beyond the so-called Sabbath boundary, riding and traveling if the purpose be not the transaction of business, but the attendance at divine service or some similar high aim. The conference declares the fiction of עירובי תחומין[113] as inadmissible if for industrial purposes or as unnecessary if for religious purposes; it declares the prohibition to carry things, in as far as this is not done for business purposes, hence also the fiction of עירובי חצרות[114] as abolished.

4. That the conference declares that the observance of the Sabbath may not ignore considerations for the preservation of life and the temporal welfare; in cases where life is threatened or is in danger any deed to avert this is permitted—yes, commanded; in cases where the livelihood

is at stake non-Jews may be employed, and if it should happen that the assistance of Jews is absolutely necessary in such instances, the Sabbath may be suspended by them exceptionally.

5. That the conference declare that participation in the welfare of the State is so exalted a duty that the observance of the Sabbath must yield to this in cases of collision. It declares, therefore, that the soldier is absolved from the observance of the Sabbath if military disciple demands this; it declares that the civil official must perform the duties of his office on the Sabbath if fealty to the State requires it, provided that he aims to restore the sacredness of the Sabbath in some other way, namely, in his home.

S. Adler, a member of the commission, declared himself entirely at variance with the majority in their conception of the fundamental idea of the Sabbath, and Joseph Kahn, another member, stated his disapproval of some of the recommendations.

As stated, the consideration of this report was deferred to the following conference. The amended report of the commission was presented at the first session of the Breslau Conference. The debate began on the morning of the second day of the session and continued at intervals morning and afternoon for nine days; every member of the conference expressed himself at greater or less length. I shall attempt to emphasize the more important points elucidated during the debate.

In bringing the subject before the conference Geiger, the chairman, stated that upon further deliberation the majority of the commission had determined upon some modifications in the recommendations submitted at the preceding conference. These modifications arose from the fact that while in the first report the rest through which the consecration of the day was made possible was conceived to be only the cessation from daily toil, the commission regarded the abstention from all activity requiring exertion just as necessary if the Jewish conception of the Sabbath is to be realized and the true consecration of the day to be achieved. With this in view the commission had so changed the recommendations as to read as follows:

1. That the conference declare that attention must be directed to arousing among the people an ever livelier con-

sciousness of the holiness of the Sabbath through the
means of a lofty divine service, and that it is necessary for
the proper consecration of the day to abstain from all
labor whether it be in the nature of the daily occupation or
whether it be an occasional task requiring exertion; on the
other hand any activity which is not for gain and does not
require exertion is permitted.

2. That the conference declare that the celebration of
the Sabbath by a worthy service is of such supreme importance that no activity, however much exertion it may
require, is prohibited if necessary for this purpose; hence,
any task which conduces towards dignifying the service or
makes it possible for the individual to participate in an
edifying service may be undertaken also by a Jew.

3. That the conference declare that any and everything
is permitted, nay, commanded to be done, when necessary
to avert danger to life.

4. The same as the fifth paragraph in the former
report.

The majority of the commission, whose views the report
reflected, believing that consecration is the essential factor of
the Sabbath, naturally laid greatest stress on the matter of
divine service. They felt that if the Jew could be attracted to
the house of worship, this would give the Sabbath that unique
place among the days of the week which it was intended to
have in Jewish life; by placing greater stress upon the consecration than upon the rest-idea, they cut themselves loose from
the extravagances of casuistry into which the anxiety of having
the people abstain from any and everything that even the most
refined ingenuity might define as work had led the Talmudical
doctors. The commission itself felt that the report was inadequate and was at best only the firing of the first gun in a long
campaign, as Geiger stated, when as president of the conference,
he made the opening remarks in bringing the subject before
the body.

Sabbath and holidays [said he] are the bone and sinew
of Jewish religious life; our aim must be to restore the
sanctity of these days for congregation and individual;
this purpose appears in both reports of the commission.
The matter is extremely difficult, for here if anywhere a
great conflict is apparent between doctrine and life. Lam-

entations avail not. We must face conditions as they are. Even if we do not succeed entirely in reaching a solution let us begin bravely; later conferences will continue what we have begun.[115]

A comparison of the original report of the commission to the Frankfort Conference with the amended report submitted at Breslau discloses a wide difference in spirit. The Frankfort report deals boldly with the problem and attempts to meet the situation by a readjustment all along the line of Sabbath observance; the Breslau amendments show a hesitancy to meet the situation face to face, which is absent from the original report. The amended report was due without doubt to the criticisms to which the original report had been subjected during the year intervening between the two conferences. The commission took account of the criticisms and so changed the report as to give satisfaction to none in the end, neither radicals, moderates nor traditionalists.

Space will not permit the reproduction at length of the arguments of the members of the conference on what is the essential nature of the Sabbath, nor is this necessary. Each one had his own theory of the Sabbath, and many propounded this in great detail. It was regrettable that so much time was devoted to academic discussions of the question and so little to a practical solution of the difficulty. What was desired and required was a way out; the Sabbath was not being observed as a day of rest; thousands were following their vocations, business, professional, industrial; could anything be done to relieve the strain of the situation and restore the Sabbath to the Jew? Geiger, in his résumé at the close of the entire discussion, stated that something must be done to preserve the Sabbath and that the commission's suggestions were made with that end in view, but he confessed that they could suggest no satisfactory remedy that would remove completely the collision between life and Sabbath observance.[116]

Auerbach declared, in a similar vein, "Our civil day of rest is another than our traditional Sabbath. This constitutes the chief collision. The commission has offered no suggestions how this is to be removed; I have none to offer either."[117] There were those who, like Salomon, felt that the question had better not have been taken up at all, for no satisfactory solution could be reached.

A very simple idea [he stated] lies at the foundation of the Sabbath; man, the image of God, shall not toil unconsciously like the animal, unremittingly like the slave; he should work from higher motives, viz., religion; he should rest in order that he may learn to know himself and his dear ones, that he may concern himself with spiritual matters in order to further the well-being of life and the spirit. How this simple idea has been spun out by later generations of men! How the institution of the Sabbath has degenerated! What a thousand and one fences have been erected about the Sabbath! Because of these things the deliberations on the Sabbath are the most difficult, and I still believe, despite the splendid addresses that we have heard, that it would have been better to consider the Sabbath a *noli me tangere* and not to have taken it up for the present; for whatever decision we may arrive at will anger one class and be decried as foolishness by another; the former, for whom every inherited folly is holy, will persecute us as though we have stolen their God; the latter, for whom èvery holy thing is folly will mock at us if we permit them such things as they have permitted themselves long ago.[118]

In truth, the confession of powerlessness to solve the difficulty on the part of so many able men is a very striking feature of the debate. One feels that the remedies suggested by the members of the commission and others were only makeshifts, temporary supports against the onrushing avalanche of life which was engulfing all the thoughts and activities of the emancipated Jew. All but one! The remedy proposed by Holdheim that the Sabbath be transferred to Sunday was certainly not a makeshift, whatever else it may be considered to be or not to be. It met with little sympathy on the part of the other members of the conference; but, before giving attention to this one drastic solution, it is necessary to indicate in brief the thoughts expressed on the nature of the Sabbath and the significance of the Sabbath idea.

The question that divided the members of the commission as to whether the idea of rest or of consecration was the essential feature of the Sabbath also lined up the members of the conference on opposing sides. In the course of the debate Wechsler,[119] S. Adler,[120] Holdheim,[121] Herxheimer,[122] Herz-

feld,[122] Goldstein,[124] and Sobernheim,[125] argued that rest is
the fundamental purpose of the Sabbath,[126] while Geiger,[127]
A. Adler,[128] Gosen,[129] Pick,[130] Salomon,[131] L. Lëvy,[132] and
Jolowicz[133] claimed that consecration was that fundamental
purpose; Stein[134] and Wagner[135] contended that both rest
and consecration were fundamental to the Sabbath idea. The
practical outcome of this difference of opinion naturally was
that those who considered the rest idea fundamental laid greatest stress on the observance of the day as a time of cessation
from all work, while such as claimed the consecration idea to
be fundamental contended that the Sabbath observance culminated, not in idle abstention from work, but in sanctifying
thought and sentiment by worship and prayer. There is no
justification in making this broad distinction. There can be
no doubt that both rest and consecration are inherent in Sabbath observance; the word שבת (Sabbath) itself means rest,
and the resting from toil was to be combined with acts of
consecration and sanctification, but it was to be applied positively to make of the Sabbath a delight, the honorable and
honored day of God, as the prophet declares. Holdheim drew
the picture of the development of the Sabbath idea so clearly
that his argument may well be reproduced:

In the Bible, especially in the Pentateuch, שבת means rest
from earthly toil; hence the cessation from usual work and not
the active celebration is the chief moment; rest is commanded,
but not religious observance, unless it be the double sacrifice.
But "rest" connotes not only the intermission of all disturbing
toil, but also the positive realization of the Sabbath idea
through consecration. This positive side is in truth the more
important; to find this we must only bear in mind in what the
essence of time exists and what God's relation to it is. Time
is absolute motion; its birth is also its passing; it is constant
change; hence one might say that its being is non-being.
Opposed to this essence of time is the being of God as the true
existence יהוה and at the same time the absolutely constant
unchangeable, immovable being, i. e. the conception of rest as
over against motion or restlessness. Therefore, if a season is
to be considered a season of God (Gotteszeit), it must be conceived as a rest-time (Ruhezeit). Rest gives it the appearance
and character of the divine and thus imparts to it the higher
sanctity. Hence, rest is the symbol employed by man to designate the day of God; and in this manner the rest on the Sab-

bath became an actual recognition of God in his relation to time, a serving of the Eternal in his infinite exaltation over all that is transient, changeable, and vain. It is, however, a mistake to think only of the negative side of the Sabbath conception, viz. the cessation from labor; the Sabbath aims to take man out of the transitory and ungodly and lead him to true existence and life, to יהוה ; hence the Talmud is correct when it defines the rest on Sabbath and holidays, the שביתה as the positive command (מצות עשה) and the abstention from labor as the negative (מצות לא תעשה).

Since rest is the fundamental idea in the Mosaic conception of the Sabbath, the reason for its institution is connected with the highest and most important things, viz. God's rest after creation, the covenant of God with Israel and the deliverance from Egypt. The conception of God's resting after creation points to the absolute difference between God and the world he created, between the Creator and the creature, and accentuates the true meaning of rest as the eternal element over against the mutability of time (see above) (Ex. xx. 8-11; Gen. ii. 2, 3; Ex. xxxi. 17).

The covenant of God with Israel is mentioned as the reason of the Sabbath (Ex. xxxi. 13, 17). The recognition of God as Creator is the revelation of the absolute difference between God and the world; it includes the recognition of his unity and personality as well as holiness. This characterizes the difference between Mosaism and other religions; since the Sabbath in its fundamental idea refers to this revelation, its celebration is the actual recognition of it. He who observes the Sabbath becomes the bearer of the sign of this relation; the non-observance of the Sabbath had to appear as a violation of the covenant and was an actual falling away from the one true God, Creator of heaven and earth; hence it implied idolatry and therefore the command to observe the Sabbath is joined with the warning against idolatry and backsliding (Lev. xix. 3, 4; Ezek. xx. 16-20; xxiii. 36-39). The deliverance from Egypt is mentioned as the reason for observing the Sabbath in Deut. v. 12-15; this was also conceived as a creative act, the creation of a people. God is called בורא ישראל, and the object of this creative omnipotence was the sanctification of the people; hence there is here the same general idea upon which Sabbath rests in the other cases, viz. creating and sanctifying.

From all this it grows clear why such stress was laid upon

the observance of the Sabbath. Those truths on which the religious and political existence of Israel rested were concentrated in the Sabbath idea, and its non-observance therefore implied the denial of those truths; for this reason extermination (כרת) was the punishment for the Sabbath breaker. (Ex. xxxi. 14.) Proceeding with his argument, he proved this from the philosophers and commentators.

Hence traditionally rest is the symbol or ceremony and the presentation of the Sabbath idea is intimately connected with the whole symbolism of the Mosaic law. Therefore all work which disturbs rest is forbidden in the Bible on the Sabbath; were the observance the chief moment, as the commission asserts, then only such work would be forbidden as disturbs the observance; but rest is the chief moment and everything opposed to it is forbidden.

In the later historical development of Judaism in the Talmudical era and in all likelihood already in the prophetical age (as seems likely from some hints), there was developed besides the rest as the negative side of Sabbath observance, the positive element which aimed at the religious refreshment of the spirit by reading from the law and by divine service. That this involved a conflict between Mosaism which regarded rest as the chief moment and a new conception which gave an ethical and moral interpretation to the Sabbath was not recognized, but the two were accepted together; the Sabbath continued to be considered the chief symbol representing creation and all other ideas; the Mosaic Sabbath-rest and the later Sabbath-sanctification existed on together.

How is it with us? Can we with our modern culture accept the notion of antiquity that the Sabbath-rest in itself implies all these fundamental doctrines of God as Creator, Israel as the covenant-people, etc., and that by resting we confess these things, and that not resting is equivalent to a denial of these most important religious truths? We must certainly answer no! if we wish to be honest. We have left behind us the symbolic age. A religious truth is significant for us not because we symbolize it by some ceremony, but because we grasp it intellectually and it becomes a very part of our nature. Hence we cannot consider that he really observes the Sabbath who passes the day in indolent rest, although according to Biblical and later ideas he would be doing so. Rest in itself contains nothing positive, and is significant for us only as the negative condition, and means making possible the observance of the Sabbath by spiritual uplifting.

If we ask, then, what work is forbidden, the answer is easy; as from the Biblical standpoint, where the rest is the chief thing, all activities are forbidden that disturb rest, so from our standpoint where the observance (*Feier*) is the essential and rest only a condition, any activity is forbidden that disturbs the observance.[136]

In this statement of Holdheim reference is made to the Sabbath as a symbol. On this point, too, some of the leading spirits of the conference differed absolutely; thus Einhorn claimed that throughout the Bible the Sabbath is designated (אות) a symbol; it symbolizes freedom from labor (Deuteronomy) and rest from creation (Exodus) שבת מורה על חדוש העולם; all productive labor must be intermitted; in post-Mosaic Biblical writings the Sabbath is emphasized as the symbol of Israel's holiness as contrasted with the peoples of the world; in the Talmud it is held to be the symbol of creation.[137] Geiger, on the other hand, declared flatly that the Bible does not consider the Sabbath a symbol.[138]

Formstecher also contended that "the Sabbath is not a symbol, but an end in itself. Each of the Ten Commandments is an end in itself, and not a symbol; hence, also the Sabbath. Further the pre-Exilic prophets who urge that symbols, like sacrifices, fasting, etc., must yield to Godfearing conduct, all insist on the observance of the Sabbath; hence, they could not have looked upon it merely as a symbol.[139]

Auerbach, too, held that the Sabbath was not a symbol, but he did not rest content with this negative statement, but injected a new thought into the discussion when he designated the Sabbath to be an institution.[140] "Judaism lives not in an abstract creed, but in its institutions," he said; "it is not merely doctrine, but a religion of deed. Israel itself is a divine institution, standing forth prominently in history, effective through its very existence. The Sabbath institution permeates all of Mosaism, hence the sanctification of the seventh week, the seventh month, the seventh year and finally the jubilee year."

It would be interesting to reproduce more of the exhaustive, learned and spirited discussions that occupied so many of the sessions of the conference, but enough has been given to indicate the chief thoughts that were brought forth in the academic and theoretical consideration of the subject. What, however, about the practical suggestions for the solution of this vexed problem of Sabbath observance? Were there any such suggestions? As noted above, both the commission and individual members of the conference confessed their inability to offer a complete remedy. The best they could do was to claim that a beginning was made at this conference and that future conferences must continue considering the question until a final and satisfactory solution should have been reached. The commission itself, basing upon the thesis that the consecration of the day was its essential feature, believed that if the services in the synagogue were made of such a character as to attract and edify the people this would gradually react upon life and the people would be so impressed with the consecrated character of the day that they would sacrifice material considerations, desert the business marts, interrupt economic and industrial pursuits and give the Sabbath its proper place as the weekly season of religious consecration. Time has demonstrated how fallacious was this argument and how delusive this expectation. Another practical suggestion was that of Formstecher's advising the formation of Sabbath associations in various communities whose object it was to be to foster the spirit of Sabbath observance among such as could be induced to enroll themselves as members. The recommendation was embodied in the report as finally adopted by the conference. The third practical suggestion was that suggested by Holdheim and Hirsch, viz. the transfer of the Sabbath to the civil day of rest. The Breslau Conference will remain notable, if for no other reason, for the fact that it was during its sessions that this drastic measure was first suggested as the only solution of the Sabbath difficulty. Hirsch hinted at it when he moved for the appointment of the commission at the Brunswick Conference. He was unable to attend the Breslau meeting, but he sent a communication in which he stated that the conflict between religion and life in the matter of Sabbath observance could be removed only by a transfer to Sunday; he closed his communication by offering as a motion that "the conference should declare that the Sabbath idea can find expression on any other day. Therefore no community steps out of Judaism which celebrates the Sabbath on a day other than that observed up to this time." [141]

At the close of his lengthy address [142] at the fourth session of the conference Holdheim declared his position in the matter in unambiguous terms. He stated that he would not offer a

resolution recommending the transfer to Sunday because he
was convinced that this would be rejected with indignation by
the great majority of the people, and hence it could not be
expected that it would be concurred in by the religious guides,
but he felt that he must express his views because freedom of
expression was and must remain the prerogative of every member of the assembly. He then declared unreservedly, "all our
effort for the restoration of a worthy celebration of the Sabbath is fruitless and there is unfortunately no thorough remedy whereby the conflict between the Sabbath and the demands
of daily life can be removed other than the transfer of the
Sabbath to a civil day of rest. I deny that this is a concession
to Christianity; I have in view the only possibility of a worthy
celebration of the Sabbath. The wounds from which our religious life is suffering affect us all most powerfully, and per-
plexity will be the result of all our endeavors until the time shall
come when the only possible remedy for the disease will be
applied." He then continued by saying that the difficulty of
the transfer lay not so much in the purely religious as in the
symbolical significance of the Sabbath, viz. the Biblical statement that God had rested on the seventh day after the completion of the creation and had sanctified and hallowed it, as well
as in the later reference of the command of Sabbath rest to
this fact whereby it becomes certain that this command to rest
refers to the seventh day (שבת בראשית). The celebration of a
definite seventh day is therefore closely connected with its symbolical significance. The celebration of this definite day sym-
bolized in an earlier time distinctive Jewish ideas in contrast
with heathenism; it can have no significance for us in itself
apart from these ideas which have become our property. If
we wish to avoid anthropomorphism, we can understand the
story that God rested on the seventh day in no other way than
that God manifested thus the absolute difference between himself and the world which he created. Since we claim that this
and all cognate beliefs are no longer realized by man through
rest, we must observe the Sabbath hereafter not through mere
rest, but through active consecration and the sanctification of
life; for the Biblical phrase, "man shall sanctify the Sabbath,"
we must substitute the words "man shall consecrate himself on
the Sabbath"; every reason for the observance of the definite
day falls away and the purely religious significance of the day
cannot contain any religious obstacle to the transfer if this is

demanded by other religious reasons. Since the Sabbath is of decisive influence for the preservation of religion, the reasons for a transfer of the same must be sought and found exclusively in the interest taken in the preservation of the religion. The Sabbath is in conflict with life, and experience teaches that it is losing ground daily in this conflict, and that there is no hope for its issuing victoriously from the conflict. The rabbinical conference has undertaken the peaceful adjustment of this conflict. If it succeeds in this there can be no talk of a retreat of the Sabbath. If, however, there is no other manner of settling the conflict peaceably, then the religion is threatened by the greatest danger and it must demand dictatorially for its self-preservation the transfer of the Sabbath to another day as the only effective remedy. Hence the religious reason for the transfer is no other than this, viz. to save the religion from certain destruction.

He then said that he forbore to give other reasons because these were of a subjective and individual nature. If those who truly observe the traditional Sabbath protest against a transfer, they are quite right and consistent, since for them the religion is in no danger inasmuch as the Sabbath asserts itself as victor in the conflict with life. If these, however, deny the right of such as really no longer observe the Sabbath to make this transfer, they are in the wrong, for here there is really danger, and for religion's sake energetic action must be taken. This non-observing section of Jewry has concurred thus far only in the negative aspect of the transfer, viz. the non-observance of the historical Sabbath; the positive observance made possible through the transfer must be given them if they are not to be entirely alienated from the religion and the religion be lost for them and they for it.

He concluded by calling attention to a Biblical precedent, viz. the permission given to such as were prevented from celebrating the Passover at the prescribed time to do so a month later.

The religious purpose of the Passover feast could be attained through the postponed celebration, so can also the religious purpose of the Sabbath be attained on another day. Such as believe or fear that the preservation of Judaism is conditioned by ceremonial externals rest under a delusion. . . . We wish to save the Sabbath for

Judaism and Judaism through the Sabbath even at the cost
of surrendering the symbolical shell of transitoriness.[143]

This suggestion of Hirsch and Holdheim found no place in
the official resolutions of the conference,[144] but it was referred
to time and again in the course of the debate.[145]

With the exception of Hess,[146] all who touched the subject,
viz. A. Adler,[147] Salomon,[148] Stein, [149] Philippson,[150] Wagner,[151] and Formstecher,[152] disapproved strongly. Salomon, in
concluding his remarks, said:

> So much is certain, we must alleviate the Sabbath
> observance for the people if the Sabbath is not to fall in
> the background altogether and it be found necessary then
> to transfer the Sabbath to Sunday. God forbid. For
> to transfer the Sabbath to Sunday would mean to serve
> two masters; it would mean coquetting with Christianity!
> That would signify the destruction of Judaism!

Stein expressed himself similarly:

> I am firmly convinced that Holdheim is actuated by the
> purest motive and the sincerest desire to help our sick
> Judaism (by his plea to transfer the Sabbath to Sunday);
> but I beg him to consider, as a faithful physician, whether
> the medicine which he prescribes is not a dangerous potion
> the imbibing whereof will mean either life or death; and
> whether he who has said so truly elsewhere that we are
> gardeners who cut away the dead branches but must
> beware lest we cut into the living wood, really considers
> our Sabbath so dead that he does not fear that he is cut-
> ting into the living wood! . . . . If we transfer the Sab-
> bath to Sunday, we will bury Judaism on Friday evening
> to permit to be resurrected on Sunday morning as another
> religion!

Philippson gave voice to his unqualified opposition in the
statement:

> All history declares against the transfer of the Sabbath.
> Christianity and Islam have transferred the Sabbath to
> Sunday and Friday respectively in order to have nothing
> in common with the Jews, and to obtain their autonomy.
> And Judaism shall now surrender its autonomy and we

shall go and say: we wish to celebrate the days that you celebrate! [153]

S. Adler offered a resolution on this subject of the following tenor:

> Resolved that the Conference, while recognizing the purposefulness of Associations for the Reform of Judaism [154] in general and of Sunday services because they are held on that week-day on which the German Jews of to-day have more leisure than any other, still declares that the conducting of a *Sabbath service on Sunday,* whether this be the only service of the week or the conducting of a similar service on Saturday be suffered in connection therewith, contradicts the teaching and the spirit of Judaism, and as such is unwarrantable.

The Sabbath commission to whom this resolution was referred reported as follows:

> The commission is of the opinion, with which the mover of the resolution agrees, that since it has appeared most emphatically and impressively from the debate on the Sabbath that the conference attaches a Sabbatical character to Saturday, the chief contention of the resolution is thereby upheld; but the need for Sunday services is not so widespread that deliberation on the subject is necessary, and for this reason action on this subject be postponed. [155]

The main purpose of Adler's resolution was to place the conference on record as opposed to a transfer of the Sabbath to Sunday; the resolution was called forth undoubtedly by the acts of the recently formed Reform Society of Berlin, which held its service on Sunday. The mover of the resolution evidently wished to have it understood that he approved of organizations like the Berlin society which were formed to advance the cause of reform Judaism, and further that there could be no objection to a service on Sunday, the day on which the Jews were at leisure, but that there was a decided objection to giving this service the character of a Sabbath service. [156]

In the discussion that ensued Philippson stated that he considered a service on Sunday to be an urgent need of the time

and desired a division of the two suggestions in Adler's resolution and a separate vote on each. This was not agreed to.
Holdheim urged that the conference contradicted itself by this
declaration; it had adopted no resolution on the subject of the
transfer of the Sabbath, and yet declared by this statement
that only the seventh day has a Sabbatical character.

Further debate was disallowed, but each member was permitted to make a personal explanation in giving his vote. Philippson, Holdheim, and Hess did so. The remainder of the
members voted in favor of the resolution postponing further
consideration of the question; as it happened this postponement proved the final action on the subject, for the fourth
conference never convened. The Sabbath question was not
broached at a rabbinical conference until fifty-six years later,
when it was discussed at the New Orleans meeting of the Central Conference of American Rabbis.[157] The Breslau Conference was bitterly criticized and stigmatized as cowardly by the
radical wing in Jewry for this action. Geiger took notice of
this criticism in the publication already referred to a number
of times, and defended the conference.[158]

As finally adopted by the conference, the resolutions on the
Sabbath read as follows:

The conference declares—
1. That the restoration of a worthy celebration of the
Sabbath as a day of rest and sanctification is one of the
most sacred tasks, both of the Israelitish teacher and of
each individual Israelite, and that therefore attention must
be devoted particularly towards arousing an ever livelier
consciousness of the holiness of the Sabbath by an edifying divine service and by the furtherance of Sabbath consecration in the home.
2. That the celebration of the Sabbath by a worthy and
dignified divine service is of such marked importance that
activities otherwise prohibited may not be forbidden in
connection therewith, and that therefore everything which
conduces towards a worthy celebration of the service and
makes the participation of the individual in an edifying
service possible is permitted.
3. That no spiritual activities detract from the Sabbath
celebration.

4. That if a cessation of one's occupation jeopardizes his livelihood, the attending thereto on the Sabbath by non-Israelites is permissible.

5. That in cases where the entire temporal well-being, where property and possessions, where the means for future livelihood are threatened, no religious duty is violated if precautions to save these are taken on the Sabbath; nay, if even the actual work of saving is done on the Sabbath.

6. That in case of danger to life, whether of self or others, of Israelites or non-Israelites, everything is permitted—yes, commanded—to be done to avert this danger.

7. That the over-great rigor of existing commands for the observance of the Sabbath is injurious to such observance. Therefore those far-fetched hedges which are intended to produce complete leisurely rest are not binding.

8. That the devices which were invented by former authorities with the purpose of alleviating the rigor of Sabbath observance, but which seem to be evasions, like Erube Chazerot and Erube T'chumin, are inadmissible for us; nay, superfluous—notably the latter in the matter of short journeys undertaken not for industrial purposes.

9. That the Jewish soldier is obliged to perform his full military duties on the Sabbath.

10. That the Jewish official may perform the duties of his office in as far as he is obliged to do so on the Sabbath, with the understanding, however, that he strive to have the spirit of consecration permeate his home on the Sabbath.

11. The conference is of opinion that societies for the restoration of a worthy celebration of the Sabbath are of benefit under certain circumstances.

These resolutions were lamentably inadequate. True, they declare against the Talmudical casuistry of the Erube Chazerot and Erube T'chumin, but they substitute a new casuistry. There is no bold position taken; a painful hesitancy is apparent. At the Frankfort meeting the conference in its resolutions on the liturgy had opened a new path and had broken with such Talmudical standpoints as were outgrown; but at Breslau an altogether different spirit seemed to pervade the meetings; a confident consciousness of strength and ability to cope with the situation marked the Frankfort gathering; a halting fear to grapple with the problem as though it demanded a prowess greater than theirs lamed the powers of the participants in the Breslau meeting. It was undoubtedly too much to expect that a way out of the difficulty would be found; but the disappointment was none the less keen, and the Breslau Conference, as will be shown later on, evoked a storm of criticism from both the liberal and the conservative sides.

Although the Sabbath discussion was the all-absorbing incident of this conference, other questions were discussed to which reference must now be made.

Festivals.—The commission to which the Sabbath question had been referred also reported on various points in connection with the observance of the holidays, notably the question of the observance of the second day. Wechsler reported for the commission;[158] several recommendations were made which were preceded by a preliminary address which set forth the reason for these recommendations somewhat in the following language:

The observance of the second day lacks all reason in our time whatever may have been its justification in an earlier day. The reason given in the Talmud for this observance because this may be necessary in the future when the restoration to Palestine takes place and the temple will be rebuilt does not impress us very deeply.

Although the original reasons for the institution of these second days no longer obtains, still it cannot be denied that the people look upon them as holy and assign to them religious significance. As long as this remains the case, no good reason can be advanced for abandoning them; but if, because of their frequency, they become a burden or detract from the fervor wherewith the first days are observed, then the time has come to abolish them. It may be that this is the case with some of these second days and not with others. At any rate, circumstances may differ in different communities, and it should be left to each congregation to determine this according to these circumstances, we merely giving the assurance that if any congregation determines to abolish the observance of these days there is nothing in Judaism to prevent it.

The report was debated at length,[159] and the resolutions as finally adopted read as follows:

1. The second days of the holidays, viz., the second and eighth days of Passover, the second day of the Feast of Weeks, of New Year, of the Feast of Tabernacles, and of the Feast of Conclusion, have no longer any significance for our time according to our religious sources; the second day of the New Year, however, deserves special consideration.

2. Therefore, if any congregations abolish some or all of these second days, they violate no religious ordinance and are thoroughly justified in their act.

3. If there be serious objection on the part of some members of a congregation to such abolition, a holiday service may be held on the second day, but the prohibition to work on that day is not binding.

4. The prohibition to eat leavened bread on the twenty-second of Nissan (the eighth day of Passover) is not binding.

5. It is permitted to blow the *shofar* on New Year's Day and to use the four prescribed fruits on the first Day of Tabernacles when these days fall on a Sabbath; in such congregations as observe only one day these features of the observance of the holiday must be observed when the holiday falls on Sabbath.

6. The custom of abstaining from eating leguminous plants, inclusive of rice and hirse, on Passover is absolutely unfounded and is therefore not to be observed.

Liturgy.—At the Frankfort Conference a Commission on Liturgy had been appointed to prepare a plan for a prayer-book along the lines of the ideas developed in the discussion and contained in the resolutions adopted. This commission failed to agree on a great number of special points; in its report to the conference at Breslau these points to the number of thirty-one were mentioned.[161] It was found impracticable to discuss these points in open meeting; it was therefore resolved to refer the report to a special committee, which was to confer with the Commission on Liturgy and report during the session. This committee consisted of Einhorn, S. Adler, Wechsler, Holdheim, and Philippson. At a later session it was resolved that the report of this committee be printed and sent to each member of the conference with the request that objections and suggestions be communicated to the committee, which should report a definite plan for a prayer-book to the next conference.[162] In this connection mention may be made of a communication addressed to the conference by the congregation of Cöslin stating that this congregation had adopted the resolutions touching the liturgy passed at the Frankfort Conference. In this communication the following words were used, which are reproduced because they express exactly the status of the conferences in their relation to the congregations:

> All your resolutions, both those which have been adopted and those which are still to be adopted, are to be considered not as irrefragable legislation, but only as deliverances founded upon the spirit and the pure principles of Judaism, which every individual congregation can modify in accordance with its particular religious needs and its condition of culture.[163]

Circumcision.—At the opening session of the conference a communication was received from Dr. Adolph Arnhold, of Breslau, in which he set forth in detail the sad experience he had had in having his two children circumcised. The first had almost bled to death; the second had died from the effects of circumcision. He asked the conference, not for a decision of the question as to whether circumcision was necessary and indispensable for the Jews, but for an opinion as to how he should act in the future.

> Should a son be born to me hereafter, will it not suffice if I have him named in the synagogue and have the customary benediction pronounced? Can the state, can the congregation, raise any objection to such an initiation of my sons into Judaism, considering the experiences I have had?

This communication, together with others on the subject of circumcision, was discussed in executive session. Philippson urged the necessity of reforms in the method of circumcision; he declared that the operation must be so safeguarded as to exclude the possibility of fatal results. The entire matter was referred to a commission of three, consisting of S. Adler, Holdheim, and Philippson, with instructions to report during the sessions of the conference. The commission reported on July 19th, and after a lengthy discussion the conference adopted the following resolutions on the subject of circumcision:

1. It is necessary that every *mohel* take a thorough course of instruction from a competent physician in all matters touching the operation, pass an examination, and have a license (legitimation).

2. Any *mohel* who, because of any bodily defect, such as trembling of the hands, nearsightedness, etc., is unfit to perform the operation, shall not be permitted hereafter to fill the office.

3. The operation of the *P'riah* with a surgical instrument is not ritually forbidden; it is therefore to be left to the judgment of the operator or the assisting physician which method is to be used whether with the nail, as is the traditional custom, or with a surgical instrument.

4. The *mezizah* is to be discontinued.

5. It is desirable to leave the after-treatment to a physician or surgeon.

6. It is necessary that a medical examination take place before the circumcision in order that it be determined whether any bodily suffering or defect make a deferring of the act advisable or necessary.

7. In such cases in which, according to a physician's declaration, a child has died or has sustained lasting injury from circumcision, and it is therefore a fair supposition that danger to life and health threaten a second child of the same parents, the act of circumcision is to be suspended until a medical declaration has been given that no danger of any kind is to be feared as a result of circumcision.

The conference did not discuss for a moment the question whether circumcision is a *conditio sine qua non* of admission into Judaism. The resolutions adopted at Breslau had the purpose simply of reforming certain abuses and of preventing as far as possible any ill effects from the operation.[164]

Mourning Customs.—Another matter in Jewish life that called loudly for reform were the customs observed in connection with death and mourning. The subject was broached at the last session of the Frankfort Conference, but was considered of too great importance to be disposed of in the hurry of a closing session; it was postponed, therefore, to the next conference. Stein reported for the commission at the Breslau Conference, whose final action resulted in the adoption of a number of important reforms.[165] The conference declared that the following customs which were survivals from earlier periods of Jewish life, viz. the tearing of the clothes (קְרִיעָה), the abstention from shaving the beard, the sitting on the earth, the dispensing with leather footwear, as well as the prohibitions to wash, bathe, and greet acquaintances have lost all significance and religious meaning for our time, nay more, they are inconsistent with our religious sentiment, and are therefore to be abolished. The conference declared it to be advisable that the mourner remain at home during the first three days, counting from the day of burial (instead of the first seven as hitherto), in as far as this is compatible with the higher duties of life and considerations of health. Further, the conference advised that the mourner close his business altogether on the day of burial if at all possible, and that on the two following days he himself abstain from participation in his business, although others may conduct it for him.

Reform of Marriage Laws.—At the Brunswick Conference a commission had been appointed to revise the Jewish marriage laws. This commission did not report at the Frankfort Conference, but a question propounded to this conference for solution by the congregation of Bingen was referred to it. The question touched the method of reconciliation of the Jewish and the civil marriage and divorce laws.[166] Also at the third conference the commission did not report, except briefly at the last session, when they craved the indulgence of the conference for longer time because of the importance of the work submitted to them. However, several times during the session the subject of the marriage laws came to the fore. At the opening meeting Holdheim submitted a resolution[167] to the effect that the conference devote attention to a number of points in the traditional marriage laws which required reform, revision and change.[168] At the closing meeting the commission on marriage laws recommended that the old institution of *Chalitzah* be declared unsuited to modern conditions, because "the levirate marriage and the *Chalitzah* were instituted in a time when the views on the position of woman, the family rights, and the perpetuation of the individual were entirely different from what they are now. They had their origin under different social conditions, and they are not only improper, but unjustified, under the entirely different views and conditions of to-day—nay, they are an insult to the free personality of woman, an insult to the religion; they are dangerous fetters which must be loosed." The commission therefore offered the resolution, "That the conference declare that no other conditions are necessary for the remarriage of a childless widow than for any other Jewish marriages." [169] No definite action, however, was taken on this recommendation.

The Position of Woman.—At the Frankfort Conference a commission had been appointed to report on the religious duties of woman in the light of the change of modern thought on her position. The commission reported at the Breslau Conference as follows:

> We recommend that the rabbinical conference declare woman to be entitled to the same religious rights and subject to the same religious duties as man, and in accordance herewith make the following pronouncements:
>
> 1. That women are obliged to perform such religious acts as depend on a fixed time,[170] in as far as such acts have significance for our religious consciousness.
>
> 2. That woman must perform all duties towards children in the same measure as man.
>
> 3. That neither the husband nor the father has the right to release from her vow a daughter or a wife who has reached her religious majority.
>
> 4. That the benediction שלא עשני אשה (Praised be thou, O Lord our God, who hast not made me a woman), which owed its origin to the belief in the religious inferiority of woman be abolished.
>
> 5. That the female sex is obligated from youth up to participate in religious instruction and the public religious service and be counted for *minyan;* and, finally,
>
> 6. That the religious majority of both sexes begin with the thirteenth year.[171]

Unfortunately this important and interesting report could not be discussed owing to lack of time. It was merely read at the last session but one. In practice, however, these first recommendations on this subject in the history of the reform movement have been carried out in reform congregations notably in the United States, where, with the abolition of the woman's gallery in the synagogue and the introduction of family pews, much more decided steps forward have been taken. Woman's

religious equality with man is fully recognized in reform congregations. Einhorn in presenting this report reviewed the
whole subject of the position of woman in Judaism, pointing
out her inferiority in the public religious functions from the
Biblical, Talmudical, and rabbinical standpoint, and closed char-
acteristically as follows:

> It is our sacred duty to declare with all emphasis the
> complete religious equality of woman with man in view
> of the religious standpoint that we represent according to
> which an equal degree of natural holiness inheres in all
> people, the distinctions in Sacred Writ having therefore
> only relative and momentary significance. Life which is
> stronger than all theory has already accomplished some-
> thing in this respect; but much is still wanting for com-
> plete equality and even the little that has been achieved
> lacks still legal sanction. It is therefore our mission to
> make legal declaration of the equal religious obligation and
> justification of woman in as far as this is possible; we have
> the same right to do this as had the synod under Rabbenu
> Gershom eight hundred years ago which passed new reli-
> gious decrees in favor of the female sex. The Talmud says
> in reference to the מזוזה command גברי בעי חיי נשי לא
> בעי חיי; let us interpret this principle in a much higher
> sense by applying it to the religious life and thus enable
> our congregations to make use of powers that have been
> alienated only too long.[172]

Rabbinical Seminary.—The commission appointed at the
Frankfort Conference to present a plan for the foundation of a
rabbinical seminary reported at this conference that an event
had taken place during the past year which promised to make
possible the opening of such an institution much sooner than
any of them had hoped would prove the case. Mr. J. Fränkel,
a wealthy Jew of Breslau, who had died recently, had left provision in his will for the foundation of a rabbinical seminary;
upon being apprised of this the commission had addressed a
communication to the executors of the will informing them of
the step the conference had taken in this matter and offering the
assistance of the conference in carrying out the work.[173] The
commission reported further that they had had a personal inter-
view with the executors, and had received the assurance from
the latter that they would take pleasure in giving the fullest

consideration to the suggestions of the conference. The account of the well-known rabbinical seminary of Breslau, the institution which Fränkel's munificent bequest called into being, does not belong here; sufficient to say that the first practical suggestions for such an institution emanated from the rabbinical conferences upon the initiative chiefly of Philippson and Geiger.

As was the case with the two preceding conferences so also did the Breslau Conference arouse a storm of opposition, with this difference, however, that while the Brunswick and Frankfort Conferences had been denounced chiefly by the orthodox, the Breslau Conference called forth the scorn of the radicals; truth to say, the third conference seemed to satisfy no party; its compromising attitude put it out of favor with both extremes;[174] it was notably the Sabbath discussion and resolutions which were made to bear the brunt of the attacks; the other discussions and resolutions were passed over almost altogether. The conference had scarcely adjourned ere the public press began to teem with denunciatory articles, notably the *Deutsche Allgemeine Zeitung,* the *Frankfurter Journal,* and the *Oberpostamtszeitung;* most of these articles were republished in the Jewish press. The first gun was fired from Frankfort; the issue of the *Frankfurter Journal* of August, 1846 (No. 219),[175] contained a bitter arraignment of the Breslau Conference by twelve Jews of the city on the Main; it opened with the words, "the third rabbinical conference has lost the confidence of the German Jews, and it is time that the friends of progress in Judaism assemble and declare openly and freely this fact, felt by all and denied by none." The letter called the rabbis reactionary, not representative of the progressive spirit ruling in German congregations, desirous of assuming hierarchical authority, etc. The neglect of the conference to declare for the transfer of the Saturday to the Sunday as the only solution of the problem was the cause of this diatribe, as appeared from the close of the communication.

This arraignment called forth a number of answers in defense of the conference, viz. from Leopold Stein, the rabbi of Frankfort;[176] from the congregation of Alzey,[177] and from B. Wechsler, the rabbi of Oldenburg in the *Bremer Zeitung* of August 18.[178]

A second attack by Frankfort Jews, supposedly members of the defunct Reform Society, declared that the Breslau Conference had gone backward; that whereas the first two conferences were animated by the reform progressive spirit, the Breslau Conference was characterized by rabbinical casuistry; [179] this, too, was answered by Stein. [180]

Holdheim, too, voiced the dissatisfaction of the radical element in a number of open letters. [181] He stated that the dissatisfaction on the part of the liberals was justified, but that this dissatisfaction was due, not so much to the results, as to the spirit that pervaded the transactions; . . . the conference had lost its place as a guiding influence in Jewish life which it had maintained in the two former meetings. At Frankfort it had taken the bold position that the Hebrew language was not an absolute requirement for the services although it had stated that its partial retention was advisable under present conditions. It had not said that it must wait with a declaration on this question until the whole community of Israel had come to this conclusion; it led. How different its attitude on the Sabbath question at Breslau! Here it feared to take the initiative by declaring for the only possible solution, the transfer; what if the community at large was not ready for it; it had to come if Judaism was to be saved. The conference should be the organ, not merely of present-day but also of future Judaism, and should give voice not alone to present convictions, but point the way to the future.

Geiger, the president of the conference, was moved, chiefly because of these attacks, to write two lengthy defenses of the work of the conference before the official publication of the proceedings appeared. Occasional references have already been made to both these pamphlets. [182] In the former of these pamphlets he reviewed the work of the rabbinical conferences in general; of this he said that they sought "to tear away abuses, to breathe into Judaism the living spirit and make it susceptible of forms suitable for our time; further, the conferences stand also for the historical development of Judaism, building on the past and preparing for the future. In this spirit the Breslau Conference worked also." In the second pamphlet he met the attacks on the attitude of the conference on the Sabbath question. He stated that it was the most pressing question of the time, and the conference had to consider it. It would have been cowardly to evade it as many say the conference should have done. The conference could not possibly suggest the transfer to Sunday; an institution of Judaism that has existed for thousands of years and is one of its very fundamentals cannot be legislated out of existence by a rabbinical conference. As for a service on Sunday, there can certainly be no objection to a supplemental service as long as it is not a Sabbath service, and any congregation can institute it; but many fear that it is only the opening wedge to a complete transfer. The conference, although asked to pronounce upon the permissibility of a service on Sunday for the benefit of such as do not attend on Saturday, postponed consideration of this question; but it is only postponed; the conference will have to take it up next year or some other time.

However, this was not to be; no further conference was convened. When the Breslau Conference adjourned, it was with the full expectation that the yearly meetings would continue. Geiger, in a letter to the dissatisfied radical element, said: "Let us prepare for future conferences; the task before us is great; let us aim to accomplish this in unity and mutual understanding." [183] The executive committee appointed at the Breslau Conference took steps toward convening the next conference at Mannheim. This conference was not held, because the consent of the government was not received in time to convene the meeting on the appointed date. [184] The executive committee requested opinions from members whether they would attend a meeting to be held at a later day in that year. After receiving a negative reply from twelve, the committee issued a notice that the next conference would be held July 17, 1848. [185] The permission to hold the conference at Mannheim was received from the government of Baden on March 3, 1848. The executive committee, consisting of H. Wagner, S. Adler, A. Adler, S. Formstecher, and L. Stein addressed a communication to the members of the conference dated Worms, July 24, 1848, in which they say, after mentioning the fact that they had received the consent of the government of Baden to hold the conference at Mannheim, that they did not consider it feasible to take advantage of this belated permission, since they were of the opinion that the rabbinical conference no longer met the needs of the Jewish situation; "the people should and must have a voice in the deliberations and decisions"; therefore they proposed that a synod be convened to take the place of the conference, and that both rabbis and laymen participate in this synod. [186] Hence, the conference at Breslau proved to be the last reform rabbinical conference to be held in Germany till 1868, when the Cassel Conference took place.

The rabbinical conferences of 1844, 1845, and 1846 will remain for all time among the most remarkable gatherings in the history of Judaism. It was here that the great truth received public expression that Judaism contained in itself the power of adaptation to changing needs and conditions of life in the successive ages of the world's progress. It was here that the spirit of Jewish tradition and the spirit of modernity met each other face to face in public view and became welded in firm embrace. The conferences pretended to no hierarchical authority; [187] they furnished the platform for the discussion of the vexing problems in Jewish life. That they did not solve all these problems does not militate against their importance and usefulness, for indeed Geiger was correct when, toward the close of his defense of the Breslau Conference. he wrote: "The rabbinical conference is the most powerful agent for progress in Judaism, the institution which will show itself more and more capable of meeting the needs of our religious conditions." [188] It is an eternal pity that circumstances prevented their perpetuation; true, it is vain to attempt to describe what might have been; but this much may be said, that of all the early results of the reform movement the rabbinical conferences of the fifth decade have gone down into history as the most characteristic expression of that task at which the present generation is still laboring, viz. the interpretation of the principles of Judaism in the light of modern conditions and the garbing of its eternal truths in expressions and institutions that are of the age and generation; in other words, the emphasizing of the all-important truth that Judaism spells development and not stagnation, for this is the intent and content of the reform movement.

CHAPTER VIII

THE governmental edict of December 9, 1823, forbidding all changes and innovations in the ritual and liturgy, had checked effectively all efforts among the Jews of the Prussian capital to institute reforms.[1] During the twenty years following the closing of the Beer reform synagogue [2] the progressive religious tendencies received no public expression. The voices of the new time were given heed to in many a small community, but the official heads of the metropolitan congregation of Germany disregarded their insistent cry. And that, too, though it was very apparent that the religious affairs were in a chaotic condition. Hundreds were alienated from the synagogues. Indifference and irreligion ran riot. The tragedy of the conflict of the old with the new appeared in many ways; thus the representatives of rabbinical Judaism discountenanced not merely liturgical reforms in the public service but resisted every innovation demanded by the new outlook of latter-day man; *e.g.* they refused to countenance such things as the vaccination of children, attendance at secular schools, abolition of rabbinical courts, military service, the elapsing of an interval of more than twenty-four hours between death and burial, and the like; they even took stand against political emancipation because it did not comport with the traditions.[3] No wonder that alienation was the result of this policy of the powers that were in Jewry. Nowhere in Germany were the Jews swept along by the currents of the new time as they were in Berlin. There can be no doubt that the reform movement would have found strong and unequivocal public expression there long after 1845 had it not been for the reactionary attitude of the government. The indifference of the cultivated Jew of Berlin was due without question in great part to the fact that adaptation of the Jewish cult to modern conceptions was made difficult, not only by this attitude of the Jewish religious authorities, but also by the policy of the state. In the fifth decade a more liberal spirit actuated

225

governmental circles,[4] and the result was that the reform movement, smothered for twenty years, broke forth into flaming activity.

In 1840 and thereabouts the Jews of Berlin might have been divided broadly into three classes: the orthodox, who observed every minute command of the rabbinical traditional code and arranged their life accordingly; the hypocrites, "official Jews," who in their private lives disregarded the ceremonies, but demanded that they be observed publicly and officially,[5] and the indifferentists who had drifted from Jewish moorings because there was nothing in the synagogue to hold them.[6] True, all Jews who had not renounced their faith were *ipso facto* members of the congregation; but hundreds were Jews only in name. They never attended the services, though by the law they were compelled to contribute to the congregation; no trace of Judaism was visible in their homes or in their lives. The officials of the congregation had been very derelict in neglecting to take any steps that might have prevented, or if not prevented this condition, at least have given no justification for it. There was no provision whatsoever made for presenting the teachings of Judaism in an intelligible manner. A sermon in the vernacular was an unknown quantity in the Berlin synagogue. No school was supported by the congregation for the religious instruction of the children.[7] What wonder, then, that Judaism was foreign to the lives and thoughts of many who might have been actively concerned in its welfare had proper efforts been put forth to reach them. But even the directory of the Berlin congregation could not remain altogether blind to the necessities of the situation. In the opening years of the 'forties they endeavored to secure a rabbi of modern training and education; after negotiating with a number of men of prominence, notably Zacharias Frankel[8] they finally elected M. Sachs, of Prague, in 1844 as assistant rabbi and preacher. Sachs was a superb preacher, and the hope was entertained that his coming to Berlin would weld the discordant elements into unity and give the congregation that standing among the congregations of Germany which it should have had owing to its commanding position. But Sachs' coming, far from making for the peaceful amalgamation of all parties in the community, became the occasion for the accentuating of the well-nigh irreconcilable differences.[9] Sachs was strongly conservative; for him Talmud and *Shulchan Aruk* were norm and authority. His influence and his magnificent pulpit gifts were arrayed on the side of tradition; he had no sympathy with the reform tendencies that were so strong in Germany at that time. His decided stand for traditionalism and the retention of the rabbinical *status quo* in Judaism [10] aroused to active effort the men in whom the spirit of Jacobson, Jacob Herz Beer, Kley, and Auerbach, the promoters of the earliest efforts at reform in Berlin before the year 1823 was renewed. As that earlier movement was allied intimately with a society for the advancement of Jewish culture,[11] so was the second effort at the establishment of a reform congregation in Berlin connected with a similar society; although this connection was not intended consciously at the time of the formation of the society, still, as will be seen, the society offered the forum where were presented the thoughts that led to the organization of the reform congregation.

On January 1, 1841, a number of men issued a pamphlet containing the statutes and a description of the aims of the recently formed *Cultur Verein*. These aims were said to be the encouragement and the furtherance of literary and artistic efforts among Jews and by the offering of prizes for essays upon such subjects [12] to assist in the solution of the contemporaneous difficulties that were perplexing Jewry. The governing board of this society included names which were already famous or destined to become so in future years, viz. Dr. I. L. Auerbach, A. Bernstein, Dr. M. Joel, Dr. Rubo, Dr. H. Steinthal, Dr. S. Stern, Dr. M. Veit, Dr. L. Zunz. The first subject selected by the society for prize competition indicated the trend of thought of its guiding spirits. This subject was "What was, what is and what should the rabbi be?" [13] Undoubtedly the agitation in the Berlin community that culminated in the selection of Sachs was the cause for the choice of this subject. The "Culture Society" desired to mold the thought of the community. The very form in which the subject was put shows that the officers of this society recognized that the functions of the rabbi of aforetimes and the rabbi of the present were not the same. Further, it is not a mere coincidence that some of the foremost organizers of the reform congregation were officers of this culture society, viz. A. Bernstein, S. Stern, I. L. Auerbach, Carl Heymann, Philip Heilbronn, and Ludwig Lesser. This society in its manifesto had declared that one of its purposes was "to offer any one the opportunity to show actively his interest in the progress of Judaism, which was apparent everywhere of recent years." It became the center for the intellectual elite of Berlin Jewry. The account of its doings does not belong here. In 1844, however, an event took place under its auspices which led to unexpected results. This was the delivery of the course of lectures by Dr. Sigismund Stern on "The Task of Judaism and the Jew in the Present." [14]

Before these lectures, which brought the renewed efforts of the reformers to a focus, were delivered, it was apparent that the same conditions which led to the formation of the reform society of Frankfort were prevalent in Berlin; a reconciliation of Jewish life and profession was longed for; a casting of the teachings of Judaism in a modern mold was passionately desired. The indifference of so many of the cultured class was due, not always to lack of interest in the religion, but to the impossibility of accepting Judaism in its Talmudical and rabbinical garb. The sentiments and longings of this element of Berlin Jewry were given expression to by two of its number [15] in the remarkable essays, "Our Present Age," [16] by A. Rebenstein, and "The Task of the Jewish Congregation of Berlin for the Present," by S. Stern.[17] Rebenstein's [18] essay is a keen diagnosis of the conditions among the Jews; he pleads passionately for a true reform of Judaism, a reform which should be neither revolution nor restoration.

> The moral-religious standpoint is that upon which theology must be based. In accordance with this standpoint theology can and must preserve and fortify in the life of the Jews such ceremonies and symbols as still testify to the God-consciousness of the people and fortify and strengthen this; it must remove such ceremonies as have ceased to further the life of Judaism and must change that which has been distorted in the course of the ages. This is the standpoint upon which theology can repel with justice all violent attacks upon the living organism, and can with no less justification accept for itself reform and reorganization.

Stern deplores the chaotic condition of affairs in the congregation and the lack of communal spirit; he bewails the fact that no activity is apparent in this great congregation when so many smaller communities had taken steps to introduce reforms; he argues that it is the mission of the community as a community to overcome the disintegrating effects of the rampant individualism that was apparent and to take its legitimate place as the leader in German Jewish life. In the light of later events it is interesting to note that Stern discountenances in this essay the action of the reformers of the second decade in leaving the main congregation and forming a separate congregation. Their duty was to remain with the main body and to insist on their right to have their religious needs satisfied by a service that was expressive of their religious conceptions. In this manner the two important questions would have been decided for all Jewry as to the right of the individual in the congregation to which he belonged and in what manner in general a reform of the cult was possible. These essays may be considered in the light of forerunners of the later activity of these two men who became the leading spirits in the organization of the congregation which cut out for itself a new channel.

The eight lectures delivered by Stern during the winter of 1844-45 before the *Cultur Verein* were the galvanic spark that roused into life the seemingly moribund Jewish community. Stern made no pretentions to theological learning; [19] his lectures, gauged by the measure of erudition, fall very short; but they were a lucid and thoughtful presentation of the conditions in the Jewish community and brought home to many of the hearers thoughts that had not occurred to them before. The hall in which the lectures were delivered was thronged, and they were the sensation of the hour in the Jewish community. The speaker had seized the psychological moment, and hundreds to whom Judaism had become merely a name or a memory and for whose lives it had ceased to have any significance were electrified by the suggestion that this faith of their fathers might become also a living force in their lives and the lives of their children. [20] In summing up he said:

> If you ask me what we have to do to prepare for and finally inaugurate this new age in Judaism, I say to you, Nothing more than to banish that dull indifference which bade us look upon the disintegration and ruin of Judaism without concern, that indifference wherewith we renounced our rightful claim to the life and development of Judaism, with which we suffered the ever growing alienation from our faith on the part of hundreds who are its children until even we appeared to be recreant and faithless sons of Judaism, and some few of our brethren designated them-

selves as its only true and rightful heirs. We wish to
banish this indifference and step forth with the full and
incontrovertible demand upon our faith that it recognize us
and our children as the rightful bearers of its name. We
wish to substantiate our right to live like unto our brethren
in the house that it has erected, and if its space is too
narrow to receive us, we would take steps in its name to
extend it so that it give us and our children protection and
shelter. Above all, we wish to come forth publicly with
our conviction and our striving and to claim before the
court of the present the rights which have been withheld
from us. We wish to bring suit before the tribunal of
history in our name and the name of our children for the
right to be recognized as the true sons of Judaism; and
finally we wish to work unitedly for the attainment of
the aim which we feel called upon to reach, for the realization of the mission which we have recognized as the
mission of Judaism."[21]

This was an inspiring call to the indifferentists to throw off
their lethargy and band themselves together for work in the
name of a living faith; it was a rebuke to the arrogant claim
of the traditionalists that all such as did not adhere to the
Judaism of the codes must be read out of the faith; it was a
dignified assertion of the right to residence within the household
of Judaism on the part of such as reinterpreted the truths of
the faith in the light of the new life which had superseded
medieval darkness and ghetto conditions. It was a mistake,
however, as was done by enthusiastic admirers at the time,
to claim for Stern the credit of having been the creator through
these addresses of the Berlin reform movement. It was not as
though reform in Judaism had been unknown and unthought of
before these addresses were delivered. The same conditions
prevailed in Berlin as in Hamburg, Frankfort, Breslau, and
other cities. The new spirit which had come upon Israel had
made itself felt in Berlin long before, but it was suppressed
owing to untoward circumstances. Now, again, it was coming
to the fore, and Stern was the spokesman whose words reflected
the thoughts of hundreds in the community. He himself discountenanced all claim to being looked upon as the creator of
the movement.[22] He was but one of a number of men of
similar thoughts, strivings, and tendencies. He had the courage

to give voice publicly to these thoughts and tendencies, and his addresses thus furnished the impulse that brought the men of knowledge, thought, and activity together and supplied the guaranty to each one that there would be no lack of sympathizers were they to take active steps toward realizing their ideals.[23] And the first active step followed closely. On March 7, 1845, Ludwig Lesser invited a number of men to confer together concerning important affairs in Judaism at a meeting to be held on March 10 in the rooms of the "Culture Society."

The outcome of this first meeting was the adoption of a resolution to the following effect:

> We declare that rabbinical Judaism as a whole and in its separate commands is not in harmony with our scientific conviction and the demands of life. Resolved, therefore, that we elect a committee to make propositions to us whether and how progress in this respect is possible.[24]

The results of the numerous deliberations of the committee of eight appointed in accordance with this resolution were embodied in the famous "Appeal to our German Coreligionists" (*Aufruf an unsere deutsche Glaubensbrüder*), which appeared in the various newspapers of Berlin in the beginning of April, 1845. This document was as follows:

> From the time that we ceased to suffer from political oppression in our German fatherland and the soaring spirit cast off its fetters; from the time that we became identified with our surroundings in culture and custom, our religion failed gradually to give us that satisfaction which was the comfort and the happiness of our ancestors. Our religion clung to the forms and prescriptions that had been handed down for centuries, but our convictions and our sentiments, our *inner* religion, is no longer in harmony with this interpretation. Hence we are in a state of conflict with ourselves, and there is a contradiction between our inner life and faith and the external life, the given law.
>
> True, our savants and teachers are engaged in a combat in the field of theology for and against a reconciliation of this contradiction; but how long has this been the case! and the end of the combat is not in sight. In the meantime, however, life has superseded science; in the mean-

time the overwhelming majority of the cultured members
of our community has renounced the greatest portion of
our religious prescriptions, and even those which they still
keep are observed without belief and without enthusiasm.
The confusion is great. Nowhere union, nowhere a support, nowhere a limit. The old rabbinical Judaism with
its firm basis has no basis any longer in us. In vain are the
efforts of those who aim to preserve it artificially. The
petrified doctrine and our life are divorced forever. The
doubt which has begun to negate threatens to transgress
all limits. It begets indifference and unbelief and delivers
us over to a state of helplessness in which we are compelled
to witness with pain how, together with the antiquated
forms, the eternal holy kernel of true Judaism threatens to
be lost for our descendants.

These are facts which speak for themselves, which only
those do not see who will not see—facts which fill our
hearts with glowing zeal, which call forth all our energy
and embolden us to issue the call to you, our German
coreligionists who feel as do we, who feel that it is incumbent on us not to view idly the ruin and the vain artificial
varnishing of the breach but to take steps together after
coming to a mutual understanding, to save out of the
chaos what can continue to exist in our spiritual development and in our German life, and to repudiate openly
what has died in us.

With this sentiment we have come together, feeling our
justification to declare openly and decidedly the necessity
of a change, a justification which we assume and may
assume because our holiest interests are threatened with
immediate danger, although we are conscious at the same
time that we are not the elect who are to carry out this
change. Therefore we wish to assure ourselves of the sympathy and agreement of our German coreligionists and in
conjunction with them convene a synod in order to fix
that aspect of Judaism which corresponds with our age
and the sentiments of our heart.

We desire: *Faith;* we desire: *Positive Religion;* we
desire: *Judaism.* We hold fast to the spirit of Sacred
Scripture, which we recognize as a testimony of divine
revelation by which the spirit of our fathers was illumined.
We hold fast to everything which is necessary for the true

worship of God, rooted in the spirit of our religion. We hold fast to the conviction that Judaism's doctrine of God is eternally true and to the prediction that the knowledge of God as proclaimed by Judaism will at some time become the possession of all mankind. But we desire to interpret Holy Writ according to its divine spirit; we cannot sacrifice our divine freedom to the tyranny of the dead letter. We cannot pray sincerely for an earthly Messianic dominion which is to lead us to the home of our ancestors out of the fatherland to which we cling with all the bonds of love as though this were a strange land to us. We can no longer observe commands which have no spiritual hold on us and can no longer recognize a code as immutable lawbook according to which the essence and the mission of Judaism consist in blind adherence to forms and prescriptions which owe their origin to a time long past and forever vanished.

Permeated with the holy content of our religion we cannot preserve it in the bequeathed form, much less bequeath it in this form to our descendants and so, placed between the graves of our ancestors and the cradles of our children, the cornet-call of the age thrills us, the *latest* recipients of a great heritage in its antiquated form to be also the *first* who, with undaunted courage, with true fraternization by word and act, lay the foundation of this new structure for ourselves and the generations which come after us.

However, we do not wish to dissociate ourselves by this step from the community to which we belong; nay, we extend the hand of brotherhood in love and tolerance to all, also to those of our coreligionists who differ with us. We desire no schism. But upon you, who sympathize with us, we call confidently for the closest union that shall make for truth within, indulgence without, endurance in the fight with others and faithfulness towards ourselves.

And thus our appeal goes forth to you, German coreligionists, far and near,

That you associate yourselves with us by name and assure us by word and act of your support and aid in order that we in great number can convene a synod which shall renew and establish Judaism in the form in which it is

capable and worthy of continuing as a living force for us
and our children."

Berlin, April 2, 1845.

The Berlin reformers had taken to heart the lessons taught
by the experience of their forerunners in Frankfort and avoided
the mistakes that the latter had made. In comparing this appeal
with the program of the Society of the Friends of Reform of
Frankfort [26] one cannot but be struck at once by the warmer
religious sentiment, the more positive tone, and the more
intense Jewishness of the Berlin document. It was therefore
not assailed with the violence and virulence that the other had
called forth.[27] As at Frankfort, so at Berlin, the movement
for reform had emanated from the people; among the signers
to the appeal there is not one theologian by profession, although
one of the number, A. Rebenstein, possessed theological knowledge [28] but there was a marked difference in the attitude toward
the rabbis; the Frankfort reformers assumed an attitude of
opposition, nay, almost of contempt; [29] the Berlin reformers
acknowledged that the theoretical guidance of the movement
must be in the hands of trained theologians; therefore, they
sought to enter into friendly relations with the rabbinical conference [30] and asked the advice of members of the conference [31]
who stopped at Berlin on their way home from the gathering at
Frankfort. The Frankfort reformers had set up a creed—
though a creed of negations—while the signers to the Berlin
appeal were careful not to close their document with a declaration of principles. Most of the signers in truth were opposed
to a creed. One dogmatic point only was touched, viz. the
Messianic belief. The reason for this grows apparent when
we remember that the time when the appeal appeared was also
the time when the Jews were still struggling for full civil and
political emancipation. Every opportunity therefore was seized
to testify to their love for the fatherland.[32] Had it not been for
this accident of the time, not even this special point of Messianic
interpretation would have been mentioned, for it was the sense
of the preparers of the appeal that this should be a glowing call
couched in general terms, picturing the religious conditions
among the Jews and making clear what they desired, viz. faith,
positive religion, Judaism, while the determination, interpretation, and definition of all special points should be left to the
synod provided for in the concluding paragraph.

This suggestion to call a synod to be composed of representatives delegates from the various reform societies was a new idea injected by the founders of the Berlin Reform Society into the religious thought of the time. This synod was to take into consideration the changes which had come upon Jewish life and thought in the new environment of the nineteenth century, reinterpret the truths of Judaism in the light of these changes and give authoritative expression to what constituted the fundamentals of Jewish thought and practice, this expression to be the rule of guidance for congregations and individuals and to form the point of union for the different forces that were pulling this way and that among the Jews who had renounced in practice the authority of the rabbinical code. In time past this code had been the authoritative voice; the Jew who was lax in his observance of its prescriptions was considered a renegade. True, there was always freedom of thought in Jewry, but not freedom of practice; heresy trials for repudiation of belief in an authoritative creed were foreign to the Judaism of rabbinical times, because Judaism was primarily a system of ceremonial observance; departures from this latter, however, were as severely frowned upon as was laxity of belief in the orthodox creed in Christianity; the code which prescribed the requirements of ceremonial observance was as binding upon the Jew as was the apostolic creed upon the Christian. As long as free thought did not result in neglect of performance of the prescribed observances and ceremonies, there was the widest lattitude of thought permitted. We must be clear upon this point for much confusion exists here. The much-discussed declaration of Mendelssohn that Judaism is not a doctrinal system (*Glaubenslehre*), but legislation (*Gesetzgebung*) is not far from the mark from the point of view of rabbinical tradition; and the great advance of the reform position beyond this standpoint of rabbinism expressed by Mendelssohn in his famous dictum lies in the fact that it has repudiated the ceremonial law as the practical confession of Judaism because the bond between this ceremonial law and the belief which it was supposed to express had been broken, and Judaism had become slavish practice without conviction; for it the reform movement had substituted the moral law as fundamental, making truth synonymous with individual holiness, and thus assuring the real freedom to the individual, for in the realm of Judaism's moral law freedom reigns.[33]

However, the individualism which followed in the train of breaking loose from the fetters of code observance threatened disaster in the view of many. In the place of the fixed anchor— the ceremonial law—to which Jews had clung aforetime, there was now no support; reform went to greater or less lengths according to individual caprice. Little wonder, then, that the idea arose to convene a synod to deliberate upon present conditions and to furnish, if not a body of authority, at least a representative organization to which there could be referred for deliberation, discussion and decision the many problems that were troubling earnest Jewish spirits. True, synods were not unknown among the Jews since their dispersion among the nations; such had been convened at crises in the history of the Jews; [34] but these synods, *e.g.* Usha in 138 A.C.E., the synods of *Shum* (Speyer, Worms, and Mayence) in the thirteenth century; the synods of Erfurt and Nuremberg in the fifteenth, of Frankfort in the seventeenth century, etc., etc., had been concerned not with determining points of belief, but of practice, or of meeting critical situations in the external fortunes of the Jewish people; the French synod or synhedrin of 1807 was different from all the others, inasmuch as it was called by the secular power and not convened by the Jews themselves. The synod, however, which was agitated for by the Berlin reformers was intended to be different from all these; it was to concern itself with determining the significance and the essence of Jewish belief and practice, to pronounce upon the relation of modern reform Judaism to the traditions, to interpret the present attitude upon all vital points, as the liturgy, marriage and divorce, the ceremonies, the position of women, the dietary laws and the Sabbath; it was to be different from the rabbinical conferences, inasmuch as the discussions in these latter were largely academic, while the declarations of the synod composed of accredited delegates from the congregations were to be binding upon these.

Simion who was its strongest advocate pleaded for it as the corrective of the evils of congregational autonomy. It was to be the center of the circle of Judaism and the congregations, the radia drawing their life from this center. [35] Stern advocated the synod as the capstone of the reform movement. He set forth the plan of its organization and its method so clearly that his words may be reproduced:

The synod will consist of representatives elected by the congregations; its chief duty will be to realize in its resolutions the conviction of the community and to furnish means for its adequate expression. It shall not regard itself as an authority which has the right to pass laws that are binding upon the community because it has passed them, but the synod will consider itself the only and highest organ in which the conviction and the will of this many-membered community find expression. For the new form of our religion is not to be inspired from without, but is to spring from the real and well-understood need of the present; for only thus will it satisfy this need fully and properly. The synod then will be composed of true representatives of the congregations, *i.e.* of men, who not only know the conviction of the congregation, but have imbibed it in the deepest and purest sense. The synod is not a rabbinical conference; still, an essential feature of its work will be that the learned and theological element will have strong representation in it; on the other hand, the practical element is to be represented by men who have understood thoroughly the soul of the people. The resolutions of the synod must be decisive and binding for the congregations which have joined the religious union. I say, binding but not eternal, binding for the present but not for all time. The essential feature of the present movement is the deliverance from the stability of the traditional religious forms of Judaism, and we cannot call forth new creations which presume upon a like eternal authority. Therefore the resolutions of this synod must not be looked upon as authentic interpretations of the divine Will, but as the most complete expression of the present religious consciousness and as the realization of the religious need evidenced in modern Judaism. Therefore, also, provision must be made for periodical meetings of the synod, not at too close intervals, as a matter of course, in order that the element of uninterrupted development in the life of Judaism may not perish.[36]

Regarded from this point of view, it is difficult to understand the opposition of even the most pronounced advocates of individual religious freedom. The synod as thus conceived arrogates to itself no hierarchial authority; it would not hamper individual freedom of opinion; it would be simply a central religious organization of a character so representative that its pronouncements and decisions would carry weight from this fact alone. It is not to be believed that any of the advocates of the synod among the Berlin reformers would have countenanced for a moment the formation of such an organization to be an ecclesiastical court with the power to try for heresy and to pronounce the individual guilty or not guilty on the score of religious belief. This was the bogy that the opponents of the synod conjured up, notably Holdheim; he and his sympathizers constantly discountenanced the calling of a synod on the score of individual freedom or because it was not practical in Judaism.[37] However, even Holdheim was impressed with the need of a central organization or *Religionsbehörde,* as he calls it; the lack of such an organization in Judaism now should not lead us to justify our course in the name of unbridled individual license, he writes; but we should be guided by the spirit of true freedom which penetrates into the historicity of Judaism in order to discover those fundamentals which a constituted religious authoritative body, were it in existence, would have to determine upon for the ordering, forming and developing of Judaism according to its present needs; only in this sense are we justified in considering ourselves as taking the place of such a body. He predicts that a *Religionsbehörde* of this kind, understanding the needs of the present, will be formed; it will not stand in the way of free religious development but rather further it. Only when the Talmud, the letter, took the place of the living authoritative body, did development cease in Judaism. "Unless my reading of the future deceives me, such a living religious authoritative organization will be formed. The historical spirit of Judaism sways and rules in spite of all chaotic confusions and this will not fail to create its organ."[38] This was, after all, what the advocates of a synod desired; and at bottom, then, Holdheim agreed with them, although he expressed himself so frequently against the conventional idea of the synod, in fear possibly that its formation might result in an organization similar to the synod in the Christian churches. Such an eventuality was impossible, however, for two reasons: first, it is against the spirit of Judaism, which, except in the rarest instances, when it was affected by Christian surroundings and example, as in the Uriel Acosta and Spinoza cases, never

instituted heresy trials and excommunicated the holders of
unorthodox opinions; and secondly, because this is contrary to
the trend of thought in the modern world. These two great
forces, viz. tradition and environment, minimize to the last
degree the danger that any religious organization in Jewry
would interfere with individual freedom of opinion.[39]

The Appeal struck a popular chord. It called forth responses
from Jews in a number of communities outside of Berlin, such
as Kulm,[40] Frankfort,[41] Elbing, Lissa, Mannheim.[42] Hundreds
in the city of Berlin declared themselves in sympathy with the
thoughts and aspirations therein expressed.[43]

The meeting for the organization of the society was called
for May 8, four weeks after the publication of the address. By
this time two hundred and forty-eight Jews of Berlin and sixty-
nine without the city had declared their desire to join with the
framers of the address in the movement they had set afoot. The
Appeal formed the constitutional basis of the society which was
formally organized at this meeting under the name "Association
for Reform in Judaism" (*Genossenschaft für Reform in
Judenthume*). The meeting was attended by from four to five
hundred people, and was presided over by Carl Heymann, one
of the signers of the Appeal. In calling the meeting to order
the presiding officer set forth the purpose of the gathering:

> We do not wish to tear down and undermine, but to
> preserve and perpetuate, the glorious, noble foundations
> of our religion. We desire to free it from the moldy and
> weatherworn walls which surround it, in order that the
> bright light of God may shine upon it and the sun of
> heaven warm the inhabitants within, as formerly in the
> days of our fathers.[44]

Fifteen trustees were elected who were to conduct the affairs
of the association. It will be noted that the meeting did not
organize itself into a congregation, but a society; all those who
enrolled themselves as members of the society were as a matter
of course members of the main Berlin congregation, even
though they were out of sympathy with the principle and practice of the congregation. It is unlikely that any one of the
original movers in this new departure had any thought at this
time of organizing a distinct congregation. In truth, such a
congregation could have no standing in law; the government
recognized only the one central Jewish body; the organization

of the society was for the purpose of crystallizing the opinions
of that great number of Jews throughout Germany who felt
the inadequacy of the inherited traditions to satisfy their religious needs and longings. This Berlin society was to be but one
of many similar organizations throughout Germany, all of
which were to send delegates to the synod, which was to determine the status of the new movement. The Berlin society
intended merely to give the impulse; its founders were sincere
in their purpose of making this a general and not a local movement. However, many months, perhaps years, would elapse
before the preliminaries for the convening of a synod could be
perfected, viz. the formation of reform societies everywhere,
the election of delegates and the like. Hence, at the very first
meeting of the trustees the question was earnestly debated
whether they should take immediate steps toward instituting a
service to satisfy the local need or wait with this until after the
convening of the synod. The signers of the Appeal, a number
of whom were among the trustees, viz. Stern, Rebenstein,
Simion, Lesser, and Heymann, naturally advocated the latter
course, for the Appeal which they looked upon as the constitution of their organization, had culminated in the recommendation that like-thinking Jews should assemble to consult together
before any definite practical steps were taken, and that therefore they were not justified in doing anything single-handed.
On the other hand, others, notably Dr. Bressler, contended that
heed must be given to local requirements. Here were hundreds
who were alienated from the synagogue because they had lost
all sympathy with the rabbinical interpretation of Judaism, and
who could be weaned back if prompt measures would be taken
for the institution of a service at which prayers and sermon
should be expressive of the thoughts and aspirations of the new
time wherein they were living. After a number of spirited
meetings, it was resolved finally to take steps to meet the present
need for a suitable service with the understanding, however,
that this was to be only provisional until the meeting of the
synod,[45] and that if the synod should declare against any portion of this service, they would bow to its superior wisdom and
authority. There can be no doubt that Holdheim is correct in
his contention that the advocates of the synod practically surrendered their whole case when they assented to this proposition,
although Stern and his confrères justified their action by the
plea that the conditions in Berlin were such as to make the hold-

ing of such a service a matter of prime importance and that, being only provisional, it could not interfere with the supremacy of the synod when once established. At any rate, the point once decided, the official machinery was set in motion to hold the first service on the great holidays in the fall of that same year, 1845.

Shortly after the organization of this reform association, the second rabbinical conference met at Frankfort. As has been stated, the Berlin movement was distinctly a lay movement; the rabbis of the city were unreservedly antagonistic; Sachs,[46] the newcomer, was almost as bitterly opposed to the forward movement in Judaism as were such pronounced and fanatic advocates of the old order as Jacob Aaron Ettlinger of Altona, Salomon Abraham Trier of Frankfort, or Hirsch Lehren of Amsterdam. In truth, it was because of the policy of the rabbis of Berlin that the laymen were compelled to take the initiative; in the opinion of the organizers of the reform society the significance of the movement lay in the fact that "it did not proceed from the rabbis nor yet from theologians, but from the people itself." [47] There was always danger at this time of a broadening of the breach between rabbi and people. In the earlier day while the Jew was still confined in the geographical and intellectual ghetto, the bond between rabbi and people was perfect; but when thousands of the people entered into the life of the world, the rabbis continued along the old traditional lines. The result was that these advanced spirits came to consider the rabbis as identified with an outgrown cause; when, therefore, as in the case of the Berlin reformers, the need for some religious nutriment different from that supplied to their fathers was experienced, they turned not to the rabbis of the community, for these were out of all sympathy with them. But yet a religious movement without any affiliation or connection with religious leaders was felt to be an anomaly; hence, it was determined to address the rabbinical conference and arrange some *modus vivendi* whereby the reform rabbis, through their official organization, and the "lay" reformers, through their societies, might come into touch with one another and work together. This was to be accomplished through the synod. A deputation of the society appeared at the conference and presented an address that had been prepared very carefully. There can be little doubt but that the primary object of this deputation to the conference was to receive from the confer-

ence an endorsement of the reform society; for even though
there were those in the society who felt that it was strong
enough to be a thoroughly independent movement, yet the
majority desired the approval of an authoritative Jewish body.
Although the conference did not claim to be such, yet was it
the nearest approach thereto. This desire was apparent from
the closing sentences of the address wherein the hope was
expressed that the conference would give some expression to
its official recognition of the fact that the reform society had
been called into being for the purpose of strengthening and
preserving Judaism, not of undermining it. The answer of the
conference was framed very diplomatically. The reason for
the formation of the society was recognized as lying in the
desire to reconcile life with Judaism; gratification was
expressed that the conviction of the need of reform in Judaism
was felt by the people as well as by the rabbis. The conference
expressed itself as willing to work hand in hand with the
reform society if the latter would be guided by the principles
which the conference considered necessary for a true reform
in Judaism. It will be noticed that the conference did not commit itself. The members present knew full well that it was
such men as had formed the Berlin society who were animated
by the sentiment that the salvation to be wrought by reform
must emanate from the people and not from the rabbis. These
had a notion that theological attainments rather hindered than
furthered reform; Stern, for example, never tired of referring
slightingly to "threshed theological straw" as incapable of
furnishing religious nourishment to the people: this must be
drawn from the perennial stream of life. The rabbis, while
agreeing that the demands of life were a primary factor in
the origin of reform, yet held that Judaism had its roots in the
soil of the past and that a true reform was not possible unless
fathered by theological experts acquainted thoroughly with the
whole development of Judaism.[48] It was only men like Holdheim, Geiger, Einhorn, the Adlers, and Hirsch, who, combining great learning with practical acumen, could formulate the
principles of reform Judaism; others not theologically trained
might and did recognize the need, but they were incapable of
more than a superficial statement.[49] The rabbis felt, and rightfully so, that they could not indorse the Berlin society unless
they had the assurance that the society would be guided by the
principles laid down by the conference. Still, there is no doubt

that much sympathy with the Berlin experiment was felt by the rabbis. Philippson, Salomon, Frankfurter, Hirsch, Hess, and Holdheim preached for the society on various occasions before a regular preacher was engaged: Geiger expressed his appreciation of the work and aim of the society.[50] These men who had the cause of reform thoroughly at heart could not but welcome any signs among the people of intelligent interest in the problems that were troubling them; but they could not agree that any but the religious guides should lead. The sentiment which animated the Berlin reformers was vicious, viz. that until a synod should be formed there should be these two parallel forces in Judaism, the conference representing the rabbinate, and the reform society representing the laity. This separation was artificial; it was un-Jewish.[51] The rabbi is no priest nor the rabbinate a hierarchy; the rabbi is the Jewish scholar and theologian; naturally he should lead all religious movements and the reform society though a lay movement in its inception should have accepted the guidance of religious experts, and not attempted to prepare a ritual without their aid, as it did. There was a certain presumption in this, and an apparent impatient disregard of the right of the rabbi to the first place in the meeting of the difficulties of the religious situation. There would have been excuse for this had there been no rabbis favorable to religious reform, and the laity been compelled for this reason to take the whole matter in hand; but there were so many men of supreme ability among the reform rabbis that their coöperation could have been readily secured for the preparation of the ritual and the institution of the service. A striking feature was that these "lay" leaders were constantly insisting that Judaism knew no distinction between rabbis and layman, and yet they were doing their utmost to accentuate this distinction. The differences were to be merged in the synod, where the rabbinical and laical streams were to coalesce. It is noticeable that the conference expressed no opinion on the synod, with the recommendation of which the address of the Berlin society closed, further than to say that they would follow with interest the steps that would be taken toward the convening of the synod. Further, the conference treated the address of the Berlin society in the same manner as it did the many other addresses that were sent from various places. The rabbis did not for one moment consider the advisability of entering into a special covenant with the Berlin Association or of giving its deputies representation on the floor. They were treated with no greater distinction than any of the other visitors. Theirs it was "to learn and not to teach; to receive, not to impart." It is very doubtful whether this reception quite pleased the delegation, composed of Stern, Rebenstein, and Simion, who, owing to their success in organizing the Berlin Society, regarded themselves as entitled to especial consideration.

During the year intervening between the meetings of the Frankfort and Breslau Conferences, the Berlin Association had waxed in strength, had held services of a reform character and had become more and more conscious of its importance as a factor in the religious life of the Jews of the German capital. This is apparent in the communication addressed to the third rabbinical conference held at Breslau.[52] A note of self-consciousness rings throughout the address; the two bodies are spoken of as of equal importance for the advance of Judaism —the conference from the theoretical, and the society from the practical side. The conference is also instructed as to what its functions should be, the writers of the address assuming the rôle of mentor. The conference did not reply to the address, but adopted the following resolution offered by the president, Abraham Geiger:

> Since lack of time permits our giving sufficient attention to the framing of an answer to the address of the Berlin Reform Association; since, further, this address contains neither resolution nor questions which demand an answer; and since finally it appears sufficiently from our deliberations and conclusions in regard to the Sabbath that the views of the conference differ widely from those which as we believe guide the preliminary steps of the association, the conference concludes that this communication may as well be left unanswered.[53]

Reference is made here to the attitude of the Reform Association on the question of the transfer of the Sabbath from Saturday to Sunday, which will be considered in its proper place. This resolution, which all the members present favored, with the exception of four (Philippson, Holdheim, Hess, and A. Adler), shows very clearly that the two bodies had drifted far apart. Although this is not stated in the resolution, the rabbis could not but resent the patronizing tone of the address, which read a lesson to the conference. The Breslau Conference being the last of the rabbinical gatherings, all official connection between the two bodies ceased naturally; there can be no doubt, however, that had the conference met at Mannheim in 1847, as had been intended, there would have been no further communication received from the Reform Association in view of the cavalier treatment which the address to the Breslau Conference had received.

After it had been resolved not to wait until the synod should become an actuality, but to proceed at once toward instituting a provisional service to meet local needs, matters were hurried during the summer of 1845 to perfect arrangements for holding services on the ensuing fall holidays. The presence in Berlin of a number of the rabbis who had stopped there on their journey homeward from the Frankfort Conference led to their being invited into consultation with the trustees; these rabbis were Geiger, Salomon, Hirsch, Frankfurter, and Jolowicz. The committee to whom the preparation of the service for the holidays was entrusted consisted of Stern, Rebenstein, Simion, and Lesser. This committee suggested radical departures from the traditional service of the synagogue. These suggestions were concurred in by the trustees and carried out in the service. They were:

1. The use of the vernacular in the entire service with the exception of a few passages, viz., the *Sh'ma,* the *K'dushah, W'nislach,* and the priestly benediction, which were to be read in both Hebrew and German.

2. The dispensing with the blowing of the shofar (ram's horn) on New Year's Day.

3. An intermission of several hours on the Day of Atonement between the morning and afternoon services, during which intermission addresses were to be delivered.

4. Worship with uncovered head, although the wearing of a black skull cap was to be permitted to individuals.

5. The discontinuance of the use of the *Tallith.*

6. The priestly benediction to be pronounced, not by the so-called Aaronides, but by the preacher and the choir.

7. The use of female voices in the choir; and

8. The seating of men and women on the same floor; provided only that the former occupy the left, the latter the right side of the auditorium.[54]

These were in truth radical and far-reaching changes and innovations and the boldness wherewith they were inaugurated stamps these Berlin reformers as being indeed intrepid pioneers who gave practical form to the thoughts which many were thinking, but yet did not dare translate into action. The question of the service in the vernacular had been discussed fully at the Frankfort Conference.[55] Reformers everywhere were quite agreed that German must be used in the public services; the Hamburg temple congregation had taken the first steps in introducing German prayers, although a large portion of the service was still read in Hebrew; the Berlin reformers made their service a German service with the very smallest sprinkling of Hebrew phrases, these being rendered also in German. The principle whereby they were guided was to have a service that could be understood and participated in by the people; Hebrew had become unintelligible to the great majority. Man must pray in a language he understands if his prayers are to be not mere lip service; the retention of the Hebrew in such phrases as the *Sh'ma,* the *K'dushah* and the like was for the purpose of reminiscence; the Jew should be able to speak in the original tongue the great watchwords. The principle involved has been acknowledged to be correct; even in conservative congregations prayers in the vernacular have been introduced quite generally; it is now merely a question of how much.

The abolition of the blowing of the *shofar* (ram's horn) on the New Year's Day was a startling change. The step was taken not because a principle was involved, but for æsthetic reasons. Awe-inspiring as was the sounding of the *shofar* for the Jew of old, to whom its reverberating tones brought thoughts of God's judgments, it aroused no such emotion in the breast of the Berlinese Jew of 1845; it called forth a smile rather than heightened devotion. Sentimental reminiscence bore little weight with these reformers of Berlin; they aimed for an intellectual service—mind rather than heart was to be satisfied.[56] The *shofar* aroused no response in the modern worshiper; therefore let it go by the board. One of the rabbis who was present at the meeting justified the abolition of the blowing of the *shofar* on the ground that it is no longer fitting at this day, and that we no longer know exactly what the Biblical *shofar* was. The Berlin reformers were brave enough to refuse to hide behind such a subterfuge:

Not because the real Biblical *shofar* is no longer known to us, but because the religious idea upon which its use in the service is based no longer appeals to us, and because the whole psychological mechanism, thanks to which the *shofar* was so essential a portion of the service in Biblical times, has passed away forever, the *shofar* has become impossible for us. If the prophet Elijah were to appear among us and show us the Biblical *shofar*, we would say with the Talmud אין שומעין לו, because the people have lost all sense of receptivity for it. If this sense could be resurrected, it would be different. But as long as this is not the case, it makes no difference what the Biblical *shofar* really was, nor what the Biblical idea was whereon it was based. The only point to be taken into consideration is that, as far as we are concerned, no religious idea can be connected in a natural, *i.e.* psychologico-æsthetic way, with the conventional blowing of the *shofar* in the synagogue on New Year's Day.[57]

Some of the most significant and characteristic portions of the liturgy of the New Year's Day are connected with the blowing of the *shofar*. The Berlin reformers were as extreme in their position as were the strict traditionalists in theirs. The past and the ceremonials that grew up therein cannot be disregarded entirely in any religion which, like Judaism, has existed for many centuries. If a ceremony has lost all power of arousing religious emotion, its day is certainly over; but if it can be so reinterpreted as to comport with the religious outlook of later man, it should be used and retained. This is possible with the blowing of the *shofar*, as was made evident by David Einhorn in his service for the New Year's Day,[58] and by the American reform rabbis, who compiled the Union Prayer-Book. These combined past and present in this matter in a felicitous manner and showed a truer grasp of the problem than did the Berlin reformers of 1845.

Another startling innovation was the worshiping with uncovered heads. Although this has become general in the reform congregations in the United States,[59] the Berlin reform congregation remains in solitary isolation among the congregations of Europe.[60] At best this is an Oriental custom and accentuates the Oriental, national, particularistic interpretation

of Judaism. The chief argument advanced against the worship
with uncovered heads is that it is an imitation of *Chuqqath
Hagoyim* (the custom of the Gentiles). But even a medieval
rabbi said that it is forbidden only to imitate the degrading
and disgraceful customs of surrounding peoples, not such as
are of a contrary character. Our Occidental habit is to show
respect by the uncovering of the head, as it is the Oriental habit
to keep the head covered, and to have laid so much stress upon
this one custom as has been the case in the controversies
between reform and orthodoxy, showed a singular misapprehension of the significance of reform, whose program from
the very start was to reconcile the religion, its services, its
ceremonies, and its practices with the life the Jew was living
and the thoughts he was thinking in the modern world. To
keep the synagogue Oriental with an entire Hebrew service,
worship with covered heads, separation of the sexes, while the
Jew in all things outside of the synagogue was Occidental,
was to institute a divorce between the synagogue and life which
could not but be detrimental to the best interests of Judaism.
This the reform movement wished to avoid, and this it has
avoided in the one land where it has had the opportunity for
free and unrestricted development—the United States.

The reform involved in having the priestly blessing pronounced by the preacher in place of by the so-called Aaronides
was very significant. It severed the only link [61] that bound the
service in the synagogue to the sacrificial priestly polity of the
ancient Temple of Jerusalem, and was the practical demonstration that these reformers had repudiated in practice as well
as in thought the expectation of the restoration of the hereditary Aaronic priesthood as ministers at the altar of a temple
to be rebuilt on the site of the erstwhile temple on Moriah's
hill at the time of the rehabilitation of the Jewish state under
the leadership of a personal Messiah. In honesty they could
not do otherwise. The Aaronic priesthood was part and parcel
of the sacrificial system which even Maimonides had declared
to have been merely preparatory and educative. True, the
Mussaf prayers in the traditional liturgy had contained the
petition for the restoration of the sacrifices; but the reformers
in the discussion on the liturgy at the Frankfort Conference
had agreed that this must be eliminated as no longer expressive
of the faith and hope of the Jew. With the sacrificial system
the priesthood in Judaism rose and fell. If, after the destruc-

tion of sacrificial altar and temple, the descendants of the old priestly families still retained the prerogative of coming forward to the raised platform in the synagogue and pronouncing the priestly blessing (Num. vi. 24-26), this was because the expectation abided with the people that at the time of Israel's return to Palestine these priestly families would again resume their ancient position as the religious aristocracy of the nation with special duties and privileges. But reform emphasized that other traditional doctrine of Judaism, viz. the priesthood of the whole people (Ex. xix. 6) as over against the priesthood of a hereditary class. To the sacrificial system, the Aaronic priesthood, the Palestinian state, the personal Messiah, reform opposed the service of prayer, the priesthood of the whole people, the countries of the world as fatherlands, the Messianic era. For this reason the Berlin reform congregation, and in its wake all the reform congregations, removed the last vestige of priestly prerogative from the public service by eliminating the pronouncement of the priestly benediction by the reputed descendants of Aaron, found among the Jewish communities everywhere. The rabbi had taken practically the place of the priest as the religious guide in Jewry since the destruction of the Temple of Jerusalem. The few distinctive traits and functions which continued to adhere to the Aaronides were mere survivals. As long as the Messianic hope of Israel culminated in the return to Palestine, the restoration of the Jewish state and the ancient service in a reconstructed Temple, there was reason for the continuance of these priestly distinctions; but when the Messianic doctrine was interpreted in its universalistic significance, this reason fell away;[62] hence this change introduced by the Berlin reformers rested on the basis of a far-reaching principle, and was an indication of the different point of view assumed by reform in this all-important matter of the Messianic outlook.[63]

The other point wherein this congregation was a pioneer was in the action taken in reference to the religious position of woman. When the reform was introduced of seating men and women on the same floor of the house of worship, the first step was taken toward the religious emancipation of woman. True, the rabbinical conference of Frankfort had considered the subject, and Einhorn there had spoken lofty words in behalf of woman's equality with man in the religious life of the synagogue.[64] The Berlin congregation by its resolution gave practical effect to such suggestions. In man's complete assumption of all public religious functions the Oriental origin of the synagogue was apparent. The gallery, to which woman was relegated, was a survival of the Oriental notion of woman's inferiority. Yet although woman was excluded from all active participation in public religious functions, and had to content herself with being a silent spectator and auditor in the gallery, still in the Jewish home her sway was supreme.[65] But this contradiction between woman's position in the synagogue and in the home was unnatural under Occidental conditions. The segregation of the women in a gallery was repugnant to the ideas and ideals of an age of emancipation and strivings after equality. Here again the Orientalism of the synagogue had to give way to the stress of the new thought and the new life. The truth of the matter was that the Jewish woman had entered a new kingdom. She as well as the man was affected by her surroundings. To her as well as to her father, her husband, and her brother, the new voices were calling and she desired to take active part in the new forward movement. To refuse to heed this desire was to extend the already wide breach between the synagogue and life in this regard. And what a precious ally has not woman become in the religious life of such communities where she has been given the opportunity to serve in the cause of Judaism! In the Berlin congregation the men and women are not seated together, simply because this is not the Continental custom; family pews in the synagogue were introduced by a congregation on the other side of the Atlantic.[66] This innovation has been followed by all the reform and many conservative congregations in the United States, while the Berlin Reform Congregation and a few others like the Liberal Jewish Synagogue of London, the liberal congregation of Frankfort, the *Union liberale israélite* of Paris, all of which were organized much later, have dispensed with the woman's gallery.[67] In theory the congregations of the Old World hold to the Oriental conception of woman's religious inferiority as codified in the *Shulchan Aruk;* but do the paragraphs of the *Shulchan Aruk* on the position of woman express the view of modern man? This is the only test. Here again so-called orthodoxy makes the unpardonable error of professing what it does not practice. Only *within* the synagogue does it continue Oriental, *without* it clasps hands with all the interests of Western life; only *within* the synagogue does it relegate woman to the gallery, *without* she asserts her place; surely here again reform has followed the truer way and has solved correctly the question of woman's place in the synagogue in the new life whereupon Jewry entered after the emancipation from medieval conditions had been achieved.

During the summer of 1845 the ritual committee was diligently at work preparing for the first services to be held by the association on New Year's Day and the Day of Atonement (October 1, 2, and 10). The prayer-book arranged by the committee for these holidays differed radically from the traditional ritual and the plan by which they were guided in their work was set forth in an explanatory statement which accompanied the prayer-book when it was placed in the hands of the members of the association; the salient paragraphs of this statement were as follows:

> We have departed radically from existing forms, varied though they be; but we have been concerned all the more to have our prayers express definitely the religious conviction that is characteristic of Judaism and to make clear the significance of these holy days in a manner to appeal to the consciousness of living men. Our religious service should not be of such a general character as to attract any and all men; but it should be such a one as is rooted in the definite religious experience of Judaism. Although it attempts to free itself from all traces of national separatism, yet it does not surrender its peculiar religious development, and therefore looks back just as joyfully to its past, in which it was called to be the bearer of an eternal truth, as it looks forward confidently to the promise of the future when all mankind will recognize and worship the one invisible God. We have borne in mind the need and the outlook of our generation in our arrangement of the external form of the service and at the same time have attempted in the content of our prayers to give full and just recognition to the unchanged spirit of Judaism.[68]

The coöperation of Dr. Ludwig Philippson of Magdeburg was enlisted to the extent that he consented to deliver the sermons at the holiday services for which this first provisional prayer-book was prepared.

Not only the ritual for this opening service of the association, but also for other holidays and for the weekly service which was instituted in the course of time, was arranged, because of the pressing and immediate need; the prayer-book therefore was not the result of slow growth but a birth of the hour. Therefore it experienced frequent changes and revisions.°° As has been stated, the earliest edition of the prayer-book (1845-6) was the result of the labors of four members of the congregation. After Holdheim was elected rabbi he subjected the first draft of the prayer-book to a thorough revision, in the introduction to which he set forth the principles whereby he was guided in constructing the new edition.

Everywhere the national and dogmatically narrowing point of view had to yield to the living flow of the purely human and truly religious thought [he wrote in this introduction]; for a noble, truly pious nature, belief in the universal Father of mankind has more attractive force than the belief in the God of Israel, the doctrine that all men are created in the image of God is of higher poetic worth than the election of Israel. The teaching of a universal law of human brotherhood and love for the neighbor has greater potency than a particularistic ceremonial legislation. The belief in the all-inclusive covenant with man as man has a more sanctifying effect than that in an exclusive covenant between Jehovah and his first-born son Israel. All these ideas subjectively present in the heart of the Jewish people have their great historical significance preparatory to the later course of the development of the human race; as such they offer the preacher a treasure trove of religious thoughts and truths as well as significant points of departure. But they should not be permitted to confuse the simple notions of the worshiper; prayer ought to be a clear, transparent mirror in which the nature of the worshiper is reflected. Above all else, man lives in the present in whose mode of thought and expression he feels most at home. Whatever is offered him from out the past should aim to make the comprehension of the present easier and not more difficult.

As for the newly composed prayers, they partake altogether of the religious spirit of the present age, to which Judaism owes its reawakening and resuscitation—the genius of our day, which has regenerated and reconstructed Judaism completely. If Judaism has passed through this refining process and has retained its power, despite all the destructive campaigns which were undertaken against it from various quarters, such as stagnation and negation, then indeed we may be proud and glad to be its followers. This is the proper place to declare openly and unreservedly that Judaism contains a treasure of ideas and sentiments which has not been exhausted by far, and that these are clothed in forms and symbols which must be brushed aside altogether in order that those deeply-hidden ideas and sentiments may reappear in their original strength. If it be thought that these forms and symbols must be piously preserved in order that the kernel hidden in them may be gained through observing them, we must call attention to the fact that the standpoint of reform is this, viz., to appreciate the kernel at its full worth and to secure it by breaking the shell; to use these symbols and forms, yes, the whole history of Judaism as means whereby to distinguish between the eternal thoughts and the transitory forms, and to attribute (relative) religious value to those forms only which are effective for the presentation of the thought and the awakening of corresponding sentiments. The diligent reader of these prayers, who is not unacquainted with the reform strivings of the recent decades, will find that most of the acquisitions in this territory, the lofty thoughts and sentiments which proved themselves to be truly Jewish (*echt jüdisch*) in the refining process of scientific investigation, have been combined here into a beautiful bond. We call particular attention to such prayers as have for their themes the holiness of God and of man, the priestly mission of Israel, the purified Messianic idea, etc., etc.

After the initial service on the holidays in the autumn of 1845 the leading spirits of the association met frequently during the ensuing winter to secure a permanent home for the association and to arrange for a regular weekly service. The most animated and heated discussion centered about the question of the day of the service, whether this should be the traditional Sabbath or the civil day of rest. The resolution as finally adopted at the general meeting of the association on November 19, 1845, was that steps be taken "to hold services twice a week, on Saturday and on Sunday." [70] Eventually [71] the congregation conducted services only on Sunday, and still does so, being the only congregation in Europe where this is the case, and with the exception of Sinai congregation of Chicago and the Free Synagogue of New York, the only Jewish congregation in the world.

The active steps taken to secure a place of worship were crowned with success, and on April 2, 1846, the anniversary of the day of the promulgation of the famous "Appeal," the synagogue was dedicated. Dr. Samuel Holdheim, rabbi of Mecklenburg-Schwerin was invited to deliver the dedicatory sermon. The sermon was an exposition of the standpoint of reform Judaism; the preacher contended that to remove the outworn and outgrown was not enough; this was merely the negative side of reform. It was necessary to nurse the positive spirit, to retain such forms as still had power to satisfy the religious nature of modern man, and to substitute for the abrogated forms new ones expressive of the new thought. Man can be freed from error only by truth, not by another error; superstition can be uprooted only by pure faith, not by unbelief; the fetters of the dead letter can be loosened only by the living spirit. Only a sincere higher degree of inner religion justifies the giving up of that which is a requirement and a duty in a lower stage.[72]

The dedicatory exercises attracted a large and enthusiastic assemblage.[73] The hostile attitude of the chief congregation of the city to the movement became known definitely when it was noted that the elders, though invited to attend, were not present.[74] The members of the Reform Association (it was not yet called a congregation) were perforce also members of the chief congregation from the very fact that they were confessing Jews and had to contribute their quota toward its maintenance; they had assumed the additional burden of organizing and maintaining the reform association because of their conviction that unless some such steps be taken Judaism was in danger of extinction. At this point the various attempts made by the association to define the relation to the chief congregation and to secure corporate powers as an institution recognized by the state may be mentioned. Before the first service in October, 1845, could be held the permission of the government had to be secured. The Minister of Spiritual Affairs (*geistige Angelegenheiten*) at this time was Eichhorn, a man of liberal spirit. The permission to hold this service and also the subsequent services was obtained. It was furthermore known that the Prussian government was contemplating the promulgation of a new edict *in re* the Jews and Judaism. Inasmuch as the liberal spirit seemed uppermost in government councils, it was hoped by the organizers of the reform association that the new decree would contain some paragraph making provision for the permission to form progressive congregations and thus nullify the effects of the notorious rescript of December, 1823, which had stifled the reform movement in Berlin. When this new decree of July 23, 1847, was published,[75] it seemed to justify the hopes of these reformers, for the fifty-third paragraph took notice of just such a condition of affairs as existed in the Berlin community. This paragraph read:

> If disputes touching religious conviction and worship arise in any synagogue which have for their aim the formation of a new synagogue, the Minister of Spiritual, etc., Affairs and the Minister of the Interior are empowered, upon the petition of the parties interested, to appoint a commission which shall aim to arbitrate the existing differences. If the conflict cannot be settled by the decision of the commission, the Ministers, guided by the opinion of the commission, shall decide under what conditions either the inauguration of a separate service or the formation of a new congregation is to be granted.[76]

This decree aroused the utmost satisfaction among the members of the Reform Association, and finally, after a number of meetings, a resolution was adopted at a meeting on March 21, 1848, to the effect that it was most desirable that they form an autonomous congregation, and not be considered, as hitherto, merely a society composed of members of the chief congregation. The stirring political events of March, 1848, prevented the calling of a meeting for consultation with the officials of the government at which this resolution of the society was to be discussed. In fact, the matter had to be postponed for some time owing to the political crisis and the association suffered from being in a state of uncertainty. At a meeting held two years later,[77] on March 30, 1850, it was resolved to form an independent Jewish congregation and to petition the government to grant papers of incorporation to them as such an independent congregation. At this meeting, too, the name of the organization was changed to Jewish

Reform Congregation (*Jüdische Reformgemeinde*), in place of Jewish Reform Association. The petition for incorporation was refused by the government on the ground that the congregation had no confession of faith, and the state could not recognize officially any religious body that had no positive confession of faith. When this answer was returned, a most spirited and interesting debate took place at the meeting of the directorate on the point as to whether Judaism has a fixed creed or no.[78] The "lay" members held that the state officials should be informed that the request for a confession of faith could not be complied with, since Judaism lacks this. One of them (Dr. Bressler) stated that "the positing of principles is altogether un-Jewish. Formerly he, too, had considered this necessary, but he had seen the error of this view and had repudiated it." Another (Dr. Stern) declared that "the fixed definition of principles contradicts entirely the idea of development which lies at the very basis of our reform." Stern was empowered to frame an answer to the government along these lines. Holdheim took issue with the "lay" members on this point; he held that the belief in definite principles did not exclude the idea of development and that "our reform touches only the dead forms of Judaism, but not its inner essence and the content of faith." Holdheim was as much opposed as any of the laymen to the acceptance of a fixed creed as a condition of salvation.[79] This is the Christian, not the Jewish, point of view, and therefore, the Christian officials took the attitude they did. The point on which Holdheim differed with the laymen was that principles were absolutely necessary of statement, and that Judaism having such principles, they could, should, and must be stated. There is a wide difference between a creed as a fixed and necessary condition of salvation and a declaration of principles.[80] In spite of Holdheim's protest the trustees adopted as the answer to the government Stern's formulation, as follows: "Judaism has no binding creed; we who have taken as our motto Judaism's capacity for development deem it out of the question to disregard the inmost essence of Judaism for the sake of obtaining papers of incorporation." Holdheim now framed another answer on his own initiative; his statement so impressed Simion that he, although agreeing with Stern's view, recommended that Holdheim's arguments be taken into consideration and another answer be framed. The form of the answer finally adopted attempted to satisfy both views by declaring that Judaism has no set creed, and monotheism was an incontrovertible principle of the faith. This statement did not seem to satisfy the government and the request for incorporation as an independent congregation was denied.[81]

This refusal of the government to incorporate the reform congregation as an independent religious organization tacitly acknowledged the claim of the chief congregation of being the only recognized official representative Jewish religious organization. Strife had been waging for some time between the members of the reform congregation and the officials of the chief congregation; in June, 1848, the former had resolved not to pay any further dues to the chief congregation on the ground that they never attended the services there and were maintaining one congregation; in spite of the repeated demands of the central body, they persisted in this attitude, until the aid of law was invoked by the officers of the chief congregation and the delinquents thus brought to terms.[82] Since then the members of the reform congregation had to contribute to the support of both organizations, thus making material sacrifices in the upholding of their convictions.[82a] This hardship undoubtedly was one of the causes why the reform congregation did not grow to greater proportions. By the law of the State every confessing Jew was, *ipso facto,* a member of the chief congregation of his community, and had to contribute to its maintenance; if he wished to belong to an independent congregation he had to bear the additional burden of supporting this and thus contribute to two organizations. This was manifestly unjust, but it was the law of the land in Germany. This was the chief reason why reformers in other German cities like Dresden, Leipzig, Frankfort, and smaller places were not able to organize reform congregations, and why, on the other hand, in the United States, where there is full freedom in this matter, the reform movement has grown to such generous proportions.[83] The Berlin reform congregation remains to this day the only official reform congregation with the exception of the Hamburg Temple in Germany, although a number of other congregations miscall themselves liberal.[84] It was organized at a time of great exuberance of thought and high enthusiasm of feeling. Its creative period extended over some ten years; but since 1854, when the synagogue in the Johannesstrasse, which the congregation still occupies, was dedicated (September 10), the congregation has remained well-nigh stationary. Holdheim

had been elected preacher in September, 1846; a year later, in
September, 1847, he was duly inaugurated as such, and continued in office until his death in 1860. In the religious school
which was established in October, 1846, the youth were
instructed in the principles of pure Judaism as set forth in his
Religionsprinzipien des reformirten Judenthums and in his
catechism.[85] From the pulpit he preached those great sermons
which are a mine containing the treasures of religious truth as
conceived by the greatest theologian of the Jewish reform
movement. In 1856 he commenced the agitation to revise the
prayer-book, and submitted suggestions for changes and revisions. He claimed that the prayer-book was too negative, and
required more positive features; true reform and development
consist, not in ignoring the past, but in the reinterpretation of
old institutions and ceremonies. However, he did not live to
see the revision of the prayer-book; in 1878 a revised edition
of the holiday services was issued,[86] but it was not till 1883
that a new edition of the whole appeared. This edition of the
prayer-book reverted to the order of the traditional liturgy of
the synagogue; psalms set to music were substituted for the
introductory chorals, and the services for the holidays were
characterized not only by prayers which set forth the ideas
connoted by these days as had been the case hitherto, but also
by appropriate Jewish music in place of the nondescript music
that had been used. The fiftieth anniversary of the congregation in April, 1895, was the occasion for another revision of
the prayer-book. This revision was directed chiefly to the hymns
which were made to express the peculiar character of the Jewish service. The prayer-book was completely in the vernacular,
with the exception of a few sentences, and in the various
prayers expressed the ideas and aspirations of pure religion as
embodied in the Jewish reform movement, maintaining, however, the framework of the traditional liturgy of the synagogue.

The most recent revision of this prayer-book took place in
1929.[87] The ritual for the entire year comprising the services
for Sunday morning, the feasts of Passover, Weeks and Tabernacles, New Year, the Day of Atonement, Chanukkah, and
Confirmation is contained in a small octavo volume of sixty-
three pages. The public service has been reduced to a minimum.
This is the most radical of all the Jewish prayer-books. While
it retains a few features of the traditional ritual like the שמיע
the קדושה in abbreviated form, the reading from the Torah,

the Haftarah, and the Kaddish, it has so attenuated the content of the prayers that they are little more than recognizable. True, the spirit of devotion shines throughout the booklet and the universalism of the religion is stressed. But the distance between this radical book and a liberal ritual like the Union Prayer-Book in the United States, the Liberal Jewish Prayer-Book of the Liberal Synagogue in England, and the most recent of all liberal prayer-books that of the Liberal German congregations, is very great. Still it is the glory of Judaism that it gives a place in its sun to the most varying interpretations of the faith ranging from extreme orthodoxy to extreme radicalism. So long as a congregation professes the fundamentals of Judaism, namely monotheism, the mission of Israel, and faith in the coming of the golden days of universal peace, so long as a congregation attests its Jewish allegiance it is a part of the universal congregation of Israel. The *Berlin Reformgemeinde* during its existence of eighty years has upheld the banner of Judaism. It has traveled a long way, because its founders and their successors would not compromise their convictions. It has been and is the left wing of German Judaism. It has done valiant service in the cause of liberal thought and worship.

The prime reason for the formation of the Berlin reform congregation lay in the circumstance, as has been already stated, that the chief congregation would take no steps through its rabbis and official representatives toward instituting such changes in the services and in the interpretation of Jewish doctrine as were necessary if the religion was to continue as an influence in the lives of men and women reared in an atmosphere altogether different from that in which their fathers had moved and breathed. The organization of the reform congregation affected without doubt the course of the chief congregation, where, too, reforms have been introduced gradually.[88] Sermons in the vernacular were instituted as a regular feature of the services with the election of M. Sachs as rabbi and continue to this day in the various synagogues built in different sections of the city by the chief congregation (*Hauptgemeinde*). The organ has been introduced, and although the service continues to be in Hebrew, still is it very apparent that a strong liberal or reform element exists among the members of the chief congregation and in the directory. The contest at the annual election of representatives is occasionally very spirited as between the liberal and the conservative elements; this appeared notably in the election of November, 1901, when the question of having discourses on Sunday [99] for the benefit of the great numbers who cannot attend on Saturday was agitated. Although the conservatives succeeded in electing a majority on the board of representatives, still was the liberal vote surprisingly large. True, official Judaism in Berlin, as throughout Germany, has the conservative stamp, and this may be one of the reasons for the many defections among the Jews of the German capital from their ancestral faith. The religion in its traditional guise, as represented by the synagogue, means nothing to them as men of modern thought and culture; were there a serious attempt in the synagogue to build up a theological system of Jewish thought along the lines of latter-day acquisitions in the domain of human knowledge hundreds and thousands to whom Judaism is merely an antiquated tradition would see in it a living faith with a powerful message to living men. [100] What is needed in Berlin to-day, yes, throughout Germany, is a return of the spirit of the reformers of the fifth decade with the result that the message of Judaism be interpreted in terms of vital significance to the present generation; *officially* the laws as codified in the *Shulchan Aruk* are taught as the summum of Judaism; *really* these laws are disregarded constantly and continually; there can be no healing until the official and the real reading of Judaism's significance square with one another. True, tradition must be reckoned with and the historical forces that have fashioned the development of Jewish life must be considered; but above all, present conditions must be the determining factor, and some harmonious solution which shall combine the living elements in inherited views and customs with the religious viewpoint of the present must be found; this is the purpose of the reform movement. Mistakes have been made; many reformers, notably those of the Berlin type, whose work has been discussed in this chapter, have broken too suddenly and completely with tradition; much had been cast away as mere rubbish that still had vitalizing power; more attention was given to lopping off abuses than to reconstructing the heritage of the past in the light of the present's needs; but whatever the mistakes in the practical cause of reform may have been, the principle at the heart of the reform movement is sound, and the issue between the traditionalists and the reformers is clear. For the former the authority of Judaism lies in a written code, for the latter in the progressive revelation of God in all the ages, the present included. For the former the creative energy of Judaism is a closed incident, for the latter it still operates and will so operate through all time. The wheels of progress cannot be turned backward, and true reform, as the progressive movement, must finally reconcile differences. Basing upon and teaching the essentials of the religion as the all-important, it shall also do justice to the historic spirit, and by a judicious welding of these two elements become indeed the true exponent of Judaism's eternal message as it addresses itself to successive ages.

CHAPTER IX

THE BRESLAU "FRIENDS OF REFORM"

How similar conditions were in different communities at this time is demonstrated strikingly by the fact that almost simultaneously with the publication of the Berlin "Appeal" a like document was issued in Breslau. Although Geiger, the rabbi of the Breslau community, had expressed himself frequently and constantly in favor of reform, yet had he up to this point not been able to give practical expression to his ideas; his position was delicate and difficult; the congregation, like many of the congregations in Germany, was composed of many elements ranging from uncompromising rabbinism to outspoken radicalism. Geiger, reformer though he was, felt that he was the rabbi of the whole community, and made haste slowly; he instituted societies like the *Lehr und Lese Verein* for the education of the participants in the true significance of Judaism, and delivered occasional lectures with the like object in view. After his decided victory over the Tiktin party [1] his hands were freer, but yet in the practical administration of his office he lagged far behind the advanced standpoint which it was known that he occupied theoretically. For the radical Hotspurs in the community his pace was too slow altogether. A number of these published a Declaration in the *Breslauer Zeitung* of April 4, 1845, [2] in which they set forth their absolute lack of sympathy with the legalistico-nationalistic conception of Judaism, as officially represented by the synagogue and their desire for an interpretation of the fundamental principles of the faith in accordance with the outlook of the men of their generation. They called for the elimination from the ritual of the prayers for the coming of a personal Messiah and the return to Jerusalem, because they were attached with all their heart and soul to the German fatherland and its interests, and had no desire to form a separate state in the land of Palestine.

It is also our conviction that the lofty religious command to observe a weekly day of rest will be of significance only if such a day does not conflict with the duties towards the state and the demands of daily life; the separatistic dietary laws have no meaning for us, since they no longer connote any religious idea, nay, they convert true religion into something purely external and lay stress upon the appearance rather than the reality.

They then call attention to the forthcoming rabbinical conference and urge that they owe a statement of their religious beliefs and convictions to the rabbis in order that these may know that they have the support of the members of the congregations if they take steps toward reconciling religion and life, and thus removing the conflicts that were becoming sharper and more pronounced day by day. By means of such a communication to the conference they hope to attain their aim. They have no desire nor purpose of leaving the existing congregations and forming a separate congregation. They are convinced that the same beliefs that they hold touching the needs of the hour in Judaism are shared by many others and that the reform can be achieved from within and become general. Therefore they feel it a holy duty to address the conference in the spirit of this declaration, assured that they speak for many, many others throughout Jewry.[3]

This publication stirred the Jewish community of Breslau profoundly, notably the bold pronouncements in reference to the Messiah, the Sabbath, and the dietary laws. The excitement was not allayed by an article of Geiger's in a succeeding issue of the *Breslauer Zeitung,* giving the meed of recognition to the bold and unequivocal statements, but advising the writers to proceed cautiously; he also commended their purpose to address the rabbinical conference. Geiger's article added fuel to the flame, because he apparently approved the radical measures; the congregation was so agitated that the directory felt compelled to address Geiger on the subject; he answered by saying that he did not approve radical measures (*meine Erklärung die es bestimmt aussprach, dass ich auf dem Wege des allmähligen Fortschrittes, wie bisher fortfahren werde*), and that as rabbi he held himself above party; the rabbi must have the whole community in view, and in an age of dissension and party strife must aim to compromise, teach and stimulate.[4]

The "Friends of Reform" sent the communication to the conference, and with this their activity ceased for the time.

In the spring of 1846 a committee of the Berlin Reform Association appeared in Breslau to present to Geiger a call from the association to fill the rabbinical position for the organization. Geiger asked for time to consider the matter, and promised an answer in the summer after the meeting of the rabbinical conference at Breslau. On March 19 he addressed a communication to the directory of his congregation mentioning these facts. He wrote in detail of the discouraging conditions in the Breslau congregation; how his every effort toward a true reform had met with the fiercest opposition, not only from the orthodox bigots (this was to be expected), but from men from whom he was justified in expecting support and encouragement. Constant efforts, too, were being put forth to undermine the confidence of the congregation in him. All this made him doubt the wisdom of his continuing his work there: "A position without honorable recognition, an activity without influence has no charm for me." [5]

On March 28, he delivered a lecture on the subject "From Whom Shall Reforms Proceed?" (*Von Wem sollen Reformen ausgehen?*) in which he stated that reforms must issue from both rabbis and people. Now the rabbis had held two conferences and had suggested various reforms, but the congregations had not carried them out; or rather none except the Berlin Reform Association; he therefore urged that its example be followed. After Geiger had finished, Dr. William Freund [6] arose and arraigned sarcastically the rabbis who attempt to reform; the rabbis are like the enthusiasts for freedom, but the rabbis will succumb, just as did the Shill Corps; the Reform Association of Berlin is composed of persons who know nothing of religion; for thirty years they have had no religion, but now that it is fashionable to be religious, they cut a religion to order. Judaism must be left to time which will remove that which is unnecessary; reforming is dangerous since there is practically no limit. Geiger answered him pointedly and carried the assembly with him. [7]

As a result of these three occurrences—the call to Berlin, the letter to the directory, and the lecture—the outspoken reformers were roused into activity a second time. [8] A Reform Association similar in purpose to the Berlin Society was formed, and on March 30 issued an address calling for sympathizers to join with them. In this address attention is directed to the fact that whereas formerly the rabbis opposed strenuously every reform, now there are in Germany a number of learned and earnest religious leaders who recognize the great requirements of the time and whose hands must be strengthened by the support of the people. These rabbis, too, had been reproached with having outraged the popular sentiment by their discussions and proposals at the Brunswick and Frankfort Conferences. It is time now for the people to declare their confidence in these leaders to carry into practical effect the recommendations of the conference. The address closes with an indorsement of the synod proposed by the Berlin Association in which rabbis and laymen are to deliberate together to the end that Judaism may become again a living, actual, religious force. "Pure Judaism, it is true, requires no reform, but present-day Judaism, with its abuses accumulated during centuries, requires a thoroughgoing reform."

The adherents of the society numbered one hundred and fifty;[9] at a meeting held April 5, it was resolved to send representatives to the Assembly of Deputies, to be held in Berlin on April 14-16.[10] Sunday services were advocated and the immediate carrying into effect of the reforms suggested by the rabbinical conferences.

During the course of the next three months five anonymous pamphlets appeared attacking Geiger. These were published together in June under the heading *Five Epistles of the Great Majority of the Breslau Israelitish Congregation to Dr. Geiger and to themselves.*[11]

The writer of these epistles was soon known to be Freund. It was pure presumption on his part to claim to be the mouthpiece of the majority of the congregation, and the directory promptly repudiated this claim.

The first epistle was a bitter arraignment of the Berlin Reform Association, followed by a personal attack on Geiger. The epistle was of the following tenor:

After attentive and careful examination of the character and views of the Berlin Reform Association the Breslau congregation in all sincerity and with full heart must declare this reform movement pernicious and condemnable, for the reason that of all religious movements whereof history tells, none has appeared in so perplexing and misleading a guise as this latest reform in Judaism. . . . In all the declarations and manifestoes of the Reform Association no definite nor clear statement can be found of what its members believe or do not believe; everywhere indefinite generalization about needs of the age, prayers, positive belief, spirit of revelation, and similar religious catch-words which every one can understand and interpret at will.

If the complete lack of definiteness and clearness in the manifestoes of the Reform Association were the result of a confused religious conviction, no justifiable objection could be urged thereagainst. But is not that lack of definiteness rather a carefully considered and skillfully wrought-out plan to compass a double purpose: first, to gather under the broadly extending roof a very large number of participants with whose coöperation it is hoped to reach the desired goal the more surely, and secondly, not to alienate immediately the direct coöperation and sympathy of the rabbis by a definite and open declaration of their true religious convictions, for the Berlin reformers believe it indispensable to secure the participation of the rabbis or the spiritual authorities if they would gain the mass of the people and if they would indeed reach the desired aim?

The agitators and leaders of the Jewish Reform Association consider as the true and real purpose of their organization the reconciliation of Jewish doctrine with life, so that the religion may put the seal of its approval upon the life which has been or is being divorced from the ceremonial law. If the leaders of these reform associations were to declare this their object in definite unequivocal terms, the rabbis would hesitate indeed to appear as sympathizers with and leaders of such a program.

The remainder of the document is a personal attack on Geiger.

At the same time (April, 1846), but independently of this *Epistle,* Geiger issued a pamphlet *Nine Years Ago and To-day: A Word from that Time for the Better Understanding of the Present.*[12] In this he reprinted his article in the opening volume of the *Jüdische Zeitschrift für Wissenschaftliche Theologie* on the need of a rabbinical conference and portions of another article on Jews and Judaism, and added:

What my heart longed for nine years ago was no will-o'-the-wisp of the fantasy. Time has verified it; it stands clearly accomplished before us. The sincere rabbis of Germany meet in conference in order to deliberate upon what is necessary for sick Judaism, and on the other hand practical men form associations in order to satisfy these religious needs and to seek appropriate expression for their innermost convictions. The day of struggle is not yet over, but the issue is no longer lost in the solitary desert; the echo resounds.

I greet, therefore, joyously and openly the beautiful productions of our age, the conferences of German rabbis, and the associations for reform; . . . May they live and work together in peace! Even though they be antagonized at the start, they will maintain themselves as the only means for the restoration of a pure and living Judaism.

Geiger did not answer Freund's *Epistle*.[13] But a few days later a second anonymous pamphlet appeared entitled *The Israelitish Congregation of Breslau in its Disintegration: A Voice from the Congregation*.[14] The writer accused Geiger of vacillation and incapability of self-sacrificing devotion in the cause of reform. He claimed that those who desire reforms cannot place implicit confidence in Geiger, but must search and examine for themselves. They would then find that some things that Geiger commends are condemnable; others that he opposes are commendable. Of all things, the desire to imitate must be shunned. Among such things is the worship with uncovered head, instituted by the Berlin Reform Association, and strongly recommended by Geiger. Reform in Judaism must come from within Judaism and not be mere imitation. Judaism often conceals within an unsightly shell a living kernel, which the self-appointed reformers throw away with the shell. Not every step is progress, nor every change improvement (*nicht jeder Schritt ist Fortschritt, nicht jede Veränderung eine Verbesserung*). In conclusion, the writer called on Geiger to resign as rabbi of the congregation and accept the leadership of the Berlin Reform Association which had been tendered him. Hereupon Geiger inserted a communication in the local Breslau press in which he definitely declined the call of the Berlin Reform Association and refuted the statements of the pamphlet.

Three other anonymous pamphlets of a similar tenor followed. The result of these writings of Freund was that the reformers became disheartened, and, as was the case in 1845, their activity ceased this time also with the publication of a high-sounding manifesto—words, words, words; no acts.

Geiger refused the call of the Berlin Reform Congregation on the ground that he could not become the rabbi of a portion of the community; he preferred to remain in Breslau as rabbi of the whole Jewish community with all its inner contentions rather than stand at the head of a separatistic congregation, even though this insured peace and congeniality.[15] Jewish affairs in Breslau continued in an agitated state; although the ultra-radical party did not succeed in this city as they did in Berlin in forming a congregation, and their public activity ceased with the incident narrated above, still agitation continued to be fostered within the community by the party occupying the other extreme—the Tiktin sympathizers. Geiger, it is true, had issued as victor from his combat with S. A. Tiktin, yet the orthodox element under the leadership of Tiktin's son was so irreconcilable that after several years of continuous conflict due primarily to the fact that Geiger had been named the chief rabbi of the community, it was decided in 1849 that the only method of insuring peace was to divide the Jewish community into two congregations—the one, under Geiger's leadership, to be known as the *Cultusgemeinde;* the other, under Tiktin's headship who was to be called by the title *Schlesischer Landrabbiner.* This arrangement continued until 1856, when the two congregations were merged with the understanding that the two rabbis were to be on an equal footing, Tiktin to have the same title as Geiger as rabbi of the community. In 1854 the congregation adopted as its official ritual the prayer-book prepared by Geiger along the lines of a plan which he had formulated in 1849.[16] The agitation for thoroughgoing reforms did not then bear fruit in Breslau as it had in Berlin; no separate reform congregation was organized; moderate reforms were introduced into the service of the main congregation, which like the congregations throughout Germany showed the effects of the reform spirit, but was not able to carry out fully the theories of reform. Privately hundreds thought and lived in accordance with the program of the Breslau reform society of 1846; publicly and officially Judaism in Breslau as elsewhere, in Geiger's congregation as in others, was ultra-conservative, not venturing to give practical evidence of the acceptance of even such moderate expressions of the modern spirit as the full equality of woman with man by the removal of the woman's gallery from the synagogue or the abolition of the second day of the holidays, to say nothing of more radical measures. Geiger continued in office in Breslau till 1863, when he was succeeded by M. Joel, famous for his studies in Jewish philosophy, who was far from proceeding even to the theoretical lengths that Geiger did. The religious atmosphere of this community was never again disturbed by storms of such violence as passed over it in the fifth decade. The days of *laisser aller* succeeded the period of storm.

CHAPTER X

REFORM IN HUNGARY

QUITE as intense, if not as widespread as in Germany, was the agitation for religious reform among Hungarian Jews in the fifth decade. The history of the beginnings of the movement in Germany as portrayed in the opening chapter of this work repeated itself in the Magyar realm fifty years later. The civil, educational and religious emancipation ran along parallel lines. The Diet of 1839-40 had passed some laws of an emancipatory character touching the position of the Jews;[1] that of 1843-44 evaded enacting any legislation. The party in power had given as a reason for this neglect the fact that the Jews had not Magyarized themselves sufficiently and therefore were not worthy of full emancipation. This statement was all that was needed for the Jews to redouble the efforts that they had put forth in this direction during the three years which had elapsed since the adjournment of the first parliament which had shown itself favorable to their emancipation. In synagogue, school and home the process of Magyarization became a matter of serious occupation. Schools were established in which instruction was given in the language of the country. Looking toward this end, Moritz Bloch (known later as Professor Ballagi) translated the Pentateuch and the Book of Joshua,[2] and Salomon Rosenthal and Marcus Bauer other Biblical books and the prayer-book into Hungarian; Salomon Neumann wrote Hebrew-Hungarian school books in order to facilitate the task of teachers who were aiding in converting the *cheder* into a modern school.[3] As the orthodox rabbis had pronounced the ban upon Hartwig Wessely in 1789 for having urged Jewish parents to give their children a modern German education, so now the Hungarian orthodox rabbis opposed the institution of schools for modern learning. They threatened to drive away any *bachur* (Jewish rabbinical student) who touched a German book;[4] from their standpoint they were quite right because it had become evident that orthodoxy was

270

doomed as soon as the Jew acquired a modern education. A similar instinct of self-preservation induced the orthodox rabbis of Pressburg to prevail upon the Jewish community of that city to issue a petition calling upon the Jews of Hungary to refuse the gift of emancipation if offered to them; they characterized the desire of the Jews for civil emancipation as sinful and as inconsistent with Israel's hopes for the future.[5] Here, again, they were consistent from their standpoint. In their view the Jews were a nation, exiled from their land; the countries of their sojourn were simply temporary dwelling places; they were living under their own legislation. To become merged in the body politic of the land meant the surrender of all their hopes for the future restoration of Israel to the land of Palestine. They made no distinction between the political and religious elements in Judaism; they were in the land, but not of it; among the people, but not of them—nor did they wish to be. In no country, possibly, was the opposition to reforms of any kind more bitter and constant than in Hungary, and nowhere did the rabbis of the old school present more solid ranks to the onslaughts of the modern spirit.[6] A few rabbis, however, helped along the process of Magyarization by preaching in the vernacular, notably Leopold Löw in Kanischa, Jacob Steinhardt (*Streinka*) in Arad,[7] Maier Zipser in Stuhlweissenburg, Edward Ehrlich in Lengyeltoth, Daniel Pillitz in Szegedin, and Leopold Rosenstein in Grosswardein.[8] Feeling ran very high, and the orthodox rabbis stormed with fanatical rage against the "innovators." To what extremes men permitted themselves to be carried appears from the words spoken by Phineas Hurwitz, rabbi in Papa, at the grave of his son in 1844; he said that he felt himself responsible for the son's early death because he had not opposed the innovators with sufficient zeal and holy wrath.[9]

The majority party of the parliament of 1843-4, which had justified its withholding of full emancipation from the Jews because they had not assimilated themselves sufficiently to the Hungarian people in language and education, had also in an address to the king touched this subject. In this address they suggested that if the Jews abolish "forms, antiquated customs and ceremonies that do not affect the essence of their religion," the path to emancipation would be greatly smoothed. Ignatz Einhorn,[10] who played a prominent part in the revolution of 1848 and in the Jewish reform movement, called these words

"hollow phrases intended to excuse the indefensible refusal
to emancipate the Jews." [11] However, although there is no
likelihood that religious reform was entered upon with the
thought to secure civil emancipation thereby, still there can be
no doubt that the movement for civil emancipation gave an
impetus to the institution of religious reforms. These things
have proceeded *pari passu* everywhere among Jews. During
these years there were many evidences of the working of the
reform spirit in Hungary. Thus in 1845, when the new synagogue in Papa was nearing completion, some Jews of that city
addressed five questions to a number of rabbis within and without Hungary; twenty-one rabbis answered. Their answers were
published in a pamphlet entitled *Permissibility and Urgency
of Synagogal Reforms; Responses of Prominent Native and
Foreign Rabbis.*[12] The questions were:

1. Is it permitted to place the *almemor* next to the ark
and to introduce the prayers with choral accompaniment
as is the custom at present in some large congregations?
2. Is not the placing of the marriage canopy and the
performance of the marriage ceremony within the synagogue in front of the ark contrary to the principles of our
faith?
3. May the officers of congregations sit with uncovered heads at their public deliberations?
4. Are the commands to dispense with leather shoes,
and to wear the shroud on the Day of Atonement so
important that if disobeyed this would imply a desecration
of the holiday and an action contrary to the spirit of the
day?
5. Is the spirit which actuates these and similar reforms
conducive to the preservation and uplifting of Judaism?

All the rabbis, including men of such differing views as
Geiger, Frankel, Stein, Philippson, and Schwab of Pesth,
answered the first, second, third, and fifth questions unanimously in the affirmative; on the fourth opinions were divided.
The reforms indicated by these questions appear insignificant,
it is true; but still they were reforms, and even the minimum of
reform meant a recognition that a new order of things had
come to pass. The Papa congregation became very prominent
during these years because of the activity of Leopold Löw, who
was a man of unusual attainments and for many years was the

foremost rabbi of Hungary. He gave himself to the emancipation movement heart and soul; after the fall of the short-lived Hungarian republic he was imprisoned for a brief period. Among his own people he was an uplifting influence. In Kanischa, where he was rabbi from 1841 to 1846, he preached in the vernacular; in Papa his reform tendencies brought him into conflict with the fanatics of the orthodox party who denounced him to the government. His enemies did not succeed in displacing him. He organized a Young People's Reading Union in Papa whose purpose it was to spread the use of the national language, and to arouse interest in questions of the day; in 1847 he established a quarterly, *A Magyar Zsinagoga* (The Hungarian Synagogue), whose aim he defined to be the spread of pure religiosity, lofty morals, and zealous patriotism.

In 1846 a service with choir and sermon was instituted in Buda (*Ofen*) under the auspices of "The Society for the Beautifying of the Israelitish Traditional Divine Service" (חברת תפארת הדת). Philip Schuler was the directing spirit, and the movement was encouraged by the rabbi of Pesth, L. Schwab.[13] Schwab favored æstheticization of the service by such means as music and sermon in the vernacular, but he was not a reformer in the sense that the German rabbis were who placed a new interpretation upon the religion in its ceremonial and its spiritual aspects. This appeared later in Schwab's hostile attitude to the Reform Society of Pesth, which was founded on German models. He believed in modern culture and education for the Jew, but he clung to the traditional standpoint, and further than countenancing efforts to bring decorum into the public service he would not go.

It was in Pesth, the Hungarian capital, that the reform party made its greatest show of strength and put forth its chief efforts. Here, as in the large cities of Germany, the cultural movements were particularly strong and drew hundreds of Jews within the circle of their influence. Participation in these cultural movements was always the forerunner of religious reform. There had been a so-called *Cultustempel* in Pesth since 1826, where sermons were delivered and a choir sang, but that continued to use the traditional ritual. In the fall of 1847 J. Bach, the preacher, advocated the introduction of German prayers and the organ. A society was formed to carry these suggestions into effect.[14] It was not, however, until after the events of the fateful revolutionary month—March, 1848—

that the movement came to a head. We note here a remarkable difference between the fortunes of the progressive religious movement in Germany and Hungary. In Germany the political excitement attendant upon the revolutions of 1848 absorbed attention to such a degree that interest in the progressive religious movement, which had aroused great enthusiasm in the pre-revolutionary years, waned, and a feeling of apathy, in striking contrast with this former enthusiasm, ensued. In Hungary, notably in Pesth, on the other hand, the free religious movement among Jews breathed in inspiration from the circumambient atmosphere of liberty that enveloped all. Ignatz Einhorn, a young man twenty-three years of age, who had already directed attention to himself by his publication, *The Jewish Question in Hungary,*[15] called upon the Jewish student youth in March, 1848, to coöperate in the effort to introduce religious reforms. These young men who succeeded soon in enlisting the sympathy and active aid of some men of mark in the Jewish community, addressed the directory of the congregation on the subject. They wished to avoid a split in the community by forming a separate reform congregation, and desired if possible to induce the directory of the main congregation to make provision by the institution of a reform service under their auspices for such as were no longer edified by the traditional mode of service. This seemed possible of ready fulfillment, because for years the congregation had supported two synagogues, in the one of which the service had been conducted along traditional lines, while in the other (the *Cultustempel*) a few external reforms had been introduced. The principle had thus been granted that the various religious needs of different sections of the community should be provided for, and therefore they would be merely following the path already marked out if they were to institute a reform service for such as found no religious satisfaction in either of the two existing synagogues.

The directory expressed its agreement with this presentation of the case, and appointed a commission of ten to prepare a definite plan of procedure. An insurmountable obstacle was met in the opposition of the rabbi, L. Schwab, to the introduction of any reforms other than external, even in a separate congregation to be formed under the auspices of the main congregation.[16]

While these negotiations, which culminated in failure, were

proceeding, the reformers moved rapidly toward a practical realization of their program. On April 15, 1848, Ignatz Einhorn began the publication of a newspaper, *Der Ungarische Israelit*. In an early number of this paper an address to the Jews of Hungary appeared signed "The Student Youth of the Jewish Faith." The spirit that animated these young men who were led by Einhorn can be best understood by a brief extract from that address:

> The time long since prophesied has come at last; a beneficent thunderstorm has cleared the political atmosphere; millennium-old systems are destroyed mercilessly and ruthlessly; age no longer sanctifies abuses; whatever mocks the spirit of our time, is in its turn now scorned and despised; the eternal truths appear pure and unencumbered on the horizon of our achieved freedom; we have taken the giant leap from pupilage to full and responsible manhood in the course of a few weeks, and shall only the golden content of our religion continue encrusted with moldering mediæval ceremonies? Is this possible at a time when everything blossoms and decks itself with the fresh apparel of the new age; is our faith alone to declare itself absolutely incompatible with the new age? No! no! say we!

Events moved rapidly. A reform society was formed in Pesth; it was hoped that similar reform societies would be organized throughout Hungary in response to appeals sent broadcast. However, the hold of traditionalism was too strong, and favorable responses were received only from Arad, Lugos,[17] Fünfkirchen, Grosswardein, and Nagy-Becskerek. The Pesth reformers, however, were not discouraged, despite the meagerness of the response; they called a meeting of all interested in the reform cause for July 8, 1848, when "The Central Reform Society of Hungarian Israelites" was formed. But the activity of the new movement was practically limited to Pesth, where the reformers displayed great energy and activity. Since the directorate of the main congregation wavered in its attitude and gave no satisfaction on the point of instituting a reform service, as requested by the reformers, these latter determined to form themselves into a separate organization, and the Pesth Reform Congregation was formally constituted on August 10. Ignatz Einhorn was elected rabbi of

the congregation, and it was determined to acquire a building
wherein to hold services as soon as possible; by the end of
September the building was ready for occupancy, and the first
reform service modeled upon the service of the Berlin Reform
Congregation was held on New Year's Day (September 28,
1848). Einhorn preached the sermon, in which he dwelt upon
the principles that underlay the reform movement. The congregation adopted a radical program advocating such extreme
reforms as the transfer of the Sabbath to Sunday, the abrogation of circumcision and the dietary laws; the services were
held on Sunday, the men worshiped with uncovered heads, and
the prayers were in the vernacular. Holdheim was the authority
to whom these Hungarian radicals looked for guidance, and the
Pesth congregation was the only one in Europe outside of his
own Berlin congregation which carried into practice the ultra-
teachings of this arch-radical among the reform leaders.

Only in Pesth did the Hungarian reformers succeed in
organizing a congregation, although there were individuals in
other cities who sympathized fully with the views of the Pesth
radicals and who like these drew their inspiration from the
writings of Holdheim. An interesting document that throws
into vivid relief the position of this extreme left wing of Hungarian Jewry has been preserved in the form of a communication addressed to Holdheim on April 23, 1848, by a group of
Jewish radicals of Arad, where, through the influence of Aaron
Chorin, reform ideas had found sympathetic lodgment in the
congregation from very early days. In this communication
Holdheim was requested to render an opinion as to whether the
signatories to the document and others who thought as they
did could continue as Jews if, taking the Ten Commandments
as the basis of their faith, they would give outer expression to
this through the following measures: 1. The transfer of the
Sabbath to the Sunday. 2. The abolition of the dietary laws.
3. The abolition of the second days of the holidays. 4. A short
service in a living language together with the abrogation of all
marks of separation and the covering of the head. 5. The
declaration that circumcision is not absolutely required of
Israelites; and finally, the definite declaration that only the
Ten Commandments are binding as the revelation of God to
Moses; therefore the Talmud and old religious observances,
both such as are contained in the Bible and such as were introduced in earlier days, fall away."[18]

These questions go to the very heart of Jewish teaching; they give evidence, too, of the fact that these radicals did not comprehend the basic principles of the reform movement. By repudiating the whole Jewish tradition, they cut themselves loose from the house of Israel; by accepting only the Ten Commandments and not the authority of the Mosaic code, they out-Karaited the Karaites. All the great reformers insisted upon the validity of the principle of tradition, however many special traditions they may have repudiated; otherwise they would have cut the cord that bound them to the century-long religious experience and development of Israel. They taught that reform was interpretation and application of the principle of tradition in the light of the changed conditions of the nineteenth century, just as the *Shulchan Aruk* was such an interpretation and application in the light of the conditions of former centuries. For them the whole history of Judaism was eloquent with the searching after God, and they saw the revelation of God, not only in the Ten Commandments, but in the whole long unfolding and growth of the spirit of man through historical time. However much the great leaders may have differed on some points, in this they were all agreed, even Holdheim. In his answer to the Arad questionnaire he explained this and other points so clearly and concisely that it appears necessary to set down here his words:

To the question whether the observance of the Ten Commandments alone is sufficient for the Israelitish confession, I answer:

(*a*) The definite God-cognition and moral content of Judaism as they are expressed briefly and sharply in the Ten Commandments, as they are more fully explained and developed in the whole Bible, the post-Biblical writings, and particularly in the whole history of Judaism, together with the historical mission of Judaism, compose the exclusive unchangeable foundation and the essential and only binding principles of Judaism. This mission means the preservation in all its purity of this God-cognition and this body of moral doctrine, which is based on justice and universal brotherly love, and the promulgation thereof among men by the moral force of example; so that, in accordance with the prophetical Messianic idea, justice and brotherhood may become dominant in all the earth.

(*b*) Now that the Jews have become integral elements of other peoples and states, in conjunction with whom they are determined to further the moral aims of society, all laws and institutions of Judaism which base upon the election of a particular Jewish people—yes, of a particular Jewish state—and hence by their very nature implied exclusiveness and particularism, and served merely to strengthen the nationalistic sentiment, as was the case among all ancient peoples, have lost all religious significance and obligation, and have given way to the national laws and institutions of such lands and peoples to which the Jews belong by birth and civic relationship. As an example of such a political law of the Jewish Palestinian state, I instance the prohibition to take interest from the native and the permission to take such interest from the foreigner (Deut. xxiii, 20-21).

(*c*) All laws which deal with the temple, the sacrificial, the priestly or the Levitical service, in which category also the many dietary laws, as well as the laws of clean and unclean, belong; in a word, all laws which grew out of the idea of a particular theocratical sanctity of the Jewish people and base upon the conception of a particular union between God and Israel, the chosen people of God, and closer than that with other peoples, have lost altogether their religious truth and significance for us now that these representations have became foreign to our whole mode of thought and we look upon God as the one and only Father, and consider and love all men as his children and our brethren.

(*d*) All other ceremonies and customs—whether they are contained in the Bible or are the products of later times—which at one time had and fulfilled the purpose of nourishing the religio-moral sentiment, but have lost all such power owing to the complete change in the position and culture of men and have for their reason sunk into mere external forms, can and may not be performed by us any longer as religious practices. We must rather strive earnestly for inner religiosity and not outer formalism, in accordance with the words of the prophet Hosea (vi, 6), "I desire mercy and not sacrifice"; we must use only such ceremonies as are efficacious in working as a religious influence upon men of the present day.

B. The special questions, notably:

1. That touching the transfer of Saturday to Sunday, I answer thus: Since we cannot assume that God pronounced one particular day holy once for all, and since we consider the Biblical account of the exclusive sanctification of a special day merely as the mythical expression for the sanctification of man on a special day, naturally no religious reason prevents the transfer of the historical Sabbath to any other day of the week, notably if such a transfer is urgently demanded by the conditions of civic life, yea, even in the interest of the preservation of the Sabbath-institution and its influence on the religious life of the congregation; hence in the interest of religion itself.

2. As I have demonstrated scientifically elsewhere, the dietary laws belong to the Biblical laws of cleanliness, which have long since lost all significance. Inasmuch as the dietary laws were given to the Israelites alone, they are part and parcel of the conception of a special theocratical sanctity of the Jewish people and therefore have lost all significance. Whatever, however, may have once been the reason for the dietary laws, this much is certain, that this reason no longer exists for us, and has no religious efficacy; every irrational practice, every belief in talismanic power is opposed to the spirit of religion. Therefore the abrogation of the dietary laws is highly desirable, since, in addition to being a disturbing feature in the civic and social life of the Jews, these laws are particularly prone to continue the differences between them and the other inhabitants.

3. The abolition of the second days of the holidays, as well as the abrogation of all fast days except יום כפור, has been recommended by the German rabbinical conference. To my mind not only is there no objection to such abolition, but it is highly desirable in the interests of the religion.

4. The abbreviation of the service, the excision of all prayers unsuited to our age as, e.g. the sacrificial and Messianic prayers of a Jewish national character, as well as the use of the vernacular in the public service, have also been recommended by the second rabbinical conference. The removal of all disturbing ceremonials has taken

place in very many Jewish congregations in Germany, and not even from the orthodox standpoint can any objection be raised to praying with uncovered head.

5. Circumcision is the sign of the covenant concluded between God and Abraham, and *eo ipso* his descendants (from which, however, the older lines of Ishmael and Esau are excluded), and its seal on the body of every Israelite. As long as such a covenant had significance for the religious consciousness of the Jews, as long as the idea of a close covenant of love excluding the nations (upon which the whole theocratic relationship was based) was deeply rooted in the people's thought, the circumcision was the characteristic symbol of this covenant, and was therefore clung to with particular zeal in Israel. But after this idea of the particular covenant which underlies circumcision has ceased to be a religious truth and an object of faith protest must be lodged against circumcision, the expression of an outlived idea. It testifies to something which is not true— yes, to something which is, in fact, denied by all Israelites who have become self-conscious. The Jew to-day believes by no manner of means that he through the accident of descent from Abraham stands in a close special relationship to God, and that he is obligated to give visible evidence of this closer relationship by a sign in the flesh. I am opposed to circumcision on principle and declare every Jew who confides in my religious insight and conscientiousness, absolved from all obligation in this matter. Yes, I declare every Jew who neglects to have his son circumcised because of his larger belief to be a true and complete Jew. Finally, I declare righteousness in the fullest sense of the term, *i.e.* equality for all men, humanity and brotherhood together with the living, stirring zeal to realize these things in all circles of life to be the practical realization of the God-cognition of Judaism and hence the true and pure Judaism.

The extreme program outlined in this response of Holdheim was carried into practice nowhere in Hungary except in Pesth, as has been stated. The career of the Pesth Reform Congregation was troubled and brief. Its rabbi, Ignatz Einhorn, left the city after the downfall of the Hungarian republic, served as chaplain to the garrison of the fortress of Komorn, was amnestied after the capitulation of that fortress, but soon after retired to Germany, where he lived in exile many years.

During the ensuing two years (1849-1851) the directory of the congregation strained every effort toward obtaining rights of incorporation as a separate congregation. Their experiences were similar to those of the Berlin congregation.[19] The government finally rendered a decision refusing the petition of the directory on the ground that the congregation had no positive dogmas which had to be accepted as the condition of membership, and it was the purpose of the Minister of Public Worship to prevent the multiplication of religious organizations of this character.[20] As was the case with the Berlin reformers, their Pesth brethren in spirit conceived Judaism to be non-dogmatic in the sense of not requiring subscription to a creed as a condition of salvation. This point has been discussed fully in a previous chapter and may therefore be dismissed with this mention.[21]

The directory of the congregation had been negotiating for sometime with David Einhorn, chief rabbi of Mecklenburg-Schwerin, one of the best known of the reform leaders, with a view to his accepting the position of rabbi. Einhorn signified his acceptance in October, 1851, and in January, 1852, preached his inaugural sermon. In this sermon he declared that reform meant a great deal more than the introduction of external changes in the worship; the organ, worship with uncovered heads and the like are mere accompanying incidents; reform is "nothing less than a Jewish-religious transformation." He set forth the ideas and purposes of the reform movement; he denied that reform breaks with the past and Jewish tradition; he defined the attitude of reform toward the Mosaic law, the eternal elements of which must be distinguished from the transitory. "If the transitory nature of certain Mosaic laws is granted on all sides, who will deny that we stand on Biblical ground if we contend for the capacity of development and change in ceremonial institutions?" Speaking of the Talmud, he said that although the reformers were far from considering it divinely inspired, and although its interpretation of the Mosaic law is different from theirs, yet they recognize that it has developed their sacred heritage in several directions—*e.g.* the doctrine of the immortality of the soul—and that many a nugget of truth is to be found in it. "Judaism may not be deprived of the least of its precious possessions," he declared;

"it is the mission of the present to continue its development; by no means to break with the past, but to enlist the old in the service of the new and to preserve it in transfigured form." [22] Einhorn's assumption of the rabbinical office aroused the opposition to greater activity than ever. After the suppression of the revolution and the collapse of the Kossuth movement the reactionary elements were in power, and reform of whatever kind found little favor with the government; hence, the orthodox party by representing to the government that the reform congregation was revolutionary in character, as far as its attitude toward Judaism was concerned, succeeded in having the reform temple closed by order of the government within a short time after Einhorn's coming; the congregation dissolved, and several years later Einhorn emigrated to the United States, where he assumed charge of the Har Sinai Congregation of Baltimore. True, the Pesth reformers did go to extreme lengths. Their program was ultra-radical; but it is likely that even a moderate reform congregation would have met the same fate, for the temper of the authorities was unfavorable to any movement anywhere that differed from the traditional *status quo*.

Orthodoxy prevailed in Hungary; individually thousands of Jews had broken with rabbinical tradition, but officially Judaism continued along the traditional lines. A few congregations introduced such innovations as the sermon in the vernacular and music by a choir, and this remains the extent of reform to this day; a reinterpretation of Judaism in the light of modern culture and the outlook of modern man has not taken place in the Magyar land.

The celebrated Hungarian Jewish Congress which met from December 14, 1868, to February 23, 1869, for the consideration of the internal affairs of the Jewish communities avoided the discussion of purely religious points for fear of interfering with the project of union. Still, the emancipation spirit which marked the majority of the delegates to this congress and caused them to view educational and civil questions in the light of modern development, even though they scrupulously evaded all matters of religious belief and practice, aroused the bitter animosity of the uncompromising orthodox party, who seceded from the congress in a body. The state of Judaism in Hungary after the Congress was worse than before, for the Jews were split into four irreconcilable factions—the "Congress" party, the orthodox, the so-called "Status ante quo" party, and the Chasidaic communities that called themselves *Sephardim.*[23] These factions divided on educational and emancipational issues; religiously they are practically on the same footing. Religious reform as conceived by the German theologians and as realized in the United States is unknown.

The chief practical achievement of the "Congress" party was the establishment of the rabbinical seminary at Buda-Pesth from the fund administered by the government for purposes of Jewish education; although the religious standpoint of the seminary is rabbinico-traditional, still it differs radically from the *Yeshibot* in that its students are permeated with the modern spirit as far as education in secular branches is concerned. The establishment of this seminary aroused the bitter wrath of the orthodox party, not alone in Hungary, but in Germany.[24]

In 1889 the orthodox rabbis denounced the reformers in an address to the government. By the reformers they meant the Congress party, although this party was as little a reform party in the religious sense as the ultra-orthodox. The occasion of this denunciation was the order of the government requiring the proper registration of the Jews.[25]

Many vital changes in the social and political position of the Jews, including civil emancipation and the recognition of Judaism as one of the religions in the state, have taken place, it is true; but this lies without the scope of this investigation. The Jewish religious situation in Hungary to-day presents the same tragical spectacle as in other European lands—a complete break between practice and official profession. Had reform succeeded in its purpose, a reconciliation would have taken place, and the Jew's religion would have been a present living force, instead of something foreign to his life, which it now is so generally in Hungary as well as in the other European countries.

CHAPTER XI

Up to the time of the rise of the reform movement there had been no question as to what was valid or invalid in Judaism. The Talmudical and rabbinical decisions as codified in the *Shulchan Aruk* were the norm of authority. This was, and among orthodox Jews still is, the official standard of religious soundness. All the laws were of equal weight; the purely religious and moral injunctions had no greater sanction than the dietary laws or the minutiæ of rabbinical dialectics in the matter of Sabbath observance; no discrimination as to greater or less validity of any of the laws was entertained.[1] Even though it was notorious that thousands of Jews disregarded the injunctions of the codes, and that life in the world made the observance of many of the traditional laws almost impossible, yet rigid orthodoxy would not yield an inch; it did not even attempt to reinterpret and reshape the traditions to meet the changed situation. Many, too, there were who took the position that individual Jews might disobserve the traditional laws, but official Judaism as represented by the officiating rabbis and the congregations must cling to the Talmudical traditions as delivered from the past.[2] The reformers, however, were not content to rest in such an inconsistency. For them the *Shulchan Aruk* had ceased to speak with authoritative voice; but men always long for some authority, or at least for some guidance. Since they had broken away from the old moorings, the reformers were greatly at sea; individualism was rampant; the rabbinical conferences had been instituted with the purpose of stemming this individualistic tide and of constituting some body of agreement as to the teaching of the new movement. True, the conferences did not arrogate to themselves any binding authority, but there can be little question that many had hoped that the decisions reached and the resolutions adopted by the conferences would serve at least as a new "guide of the perplexed" in the constant clashings which were taking place between the

requirements of life and Jewish practice and belief. The conferences did not succeed in fulfilling this expectation. When
this became apparent, voices were heard to the effect that the
conferences had failed in this respect because they were not
representative popular assemblies; they did not originate from
among the people, and the people had no voice in their deliberations; therefore, let synods be convened to be participated in by
rabbis and laymen, scholars and teachers, theologians and men
of practical affairs. Judaism had never known the distinction
between clergy and laity; not sacerdotalism, but knowledge, was
the mark of distinction between Jew and Jew; therefore, the
rabbinical conferences which had had only officiating rabbis as
members were not truly representative of the Jewish spirit;
only a synod would be such. The synod would be the authoritative organization. It would determine the position to be
taken on the many vexed points of belief and practice among
the Jews. Notably in the fifth decade of the nineteenth century
was the call for a synod frequent and insistent. The introduction of reforms in various congregations was largely a matter
of caprice—here more, there less; there was no authority to
declare how far congregations should go. Many felt that this
unsettled, indefinite condition was causing untold harm; they
felt no less that a clear presentation of what constituted the
principles of Jewish belief and procedure on the basis of the
changes that the modern era had brought would reconcile the
contending opposites in Jewish life. As stated in a previous
chapter,[3] the recommendation that a synod be convened
emanated from the founders of the Berlin Reform Congregation; in that chapter the pros and cons of the synodical idea
were discussed, and to expatiate upon them here is therefore
unnecessary. It is worthy of note that the demand for a synod
at this time (1845-50) issued from a number of independent
quarters; the *Breslau Reformgenossenschaft* seconded the suggestion of the Berlinese;[4] a French writer, Jerome Aron, advocated its organization in the columns of the newspaper *L'ami
des Israélites* in 1847.[5] When it was found impracticable or
unfeasible to continue the rabbinical conferences the executive
committee that had been entrusted with the duty of convening
the fourth conference, recommended that a synod to be participated in by both rabbis and laymen be called into being to take
the place of the conference;[6] a number of Jews of Worms
styling themselves Friends of Reform, addressed and published

a communication to their coreligionists in 1848 setting forth a reform program and closing with the demand for a synod;[7] so also a society in Munich (*Israelitischer Fortschrittsverein*) advocated the same at this time;[8] on August 31, 1848, a self-formed committee of Frankfort Jews issued a call for a preliminary meeting, preparatory to the convening of a synod. At this preliminary meeting, which was held on October 23 and 24, it was resolved to call a synod in the spring of 1849.[9] This was a paper resolution, for the synod was not convened. Three prominent rabbis, Philippson, Formstecher, and Stein advocated the advisability of the movement.[10] In 1849 Ludwig Philippson called upon the directorate of the Berlin Jewish community to take the initiative in creating a Prussian synod.[11] However, no action resulted from all this agitation. In fact, the energy that had flamed into such remarkable activity in the cause of religious reform during the years 1837-1848 had consumed itself and was followed by a lassitude that endured for well-nigh twenty years. The tremendous political upheaval of the year 1848 may have, nay, undoubtedly did have, much to do with this, for there was little time or attention for anything but the revolutionary changes wrought by the agitations of that year of struggle in the cause of liberty. Notably did this hold true of the Jews, for there was no section of the people for whom the changes then wrought in the constitutions of states were of greater significance in the securing of civil and political rights. There is little cause for surprise, then, that all other interests fell into the background and were overshadowed completely by the political issues; but even after the excitement had toned down and the political stream was flowing smoothly through the new channel which the revolutionary year had cut, the interest of the Jewish communities in religious matters could not be aroused to a high pitch.[12] It seemed to be impossible to convene a gathering for the discussion of Jewish religious concerns.[13] True, there were not lacking individual voices which called for action.[14]

Still, it may not be forgoteen that although there were no such gatherings, and although, further, there were no striking occurrences in the Jewish world directing attention to the reform cause, as had been so constantly the case in the years preceding the March revolutions of 1848, yet reform had conquered in so far as in scores of congregations reforms had been and were being constantly introduced. These reforms were not far-reaching, it is true; but they were evidential of the fact that the spirit of progress had touched the Jewish communities.[15] During this period, however, a tendency toward romanticism showed itself and through the influence of the Breslau theological seminary, which had been founded in 1854, a conservative reaction set in;[16] but even more than this must be accounted the activity of the Neo-orthodox party which largely, under the leadership of Samson Raphael Hirsch, sought to stifle every effort toward reform and religious progress. Notably through the influence which he wielded by means of his organ, the *Jeschurun*, did Hirsch administer many a body blow to the cause of reform; on the other hand, the reformers began to bestir themselves actively, and in the "sixties" new signs of life began to appear.[17] In 1865 Abraham Geiger, in an essay entitled "What is Needed?"[18] described the unsettled condition of affairs in Judaism. He showed how in practice the Jews had wandered far from orthodox lines, and that the great majority of the people had no conception of the true inwardness of Judaism. Although the life of the people was in total contradiction with Talmudical and rabbinical dicta, yet these still stood as the official teachings of the synagogue; hence an insufferable state of inconsistency and contradiction. One of the great needs of the time, therefore, was "large gatherings for the discussion of Jewish questions." Geiger's suggestion was received sympathetically.[19] Many rabbis felt as he did, and again it was the rabbis who in this time of renewed agitation and discussion assembled for the consideration of the problems arising from the conflicts between life and tradition. On August 11, 12, 13, 1868, twenty-four rabbis gathered at Cassel to confer together. These rabbis were L. Adler, of Cassel; J. Aub, of Berlin; Ben-Israel, of Coblentz; J. Kahn, of Trier; A. Cassel, of Schwerin a. d. Warthe; T. Cohn, of Potsdam; H. Engelbert, of St. Gallen; S. Formstecher, of Offenbach; Friedman, of Mannheim; Fürst, of Bayreuth; A. Geiger, of Frankfort; Goldmann, of Birkenfeld; A. M. Goldschmidt, of Leipzig; S. Herxheimer, of Bernburg; B. Hochstädter, of Ems; M. Joel, of Breslau; M. Kayserling, of Lengnau; B. Levi, of Giessen; J. Mayer, of Hechingen; L. Philippson, of Bonn; G. Philippson, of Dessau; J. Rothschild, of Alzey; B. Wechsler, of Oldenburg; A. Wiener, of Oppeln.

L. Philippson submitted for consideration thirty points touching the liturgy; these liturgical questions called forth a lengthy debate. All expressed themselves to the effect that it was advisable to prepare a union prayer-book [20] for congregations desiring reform. The only resolutions adopted in reference to the liturgy, however, were the recommendations to the congregations that the Torah be read through every three years (the triennial cycle); that the Tefillah (the eighteen benedictions) be recited but once during the service, except on New Year's Day and the Day of Atonement, and that the sections between *Bor'ku* and *Sh'ma* and between *Sh'ma* and the *Tefillah* be cast into the vernacular; that the *haftara* be read in the vernacular, and that the Commission on Liturgy make a new selection of *Haftarot* agreeably to the Torah readings arranged for the triennial cycle, in which selection passages from Hagiographa were to be included. The feeling among those present was that no definite action should be taken on any of the other subjects presented in order to disprove the frequently preferred charge that the rabbis had hierarchial ambitions; this conference was to be considered merely preparatory to a synod. It was therefore resolved that "the rabbis assembled at Cassel constitute themselves into a preliminary assembly, in order to prepare for periodical gatherings, to which also Jewish scholars who are not officiating ministers and the representatives of the congregations are to be invited." [21] They resolved, further, that all the resolutions which were offered at the conference should be referred to commissions who were to prepare reports to be submitted to the synod, which was to be called in accordance with the above resolution. The formation of local or provincial synods preparatory to the general synod was advised. [22] The need for a synod was felt particularly because many congregations were divided into reform and orthodox factions; there was also prevalent the fear lest the indifferent would withdraw from the congregations and thus evade contributing their share toward the maintenance of the congregations. Since the laity were especially concerned in the composition of the congregations, it was concluded that they should be asked to assist in the solution of the difficulties presented by the situation by participation in a synod to be composed of rabbinical and lay delegates. [23] L. Adler, L. Philippson and J. Aub were appointed the committee to call the synod. Four additional commissions were elected to prepare the work for the synod, viz.: On the Liturgy—L. Adler, L. Philippson, and M. Joel; on Ritual Laws—J. Cohn, A. Wiener, and L. Adler; on Marriage Laws—

Friedman, J. Aub, and A. Geiger; on Schools and Religious
Education—S. Herxheimer, J. Hochstädter, and G. Philippson.
This conference, then, has a place in the history of the reform
movement merely as preliminary to the Leipzig Synod.[24]

As might have been expected, the opponents of reform broke
forth in harsh diatribes against the conference, as had their
predecessors twenty-five years previously; [25] but, nothing
daunted by the opposition, the committee to whom had been
entrusted the chief task, viz. to take steps to convene a synod,
went to work at once, and in February, 1869, published to the
Jewish world a document under the heading "Invitation to the
rabbis, Jewish scholars, and congregational boards to the Synodal Assembly." This document was as follows:

> At the close of the past century the European Jews
> began to participate in the general activity of the world,
> owing to the gradual removal of the barriers which had
> excluded them from industrial life, social amenities, gen-
> eral and scientific culture and public service. Under the
> influence of these completely changed conditions new and
> fresh life awoke in our midst in the province of religion,
> with the result that different views and many conflicts
> arose in the religious field. In spite of the indestructible
> fealty of the Jews which is as ready to-day as at any time
> in the past to bring all sacrifices in act and suffering, there
> yet arose a growing confusion and an almost indescribable
> diversity among individuals and in congregations. Every
> individual was a law to himself as far as religious prac-
> tices went, and the same was the case with congregations
> in their religious institutions. From these conflicts parties
> issued which called into being inner divisions, and in many
> places violent conflicts took place whereby the condition
> of Judaism became ever more confused and precarious. A
> religion of the minority, a religion of scattered small divi-
> sions, can be exposed to no greater danger than to become
> internally divided, conflicting, hesitating, and agitated by
> violent party strife. It is readily comprehensible that such
> a condition can be cured only by organization and united
> action. Real improvement and betterment of the conditions
> can be accomplished only by the union of many, and such
> a union alone can obtain a true and sufficient authority.
> With this in mind, twenty-four rabbis from all parts of

Germany and Switzerland met at Cassel on August 11, 12, and 13 of last year. These rabbis recognized that the most effective remedy for the present conditions in Judaism lies in the creation of a union of the best-intentioned and ablest elements, but that such a union was not to be found in the assembling and the resolutions of a smaller or greater number of rabbis, but must be formed by the joining with the rabbis of the ripe scholars of Judaism and especially of the representatives of the congregations themselves. The conference at Cassel therefore resolved unanimously: (1) to convene a synodal assembly of rabbis, Jewish scholars, and representatives of the congregations; (2) to choose committees who are to formulate propositions for the synod.

It is apparent that nothing further could be done by the rabbinical conference than to determine of what class of men the synod shall be composed, while all more explicit measures concerning the future composition of the synod, the order of business, the manner of voting, etc., had to be left to the first synodal gathering.

The committees on the cult, the schools, the marriage laws, and other ritual matters, promised to publish their reports sufficiently long before the meetings of the synod to enable all who expect to participate in the meeting to become thoroughly acquainted with and to examine them. Furthermore, it is scarcely necessary to state that by their participation in this first synod, the congregations assume no responsibility for its resolutions and results. The object, above all else, is to lay the foundation for a large and more intimate, but altogether free union devoid of all outer coercion—yes, for a visible and more effective organization and coöperation.

We therefore approach the Jewish congregations in general, and the governing boards in particular, with the request to participate through one or more representatives in the synodal assembly that is to be convened during the summer of 1869. We do this with the consciousness that the honorable board is fully able to appreciate the real significance, the beneficial bearing, of the proposed assembly. We do not doubt that you have no wish to dissociate yourselves from the community of Israel, and that you will contribute with pleasure toward ensuring its well-being and providing for its future. We see no other means whereby, in the spirit of our religion, whose loftiest principle is brotherhood, as well as in the spirit of faith and freedom of conscience, we can effectually prevent further ruin. We can think of no cogent reason for refusing to participate in this gathering. Every view, every tendency, will have the right to express itself. Verily only that peace is upright, only that union real which results in mutual understanding and agreement, even though these involve much contention and struggle. All these things we submit to you for consideration and beg you to let any one of the undersigned committee know within four weeks whether you will participate in the synod.

May we all, mindful of what we owe to the glorious heritage of our fathers, the religion of four thousand years, soon see the work of union take shape before our eyes under the providence of God!

A large number of congregations responded favorably to this call for a synod, which seemed to have struck a responsive chord; most of the public Jewish organs [26] wrote favorably of the plan. When the synod convened at Leipzig on June 29, 1869, sixty congregations were represented by eighty-three delegates. Many congregations that had expressed their sympathy with the movement were not represented. Most of the delegates were, as was to be expected, from Germany, although a number of foreign countries were represented, as e.g. Austria (through Joseph von Wertheimer, Dr. Maximilian Engel, E. Brach, Solomon Sulzer, and Simon Szanto, all of Vienna), Belgium (through Grand Rabbi E. A. Astrue and E. Lassen, of Brussels), Bohemia (through George Feigl, of Prague), England (through Dr. G. Gottheil, of Manchester), Hungary (through Dr. L. Löw, of Szegedin), Galicia (through Abraham Gumplowicz, of Krakau), Roumania (through Samuel Marcus, of Bucharest), Switzerland (through Dr. M. Kayserling, of Endingen-Lengnau), the United States (through Simon Herman, of New York), and the West Indies (through Reverend M. N. Nathan, of St. Thomas). Among the German representatives were many rabbis and laymen of note as e.g. (among the rabbis), J. Aub, of Berlin; S. Herxheimer, of Bernburg; L. Philippson, of Bonn; M. Joel, of Breslau; L. Adler, of Cassel; W. Landau, of Dresden; A. Geiger, of

Frankfort-on-the-Main; A. M. Goldschmidt, of Leipzig; B. Wechsler, of Oldenburg; A. Wiener, of Oppeln; Tobias Cohn, of Potsdam and (among the laity) Professor M. Lazarus, of Berlin; David Honigmann, of Breslau; Emil Lehmann and Joseph Bondi, of Dresden; Professor C. Munk, of Glogau; Professor Julius Fürst and Moritz Kohner, of Leipzig; and Dr. G. Josephthal, of Nuremberg. The lay element was far in the majority, there having been forty-nine lay and thirty-four rabbinical delegates, including religious educators and cantors. The synod was opened with an address by Dr. A. M. Goldschmidt, the rabbi of the Leipzig congregation, who declared this synod to be the successor of the conferences of the fifth decade. He referred to the reaction after 1848, but declared that now there were signs of renewed life and activity in the cause of progress, and of this the present gathering gave eloquent testimony. Jews are of many nationalities, but they are all united in their faith, which rises above national boundaries. In the interest of that faith and its universal teachings they had assembled. He was followed by Dr. L. Adler, rabbi of Cassel, the chairman of the committee appointed by the rabbinical conference of Cassel to call the synod. Dr. Adler referred to the unfortunate conditions in Jewry, the dissensions, and the indifference. He claimed that reforms were necessary, and referred with words of scorn to "such as have arranged religious affairs for their own ease and convenience; they have thrown off all allegiance to religious enactments and have reconciled life with religion very easily, inasmuch as they have renounced religion and enjoy life. Let every individual satisfy his conscience in this matter; but if such persons want to take a prominent part in congregational councils in order to secure the reputation of belonging to the conforming party, then must we bend all our energies to make such inconsistency impossible, for so palpable a break between official religion and private practice can result only in detriment to true religion."

The synod organized by electing the most celebrated layman in the gathering, Professor Moritz Lazarus as president, Dr. Abraham Geiger and Joseph von Wertheimer, of Vienna, vice presidents, and Dr. M. Engel (physician), of Vienna, and Dr. Emil Lehmann (advocate), of Dresden, as secretaries. In his address of acceptance Lazarus pleaded for tolerance; that every one, no matter what his views, should concede to others the same rights of opinion which he demanded for himself.

He urged further that all should have in view only the desire to serve the truth and that they be open to conviction.

The synod being composed of men of many shades of opinion ranging from the progressive standpoint of Geiger and Lazarus, to the conservative attitude of Joel and Landau, it was meet that at the very first session after the organization of the body some declaration should be made of a standpoint on which all agreed. This was done by the adoption of a statement of principles submitted by Ludwig Philippson, which in their final form as concurred in by the synod read as follows:

> The synod declares Judaism to be in agreement with the principles of modern society and of the state as these principles were announced in Mosaism and developed in the teaching of the prophets, viz., in agreement with the principles of the unity of mankind, the equality of all before the law, the equality of all as far as duties toward and rights from the fatherland and the state are concerned, as well as the complete freedom of the individual in his religious conviction and profession.
>
> The synod recognizes in the development and realization of these principles the surest pledges for Judaism and its followers in the present and the future, and the most vital conditions for the unhampered existence and the highest development of Judaism.
>
> The synod recognizes in the peace of all religions and confessions among one another, in their mutual respect and rights, as well as in the struggle for the truth—waged, however, only with spiritual weapons and along strictly moral lines—one of the great aims of humanity.
>
> The synod recognizes, therefore, that it is one of the essential tasks of Judaism to acknowledge, to further, and represent these principles and to strive and work for their realization.

In the debate upon these paragraphs a number of interesting views were given expression to by Grand Rabbi Astrue, of Belgium, who spoke in French (it having been voted that each delegate speak in his own language and that his remarks be then translated into German) to the effect that "Judaism bases upon the principle of the Divine Unity, which signifies human unity and the equality of all before the civil as well as the moral law; Judaism bases upon the liberty of the individual conscience, and from all its principles, as well as from its history, there results an energetic condemnation of all religious constraint and the affirmation that mankind ought to march onward to fraternity and universal peace under the banner of knowledge and love." [27]

It will be noted that not a word is mentioned in this statement of principles concerning the special religious tendency of the synod. The question of reform or orthodoxy was purposely avoided. The synod was supposed to be catholic in character and was intended to furnish the forum for the expression of every possible view. However, although it was the hope of its promoters to engage the interest and sympathy of all Jews, the entire absence of representatives of extreme traditionalism was very significant; the orthodox would have none of it; there was not a delegate from Russia or Poland, but one from Galicia; the most noted leaders of orthodoxy in Germany, especially Samson Raphael Hirsch, assumed a most hostile attitude to the synod from the very start. And in truth they were right in their claim that the synod was of a reform character. Although this was not stated in so many words in formal resolution or declaration, it cropped out constantly in debate and in the character of the work mapped out in the program of the meetings. Thus immediately after the adoption of the above declaration proposed by Philippson, Dr. Wollner of Gleiwitz and others proposed "that in connection with the first resolution of Dr. Ludwig Philippson and immediately after its dispatch, the synod declare:

"That in the attempts to remedy the evils now existing it will be concerned first of all to keep intact the connection with the Bible and the traditional literature." The purpose of this resolution naturally was to commit the synod to the traditional or rabbinical standpoint. It was feared by some that this resolution if discussed at this early stage would prove the apple of discord that would disrupt the synod. Wollner disclaimed any such purpose, but declared that since all congregations had been invited to participate, also such as base upon the standpoint of rabbinism, he felt it proper to reassure such that the synod would not break with the rabbinical tradition. The issue was avoided by the referring of the discussion to a later session. [28] At the last session Dr. Wollner withdrew his resolution, with the explanation that he had introduced it at the beginning because he wished the discussion thereof to make clear whether

the synod was destructive in its tendency, but that he was constrained to confess now that the synod had not abandoned the
positive standpoint.[29] Its whole spirit was to bring the interpretation of Judaism into harmony with the modern outlook.
In the debate on the question of Torah readings Dr. Gottheil
of Manchester (later of New York) received approbation for
his statement: "If we want to reform from formalism into
formalism, we will miss the true purpose, we must reform
toward the living spirit;[30] . . . let us keep in mind the true
and real need of men, and not always a false piety toward
antiquity." The reform character of many of the speeches
induced Joel to warn the synod not to discriminate against the
orthodox nor throw down the gage of battle to them.[31] Aub of
Berlin found the object of the synod indicated in the old prohibition not to touch the dead lest it make unclean: "This is a
warning for the synod not to make itself unclean by touching
the dead, but to bury this quietly. We wish to support life
and, while remembering the dead, to purify what still has life
and vitality." In the effort to satisfy the various views represented in the synod, there had been rather much casuistry in
the proceedings; this led Dr. Wiener of Oppeln[32] to demand,
when a proposition of a distinctly reform character was before
the synod that it be adopted "in order that the delegates who
constitute the progressive element receive consideration, there
having been so much subtlety in the settling of many other
points."[33] But the reform tendency of the synod found clearest
expression in the superb address with which the president closed
the sessions, in the course whereof he said: "There is much
in the synagogue that requires reform, therefore we devoted
ourselves here to the consideration of these reforms within the
synagogue. Opponents will ask, What have they abolished
again, what will they put in its place? Gentlemen, certainly we
wish to abolish; we wish to abolish first of all, indifference; we
wish to abolish—to abolish, I say—ignorance. But this is not
sufficient; we need also reform. We honor the old; but the true
honoring of the old consents in our nursing it, not in our permitting it to decay. A wine dresser knows that if his vine is to
bring forth fruit, much and good fruit, he must cut away the
rank sprigs of the vine lest it shoot into wood. But he knows
also that if he cuts away all twigs the stem withers."[34] If
anything, this reform spirit found even stronger and more frequent expression at the Augsburg Synod. Thus in the discussion

on the reform of the marriage laws, Dr. Leopold Löw of Szegedin, in condemning the timorous attitude of a previous speaker, advised the synod: "I beg of you not to fear the opposition of the orthodox, for the orthodox party will hesitate to shoot the arrows of defamation from fear that these arrows might hit many a one whom it counts among its protectors, advocates and defenders." [35] The seasoned reformer, Dr. B. Wechsler of Oldenburg, who had been a member of the rabbinical conferences of the fifth decade, gave voice to the convictions of a lifetime when he declared in the course of his remarks on the necessity of abolishing the *chalitza* ceremony "we may and must say that we have the right and the power to abrogate an institution which has no significance to-day and in its form and content is no longer worthy of our age and of ourselves." [36] Similarly in a discussion on the proposition to revise the *Shulchan Aruk* [37] Dr. Wassermann laid down the general proposition: "The worst demoralization of nations and individuals; yes, let me add, of congregations, arises from the circumstance that they habituate themselves to the contradiction between their theoretical convictions and their practical existence and mode of life. This contradiction between theoretical conviction and the practical mode of life should and must be removed." [38] Again, in the Sabbath discussion, Dr. A. Wiener stated unqualifiedly, "We do not desire to hold fast to all old petrified formulæ, but to preserve the living element" [39] and finally a strong utterance of Geiger in the course of that same discussion must be cited: "We cannot take cognizance in all their details of the words of ancient teachers—men, it is true, of the deepest insight; men whose memory we revere, but who lived in their age and not in ours; in an age of altogether different views, circumstances, and conditions." [40]

On the important question as to the character of the synod, opinions were divided. Philippson contended, as he had twenty-five years previously in regard to the rabbinical conferences, [41] that the synod must be of a practical character; not theoretical discussions, but practical suggestions and resolutions, should be its main feature. [42] Geiger held quite the opposite view: "The purpose of our gathering is to encourage, enhearten and enlighten the congregations and not to take in hand practical undertakings." [43] The president took an intermediate position when he declared that the synod was of a mixed nature, being both theoretical and practical; that it was an assembly in part scientific and in part resolutatory;[44] the actual work of the synod substantiated this view. As to the authority of the synod, always the most important question in a gathering of this kind, there was no thought that the synod should have the power to loose or to bind, to exercise ecclesiastical control, to coerce or to excommunicate; its sole authority was to arise from the confidence of the people. It was not to gain its authority by the conventional methods of hierarchical assumption, but by arousing conviction. Being a body of notables in whom the people trusted, its deliverances were to gain authority simply through this and not by any external measures or force of any kind.

All reform in Judaism is obligated to win the people, to plant convictions. There is no authority, no one possesses it, nor may any one be permitted to possess it. We do not speak of that small party which declares that there is an absolute authority, namely, the written word, which one need only read in order to know what Judaism is and what constitutes Judaism; this requires no consultation, no speech, merely dumb acquiescence; it requires merely that one read and accept what is printed in the *Shulchan Aruk.* . . . Our object must be to convince; let us aim here in the synod to win through the thoughts themselves those who wish to accept our standpoint.[45]

The synod, then, was, in the view of its most distinguished participants, to be an organ for the formation of Jewish opinions on important questions, a gathering of enlightened thinkers who were to grapple with the perplexing questions that were distracting Jewry—not a heresy-hunting theological police nor an ecclesiastical court with all its attendant evils.

With this aim in view, the synod addressed itself to the consideration of a number of important issues in Jewish life, the most salient points in the discussions, deliberations, and decisions of which follow.

Religious Education.—From the time that Jewish children had begun to attend the common schools the question of their religious instruction had assumed a serious aspect. In ghetto days, the Jewish child had received all its instruction in the *cheder,* and this instruction had been altogether in Hebrew branches. There was no such thing as a distinction between secular and religious education. Necessarily when Jewish children attended schools in common with children of other faiths, the matter of religious instruction became acute. Two courses were now possible—either that hours should be set aside in the curriculum of the day school when religious instruction should be imparted by teachers of the various faiths to the children of these faiths, or that special religious schools should be instituted whereat the religious education could be received. As a matter of course where Jewish children attended Jewish day schools the problem did not arise. Even to this day the problem of the religious education of the young is one of the most serious in Jewish life. Where the public school is altogether secularized, as in the case in the United States, individual congregations must make provision for the religious instruction of the children; where Christian religious influences prevail in schools, as is the case in a number of European countries, Jewish societies and congregations have largely succeeded in having regular hours indicated in the curriculum in which religious instruction is imparted to Jewish children by a teacher of their faith. The first deliverance by any constituted body on this whole subject of religious education was made by the Leipzig Synod. Dr. S. Herzheimer of Bernburg, the chairman of the Committee on Religious Education that had been appointed by the Cassel Conference to prepare a report to be submitted to the synod, presented an exhaustive paper on the subject [40] of religious instruction, closing with a number of recommendations; among others, that every congregation should make attendance at the religious school compulsory for every child unless the parents of the child can prove that the child receives such instruction from a qualified teacher; that, to ensure unity in religious instruction, a Union Book for Religious Instruction be introduced in all congregations, and that the examination in religion and confirmation constitute the ceremony of graduation from the religious school at an age ranging between the thirteenth and sixteenth year. In the discussion which ensued, a number of moot points were discussed, such as the possibility of a union religious textbook; here two distinct views appeared, the one suggested by Herxheimer and the other championed by Geiger, who declared that owing to the differences in opinions among various congregations a Union Catechism was an impossibility, and that for the majority to attempt to foist such a book even upon the smallest dissenting minority would be disastrous. It must always be left to the free choice of any school to adopt or reject such a book. Another interesting discussion turned upon the question of Biblical criticism; were the Bible stories and incidents to be taught literally, or was the critical method to be applied? This was precipitated by the resolution offered by Dr. Szanto, of Vienna, who called upon the synod to declare that "the fundamental principles of the Jewish creed are not antagonized by a teacher who explains all the natural and historical events narrated in Sacred Scriptures in accordance with the teachings of the sciences, so long as he does not deny the fact itself, and that a teacher should not be removed from his position who explains a miracle naturally, provided he casts no doubt upon the veracity of the Bible." The members of the synod were not prepared to assume so outspoken an attitude but, with four exceptions, declared without further debate against the critical method in the teaching of the Bible. The resolutions on the subject of religious education as formally adopted by the synod are as follows:

1. The assembly recommends most urgently to the congregations the establishment and support of good religious schools for the youth of both sexes.

2. The assembly recognizes it to be the task of the congregations, yes, of all the Jews of each and every state, to put forth every effort to have Judaism obtain its rights in the higher institutions of learning which are intended for all confessions by having it made possible for the Jewish students to receive there higher religious instruction.

3. The assembly hails with joy the tendency of our age which strives for the general establishment of non-sectarian schools; it recognizes in this tendency no danger for Judaism, but considers it all the more important that in addition to these non-sectarian schools there should be institutions which inculcate in the rising generation the knowledge of and love for their inherited faith.

4. The assembly recognizes as inalienable portions of religious education, not only the usual instruction in Biblical history and the compilation of the deeply ingrained religious principles, but also the firm grounding in the content of all the Biblical books, the cultivation of the Hebrew language as the language in which these books are written, in which the religious idea finds its uniquely deep and intense expression, the language which has been and should remain the fresh spiritual source of all succeeding

centuries and likewise the firm spiritual bond between all parts of Jewry. Especial stress, however, should be laid upon acquainting the young with the whole of Jewish history, including the post-Biblical, as the richest source for confirmation in the faith, and the fortifying of the religious sentiment.

5. The assembly declares that religious instruction in the school must avoid the critical method; the idealistic outlook of the young should not be blurred by the suggestion of doubts. For this very reason, however, the assembly expects our teachers to be wisely discreet in not ignoring the results of science, but to anticipate and prevent a conflict which may arise later in the soul of our growing youth between religion and the commonly accepted scientific point of view.

6. The assembly recognizes the need of special training schools for Jewish teachers, notably religious teachers. It appreciates the existing worthy institutions of this character and desires eagerly their increase. But it does not fail to recognize the great difficulties in the way of establishing a sufficient number of such seminaries. Therefore, the assembly considers it an urgent duty to strive towards having capable Jews who understand how to train Jewish religious instructors in their future profession appointed at the general public seminaries because of their specific sectarian character.

7. Finally, the assembly regards the establishment of one or more higher institutions of learning for the science of Judaism (theological faculty) as the highest task in the interest of the scientific knowledge of Judaism, and considers it to be one of its essential objects to arouse general interest in this matter. The assembly declares that the significance of such institutions consists primarily in their becoming the nurseries of free scientific knowledge and that their mission is to strengthen Judaism spiritually and to secure for it its justified influence upon general spiritual development. The assembly therefore names a committee which is to unite with all efforts already put forth for the establishment of such higher institutions of learning.

The committee appointed in accordance with this resolution consisted of Philippson, Geiger, Astrue, Joel, and Lazarus. To

this committee was referred the resolution of Dr. Löw that
a curriculum be prepared for such institutions of learning, in
which especial attention be paid to introducing a proper method
for instruction in the Talmud. The synod indorsed the suggestion of Grand Rabbi Astrue of the advisability of an international union of the various higher institutions of Jewish
learning (Paris, Padua, Breslau), but concluded that the initiative for such union must come from the institutions themselves.[47] Already at this time plans were under way for the
foundation of a theological seminary of a progressive character
at Berlin.[48] These plans found fulfillment in the establishment
of the *Hochschule* (now *Lehranstalt*) *für die Wissenschaft
des Judenthums* in 1872.

Liturgy.—The question of the reform of the prayer-book
and all matters germane thereto had been prominently before
the Jewish people ever since the inception of the reform movement, as has appeared abundantly throughout these pages. All
the agitation on the subject had not resulted in any united
action. The conferences of Brunswick, Frankfort, and Breslau
had made a number of pronouncements, but these had remained
largely paper resolutions. Therefore it must not cause surprise
that the synod, too, addressed itself to this subject. The preliminary conference at Cassel had appointed a commission that
was to prepare a report on the liturgy for consideration by the
synod.[49] At that conference Dr. Ludwig Philippson had proposed thirty points for discussion and decision. In the meantime Dr. Geiger had formulated a number of theses for the
deliberations of the synod on this subject.[50] When the matter
came before the gathering for consideration, the report prepared by the commission appointed at Cassel, consisting of
Drs. L. Adler, L. Philippson, and M. Joel,[51] formed the basis
of the discussions. At the very outset of the debate, the old
question as to whether the principles or practical points should
receive prime attention, divided the members. Geiger claimed
that the synod should lay down the general principles and leave
it to individual congregations to make the special applications
of these principles to such practical reforms as they deemed
necessary.[52] Philippson, on the other hand, held that the principles had been discussed for half a century, and that it was
supremely necessary for the synod to express itself on such
practical and special questions as were troubling the congregations.[53] L. Adler agreed with him, calling attention to the

fact that the present gathering was a synod and not a rabbinical conference; a rabbinical conference was expected to discuss theoretical questions and principles; a synod to make practical application of these principles. Aub spoke in a similar vein, and used the significant words: "Of all things, posit no principles, manufacture no creed. The safety and guaranty of our religion depend upon this very fact that its professors never quarreled about or had differences concerning articles of faith. The Bible is our basis, not any individual synod." [54] Geiger stood almost alone in his contention that the principles or doctrines which were to find expression in the prayers should first be decided upon. The assembly determined to devote itself to the consideration of those practical issues in the public service which the commission had incorporated in its report. Inasmuch as the debate on the various points brought before the synod elicited no arguments that had not been adduced in the remarkable discussions on the prayer-book and the liturgy in general at the Frankfort Conference, which discussions have been reproduced at length in a former chapter, it will be unnecessary to set down here anything more than the resolution adopted by the members of the synod.

Sabbath Morning Service.—All readings from the Torah are to be in Hebrew. The weekly portions on Sabbath morning and afternoon are to be read in accordance with the one-year cycle. [55] On the afternoon of the Day of Atonement Lev. xix, 1-23, shall be read in place of Lev. xviii. [56] In reading the Torah, the traditional cantillation (*trop*) is to be displaced by intelligible reading. [57]

The *Haftarot* are to be read in the vernacular. Portions from Hagiographa may also be used for this purpose. [58] The *Tefillah* (eighteen benedictions) is to be read only once in each portion of the service. [59]

In the recasting of traditional prayers and in the new prayers all expressions which savor of bitterness or revenge are to be avoided. All petitions which are not of a confessional character are to be so framed as to include all mankind and all prayers of thanksgiving for the spiritual benefactions of God to Israel, such as the election of Israel, the Sabbath, etc., are to be expressed in a positive manner, and in such a way as not to offend our brethren of other faiths. On the other hand, especial stress is to be laid on the following points, as is in truth already the case in a number of prayers, viz. the religious mission of

Israel, the providential guidance of Israel, the great principles of Judaism, *e.g.* progressive development, the eventual universal rule of the knowledge of God, justice and peace (the Messianic age) love of the neighbor, etc., etc.[60]

The Three High Feasts.—The services on the holidays are to be similar to the Sabbath services, with the addition of the festival *Tefillah*,[61] the *Hallel*[62] (in Hebrew or the vernacular according to the need of the congregation) the assigned Torah-lection, the special *haftara* and songs appropriate to the holiday.[63]

All *piyyutim,* whether for Sabbath or holidays, are to be abolished. On holidays a meditation on the special significance of the holiday is to be inserted between the *Tefillah* and *Hallel.*[64] The petition for *geshem* and *tal*[65] is to be replaced by a German prayer. The *hoshanahs*[66] are to be retained in Hebrew for the Feast of Tabernacles and to be shortened for *Hoshana Rabba.*[67]

The Morning Service of Rosh Hashanah.—On *Rosh Hashanah* a number of especially lofty *piyyutim* in Hebrew and meditations in the vernacular are to be added in order to bring the high significance of this holiday home to the consciousness of the individual.[68]

Yom Kippur.—A meditation in the vernacular and penitential prayers in Hebrew or the vernacular are to be introduced in each of the four services on *Yom Kippur* as time permits.[69]

The impressive *Hazkorat Neshamot* (Memorial Service for the Dead)[70] shall take place between Shaeharit and Mussaf or between Mussaf and Mincha.[71] The *aboda*[72] is to be retained, but the intermediate sections are to be recast and shortened.[73]

General.—Unison congregational singing is recommended. Chorus singing and other musical performances are in place only when the singing material is adequate; all profane music is to be banished from the synagogue.

The introduction of the organ in the synagogue is commendable and there is no religious objection to its use on Sabbath and holidays.

A resolution to abolish the custom of calling members of the congregation to the Torah (*Aufrufen*) was defeated as was also Geiger's motion that the portions assigned for reading on the so-called Sabbaths *Parah* and *Zakor* be dispensed with.[74]

Circumcision.—Dr. Maximilian Engel, of Vienna, a physician, and Professor Julius Fürst, of Leipzig, offered resolu-

tions on the subject of circumcision. Dr. Engel desired the
reference to a committee for consideration and report to the
synod of the following two questions:

> (*a*) Is a child born of a Jewish mother which for what-
> ever reason has not been circumcised to be considered a
> Jew in the light of the rules now existing and considered
> binding for the Jew, and (*b*) How in case the first ques-
> tion is answered in the affirmative is such an individual
> to be treated subjectively as well as objectively in ritual
> matters in view of the rules indicated above?

Professor Fürst's resolution was to the effect that "the synod
should declare, that according to the express dictum of the
Talmud, every child born of Jewish parents belongs to the
Jewish community by the very fact of its birth and not primarily by virtue of circumcision. Therefore a boy born of Jewish
parents is to be registered as a Jew without any further consideration as to whether he is circumcised or not. The neglect
on the father's part to have his child circumcised is placed in
the same category with all other commands, the neglect of
which entails the punishment of *Karet* and is beyond all human
jurisdiction. One that is uncircumcised may not be slighted
either in the deposition of the oath or in being called to the
Torah" (*Aufrufen*).

As the reasons for submitting the two questions to the synod
Dr. •Engel called attention to several cases in Vienna and
Prague which had caused much confusion. Jewish fathers were
unwilling to circumcise their children, but were desirous of
rearing them as Jews. They demanded the registration of the
children as such. The rabbis refused. In Vienna the father
had appealed to the civic authorities, who ordered the rabbi to
enter the child's name on the registry. In Prague a similar
order was given with the supplementary suggestion, however,
that the rabbi could keep a private record in which he could
indicate whether the child was circumcised or not. The next
step was taken by the directorate of the Viennese Jewish community who informed the magistrate of the city that they would
enter the order among the legislative acts, but would not obey
it. They claimed that the decision in the matter lay with the
religious authorities of the Jews; they therefore called upon
the rabbis of the city to meet with them for consultation. After
lengthy debate, they decided that such a child must be consid-

ered a Jew. But the directorate wanted to know, further, what the standing of such a boy would be in the future as a Jew, *i.e.* they wanted enlightenment on the practical, not the theoretical aspect, of the matter. The answers were so involved that the directorate could not comprehend them, and even now do not know whether such a person is to be considered a Jew in the performance of ritual functions like being called to the Torah, whether he can be married as a Jew, etc., etc. Only one of the rabbis gave a clear answer, inasmuch as he said that he distinguished between the subjective and the objective aspects of the case. Subjectively he considered such a one a Jew, *e.g.* he would marry him; on the other hand, such a one could never be a rabbi or cantor. The directorate was therefore at sea, and he had come to the meeting with the hope that these questions would receive the fullest consideration; this could not be done were they to be discussed at once; he, therefore, urged that they be referred to a committee for thorough investigation along the lines of Jewish regulations. This proved to be the sense of the meeting and both resolutions were referred to a committee consisting of Drs. Landau, Aub, Joel, Löw, and Wechsler. This committee was well balanced—Landau representing the orthodox, Joel, Aub, and Löw the conservative, and Wechsler the liberal tendency.

Many resolutions on various subjects were submitted to the synod, but were not acted upon; some were referred to the proper committees for report at the next synod, while others were merely printed in the appendix to the proceedings.[75]

The synod adjourned on July 4 after listening to the inspiring closing address of the president, some significant paragraphs of which have been already given. It will suffice, therefore, to reproduce here merely those words wherein the speaker set forth the importance of the gathering for the history of Judaism:

> The guiding principle which, in various guises, has animated our proceedings has been the golden mean: we would not be of those who press the hand to the dial or set it back and believe that the clock has stopped running; nor would we be of those who are constantly winding the clock. It is a well-known fact that the clock stops running while it is being wound, hence such as constantly wind the clock do not know at all what is the time. In conclusion,

let me give voice to the emotions which sway and should sway us here and now ויום טוב היה עושה כהן גדול ביום הכפורים כשנכנס בשלום ויצא בשלום בלי פגע. We are in a holiday mood; for we, too, have [76] been in the Holy of Holies. We have been serving in the Holy of Holies of mankind—the development, the beautifying and the clarifying of our own religion and its institutions. You who are theologians know well that the service in the Holy of Holies was consecrated but dangerous. Consecrated but dangerous is also the service which we have performed here; but that which was sought in the Holy of Holies we also desire to find, namely, reconciliation.[77]

The Leipzig Synod was characterized by the spirit of moderate and gradual progress. Although of a reform tendency, its proceedings and resolutions were in no single instance radical in character.[78] It took up for action such subjects as had been discussed publicly and privately for many years and concerning which the views were clear, but for which some authority was desired. It did not call forth acrimonious discussions to the degree that the rabbinical conferences of the fifth decade had done; this was largely due, in the first place, to the fact that in the intervening quarter of a century reform had made quiet headway; and secondly, to the circumstance that none of the changes advocated were of such a nature as to fan the smoldering fires of theological passion into flame. The proceedings had been conducted on so high a plane and were so peaceful in character that Lazarus was apparently justified in the prophetic utterance which was the concluding sentence of his closing address: "Our synod forms the foundation of future synods." The men who had gathered at Leipzig departed for their homes animated by the high feeling that they had builded lastingly and had assisted at the inauguration of a perennial institution which in time would become the body of authority for Israel. A good beginning had been made. A large number of representative and earnest men had gathered together. Much work had been projected for the next synod; important resolutions had been referred to committees for report at the next synod, and it had been resolved that these various reports should be distributed broadcast in the spring, so that when the synod met in the summer, the delegates might come fully prepared, inasmuch as ample opportunity would have been had for the consideration and discussion of the various matters to be acted upon. The following year the Franco-Prussian War took place; there was neither room nor thought in Germany for anything but this war; it was not to be expected that any synodal gathering could take place during this period of national excitement;[78] but in the following year the work begun at Leipzig was continued in the second synod which convened in the south German city of Augsburg.

The Augsburg Synod

This synod was composed of fifty-two delegates from thirty congregations, a noticeable falling off from the attendance and the representation at Leipzig. True, among the delegates were quite a number of distinguished rabbis and laymen. The large cities, such as Berlin, Vienna, Frankfort, Leipzig, Munich, again participated, as well as a number of smaller communities, notably those in the neighborhood of Augsburg. The hope that the synod would become Pan-Jewish was not realized, for only Jewish communities of Germany were represented, with the exception of Vienna for Austria, Szegedin for Hungary, Krakau for Galicia, and St. Gallen for Switzerland.[80] The delegates at the Leipzig Synod had parted from that meeting animated by great enthusiasm, the synod at Augsburg was permeated with a spirit of discouragement from the start, because many communities that had been confidently expected to participate had failed to do so. It was evident that the results of the meeting at Leipzig had not been of such a character as to assure the congregations that the synod as there constituted was able to solve the problems that were vexing Judaism. The radicals ridiculed it for devoting attention to matters which they had long since ceased to consider of paramount importance, the orthodox had assumed a hostile attitude from the start because of the reform tendency of the movement, while the thousands who were in sympathy with a project whose avowed purport was to solve the perplexities arising from the conflict of rabbinical Judaism with the modern environment and outlook were disappointed in the Leipzig Synod because of the fearsome timidity which marked its proceedings. Even had it been possible to convene the second synod in 1870 it would have been altogether likely that the effect of these views would have been felt; and when the synod did actually convene at Augsburg this was found to be the case. In his opening address Lazarus, who was elected president of this synod also, contrasted the Leipzig assembly with the present. There they had met as at a festive gathering; here they had come together primarily for work; they had not assembled in a spirit of great encouragement, for the synod was not sustained generally by the congregations as it should have been.[81]

The Augsburg Synod met from July 11-17, 1871. The more notable rabbis present were Geiger and Aub, of Berlin; Löw, of Szegedin; Nehemias Brüll, of Frankfort-on-the-Main; Grünebaum, of Landau; Adler, of Cassel; Goldschmidt, of Leipzig; Wiener, of Oppeln, and Wechsler, of Oldenburg. Of lay delegates the most distinguished were Professor M. Lazarus, of Berlin; Joseph von Wertheimer, S. Szanto, and Leopold Kompert, of Vienna; Dr. Jacob Auerbach, of Frankfort; Professor Julius Fürst and M. Kohner, of Leipzig; and Dr. Gustav Josephthal, of Nuremberg. The synod organized by electing Professor M. Lazarus president, Dr. Abraham Geiger and Leopold Kompert vice presidents, and A. Wertheim, of Berlin, and G. Josephthal, of Nuremberg, secretaries.

The president, in taking the chair, delivered a lengthy address. He declared that the object of the synod was not only to pass new resolutions for the delegates to take home, but to imbue them with new life and new energy for Judaism; to give them not only new thoughts but new courage for the cause. It was incumbent upon them to deal not only with practical questions, but with the whole higher outlook of Judaism, for it was quite possible that a synod might meet at some future time when there were no burning problems to solve. In such case the synod would be no less significant and necessary as the ideal assembly in which men met together to celebrate as it were the feast of loyalty, unity and harmony in spirit; the synod would then be as a place of pilgrimage in the newer time and in accordance with the newer spirit. True, it is necessary that at every synod certain minor reforms be achieved, certain institutions modified, certain forms and traditions abrogated. But this is not enough—"The more ideal, the more practical"; we cannot live from hand to mouth; we must keep constantly in view the great and eternal truths of our religion and strive to have these understood ever better. Nor is it enough for the synod to recommend only such things as it is sure the congregations will accept; it must teach and lead and be a true guide.

Marriage Reforms.—In no province of Jewish life was reform of traditional institutions more necessary than in the marriage legislation. Here the Oriental origin of Judaism was apparent in a number of institutions that were repugnant to the Occidental view; the relation, too, of the Jewish marriage law to the civil law had to be regulated; before the Jews acquired rights of citizenship in the countries of their birth and residence they had their own ecclesiastical jurisdiction; marriage and divorce were governed altogether by the dicta of the rabbinical law. How regulate the relation between the Jewish laws and the civil statutes on the subject? Further, in the modern view of the universalistic character of Judaism as opposed to the nationalistic, what was the status of much of the traditional marriage legislation which was of a distinctly nationalistic character? At the rabbinical conference of Brunswick in 1844 a commission had been appointed to revise the marriage laws, but it did not report at either of the two succeeding conferences. At the first session of the Breslau Conference in 1846 Holdheim had presented a lengthy communication suggesting many reforms in the laws of marriage and divorce, but no action was taken;[82] since then there had been no Jewish gathering of an authoritative character in Europe where these subjects could be discussed.[83] Presumably the rabbinical legislation was still the norm of Jewish practice here; but, as in so many other things, modern life had decided many of the points involved contrary to the spirit of this rabbinical legislation. Tradition and practice had parted ways, and it was necessary that there be a reconciliation; hence the synod at Augsburg made the subject of the marriage legislation its first order of business. The action of the synod on this all-important subject cannot be considered adequate, for no general principles were laid down, but merely special points were discussed and acted upon. The resolutions adopted were these:

1. It is permissible during the marriage ceremony for the bride to give the bridegroom a ring accompanied by some appropriate words after the bridegroom has placed the ring on the bride's finger while speaking the traditional formula הרי את מקודשת.[84]

In the traditional marriage ceremony the bride was passive. The ring was the symbol of her acquisition by the groom. The significance of this action of the synod permitting the exchange of rings, and the active participation of the bride in the ceremony by the utterance of some appropriate words (Geiger suggested the phrase in the Song of Songs, אני לדודי, I am my beloved's and my beloved is mine) lay in its designating hereby the equality of the sexes. "The old juridical view, according to which the woman was a chattel that the man acquired, has disappeared entirely from among us," said Geiger, the chairman of the commission. "We do not wish to retain any form whatsoever which was symbolical of this view in earlier days. This is the significance of the resolution that two rings be used in the ceremony, in order that it become known thereby that the man and the woman marry one another, as responsible moral personalities, or if only one ring be used, Judaism protests decidedly against the imputation that an old Oriental view still holds in its midst whereby the worth and dignity of woman are discriminated against legally in any way, even though this was not the case in life." [85] The truth of the matter was that in a number of congregations like Berlin and Frankfort the ceremony of exchanging rings had been in vogue for some time; the synod by recommending it, or rather declaring it permissible, simply added the weight of its authority to an accomplished fact; but the action was important in view of the implication of woman's parity with man; the rabbinical standpoint of woman's inferior position legally and in public functions was abandoned and the reform position in this matter endorsed.

2. The synod recommends that in those countries in which the civil marriage is given in charge of the rabbis, questions asking if they consent to the marriage be put to the high contracting parties at the religious ceremony analogous to the prescribed formula used in the land of Wurtemberg.

The point of this resolution lay in the fact that in some countries a civil ceremony performed by a civil officer had to precede the religious ceremony performed by the rabbi; in such cases there would be neither rhyme nor reason in the rabbi's asking the couple if they consented to the marriage since they were already civilly married; in countries where the religious ceremony was considered also the civil ceremony the questions had point; again, by putting the question also to the woman, her equality with the man was emphasized once more.

3. No one may be objected to as a witness at marriages and divorces on the score of the non-observance of a ritual law.

From the traditional standpoint no Jew who failed to observe

all the ritual laws was permitted to give testimony before the
Beth Din or to serve as a witness at marriages or divorces. A
number of speakers, notably Dr. Vogelstein,[86] urged that this
resolution be laid on the table on the ground that no rabbi who
was guided by rational principles would in the present day
make the observance of the ritual law a condition *sine qua non*
of a man's availability as a witness, and that, further, such a
resolution would lessen whatever confidence the orthodox party
might repose in them. Löw and Geiger especially insisted on
the adoption of the resolution, the former on the ground that
in Hungary instances had occurred very recently where rabbis
had ruled out men as witnesses for this very reason; the latter
on the score of principle, because this involved a vital distinction between the rabbinical viewpoint and the modern.

> The question here is, Are men trustworthy as witnesses
> if they act in accordance with their conscience and their
> conviction, considering this or that as unessential, or are
> they to be stamped as unreliable on this account? Are they
> not to be accepted as witnesses in general and at marriages
> in particular on this account? It is of great importance
> to declare ourselves on this point. In former days all
> things hung together; if an individual disregarded the
> ritual laws it was assumed that he did this from frivolity
> and levity, hence, he could not act as a witness. We do
> not accuse our ancestors of narrow-mindedness on this
> account; nay, this principle was not an established rule in
> the ancient days, it became such only in the hard dark
> ages.
> Why, I ask, then, shall we not make this declaration?
> Modern Judaism recognizes the conscientiousness and
> credibility of every person even if he has his own individ-
> ual views. This must be declared openly and may not be
> evaded.[87]

The synod adopted this resolution unanimously and repudiated by this act the fundamental principle of rabbinism of the
eternal validity of every regulation of the traditional law.

4. The synod declares that the custom of not having marriage ceremonies performed on certain supposedly unlucky
days, viz. during the interval between Passover and the Feast
of Weeks, as well as during the so-called three weeks,[88] with
the exception of the week in which the ninth of Ab falls, con-

duces to superstition and corresponds to no true pious sentiment. Hence, the synod regards this restriction as abolished.

The custom prevalent among Jews of not marrying during
the weeks between the feasts of Passover and Weeks (excepting on the thirty-third day) was attributed commonly to the
tradition that during this period the thousands of pupils of
Rabbi Aqiba died from a plague, and that therefore this was a
time of mourning during which it was improper to celebrate
so joyous an event as a wedding. This was, however, only an
ostensible reason; the real origin of the custom lay in the Roman
avoidance of marriage during the month of May, during which
month the spirits of the dead were supposed to return to earth
and bring misfortune to the living unless exorcised by prescribed formulæ.[89] The synod rightly condemned this superstition, which is still widespread. As for the second custom
mentioned, viz. the intermission of marriage ceremonies during
the so-called three weeks, it is readily comprehensible that Jewish nationalists should consider these weeks as a period of
mourning par excellence, for in their view the destruction of
Jerusalem was the beginning of Israel's great travail in the
world and the most tragical of all occurrences; but the synod,
representing the view that the old Jewish political existence had
passed altogether and the Jews were incorporated in the modern nationalities, could not acquiesce in this feeling. In the
view of modern Judaism the destruction of Jerusalem was the
end of the preparatory national existence of the Jews and the
beginning of their larger mission as missionaries of the truth
of the One God in all parts of the earth, whither they were
scattered. However, although disenthralled from Palestinian-
ism though many of the synodians were, yet was the spell of
the mournful significance of the month of Ab, the anniversary
of the actual destruction of Jerusalem, still too potent to be
discarded altogether. This day was still quite generally observed
as a fast day and in deference to this widespread custom the
resolution excepted the week in which the ninth of Ab itself
fell, and declared that the prohibition to marry still held for
this time. Dr. J. Aub, of Berlin, expressed the views of the
majority when he said:

> Although we have long since been comforted for the
> destruction of Jerusalem, although we entertain no longer
> the wish to return to Palestine to found our own state,

since we are citizens of our fatherland, and love it with all
our heart and all our might, still, the first and second
destructions of Jerusalem were sad events, which cost so
many lives and led our people into captivity; let the memory thereof be sacred to us. But let us thank God that
we live in better times, without, however, forgetting that
catastrophe; but the observance of this day is quite sufficient; at most we will not officiate at marriages during the
one week in which this day falls. If we extend the time
of the prohibition we will weaken the impression of the
memory of the event.

The out-and-out reformers went much further than that; in
place of the traditional service of lamentation on this day, they
suggested the substitution of a service which, while it dwelt
upon all that was precious and dear in the memory of Palestine
and Jerusalem, laid the chief stress on the universalistic prophetic teachings of the faith which stands out all the more
clearly since the fortunes of the religion are no longer bound
up with the petty politics of a small country.⁹⁰ This to-day is
the vital distinction between reform Judaism, the interpreter
of the universalistic outlook of the faith, and political Zionism,
the reincarnation of narrow nationalism.

5. A widow, who has been left with a child, need not wait
longer than a year before contracting a second marriage. In
cases where the interests of the widow or the child make it
desirable that the marriage be not delayed so long, it may take
place sooner.

The traditional law was that no widow could remarry until
her youngest child was two years old on the ground that a
child requires nursing until it reaches that age. The unanimous
adoption of this reform of a traditional law is indication sufficient of the fact that the synod considered itself empowered
to make such changes in the existing Jewish marriage laws as
were made necessary by the different conditions under which
the Jews were living. In the opinion of all the men present the
state of affairs which made a two-year interval in these cases
necessary and feasible had passed, and hence a change was
necessitated in the law. This, when all is said, is the underlying
principle and justification of all reforms, be they small or great.

6. The civil marriage has full validity and sanction, according to the view of Judaism, provided that the prohibitions

enumerated in the Mosaic law are not transgressed. Still the religious ceremony is necessary to give marriage that consecration which its importance requires.

This resolution called forth a lengthy discussion. It in truth struck at the root of the whole question of the relation of Judaism to the state. Before the Jews became citizens of the lands wherein they were born or were living, the Jewish marriage law was alone valid for the Jew who desired to enter the matrimonial relation, but when he became a citizen of the state, the laws of the state became operative for him in the marriage relation as in all things. Now, in some states there were civil officers empowered to contract marriages—were such marriages legal from the Jewish standpoint, or must they be supplemented by the Jewish ceremony? There was no question with any of the members of the synod that such marriages were legal. But this was not the most serious point at issue. How about marriage ceremonies performed by a rabbi without a civil marriage having been performed or a license having been secured where this was demanded by the law of the land? Were these illegal? Was such a couple living in concubinage? The whole matter of marriage legislation had to be recast to conform with the changed relationship of Judaism to the state. The law in Prussia required civil marriage for Jews and dissenters. Hence Dr. Geiger desired a declaration on the part of the synod that a marriage contracted only according to Jewish rites in lands where a civil marriage was demanded by the law was illegal. This raised a storm of protest on the ground that to adopt such a resolution would be a reflection on Judaism, and that it was unjustifiable for a Jewish synod to declare that a marriage performed according to Jewish rites was illegal under any circumstances. Should such a marriage have been performed without compliance with the law of the land, then a divorce should be declared necessary before either party could marry again, for the ceremony had been performed in good faith. This was the overwhelming sentiment, and Geiger, in consideration thereof, surrendered. The resolution as finally adopted seemed to satisfy the many varying opinions. Although anxious and desirous of declaring their fealty to the state, the delegates were equally anxious to emphasize the religious aspect of the marriage ceremony and the high moral significance of the marriage relation. They did not wish to have marriage looked upon in the light of merely a civil contract; hence, while declaring the validity of the civil marriage, they added the further clause that marriage, being so sacred a relation, it was greatly to be desired that it receive the sanction of religion through the ceremony performed in accordance with religious rites.

7. A legal declaration of the courts concerning the identity of a deceased person and a legal certificate of death has sanction also for ritual cases.

Here, again, the synod placed itself in a line with modernity. If the courts of the land declared that a man who had disappeared was dead, or if they identified a dead body as that of such a one, the wife was to be looked upon as in the widowed state, and be permitted to remarry. The means of identification in modern days were so much better than of old, that the legislation of the Talmud in this matter necessarily had to give way to the legislation of the courts of the land.

> Unfortunately [said Dr. Aub the referee], cases still occur in which rabbis pay no regard to the voice of the age, are not cognizant of the progress that the world has made, and are still guided by the old laws which were of import in their time, because in that time it was not possible to identify people as readily as is now the case, and because, furthermore, judicial procedure in those days was not always impartial as far as Jews were concerned. Such rabbis still wish the antiquated laws to be observed, and thereby misfortune attends the life of many a woman because she must remain a widow forever. The court declares: the husband is dead, his wife is a widow. The rabbi says, "We do not know if the man was he whose identity is here declared but whose body is missing.

Therefore the commisson recommended that identification by the courts was sufficient and final."[1]

8. The provision of the Torah concerning *chalitzah* has lost all significance for us, since the conditions which gave rise to the levirate marriage and *chalitzah* no longer exist, and the idea which underlies the whole institution is foreign to our religious and social consciousness.

The non-performance of the *chalitzah* is no impediment to the widow's remarriage. Still, for the sake of freedom of conscience, no rabbi will refuse, at the request of the parties, to conduct the act of *chalitzah* in a proper form."[2]

The synod, in declaring this Mosaic institution (Deut. xxv, 4-13) without significance, merely declared officially, it is true, what had long been the case actually; but yet the resolution was significant, inasmuch as a body of Jewish notables made this public utterance regarding the invalidity of a Mosaic institution. It abandoned the orthodox position which held in regard to all such laws and institutions which were impossible of observance by the people scattered through the world that these were only suspended and not abrogated, and would be in force again when Palestine would be regained and become the home once more of the restored Jewish nationality. It was in the debate on this subject that Dr. Vogelstein drew sharply the *either-or* of the attitude toward the Biblical legislation:

> Either we say that the Biblical legislation must endure simply because it is in the Bible, although the reason for it has ceased (in that case the letter of the Bible is our sanctuary, even if the spirit has departed), or we say, we revere the Bible and we consider every word in it as wise and holy. We do not fail to recognize that through this law, which is contained in the fifth book of Moses, a beneficial institution was founded for that age; but we know that the reasons that gave rise to that law do not exist for us. We know, further, that its observance would no longer be a benefit for us, but a frightful calamity; we cannot do otherwise than abrogate it altogether. Thus we will be true to our conscience, and at the same time will assume the proper attitude of reverence toward the Bible.

9. In consideration that the tenets of Christianity and the laws of modern states are possibly even more strict than the Jewish marriage law on the subject of prohibited marriages, that they regard marriage as an ethical union, and consequently forbid in connection therewith everything that offends morality, the Israelitish synod of Augsburg declares:

That the Talmudical marriage laws touching heathen proselytes have no reference to such persons as are converted to Judaism from any one of the Christian sects.

This resolution which was offered by Dr. Adolf Jellinek, of Vienna, through Joseph von Wertheimer, was adopted unanimously without debate; after the vote, the president, Professor Lazarus, said:

In an assembly like this much appears in the transactions which is self-evident. But it is well to know many self-evident things. Twice two is four, and the multiplication table is also self-evident; but it is bad if one does not know it. So also with the content of such resolutions like the present. Let us rejoice that this is self-evident for us and that it was adopted unanimously; yet it is not unnecessary that it be adopted.

The reason for the offering and adoption of this resolution lay in the charge made so constantly by enemies of the Jews that the Talmudic legislation concerning the *nokri* and the *Akum* (heathen) refers to the Christians. This is still a favorite weapon in the hands of anti-Semites; the unanimous declaration of the Augsburg Synod is the answer of all Jews to this charge.

10. The synod resolves to appoint a commission to report to the next synod on the jurisdiction in divorce cases, viz. on the relation of rabbis to divorce and on the grounds of divorce which are still to be considered valid, keeping in view the equality of both parties to the divorce.[93]

The subject of divorce was not discussed at all at this synod. In the pre-emancipation days the rabbinical divorce had full validity among Jews; at present this is not regarded as valid in such lands where the granting of divorce is a function of the civil courts.

Intermarriage.—Dr. Emil Lehmann, of Leipzig, who was prevented from attending the synod through illness, had proposed a number of recommendations on various subjects, one of which touched the matter of intermarriage, and was as follows:[94]

> The declaration of the rabbinical conference at Brunswick in 1844 that there is no objection in Judaism to marriage between Jews and Christians, provided that the state does not demand that the children be reared in the Christian religion, still meets the views of the members of the synod to-day in accordance with the experiences of the intervening years.

The commission on the reform of the marriage law to whom this recommendation was referred suggested that it be laid on the table because it was premature in view of the existing laws in various states and that, therefore, nothing would be gained by any resolution they might pass. Geiger amended this suggestion by moving that instead of laying the matter on the table, which was equivalent to shelving it altogether, it be deferred to a later time; this would mean simply that they were not prepared to deliberate upon it at present, but would in the future. This was concurred in.

The Sabbath.—At the Breslau Conference in 1846 the Sabbath question had been discussed in all its phases; as a rather full résumé of the discussions there held has been given in a former chapter, it is unnecessary to reproduce here the arguments employed at this synod. In truth, the discussion was by no means as thorough as at Breslau; there were only some few special points which the commission submitted to the synod; these did not embrace the consideration of the whole question of Sabbath observance; the spirit at Augsburg was much more conservative than at Breslau, and there was absent all evidence of a broad comprehension of the subject in all its details. The only members of the Breslau Conference who were present at Augsburg were Geiger and Wechsler. Their remarks showed some of the spirit of the first rabbinical conferences. The particular question under discussion was whether it was permitted to ride on the Sabbath, doing away at the same time with the Talmudical casuistry of the "Sabbath boundary." The discussion had moved largely along casuistical lines, when Geiger arose and said:

> Let us not forget that we do not wish to open a casuistical discussion here, but that we must have in mind the consecration of the Sabbath and the efficacy of the religious institutions of Judaism. . . . The whole method and manner in which the Sabbath observance has been developed during the past fifteen hundred years is clearly and decidedly contradictory of the true idea of the Sabbath; the scrupulous prohibitions of a hundred and one tasks, the forced externalism—this is no longer the significance of the Sabbath. The significance of the Sabbath lies in the composure of the spirit and of our whole nature. This it is which we have constantly in view, and this cannot be achieved by paragraphs nor by combinations and comparisons of passages from the writings of the casuists. Thereby nothing is accomplished for our time.

Let us leave this alone, if we have not the courage to throw the whole casuistical legislation overboard; that were truly the best thing to do. But let us approach only the question before us and express ourselves briefly and simply. This is very clear: if it has become evident that riding on the Sabbath will enable many to attend divine services who would be otherwise prevented, it may be taken for granted that this will be decided in the affirmative by an almost unanimous vote. But it is impossible to discuss the various minutiæ of this and similar questions, viz., what the old teachers taught—men, it is true, of the deepest insight; men whose memory we revere, but who lived in their age and not in ours, in an age of altogether different views, circumstances, and conditions. Let us be concerned, then, not with this in our decisions on the points before us, but with the idea of the Sabbath, with the needs of our age.

The pronouncements of the synod on the subject of Sabbath observance were these:[95]

1. If the distance from the residence to the house of worship, or age and delicate health, prevent attendance at divine service, notably if this be of an elevating and edifying character, it is permissible to remove this obstacle by riding on Sabbath and holidays, either on the railroad or in a vehicle to the place of communal worship.

2. This permission extends also to the practice of charitable acts in such cases where delay would be dangerous.

3. The same permission holds where the purpose is educational or recreative.

An Israelite is permitted to play the organ in the house of worship on the Sabbath.[96]

The resolution offered by Dr. Wiener and adopted unanimously, on the subject of the attendance at divine service by school youth properly belongs in this place, although it did not form part of the Sabbath discussion:

In consideration of the fact that the reforms in the public services are intended for the benefit of the younger generation, but our youth remains away from the house of worship because of attendance at school, the members of the synod resolve to bend all their efforts towards inducing parents to have their children, girls as well as boys, excused from school for one hour in order to enable them to attend divine service. Only by this means can a choir be formed and maintained in small congregations. The members of the synod shall also request the school authorities to have instruction imparted only in the less important subjects during the hour of divine service on the Sabbath, so that the Jewish children will not miss much during their absence.

Circumcision.—The resolutions submitted to the Leipzig synod on this subject had been referred to a committee to report at the next synod. The subject was not considered in open session at Augsburg, but at an executive session at which nearly all the members were present. One deliverance was made on the subject, viz. the president having declared that the question had been thoroughly discussed in an executive session attended by most of the members of the synod at which session the great importance of this sign of the covenant and its maintenance as a symbol among Jews was dwelt upon and the fact deplored that it had been neglected in a number of instances, the assembly unanimously resolves:

> Although the synod premises without any reservation the supreme importance of circumcision in Judaism, it yet declares in answer to the question propounded [97] that a boy born of a Jewish mother who has not been circumcised, for whatsoever reason this may have been, must be considered a Jew, and be treated as such in all ritual matters, in accordance with the existing rules regarded binding for Israelites (Talm. Bab. Jeb. 70b, Jore Dea 264, 1).

The Proselyte Bath.—The traditional Jewish law prescribed the ritual bath as one of the conditions for entrance into Judaism, to be taken in presence of witnesses. Since women were not admissible as witnesses in ritual cases, they being in the same category as minors and incompetents from the rabbinical standpoint, it became necessary, in view of the fact that it was not uncommon at this time for women to proselytize to Judaism, for the synod to make some declaration asserting the capability of women to act in the rôle of witnesses to this act. By doing so it practically emancipated woman from the inferior position that she held under the Talmudical legislation.

Here, again, as in so many cases, it became evident that a reinterpretation of Judaism was necessary in the spirit of modernity; the resolution of the synod was:

> The assembly declares that the validity of the proselyte bath after all other prescribed preliminary conditions have been fulfilled by a woman desiring to become converted to Judaism, is made contingent upon the presence of two trustworthy Jewish women.

The Education of Cantors.—Sulzer, the great Viennese cantor, had presented a resolution at the Leipzig Synod advocating the need of a course of instruction for cantors. The idea seems to have been to train cantors with a view to enabling them to make the services which they conducted as impressive as possible. It could not be denied that a tendency of the reform movement was to make the service cold by depriving it of color. There was too much appeal to the intellect, too little to the sentiment; too much stress came to be laid on the sermon, too little on the service. "The more that religious ceremony disappears from life, the more care must be exercised to have a service in the synagogue that furthers religiosity," said Dr. Adler in discussing the subject. Hence, the synod recommended that "steps be taken to arrange courses for the training of cantors in existing teachers' seminaries, and further that institutions be called into being for the especial purpose of training Jewish cantors."

The Celebration of Chanukkah.—A noticeable constructive spirit was apparent among the delegates at this synod. They were reformers for the most part, but they wished to conserve as far as possible and to strengthen traditional institutions if these could be brought into harmony with the contemporaneous outlook. A case in point was the resolution of Dr. Szanto, of Vienna, on the question of the celebration of *Chanukkah*, the midwinter festival commemorative of the Maccabean exploits. The Viennese congregation had revived the celebration which had fallen into strange neglect, and the remarks of the mover of the resolution were directed toward the need of a general and united effort in Jewry to invest the celebration of this feast with its proper spirit. One of the delegates, Dr. Silberstein, rabbi in Buttenhausen, referred to the extensive celebration of Christmas by Jews and the corresponding neglect of their own feast that falls at the same time of the year. This matter of the celebration of *Chanukkah* first agitated at this synod has since engaged the attention of Jewish congregations touched by the modern spirit. The truth of the matter is that reform Judaism has given the *Chanukkah* feast a place in the public religious life such as it never had in the heyday of rabbinical Judaism. Not being a Biblical feast, it was given but a small place in the code, and was not of great significance in the life of the people; compared with the celebration of *Purim*, for example, *Chanukkah* was a veritable Cinderella. Now all this has quite changed, and the Augsburg Synod must be credited with having been the first public gathering to bring the subject to the attention of the people.[98]

The Revision of the Shulchan Aruk.—Although no definite action was taken on the subject, yet one of the most interesting episodes of the synod was the discussion called forth by the resolution of Dr. Wassermann, rabbi of Mühringen, declaring the necessity of a revision of the *Shulchan Aruk*. In his argument he spoke of the many discrepancies between laws of the *Shulchan Aruk,* the authoritative code of Judaism, and the life of the Jews. "This contradiction between theoretical conviction and the practical life should and must be removed." He declared, further, that this revision should be undertaken, not only with a negative, but a positive purpose. He explained this by saying that the *"Shulchan Aruk* is a pure *corpus juris;* moral injunctions are only incidental in it. I beg to call the attention of the assembly to the fact that the highest injunction of our religion after the 'Hear, O Israel,' viz., 'Thou shalt love thy neighbor as thyself,' is not to be found in the *Shulchan Aruk.* The command, 'Thou shalt love the stranger,' is in the *Torah,* but not in the *Shulchan Aruk."* "For this reason our religion has been reproached with being merely legislation and not moral teaching." We know how untrue this charge is but it has arisen from the character of the greater portion of the *Shulchan Aruk.* A commission, or call it what you will, should be appointed that has the confidence of all Israel, a new "Great Assembly" should be created which should give us a revised *Shulchan Aruk* such as our age needs and such as alone will have validity in our age. The revision and amendment of this or that provision of the *Shulchan Aruk,* as has been proposed and in instances resolved upon in this assembly, is only a makeshift; what is necessary is a thorough, broad and comprehensive treatment of the whole subject, the compilation of a code in consonance with the religious conceptions and needs of our age.

Szanto declared himself as opposed to the suggestion, because if a revision of the code were undertaken, there would be an acknowledgment of the authority of the code. "I am a conservative Jew . . . yet in my orthodoxy I concede no such authority to the *Shulchan Aruk*. I believe in verbal tradition, I am no Karaite. . . . No man has the right to lay down a law or to codify it; God alone has that right. What God has said is in the Bible; and of whatever is not in the Bible I say, with Omar, that is not of God, else God had said it." He declared, further, that there had always been free discussion and development in Judaism. When Maimonides codified the laws of the Talmud he had no idea of making this an authority, but merely a compendium. The same is the case with the *Shulchan Aruk;* it is a compendium like any other handbook that one refers to whenever he wishes to know the exact wording of the law. "If we undertake a revision, we declare ourselves Karaites, worshipers of the letter, who obey not the holy word of God, but the word of man. . . . The *Shulchan Aruk* cannot be revised because it is not our lawbook." This argument is most interesting because of its casuistical character. It is in part true and in part not. True, in the statement that there was always development in Judaism; not true in the declaration that the *Shulchan Aruk* is not the authoritative law-book for orthodox Judaism. The acceptance of the authority of the *Shulchan Aruk* was the cause of the cessation of any development in Judaism after the sixteenth century, when it was compiled, to the beginning of the nineteenth, when the reform movement arose. Szanto belonged to that school of conservative Jews who were in reality reformers, but were not clear in their own thought. His statements just quoted are an excellent gauge of the confusion of thought of so many who have not grasped the essential fundamentals of the reform movement, but are far removed from the true traditionalists for whom the rabbinical codes are absolute norm and authority.

Adler, rabbi of Cassel, stated that so much commanded in the *Shulchan Aruk* had fallen out of the life of the Jews that were they to begin to revise the code very little would be left. "Let us point to the Bible, let us say, the spirit of religion, the spirit of eternal truth, which is in the Bible is also the spirit of the moral laws; the Decalogue is our foundation, and whatever has grown out of this is the kernel of our religion. Then we will have a spiritual revision and every revision of the *Shulchan Aruk* is unnecessary."

Klingenstein, editor of a newspaper, *Der Israelitische Lehrer,* opposed the suggestion on the very good ground that were a new *Shulchan Aruk* to be codified, this would mean simply that development had ceased; in two or three centuries this codification would be petrified, as is the case with the *Shulchan Aruk* now, and a new revision would be necessary then. No bibliolatry; the synod has been created in order that our religious life remain fluid.

Dr. Nehemias Brüll, the learned rabbi of Frankfort, spoke but a few words, but they were remarkably to the point: "We regret that the fluid word of the Talmud codified in the *Shulchan Aruk* has become fixed, and we would not like to see a new edition and revision of this book, a proceeding which could only be injurious to the development of Judaism. Every new revision is a recognition of the book, which, as a religious codex, has no value for us. I move that we should declare openly that the *Shulchan Aruk* has no significance for us as a religious codex, the views written down in the *Shulchan Aruk* never were our theoretical conviction and never should be such." Had the synod acted upon this suggestion, what a service it would have rendered! To have declared in open assembly that the *Shulchan Aruk* had no significance for the Jew as a religious authority would have been sufficient to have made this synod ever memorable in the history of Jewish thought. But the delegates did not rise to the occasion. The incident closed with Wassermann's withdrawal of his resolution.

The Augsburg Synod is of little real significance; the discussions for the most part were commonplace and lacked strength and power. The best utterance of the synod was the declaration of what it stood for, a document of seven paragraphs adopted just before final adjournment on July 17. This was really the valedictory of the German synods, since no other convened; it was concurred in unanimously, with great acclaim, and was couched in these terms:

The synod declares—

1. Since the days of its inception in hoary antiquity, Judaism has passed through many phases of development,

and in them has unfolded its inmost being more and more. A new and highly significant crisis has occurred in its history. The spirit of the true knowledge of God and of pure morality is filling more and more the consciousness of mankind and is impressing itself constantly on the life of the nations, on state and people, on art and science. Judaism joyfully recognizes in this phenomenon an approach to those aims which have at all times guided its course through history.

2. The essence and mission of Judaism remain unchangeable in themselves, but the mighty change which is taking place constantly in the views of all mankind, and of the followers of Judaism in particular, as well as the entirely new position of the latter among the nations, has called forth an urgent necessity for reorganization of many of the forms of Judaism.

3. Judaism from its inception always stood for knowledge, and has likewise constantly premised and demanded harmony between thought, feeling, and deed. Along this line it seeks courageously and confidently to effect the above-mentioned change. It follows only its innermost instincts when, with full esteem for the higher and eternal possessions of life, and with due recognition and reverence for the past, guided by the results of earnest, scientific research, it strives to do away with antiquated and inappropriate customs and to forge ahead in consonance with the spirit of the times.

4. The synod aims to be the organ of this development. In it the living convictions and efforts of Judaism of to-day are to find decided expression. With clear purpose, it aims to bring about the result that the reorganization striven for during several decades should be as widely acceptable as possible and should be carried to a successful conclusion with due regard to the needs of all our co-religionists. It would protect the bond of unity, which twines about all our coreligionists, against disintegration, and would further with all its power the common higher interests in life and science.

5. The synod claims for its resolutions no other validity than that which the force of truth, of sacred earnestness and of firm conviction imparts. It knows, however, that this power, the only one which should be effective in

the realm of religion, is irresistible and must finally gain the victory in spite of all difficulties and obstructions.

6. While the synod seeks to meet the demands of the times, it is convinced of the fact that it is working for the maintenance of Judaism. Thus it feels itself in unison with the spirit of Judaism in its whole historical development, at one with all its coreligionists of whatever tendency, and hopes to bring about reconciliation, not immediately, it is true, and not through the denial of convictions, but through the spirit of truth which, according to our old teachers, is the essential condition of peace.

7. The mission of the synod is not to be confined to the above declarations. Considering the intimate relation existing between religious life and social and political conditions, it seems rather to the synod to be a peremptory duty that in the matters which will come before it fitting expression be given to the consciousness of relationship in the matter of the political and social standing of our coreligionists.

The tendency of the Augsburg Synod was of a decidedly reform character, as appeared constantly during the discussions. The synodal declaration of the non-validity of even such impossible institutions as *chalitzah,* and the official permission to disregard the refinements of Talmudical casuistry on the subject of Sabbath legislation, as well as the entire spirit of this gathering, enraged the rabbinical orthodox party from whose midst emanated shortly after the adjournment of the synod a protest signed by one hundred and thirty-three rabbis of Germany, Holland, Austria, Hungary, France, and Denmark, which contained the following pronunciamento:

1. Rabbis, preachers, and other Israelites who officiate at a marriage prohibited in the Bible or in the rabbinical legislation; also such as declare this or that Biblical or rabbinical marriage prohibition as no longer obligatory; finally such as join assemblages which question the validity of Jewish marriage prohibitions, all these are unfit to perform any rabbinical functions whatsoever.

2. Therefore, every God-fearing Israelite is warned not to have such individuals officiate at marriages, divorces, *Chalitzah,* and so forth.

3. *Shochtim* and *Soferim* (ritual slaughterers and

scribes) who obtain their authority from such rabbis without having their worthiness and capability attested to by a rabbi faithful to the law are to be considered as unauthorized.

4. Israelitish congregations are obligated to lend their energies towards turning out of office all such rabbis and preachers as are designated in paragraph 1. Should the observant members of a congregation be in the minority, and therefore be unable to secure the removal of such rabbis from office, they are obligated to provide for the proper administration of rabbinical functions, in accordance with the strict requirements of the law, even though this compel them to sever their connection with the congregation.⁹⁹

This protest is animated by the same spirit as appeared in the condemnation of Geiger by the Lissa rabbinate and in the famous protest of the one hundred and sixteen rabbis against the Brunswick Conference, well-nigh thirty years previously; nor is it surprising. The standpoint of orthodoxy is fixed. Thirty years, or thirty centuries bring no change. Any infringement is illegal. But protests like this are vain. They are mere card-houses erected against the onrush of the forces of progress. The rabbinical marriage and divorce legislation is Oriental and out of all harmony with Western life. This legislation must be largely the concern of the civil courts; the rabbinical tribunals must give way to these courts wherever Jews have become incorporated in the body politic of the State. Holdheim struck the true note when, as early as 1845, he insisted on a reform all along the line of the Jewish marriage law and an adjustment thereof to the laws of the land. This has been practically accomplished. Occidental life has legislated *chalitzah* and the rabbinical divorce out of existence, all protests to the contrary notwithstanding.

When the Augsburg Synod adjourned, many present must have felt that it would have no successor.¹⁰⁰ The two synods failed to realize the hopes of their projectors. The time was evidently not yet ripe for such a movement. There were too many differences among Jews. No steps were taken after adjournment of the synods to spread actively the resolutions adopted. True, the proceedings were printed after the lapse of a considerable interval, but beyond that no active propaganda were made. Yet although as far as permanent results are concerned these two German synods must be written down a failure, still has the synod idea persisted and come to the fore frequently since then. At that very time (1871), American leaders of religious thought were agitating for a synod; again, in 1881, Isaac M. Wise submitted a report to the Rabbinical Literary Association advocating the formation of a synod. The most recent agitation of the subject has been witnessed at three sessions of the Central Conference of American Rabbis (1904-05-06).[101] Opinions are still divided as to the advisability of the establishment of such an institution. Its opponents fear that it will resolve itself into an ecclesiastical court that will institute trials for heresy if its behests are not obeyed. This is a vain fear, for heresy trials are un-Jewish in the first place, and in the second place they belong to the Middle Ages, not to the twentieth century. There can be little doubt that in the present unsettled state of Jewish opinion on many vital points, owing to the transition from the old to the new, there is great need for a central organization of this kind composed of rabbinical and lay delegates, whose power shall be not to loose or to bind, but to pronounce judgments on controverted points of doctrine and practice. The synod "shall not be an ecclesiastical court with power to dictate to the individual conscience, to restrict or interfere with freedom of either belief or conduct. The purpose of such a synod in our judgment is to guide by a consensus of academic and practical wisdom and thereby educate Jewish public opinion."[102] Some such purpose undoubtedly animated the rabbis who convened these German synods; Jewish life is tending toward centralization and organization, and the institution of a synod on American soil would but carry out established precedents in the history of the reform movement, so many of whose ideas and plans, born in German Jewish brains, have found their realization in the United States. It is indeed not beyond the bounds of probability, judging from the development of Judaism in the great Republic, that a latter-day *Keneset Haggedolah,* a new Great Synod, will greet the light of day within its boundaries.

CHAPTER XII

REFORM IN THE UNITED STATES

ALTHOUGH the Jewish reform movement had its inception in Germany, and that country will always be looked upon as its birthplace, yet has this movement found its full, free, and logical development in the United States. It was, in most instances, German preachers and thinkers who, in the early days, shaped the course of the American congregations in their adoption of the principles of reform. There is therefore a direct connection between the practical outworking of these principles in the United States and their primal enunciation in Germany. The very first effort at reform, made some years before any of the great European leaders arrived in the United States seems to indicate this. In the year 1824,[1] forty-seven members of the congregation Beth Elohim of Charleston, in the State of South Carolina, being dissatisfied with the services, memorialized the vestry to have the ritual reformed. This memorial contains a lengthy quotation from the *Frankfurter Journal,* thus showing that the Americans were influenced by the religious agitations that were stirring the Jews of Germany so profoundly at that time.[2] As the first document of this kind it is interesting, and the main portions are herewith presented:

Your memorialists seek no other end than the future welfare and respectability of the nation. As members of the great family of Israel, they cannot consent to place before their children examples which are only calculated to darken the mind and withhold from the rising generation the more rational means of worshiping the true God.

It is to this, therefore, your memorialists would, in the first place, invite the serious attention of your honorable body. By causing the *Hazan* or reader to *repeat* in English such part of the Hebrew prayers as may be deemed necessary, it is confidently believed that the congregation generally would be more forcibly impressed with the

329

necessity of divine worship, and the moral obligations which they owe to themselves and their Creator; while such a course would lead to more decency and decorum during the time they are engaged in the performance of religious duties. It is not every one who has the means, and many have not the time, to acquire a knowledge of the Hebrew language, and consequently become enlightened in the principles of Judaism. What, then, is the course pursued in all religious societies for the purpose of disseminating the peculiar tenets of their faith among the poor and uninformed?

The principles of their religion are expounded to them from the pulpit in language that they understand; for instance, in the Catholic, the German, and the French Protestant Churches; by this means the ignorant part of mankind attend their places of worship with some profit to their morals, and even improvement to their minds; they return from them with hearts turned to piety, and with feelings elevated by their sacred character. In this consists the beauty of religion—when men are invoked by its divine spirit to the practice of virtue and morality. . . .

With regard to such parts of the service as it is desired should undergo this change, your memorialists would strenuously recommend that the most solemn portions be retained, and everything superfluous excluded; and that the principal parts, and, if possible, all that is read in *Hebrew,* should also be read in *English* (that being the language of the country), so as to enable every member of the congregation fully to understand each part of the service.

In submitting this article of our memorial to your honorable body, your memorialists are well aware of the difficulties with which they must contend before they will be enabled to accomplish this desirable end; but while they would respectfully invite the attention of your honorable body to this part of their memorial, they desire to rest the propriety and expediency of such a measure solely upon the reason by which it may be maintained. . . .

Your memorialists would next call the particular attention of your honorable body to the absolute necessity of *abridging* the service generally. They have reflected seriously upon its present length, and are confident that this is one of the principle causes why so much of it is hastily and improperly hurried over. . . .

According to the present method of reading the Parasa (Pentateuch), it affords to the hearer neither instruction nor entertainment, unless he be competent to read, as well as *comprehend,* the Hebrew language. But if, like all other ministers, our reader would make a chapter or verse the subject of an English discourse once a week, at the expiration of the year the people would, at all events, know something of that religion which at present they so little regard.[3]

This memorial was signed by forty-seven members of the congregation. It was emphatically rejected by the vestry without discussion. This summary action caused some who had signed the petition to resign from the congregation. Twelve of their number founded a new congregation, on November 21, 1824, which they styled "The Reformed Society of Israelites."[4] By July, 1826, the number had increased to over fifty. The formation of this first reformed congregation on this side the Atlantic, then, had its cause in the feeling that the expression of the faith was not in accord with the changed needs and conditions of the people. It was a movement from within; it was the people themselves who, longing for an intelligible service, sought to change the established form of worship. In the statement they issued, after the secession from the congregation, they declared that it was their purpose to discard the observance of all such ceremonies as had their origin altogether and alone in rabbinical Judaism, such as are not founded on the moral legislation of Moses, but, on the other hand, flatly oppose in many respects the spirit, the beauty, and sublimity which so singly distinguish that legislation and the lofty piety and virtue that it teaches.[5]

It was not merely an æsthetic impulse that swayed these men in their desire for a reform of the public worship, but there was also a question of principle. There were certain articles in the commonly accepted creed to which they could not give assent. In formulating the creed that expressed their beliefs they omitted the sections of the traditional Maimonidean creed that declared the belief in the coming of the personal Messiah, and the bodily resurrection. The creed, as by them adopted, consisted of ten articles, as follows:

I believe, with a perfect faith, that God Almighty (blessed be his name!) is the Creator and Governor of all creation; and that he alone has made, does make, and will make, all things.

I believe, with a perfect faith, that the Creator (blessed be his name!) is only One in Unity; to which there is no resemblance; and that he alone has been, is, and will be God.

I believe, with a perfect faith, that the Creator (blessed be his name!) is not corporeal, nor to be comprehended by any understanding capable of comprehending only what is corporeal; and that there is nothing like him in the universe.

I believe, with a perfect faith, that the Creator (blessed be his name!) is the only true object of adoration, and that no other being whatsoever ought to be worshiped.

I believe, with a perfect faith, that the soul of man is breathed into him by God, and is therefore immortal.

I believe, with a perfect faith, that the Creator (blessed be his name!) knows all things, and that he will reward those who observe his commands, and punish those who transgress them.

I believe, with a perfect faith, that the laws of God, as delivered by Moses in the Ten Commandments, are the only true foundations of piety towards the Almighty and of morality among men.

I believe, with a perfect faith, that morality is essentially connected with religion, and that good faith towards all mankind is among the most acceptable offerings to the Deity.

I believe, with a perfect faith, that the love of God is the highest duty of his creatures, and that the pure and upright heart is the chosen temple of Jehovah.

I believe, with a perfect faith, that the Creator (blessed be his name!) is the only true Redeemer of all his children, and that he will spread the worship of his name over the whole earth.

From the very beginning the members of the congregations gave public evidence of the faith that was in them. In their services they made radical departures from the traditional ritual. On the Sabbath eve the service opened with the reading of the ninety-second and ninety-third Psalms in English; then followed the recitation of the שמע in Hebrew and English; the ברכת שבע, greatly abbreviated, in English, with the exception of the אלהי נצור, which was recited in Hebrew and English; the עלינו prayer in English. Thereupon a chapter from one of the prophetical books was read, the congregation sang a hymn, the reader offered an original prayer, and closed the service with the priestly benediction.

The Sabbath morning service was opened with an English hymn and a prayer by the reader; then followed the thirty-third Psalm, the prayers אלהי נשמה and אתה קדשת in English, the שמע, the ברכת שבע, and selected verses from the Psalms in Hebrew and English; the prayer for the country, the reading from the scroll of the law, the sermon, an English hymn, a prayer, and the priestly benediction. On the holidays special prayers, appropriate to the occasion, were inserted.° There was instrumental music. The congregation worshiped with uncovered heads.

This first reformed congregation existed but a few years. It had no leader. Laymen delivered the address and conducted the services. Good as were their intentions, and talented as some of them were, yet they had not the training to carry on the work; besides, there was bitter opposition from without. These reasons led to the dissolution of the society; but the cause of reform, though temporarily in abeyance, was to awaken into stronger and fuller life in the mother congregation itself, to which a number of the reformers returned.

In the year 1836 the Reverend Gustav Poznanski was elected preacher and reader of the congregation Beth Elohim. While in Hamburg he had been imbued with the spirit of the Hamburg Temple congregation, the foremost exponent of the reform movement in Europe, and after entering upon his charge in Charleston, he bent all his energies toward introducing reforms into the service. The synagogue having been destroyed by fire in the great conflagration of 1838, which laid a large portion of the city waste, a new building—at the time the finest Jewish house of worship in the country—was erected. While it was building, a petition signed by thirty-eight members, and requesting that an organ be placed in the new structure, was granted by the congregation in meeting assembled. The petition was accompanied by the written opinion of the minister to the effect that such a step was lawful. As is unfortunately always the case, the innovation caused strife and contention. Opposition on the part of those wedded to the old order of things was a feature in all the reform movements in the congregations. Religious reforms always arouse the bitterness of bigotry and kindle the flame of fanaticism. This is deplorable enough when confined to inner contentions, but at times the quarrels engendered were referred to the civil courts, as was the case in Charleston,[7] a חילול השם indeed.

At the dedication services held on March 19, 1841, the minister in his sermon said: "This country is our Palestine, this city our Jerusalem, this house of God our temple." When, two years later, Mr. Poznanski advocated the abolition of the second day holidays, as not being Biblical in origin, a bitter contest was again precipitated, which lasted for a number of years. The outcome of the struggle was a victory for the reform party; the second day holidays were abolished, and other minor reforms introduced into the service.

The story of the Charleston movement has been given somewhat at length, since that congregation inaugurated Jewish reform in the United States. Reforms in greater or less degree have been so commonly introduced by the congregations of the country that all that is possible here is to give the account of the movement in its general aspects rather than the history of special congregations. However, it will not be amiss to state at what time and under what circumstances, the older congregations ranged themselves on the side of reform, particularly since Judaism in the United States is congregational. The congregation is autonomous. There is no chief rabbi, no consistory, no synod, no assembly;[8] each congregation is responsible to itself, and hence it lies with the congregation, and it alone, to determine what its policy shall be.

The Early Reform Congregations

With the exception of the Charleston congregation, there were no steps taken anywhere in the country in the interest of the reform movement before the year 1840. In all the congregations the services were conducted along traditional lines.[9] In truth, with but few exceptions, the reform congregations represent a growth, a gradual adoption of various reforms, in the ritual and the congregational polity.[10]

It is noticeable that such early congregations as have from the date of their organization been reform, grew out of societies, "Reform-Vereine," which were formed for the purpose of giving expression to the doctrines of reform. When these societies became strong enough they organized themselves into congregations. Such societies were the foundation of the congregations Har Sinai of Baltimore, Emanuel of New York, Keneseth Israel of Philadelphia, and Sinai of Chicago.

The first congregation organized as a reform congregation was the Har Sinai of Baltimore. In April, 1842, a number of young men, influenced by the Hamburg Temple movement, formed themselves into a society known as the Har Sinai Verein; they adopted the Hamburg Temple Prayer-Book for their services, which were conducted by several of their own number. Three years later, in 1845, the Emanuel congregation of New York,[11] at present the largest congregation in the land, was organized by a number of young men whose purpose may be gathered from the following words addressed to Mr. Poznanski:

> We fully recognize the necessity of a complete reform of the Jewish service, as at present conducted in the local German congregations; we have therefore formed ourselves into a society which we have called "Cultus-Verein," and have resolved to provide ourselves with such means and to seek such instruction and information as shall enable us later to conduct, in a congregation to be formed from our society, such a service as, freed from abuses tolerated hitherto, shall arouse and quicken devotion, and thus uplift the heart to God.[12]

The congregation was the direct outgrowth of the "Cultus-Verein." Its first service was conducted on the eve of Passover, 5605 (1845), in a room in a private house; the sermon was preached by the Reverend Dr. Leo Merzbacher, who continued as the rabbi of the young congregation until the time of his death in October, 1856. The next congregation to place itself in line was that of Albany, New York. In the year 1846 this congregation had elected as its minister Isaac M. Wise, who had recently arrived in the country. Under his leadership a number of reforms were introduced, notably the mixed choir, family pews and the confirmation ceremony. At the service on New Year's Day, 1850, Dr. Wise was forcibly ejected from his pulpit by some opponents of his reform ideas. The primary cause of this act of violence lay in the following circumstance.

In the spring of 1850 a public debate had been arranged to take place in Charleston between Mr. Poznanski and the Reverend Dr. Raphall of New York, a champion of orthodoxy, on the subject of the justification of the reforms that had been introduced by the former. Dr. Wise, who happened to be in Charleston at the time, was present, and took part in the discussion. Dr. Raphall put the direct question to him as to whether he believed in the coming of the Messiah and the bodily resurrection. Dr. Wise answered, "No." When he returned to Albany the orthodox element in his congregation was not slow in making its dissatisfaction felt. The opposition culminated in the act of violence mentioned. As a result, the friends and supporters of the rabbi withdrew and organized themselves into a reform congregation, the Anshe Emeth.[13]

For the next step in the story of the reform congregations we must direct our attention to what was then the western settlement of the country. The oldest congregations in the West were those of Cincinnati. In 1824 a number of young Englishmen organized the first Jewish congregation west of the Alleghanies, the Bene Israel;[14] in 1842 a company of young Germans formed themselves into the congregation Bene Yeshurun.[15] Both these congregations were at their origin orthodox, but with the election of Dr. Wise as rabbi of Bene Yeshurun in 1854, and of Dr. Max Lilienthal as rabbi of Bene Israel in 1855, these two congregations designated their sympathy with the reform movement.

The city of Philadelphia was, in the fifth and sixth decades the century, the stronghold of orthodox Judaism, owing largely to the prestige and influence of the Reverend Isaac Leeser, minister of the Mikveh Israel congregation of that city, and the foremost representative of orthodox Judaism in the country. Any effort at reform in that community naturally met with the greatest obstacles, and the pages of the *Occident,* the organ of Mr. Leeser, present a vivid picture of the opposition superinduced by every step toward reform anywhere in the country. Yet the spirit was aroused, and made itself felt even in Philadelphia. There, too, as in Baltimore and New York, some young men had organized a "Reform-Gesellschaft." Few in number, but strong in purpose, they maintained their organization for some years, until in 1856 they united with one of the existing congregations of the city, the Keneseth Israel, which had been formed in 1847, and in the intervening years had also introduced a few minor reforms into its service. From the union of this congregation with the Reform-Gesellschaft in 1856 the persent Keneseth Israel Reform Congregation sprang.[16]

In 1858 some members of the Anshe Maarab congregation of Chicago, being dissatisfied with the services and the course of the congregation, formed a society which they called the "Reformverein," with the avowed intention of organizing themselves into a congregation as soon as their number reached thirty. At the first public session of the society held on April 17, 1858, the secretary, B. Felsenthal, afterwards the first rabbi of the newly formed congregation, addressed the company on the object of the society. In the course of his remarks he said:

How can the abuses which have crept into our religion be corrected? We must separate the eternal and indestructible kernel of Judaism from its tattered encasings, must remove the antiquated notions, and make the service fruitful and intelligible by the use of a language understood by all. Not two per cent of the members of any Jewish congregation are sufficiently conversant with the Hebrew language to invest the service with dignity or to clothe it with intelligibility; the whole service has been degraded to the level of a dead formula. . . .

A small number of men have here combined to arouse new life in Jewish hearts. A spark at least is still smoldering beneath the ashes of indifference, and this spark must be fanned into flame. The Jews will not permit the work of their fathers, that has existed thousands of years, to be destroyed: they will show the world by new progressive movements that they are still the chosen people, destined to become the Messiah of the nations of the earth.[17]

Two years later, in 1860, the society formed itself into the Sinai congregation. The preamble [18] to the constitution adopted by this congregation expresses the purpose and object of a reformed congregations so clearly that it may well be given at length:

Whereas, there appears to exist among Israelites a large degree of indifference in religious matters, threatening to drag life more and more to materialism and degradation, and stifling all nobility of sentiments, all sympathy for higher pursuits, all appreciation of the more sacred boons of humanity, while, on the other hand, Jewish religious life, clinging to obsolete ideas and maintaining antiquated usages, has taken its course in a direction of which we cannot approve; and,

Whereas, we share the conviction that a truly religious life is the most powerful agent to create noble thoughts and good morals; and,

Whereas, especially the Jewish religion, having a past of four thousand years, most glorious and eventful, is evidently destined in the future too to act a most important part in the development of mankind, and in its onward course to the lofty position of the Messianic time coming:

Therefore, a number of Israelites have associated with the avowed intention of fostering the inestimable inheritance of our fathers, of restoring the original spirit of simplicity, purity, and sublimity in Judaism, and thus to perpetuate the same and secure its duration.

The means of attaining this sacred object are chiefly as follows:

1. A divine service, which, without divesting the same of its specific Jewish character, shall be in consistence with the laws of reason and truth, and which, in its form, shall be such as will meet the demands of our time, claiming public instruction from the pulpit as a part of the same.

2. A sound religious education for the rising generation, by maintaining a school in which at least a thorough instruction in religion, Hebrew, and the branches connected therewith, be imparted—a school inspiring the tender hearts of the children for Judaism, and for everything that is good, just, and noble.

3. The removal of usages and ceremonies partly outlived and partly based upon erroneous conceptions, and the substitution of others more vital, more truthful, and more apt to produce blissful effects, and the formation of such agencies and institutions which tend directly or indirectly to promote and fulfill the objects of religion and to advance its professors to a higher stage of perfection.

These are the most important congregational movements in the early history of Jewish reform in the United States. Since

1860 the movement has made great progress; there are but few older congregations of influence that have not adopted reforms of some kind, some to a greater, some to a less extent. Even such congregations as are considered conservative in this country would in European lands be regarded as reformed.

The great recent influx of Russian Jews has increased the number of orthodox congregations; this accounts for the increasing number of such congregations during the past four decades. However, even many of these immigrants, after living in the country for some time, affiliate themselves with reform congregations. The free spirit of American institutions is impatient of the restraints of rabbinical legislation as embodied in the *Shulchan Aruk*. The descendants of the immigrants, even in the first generation, are so affected by the free school, the free state and the free atmosphere in which they live and move and have their being, that they can impossibly entertain the religious views of their orthodox forebears. Frequently they swing to the opposite extreme and become outspokenly irreligious and atheistic. The saving religious influence in their life are the teachings of reform that harmonize the faith with the free surroundings.

The Leaders of the Reform Movement

Every movement among men, in order to issue successfully, requires ability, conviction, and enthusiasm in its leaders. Without any doubt, the reform movement took such firm hold in the United States because in its early days it was led and directed by men of great ability, strong purpose, deep conviction, earnest enthusiasm, and scholarly aims. The first attempt in Charleston collapsed because it was not headed by a capable leader. The earnest men who composed that first "Reformed Society of Israelites" failed to succeed because there was no one to direct them. It was fortunate for the success of the movement elsewhere that a number of strong men, dissatisfied with conditions in Europe and despairing of accomplishing their cherished aims there, emigrated to America and shaped the policy of the congregations. The people themselves were ready for the reforms; they had organized reform societies, but these languished until they were taken in hand by the men who stand as the true and tried leaders of those formative days. Mentioning them in the order of their appearance in American Jewish life, these will ever be regarded as the great pioneer preachers and workers in the cause of reform; Max Lilienthal, who arrived in New York in 1845; Isaac M. Wise, who came the following year, in 1846; David Einhorn, whose work began in Baltimore in 1855; Samuel Adler, who was called to New York in 1857; Bernard Felsenthal, whose *Kol Kore Bamidbar,* "the voice in the wilderness," was raised in Chicago in 1858; and Samuel Hirsch, who took charge of the congregation in Philadelphia in 1866.

How clearly these men understood and defined the issues, will appear from words spoken or written in those early years of their American sojourn. In one form or another, they express what to them are the essentials and characteristics of the reform movement. In sermons of burning eloquence, or in disquisitions of calm reasoning, they published forth the faith that was in them.

Max Lilienthal [19] (1814-1882) arrived in America in 1845. He was elected rabbi of three orthodox congregations of New York City, in which capacity he served for several years, but severed the connection on account of the differences that had arisen between his views and those of his constituencies. His opinions were changing and taking a decided trend toward the principles of reform. He was one of the most active spirits in the organization of the "Verein der Lichtfreunde," a society formed in 1849 for the discussion and the spreading of the teachings of the reform movement. In a lecture delivered before this society in that year, he said: "The bridge between the past and the present is broken off." He retired from the ministry for a number of years, and opened a school. In the year 1854, however, he again entered the arena of active Jewish life by writing for *The Asmonean;* in a number of articles published in the columns of this paper, and in *The Israelite,* shortly thereafter, he declared strongly for reform. In 1855 he was elected rabbi of the congregation Bene Israel, Cincinnati, which office he filled to the day of his death. He led the congregation along the path of reform. Characteristic was the statement he made shortly after assuming office in Cincinnati, when refusing to conduct the traditional service of lamentation on the ninth day of Ab; he said that he considered the destruction of Jerusalem a reason for rejoicing rather than mourning, as it was the cause of the Jews spreading all over the world and carrying the light of monotheism everywhere. In one of the early articles on reform, alluded to above, he wrote: [20]

We are tired of seeing men violating the Sabbath until they have accumulated an independent fortune, and calling themselves orthodox nevertheless; we are disgusted at seeing men transgressing every religious ceremony in public life, and yet clothing themselves with the halo of sanctification. We wish to see this contradiction solved: we wish to know when religious ceremonies have to yield to the necessities of life and when they have to be kept at any price, subjugating life and its exigencies. In a word, we wish to know what in our law is God's command and what is the transient work of mortal man. Such an investigation will solve the contradiction between life and religion; will raise the Mosaic law to its divine purity; will do away with all the unfounded conglomerations of different ages; and will surely reunite the now distracted body of Israel in peace and harmony. . . .

Reform has tried and tries to raise the dignity of our worship. No one will deny that the worship as conducted in the old synagogues is unsatisfactory. . . . How many prayers are there unbecoming the country we live in; unfit for our mode of thinking, totally antagonistic to the changed views and feelings! Reform tries to find a remedy for all these abuses and to make the house of the Lord a house of true prayer and devotion. . . .

Whether agreed to or not, it is a fact that the belief in a great many things, that fifty years ago were considered holy and sacred, has been greatly shaken. No one will be quieted by such sentences as "the Minhag of Israel is as binding as the law of Moses." Men of learning and profound reasoning have clearly shown the historical development of so many of our ceremonies, and the belief that the rabbinical law, from A to Z, has come down from Sinai, has totally disappeared. Scientific researches have proved that all nations and times have added to the store of our religious observances, and that all therefore cannot be as holy as the Bible. Further researches will restore our religion to its primitive purity and simplicity; will remove each and every contest; and unite us again in the firm belief in the Holy One, for whom our fathers suffered and for whom also we, their descendants, are ready to make every sacrifice. . . . We are no reformers from inclination, no reformers for fashion's sake, but reformers from conviction. We do not belong to that frivolous or arrogant class that do away and abolish because it suits them just now. No; what we assert we intend to prove; and where we shall move the abolition of any ceremony, we shall not do it without showing that the religious codes themselves entitle us to demand such a change and such a reform.

Isaac M. Wise [21] (1819-1900) was the great organizer and unifier. His mind was eminently of the constructive order; he translated theory into actuality and called institutions into being which attest the living power of progressive Judaism. From the moment almost of his landing on these shores he became a power in American Judaism. It is not too much to say that, more than any other man, he stamped his individuality upon the history and development of Jewish life in the United States. His is the most prominent rabbinical name in American Jewry. His activity of over half a century as organizer, editor, preacher, educator, is part of the history of the reform movement whose untiring advocate he was from the very beginning. He was the embodiment of the free democratic spirit. For over fifty years he was tirelessly active in the cause of freedom in religion. For him American Judaism represented a new phase in the history of the ancestral faith. Undismayed, unafraid, idealistic, optimistic, he preached, wrote and taught the ultimate triumph of the principles of prophetic Judaism as reinterpreted by the theology of the reform movement. In an article written in the year 1854, he said: [22]

Our religion contains better elements than a mere controversial and casuistical rabbinism, and these better elements must be considered the primary cause of its self-preservation. The Jew had the consciousness that he alone possesses the most philosophical views of the existence and nature of the Deity; of the nature, duties, and hopes of mankind; of justice, equity, and charity; of the several relations between God and his creatures, and between man and his fellow-man. With this sublime conviction he first stood in the midst of degraded and superstitious heathenism, then by the side of persecuting Catholicism, and finally opposed to a ridiculous mysticism. . . . The Jew, however, felt conscious of the verities of his religion, and therefore he loved them better than his life and worldly interests; he saw himself alone in the world, alone with his sublime ideas, and therefore he lived in his faith and for it, and the thousand forms which he observed only led him to his sublime ideas. It was this elevating and inspiring consciousness, and not rabbinism, which preserved Judaism. But now the idea, the sublime cardinal elements, are almost lost sight of in the multitude of thoughtless observances of rabbinical forms. . . . Judaism has become a set of unmeaning practices, and the intelligent Jew either mourns for the fallen daughter of Zion or has adopted a course of frivolity and indifference. Therefore we demand reforms. All unmeaning forms must be laid aside as outworn garments. The internal spirit of Judaism must be expounded, illustrated, and made dear again to the Jew. We must inform our friends and opponents that there is a Judaism independent of its forms, and that this is Judaism emphatically. It is therefore our principle of reform: "All forms to which no meaning is attached any longer are an impediment to our religion, and must be done away with." Before we propose to abolish anything we should inquire, What is its practical benefit? If there is none it is time to renounce it, for one dead limb injures the whole body. Another principle of reform is this: "Whatever makes us ridiculous before the world as it now is, may safely be and should be abolished," for we are in possession of an intelligent religion, and the nations from our precept and example should be led to say, "This is a wise and intelligent people."

A third principle of reform is this, "Whatever tends to the elevation of the divine service, to inspire the heart of the worshiper and attract him, should be done without any unnecessary delay," for the value of divine service must be estimated according to its effect upon the heart and understanding.

A fourth principle of reform is this, "Whenever religious observances and the just demands of civilized society exclude each other, the former have lost their power"; for religion was taught for the purpose "to live therein and not to die therein"; our religion makes us active members of civilized society, hence we must give full satisfaction to its just demands.

Last, or rather first, it must be remarked, the leading star of reform must be the maxim, "Religion is intended to make man happy, good, just, active, charitable, and intelligent." Whatever tends to this end is truly religious, and must be retained or introduced if it does not yet exist. Whatever has an effect contrary to the above must be abolished as soon as possible.

David Einhorn (1809-1879), whose name has appeared frequently in these pages as one of the foremost reformers in Germany, easily sustained his prestige as one of the leading spirits of the liberal movement after his arrival in the United States. In many an inspiring sermon and in many a learned article he expressed the fundamental principles of reform. His words ring with the earnestness of conviction, and are eloquent with the enthusiastic outpourings of a spirit akin to that of the prophets of old. Israel's Messianic mission, Judaism's true inwardness, these form the constant refrain of the remarkable utterances of this man, whose lips were touched with the coal of living fire taken from the altar of God. In the very first sermon that he preached in the United States, his inaugural address before the Har Sinai congregation in Baltimore, he stated in broad and clear lines his conception of Judaism. From that sermon the subjoined paragraphs are taken as indicative of his thought:

Like man himself, the child of God, the divine law has a perishable body and an imperishable spirit. The body is intended to be the servant of the spirit, and must disappear as soon as bereft of the latter. This spirit is the doctrinal and moral law of Scripture, whose fundamental principles the Ten Commandments set forth exclusively; to them belongs also the Sabbath, which has a symbolical significance only in reference to the choice of the day. The Decalogue is the essence of the covenant between God and man; it is therefore binding for all times, places, and peoples, and was destined to become from the very beginning the common possession of mankind through Israel. . . . All other divine ordinances, on the other hand, are only *signs* of the covenant—guards and protections of the eternal and universal law . . . ; these, from their very nature, cannot remain always and everywhere the same, nor acquire the force of eternal or general obligations. Not that man will ever be able to dispense altogether with visible signs, but the expression and form of these must necessarily change with different stages of culture, national customs, industrial, social, and civil conditions, in short with the general demands of the inner and outer life. As little as the ripe fruit can be forced back into the bud or the butterfly into the chrysalis, so little can the religious idea in its long process from generation to maturity be bound to one and the same form. And if the inner growth of the religious idea in Judaism demands such a transformation, the contact with the world calls for it none the less urgently. . . . The Israel which nestled on Mount Zion, more or less isolated among the neighboring peoples, that, ocean-like, surrounded it, could and did fortify itself with quite different bulwarks than the Israel which traverses this ocean in all directions, which wanders through all districts with its spiritual possessions, and, willy nilly, cannot but recognize the demands made upon it to coalesce with the peoples round about. And, in truth, the historical development of our religion has effected so great a change in the biblical ordinances, that during the space of two thousand years the observance of the greater portion of them has disappeared from Jewish life.

It is true, the piety of our fathers sought to retain a hold on these forms as long and as well as it could possibly be done; they lamented sore as though in their loss Judaism had sustained a fatal wound, and they comforted themselves with the thought that these laws were only in a state of suspended animation. Not forever and for aye, so mused they, would the glorious house of David, the magnificent temple with its sacrifices, and priests, and Levites be sunk into the dust; not forever and for aye would Israel remain an outcast from its ancestral home! At some future day the Lord would once again erect the fallen tabernacle of David, gather the scattered tribes of Israel into the old home, and let the sanctuary of Zion rise in all its glory! But the lamentation as well as the consolation rested on the same untenable foundation, viz., the *equalization,* or more correctly the *confounding,* of the religious form with the religious spirit. Hence both were invested with immutability, and instead of striving to spiritualize the form, the spirit was formalized and a ceremonial standard applied even to the moral law.

Long ago those prophetical voices had been silenced which, with unwearied enthusiasm, had extolled the *spirit* of the divine law as the true banner of Israel, about which all people would some day rally, and, compared with which, all sacrifice and fasting would appear worthless. Those prophets would have proclaimed at the destruction of the second temple: "Comfort ye! the old forms are and will remain dead, but out of their grave the freed spirit rises to spread its pinions over all the earth; out of the ashes of the destroyed temple of isolated Israel will gradually emerge that gigantic temple, whereof the Lord hath said ביתי בית תפלה יקרא לכל העמים 'My house shall be called a house of prayer for all peoples'; from the ruins of Judah a Messianic world will arise! Yes, often will you be forced to cement the stones of this structure with your heart's blood; but such a mission merits such sacrifices, and these sacrifices are worth more than thousands of rams and goats!" Thus, I claim, our old prophets would have spoken; and truly at the present time we are called upon most urgently to work earnestly and effectively in the spirit of the prophets, to proceed to make the proper modification of our outer and our inner religious life. Judaism has reached a turning-point when all such customs and usages as are lifeless must be abolished, partly with the object of retaining its own followers, partly to protect from moral degeneracy. In consequence of the insuperable conditions of life there has set in a violent antagonism between practice and religious conviction which will eventually cease to distress the conscience. The continuance of such a state of affairs would be the greatest misfortune that could befall Israel. On the one hand, the most important ceremonial laws are violated daily, laws which are still considered incumbent upon the Israelite; on the other hand, religious wishes and hopes are expressed in prayer which do not awaken the least response in the heart, and stand in absolute contradiction to the true spirit of the Sinaitic doctrine. This must necessarily lead to one of two things, either that the religious sentiment will become completely dulled or take refuge in the bosom of some other faith. Experience has shown the futility of all attempts to breathe life into the obsolete and dead. Even those praiseworthy attempts to win back for the public service some of the old attractiveness by establishing an outward harmony must and will remain fruitless as long as, at bottom, they

serve merely to hide the inner decay. There is at present a
rent in Judaism which affects its very life, and which no
covering, however glittering, can repair. The evil which
threatens to corrode gradually all the healthy bone and
marrow must be completely eradicated, and this can be
done only if, in the name and in the interest of the religion, we remove from the sphere of our religious life all
that is corrupt and untenable, and solemnly absolve ourselves from all obligations toward it in the future; thus we
may achieve the liberation of Judaism for ourselves and
for our children, so as to prevent the estrangement from
Judaism.[23]

The renunciation of antiquated religious notions and
customs must direct our attention the more singly and completely to the essence of God's word, which is exalted above
the change of times and places, and will be potent even
though the earth wax old as a garment and the heavens
vanish like smoke. No, no! we do not desire a self-made
cult, our wish is not for a Judaism manufactured to meet
the demands of æstheticism; no planing off of the Israelitish emblem, no excursions into the empty void; but, on
the contrary, an Israelitism that is rooted in Sinai and
wishes to bring forth new blossoms and fruits on the
mighty height of a history of four thousand years. . . .
The more ceremonialism loses its import and extent among
us, the more necessary it becomes to grasp the Jewish belief
in its uniqueness, a uniqueness which separates Judaism
from all other faiths, even after the abolition of its whole
ceremonial law.

These, then, are the beliefs which are the source of our
strength, the fundamental reason of our unexampled
endurance, the trophy of our historical struggle—the belief
in the one and only God, who, eternal, invisible and incor-
poreal, reveals himself to man alone in his wonderful
works, but especially in man himself, pervading everything
alike, the earth and the heavens, the perishable and the
imperishable, the body and the spirit; the belief in the
innate goodness and purity of every created thing, and
especially of the godlike creatures gifted with reason,
whose free self-sanctification no original sin prevents, and
whose redemption and salvation no other mediation than
their own free activity can effect; the belief in one

humanity, all of whose members, being of the same heavenly and earthly origin, possess a like nobility of birth
and a claim to equal rights, equal laws, and an equal
share of happiness; the belief that all will partake of this
happiness here on earth by the eventual amalgamation of
all peoples into one people of God, from whose midst the
Lord, according to the prophetical promise, וגם מהם
אקח לכהנים ללוים, will choose also non Israelitish priests
and Levites; this people will recognize the Lord of the universe alone as its king והיה יי למלך על כל הארץ. Then
shall the blood-stained purple of earthly dominion be buried
forever, and with it the whole illusion of glittering falsehood, selfishness, and persecution. These and like teachings, whose first promulgation had to take place within the
pale of the narrow Jewish nationality for fear lest mankind
at large might have been blinded by their splendor, are
Israel's still to-day; the possession thereof is its pride, their
future acknowledgment its only hope. Each of these doctrines contains treasures of world-redeeming thoughts, and
it is our sacred mission to draw forth these treasures more
and more from out the deep mine of our literature, to show
them forth in all their glory, to make them practicable for
active life, and through them enrich heart and soul.[24]

Samuel Adler (1809-1891), the student and scholar, an
active participant in the German rabbinical conferences of the
fifth decade, was active in the city of New York, where he served
as rabbi of Temple Emanuel for nineteen years. He came to
this country from Alzey in 1857. His sermon on the last day of
Passover in that year clearly indicated that a new leader had
been gained for the cause of Reform Judaism in America.

Our situation is like unto that of the Israelites immediately after their deliverance from Egypt. Behind us lies
Egypt, the Middle Ages, before us the sea of Talmudic
legalism, whereof it may truly be said, all streams and
rivulets discharge themselves into the sea, which is nevertheless never filled nor yet ever cleansed through flood.
Let, then, the rod be raised to cleave it! backwards we cannot go, to stand still means death. Then let us forward,
forward across the sea. Reason holds the rod, reason is
the leader. The Torah itself calls itself our wisdom and
our understanding in the eyes of the nations. A violent

east wind is being wafted, and dries up the sea in this land of freedom. The spirit indwelling here in the West, the spirit of freedom, is the newly-born Messiah."

Shortly before the Sinai congregation of Chicago was organized," its promoters addressed a series of questions to Dr. Adler, one of which was, "What course should a reformed congregation pursue?" His answer in part was as follows:

> The answer to this question would quite fill a book, and cannot be even fully indicated in a letter. However, in order not to leave you without any satisfaction, I would state that the first and most important step for such a congregation to take is to free its service of shocking lies, to remove from it the mention of things and wishes which we would not utter if it had to be done in an intelligible manner. Such are, the lamentation about oppression and persecution, the petition for the restoration of the sacrifical cult, for the return of Israel to Palestine, the hope for a personal Messiah, and for the resurrection of the body. In the second place, to eliminate fustian and exaggeration; and, in the third place, to make the service clear, intelligible, instructive, and inspiring."

Samuel Adler was essentially a scholar, and preferred the quiet of the study to the excitement of active life. He spent the last sixteen years of his life in honored retirement.

Bernard Felsenthal (1822-1908) was the most active spirit in the inauguration of the reform movement in Chicago. As rabbi of Sinai and later of Zion congregation of that city, his voice and his pen were ever active in the service of reform. In the pamphlet *Kol Kore Bamidbar*, which, a clarion call, he addressed to the friends of reform in the year 1859, he speaks with no uncertain tone. From this pamphlet a number of paragraphs are herewith taken:

> There is a time to tear down and a time to build up. Thus speaks the holy book imbued with the spirit of God. Our age, in as far as it concerns itself with Jewish religious life, is evidently intended rather to build up than to tear down. But what shall be built up, what shall be constructed anew? The inner, deep-seated belief in God, the moral sense in all the relations of life, the attachment to

and love for Judaism, the teaching of Moses freed of all heathenism and foolishness; with this must be combined the excision of all statutes and observances intended for other times, places, and conditions.[28]

There is but one class of laws which, biblical or post-biblical, have eternal validity, and these are the moral laws, engraved by the finger of God with ineradicable letters in the spiritual nature of man.[29]

A religious law, which has not its root in the spiritual or physical nature of man, is of binding force only so long as it is able to exert a hallowing influence on mind and heart, on the sentiments and actions of the devotee.[30]

By virtue of our mind, which we recognize as a revelation of God in common with the rest of nature, we distinguish the treasures of eternal truth in sacred Scripture from that which is the result of the deficient conceptions of early times and the incorrect ideas concerning the world and life, as well as from those laws which were intended for past and transient conditions.

Holding this doctrine concerning the Bible, we the more certainly assume the right to subject the post-biblical religious sources and institutions to investigation, and to separate that which we consider true in principle and worthy of retention from that which is evidently unsound in doctrine and antiquated or irrelevant in practice. But we recognize our mission to consist much more in nurturing and building up than in abolishing and removing. Doctrines which we have recognized as true, but which have lost in great part their hold on our contemporaries, must be implanted anew and more firmly; institutions which have a hallowing influence on the religious nature, and which are likely to enhance the religious life, must be retained, suitably changed, or, when necessary, created anew, according to the needs and circumstances.[31]

Samuel Hirsch (1815-1889) was the philosopher of the movement. Although he did not come to the United States till 1866, yet, with his clearness of purpose and positiveness of conviction, he became a strong factor in the work of Reform Judaism, not alone in Philadelphia, but in wider circles. In his various books, *Die Religionsphilosophie der Juden,*[32] *Die Messiaslehre der Juden in Kanzelvorträgen,*[33] *Das Judenthum, der christliche Staat und die moderne Kritik,*[34] *Die Humanität als Religion,*[35] he had fully and explicitly expounded his views on religion, explained the principles of Judaism, and set forth his interpretation of the meaning and symbolism of the ceremonies and laws. As an expression of his thought, selection has been made of the closing paragraphs of his dissertation *Die Reform im Judenthum,*[36] where he gives the conclusions of his reasoning:

The need of the time is the highest law in Judaism; all ceremonies are but means for the fulfillment of this highest law; the means must however everywhere be subservient to the end, therefore also in Judaism. The demand that everything which hinders us from working for the maintenance and prosperity of civil society, with all our spiritual and material powers, be removed from our ceremonial practice is therefore religiously justified. . . . It is a serious misdemeanor against, and not an indifferent action towards, the spirit of Judaism if anything be retained which in any way prevents us from the fulfillment of duties incumbent upon the citizen as such. It matters not whether any ceremony which is not to be retained for the above-mentioned reason be prescribed in the Bible or the Talmud. . . . Even the most biased cannot deny that in the regulation of the ceremonial law the Bible had only the Jewish state in view. True, it forsees the downfall of the Jewish state as a divine punishment, but it conceives the event to have been possible of prevention by the Jews through a change of conduct, and therefore it gives no precepts as to how the religious life was to be arranged thereafter. When the Jewish state disappeared, the people, as Holdheim correctly remarks, had no guiding principle to determine what, under the changed circumstances, should be retained and what must be abrogated. . . .

The ceremonies became meaningless, *i.e.* their meaning was no longer understood, and they passed current as the incomprehensible commands of God. Therefore to observe as many of the prescribed ceremonies as possible became the one and important principle. What was no longer possible of observance, as the temple service and everything connected with the possession of Palestine, naturally had to be relinquished. Yet this was regarded only as a punishment of God. God had abolished our sacrifices, our Sabbath and jubilee-years, because we are unworthy to fulfill these commands. Therefore the ever-repeated sigh, "Lead us back to Palestine in order that"—possibly to found there a state that should serve for the glorification of God? No, but—"we may pay our penalty there, that we may offer the prescribed number of sacrifices, etc." This is always and again the heathenish conception (so opposed to our time as well as to the Jewish spirit), that by the practice of ceremonies a service is rendered to God, and as though only the service in the temple at Jerusalem could be perfect because only there everything that God commands could be carried out. But our standpoint to-day is entirely different. We, and the world with us, have arrived at the threshold of the future that the prophets foresaw. A world-temple must be built unto God, for His name shall be praised from the rising of the sun to the setting thereof. The freedom of every man must be not merely proclaimed but realized, for all were created in the image of God. The sanctity of labor must be declared, for man has been placed on earth to work, to employ and develop his powers. God's activity in the history of the individual and of nations must be recognized and acknowledged. God gives the individual and nations the opportunity to use their powers rightly. If they undertake this high task they will live; if not, and they prefer mental sloth and material luxury to hard work, they will go to ruin.

Finally, we must bear testimony to the world, through our cult and through appropriate symbols and ceremonies, that this truth is confirmed in sacred history, inasmuch as there is shown in it how, in a rude, material age, a people, ruder and more sensual than others, was trained until it recognized and taught for all time to come the rule of spirit over nature, and how the spirit can retain this superiority only by free, spiritual activity. Therefore symbols must be retained in Judaism, symbols which shall give this testimony in a fitting manner both to the Jews and to the world. But the Jews of the present day must, before all else, participate in the work of the age with all their powers; for this work is the object of Jewish history, yes, it is the be-all and the end-all of Judaism. The high aim sanctified by time and by Judaism is, that all men be free, all recognize God, all employ their spiritual and material powers with full and free desire, so that a throne be built for truth and justice on this earth, a throne which shall adorn the lowliest hut as well as the most glorious palace. Therefore no symbol can hereafter pass as Jewish which prevents the Jew from participating in and working towards the fulfillment of this object with all his powers. He may not be a mere spectator of the work of the modern age, but must give himself heart and soul to it, for this is the command of the God of his fathers, who only wishes to have right and love realized on earth, and therefore called Abraham from the other side of the river, and desired to make him and his descendants a blessing for the world through their deeds and their sufferings.

These men were the leaders to whose influence is due the decided trend that Judaism in this country took toward reform. Their work was, in the nature of the case, largely individual, but in one instance they, with others, met in conference and gave expression to a declaration of principles. It is this and other conferences of rabbis that will now engage our attention.

Rabbinical Conferences

The first conference of rabbis of the reform school in this country was held in the city of Philadelphia, November 3 to 6, 1869. Fourteen years before that, in 1855, there had been a conference at Cleveland, Ohio; this, however, aimed to be a conference of all the rabbis of the country of all shades of opinion. The articles upon which the rabbis assembled at Cleveland agreed were:

1. The Bible, as delivered to us by our fathers, and as now in our possession, is of immediate divine origin, and the standard of our religion.

2. The Talmud contains the traditional legal and logical exposition of the biblical laws, which must be expounded and practiced according to the comments of the Talmud.

The second article called forth strong protests from the Har Sinai congregation of Baltimore and the Emanuel congregation of New York; on the other hand, the conference did not go far enough for the rigidly orthodox. The results of this conference were most unfortunate. The house of the reformers was divided; two factions arose, one in the eastern, the other in the western, part of the country. This division continued for years with resultant controversies and dissensions, but the breach has been happily healed, as shall be seen later on.

The decade following the Cleveland Conference, being the years of the Civil War and intense political excitement which overshadowed all other interests, witnessed no further effort at a meeting of this kind. In the years 1867-1868, however, the subject was reagitated in the columns of the *Israelite,* but before the meeting was called a conference was convened by the Eastern reformers in Philadelphia in 1869. This conference was attended by the leading reformers from both sections of the country. The conference adopted the following principles, the first public statement made by a body of reformers on this side the Atlantic:

1. The Messianic aim of Israel is not the restoration of the old Jewish state under a descendant of David, involving a second separation from the nations of the earth, but the union of all the children of God in the confession of the unity of God, so as to realize the unity of all rational creatures and their call to moral sanctification.

2. We look upon the destruction of the second Jewish commonwealth not as a punishment for the sinfulness of Israel, but as a result of the divine purpose revealed to Abraham, which, as has become ever clearer in the course of the world's history, consists in the dispersion of the Jews to all parts of the earth, for the realization of their high priestly mission, to lead the nations to the true knowledge and worship of God.

3. The Aaronic priesthood and the Mosaic sacrificial cult were preparatory steps to the real priesthood of the whole people, which began with the dispersion of the Jews, and to the sacrifices of sincere devotion and moral sanctification, which alone are pleasing and acceptable to the Most Holy. These institutions, preparatory to higher religiosity, were consigned to the past, once for all, with the destruction of the second temple, and only in this sense— as educational influences in the past—are they to be mentioned in our prayers.

4. Every distinction between Aaronides and non-

Aaronides, as far as religious rites and duties are concerned, is consequently inadmissible, both in the religious cult and in life.

5. The selection of Israel as the people of religion, as the bearers of the highest idea of humanity, is still, as ever, to be strongly emphasized, and for this very reason, whenever this is mentioned it shall be done with full emphasis laid on the world-embracing mission of Israel and the love of God for all His children.

6. The belief in the bodily resurrection has no religious foundation, and the doctrine of immortality refers to the after-existence of the soul only.

7. Urgently as the cultivation of the Hebrew language, in which the treasures of divine revelation are given and the immortal remains of a literature that influences all civilized nations are preserved, must be always desired by us in fulfillment of a sacred duty, yet has it become unintelligible to the vast majority of our coreligionists; therefore it must make way, as is advisable under existing circumstances, to intelligible language in prayer, which, if not understood, is a soulless form.[37]

The conference, after adopting a number of resolutions reforming rabbinical legislation on marriage and divorce,[38] adjourned to meet in Cincinnati the following year. The meeting, however, did not take place, because some of the men who were most prominent in the Philadelphia Conference failed to appear. In the year 1871 a conference did take place in Cincinnati, after preliminary meetings in Cleveland and New York; this conference is chiefly memorable because it gave the impulse to the organization of the Union of American Congregations and the subsequent founding of the Hebrew Union College.

In the year 1885, in the month of November, from the sixteenth to the eighteenth days of the month, the memorable Pittsburg Conference (called by Dr. K. Kohler) was held. It adopted the following declaration of principles, the most succinct expression of the theology of the reform movement that had ever been published to the world:

1. We recognize in every religion an attempt to grasp the Infinite, and in every mode, source, or book of revelation held sacred in any religious system the consciousness of the indwelling of God in man. We hold that Judaism

presents the highest conception of the God-idea as taught in our Holy Scriptures and developed and spiritualized by the Jewish teachers, in accordance with the moral and philosophical progress of their respective ages. We maintain that Judaism preserved and defended, midst continual struggles and trials and under enforced isolation, this God-idea as the central religious truth for the human race.

2. We recognize in the Bible the record of the consecration of the Jewish people to its mission as the priest of the one God, and value it as the most potent instrument of religious and moral instruction. We hold that the modern discoveries of scientific researches in the domain of nature and history are not antagonistic to the doctrines of Judaism, the Bible reflecting the primitive ideas of its own age, and at times clothing its conception of divine Providence and Justice dealing with man in miraculous narratives.

3. We recognize in the Mosaic legislation a system of training the Jewish people for its mission during its national life in Palestine, and to-day we accept as binding only its moral laws, and maintain only such ceremonies as elevate and sanctify our lives, but reject all such as are not adapted to the views and habits of modern civilization.

4. We hold that all such Mosaic and rabbinical laws as regulate diet, priestly purity, and dress originated in ages and under the influence of ideas entirely foreign to our present mental and spiritual state. They fail to impress the modern Jew with a spirit of priestly holiness; their observance in our days is apt rather to obstruct than to further modern spiritual elevation.

5. We recognize, in the modern era of universal culture of heart and intellect, the approaching of the realization of Israel's great Messianic hope for the establishment of the kingdom of truth, justice, and peace among all men. We consider ourselves no longer a nation, but a religious community, and therefore expect neither a return to Palestine, nor a sacrificial worship under the sons of Aaron, nor the restoration of any of the laws concerning the Jewish state.

6. We recognize in Judaism a progressive religion, ever striving to be in accord with the postulates of reason. We are convinced of the utmost necessity of preserving the historical identity with our great past. Christianity and Islam

being daughter religions of Judaism, we appreciate their providential mission to aid in the spreading of monotheistic and moral truth. We acknowledge that the spirit of broad humanity of our age is our ally in the fulfillment of our mission, and therefore we extend the hand of fellowship to all who operate with us in the establishment of the reign of truth and righteousness among men.

7. We reassert the doctrine of Judaism that the soul is immortal, grounding this belief on the divine nature of the human spirit, which forever finds bliss in righteousness and misery in wickedness. We reject as ideas not rooted in Judaism, the beliefs both in bodily resurrection and in Gehenna and Eden (Hell and Paradise) as abodes for everlasting punishment and reward.

8. In full accordance with the spirit of Mosaic legislation, which strives to regulate the relation between rich and poor, we deem it our duty to participate in the great task of modern times, to solve, on the basis of justice and righteousness, the problems presented by the contrasts and evils of the present organization of society."[39]

This platform aroused the usual storm of opposition in the conservative and orthodox camps, but it still stands as the utterance most expressive of the teachings of Reform Judaism.[40]

In July, 1889, the Central Conference of American Rabbis was organized in the city of Detroit. It has met in regular session every year since then. It comprises in its membership, with scarcely an exception, all the rabbis of the reform school in the country. Although it does not exclude from membership any rabbi, the third article of its constitution reading, "All active and retired rabbis of congregations, and professors of rabbinical seminaries, shall be eligible for membership," yet it is a well-known and accepted fact that it is a body of reform rabbis.[41] It is truly representative, including as it does in its membership, according to its last report, three hundred and thirty-six rabbis [42] located all over the country, from ocean to ocean and from lakes to gulf and in Canada, England, Palestine and Cuba. The president from the beginning to the day of his death, March 26, 1900, was the founder, Isaac M. Wise. In his annual address delivered at the meeting of the conference held at Milwaukee, Wisconsin, in July, 1896, the president summed up what the Central Conference had accomplished. At the Cincinnati Conference held in March, 1899, in honor of his eightieth birthday, Dr. Wise spoke in the following words of the work of the conference in the last presidential address which he delivered: "By this God-blessed organization, the American Rabbis were united in a bond of brotherhood, all feuds, strifes, quarrels and animosities which raged among us for many years vanished like the fog before the sun." [43]

The notable achievements of the conference are the production and publication of the *Union Prayer-Book for Jewish Worship,* its success in representing Judaism at the World's Parliament of Religions held at Chicago during the World's Fair, [44] its declaration on the requirements for the admission of proselytes, [45] and, above all, its uniting in one body the reform leaders of the country. It has even extended into Canada, and the meeting of 1897 was held in Montreal. It has published thirty-nine year-books, which contain, besides the record of the proceedings, a large number of addresses and learned papers read at the sessions.

The principles of the men forming the conference were so well known that there was not thought to be any necessity for making a declaration of principles, notably as at its second meeting the conference passed a resolution to the effect that all the declarations of reform adopted at previous rabbinical conferences in Europe and this country be collected and recorded in the year-book, and be considered the working basis of this conference. [46]

At the meeting held in Rochester, N. Y., in July, 1895, the president, in his address, proposed for discussion and decision several questions, one of which, bearing on the attitude of Reform Judaism, must be referred to here, notably as it involved a far-reaching issue and concerned a question of principle. "What is our relation in all religious matters to our own post-biblical, our patristic literature, including the Talmud, casuists, responses, and commentaries?" The committee to whom this was referred reported as follows:

> Your committee, to whom that part of the president's message was referred which reads, "What is our relation in all religious matters to our own post-biblical, our patristic literature, including the Talmud, casuists, responses, and commentaries," begs leave to report that, from the standpoint of Reform Judaism, the whole post-biblical and

patristic literature, including the Talmud, casuists, responses, and commentaries, is, and can be considered as,
nothing more or less than "religious literature." As such
it is of inestimable value. It is the treasure-house in which
the successive ages deposited their conceptions of the great
and fundamental principles of Judaism, and their contributions to the never-ceasing endeavor to elucidate the
same. Consciously or unconsciously, every age has added
a wing to this great treasure-house, and the architecture
and construction of each wing bear the indelible marks of
the peculiar characteristics of the time in which it was
erected. Our age is engaged in the same task. We, too,
have to contribute to the enlargement of this treasure-
house; but we have to do it in our own way, as the spirit
of our time directs, without any slavish imitation of the
past.

To have awakened the consciousness of this historic fact
is the great merit of Reform Judaism; and the more this
consciousness grows upon our mind, the more the conditions and environments of our modern life force it upon
us, the more persistently we have to assert: that our relations in all religious matters are in no way authoritatively
and finally determined by any portion of our post-biblical
and patristic literature.[47]

This report was considered at the last session of the conference. Many of the members had left for their homes, so that
only twenty were present. The report called forth long and
warm discussion. A number of the most pronounced reformers
took the ground that the report did not go far enough, and that
it ought to have stated the attitude also in reference to the biblical books. They declared that in the stream of tradition the
biblical books must be considered with the post-biblical, that
the two cannot be separated. Therefore they voted against the
report of the committee, which was carried by the narrow
margin of eleven to nine. This action of the conference called
forth great excitement. The conservative press naturally interpreted the vote as an almost equal declaration in favor of the
binding authority of the Talmud, misrepresenting altogether
the opinions of those who had voted in the negative. In his
address at the opening of the next conference in July, 1896, the
president referred to the matter as follows:

The vote of eleven to nine "placed the conference on record that nine out of twenty hold the post-biblical or patristic literature as authoritative and final for us in all religious matters. So the vote was generally understood by outsiders, and this placed the conference in a ridiculous position of inconsistency, the same which I. M. Jost charges on German conferences in his time. As this was positively not the import of that vote, it places the nine of the opposition in a false light before the world as being adherents and advocates of orthodox rabbinism. It will therefore be necessary that a reconsideration of the said vote be moved by some one who voted on it in the affirmative. We must sustain the position we took from the beginning: that this conference consists of the reform element only and exclusively, and its standpoint is historical Judaism, that is the Judaism of all ages, and not that of one period, class, or people. We cannot submit to the legalism of the Talmud, the Kabbalism of the Sohar, the literalism of the Karaites, or even the rationalism of Maimonides and Mendelssohn, because either of them was a child of his respective age and not of the Judaism of all ages. And this only and exclusively is our basis." [48]

The president's address was, as usual, referred to a committee of three; two of these were among the nine that had voted in the negative at the preceding conference. In their report they stated in reference to this part of the address:

Those who were present at the conference held last year in Rochester, and who heard the discussion of the report of the Committee on Post-Biblical Literature, know full well that the nine who voted against it as it was presented and adopted had no intention of declaring in favor of the Talmud and the later codifications as an authority in religious matters, and if their vote was so construed, it was certainly misunderstood. [49]

This was unanimously adopted by the conference, and thus its tendency of thought as a reform body once again emphasized. In his presidential address at the Montreal Conference in 1897, Dr. Wise made reference to the Zionistic movement which was then beginning to agitate the Jewish world and declared that "the honor and position of American Israel demand imperatively that this conference, which does represent the sentiment of American Judaism, minus the idiosyncrasies of . . . late immigrants, do declare officially the American standpoint in this unpleasant episode of our history." [50] In accordance with this suggestion, the conference, by a unanimous vote, put itself on record as follows: *Resolved,* That we totally disapprove of any attempt for the establishment of a Jewish state. Such attempts show a misunderstanding of Israel's mission, which from the narrow political and national field has been expanded to the promotion among the whole human race of the broad and universalistic religion first proclaimed by the Jewish prophets. Such attempts do not benefit, but infinitely harm, our Jewish brethren where they are still persecuted by confirming the assertion of their enemies that the Jews are foreigners in the countries in which they are at home and of which they are everywhere the most loyal and patriotic citizens.

We reaffirm that the object of Judaism is not political nor national, but spiritual, and addresses itself to the continuous growth of peace, justice, and love in the human race, to a Messianic time when all men will recognize that they form one great brotherhood for the establishment of God's Kingdom on earth.[51]

Nine years later, an affirmation similar in spirit was made when the members present at the Indianapolis Convention in 1906 declared, "We, herewith, reaffirm that religion is the tie which unites the Jews; the synagogue is the basic institution of Judaism, and the congregation, its unit of representation," and in terms equally strong the standpoint of the conference in this matter was reaffirmed in 1911 when at Baltimore the statement in the report of the Committee on Church and State was endorsed to the following effect:

> Inasmuch as we are unqualifiedly committed to the total separation of Church and State, we discountenance any movement in Jewish communities on other than the religious basis which would violate this principle and tend to create the impression that the Jews are an *imperium in imperio.*

In his presidential message delivered at Buffalo in 1917 Rabbi William Rosenau, while stating that he had no desire to quarrel with Zionists, yet urged that the conference publish the statement that "it stands for an Israel whose mission is religious and that, in the light of this mission, it looks with disfavor upon any movement, the purpose of which is any other than religious."

The committee on president's message presented a majority and two minority reports on this recommendation; the majority report was signed by twenty-one members of the committee and each minority report by one member of the committee. The majority report which was adopted by a vote of sixty-eight to twenty reads as follows:

> We herewith reaffirm the fundamental principle of reform Judaism, that the essence of Israel as a priest-people, consists in its religious consciousness, and in the sense of consecration to God and service in the world, and not in any political or racial national consciousness. And therefore, we look with disfavor upon the new doctrine of political Jewish nationalism, which finds the criterion of Jewish loyalty in anything other than loyalty to Israel's God and Israel's religious mission.

On November 2, 1917, the Right Honorable Arthur J. Balfour, Secretary of Foreign Affairs, of the government of Great Britain, in a letter to Lord Rothschild conveyed the information that "his majesty's government views with favor the establishment in Palestine of a national home for the Jewish people, it being clearly understood that nothing shall be done which may prejudice the civil and religious rights of existing non-Jewish communities in Palestine, or the rights and political status enjoyed by Jews in any other country."

This historic document known as the Balfour Declaration created a great stir in the Jewish world. At the meeting of the conference held in Chicago in June, 1918, a resolution was introduced on the subject. This resolution was referred to the committee on President's Message which reported as follows:

> The Central Conference of American Rabbis notes with grateful appreciation the declaration of the British Government by Mr. Balfour as an evidence of good-will toward the Jews. We naturally favor the facilitation of immigration to Palestine of Jews who, either because of economic necessity or political or religious persecution desire to settle there. We hold that Jews in Palestine as

well as anywhere else in the world are entitled to equality
in political, civil and religious rights but we do not subscribe to the phrase in the declaration which says, "Palestine is to be a national home-land for the Jewish people."
This statement assumes that the Jews although identified
with the life of many nations for centuries are in fact a
people without a country. We hold that Jewish people
are and of right ought to be at home in all lands. Israel,
like every other religious communion, has the right to live
and assert its message in any part of the world. We are
opposed to the idea that Palestine should be considered *the*
home-land of the Jews. Jews in America are part of the
American nation. The ideal of the Jew is not the establishment of a Jewish state—not the reassertion of Jewish
nationality which has long been outgrown. We believe
that our survival as a people is dependent upon the assertion and the maintenance of our historic religious rôle
and not upon the acceptance of Palestine as a home-land
of the Jewish people. The mission of the Jew is to witness
to God all over the world.[52]

The San Remo Conference of the Allied Powers who had
been victorious in the World War issued to Great Britain the
mandate over Palestine. The president of the conference Rabbi
Leo M. Franklin had declined the invitation of the Zionist
Organization of America to appoint a delegation to participate
in a meeting to be held in the city of New York on May 9,
and 10, 1920, to celebrate this event. In his message read at
the meeting of the conference held in Rochester in June, 1920,
he reported that he had refused the invitation on the ground
that the conference had placed itself on record very definitely
in this matter. He quoted the resolution adopted at Chicago
in 1918. But he stated at the same time that he believed the
conference would lend its coöperation to any movement for
the rehabilitation of Palestine, so that it be made not only a
"refuge for the down-trodden Jew but as a place where a fuller
expansion may be given to the spiritual genius of the Jew."
He asked that the conference endorse this letter. The committee on President's Message in response to this request submitted a majority and a minority report, the former signed
by fifteen members and the latter by two. The majority report
which was adopted by a vote of fifty-eight to eight declared:

We endorse the action of the president in declining the invitation of the Zionist Organization of America to appoint a delegation to participate in the Extraordinary Convention of delegates representing the membership of the Zionist Organization held in the city of New York, May 9 and 10, to celebrate the issuance by the San Remo Conference of a Mandate over Palestine to Great Britain.

We rejoice, indeed, at the present decision of the San Remo Conference to give to Great Britain, a mandate over Palestine in line with the Balfour Declaration. But, we hold today what the conference declared anent the Balfour Declaration two years ago. We do not subscribe to the phrase in the declaration which says, "Palestine is to be a national home land for the Jewish People." We believe that Israel, the Jewish people, like every other religious communion, has the right to live, to be at home, and to assert its message in every part of the world.

With confidence in the free institutions of Great Britain, we rejoice in and recognize the historic significance of such a British Mandate for Palestine, in that it will offer the opportunity to some Jews who may desire to settle there to go there, and to live full, free, and happy lives. And if facilities are offered for an appreciable number to go there from lands in which they suffer from religious, political, or economic persecution they may be enabled so to shape their communal life that, inspired by the hallowed associations of the land in which Israel's Prophets announced world-redeeming ideas, they may become a great spiritual influence.

While we thus rejoice, we do not, however, admit that this historic event is what it has been called, the *Geulah* or the Redemption of Israel. Convinced that the mission of the Jew is to witness to God all over the world, emphasizing the religious function of Israel, and rejecting any assertion of Jewish nationality, which it has long ago outgrown, we hold that Israel's Redemption will only be realized when the Jew will have the right to live in any part of the world, and, all racial and religious prejudice and persecution ended, Israel will be free as a religious power and integral part of all nations to give world service.**

It was abundantly evident in these resolutions on Zionism and on Palestine that the great majority of the members of the conference, though opposed to the political agitations of Jewish nationalists, are yet heartily in favor of coöperation in all efforts for the physical rehabilitation of Palestine. And this appeared in the action taken at the meeting held at Cedar Point, Ohio, in 1924, when the report of the committee on the Message of the president, Rabbi Abraham Simon, on this point was adopted unanimously as follows:

Your committee having studied with the greatest care the president's review of our coöperation in the social-economic rehabilitation of Palestine, the account of his contacts with the non-partisan group which is studying the same problem, his recommendation that the conference accept the tentative outlined program of the newly contemplated Jewish agency as suggested by the non-partisan group, and his recommendation that a committee be appointed to coöperate with this group or with a more inclusive body in the further development of this program recommends:

(a) That the conference reaffirm its agreement to coöperate in the rehabilitation of Palestine.

(b) That the conference favors the formation of a non-partisan group for the development of Palestine, that the president continue his unofficial coöperation with the non-partisan conference mentioned in the message, in the further development of its program, but that no final action be taken until approved by the members of our conference in convention assembled.

(c) In view of the fact that at a recent conference held in New York City in which representatives of Jewish organizations of national scope including our conference participated, an emergency committee was organized to study the problem of migration of our brethren, your committee recommends that the conference coöperate in the study and solution of this great problem which confronts the Jews of the world.

The Prayer-Book [54]

The public expression of a faith is its public service. That reforms were necessary here was the conviction of all the early reformers. The language of prayer, albeit the sacred tongue,

was unintelligible to most of the worshipers. Customs were
in vogue at the service that detracted much from making it
devotional and reverential. In the prayers hopes were given
expression to, and petitions directed to the throne of divine
grace, which were not living hopes and petitions. Doctrines
were expressed that were no longer the beliefs of the people.
Naturally, attention was almost immediately given to making
the public service a true reflection of the changes that had
come upon men's thoughts. The traditional service was modified and changed. We have seen how from the very beginning
this matter engaged the attention of the reformers.[55]

The prayer-book compiled in 1830 by Isaac Harby, Abraham Moise, and David N. Carvalho, members of the Reformed
Society of Israelites, and entitled "The Sabbath Service and
Miscellaneous Prayers," was adopted by the Reformed Society
of Israelites, founded in Charleston, South Carolina, November
21, 1825.[56] In 1854, the Reverend Dr. L. Merzbacher prepared
a prayer-book which was adopted by the Emanuel congregation of New York whose minister he was, as its ritual. This
prayer-book greatly abbreviated the traditional service, and
although not as thoroughly and consistently reformed as it
might have been, was yet a great step forward at the time.
In the year 1856, shortly after landing in this country, Dr.
David Einhorn published the first part of his *Olath Tamid: a
Prayer-Book for Jewish Reform Congregations*. At the same
time he set forth clearly the principles that had guided him in
writing the book.[57] He expressed the matter well when he
wrote:

> It is a clear and undeniable fact that the traditional serv-
> ice has no charm for the present generation; the old
> prayers have become for the most part untruths for pres-
> ent conditions and views, and neither the organ nor the
> choir, nor yet youthful memories that cluster about the
> synagogue, are sufficient to cover the bareness, to banish
> the lack of devotion, to fill again the vacant places. Salva-
> tion will come only from a complete reform of the public
> service which, founded on principle, will enable the wor-
> shiper to find himself and his God in the sacred halls.
> . . . Dogmatically, this prayer-book is differentiated from
> the traditional order by the omission of prayers for the
> restoration of the sacrificial cult and the return to Pales-

tine, *i.e.* the reinstitution of the Jewish kingdom, as well as the change of the doctrine of bodily resurrection into the idea of a purely spiritual immortality.

Although the book followed the traditional order of prayers in a measure, and retained a number of prayers in the Hebrew, yet the greater part of the ritual was in the vernacular. In the Hebrew text, too, such changes as were necessitated by the changes of belief indicated above were made.

There now appeared from time to time a number of prayer-books, such as the *Minhag America,* by Isaac M. Wise, adopted by most of the congregations in the southern and western sections of the country; the *Abodath Yisrael,* by B. Szold and M. Jastrow; the *Hadar Hattefillah,* by A. Huebsch; besides these, quite a number of congregations had individual prayer-books prepared by their ministers for their use. There was thus a wondrous variety. As time wore on it was felt that there was a great need for a prayer-book that could be adopted by the reformed congregations everywhere. There were obstacles in the way of taking any one of the existing books. At the meeting of the Central Conference of American Rabbis held in Baltimore in 1891, the subject of a Union Prayer-Book was first broached. A ritual committee was appointed that labored for three years, and at the meeting in Atlantic City in July, 1894, the book as submitted by the committee was ratified. This book expresses in its prayers and meditations the doctrines of Reform Judaism. In the report accompanying the manuscript of the second part of the prayer-book, the services for New Year's Day and the Day of Atonement, the Ritual Committee stated the principle that had guided it in its work:

> Imbued with the earnestness of the task that was laid upon us, we endeavored to conform the ritual for these two great holidays to the spirit and principle of the first part of our Union Prayer-Book, to unite the soul-stirring reminiscences of the past with the urgent demands of the present, and to enhance the solemnity of the service by combining the two essential elements, the ancient time-honored formulas with modern prayers and meditations in the vernacular.[58]

With the passing of the years the call became quite insistent for a revision of the prayer-book. Finally at the meeting at

Detroit, Michigan, in 1914, the conference decided that the work of revision be proceeded with and that such revision be "more than verbal yet shall retain the structure and framework of the present book." [59] The revision was entrusted to a committee consisting of David Philipson, chairman, H. G. Enelow, Henry Englander, Maurice H. Harris, Max Heller, Kaufman Kohler, Julian Morgenstern, I. S. Moses, William Rosenau, Samuel Schulman, and Joseph Stolz. In revising the first volume of the prayer-book containing the services for the Sabbath, week days and the three festivals, Passover, Weeks, and Tabernacles, new prayers were substituted for the special prayers for the particular days, and more provision was made for congregational participation through responsive readings and collective readings with the minister. The various services were harmonized and the needs of contemporary life were given consideration. The words of the expert authority in English to whom the manuscript was submitted for examination and suggestion, written to the chairman of the committee may be quoted:

> Coming to this work as a stranger and with a mind unprejudiced in its favor by sectarian training, I find myself deeply impressed by its literary and spiritual qualities. Its language is simple, rich, sincere and beautiful and its sentiments are such as any intelligent and reverent person must respond to with quickened faith in "the power not ourselves that makes for righteousness." . . . Especially to be commended from a literary point of view are the modern prayers and meditations, since without sacrificing applicability to our contemporary life, they retain the fine cadence and flavor of the best biblical language. [60]

The revised edition of the first volume was published in the fall of 1918.

When the report on the second volume containing the services for New Year's Day and the Day of Atonement was discussed at the Rochester meeting of the conference in 1920, it became apparent that there was dissatisfaction with the work of the revision on the part of a number of members of the conference. It was stated that the prayer-book as revised did not reflect the modern spirit sufficiently, and that it did not express satisfactorily the spiritual longings and yearnings of the present generation. The criticism that the book contained outgrown points of view was also hurled. In short, it appeared that a socially minded group desired that place be given in the prayers to the industrial and social tendencies of the age. It was decided to give this group representation in the revision committee so as to afford them the opportunity of bringing their views forward. The personnel of the committee as reconstituted was David Philipson, Chairman, Israel Bettan, Edward N. Calisch, Hyman G. Enelow, Harry W. Ettelson, Ephraim Frisch, Samuel Goldenson, Louis Grossman, Kaufman Kohler, Isaac E. Marcuson, Julian Morgenstern, William Rosenau, Samuel Schulman, and Joseph Stolz.

As finally revised, this volume was coördinated with the first volume. The same principles that guided the revision of the first volume were applied also here. The book retained the framework of the traditional Siddur but there were many marked changes. The social mindedness of the generation was given recognition in the so-called social justice prayer which was placed in the afternoon service of the Day of Atonement. Many new prayers and meditations were introduced. Besides passages from the Bible, selections from Talmudic and medieval literatures were included in the section of extra readings. The book appeared in the fall of 1922 and is used in practically all the reform congregations of the country. It may be said that this prayer-book represents the most decided step toward real spiritual union that the reform congregations of the country have ever taken. At the session of the Conference held at Detroit, Michigan, in 1929 a resolution to subject the prayer book to another revision was adopted, but at the time of this writing no active work toward such revision has been done.

The Proselyte Question

Is Judaism a missionary religion? Shall Judaism put forth special efforts to induce men and women not born in the faith to become identified with it? These questions have often agitated Jewish thinkers, and there are the two well-defined positions, the advocates of the one claiming that Judaism's truth will eventually prevail without active efforts being put forth to gain adherents to its doctrines, while others hold that there are at present great opportunities for Judaism, and that if the proper steps were taken, many who are dissatisfied with other creeds will eagerly take refuge within its ranks. If, then, there be those who desire to become Jews, what shall be the requirements for admission into the faith? Is a simple expression of this desire and a confession of faith sufficient, or shall initiatory rites be required? Notably has it been the question of circumcision about which the controversy has turned. If true to its own professions, must not Reform Judaism declare that the expression of belief in the distinguishing doctrines of the faith on the part of the would-be proselyte is all-sufficient for entrance into the religion? This question has come up time and again for discussion, both privately and in rabbinical conferences, in the United States, and decided expression has been given and decided action taken.

The first public statement in the matter, though it did not touch the question proper, was the resolution passed by the Philadelphia Conference in 1869:

> The male child of a Jewish mother—in accordance with a never-disputed principle of Judaism—is no less than her female child to be considered a Jew by descent, even though he be uncircumcised.

In the discussion precipitated by this resolution the question of the circumcision of proselytes was debated; although the greater number of the rabbis present expressed themselves to the effect that circumcision should not be considered a *conditio sine qua non* for admission into Judaism,[1] yet there was no further action taken than that indicated by the resolution.

In 1878 the Reverend M. Spitz, of Milwaukee, Wis., addressed a letter to the rabbis of the country, requesting their opinion as to the right and advisability of accepting a proselyte without circumcision; a case in point had occurred in his city, and as he did not desire to act on his own responsibility he took this course. The letter called forth a lengthy response from Dr. B. Felsenthal, published as a pamphlet, *Zur Proselytenfrage im Judenthum,* in which the position was taken and defended from the historical standpoint that circumcision is not necessary. Dr. M. Mielziner took the opposite view in an article which appeared in the *Jewish Messenger.*[2] No further opinions were elicited. Rabbi Spitz refused to admit the young man without the initiatory rite. The next public step in the matter was the action taken by the Sinai congregation of Chicago (which, under the leadership of Emil G. Hirsch, became known as the most radical of American Jewish congregations), at its meeting held on April 9, 1885, when it was resolved:

That the Abrahamitic rite is not an essential condition, the compliance with which must precede or follow admittance to membership in Sinai congregation.[63]

At the Pittsburg Conference held in November, 1885, the question was again up for discussion, and the following resolution was adopted:

Inasmuch as the so-called Abrahamitic rite is by many, and the most competent, rabbis no longer considered as a *conditio sine qua non* of receiving male gentiles into the fold of Judaism, and inasmuch as a new legislation on this and kindred subjects is one of the most imperative and practical demands of our reform movement, be it

Resolved, that a committee of five, one of them to be the president of this conference, be entrusted with framing a full report to be submitted for final action to the next conference.[64]

This resolution clearly indicates the temper of the conference in the matter; but, since the next conference, called to meet in Cincinnati in June, 1886, did not, because of unforeseen circumstances, convene, the resolution of the Pittsburgh Conference came to naught.

On July 23, 1890, Rabbi Henry Berkowitz, of Kansas City, Missouri, being applied to by a Christian, who did not wish to submit to circumcision, for admission to Judaism, also addressed a circular letter to the rabbis of the country, asking for their opinion and advice. He received a number of responses; some rabbis had expressed their opinions on the subject before this; in published views or in responses the following had declared that proselytes could be admitted without circumcision: I. M. Wise, B. Felsenthal, G. Gottheil, K. Kohler, A. Moses, E. G. Hirsch, M. Landsberg, E. Schreiber, S. Hecht, M. Samfield; of an opposite tenor were the views of M. Mielziner, M. Spitz, and H. Iliowizi.[65] Dr. Berkowitz received the young man into the faith without his having submitted to the initiatory rite.

At the meeting of the Central Conference held at Baltimore in July, 1891, these responses were submitted and several papers read on the subject. The whole matter was referred to a committee of five.[66] At the meeting of the conference held the following year in the city of New York the report of this committee was submitted, and the whole subject was again thoroughly discussed.[87]

The resolution, as finally adopted at the meeting, reads thus:

> Resolved, that the Central Conference of American Rabbis, assembled this day in this city of New York, considers it lawful and proper for any officiating rabbi, assisted by no less than two associates, and in the name and with the consent of his congregation, to accept into the sacred covenant of Israel, and declare fully affiliated with the congregation לכד דבר שבקדושה, any honorable and intelligent person who desires such affiliation, without any initiatory rite, ceremony, or observance whatever; provided such person be sufficiently acquainted with the faith, doctrine, and religious usages of Israel; that nothing derogatory to such person's moral and mental character is suspected; that it is his or her free will and choice to embrace the cause of Judaism, and that he or she declare verbally, and in a document signed and sealed before such officiating rabbi and his associates, his or her intention and firm resolve—
>
> 1. To worship the One Sole and Eternal God and none besides him.
>
> 2. To be conscientiously governed in his or her doings and omissions in life by God's laws, ordained for the child and image of the Father and Maker of all, the sanctified son or daughter of the divine covenant.
>
> 3. To adhere in life and death, actively and faithfully, to the sacred cause and mission of Israel, as marked out in Holy Writ.

In the course of the next thirty-five years, this matter of the conversion and reception of proselytes was brought upon the floor of the conference a number of times, but the vital action on the subject of the requirement of circumcision for male proselytes has not been reconsidered nor changed. At the Charlevoix Conference in 1910, a certificate of conversion was adopted.[88] In 1925, a committee was appointed to prepare a manual for the instruction of proselytes. This manual which was formally adopted by the conference in 1927, contains the latest expression of Reform Judaism through its accredited representatives on this important subject. At the end of the small volume, seven questions which are to be put to and answered by the intending convert are printed. The last of these questions, by implication, touches the matter of the circumcision of proselytes wherein Reform Judaism by the action of the reform rabbis made so radical a departure from tradition. After the question, "Should you be blessed with children do you agree to rear your children according to the Jewish faith?" the final query is put, "Do you also agree to have male children circumcised?" [69] This means as a matter of course, that though circumcision is not a requirement for conversion to the faith, and the members of the conference have here departed from the traditional requirements, still as far as the circumcision of newly born children is concerned, they adhere to the age-old tradition.

Thus this vexed question was finally disposed of, and the Central Conference of American Rabbis has placed itself on record, acting in the true spirit of that larger interpretation of the faith which is the only consistent course for the exponents of Reform Judaism to take.

The Sabbath Question

As in Europe, so also in the United States, the question of Sabbath observance has long been acute. Economic and social conditions compel the great mass of people engaged in mercantile pursuits to follow their ordinary vocations on the Sabbath. The conflict between the religious observance and life is constant here. In a foregoing chapter [70] the subject has been treated in all its phases, hence nothing further is now necessary than to indicate the practical steps that have been taken in the United States to solve the difficulty presented by the Sabbath problem.

In 1866 Rabbi Isaac M. Wise, having noted that many could not attend the services on Saturday morning, instituted a late service with lecture on Sabbath eve. This innovation made rapid headway, for it seemed to meet the double desire of retaining the Saturday Sabbath and to furnish the opportunity for all to attend divine worship at a leisure hour. There have always been those, however, who have felt that a late Friday evening service is harmful rather than helpful in the preservation of the Sabbath spirit, since it induces a feeling that by the attendance at this service the whole duty to the Sabbath has been performed, and the day itself can be spent in accordance with individual pleasure.[71] The other remedy applied to meet the situation is the Sunday service. This has assumed two aspects, the advocacy of a transfer of the Sabbath to Sunday on the one hand and the retention of the historical Sabbath, with a supplementary service on Sunday, on the other. The only congregations which have carried out the former program are Sinai, of Chicago, which introduced services on Sunday on January 18, 1874, and the Free Synagogue of New York under the leadership of Stephen S. Wise. For thirteen years Sinai congregation held services on both days, but in 1887, under the leadership of Emil G. Hirsch, services on Saturday were discontinued.

The first attempt to hold services on Sunday was made in Baltimore in 1854 by a society calling itself "The Hebrew Reformed Association"; after a brief trial of six months the attempt was abandoned. It was in the same city that Sunday services were again instituted twenty years later by the Har Sinai congregation, where, with occasional lapses, they have continued to this day. As already stated Sinai congregation of Chicago instituted Sunday services in 1874, and on October 13, 1881, the Board of Trustees of Keneseth Israel congregation of Philadelphia adopted a resolution to make provision for a service on Sunday. This resolution was indorsed by the congregation; the rabbi of this congregation, Samuel Hirsch, had been the first to broach the subject in a public Jewish forum,[72] and had been a consistent advocate of the transfer of the Sabbath to Sunday throughout his career. The services on Sunday since 1887 have been a feature of the congregation's activity.

Since then Sunday services have been instituted in many other congregations, among which may be mentioned: Emanuel, New York City; Berith Kodesh, Rochester, New York; Bene Israel and Bene Yeshurun, Cincinnati, Ohio; Adath Israel, Boston, Mass.; Tiffereth Israel and Anshe Chesed, Cleveland, Ohio; Isaiah and Anshe Maarak, Chicago, Illinois; Adath Israel, Louisville, Kentucky; Bethel, Detroit, Michigan; Rodef Shalom, Pittsburgh, Pennsylvania.

The Sabbath question has also been debated at rabbinical conferences. At the session of November 18, 1885, of the Pittsburgh Conference the following resolution was unanimously adopted:

Whereas we recognize the importance of maintaining the historical Sabbath as a bond with our great past and a symbol of the unity of Judaism the world over; and whereas, on the other hand, it cannot be denied that there is a vast number of workingmen and others who, from some cause or other, are not able to attend the services on the sacred day of rest; be it resolved that there is nothing in the spirit of Judaism or its laws to prevent the introduction of Sunday services in localities where the necessity for such services appears or is felt.

At the New Orleans Meeting of the Central Conference of American Rabbis in May, 1902, Dr. Jacob Voorsanger, of San Francisco, presented an exhaustive paper on the Sabbath question in which he set forth at length the difficulties connected with the observance of the Sabbath, although he argued strongly for the retention of the historical Sabbath.[73] The discussion which followed centered mainly about the question of the transfer of the Sabbath to Sunday. The sentiment of those present was almost unanimously against such transfer, although the advisability and even necessity of a supplementary service on Sunday was conceded by most.

The crux of the lengthy and at times heated discussion was the matter of Sunday services. In the resolution which was finally adopted the question was not included except by inference. The resolution read:

The conference declares itself in favor of maintaining the historical Sabbath as a fundamental institution of Judaism and of exerting every effort to enforce its observance.[74]

This action places the conference on record as favoring the retention of the historical Sabbath. However, this proceeding should not be understood as implying objection to a service on Sunday, since a number of the men who voted for it held such services. The conference took a definite stand in this matter of Sunday services when a committee was appointed to prepare a ritual for use at such services. Although the committee was designated "Committee on Week-Day Services," it was definitely understood that its work was to be the preparation of a ritual to be used in such congregations as conduct services on Sunday. The committee was so named to give point to the stand of the conference that not Sunday, but Saturday, is the Sabbath, while the first day of the week has no sacred character from the Jewish point of view.

The following year at Louisville, the Reverend Dr. Joseph Krauskopf in his presidential message called attention to economic and business conditions which make the observance of the historical Sabbath practically impossible for thousands and urged the need of a service on the civil day of rest for the benefit of such as cannot attend on the historical Sabbath. In response to this presentation of the matter the conference placed the seal of its approval upon the resolution adopted by the Pittsburg Conference by concurring in the recommendation of the committee on President's Message, which reported on the subject in this wise:

We recommend that the principle expressed in the resolution adopted at the Pittsburg Conference in November, 1885, presenting it in the following form:

> Whereas, we recognize the importance of maintaining the historical Sabbath as a bond with our great past and a symbol of the unity of Israel the world over; and,
>
> Whereas, on the other hand, it cannot be denied that there is a very large number of Jews who, owing to economic and industrial conditions, are not able to attend services on our sacred day of rest; be it
>
> Resolved, that in the judgment of this conference there is nothing in the spirit of Judaism to prevent the holding of divine service on Sunday or any other week day where the necessity for such service is felt.[75]

At the Cleveland Conference in 1905 a committee was appointed to gather data on the influence of Sunday services for good or ill to the cause of Judaism. The burden of the exhaustive report of the committee which was presented to the Indianapolis Conference in July, 1906, was to the effect that these services had done much in nearly every locality in which they had been introduced toward reviving interest in Judaism and its teachings.[76] The conference has taken official recognition of the Sunday service. The members, with the fewest exceptions, believe that the Saturday Sabbath is the only Sabbath for the Jew; but many of them likewise believe that by an additional service on Sunday hundreds and thousands can be reached who would otherwise stand altogether outside of

Judaism's influence. Not the transfer of the Sabbath to the Sunday is advocated, but a way out of the supreme difficulty presented by the conflict between Sabbath observance and the demands of life, and this, it is believed, is achieved by a supplementary service on the civil day of rest. However, most of the congregations in the land hold the extra service on Friday evening at a late hour, generally about eight o'clock.

This has been the doctrinal development, if it may be so termed, of the reform movement in the United States. Accompanying this doctrinal development there have been introduced a great number of ceremonial reforms. Each one of these reforms was adopted individually by each congregation that introduced it. Every innovation met, in most instances, with stubborn opposition, and, in some cases, was the cause of division in, and secession from, the congregation. But these things are happily forgotten now. It is unnecessary to give the account of how and when each and every one of these reforms was introduced into each congregation. Sufficient to say that now, owing to these reforms in the ritual, the service in the reform congregations is decorous, uplifting, and reverential. The chief liturgical and ritual reforms may be summed up as consisting in the reading of prayers in the vernacular, as discussed above, the introduction of the organ with mixed choirs, the abolition of the women's gallery [77] and the introduction of family pews,[78] the worship with uncovered heads, the substitution of the confirmation ceremony for boys and girls in place of the *Bar Mitzvah* for boys alone,[79] the abolition of the calling of the Torah, the selling of *Mitzwot* and like practices that had become abuses, the abolition of the second day holidays; these reforms are now accepted as a matter of course, and show how completely Judaism in America has been modernized. Its spiritual interpretation of the tenets of the faith rests on the highest plane of ethical monotheism, and is in a line with the most exalted thought on the universal character of Israel's faith and mission as first proclaimed by the great prophets of old.

The Union of American Congregations and the Hebrew Union College

Almost from the moment of his coming to this country Isaac M. Wise had urged the formation of a union of the congregations of the land and the foundation of a theological seminary. As early as 1848 he issued an appeal for a union among the congregations; in 1854 he established the Zion College Association, which opened Zion College in Cincinnati; this, however, had but a very short life. For many years he continued to advocate these his pet ideas, in season and out of season. At the rabbinical conference held in Cincinnati in 1871 the matter received definite expression in the following resolution:

> The members of the conference take upon themselves the duty to bring prominently before the congregation, to advocate and to support by their influence, the following project of coöperation of the American Hebrew Congregations:
> The congregations to unite themselves into a Hebrew Congregational Union with the object to preserve and advance the union of Israel; to take proper care of the development and promulgation of Judaism; to establish and support a scholastic institute, and the library appertaining thereto, for the education of rabbis, preachers and teachers of religion; to provide cheap editions of the English Bible and text books for the schools of religious instruction; to give support to weak congregations, and to provide such other institutions which elevate, preserve, and promulgate Judaism.
> Resolved, that whenever twenty congregations, with no less than two thousand contributing male members, shall have declared, in accordance with the preceding resolution, their resolution to enter the H. C. U., the said committee shall convoke the synod to meet at such time and place as may be most satisfactory to the coöperating congregations.

For two years after that Dr. Wise agitated the subject almost every week in his organ, *The Israelite*. His persistent efforts were finally rewarded. On July 8, 1873, the organization of the Union of American Congregations was effected at a meeting in the city of Cincinnati by thirty-four congregations, numbering eighteen hundred members. This union, which now comprises two hundred and eighty-two congregations, meets in council every two years: each congregation is represented by delegates; rabbis and laymen meet for mutual discussion and interchange of opinion. The union was originally intended to include congregations of all shades of religious opinion, and

therefore it was determined that no questions of religious belief
or practice should be discussed at its meetings, in order to avoid
dissension. However, it has now become practically a union of
the reform congregations.

Its greatest achievement has been the establishment of the
Hebrew Union College, which was opened on October 3, 1875.
This is the theological training school of Reform Judaism in
America. The first class, consisting of four, was graduated
in 1883. The number of rabbis that have gone forth from its
halls now reaches three hundred and sixteen.

In 1922, a second institution for the training of liberal rabbis, entitled The Jewish Institute of Religion, was organized in
New York City. Its founder the Reverend Dr. Stephen S. Wise,
who founded also the Free Synagogue in 1907, has served as
the acting president from the time of the organization. The
Institute held its first commencement May 26, 1926, and up
to this time has graduated forty-two rabbis who occupy pulpits
in congregations throughout the country. All these organizations and institutions testify to the activity and energy of
the reform movement in American Judaism. The Union of
Congregations, the Central Conference of Rabbis, the Hebrew
Union College, the Union Prayer-Book are notable achievements. These are warrant sufficient of the spirit that animates
the earnest workers in the cause of Judaism in the land where
it has had the fullest opportunity to grow and develop without
hindrance from government or obstacle from environment.
Judaism has celebrated a rebirth in America and Professor
Moritz Lazarus of Berlin was probably a true prophet when he
wrote that the future of the faith lies in the United States and
that the inspiration in coming days will go forth from there.

During the convention of the Union of American Hebrew
Congregations held in Cincinnati in January, 1913, the superb
new buildings of the Hebrew Union College were dedicated.
During this same convention, The Federation of Temple Sisterhoods which has now grown to great proportions was organized and ten years later the Federation of Temple Brother-
hoods was formed.

The past fifteen years have witnessed remarkable changes in
Jewish religious life in the United States. The reform group
which at one time was in the majority has become a minority.
A large number of orthodox Jews have become self-conscious.
In this self-consciousness, several of their leaders are recogniz-

ing that if Judaism is to survive in the American environment it must adapt itself to American conditions of life, and to modern outlooks. Such leaders and their adherents are differentiating themselves from the strictly orthodox group and calling themselves conservative.

Thus in his presidential address at the opening of the Rabbinical Assembly at Atlantic City in July, 1927, Rabbi Max Drob declared that the United Synagogue which stands between ultra-orthodox and ultra-reform is the hope of the religious future of Judaism in the United States.[80] At this same convention one of the foremost exponents of this so-called third party in American Judaism, declared that the Rabbinical Assembly "had put Conservative Judaism in the field of American vision."[81] Changed conditions demand new definitions of Judaism and new alignments. East European Judaism is not suited to American requirements. In a symposium on orthodox, conservative and reform Judaism, arranged by the Hebrew Union College for Teachers in New York City, in the spring of 1928, Dr. Jacob Kohn, the protagonist of conservative Judaism declared "that its chief characteristic is that it recognizes that Judaism in all its rich complexity must be subject to constant development and adaptation." This sounded so dangerously like the advocacy of Reform Judaism that the speaker anticipated the possible charge that he had become a convert to Reform Judaism by making a hair-splitting distinction in that he stated that his Conservative Judaism instead of conceding the reformation of Judaism advocates "reform in Judaism from time to time." Another leading thinker of the conservative group, Dr. Mordecai M. Kaplan, subjects the reform position to acid criticism[82] and dissents also from the program of the orthodox whom he calls Jewish fundamentalists. He calls for a distinct formulation of the principle or principles which the conservative party intends to follow in the changes they would introduce, "the bootlegging of innovations will have to be stopped." He dubs the followers of Reform Judaism, Reformists. He is dissatisfied with the policy of Conservative Judaism. He is disturbed by the attacks of the orthodox party. He repudiates the name conservative and advocates a new name for the middle of the road party, namely, "Reconstructionists." In his definition of this term he writes "what we want is that Jewish life should become as many sided as it is possible to make it in the Diaspora, with Palestine as our cultural and spiritual center. Our interest is centered in the reinterpretation and reconstruction of traditional ideas that are at the basis of our theology, ritualism, and Jewish law. Hence we should be known as the Reconstructionist Party in Judaism." [83]

Similarly Dr. Louis Finkelstein, professor at the Jewish Theological Seminary, speaking at a conference of the United Synagogue in November, 1928, likened the condition of present-day Judaism to a leaky ship; the ship that was built in the ghetto must be reconstructed for American use.

From such expressions it grows abundantly clear that the principle of adaptation to changing needs and circumstances which has been the characteristic of the Reform Movement in Judaism from the beginning is being recognized and advocated throughout American Jewry, barring the adherents of *Shulchan Aruk* Judaism. It is largely a question of more or less. As the years pass there will doubtless be an ever greater rapprochement of conservatism to the reform position.

CHAPTER XIII

THE LATEST DEVELOPMENTS IN EUROPE

THE past half of a century has witnessed many interesting passages-at-arms between Jewish traditionalists and progressionists in Europe. The unfortunate dissonance between the daily practice of the Jews and the official teaching of the synagogue is constantly apparent. What official Judaism declares binding thousands of Jews in practical life disregard. The two synods had disappointed the expectations of their projectors that the leaders of Jewry in convention assembled would succeed in finding ways and means to reconcile these differences.[1] The forward spirit among the people, however, despite the untiring efforts of the orthodox, could not be stemmed. A most significant event was the opening of the *Hochschule für die Wissenschaft des Judenthums* in Berlin May 6, 1872.[2] The purpose of this institution was the training of rabbis along liberal lines; Abraham Geiger among the rabbis, and Moritz Lazarus[3] among the laymen, were its leading spirits. As was to be expected, this action on the part of the reformers was met by a similar movement on the part of the orthodox. October 21, 1873, the orthodox rabbinical seminary was founded by Israel Hildesheimer, the uncompromising foe of each or any reform in ritual or practice.[4] The Hildesheimer brand of orthodoxy is thoroughly consistent; here there is no recognition of changed conditions and changing views. The body of tradition is sacred; he who would alter even the least among the numberless precepts is a transgressor in Israel. The Berlinese community, however, has been committed for some time to the reform position through its official mouthpiece, the main congregation (*Hauptgemeinde*). No reforms of a far-reaching character had been introduced, it is true; but still some changes had been made in the liturgy, and as soon as any change, however slight, is countenanced, the principle of religious progress is recognized, and the orthodox position is surrendered. Appreciating this fact, orthodox leaders bent their energies toward securing legislation which would permit their followers to secede from the main congregation and form themselves into separate orthodox congregations. The law in Prussia and other German states was to the effect that every Jew had to belong and contribute to the main Jewish congregation. If a body of Jews who dissented from the standpoint represented by the main congregation, desired to form themselves into a society organized on lines agreeable to their convictions, they could do so as a private enterprise, but they were compelled to retain membership in the main congregation if they wished to be considered within the pale of Judaism. The Berlin reform congregation was a case in point. Its members had to bear a double burden; although repeated efforts had been made by this congregation to obtain official standing, and thus free its communicants from bearing this double obligation, these efforts had proved unavailing.[4a]

In 1873 the orthodox, under the inspiration of Samson Raphael Hirsch, began to agitate for the passing of a law by the Legislature known as the Law of Withdrawal (*Austritts-gesetz*). This was intended so to change the existing law as to permit a Jew to step out of the main congregation and join an orthodox congregation without thereby officially forfeiting allegiance to Judaism. The German Israelitish Congregational Union, which had been organized in 1871, protested against this proposed legislation in a petition to the law-making body of the land, in which it was set forth that such a law would weaken the main congregations and give many individuals the excuse not to contribute. Hirsch had succeeded in enlisting the powerful coöperation of Eduard Lasker, possibly the leading German political leader next to Bismarck; Lasker consented to father the bill, and it was passed in 1876. The results of this law were far-reaching, not so much as it caused the formation of separate orthodox congregations (this proved to be the case only in Berlin, Frankfort,[5] and Wiesbaden), but because it forced the congregations of the various German cities to adopt a policy of accommodation for fear of a diminution of revenue; care was taken by the officers of the congregation not to permit the introduction of reforms lest this might lead to secession on the part of many to whom reform was distasteful. The Law of Withdrawal was the club which the orthodox held over the congregations to compel a maintenance of the *status quo*. In

large communities it was natural that there should be many
shades of opinion; provision should have been made as far as
possible to meet the religious requirements of the different elements, reform services with liturgical changes, organ, German
sermon, choir for reformers, and traditional services without
these changes and additions for the orthodox. But the orthodox party was generally unwilling to agree even to the principle
"like opportunities for all," and this just policy was prevented
from being put into practice. Truth to say, the anti-Semitic
movement in Germany which beginning in 1875 infected with
its virus as the years passed every phase of life, political, social,
educational, industrial, so engrossed the energy and attention
of the Jews in combating it, that all specifically Jewish interests, notably the purely religious, suffered. Thousands came
to look upon their Judaism as a misfortune because it blocked
their material advancement. Conversions became more and
more numerous,° indifference to the religion on the part of
those who did not take this extreme step grew more and more
pronounced. So desperate did the situation become that the
rabbis of Berlin deemed it necessary to convoke a conference
of the rabbis of Germany to deliberate upon ways and means
to meet the critical turn of affairs. The conference took place
at Berlin, June 4 and 5, 1884. The discussions centered about
three points: first, the relation of Judaism to other faiths;
secondly, the means to quicken the religious spirit of the people
and to further the cause of religious education; and thirdly,
the formation of a Union of the Rabbis of Germany. The pronouncement of the relation of Judaism to followers of other
faiths was called forth by the accusations of the anti-Semites
and was intended to be the official reply of Jewish leaders to
agitators of the Stöcker type. This declaration aroused so
much attention at the time it was made and has in itself so
much intrinsic value, that it will be given a place here although
its subject matter does not come directly within the compass
of this study. Said these rabbis in conference assembled:

> In the name and under the protection of the one and
> only God, the conference of German rabbis makes the
> following declaration over against the defamations which
> hatred and prejudice have heaped upon the moral teach-
> ings of Judaism of late years. The command to love the
> neighbor, which is enjoined in the third Book of Moses,

chapter 19, verse 18, in the words "Thou shall love thy neighbor as thyself, I am the Lord," and which is designated by Hillel, the great master, as being the essence of the whole Jewish doctrine, has reference not alone to the members of the Jewish race or faith, but is an unlimited statute including all men, as is also the command inculcating righteousness in the same book, chapter 24, verse 22: "Ye shall have one manner of law, as well for the stranger as for the home-born; for I am the Lord your God." Every man who demonstrates his humanity by doing justly, loving mercy and walking humbly before God, is considered truly pious in the eyes of Judaism, even though he be born in another religious faith, and will participate in future salvation as is taught in the Talmudical expression which has become engraved in the Jewish consciousness "The pious of all peoples have a share in the bliss of the future life." These teachings are the fundamental tenets defining the position of Judaism towards the followers of other faiths. If, however, in the Jewish literature which has grown up during thousands of years there occur sentences here and there which do not correspond with these fundamental principles, such sentences are to be considered the opinions of individuals, or else they were called forth by the oppression of the age and have no binding force.⁷

This conference was not a reform conference; in fact, in the call which was issued convening it, it was stated that "every religious difference of opinion will be excluded from the discussions." When the consideration of the vital matter of how to quicken the religious spirit was on the carpet, no suggestions were made similar to those offered in the conferences of the fifth decade. The means to accomplish this end were declared to be the spreading among the people of a knowledge of Jewish teachings and Jewish achievements, and the devotion of particular attention to the education of the young. True, most of the rabbis here assembled, were far removed from the orthodox type of the old school; they were men of modern culture, but for the most part had no sympathy with religious reform; they were conservative in practice, however radical they may have been in thought. This is the tragedy of the religious situation among the Jews of Germany; the religious leaders occupy an outgrown standpoint; the people look upon Judaism simply as a heritage from the past with no modern message for them. The inconsistency of officers of congregations who insist upon a religious policy in the congregations with which their whole life is at variance [8] has been bitingly but truthfully defined by the term "ham-eating orthodoxy" (*Schinkenorthodoxie*).[9] A leading thinker said, in describing the situation, "A deep cleft yawns between the religious views of the majority of German Jews and those views which receive expression in Jewish schools, from many pulpits and in most Jewish newspapers and magazines! [10]

This intolerable state of affairs, which became more and more noticeable in the closing decades of the nineteenth century, led to the formation in Berlin in 1895 of the "Liberal Society for the Affairs of the Jewish Community" (*Liberaler Verein für die Angelegenheiten der jüdischen Gemeinde*), whose purpose was stated to be "to further religious development within the Jewish community of Berlin and to strive to have the administration conducted along liberal lines." The immediate cause of the formation of this society lay in the fact that the representatives of the community administered the congregational affairs without any regard to the wishes of the liberals and without any attempt to harmonize the public expression of Judaism with the life its professors were leading. In the first address which this society issued in April, 1895, to the Jews of Berlin, attention was called to the attacks upon Jews and Judaism from without. These, however, would pass and do little permanent harm were it not for the internal ills, viz. apostasy, indifference, and the seeking for salvation in the return to inflexible forms or the acceptance of the nationalistic interpretation of Judaism.

> History is repeating itself. As has always been the case in times of oppression from without, so in these anti-Semitic days, apostasy and fanaticism are making their appearance. But history also teaches the remedy against this double-headed evil, viz. the strengthening of the religious sentiment by new inner incentives through which the outer forms also receive new significance. The cultural development in German Jewry prompted by Mendelssohn, the religious development further by Geiger, may now less than ever be permitted to come to a standstill.

The signers of the address declared they desired, not violent change, but peaceful development; that they stood on the historical ground of their faith. What they aimed for was a development of the forms, so that they be no meaningless observances, but continue as the real outer expressions of the inner belief. "Berlin has always been the center of the spiritual struggle of German Jewry. Let us not prove ourselves unworthy of our fathers."

The formation of a liberal society was declared to be a pressing need just at this time because the election of representatives would take place in the following autumn. The program of the society was thus set forth:

> We unfurl the banner of religious progress in Judaism. Liberals not only in name, but also in conviction, we will never coerce consciences. We gladly concede to our coreligionists who hold different views from ours the right to demand the continuation of institutions that express their point of view, but the watchword of equal rights may not, as has been the case of late, be so interpreted as to signify the fulfillment of every demand of the orthodox or seemingly orthodox minority. Equal rights also for us, the great liberal majority of the community! The community is still without a house of worship in which the service is conducted for the greater part in the vernacular, in which all, especially our wives and children, can participate with full comprehension and therefore with proper edification.[11] What our forefathers found to be necessary already thousands of years ago, the service in the vernacular, cannot be a mischievous innovation to-day. Our solution in all questions of the public worship is this: as we wish to exercise no coercion of conscience, so will we not tolerate any.

They also pleaded for such a religious education of the children as would acquaint them with the essentials of Judaism; but they desired the children to be animated by the same spirit that animated them, viz. love for their faith combined with love for their fatherland, so that the children should be German not only in language and education, but also in sentiment. The motto of the society, then, was "Equal rights for all." They would have the representatives of the community provide for the various tendencies of thought among Jews by synagogues

corresponding in the mode of worship to these various tendencies, reform synagogues for reformers, conservative for conservatives, orthodox for the orthodox.

In the autumn of 1895 the society issued another address
urging the election of the liberal candidates for the representative assembly; in this address the campaign cry was again
raised for the vernacular in the service; that system of religious
education was also denounced which set forth the chief content
of Judaism as consisting of such ceremonies as the children see
their parents disregard and by which course of instruction
school and home are brought into conflict.

> Apostasy and indifference will spread if there is no
> other choice but that between forced observance of ortho-
> dox demands and complete non-observance. This sad
> result can be avoided if provision is made for the satis-
> faction of the liberal religious sentiment.

In the election which took place at the end of November, the
liberal candidates were defeated by a small majority; the religious indifference of the Berlin Jewish community appears
from the fact that of 16,235 electors privileged to cast their
ballots for these officers only 4,620 voted.

It was during the incumbency of the representatives chosen
at this election that the question of a service on Sunday became
a burning issue. In August, 1897, Gustav Levinstein issued a
pamphlet entitled *The Demand for Sunday Service,* advocating
a service on the civil day of rest supplementary to the service
on Saturday. True, the reform congregation had conducted
services on that day for fifty years, but Levinstein advocated
its general introduction in Jewish congregations as the only
measure competent to solve the glaring inconsistency between
the theoretical and the practical observance of the Sabbath.
This pamphlet called forth a number of replies.[12] The matter,
however, did not end as a purely academic discussion, but active
steps were taken to give the suggestion practical effect. On
February 20, 1898, a petition signed by five thousand eight
hundred names was submitted to the representatives asking for
a supplementary service on Sunday. The debate called forth
by this petition was heated; naturally, the petition aroused the
bitter opposition of the conservative members; some remarkable expressions were used in the course of the debate which
reveal the peculiar state of mind of many so-called orthodox

Jews who are anything but orthodox in practice, and throw a flood of light upon the Jewish religious situation in Germany where the rankest hypocrisy prevails, the Judaism of the synagogue having no connection with the Judaism of daily life. Said one of the orthodox representatives unreservedly: "One can think orthodox and feel orthodox without having to practice orthodoxy." [13]

The petition was rejected by the decisive vote of nineteen to two. A resolution to hold late Friday evening services with sermon during the months between the Feasts of Tabernacles and Passover was adopted. The Berlin rabbinate had submitted to the meeting an opinon unfavorable to the holding of services on Sunday. In reply to a request of the representatives for an opinion on Friday evening services, two members of the rabbinate, Maybaum and Rosenzweig, answered dissentingly, giving as their reason the fear that such a service would detract from the attendance on Sabbath morning; they stated, further, that this would necessitate two services on Friday evening, one at the entrance of the Sabbath in accordance with the prescribed command of the *Shulchan Aruk,* and the other at the hour fixed by the representatives. The other two rabbis, Stier and Weisse, expressed their willingness to carry out the resolution of the representatives. This resolution was then reaffirmed at a meeting in March, 1898.

Levinstein now issued another pamphlet in which he criticized sharply the response of the rabbinate on the subject and the action of the representatives. A result of this agitation appeared in the election for representatives in November, 1898, when, in addition to the regular tickets of the conservative and liberal parties, a third ticket was placed in the field under the auspices of a committee for the introduction of a service with sermon on Sunday, in addition to the regular Sabbath service. The liberals elected a majority of the representatives. [14] At the meeting of the representatives held on February 18, 1900, Levinstein presented a petition for the introduction of a service on Sunday. This petition was referred to a committee of five, who at a subsequent meeting reported recommending that religious addresses be delivered on Sunday at an hour when business was suspended. This was defeated, as well as two other propositions, one of which was that a week-day service with sermon be held on Sunday in one of the communal synagogues at a business-free hour, and the other that a religious discourse

without a service, but with an opening and closing song, be
delivered at such an hour.

This question of a service on Sunday was made the issue at
the election for representatives in November, 1901.[15] The conservatives worked the community up to a great pitch of excitement on the subject, and succeeded in carrying the election.

The affairs of the community during the next three years
were administered in an altogether reactionary spirit. During
these years steps were taken to build a new synagogue. The
representatives purposed to dispense with an organ in the building.[16] This called forth an article in publication No. 17 [17] of
the Liberal Society in December, 1903, entitled "Liberalism in
Berlin." A warning note was sounded that the Jews of Berlin
should see to it lest the metropolis of intelligence, progress, and
culture in religious concerns, became the leader of the reaction.
The reactionary policy of the representatives did, in fact, arouse
the community. In October, 1904, the liberal society issued an
electoral address to the Jewish voters in which they showed
how during the past three years the needs and demands of the
liberal element had been altogether disregarded; despite the
fact that every synagogue which had been erected in Berlin
during a period of forty years was equipped with an organ, the
one that had been dedicated in 1904 was without this instrument; it was also intended to revise the prayer-book in use by
the community and include all the old prayers that had been
removed; the children's Sabbath afternoon [18] service had been
so changed as to be conducted altogether on orthodox lines;
the object of the conservatives was to stifle every liberal aspiration. At the election the liberals succeeded in returning all their
candidates. There can be little doubt that the great majority of
the Jews of the German capital sympathize with the forward
movement in Judaism, but reform there has been a matter of
shreds and patches; the synagogue, despite the organ and the
German sermon, still breathes of Orientalism, as does also the
official interpretation of Judaism, while the people in thought
and in life are thoroughly Occidentalized; until this dissonance
shall be removed Judaism cannot be the great influence in the
lives of its followers that its essential and fundamental teachings demand that it should and must be.[19]

The reform movement in Germany had its beginning in
Westphalia through the activity of Israel Jacobson. Throughout the nineteenth century the congregations of Westphalia had

taken no especially further noticeable part in the cause of religious progress. Toward the end of the century, however, the spirit again awoke in this Rhenish province, when, in 1892, the Union of Jewish Congregations of Westphalia resolved to revise the traditional prayer-book on the basis of the five following rules of procedure: the elimination of those prayers which are no longer prayed to-day; the excision of those portions wherein mention is made of sacrifices and sacrificial service; the removal of passages speaking of the return to Jerusalem; the avoidance of the many repetitions and reiterations, notably when the content of one prayer is repeated in the next following; the removal of all expressions not in consonance with the outlook of our time (by which is to be understood also the limitation of the mystical element as far as this is possible). The whole prayer-book was to be translated into German. The task was entrusted to Dr. H. Vogelstein, one of the foremost rabbis of Germany.[20] This prayer-book was issued in 1894. In accordance with the provisions just mentioned, all prayers of a national tendency were so changed as to define Israel's mission to be ליחד את שמו the spread of the truth of monotheism; the sacrificial prayers, the petition for the return to Palestine, and the restoration of the Jewish state were all recast in such a manner as to comport with the feeling and thought of the Jew for whom the mission of Judaism is religious and not political. The prayer which had been so often misrepresented by the enemies of the Jews as being a petition for the punishment of non-Jews was so changed as to read ולמלשינות, the practice being put in place of the person so as to make misinterpretation impossible. In his preface the author stated: "We desire to be truthful in all our speech, and notably when we direct our words in prayer to the God of truth." In the service for the anniversary of the destruction of Jerusalem (*Tisha b'ab*), after indulging in reminiscences of what Zion and Jerusalem were, the prayer continues: "We bear now another, a higher ideal, in our hearts—the triumph of the sublime teachings of reverence for God and pure humanity which were proclaimed on Zion by prophets, psalmists, and teachers."

The book was bitterly attacked by the orthodox leaders and press. In a reply to the criticisms the author called upon his liberal coreligionists not to be misled nor discouraged; he bade them think of their children and remove from their path every obstacle which would interfere with their proper conception of the high mission of Judaism. He disclaimed any intention of forcing the prayer-book upon any who believed that the retention of the old prayers for the restoration of the sacrifices and similar petitions conduced to the enhancement of the religious spirit. Let such who sincerely believe this continue in the old way; but,

> If you do not wish Israel to be gathered from the four corners of the earth and brought back to Palestine, if you believe that the sacrificial service was simply a concession to views now antiquated and that its restoration is not desirable, then let the truth have its place in the prayers, and be not led by fear or false considerations to utter with your lips what your heart does not share; make not of your tongue a bow of falsehood; and be assured that if as true Israelites you will speak the praise of the Highest in your houses of worship with the expressions in the new prayer-book, you will perform a service acceptable to God.

The protest of fifty orthodox rabbis against the prayer-book elicited an answer from the executive committee of the Westphalian Congregational Union, in which they declared themselves in full accord with the principles expressed in the prayer-book.

> We desire no return to Jerusalem. We desire no restoration of the sacrificial service, against which the prophets thundered with fiery zeal. What we desire not shall not find expression in our prayers; otherwise we would be guilty of hypocrisy, which would be equivalent to a mockery of the name of God. Our fundamental teachings and truths are the belief in God and the lofty morality which the Bible enjoins upon us as a duty.

They then point out the steps they had taken for the religious education of the young, and other constructive work and declare that they have no desire to tear down, but to build up and fortify, the faith which to them is dear. But,

> We publicly disavow the efforts of Jewish orthodoxy. We have nothing in common with the men whose eager longing it is to return to Palestine and whose ideal service is the offering of sacrifices. Our conception of Judaism is

different from theirs; this we wish to establish once and for all.[21]

Frankfort-on-the-Main, which witnessed many conflicts between reformers and traditionalists, the home of the radical Reform Society of 1843 on the one hand, and on the other the scene of the activity of the great pillar of orthodoxy, Samson Raphael Hirsch, and his unremitting fight against every innovation, witnessed a recrudescence of the reform spirit in 1904. On the holy days in the fall of that year, a service was held in a hall in the West End of the city at which a new prayer-book with German prayers was used. In this prayer-book many of the old prayers were shortened, a number of German prayers, selections from the psalms in German translation and German hymns were inserted; the singing was accompanied by the organ, and German sermons were preached. The prayer-book was prepared by Dr. Cæsar Seligman,[22] rabbi of the main congregation, but the service was more reformed than in this congregation. Many who had been estranged for years attended. Here the plan vainly advocated by progressionists in Berlin that provision should be made for all shades of belief was carried out, and with evident success.

On May 25, 1899, the "Union of the Liberal Rabbis of Germany" was formed under the presidency of Dr. H. Vogelstein, of Stettin; eighteen rabbis were present, although forty-eight signified their willingness to join. No far-reaching reforms were resolved upon, although the spirit of the meeting was, as the name of the society indicates, free and liberal. The few definite resolutions evince the recognition of changed conditions in Jewish life and the desire to meet them. The conference departed in a number of things from traditional usage. Thus they resolved that marriages may be solemnized during the *Sefira*, the seven weeks intervening between the feasts of Passover and Weeks; in urgent cases, during the two weeks between the seventeenth of Tammuz and the first of Ab, but in no instance during the nine days from the first to the ninth of Ab.[23]

The *Bar Mitzwah* ceremony, the official assumption by boys of the duties of Judaism on their thirteenth birthday, has except in very orthodox congregations, come to be an empty form. The boys recite the benedictions before and after reading the Torah, but the ceremony has no living force. In order to give the ceremony significance, the rabbis here assembled determined to introduce the custom in their congregations of making a short address to the boy on the meaning of Judaism and the duties of the Jew and having the boy speak a confession of faith in German before the congregation.

The question of cremation had begun to assume importance. What to do in cases when called upon to officiate in a case of cremation was of interest to every minister, notably as a number of such instances had taken place.[24] This conference made a declaration on the subject:

> Cremation is not in accord with traditional Jewish practice. It is the duty of the rabbi to strive for the maintenance of the traditional custom. Still, if requested to officiate, the rabbi should not refuse religious coöperation, but should participate in the funeral service.[25]

At the second meeting of the Association, held at Frankfort-on-the-Main, July 9, 1902, the only discussion involving reform was that concerning *chalitzah*. The very fact that German rabbis of the twentieth century seriously discussed this outgrown Oriental custom, which is altogether at variance with the practice and thought of Jews in Western lands, shows how slightly reform had touched official German Jewish practice, although life had long ago repudiated the practice. Dr. Vogelstein proposed the question for discussion "how is the rabbi to proceed if the *yibum*[26] will not permit the act of *chalitzah* to be performed or if the *yibum* cannot be reached?" All present agreed that the Jewish marriage law required reform, but the difficulty of such reform was pointed out because it would be likely to cause a split in Judaism. No resolution was passed, but the opinion was given expression to that just as in many other cases, so also here, things would so develop that those rabbinical enactments which had disappeared from the living consciousness of Judaism would gradually pass out of practice.[27]

This latter utterance expresses a great truth, and it is indeed remarkable that these rabbis were not guided by it. Truly, there were too many burning questions involving the very life of Judaism itself to engage the attention of rabbis in meeting assembled for them to waste their deliberations on such an outgrown subject as *chalitzah,* of the very existence of which few Occidental Jews knew.[28]

All in all, it appeared that in Germany the problem of the adjustment of Judaism to modern life and modern thought had been solved by no manner of means. It is true that, compared with the Berlin synagogue of one hundred years ago, its modern successor shows the effect of the liberalizing influences at work, and it is still more true that the German citizen of Jewish belief and descent is as far removed in thought and outlook from his ghetto ancestor of one hundred years ago as is pole from pole. But with the de-Orientalization and de-rabbinization has gone hand in hand a de-Judaization, because the Jew of modern education and modern views has not been made to feel and understand that the eternal principles of his inherited faith do not rise and fall with traditions, institutions, and ceremonies which have disappeared from active life, but are preserved in the mummy casket of the synagogue. Judaism has become foreign to the Jew's life in the centers of German activity, and the leaders, instead of grappling with this all-overmastering problem of the vitalizing significance of the religion, busied themselves with discussions in their gathering in the year 1904 concerning the *chalitzah*, an Oriental institution about which their constituents knew little and cared less, and at their meeting in the year 1907 debated about the prohibited marriages of the priests concerning which equally little is cared." The romanticism, too, of Neo-orthodoxy that delights in the dim half-light of medievalism contributes much toward a confusion of main issues, and the Neo-nationalist movement known as Zionism succeeded in increasing the Babel. If the reform movement teaches anything clearly, it is the repudiation of the political and national aspects of traditional Judaism and the clear declaration that Judaism is a religion with a religious mission; Neo-orthodoxy, Zionism, inconsistent rabbinism, with its canonization of the *Shulchan Aruk* in theory and its repudiation thereof in practice, the juridical interpretation of Judaism as "law," these are the backward forces that drive the Jew of modern training and life further and further from his religion and leave him spiritually bankrupt. He comes in no manner of touch with the high message of his faith; in the synagogues the prayers are uttered in an unintelligible language; in his home there are no Jewish influences, in his wordly life Judaism is a negligible factor. Reform in its interpretation of Judaism aims to meet these conditions; in actuality it has fallen far short of carrying out this program in Germany, but this must be done if Judaism is to assert its place as a potent influence. New problems face the Jew to-day different from those of the ages past; "the theology of Judaism speaks of all things except those which are of the greatest necessity, viz. the doubts and struggles, the questions and pangs which agitate present-day Israel. A dream palace of past glory is constructed, and men teach and preach as though everything were in beautiful order and no chasm yawns in contemporary Judaism." [30] Thus strongly and truly wrote one of the leaders in Germany who felt the truth of the fundamental dictum of reform, viz. that the progressive development of humanity requires a constant reinterpretation of the principles of Judaism in the light of new conditions, and new thoughts will bring the essential teachings of the faith face to face with perplexing questions and help solve them. Reform teaches that Judaism is not merely a storehouse of traditions, not merely a survival from a far past, but a living faith with a message to living men, and that it requires only "the living breath in order that it may be rejuvenated from within."

Three years after these words were written, namely, in 1908, the Union for Liberal Judaism (*Vereinigung für das Liberale Judenthum*) was formed. An organ, *Liberales Judenthum* began to be issued. At meetings held in Berlin and Frankfort-on-the-Main in 1912, the Union of Liberal Rabbis adopted a program which was indorsed by the Union for Liberal Judaism at the convention held in Posen that same year. This program which restates the principles of Liberal Judaism in a number of paragraphs may be considered the official formulation of the theoretical principles of Reform Judaism in the land of its birth at the close of the first century of its existence. [31]

A new liberal movement of great promise was launched when in 1913, the Jewish Liberal Youth Society (*Jüdisch Liberaler Jugend Verein*) was organized in Breslau. The liberal Jewish movement had lost energy; reactionism and nationalism had played havoc with it. Young men imbued with the liberal idea determined to strengthen the movement. [32] There are now a number of these Liberal Youth Societies.

In his report on Liberal Judaism in Germany submitted at the Berlin Conference of the World Union for Progressive Judaism in 1928, Dr. Herman Vogelstein, in speaking of the present situation said,

We do not deceive ourselves about the difficulties and dangers which threaten liberal Judaism. We believe in the

unity of the whole community of Jews for we stand for
the unity of the congregations which comprise it, even
while we regret any attempt to force the individual conscience into conformity. But, at the same time, we ask for
recognition and respect for our convictions; indeed reverence for our religious principles. Peace and unity in the
congregation cannot be obtained through sacrificing principles but only through giving to everybody the religious
liberty to which he is entitled.

Liberal Judaism has already achieved great things, but
there are still great tasks before it. It has to accomplish
educational work; the work of persistent creation, of preserving and making new, through rebuilding upon old
foundations. Judaism needs liberalism and liberalism will
lead to the deepening and intensifying of Judaism, if it
knows how to accomplish its task and to develop it. Liberalism and indeed the whole of Judaism must be to us what
Goethe calls the perfect form, through which a living soul
is susceptible of constant development.

Despite such brave words the actuality of the situation in
Germany demonstrates that practice lags far behind theory.
The voice of liberal Judaism through its best known and most
capable exponents, Dr. Leo Baeck of Berlin, Dr. Cæsar Seligman of Frankfort and Dr. Herman Vogelstein of Breslau rings
clear and strong, but liberalism in practice is such only in name
in the liberal Jewish circles with few exceptions. Congregational Judaism is organized on the political pattern of the ruling
democracy in Germany. Just as there are a number of parties in
German political life so also are there opposing parties in Jewish
congregational politics. Every city has its so-called Jüdische
Gemeinde or Jewish community which legislates for all Jews in
Jewish matters. To the upkeep of this community every Jew
must contribute unless he officially separates himself from the
Jewish community.[33] Such "self-excommunication" puts the
person in question beyond the religious pale of the Jewish community and deprives him of even such privileges as represent
the minimum of Jewish loyalty, namely, burial in a Jewish
cemetery and participation in the worship at the Holy Day
services.

Furthermore, all synagogues in Germany, with three exceptions, must act in accordance with the legislation of the nation-

wide central organization. These three exceptions are the
Berlin Reform Gemeinde and the ultra-orthodox congregations
Adath Israel of Berlin, founded by Israel Hildesheimer and the
Adath Jeshurun congregation of Frankfort, founded by Samson Raphael Hirsch.

The Berlin central organization or Jüdische Gemeinde may
be cited as the pattern local organization. It is run politically.
There is an upper and lower house; the upper house consists of
seven *"Vorsteher,"* the lower house of twenty-one representatives. Every four years there is an election of representatives,
for whom every Jewish adult above twenty-one years of age
may cast his ballot. No congregation, barring the three above-
mentioned can manage its own affairs. Even so-called liberal
congregations can introduce no reforms unless sanctioned by
the Jewish legislature. The elections for delegates are veritable
political campaigns. At present (1929) there are five parties,
each with its own platform, namely, the Liberal, the Zionist,
the Mittel Partei, the Orthodox, and the Paole Zion.

Every proposition fathered by liberal forces must run the
gamut of political log rolling. This political organization of the
Jews of Germany complicates the religious situation indescribably. Liberal religion in Germany finds it most difficult to
register real achievement. This was illustrated conclusively by
a recent incident in February, 1929. The liberal congregation,
worshiping in the fine new synagogue on Prinzregentenstrasse,
requested the permission of the representatives of the Jewish
community to have family pews, so that the members of the
same family, both men and women, might sit together during
divine services. With the single exception of the Reform
Gemeinde, the sexes have been separated in all German synagogues, up to this time, the women sitting in the gallery or in
a women's section on the lower floor, as was the case in a few
progressive synagogues. The request went first to the upper
house in the form of a resolution to the effect that men and
women, members of the same family, shall be permitted to
occupy adjacent pews at divine services to be conducted at the
newly constructed Prinzregentenstrasse Synagogue, Berlin.

The upper house of seven members divided in the vote, the
three liberal members in favor, the two Zionist members
opposed, the orthodox member did not vote, and the Mittel
Partei member was absent. The upper house now sent the resolution to the lower house and at the same time asked the opinion

of the rabbis of Berlin. Now appeared the amazing fact of the division of the liberal house against itself. Of the eight liberal rabbis who submitted opinions on the subject only three favored the resolution outright, three opposed it and two offered substitute resolutions. It seems almost incredible that so-called liberal rabbis, ninety years after Abraham Geiger wrote his ringing words urging the religious equality of women with men, should have declared themselves against this measure. Said one of these misrepresentatives of that liberal Judaism, under whose banner he ostentatiously marches, "Picture a man making his way through a pew occupied by women in order to participate in a ceremony before the Holy Ark. We cannot afford to dispute a tradition of hundreds of years." *Sancta Simplicitas!* The same old argument! And another of these rabbis who passes as a liberal wrote the astonishing words, "For the past few hundred years the separation of sexes at services has been a distinctly Jewish practice. This we must keep. We cannot afford to assimilate Judaism with its environment." That orthodox and conservative rabbis should defend traditional practices was to be expected, but that liberal leaders should so express themselves rather passes comprehension. A few liberal rabbis, however, favored the resolution without equivocation in such a phrase as, "The modern attitude toward woman demands the change"; others hedged and offered compromises such as this, "While members of families should be permitted to sit together, the sexes of the other worshipers should be separated by a curtain." All this bears witness to the peculiar condition of liberal Judaism in Germany. The religious leaders, though theoretically liberal, are, with honorable exceptions, fearful of decisive action.

The leading layman was, however, unreserved in his advocacy of the change. Said Dr. Heinrich Stern:

> The new place of women in modern life, the modern interpretation of the status of mother and woman in Judaism and the recognition of the non-existence of male religiosity or female religiosity must lead us to dispense with the ordinance which separates the sexes during the services in our synagogue.

The resolution was finally carried by a vote of ten to nine. As a result of this bare majority, women will the first time in any synagogue affiliated with the Berlin Jüdische Gemeinde sit in pews on the main floor of the synagogue during regular divine services.

This action seems to have been inspired by the meeting of the World Union of Progressive Judaism held in Berlin in August, 1928. Miss Lily Montagu of London, who preached the sermon in the temple of the Reformgemeinde on Johanne-strasse and thus was the first woman to occupy a pulpit in any Jewish house of worship in Germany, declared in her published impressions of the meeting of the World Union: "The German women must come down from the galleries and take part literally and in a real sense in the construction of and struggle for a living religion for the entire community." Possibly this change in the religious status of woman is only the first sign of new life in liberal Judaism in Germany, as a result of the personal contact with the American and English representatives of liberal Judaism, and that gradually the present dissonance between theory and practice will give way to a greater con-sistency and a new chapter in the story of reform Judaism in Germany will be begun.

Without doubt the most significant recent practical achieve-ment of liberal Judaism in Germany is the compilation of a union prayer-book for liberal congregations.[34] From the days of the beginning of the reform movement, the change and adaptation of the public ritual had engaged the attention of the leaders of the movement. Commencing with the issuing of the Hamburg Temple Prayer-Book in 1818 one ritual after another appeared. Well-nigh every large congregation had its own prayer-book. This made for disunion. The same condition had prevailed in the United States but this was remedied when the Central Conference of American Rabbis issued in 1894 the Union Prayer-Book.[35] It appears that this achievement made a deep impression on the German liberal leaders and gave the impetus to a similar movement in that land. After years of agitation and preparation, the definite step was taken when, in 1926, the ritual committee of the Prussian Union of Jewish Congregations commissioned a sub-committee of three, consist-ing of Dr. Cæsar Seligman of Frankfort-on-the-Main, Dr. H. Vogelstein of Breslau, and Professor Ismar Elbogen of Berlin, to prepare this prayer-book. The important task was brought to a successful conclusion when the book appeared from the press in the summer of 1929.

In their preface to the book, the compilers set forth that

inasmuch as this is a prayer-book intended for all liberal congregations, a certain choice and latitude had to be provided for. Therefore, the entire Hebrew content as well as the German equivalent or adaptation of the prayers appears in the book. Each congregation can, therefore, make its choice of what it desires to use or omit. A number of abbreviations and changes in the traditional Hebrew prayers were made. Thus repetitions of the same prayer (*e.g.* Kaddish, Ashre, Kedusha) in the same service were avoided. A number of the prayers were abbreviated. New portions were added, such as a service for the eve of Chanukkah, Purim, and Tisha b'ab. New readings from the Torah and from the Haftara are provided for; *e.g.* the Torah reading for the second day of Shabuot has been changed from the traditional section, Deut. xv, 19-xvi, 17, to the repetition of the Ten Commandments in Deuteronomy v. For the Torah reading on Rosh Hashanah, a choice is offered as between the traditional section, Gen. xxii, and a newly suggested portion, Deuteronomy xxix (atem nizzabim). For the Torah reading on Yom Kippur afternoon, the passage Leviticus xix (Kedoshim tihyu) is substituted for the traditional section, Exodus xxxiii, 12-34. The tefillah has been shortened from eighteen to seven benedictions, the first and last three as in the traditional prayer-book, while the twelve intermediate benedictions are replaced by one, Kedushat hayom, the petition for a proper sanctification of the especial day, Sabbath or holiday, as the case may be.

There can be little doubt that much conscientious effort was expended on the production of this prayer-book, but barring the beautiful German rendition of the prayers, thus enabling the use of the vernacular whenever desired, the doctrines of Liberal Judaism find little place in the book. The petition for the bodily resurrection of the dead is retained. The reference to the personal Messiah appears; the Mussaf section, which has lost all significance for the modern worshiper, is retained in every service. Surprising, too, is the retention of the Kol Nidre declaration at the beginning of the service on the Eve of Atonement, although in revised form. There was such good reason for the action of the reformers present at the Brunswick conference in 1844, who eliminated the passage entirely from the prayer-book that it is more than passing strange that a so-called Liberal Prayer-Book should reinstate it ninety years later. The resolution carried by a very small majority at the meeting of

the Central Conference of American Rabbis in June, 1930, at
Providence, Rhode Island, to incorporate a revised Hebrew
version of the Kol Nidre in the contemplated new edition of the
Union Hymnal was made the occasion by Dr. Ismar Elbogen
to explain the reason which led him and his fellow-compilers
of the new German prayer-book to retain the Kol Nidre formula even though in greatly changed form.[36]

Still this prayer-book marks a great step forward in the
process of unification of the liberal congregations of Germany.
The spirit of devotion breathes throughout its pages. The purpose of the book is finely expressed by the compilers in the
closing sentence in the preface, which makes clear their own
desire.

> The genius of the synagogue has never rested, one gen-
> eration after another has striven to renew devotion and
> piety, each has enlivened the old heritage by the mode of
> expression of its time. So may also this prayer-book
> justify itself as an expression of the faith and hope, the
> humility and gratitude of our age! May it fulfill its
> mission as the inspirer of Jewish piety and faith!

In England a number of efforts have been made during the
past forty years to galvanize the petrifying body of Jewry into
life. The West London Synagogue, which had been organized as
a reform congregation, had in the course of time become wedded
to its traditions, and its fiftieth anniversary in 1892 found it
practically occupying the very standpoint it had taken on the day
of its organization. It had not gone forward. It has ceased to be
an energizing liberal force. It lived upon its past. The United
Synagogue, with the chief rabbi at its head, was encrusted with
traditionalism, and took no note of and made no provision
whatsoever for the hundreds of Jews who were drifting away
and for whom Judaism had ceased to have a living message.
The race Jew loomed large upon the horizon; to all religion
and all Jewish spirituality he turned a deaf ear. Indifference
was abroad in the land. The public services were unedifying,
and to very many unintelligible, being conducted in Hebrew
altogether. Ritual and life were contradictory of one another.
The Sabbath had become in great part a work-day and while
its praises as a day of rest were extolled in the synagogues
thousands were engaged in their daily vocations. The prayer-
book contained doctrines in which English Jews had ceased to

believe. True, a number of individuals were awake to the sorry condition of Judaism, and gave voice occasionally in written and spoken word to the necessity of introducing such changes in the public services and expositions of Judaism as were necessary to reclaim to their Jewish allegiance a generation which had grown up under conditions different absolutely from those of the ghetto period. Moved by considerations of this character, a committee of gentlemen, of whom Mr. F. H. Harvey Samuel was chairman, took steps to introduce a service on Sabbath afternoons which should be of such a nature as would attract those who found no spiritual uplift in the existing synagogal services. This movement was inaugurated at the West Hampstead Town Hall on February 22, 1890. The movement was known as the Hampstead Sabbath Afternoon Services and continued for three years. They were conducted by the Reverend Morris Joseph, who arranged an order of service.[37] In his preface, the author who was the guiding spirit of this movement stated well the reason which led him and his associates to initiate these services:

There is much reason to fear [wrote he] that the appeal made by the liturgy of the synagogue elicits but a feeble response from the intellect and the emotions of the modern Jew. The aspect of our places of worship on Sabbath mornings tends to show that the service lacks these vital elements which are needed in order to ensure its sway over the mind and the heart. Even of those who regularly attend a synagogue, many go away unimpressed without having experienced one prayerful feeling. But besides these, there are many others whose habitual absence from the House of God is plainly attributable to the failure of the service to perform its special function. This moral divorce between the educated Jew and the synagogue is deeply to be deplored, inasmuch as it portends his eventual alienation, or that of his children, from Judaism, perhaps from religion itself. It is in the hope of aiding to avert such a danger that the services for which the present prayer-book is compiled have been initiated. In determining their form, regard has been had to modern ideas and aspirations; but care has been taken at the same time to avoid those radical changes which are calculated to rob the liturgy of its distinctively Jewish character, and to

weaken that feeling of attachment to Israel's religion which
it is its chief business to enforce.

The services consisted of the traditional *Mincha* prayers.
There were, however, certain omissions and changes. The
prayer ובא לציון was abridged. The most important change,
inasmuch as it involved a doctrinal point, was that in the benediction רצה the word שירי "songs" was substituted for אישי
"burnt offerings," making this portion of the supplication read:
"Restore Thy worship to Thy sanctuary and let the supplications and *songs* of Israel ever be acceptable unto Thee," instead
of "the burnt offerings of Israel." This changed wording of
the traditional prayer but declared what most modern Jews
agreed with. The restoration of the sacrificial worship as conducted in the Temple of Jerusalem is, it is true, still prayed
for in orthodox synagogues, but it is more than doubtful
whether such sacrifices would be restored even were the apparently impossible to happen, viz. the rebuilding of the temple on
Moriah's hill. This is one of the instances of that disagree-
ment between liturgy and belief which the reform movement
aimed and aims to remove. Other features in which these
services differed from the orthodox form consisted in the use
of instrumental music and the participation of a mixed choir.
The Ten Commandments were read at each service. These
services were an advance upon the only reform service known
in London, viz. the West London Synagogue in the following
points: the Hebrew portion of the service was followed by
prayers, psalms, and hymns in English; the sexes, though
separated, were seated on the same floor, and the utmost freedom was given the preachers.

Besides Mr. Joseph, occasional preachers at these services
were the Reverends Professor Marks, Dr. Löwy and Isidore
Harris, ministers of the West London Synagogue, and the
Messrs. Claude G. Montefiore and Israel Abrahams. In 1892,
two years after these services had been inaugurated, the Board
of Management of the St. John's Wood Synagogue expressed
their willingness to have the services conducted in their house of
worship, provided the consent of the chief rabbi could be
obtained. The negotiations failed because the chief rabbi
demanded that the following conditions be complied with, viz.
that the prayer for the reinstitution of the sacrifices be
restored;[55] that the women be relegated to the galleries, and

that the preachers be limited to such gentlemen as he approved of. The committee found it impossible to accept these conditions, although for the sake of securing the great advantage of conducting the services in a synagogue, they would have agreed to accepting the further condition imposed by the chief rabbi involving the discontinuance of instrumental music. The services continued a year longer as an independent movement. A selection of the sermons preached at these services by Mr. Joseph was published under the title *The Ideal in Judaism.*[39]

Another Hampstead movement of a more radical character was the attempt in 1899 to organize a reform congregation with services on Sunday; a call was issued on May 28th of that year, in which the signers stated "after most earnest reflection, we are convinced that whilst being determined to safeguard the observance of the seventh day, Sabbath, it is an indispensable feature of the new movement that the daily morning service shall be so adapted as to enable many persons with their children to avail themselves of public worship on Sunday mornings." True, this effort did not succeed, but it demonstrated the shortsightedness of the policy of the representatives of official Judaism in the matter of the earliest Hampstead movement. Had the chief rabbi given his sanction to the Sabbath afternoon services; had he permitted them to be held in a synagogue under his jurisdiction with the few unimportant changes desired, he would have precluded the likelihood of the formation of this much more radical sentiment that found expression in this call. Both he and the Reverend J. F. Stern preached against the introduction of Sunday services.[40] Notable in the chief rabbi's sermon was, not the position that he took in unalterable opposition to a service on Sunday (this was natural and to be expected), but his appeal to the authorities of the West London Synagogue with which the new congregation proposed to associate itself not to countenance this movement. Truly, the whirligig of time brings its revenges. In 1842 the West London Synagogue was anathematized by the rabbis and the lay authorities of the official synagogue; in 1899 it was appealed to by a successor of the chief rabbi who had pronounced the *Cherem* upon it to join hands with him in suppressing a forward movement. The chief rabbi, in his sermon, recommended the introduction of Friday evening or Sabbath afternoon services. Even he had been brought to the recognition that

something must be done to attract to the synagogue the great
number who, because of economic and other conditions, cannot
or do not attend the regular Sabbath services.

Shortly after this incident was closed a statement appeared
in the London Jewish press under the heading, "The Sunday
Movement—A Religious Manifesto," signed by O. J. Simon.[41]
In this manifesto Mr. Simon expressed his intention of
inaugurating a service on Sunday mornings at eleven o'clock,
mainly in English. The prayers were to be founded on the
Jewish liturgy; there was to be no separation of the sexes;
men were to worship with uncovered head; anyone who so
desired could kneel in prayer. He stated that he had no desire
to cause any breach in Judaism, and therefore requested all who
intended to join with him in this movement not to withdraw
from the congregations with which they were affiliated. As an
earnest of his desire to maintain the unity of the Jewish community and avoid schisms, he announced that various ministers
of the United Synagogue and all the ministers of the reform
synagogue would be invited to preach, although he himself was
to be the regular preacher. After the first service at which he
would deliver the inaugural sermon, the Chief Rabbi and the
Haham of the Portuguese community would be invited to
preach on the two succeeding Sundays. This manifesto was
the culmination of an agitation which Mr. Simon had been conducting for some years on this subject of the mission of Judaism. In the *Fortnightly Review* for October, 1896, in an article
on "The Mission of Judaism," he advocated that Judaism
assume a missionary rôle and make active propaganda to gather
within its fold those who accept the universal elements of Judaism without subscribing to such ritualistic requirements as circumcision, eating unleavened bread on Passover, etc.; he would
have a modern institution corresponding to the old "Proselytes
of the Gate." [42] He believed in the spiritual possibilities of
Judaism, but he also held that in no age was there a greater
need of spiritual revival in Israel than at present.[43] This
revival within and without the ranks of Judaism he intended
to bring about by this service at which he would preach those
elements and doctrines of Judaism that stamp it as a universal
religion; his purpose by this service was first to give opportunity to such Jews as do not observe the Jewish religion by
attending on Saturday to do so by coming on Sunday, and
secondly "to form a bridge of religious fellowship and common

worship across the gulf which so far has separated monotheists who are Jews, and monotheists who are not Jews. In other words, it is my intention to make the experiment, however inadequately, to carry out the mission of Judaism by proclaiming its divine truths to those who are not of our race; that is, to put into effect the missionary aspect of Judaism." [44] He held a service to carry out these ideas on October 29, 1899. The movement died at birth. Every one recognized the originator's purity and singleness of purpose, but a religious departure such as was proposed required for its success elements and qualities which were evidently lacking, and this plan to bridge over religious differences remained a pious and an impractical dream.

At a meeting held on November 23, 1901, by a number of English Jews the question of how to retain for Judaism many who were drifting away for some reason or other was earnestly discussed. The decision was arrived at that one of the chief means whereby this could be accomplished would be the institution of special services of such a nature as would attract those who were out of touch with the services as conducted in the existing synagogue. [45] A provisional committee was appointed which issued a circular to such as it was expected would sympathize with the movement, explaining its purpose. A number of favorable answers being received, a meeting was held on February 16, 1902, at which the Jewish Religious Union was organized and a committee elected, with Claude G. Montefiore as president. The committee comprised names of leading spirits of the Jewish community. Especially notable in the composition of the personnel of the committee was the fact that ministers both of the United Synagogue and the reform congregation were included, Reverend S. Singer being one of the vice presidents and the Reverends A. A. Green, J. F. Stern, and Morris Joseph being members of the committee. The Union hoped to gain the sympathy of the whole community and avoided attaching itself to any existing synagogue. It was an independent movement, looking particularly to the regaining for Judaism of the many who were unaffiliated with or indifferent to the synagogue; therefore it included in its committee representatives of all shades of opinion and ritual. Another noteworthy feature in the list of officers was the inclusion among the vice presidents of Miss Lily H. Montagu, by which the new religious organization evidently desired to express its departure from the traditional Jewish view of the religious inferiority of woman in the public life and services.

The object of the Union was declared to be "to provide means for deepening the religious spirit among those members of the Jewish community who are not in sympathy with the present synagogue services, or who are unable to attend them" and the methods by which this object was to be attained were "the establishment of religious services supplementary to those provided by the existing synagogues, the holding of public lectures and the issue of publications."

The committee was given power to arrange for the carrying out of this object. At the February meeting a number of members had advocated that the services of the Union be held on Sunday morning. They were not held on Saturday morning for two reasons: first, because the Union did not wish to be understood as desiring to conflict with the existing synagogue services; and secondly, because the Union desired to reach those whose vocations did not permit them to attend service on Saturday morning. In spite of the expressed opinions in favor of services on Sunday morning, the committee felt that for various reasons it would be wiser to hold the services on Saturday afternoon. The committee also resolved that the service should be of moderate length, that the prayers should be mostly in the vernacular, being in part founded on the Jewish liturgy and in part specially composed for the services. There was to be instrumental music and the sexes were not to be separated. When it came to securing a place wherein to hold the services, it was determined that the chief rabbi be waited upon in order to learn whether any one of the constituent synagogues of the United Synagogue could be secured at an hour on Sabbath afternoon when it was unused for a service conducted along the lines indicated but without instrumental music. The chief rabbi advised the deputation of the committee that waited on him that it was impossible for him to sanction the holding of such a service in any of the synagogues under his jurisdiction. The committee then determined to arrange for the services as originally intended with instrumental music and secured the Wharncliffe Rooms, attached to the Hotel Great Central, for this purpose.[46]

The first service was held on Saturday afternoon, October 18, 1902. The service was conducted by the Reverend S. Singer, and the sermon was delivered by Mr. C. G. Montefiore. The features wherein this service differed from the regular Jewish services in the English synagogues were that the prayers were almost entirely in the vernacular. There was no reading from the Scroll; there was no *chazanut;* men and women sat together, but the men worshiped with covered head; there was a choir accompanied by an instrument. In his sermon [47] Mr. Montefiore dwelt on the need of public worship; the sermon was in part a defense of the Union; the service instituted by the Union was justified because Judaism permits more than one kind of service; the prevailing form of service did not appeal to very many, who are therefore lost to Judaism; for these the Union was providing a form of service entirely Jewish in essence and likely to draw back these wanderers. On Sunday, the day following this inaugural service, a public meeting of the members of the Union was held at which Miss Lily H. Montagu read a paper on "The Objects and Methods of the Union," in which she declared that "the founders of the Jewish Religious Union believe it possible to transmit the essentials of Judaism in forms adapted to the special needs of the day." [48]

The organization of the Union and its practical achievement in inaugurating these services called forth a storm of opposition, and gave rise to a number of interesting developments. The opposition denounced the services as un-Jewish, notably because it was an extra-synagogal movement, and thus broke the link of tradition; further, because at its services there was no reading from the Scroll, because of the paucity of Hebrew prayers, and because some of the hymns were Christian in character. [49]

The Reverend A. A. Green, a minister of the United Synagogue, withdrew from the committee of the Union because he desired reform within the synagogue; he believed the Jewish Religious Union made a mistake in starting a separatist movement and not confining itself to work within the congregations and bringing them to its standpoint. On the other hand, the Reverend Morris Joseph, in a sermon on "Hebrew and the Synagogue," preached at the Berkeley Street Synagogue on October 23, 1902 (*Shemini Atzeret*), indorsed the Union as ancillary to the synagogue.

In a sermon preached at the St. John's Wood Synagogue, December 6, on "The Old Paths," the chief rabbi denounced the service of the Union as non-Jewish; he charged specifically that in the prayer *Ahabah Rabbah,* which the Union's prayer-book had included in an English version, the words, "O bring us from the four corners of the earth," are omitted and that this omission meant the discarding of the belief in the ingathering of Israel; also that in the Sabbath Psalm (xcii) verses 8-13 are omitted—to mutilate a psalm is unjustifiable; further, that the hymns were not Jewish—"one of these has been composed from so essentially a Trinitarian standpoint that two lines had to be modified." [50]

Israel Abrahams, one of the founders of the Union, and a member of the committee, answered this attack in "An Open Letter to the Chief Rabbi," [51] The criticism of the Union's form of the prayer, *Ahabah Rabbah,* he claimed, was unjustified. "The Union has formulated no beliefs, least of all has it assumed an attitude one way or the other on the Zionist question. If it had, as a body, disclaimed the belief in the ingathering of Israel, it would not have included Psalm cxlvii." He claimed that the form of the *Ahabah Rabbah* adopted in the Union's prayer-book was the older form as found by the investigations of scholars, and that the phrase in question is a later interpolation. As for the charges of the mutilation of the Sabbath Psalm, skipping verses is sanctioned by tradition; the Jewish ritual always made the freest use of the Bible. He referred the chief rabbi to his own course when, in arranging the synagogue service for the Queen's Diamond Jubilee in 1897, he used Psalm xvi, but stopped at verse 7 for good reasons, it is true; but, having done this himself, the chief rabbi had no justification in criticizing a similar act of the Union.

As for the criticism that the book is un-Jewish, the writer called attention to the distinctively Jewish ideas expressed in the prayers, *e.g.* the election of Israel. God is invoked as "God of our fathers"; the departure from Egypt is alluded to; Israel is spoken of as "God's people"; Israel's mission is dwelt upon; "the joy of living," a distinctively Jewish doctrine, is laid stress upon; the priestly blessing is a portion of every service. The object of the Union is to win back those who have strayed; if such were led to believe that the Union is non-Jewish, they would be justified in saying, "Let us cease bothering about Judaism." This may not be permitted to happen; the service must be proclaimed to be Jewish, as it indeed is, and thus win the enthusiastic devotion of those who now are indifferent, or worse.

Undoubtedly because of the pronouncement of the chief rabbi against the Union the Reverend J. F. Stern severed his connection with it. This left the Reverend S. Singer as the only minister of the United Synagogue on the Union's committee. Mr. Singer continued to serve on the committee during the first season. On Passover, 1903, in his sermon on "Art thou for us or for our adversaries?" he pleaded for charity of views, and urged that men should not regard as adversaries those who differed with them. Undoubtedly he referred to the criticism directed at the Jewish Religious Union when he said, "terms like 'un-Jewish' are flung about rather wildly nowadays, and in a spirit which to say the least, is anything but Jewish." [52] In a published correspondence between Sir Samuel Montagu and Mr. Singer, dated April 15, 1903, the former called attention to the fact that his connection with the Union was causing his friends uneasiness and would undoubtedly be subversive of his influence; he therefore asked Mr. Singer to withdraw from the Union on the ground that the welfare of his congregation demanded it. In his reply Mr. Singer signified his intention of withdrawing, although he felt that the Union was doing a great and sacred work for such in whose behalf no one had hitherto stirred a finger and who were drifting away from Judaism. He had hoped that his would be the privilege and happiness to assist in this work; still, if the welfare of the congregation, to build up which he had given the greater part of his life, was jeopardized, as seemed to be the case by his connection with the Union, he felt that he must withdraw. [53]

It was claimed by the critics of the Union that because in its prayer-book all passages petitioning for the return to Palestine had been eliminated, no minister of the United Synagogue or of the Portuguese congregation could possibly officiate there; such a one must dissolve his connection either with the synagogue or the Union. Among the members of the Union's Committee were two honorary officers of the council of the United Synagogue, A. H. Jessel and Felix Davis. At a meeting of the council held January 13, 1903, L. J. Greenberg moved a vote of censure upon these two officers on the ground that the two positions they held were incompatible, inasmuch as the Union represented a religious tendency altogether different from that of the United Synagogue. The motion was roundly defeated, the opposition having taken the ground that the two gentlemen in question acted in their private capacity in the affairs of the Union, not as officers of the synagogue; had the mover of the vote of censure desired an expression regarding the Jewishness of the services of the Union, he should have made his motion of that tenor, and not have given it a personal coloring.

The peremptory refusal of the chief rabbi at the early stage of the Union's activity to grant the use of a constituent synagogue for the Sabbath afternoon services precluded any rapprochement between the committee of the Union and the council of the United Synagogue. This was not the case, however, with the authorities of the West London Synagogue, the reform congregation. At a meeting of the council of this Synagogue held on March 1, 1903, it was resolved to recommend to the seat-holders at the annual meeting on March 29 to place the synagogue at the disposal of the Union under certain conditions. Several meetings had been held between the committee of the Union and the council of the synagogue; the advances had been made by the latter. When the Reverend Morris Joseph, the minister of this synagogue, had, in accordance with its laws, asked permission of the council to participate in the services of the Union, this was granted, and at the same time an invitation was sent to the Union asking that they come into conference with the council of the Synagogue to determine whether their services could not be held there. When, owing to the opposition aroused in the community, it became clear that it would be impossible to obtain one of the constituent synagogues of the United Synagogue for the services, and since objection was raised to holding the services in a hotel, the committee of the Union decided to confer with the council of the West London Synagogue; the conference resulted in the acceptance by the committee of the offer of the council. At the annual meeting of the seat-holders of the Synagogue the recommendation of the council was indorsed, and it was resolved to grant the use of the synagogue to the Union under the following conditions:

1. All preachers and readers shall be Jews.

2. Arrangements shall be made for the separation of the sexes during service.

3. In the course of the service the Ark shall be opened, a Scroll of the Law shall be taken out and elevated, and a portion of the Law, varied from week to week, shall be read from it in Hebrew.

4. No hymn or psalm shall be introduced into the

service of which the words have not been composed by a person of the Jewish faith.

5. Modern English prayers of Jewish authorship may be included in the ritual and prayers to be approved by the Council.

6. The Sabbath afternoon *Amidah* shall be included in the service and a portion of it shall be read each week.

7. The Hebrew portion of the service shall at least include a Kaddish (to be read once) the שמע, the prayer commencing עלינו and a Psalm or Hymn.

8. Subject to the foregoing conditions the general control of the services shall be left in the control of the committee of the Union.

9. The ritual of the Union when formulated shall be submitted, with power to approve, to the sub-committee appointed by the council to meet with the sub-committee of the Jewish Religious Union.[54]

These conditions were in part subversive of the principles on which the Union rested. The Union, by having men and women sit together at its services declared its opposition to the traditional Orientalism of the synagogue in the matter of woman's religious position; by not having the Scroll taken from the Ark and elevating it with the words, "this is the law which Moses placed before the children of Israel," the members of the Union indicated their refusal to grant the Torah a more important place in the ritual and in the development of Jewish thought and life than any other portion of the Bible. Further, the council of the Synagogue, by demanding to be the court of last resort, robbed the Union of its character of an independent movement. There is little cause for surprise, then, that the members of the Union, at a meeting held April 5 at the residence of the president, rejected the offer of the synagogue made with such conditions. True, the committee of the Union had recommended the acceptance of the offer, because they felt that the great advantage accruing from meeting in a synagogue, and thus becoming identified with the Jewish community outweighed all other considerations, and further that it was quite possible that in time the objectionable conditions migh gradually be done away with. The president, Claude G. Montefiore, in opening the meeting, before advising that the offer be rejected, stated the pros in favor of the scheme. If they accepted the offer, the harsh criticism and irritation arising from the opinion that they were bringing about a schism would be ended. If they rejected this offer, it was not likely that they would soon receive another to worship in a synagogue, and the holding of the service in a synagogue had its advantages. Further, if they accepted the offer, it was likely that some of the conditions would be relaxed, notably that in relation to the ministers of the synagogue. Still, some of their members thought they ought not to be allied to any one particular section of the community, for in that case they would not be so likely to draw members from all sections. Again, their liberties might be restricted, for they would be largely under the control of the authorities of Berkeley Street. If by going to Berkeley Street they could get more preachers it would be worth while; but it was altogether likely that there would be more difficulty in getting men like Singer or Emmanuel, of Birmingham, to preach for them in Berkeley Street than at present. Yet the only question after all was what course would most help the Jews and Jewesses who do not attend at present any place of worship. To attach these was the reason why the Union was started. It mattered not so much what people who attended existing synagogues felt. It was impossible to satisfy all. But if they rejected the scheme, then they must put forth the greatest efforts and energy to make the movement successful, for it then stood on its own feet; but if they had not this energy, then it would be better to dwindle and die within the synagogue than without.

The Reverend Morris Joseph pleaded earnestly for the acceptance of the scheme for two reasons: first, he was anxious that his synagogue perform an act of religious liberality—yes he might say, of religious justice; that his synagogue, known as the reform synagogue, should justify its title by associating itself directly or indirectly with a movement which sought to provide for the religious needs of those who could find satisfaction in no existing synagogue; secondly, he was anxious that the Union be stamped as Jewish in the eyes of the community. The members of the Union might not think this important, but it was; they were a section of Israel, and they had to set themselves right with the community, and here was the opportunity to demonstrate their Jewishness. The concessions demanded by the council of the synagogue were not so great; although the sexes were to be separated, still, the ladies were not to be relegated to the gallery, to which a stigma of inferiority was attached, but they were to sit on the same floor. True, more Hebrew was demanded in the service, but they already had some Hebrew, and a little more would not signify, notably as the greater portion of the service would continue in English. As for the reading from the Law, after all the Pentateuch was a very integral portion of Judaism. The chairman, in his book on *Liberal Judaism*,[55] had said that the Pentateuch was valuable because it stood for law and obedience to law. If this were so, why could they not pay respect to that principle by reading from the Law every Sabbath? He warned them lest, by rejecting the scheme, they give color to the cry that they were desirous of causing a schism.

The scheme was rejected by a large majority. The Union continued to hold its services independently until the end of June of that year. Its pulpit was preëminently a free pulpit, and was occupied during the year by Claude G. Montefiore, the Reverend S. Singer, Harry S. Lewis, Israel Abrahams, Oswald J. Simon, Philip J. Hartog, the Reverend Morris Joseph, the Reverend A. Wolf, Lionel Jacob, Alfred L. Cohen, and Max Herz.[56] The revised prayer-book of the Union [57] appeared in the fall of 1903. Many harsh and severe criticisms had been leveled at the first service book of the Union; some of these criticisms were taken note of as appeared in this revised edition, which not even the bitterest opponent could stigmatize as un-Jewish—the favorite charge by traditionalists against every departure from tradition. The prayers were mostly in the vernacular, the Hebrew portions consisted of ברכו, with its response, שמע with ואהבת, קדושה, אלהינו ואלהי אבתינו and שים שלום; further, a few sentences of the ובא לציון *Kaddish* and the *Ten Commandments*. A choice selection of Scripture verses, psalms, and hymns was appended.

Doctrinally the prayer-book was like the most advanced reform prayer-books; all petitions for a return to Palestine, a restoration of the Jewish state, and a reinstitution of the sacrificial worship were excluded. The election of Israel, however, is expressed time and again, while on the other hand, the universal elements of Judaism were set forth in lofty terms.

A number of sources were drawn from besides the traditional liturgy. A Sabbath prayer was taken from the Order of Prayer for Sabbath afternoon services discussed above, and a prayer for the congregation from the Sephardic Prayer-Book; beautiful liturgical productions of Jehudah Halevi were

included, as well as a selection from the Zohar; a number of the
prayers were written particularly for the services of the Union.
The book breathed devotion and the true Jewish spirit, and was
a distinct contribution to the liturgical literature of the synagogue.

On Saturday afternoon, October 17, 1903, a service similar
to that held in the West End was instituted in the East End
of London by the East End Branch of the Jewish Religious
Union, whose committee had been constituted with Harry S.
Lewis as Chairman and Emanuel Sternheim as Secretary. The
only difference between this service and that in the West was
the absence of instrumental music. A. Lindo Henry read the
prayers, and Harry S. Lewis delivered the address at the opening service. In the address the speaker dwelt upon the necessity
of a service like this in the East End of the metropolis.

During the twenty-three years which have elapsed since these
paragraphs were written in the original edition of this book the
Jewish Religious Union has made great strides and the liberal
Jewish movement in England has indeed breathed a new spirit
into the religion. This new life began to manifest itself in 1909,
when the Union at a meeting on June 23 determined to enlarge
the cords of its tent. To symbolize this enlargement the name
and title of the organization was changed so as to read "The
Jewish Religious Union for the Advancement of Liberal Judaism." Along with this, went the decision to found an independent congregational organization.

In September of that year a manifesto was issued which set
forth the enlarged policy of the Union. This manifesto aroused
great excitement. The waters of London Judaism were deeply
stirred. It was particularly the purpose to establish an independent congregation which was bitterly attacked as revolutionary and disloyal to the best interests of English Jewry.

The chief rabbi issued a statement denunciatory of the newly
to be established independent liberal congregation, to which
statement Mr. Claude G. Montefiore, the president of the
liberal synagogue, felt compelled to make respectful though
firm reply.

The acquisition of a small building on Hill Street in 1910
gave the new congregation a permanent home. Beginning
Saturday afternoon, February 4, 1911, the services which had
been held in the Wharncliffe Rooms every year from 1902 to
1911, during the months from October to June, barring a brief

interval in January, 1911, were resumed in the Hill Street building. The service was enhanced by a brief reading from the Sefer Torah. Sermons were delivered by Claude G. Montefiore, Israel Abrahams, Lionel Jacob, Charles Singer, and others.

The next important step was the engagement of a regular minister. There seemed to be no available rabbi in England who occupied the liberal standpoint represented by this congregation. The eyes of the congregation turned westward across the Atlantic to the land where rabbis had been trained in the liberal theological seminary, the Hebrew Union College of Cincinnati. As a result of a journey of Mr. Montefiore to the United States, where he consulted a number of leaders in Judaism, Rabbi Israel I. Mattuck, minister of the reform synagogue at Far Rockaway, Long Island, was invited to London to preach in the Hill Street Synagogue on June 17, 1911, and to address the members of the congregation at a meeting held the following day. Shortly thereafter, the pulpit of the liberal Synagogue was offered to Rabbi Mattuck. He accepted the offer and on January 12, 1912, assumed charge of the congregation. Under his spirited leadership the liberal Synagogue has grown exceedingly in membership until at present it is the largest Jewish congregation in England. He introduced a number of reforms among which two particularly may be mentioned, one of which was the permission given to women to preach. This permission was granted in 1918, and, two years later, women were accorded the privilege of reading prayers from the pulpit. The influence of American reform Judaism upon English Jewish liberalism was exerted through Rabbi Mattuck, not only in this instance but also in the matter of services on Sunday. The first Sunday service was held in 1920 in Mortimer Hall, and in 1926 it was introduced as a regular feature of the religious activity of the congregation. Such a service has been conducted regularly since then in the beautiful new synagogue on St. John's Wood Road, which was dedicated in 1925.

The Jewish Religious Union, whereof the liberal Synagogue is the great outcome, still continues its existence. It draws its membership from all sections. It has its own officers and a separate constitution adopted in 1911. The liberal Synagogue represents its largest constituency, but it has sections in various districts of the metropolis. The West Central section, established in 1913, instituted local afternoon services designed particularly for young people. Miss Lily Montagu conducted these services from 1913 to 1922, she having in the two preceding years led services only on the High Holidays. In 1922, the liberal Synagogue took over these services which since have been conducted in the Hill Street Synagogue on Sabbath morning. Rabbi Mattuck preached here once each month and the liberal Synagogue furnished the funds for the choirmaster and one professional chorister. In 1928, Rabbi S. E. Starrels of Lincoln, Nebraska, another graduate of the Hebrew Union College was called as an assistant rabbi to Rabbi Mattuck and was placed in charge of the West Central work.

However, four years earlier, in November, 1924, because of the expansion of the liberal congregation, an assistant rabbi was taken in the person of the Reverend Maurice Perlzweig. His first activity was in the West Central section but now he shares with Rabbi Mattuck the burden of the main congregation.

A second section of the Jewish Religious Union was organized in Hampstead in 1918. This functioned for several years but dissolved when most of its members gave their allegiance to the West Central section. A North London section was organized at Mortimer Hall in 1920, upon the initiative of Mr. M. Green. Sabbath afternoon services were established at which Mr. Perlzweig officiated. A religious school has been established and some social activities undertaken. A fourth section of the Jewish Religious Union was begun in South London on January 23, 1927, in the house of Mr. S. M. Rich of the educational staff of the liberal Synagogue.

The influence of this synagogue is not confined to the metropolis. The liberal idea is spreading in England, notably through the propaganda spread by rabbis Mattuck and Perlzweig, Mr. Montefiore, and Miss Montagu. The most recent result of this liberal propaganda has been the formation of a liberal Jewish congregation in Liverpool, which is ministered to by Rabbi Morris Goldstein, who was graduated from the Hebrew Union College in 1927.

This propaganda consists not only in the preachments by these devoted servants of the liberal cause but also through publications, notably the *Papers for Jewish People,* of which twenty-seven numbers have appeared, mostly from the pen of Mr. C. G. Montefiore. Others who have contributed to the production of these papers are Mr. N. S. Joseph, Miss Lily Montagu, Dr. Israel Abrahams, and Rabbi Israel I. Mattuck.

Despite difficulty and discouragement, the Union kept bravely on in its East End activity for the reason as stated by Miss Montagu that the founders of the Union are "deeply concerned by the growing indifference to Judaism shown by the sons and daughters of orthodox believers and we hoped that, as in the West End, a presentment of a more liberal conception might arrest the general apathy"; [58] because of this general apathy, the work in the East End was discontinued. Still, in order to continue some relationship with East End Jewry, it was resolved, May, 1907, that three members of the executive and three members of the general committee should be residents of the East End.[59] It was not until a number of years later that under the leadership of Mr. Basil Henriques, who conducted services in September, 1922, under the joint auspices of the West London Synagogue and the Liberal Jewish Synagogue, a flourishing liberal congregation in the East End began to function freely and actively.[60]

Every religious movement finds expression through its public services and prayers. The reform movement in Judaism ran true to this experience. A score and more of reform prayer-books were composed and issued by reformers.[61] In spite of the number of reform prayer-books already in existence, the Jewish Religious Union seemed to find none of these exactly suited to its purpose and therefore issued in 1903 [62] its own book entitled *The Jewish Religious Union Book of Services and Prayers.*

In 1923, a new prayer-book was issued by the Liberal Jewish Synagogue, entitled *Liberal Jewish Prayer-Book.* This book contained the services for The Day of Memorial (Rosh Hashanah) and the Day of Atonement. Although issued first, this book is now entitled Volume II of the complete ritual of the liberal Synagogue. Two years later another volume, containing the services for week-days, Sabbaths, and special occasions appeared and shortly thereafter a third volume comprising the services for Passover, Pentecost, and Tabernacles. Rabbi Mattuck has been chiefly instrumental in the compilation and publication of this ritual of reform Judaism. The book contains traditional and new prayers. In his preface, the compiler and author says on this point:

Liberal Judaism in its teaching aims to combine the spiritual permanent values in the Jewish tradition with

modern thought and to express the spiritual and moral
direction of Judaism in a way particularly suitable to the
needs of modern Jewish life: this prayer-book is the
attempt to make Jewish public worship conform with this
aim. The traditional and the new are combined, forming,
we hope, in the case of each service, a unity which shall
satisfy the historic feeling and the religious thought of
the modern Jewish consciousness.

The book has been largely successful in achieving this aim.
The services though chiefly in the vernacular follow the traditional order, particularly for the Holy Days. A notable exception, however, is the omission of the Mussaf or additional
service on the mornings of these days. The reason for this is
stated in the work. "This part of the service was so closely
associated with the sacrificial ritual that most Reform and
Liberal Jewish congregations have omitted it and we have followed the general example."
The services are mostly in the vernacular, although some
Hebrew prayers are retained, שמע and its pendant ואהבת
the Torah service (Ausheben and Einheben), the Kaddish and a few other rubrics. Where the Hebrew has been
retained, an English translation or paraphrase is printed along-
side. The retention in the Hebrew of whatever traditional
prayers have been kept caused occasional embarrassment. Particularly was this the case with the prayer אתה גבור רב להושיע
"Thou O Lord, art mighty to save," the second of
the Eighteen Benedictions. This prayer, which expresses the
belief in the bodily resurrection, surely in its original form has
no place in the ritual of a liberal congregation which has repudiated the traditional belief and has accepted in its stead the
doctrine of spiritual immortality. The author of the book felt
this difficulty, for he refers to it in the preface in apologetic
terms. After stating that the "belief in the resurrection of the
body has lost its significance for Liberal Judaism" and "that its
teaching about life after death is contained in the hope for
immortality issuing from the belief in Eternal life," he goes on
to say that "though this prayer has been retained in the ancient
Hebrew form, the paraphrase shows what meaning it holds
in this prayer-book." In other words, Hebrew and the English
which appear in parallel columns do not correspond. The
original Hebrew prayer opens with the words, "Thou art

mighty forever, O Lord, who resurrects the dead; thou art mighty to save." The English, in the parallel column omits the words "who resurrects the dead"; the same is done at the close of this prayer where the Hebrew phrase occurs twice and is omitted both times in the English. The authors of the American reform ritual, namely the Union Prayer-Book were much braver, if that word can be used. They did not hesitate to lay hands on the traditional Hebrew prayer and change its form. They omitted in the Hebrew the words מחיה מתים "who resurrects the dead" in the body of the prayer and made the closing words of the benediction read, ברוך אתה יי נטע בתוכינו חיי עולם "Praised be Thou, O Lord, who hast implanted within us eternal life," in place of the traditional, "Praised be Thou, O Lord who resurrectest the dead."

This prayer-book is featured by the extensive use made of the books of the Apocrypha and selections from later Jewish writings. The treasure trove of English poetry is also drawn upon liberally.

The book is fully expressive of the modern religious spirit and meets the needs of the modern worshiper much more adequately than does the traditional prayer-book. On this point the author refers to the penetrating thought of the late Dr. Israel Abrahams, which he expressed in these words:

> The formulation of the highest truth needs constant revision, and even more surely do the forms in which that truth is clothed. Where dogma takes the place of love, religion is dead. And a liturgy that cannot expand, that cannot absorb the best religious teaching of the age, that cannot dare to sing unto the Lord new songs, such a religion is a printed page, it is not a prayer-book for the supplicant's heart.

An enlivening breath does animate the supplications and aspirations in this *Liberal Jewish Prayer-Book*.

On February 20, 1927, the twenty-first anniversary of the Jewish Religious Union was fittingly celebrated by a special Thanksgiving service at the Liberal Jewish Synagogue. The participants in the service were Miss Lily H. Montagu, the Reverend M. L. Perlzweig who read the service, Mr. Claude G. Montefiore, and Dr. Israel I. Mattuck who delivered the addresses. Dr. Mattuck also made a special prayer suited to the occasion. The report of the service in the "Anniversary

Supplement" to the *Jewish Religious Union Bulletin* of March, 1927, contrasts this largely attended service with the small beginnings, in these words:

> Memory can condense time, making the past vividly present. For those who recalled the first service, the anniversary service must have been filled with recollections of a past, not very distant in time, but in many ways different from the present. The large congregation, the character of the service, the place in which it was held were a reminder of the developments of the Union. But, as Mr. Montefiore said in his address, though the present position of the Union could not have been foreseen twenty-five years ago, the developments followed logically out of the beginning. With Mr. Montefiore and Miss Montagu on the Almemer and with many in the Anniversary congregation who were present in the first congregation, present and past became one. The sanctity of the occasion combined joy with sadness, joy in what the Jewish Religious Union had achieved, and sadness for the absence of those who did so much for it but were called to their eternal homes without seeing the fruition of their work, or more than a part of it. The names of A. Lindo Henry, Israel Abrahams and Sidney Mendelsohn irresistibly came into the minds of those who had worked with them. . . . Little was said about the difficulties and opposition which the Union had to face and overcome and little was said about the achievements of the Union; both the achievements and the opposition were too well-known to require emphasis. The occasion was one of happy gratitude and great hope.

Toward the close of his anniversary address, Mr. Montefiore showed the potentialities of Liberal Judaism to meet the confused religious conditions in Judaism. "True orthodoxy," he said, "is losing its hold, though the shell, the framework may remain. Men are now under the influence of modern thought."

Dr. Mattuck well said that "the strength of Liberal Judaism consists in that it combines past and present, and it is the hope of the future. It aims to solve the Jewish problem in the only way by which that problem can be solved, by correlating Judaism with life."

Along with Mr. Montefiore and Dr. Mattuck, Miss Lily H.

Montagu, the real founder of the Union was enthusiastically acclaimed for the great work which she had done for the cause of Liberal Judaism in England. She had lived to see the seed which she had planted twenty-five years before, grow into a great institution. Liberal Judaism had made it possible for a woman to share so prominently in the work.

The progress made by the Jewish Religious Union and the liberal Synagogue proves the truth of the prophecy mentioned in the first edition of this book when the account of the founding of the Jewish Religious Union was concluded with the paragraph:

> The people have advanced beyond the synagogue; Judaism is of their lives and thoughts, a thing apart. Jews they are by birth; of the spiritual message of Judaism they are either ignorant, or to it they are indifferent. From out of this ignorance and indifference, they will be startled as by a trumpet call when some time (and if the official authorities are wise, not very far hence) the synagogue will speak to them in the voice of their generation and Judaism, recasting its age-old truth into modern shape will be as living an issue for them as in its rabbinical guise, it was for their fathers. "When the cloud lifted, the children of Israel went forward"; so has it always been, so shall it be again. The cloud of benumbing conservatism shall lift, even in England, and from the four winds will come the spirit and breathe upon the dry bones of the house of Israel, and they shall live.

The surface of the waters has been stirred slightly in France. In this land reform has made but slight headway; the accepted official interpretation of Judaism is the rabbinical as codified in the *Shulchan Aruk*. Of reform such as was theoretically advocated in Germany and has been practically carried out in the United States, there had been little up to a very recent time. True, there was preaching in the vernacular since 1831, the organ was in general use in the synagogues for a long time, and confirmation of the young people of both sexes was in vogue since 1841. In 1856 the grand rabbi of France, Salomon Ulmann, called a meeting of the grand rabbis of the various consistories to be held at Paris. The Synod, as it was called, considered the state of Judaism in France; a number of mod-

erate reforms of the ritual were recommended, but it was left
to each grand rabbi to use his own judgment in carrying out or
disregarding these recommendations in his own consistory. The
reforms in the ritual have been slight; *piyyutim* have been
eliminated from all services excepting New Year's Day and the
Day of Atonement; on these two days, too, the *piyyutim* have
been considerably reduced. The Long prayer והוא רחום read
at the morning service on Mondays and Thursdays, the section
אנעים זמרות and the יקום פורקן the ,שיר היחוד the ,במה מדליקין
have been eliminated. But there have been no changes other
than these. The entire service is in Hebrew, with the exception
of the prayer for the government, which is spoken in the vernacular. Likewise in communities which have a rabbi the
prayer רבונו של עולם spoken at the taking of the Scroll from
the Ark and the מי שברך read before the Scroll is returned to
the Ark are replaced by paraphrases in the vernacular.[63] At the
initiative of Zadoc Kahn, former grand rabbi, a French prayer
was introduced before the Kaddish at the service on Sabbath
eve, and another prayer likewise in French on Sabbath morning when the Law is taken from the Ark. There have been,
however, no changes in the doctrines of the old prayer-book;
here reform is unknown.

But the same conditions obtained in France as in Germany,
England, and the United States; the Sabbath was not observed;
the synagogues were sparsely attended on Sabbath morn; many
heard no word of religious instruction. To meet this condition Zadoc Kahn instituted a service with sermon on Sabbath
afternoons.[64] In 1896 a movement for a Sunday service was
started; it was suppressed. To meet the need, addresses on religious subjects were given for a short time on Sunday morning—not in the synagogue however, but in the congregational
meeting room, so as to divest them altogether of the character
of divine services.[65]

Early in the twentieth century, however, active propaganda
for reform began to be made by an association calling itself
"Union Israélite Liberale." The founders of this liberal union
were Alphonse Pereyra, Theodore Reinach, Salvador Levi,
Gaston Bach, P. Sacerdote, Max Frank, Frederic Simon, and
Mesdames Eugene Simon, Brandon, Anatole Dreyfus, Edgard
Hertz, and Heilbronner. In 1903 they set about collecting
funds for the erection of a "Temple Liberal." At this time
they promulgated the following program:

1. A service of one hour's duration to include a sermon, shall be held every Saturday and Sunday morning from ten to eleven o'clock.

2. The principal Hebrew prayers (for example, the Shemang and the Kedushah) shall be retained; the others shall be read in French.

3. The religious instruction of children preparing for confirmation shall be completely modified. They are to be taught that which will best enable them to understand the beauty and grandeur of the love of God, and the reasons which should cause them to be proud of professing the Jewish faith. . . .

7. Ladies as well as gentlemen shall be permitted to sing during the services.

8. As in our country, males uncover as a mark of respect, this practice shall be observed in our Temple."

This agitation for the establishment of a reform temple received a great impetus when the bill providing for the separation of church and state in France was passed by the legislature in 1905. As with the other religious denominations, so also with the Jews, this bill entailed a complete revolution in the administration of religious affairs. In no country in Europe was the union of church and state closer than in France—not in the sense that there was one established state church, but that all the churches received governmental support, and hence were in part subsidiary to the government. French Judaism, with its elaborate consistorial organization, was officially represented by the grand rabbi of France, who as well as all other rabbis, was paid his salary from the governmental treasury. The new law changed all this, and Judaism in France, as is the case in other countries, became a concern of the Jews only, who have to support their own ecclesiastical organizations. The complete transformation in administration involved in the new order of things called forth greater energy on the part of the French Jews, since they were made to rely entirely upon themselves, the governmental prop being withdrawn. The advocates of reform seemed to consider this an especially auspicious time for the definite carrying out of their plans. The passing of a state supported Judaism gave such scope to independence of thought and originality of action as had not been known in French Judaism since the dead weight of governmental paternalism had rested upon it. The manifesto issued by the Liberal Union in consequence of the act of separation of church and state so clearly indicates the freer spirit that breathed through French Judaism, that no words can make this clearer than the terms of the document itself, which runs as follows:

A certain number of Parisian Jews firmly attached to the fundamental principles of the Jewish religion, but persuaded of the necessity of placing the external forms of worship and the methods of religious instruction in more complete harmony with modern conditions of existence, knowledge and conscience, have conceived the project of constituting a group of the large Parisian community about to be reorganized in accordance with the law of the separation of church and state. There is no intention of provoking a secession or schism. All that we are ambitious of doing is to be enabled to hold our services and instruct our children according to our own ideas, and we ask to do this in one of the existing synagogues in order to demonstrate our strong desire to remain in communion with the co-religionists in thought, administration and communal charges. These are the general principles which we propose to apply in the realization of our reform:

1.   Besides the Saturday Sabbath, to institute a service on Sunday morning, to give to those who are not free on Saturday opportunities of instruction and edification.

2.   To reduce the length of this service to one hour, with the prayers for the most part in French and a sermon on each occasion; the latter might, on certain days, subject to the control of the executive committee, be entrusted to lay speakers conformably with an old Jewish tradition which deserves to be restored.

3.   To make religious instruction more thorough and better adapted to the assured results of modern criticism, which has done nothing but enhance the grandeur and originality of the religious progress from which Judaism emanated.

4.   To leave to all full liberty to follow the traditional practices and ceremonies, it being clearly understood that they may not eclipse nor replace the essentials of religion which consist in the communion of public worship and in the intensity of moral individual belief.

In a word, we are pursuing a task, not of separation and revolution, but of spiritual renovation, which will be of such a nature, if it is rightly understood, as to give to Judaism new youth and vigor, better to assume its character as doctrine eternally based on truth and moral strength, and finally to assure to it even from without valuable sympathy. The spirit, and not the letter; truth and life—that is our motto.

In 1907, this Union Liberale requested the Central Consistory to grant them the use of a hall in one of the temples in which they might conduct a service on Sunday morning. This request was not granted. Hence the liberal union organized themselves into an "association cultuelle," in accordance with the law of 1905. On December 1, 1907, the temple of the Union Liberale was dedicated. In 1924, this temple in the Rue Copernic was enlarged and rededicated. Louis Germain-Levi [17] has served as rabbi of the liberal congregation since its formation. Aimée Palliere, the convert from Catholicism to Judaism, whose autobiographical chronicle, *Le Sanctuaire Inconnu*, created so great a stir when it appeared in 1925, is acting as assistant to Rabbi Germain-Levi.

Services are conducted on Sunday morning in addition to the traditional service on Friday evening and Saturday morning. The congregation has its own ritual. The prayers are read partly in Hebrew and partly in the vernacular. The Torah readings on Saturday morning are in the Hebrew and French, the Haftara in French.

The official bulletin of the Union Liberale, entitled *Le Rayon*, appears monthly as does also the juvenile publication *Le Petit Rayon*. Through these organs the members of the Union and their children are kept informed not only of Jewish activities in general but of the progressive movement in particular. In 1925 an organization of the youth, entitled "La Jeunesse Liberale," was called into being. At the meetings of this organization, questions vitally affecting the religious outlook of the rising generation are discussed.

In his report on the status of Liberal Judaism in France, submitted to the meeting of the World Union for Progressive Judaism held in Berlin, August, 1928, Rabbi Germain-Levi concluded by declaring that "Progressive Judaism gains new adherents every year. It is particularly interesting to note that

Russian, Polish and Oriental coreligionists are constantly aug-
menting the ranks of the Liberal Union." The Union now
numbers four hundred families.

The World Union for Progressive Judaism

Pursuant to an invitation extended by the Jewish Religious
Union for the advancement of Liberal Judaism, through the
honorary secretary, Miss Lily H. Montagu, a number of representatives of Liberal Judaism in England, United States, Germany, Czechoslovakia, France, Sweden, and India, gathered
for the first international conference of Liberal Jews in the
world's history, at London, England, from July 10-12, 1926.

The conference opened with divine services, Saturday morning, July 10, at the Liberal Jewish Synagogue, the sermon being
preached by Dr. Israel I. Mattuck, the rabbi of the synagogue,
on the subject, "The Task of Liberal Judaism."

This task he declared to be to revitalize Judaism, wherever
it has grown weak spiritually. A great challenge confronts the
Jews in the conditions of modern world. This challenge is:

> Can Judaism live? And our answer is, it must live!
> For us, the means to insure its life is to express its teach-
> ings in a way that shall answer the longing of Jewish
> hearts, give some light to Jewish minds seeking through
> the universe its secret and satisfy the eternal hunger of the
> Jewish soul, so that it shall live.

The sessions proper began on Saturday evening with an
address of welcome by Mr. Claude G. Montefiore, the president
of the Jewish Religious Union. Among the many pertinent
observations made by this most distinguished figure in the ranks
of liberal Judaism in England, who has fought the fight for
religious enlightenment for decades, was a restoration of the
principles of Liberal Judaism which he declared "to include a
belief in progressive or continuous revelation, an allegiance to
the highest teachings of the Prophets, as applied to modern
conditions, knowledge and developments, and a willing adaptation of ancient forms and practices to present needs, requirements and life."

During the two days session, papers were presented on the
"Synagogue and Modern Life" by Dr. Samuel Schulman of
New York, "Judaism in Relation to Modern Thought and Life"
by Rabbi Dr. Max Wiener of Berlin and Dr. Israel I. Mattuck

of London. These speakers addressed themselves particularly to the attitude of liberal Jewish thought toward the Bible, discussing the subject under the headings, "Belief in the Inspiration of the Bible in the Light of Biblical Criticism" and "The Use of the Bible in Worship and Education."

Estimates of the present status of Liberal Judaism in various countries were given by different speakers, Herr Heinrich Stern for Germany, Dr. Julian Morgenstern for the United States, Professor Theodore Reinach for France, Mr. Claude G. Montefiore for England, Miss Leah Jhirad for India, and Mr. Heinrich Wolff for Sweden.

Other papers presented were on themes subsumed under the general heading, "The Practice of Judaism in Modern Times." Dr. Leo Baeck, of Berlin, was heard on the subject, "The Message of Judaism to the Individual," Dr. Maurice H. Harris, of New York, on "The Aspect of Judaism in the Home and in Private Life," and Dr. William Rosenau, of Baltimore, Maryland, on "The Value of Ceremonials."

Dr. Baeck declared that the great achievement of liberalism is that it has stressed the individual appeal of religion. He went on to say that possibly liberalism has forgotten at times that the environment is also of great importance and that it is necessary to organize the religious life of the community. If it can succeed in combining the individual and institutional ideals, *i.e.* educating the individual so that he may develop his religious forces and use them in the interest of the community, it will become the strongest force in contemporary Judaism. In a word, "Liberalism must emphasize the message of Judaism to the individual and must at the same time place the individual in an environment in which his Judaism becomes living."

The interchange of views among these representatives from various lands made it abundantly clear that while the development had proceeded differently in various countries, yet the underlying principle of liberalism, viz. that Judaism is capable of adaptation to the widening thoughts of men marks the liberals in all lands. It became apparent during the deliberations that a community of spirit made these men and women of various nationalities and cultures, kin in the religious domain.

The outcome of this first international conference of Liberal Judaism was the adoption of a name, a preamble, and a resolution that the governing body draw up a constitution and by-laws to be referred to the next convention for adoption. The Preamble to the Provisional Constitution adopted reads:

I

The World Congress of Progressive Judaism, inspired by the belief of the Prophets in the mission of Israel to spread the knowledge of God, declares that that belief lays upon Israel the duty to work for a further recognition, by Jews and by all mankind, of the religious and ethical demands of righteousness, brotherly love and universal peace.

II

The World Congress, convinced of the capacity for development inherent in the Jewish religion, declares that it is the duty of each generation of Jews to bring the religious teachings and practices of their fathers, into harmony with developments in thought, advances in knowledge, and changes in circumstances of life.

The formation of this World Union is the most significant organizational step taken by Liberal Judaism since the birth of the movement. It shows that the liberal idea has marched steadily onward and that it holds within itself that possibility of universalism which has been the enlivening hope of Judaism from the days of the prophets who predicted the coming of the day when the knowledge of God would fill the earth as the waters cover sea to the present time, when the thought of universalism or internationalism is gripping the imagination of a constantly increasing number of men and women throughout the earth.

The second meeting of the World Union for Progressive Judaism took place in Berlin, Germany, August 18-21, 1928. About one hundred delegates from England, France, Germany, Belgium, Czechoslovakia, Austria, Poland, South Africa, Roumania, Australia, and the United States were present. The conference opened with a service in the great Oranienburger Synagogue on Sabbath morning, which spacious edifice was crowded to the doors. How far the liberal movement in Germany lags behind the Jewish liberalism in the United States and England was constantly apparent throughout the sessions, but never more so than at this service which, judged by this American and English standard, was distinctly conservative, if not orthodox. A service conducted almost completely in Hebrew, men and women separated, the women being relegated to the gallery, the men worshiping with covered heads, all this seemed unreal at a liberal Jewish convocation. The situation was somewhat redeemed by the sermon preached by Dr. Cæsar Seligman of Frankfort, who in the course of his discourse said,

> Liberal Judaism has preserved Judaism during the past one hundred years, in a time of indecision and perplexity. It has been and is still the saving element and if there were no liberal Judaism, it would have to be created, if Judaism is to be preserved. Go to the countries where liberal Judaism has been unable to secure a foothold and see what has become there of the Jewish masses who could not be retained by orthodoxy; religious annihilation, the quiet of the cemetery!

The sessions of the convention took place in the *Herrenhaus,* the former Prussian House of Lords. How significant of the change that the years have wrought in the position of the Jews, was this Jewish gathering in that hall of *Junkerthum,* whose walls resounded so frequently with anti-Semitic tirades in the imperial days! And when it was brought to the attention of the delegates, who had gathered from far and near, that this palace in which they were meeting stood on the site of the home of Abraham Mendelssohn, the son of the great Moses, thought could not but be engendered on the wondrous ways in which Providence works. The liberal movement in Judaism really harks back to Moses Mendelssohn, in that he, through his service in the cause of introducing the era of modern education and culture among the Jews, sounded the knell of medievalism and paved the way for the liberal movement. When Mendelssohn translated the "Five Books of Moses" into pure German and thereby displaced the jargon, he builded better than he knew. That linguistic emancipation was the first step in the onward progress which led the Jewish youth to the colleges and universities, removed medieval disabilities from the Jew, secured for him the rights of citizenship, and culminated in the liberal religious movement. This onward progress was emphasized when an official representative of the German government cordially welcomed the delegates and the president of the World Union. Claude G. Montefiore made a fitting response.

The status of Liberal Judaism in various lands was presented by delegates from these countries, Dr. H. G. Enelow, for the United States; Dr. H. Vogelstein, for Germany; Dr. Israel I. Mattuck, for England; Rabbi Louis Germain-Levi, for France; Counsellor Heinrich Wolff, for Sweden; Mr. A. Chincholkar, of Bombay, for India; Mr. Leon Bergman, of Warsaw,** for Poland; Dr. Fritz Seifter, for the western Polish provinces, and others for Czechoslovakia, South Africa, Australia, Belgium, and Austria.

A startling feature of this convention was the first appearance of a woman in the guise of preacher in a German Jewish pulpit. When Miss Lily Montagu delivered the sermon from the pulpit of the Reformgemeinde on Sunday morning, she presented in visible form the changes which Liberal Judaism has wrought in the position of woman. Radical in its tendencies and expressions as this congregation has been from its very organization ** so revolutionary a step had not yet been taken by it in the course of its existence of eight decades.

The leading discussion of the convention was furnished by a symposium on the theme, "The Message of Liberal Judaism for Modern Life," the participants in which were Dr. Leo Baeck, of Berlin; Dr. Claude G. Montefiore, of London, England; Dr. David Philipson, of Cincinnati, Ohio, and Dr. Joseph Lehman, of Berlin.

Another symposium on the general subject, "How to Give the Message of Liberal Judaism," was held on Monday. This symposium was conducted in three sections, on "Worship," led by Dr. S. H. Goldenson, of Pittsburg, Pennsylvania; on "Home Life," led by Miss Lily H. Montagu, of London, and on "Youth," led by Ludwig Levin, of Berlin.

At this Berlin Conference, the constitution and by-laws of the World Union for Progressive Judaism were definitely adopted. The objects of the Union are stated as follows:

The object of the World Union for Progressive Judaism, shall be:
(a) To further the development of Progressive Judaism; to encourage the formation of Progressive Jewish Religious Communities or Congregations in the different countries of the World; to promote coöperation between all such, whether now in existence or hereafter formed, and to stimulate and encourage the study of Judaism and its adaptation and application to modern life.

(*b*) To make this adaptation without changing the fundamental principles of Judaism and to awaken an active interest in those Jews who, for one reason or another, do not participate in Jewish religious life.

The World Union has undertaken missionary activity for the spread of Liberal Judaism in new fields. During the year 1929 Rabbi Max Lasker worked under its auspices in this cause in Poland and Rabbi Jerome Mark is at present (1930) undertaking a similar task in Australia.

The attempt has been made in these pages to give a survey of the currents and cross-currents in Jewish liberal religious thought during the modern period, notably as these have become realized in synagogue organization and public corporate expression.[70] It has been impossible even to indicate the many individual expressions and analyses of liberal tendencies as they have appeared in literature.

It is one hundred and twenty years since the first public demonstration in the cause of Jewish reform was made in the dedication of the synagogue in Westphalia by Israel Jacobson. During this century, the most significant in the history of Jewish thought since the dispersion from Palestine, values have been readjusted, and Judaism has adapted itself to new environments in the various free countries of the world. The story of the reform movement is the record of this readjustment and this adaptation. The essentials as they appear in prophetic thought remain unchanged, it is only the interpretation and expression of these essentials as demanded by the changed conceptions of modern life that are different from past interpretation and expression. The work of the reform movement has been, in a word, to substitute for the nationalistic, legalistic, and ceremonial form of Judaism—the product of the ages of exclusion, repression, and the ghetto—the universal and spiritual teachings that accentuate Judaism's message of ethical monotheism. The modern spirit touched Judaism, and the reform movement sprang forth. Reform Judaism bridges antiquity and modernity, garbing the eternal verities in the raiment of these latter days. It proclaims the great truths that God's revelation is progressive, and that Judaism has in itself the power of adaptation to bring this revelation to successive ages.

That God reveals himself thus constantly will continue to be a fundamental principle of Reform Judaism; indeed, this much

may surely be said, the reform movement in Judaism is part
and parcel of that great change of front in the religious thought
of mankind that modernity symbolizes; part, too, of the
broader and freer outlook that came with the passing of
medievalism; and as these broader and freer forces move
majestically forward, there will keep pace therewith the liberal
religious spirit, leading men at last to God's holy hill and His
tabernacle.[71]

NOTES

ABBREVIATIONS

A. Z. d. J.—Allgemeine Zeitung des Judenthums, 1837.

C. C. A. R.—Central Conference of American Rabbis.

G. J. R. G. B.—Holdheim, Geschichte der Entwickelung und Entstehung der jüdischen Reformgemeinde in Berlin. Berlin, 1857.

I. N. J.—Israelit des Neunzehnten Jahrhunderts, Vols. I-IX, 1839-1848. Edited by M. Hess.

J. Q. R.—*Jewish Quarterly Review*. Edited by C. G. Montefiore and Israel Abrahams, London, 1889.

J. Z. W. L.—Jüdische Zeitschrift für Wissenschaft und Leben. Edited by Abraham Geiger, 1862-1875.

M. G. W. J.—Monatsschrift für die Geschichte und Wissenschaft des Judenthums, 1852.

W. Z. J. T.—Wissenschaftliche Zeitschrift für Jüdische Theologie. Edited by Abraham Geiger, 1835-1848.

Z. A. W.—Zeitschrift für alttestamentliche Wissenschaft.

Z. D. M. G.—Zeitschrift der Deutschen Morgenländischen Gesellschaft, 185.

NOTES

CHAPTER I

[1] Bousset, *Die Religion des Judenthums im neutestamentlichen Zeitalter*, 448-492. Berlin, 1903.
[2] Num. xxv. 3; I Sam. viii. 5ff.; I Kings xi. 7; 2 Kings xxiii. 11; Amos v. 26; Hosea iv. 12; Jer. vii. 18, xliv. 17, 18, 19, 25.
[3] Stade, *Z. A. W.*, xxiii. 174ff.
[4] Zimmern, "Zur Frage nach dem Ursprung des Purimfestes," *Z. A. W.*, XI, 167-169; C. H. Toy, "Esther as a Babylonian Goddess," *New World*, VI, 130-145; Bousset, op. cit., 467; Paton, *A Critical and Exegetical Commentary on the Book of Esther*, 87ff. New York, 1908.
[5] Erik Stave, *Ueber den Einfluss des Parsismus auf das Judenthum.* Haarlem, 1898; Bousset, op. cit., 473ff.; Geiger, *J. Z. W. L.*, iv. 70ff.; Jackson, *Zoroaster, The Prophet of Iran*, 142. New York, 1898.
[6] A. Kohut, *Ueber die jüdische Angelologie und Dämonologie in ihrer Abhängigkeit vom Parsismus.* Leipzig, 1866.
[7] M. Friedländer, *Das Judenthum in der vorchristlichen griechischen Welt.* Vienna, 1897; also in *J. Q. R.*, XIV, 268; Bousset, op. cit., 450.
[8] Talm. Bab. Sotah 49 b; Ab. Zara 44 b; Meg. 9 a, 18 a; Baba Qamma 83 a. Talm. Jer. Sotah VII, 1; Meg. I, 11.
[9] I. M. Jost, *Geschichte des Judenthums und seiner Sekten*, II, 143; A. Kohut, "Was hat die Talmudische Eschatologie aus dem Parsismus aufgenommen?" *Z. D. M. G.*, XXI, 552-591; E. Böklin, *Die Verwandschaft der jüdisch Christlichen mit der Parsischen Eschatologie.* Göttingen, 1902.
[10] M. Güdemann, *Geschichte des Erziehungswesens und der Cultur der Juden in Deutschland während des XIV. und XV. Jahrhunderts*, 158ff. Vienna, 1882; A. Berliner, *Persönliche Beziehungen zwischen Christen und Juden im Mittelalter.* Halberstadt, 1882; Abrahams, *Jewish Life in the Middle Ages*, 64, 424ff. Philadelphia, 1896; Salo Baron, "Azariah dei Rossi's Attitude to Life," *Jewish Studies in Memory of Israel Abrahams*, 38-40. New York, 1927.
[11] Philipson, *Old European Jewries*, 20ff. Philadelphia, 1894; Wirth, *The Ghetto*, 19. Chicago, 1928.
[12] The fourfold code compiled by Joseph Karo in the sixteenth century; this code, which contained the decisions of Talmudical and rabbinical authorities on all subjects, was the observant Jew's *vade mecum*.
[13] Num. ix. 9ff.
[14] Joshua v. 2-3.
[15] Num. xxi. 6-9 and II Kings xviii. 4.
[16] Ex. xxii. 28.
[17] *Ibid.*, xxxiv. 20, Num. iii. 11-13.
[18] Talmud Babli Baba Qama 82 a.
[19] Mielziner, *Introduction to the Talmud*, 117ff.
[20] Mishna, *Shebiit*, X. 3.
[21] Mishna, *Gitin*, IV. 3 הלל התקין פרוזבול מפני תקון העולם
[22] Mishna, *Rosh Hashanah*, IV, 1 and 2.

437

[22] Baba Batra 60b אין גוזרין גזירה על הצבור אלא אם כן רוב הצבור יכוליןלעמוד בה

[24] Leopold Löw, "Reform im Mittelalter," *Liberales Judenthum*, III. 148; J. S. Raisin, "Reform Movement before Geiger," *Year Book C. C. A. R.* XXI, 97; Finkelstein, *Jewish Self Government in the Middle Ages*, 41. New York, 1924.

[25] Geiger, "Jüdische Geschichte von 1830 bis zur Gegenwart," *Nachgelassene Schriften*, II. 265.

[26] Kohler, *Jewish Theology*, 330. New York, 1918.

[27] Philipson "Samuel Holdheim," *Centenary Papers and Others*, 74-5. Cincinnati, 1919. Though a number of reform rabbis and writers are sympathetic with Zionism, the new nationalistic movement among Jews, there can be no manner of doubt that the position stated in the text expresses the true philosophy of the reform movement.

[28] Kohler, *Jewish Theology*, 389.

[29] S. Bernfeld, תולדות הריפורמציון הדתית בישראל I, 6ff. Krakau, 1900.

[30] Jost, *Geschichte des Judenthums und seiner Sekten*, III, 317; Holdheim, *G. J. R. G. B.*, 23. Berlin, 1857; M. Levin, *Die Reform des Judenthums*, 19. Berlin, 1895; Badt-Strauss, *Moses Mendelssohn, Sein Leben und sein Werk*, XX. Berlin, 1929.

[31] Zunz, *Die gottesdienstlichen Vorträge der Juden*, 14; Geiger's *Wissenschaftliche Zeitschrift für jüdische Theologie*, V, 7; Holdheim, *G. J. R. G. B.*, 14; S. Stern, *Geschichte des Judenthums*, 184. Breslau, 1870; Ludwig Geiger, *Geschichte der Juden in Berlin*, 86-7. Berlin, 1871.

[32] The chief writers for this magazine were Isaac Euchel who translated the Prayer-Book and also the Book of Proverbs; the celebrated physician, Michael Friedländer; the ingenuous grammarian, Joel Loewe of Breslau; the philologist, Isaac Satanow of Berlin; Herz Homburg, superintendent of the Jewish schools in the Austrian empire that were founded after the formulation of the edict of the Emperor Joseph; Hartwig Wessely, and others; Jost, *Geschichte des Judenthums und seiner Sekten*, 316.

[33] As late as 1844 the orthodox rabbis of Hungary opposed the institution of schools of modern learning and declared it a sacrilege to have the Talmud and German taught in the same building. *Allgemeine Zeitung des Judenthums*, VIII, 583. Similarly, the orthodox rabbis of Pressburg counseled their constituency to issue a petition calling upon the Jews of Hungary to refuse the proposed grant of Jewish civil emancipation by the government; they declared the wish for political equality on the part of the Jews as sinful and as inconsistent with Israel's hopes for the future. *Ibid.*, 452. See also N. Samter, *Judentaufen im 19 Jahrhundert*, 16, note 1. Berlin, 1906.

[34] Bernfeld, *Juden und Judenthum im neunzehnten Jahrhundert*, 8. Berlin, 1898.

[35] Hirschl Levin's own son, Saul Berlin, was affected by the modern spirit. In 1793 he published a book, *Besamin Rosh*, which purported to be a collection of responses by Asher ben Jechiel, a great rabbinical authority of the fourteenth century. A number of reforms are sanctioned by the writer of the responses. The book and the author were assailed as spurious by Mordecai Benet, chief rabbi of Moravia, and as zealously defended by Saul Berlin's father. There seems little doubt that the publication was Saul Berlin's own, who used the name of the great medieval rabbi to voice and give weight to the ideas of his own generation.

[36] Jost, *Geschichte der Israeliten*, IX, 120.

[37] Geiger, *Nachgelassene Schriften*, I, 147. Berlin, 1875.

[38] Jost's *Israelitische Annalen*, I, 58. Frankfurt am Main, 1839.

[39] Holdheim, *G. J. R. G. B.*, 120, note.

[40] *Jerusalem*, 31; cf. the article "Ueber die von Mendelssohn im Jerusalem geäusserte ewige Verpflichtung des Ceremonialgesetzes," *Israelit des*

neunzehnten Jahrhunderts, VI, 153; also Geiger, *Jüdische Zeitschrift für Wissenschaft und Leben,* VII, 7.

[41] *Autonomie der Rabbinen,* 38, 45. *Vorträge über die mosäische Religion,* 59; *Ceremonialgesetz im Messiasreich,* 58, 68; *G. J. R. G. B.,* 94, 227; also Steinheim, *Moses Mendelssohn und seine Schule,* 22. Hamburg, 1840; S. Stern, *Geschichte des Judenthums,* 92ff. Berlin, 1870; M. Levin, *Die Reform der Judenthums,* 17ff. Berlin, 1895; Leopold Löw, *Gesammelte Schriften,* I, 138; K. Kohler, "Moses Mendelssohn," *The Jewish Reformer,* Jan. 15, 1886, 12; E. G. Hirsch, *Ibid.,* Jan. 8, 1886, 8; Felix A. Levy, "Moses Mendelssohn's Ideals of Religion and Their Relation to Reform Judaism," *Year Book, C. C. A. R.,* 1929, 353ff.

[42] Cf. Holdheim, *G. J. R. G. B.,* 120-121, note.

[43] *Sendschreiben an die deutschem Juden.* Berlin, 1788.

[44] The first Jewish liturgical book published in the United States was Isaac Pinto's English translation of the prayer-book (1766). In his preface to this book the translator says in justification of his course: "A veneration for the language *sacred* by being that in which it pleased Almighty God to reveal himself to our ancestors, and a desire to preserve it, in firm persuasion that it will be reëstablished in Israel; are probably leading reasons for our performing divine service in Hebrew. But that, being imperfectly understood by many, by some not at all; it has been necessary to translate our prayers in the language of the country wherein it hath pleased the divine Providence to appoint our lot."

[45] *Sendschreiben an seine Hochwürden Herrn Consistorialrath und Probst Teller zu Berlin, von einigen Hausväter jüdischer Religion.* Berlin, 1799. A strikingly similar proposal was made by Theodor Herzl, the founder of Zionism. His son, Hans Herzl, stated recently that at one time his father proposed the conversion of Jews to Christianity as the most expeditious way of realizing Jewish nationalism. See Joseph Brainin, "The Mystery of Hans Herzl," *Emanuel,* San Francisco, Cal., May 24, 1929. See also Sachar, *A History of the Jews,* 353. New York, 1930.

[46] "Nothwendigkeit und Mass einer Reform des jüdischen Gottesdienstes," *Nachgelassene Schriften,* I, 205.

[47] *Ibid.,* 127, 187, 204; Holdheim, *Verketzerung und Gewissensfreiheit,* passim; *G. J. R. G. B.,* Preface, iii; Löw, *Gesammelte Schriften,* II, 271; Levin, *Reform des Judenthums,* 80.

[48] Schreiber, *Reformed Judaism and its Pioneers,* 34. Spokane, 1892.

[49] Holdheim, *G. J. R. G. B.,* 79-81.

[50] Levin, *Die Reform des Judenthums,* 19; Bernfeld, *Juden und Judenthum im 19ten Jahrhundert,* 28; Jost, *Geschichte des Judenthums und seiner Sekten,* III, 317.

[51] Breslau, May 21, 1790.

[52] Jost, op. cit., III, 325.

[53] *A. Z. d. J.,* I, 240.

[54] In a communication addressed to the Westphalian Minister, von Wölfradt, in May, 1810, he set forth his "Confession of Faith." In this he speaks of three interpretations of Judaism—the ceremonial, the moral-ceremonial, and the spiritual—and declares himself in sympathy with the last named. See "Zur Charakteristik Israel Jacobsons," by L. Horwitz, *A. Z. d. J.,* LXVIII (1904), 392-3.

[55] It is of more than passing interest that the English translation of one of these sermons was the first Jewish publication printed in Philadelphia, U. S. A.; it appeared in the year 1763 under the title "A Thanksgiving Sermon for the Important and Astonishing Victory obtained on the Fifth of December, MDCCLVII, over the united and far superior Forces of the Austrians in Silesia. Preached on Sabbath, the tenth of said month, at the Synagogue of the Jews in Berlin, by David Hirschel Fränkel, Arch-Rabbi.

Translated from the German original printed at Berlin." See *Publications of the Amer. Jew. Hist. Soc.*, I, 63.

[56] "Aus meiner Knabenzeit," Reminiscences by Ludwig Philippson, a native of Dessau. *A. Z. d. J.* LI (1887), 750.

[57] Dembitz, *Services in Synagogue and Home*, 295. Philadelphia, 1898.

[58] See *Jewish Encyclopedia*, art. "Homiletics."

[59] "The reform movement emanated from the people, the living bearer of Judaism, and not from reformers. . . . The impetus to all changes proceeded from so-called laymen. It is an incontrovertible fact that the reform movement was not fathered by rabbis." Seligman, *Geschichte der jüdischen Reformbewegung*, 15, 16. Frankfurt am Main, 1922. See also the symposium on "Reform Judaism and the Laity," *Year Book C. C. A. R.*, xxxviii (1928).

[60] The first reform prayer-book used by a Jewish congregation, viz., that of the Hamburg Temple congregation, issued in 1819, was dedicated to Jacobson as the father of the reform movement. For an exhaustive study of Jacobson's career and service see Jacob R. Marcus, *Year Book C. C. A. R.*, xxxviii (1928), 386-498.

[61] Léon Kahn, *Les Juifs à Paris*, 86. Paris, 1889.

[62] Graetz, *Geschichte der Juden*, XI, 268.

[63] Guizot in *Revue des Deux Mondes* for July, 1867, 18-20. Quoted in Graetz's *Geschichte der Juden*, XI, 620.

[64] "Reform des Judenthums in Frankreich und Italien," *Sulamith*, II, 3ff. Dessau, 1807.

[65] Kahn, *Les Juifs à Paris*, 88.

[66] *Sulamith*, I, 183.

[67] *Gesammelte Actenstücke über die Verbesserung des Zustandes der Juden*. Herausgegeben von Alexander Bran, I, 342. Hamburg, 1807.

[68] Mielziner, *The Jewish Law of Marriage and Divorce*, 97. Cincinnati, 1884.

[69] An expression which had been used by Napoleon himself, *"une nation dans la nation"*; see Kahn, op. cit., 88.

[70] Quoted in *A. Z. d. J.*, III, 151, from the *Courrier de la Moselle*.

[71] Ludwig Geiger, *Geschichte der Juden in Berlin*, 145. Berlin, 1871.

[72] Graetz, *Geschichte der Juden*, XI, 317.

[73] *Ueber die durch die neue Organisation der Judenschulen in den preussischen Staaten nothwendig gewordene Umbildung ihres Gottesdienstes in den Synagogen*. Berlin, 1812.

[74] *Sulamith*, II, 66.

[75] *Ibid.*, 68.

[76] The first Jewish prayer-book entirely in the German language was issued in 1817 by two of these young men, Kley and Günsburg. It was entitled, *Die deutsche Synagoge oder Ordnung des Gottesdienstes für die Sabbath- und Festtage des ganzen Jahres zum Gebrauche der Gemeinden, die sich der deutschen Gebete bedienen*. Berlin, 1817.

[77] Geiger, *Die letzten zwei Jahre*, Nachgelassene Schriften, I, 1-51. *Ansprache an meine Gemeinde*, ibid., 52-112.

[78] *A. Z. d. J.*, I, 457; III, 244; V, 610; VIII, 259.

[79] *Ibid.*, VI, 108.

[80] *Ibid.*, XI, 251; XIII, 89.

[81] *Ibid.*, VI, 393. Geiger, *Geschichte der Juden in Berlin*, 234.

[82] Holdheim, *G. J. R. G. B.*, 17, note.

[83] Samter, *Judentaufen im 19 Jahrhundert*, 30. Berlin, 1906.

[84] This charge was hurled as late as 1911 by the Rev. Joseph H. Hertz, the present chief rabbi of England, while he was rabbi of Johannesburg, South Africa. Dr. G. Deutsch refuted this charge in a detailed communication to the *Jewish Chronicle* of June 2, 1911. This article was translated by

Benas Levy and appeared in *Liberales Judenthum*, III, 141, under the heading "Reform Judenthum und Taufe." Dr. Hertz returned to the charge when, in 1926, he delivered a series of addresses against Liberal Judaism. See *Jewish Daily Bulletin*, New York, Feb. 21, 1926. Dr. Israel I. Mattuck, rabbi of the Liberal Jewish Synagogue, London, took up the gauntlet.

[85] Because of the special meaning which the term "science" has assumed in English it is difficult to render exactly the German phrase *Wissenschaft des Judenthums;* if the word "science" be understood in its original and larger meaning of knowledge and not in the more restricted significance of natural science, the phrase "Science of Judaism" may stand as the equivalent of the German.

[86] But one volume of this magazine appeared with the title *Zeitschrift für die Wissenschaft des Judenthums*. Berlin, 1823.

[87] He had won his spurs before this as an original investigator by his study on the great Jewish commentator Rashi, which had appeared in the magazine mentioned in the previous note; his first publication was an essay on rabbinical literature. Berlin, 1818.

[88] An interesting occurrence illustrating this attitude of the Prussian authorities took place as late as the year 1847. In the columns of the *Reform Zeitung*, a paper published by A. Rebenstein (Aaron Bernstein) in the interests of the Jewish reform movement, a sermon delivered in a Jewish house of worship was spoken of in complimentary terms. The censor struck out the word "sermon" (*Predigt*) on the ground that only religious discourses delivered in a Christian church could rightly be called sermons (*Diese Bezeichnung ist der christlichen Kirche eigenthümlich und vorbehalten*) "Eine Reliquie aus der Censurzeit." *A. Z. d. J.*, LVII (1894), 424.

[89] *Die Gottesdienstlichen Vorträge der Juden, historisch Entwickelt.* Berlin, 1832.

[90] Ritter, *Samuel Holdheim*, 82. Berlin, 1865.

[91] See Zunz' interesting statement regarding the genesis of this work in "Ein Besuch bei Leopold Zunz," by Adolf Frankl-Grün. *A. Z. d. J.*, LX (1896), 487.

[92] *Gottesdienstliche Vorträge*, 477.

[93] *Ibid.*, 478.

[94] *Ibid.*, 479.

[95] *Ibid.*, 475.

[96] *Ibid.*, 481.

[97] Ritter, op. cit., 81.

[98] Rapoport's biographies of Saadia, Chananel, Nathan Hababli, Elazar Kalir, Nissim, and Hai Gaon had appeared in the periodical *Bikkure Haittim* in 1828-1831, and Luzzatto's treatise on the Aramaic translation of the Bible in 1830.

[99] Geiger, *Geschichte der Juden in Berlin*, 251.

[100] For an account of the introduction of the ceremony of confirmation into Judaism see the author's *Confirmation in the Synagogue, Year Book, C. C. A. R.*, I, 43-58.

[101] Well expressed by Holdheim, "Der Talmud spricht aus seinem Zeitbewusstsein und für dasselbe hatte er Recht; ich spreche aus einem höheren Bewusstsein meiner Zeit und für dasselbe habe ich Recht." *Das Ceremonialgesetz im Messiasreich*, 50. Schwerin, 1845.

[102] See L. Philippson's clear exposition of this point. *A. Z. d. J.*, VIII (1844), 461; cf. also Holdheim's critique of Fränkel's article on *Reformbestrebung und Emancipation*, 86. Schwerin, 1845. Freund's *Zur Judenfrage im Deutschland*, II, 30, 159, 166. Geiger, *W. Z. J. T.*, I, 349, V, 53, 234; *Nachgelassene Schriften*, I, 93, 96; Stein, *Protokolle der dritten Versammlung deutschen Rabbiner*, 117. Breslau, 1846.

[103] This was done by the Central Conference of American Rabbis at the

Rochester meeting in July, 1895; see *Year Book C. C. A. R.,* VI, p. 63.

[104] Jost, *Culturgeschichte zur neueren Geschichte d. Israeliten,* III, 23.

[105] The prayer-book was entitled *Ordnung der öffentlichen Andacht für die Sabbath und Festtage des ganzen Jahres nach dem Gebrauche des neuen Tempelvereins in Hamburg. Herausgegeben von I. J. Fränkel und M. J. Bresselau.* Hamburg, 5579 (1819).

[106] *Nachgelassene Schriften,* I, 162. This critique, it is true, was written concerning the second edition of the prayer-book issued in 1842, but it applies as well to this first edition.

[107] *Nachgelassene Schriften,* I, 148; *Infra.,* Chapter IV.

[108] Jost, op. cit., 23.

[109] *Adresse an meine Glaubensgenossen in Hamburg.* Altona, 1818.

[110] נגה הצדק, with an appendix אור נגה. Dessau, 1818.

[111] Leopold Löw, *Aaron Chorin, Eine biographische Skizze, Gesammelte Schriften,* II, 251-420. Szegedin, 1890.

[112] The last public utterance of Aaron Chorin was a communication addressed to a conference of Hungarian rabbis at Paks in 1844. He died on Aug. 24 of that year; on Aug. 13 he wrote the communication in question; I quote a portion of it because it expresses so well the ideals that led this early reformer up and on. He had passed through struggles and persecutions because of his convictions, but at the very close of his life, after he had reached his seventy-eighth year, we find him as undismayed as ever in the cause to which he had devoted himself. We may consider this final communication as his rabbinical will and testament; he wrote thus: "The permanent elements of religion must be expressed in terms that appeal to the people and are consonant with the needs of life. If our religion and life appear to conflict with one another this is due either to the defacement of the sanctuary by foreign additions or to the license of the sinning will which desires to make its unbridled greed and its false tendency authoritative guides for life. If we will show ourselves as ready to strip off these unessential additions which often forced themselves upon our noble faith as the spawn of obscure and dark ages, as we are determined to sacrifice our very lives for the upholding of the essential, we will be able to resist successfully with the help of God all wanton, thoughtless and presumptuous attacks which license or ignorance may direct against our sacred cause; the seeming conflict will then disappear and we will have accomplished something lasting for God. I need not tell you that of all the external institutions the public service demands our immediate and undivided attention. He who is faithful to his God, and is earnestly concerned for the welfare of his religion, must exert himself to rescue our service from the ruin into which it has fallen and to give it once again that inspiring form which is worthy of a pious and devout worship of the one true God. For it is not only the excrescences of dark ages which cover it with disgrace, but thoughtlessness, lack of taste, absence of devotion, and caprice have disfigured its noble outlines." *A. Z. d. J.,* VIII, 551; see Leopold Löw's exhaustive biography of Chorin in *Gesammelte Schriften,* II, 251-420. Szegedin, 1890.

[113] אלה דברי הברית. Altona, 1819. An answer to this publication was issued the same year by M. J. Bresselau, one of the organizers of the temple congregation, under the title הרב נקמת נקם ברית *Streitschrift gegen die Scrift* אלא דברי הברית *den Hamburger Tempelstreit betheidigend.*

[114] Moses Sofer was one of the luminaries of rabbinical Judaism. His fanaticism against the reform movement was intense. He was the very antipode to Aaron Chorin, and since his final utterance also contains some expressions concerning reform, I quote it as representing the other side. In his will he gives his children parting advice and instruction in these

terms: "Avoid the pernicious company of these evil-doers, the innovators who have removed themselves far from God and his law! Live not in their vicinity, and have no association of any kind with them. Touch not the books of Moses of Dessau (Moses Mendelssohn); then will your feet never slip! . . . Your daughters may read German books, but only such as are written in our spirit, in harmony with the explanations of our teachers of blessed memory. . . . Never say 'The times have changed.' We have an old Father, blessed be his name! who has never changed, who will never change." Apart from the polemical expressions against reform, the document is permeated with a fine spirit and teaches the loftiest lessons. Published in Jost's *Israelitische Annalen*, I (1839), 354; see also Abrahams, *J. Q. R.*, III, 475.

[115] Israel Bettan, "Early Reform in Contemporaneous Responsa," *Hebrew Union College Jubilee Volume*, 434-443. Cincinnati, 1925.

[116] *W. Z. J. T.*, herausgegeben von Abraham Geiger, I, 464; II, 493.

[117] Geiger, *J. Z. W. L.*, V, 241, in estimate of Kley's services at time of latter's death in 1867; *ibid.*, VII, 24, *Zu Schutz und Trutz*.

[118] A prayer for the well-being of the established government.

[119] The twelfth benediction of the *Shemone esreh* (eighteen benedictions). This prayer, originally framed against sectaries within Judaism (*Birkat hamminim*) was in medieval days claimed by the enemies of the Jews to be a petition directed against the Christians. Because of this misinterpretation many urged its elimination from the ritual. On the history of this benediction see Baer *Abodath Jisrael, sub voce*, "welamalshinim," Roedelheim, 1868; Bacher · *Agada der Tanaiten*, 83ff., Strasburg, 1903; Friedländer *Jüdische Apologetik*, 469, Zurich, 1903; Dembitz, *Services in Synagogue and Home*, 132-4, Philadelphia, 1898; on the advisability of its elimination see Salomon, *Das neue Gebetbuch und seine Verketzerung*, 22. Hamburg, 1842.

[120] *A. Z. d. J.*, II, 210.

[121] Geiger, *Nachgelassene Schriften*, I, 176.

[122] *A. Z. d. J.*, I, 101, 110.

[123] *Ibid.*, I, 25.

[124] This hymn was composed by Solomon the Levite about 1500 at Safed, Palestine. For an English rendering of the poem see Alice Lucas' *The Jewish Year*, 167. London, 1898.

[125] Psalm xcii.

[126] A Mishnaic section (Mish. Sabb. II) on the Sabbath lights, which had been incorporated in the liturgy.

[127] A similar section on the sacrifices (Mish. Zeb., V).

[128] Psalms included in the service.

[129] The peculiar chant in which the cantor read the Pentateuchal section.

[130] The verse taken from Num. x. 36, and spoken at the *Einheben*, the return of the scroll to the ark.

[131] The psalms of praise (cxiii-cxviii) read as an additional portion of the service on New Moon, the three high feasts, and the Feast of Dedication.

[132] A poetical rendition of the thirteen articles of faith formulated in the Maimonidean creed and used as a hymn at the close of the service.

[133] The ninth day of Ab, the anniversary of the Destruction of Jerusalem, observed as a day of fasting and mourning.

[134] *Rabbinische Gutachten über die Verträglichkeit der freien Forschung mit dem Rabbineramte*, 14. Breslau, 1842.

[135] *A. Z. d. J.*, II, 4.

[136] Geiger's *W. Z. J. T.*, II, 435.

[137] Cf. the striking statement in a letter written from Frankfort-on-the-Main in 1845. *I. d. N. J.*, V, 112.

[138] Liturgical poems wherewith the ritual had become overweighted.
[139] *Supra,* n. 113.
[140] Vol. I, 44.

CHAPTER II

[1] Geiger, *W. Z. J. T.,* I, 8-9; see also *ibid., Jüdische Geschichte von 1830 bis zur Gegenwart* (1849), in *Nachgelassene Schriften,* II, 264ff.; cf. also Holdheim, *G. J. R. G. B.,* 3-4.
[2] Holdheim, *ibid.,* 75.
[3] Geiger, *Der Hamburger Tempelstreit,* in *Nachgelassene Schriften,* I, 194.
[4] Geiger, *W. Z. J. T.,* II, 211.
[5] Geiger, *W. Z. J. T.,* II, 220; cf. also his definition of reform, *Nachgelassene Schriften,* II, 265.
[6] *Reformbestrebung und Emancipation* (appendix to *Das Ceremonialgesetz im Gottesreich,* Schwerin, 1845), p. 123; see, however, his definition of reform as the reconciliation of two opposing principles in *G. J. R. G. B.* Preface, v, vi.
[7] *A. Z. d. J.,* VIII (1844), 87.
[8] Philippson, *ibid.,* IX (1845), 516. Cf. also Holdheim, *G. J. R. G. B.,* 105, 200; Geiger, *J. Z. W. L.,* V, 251.
[9] Geiger, *A. Z. d. J.,* IX, 340.
[10] Cf. Geiger, *W. Z. J. T.,* I, 10, 11, 222; II, 569; *Nachgelassene Schriften,* I, 127, 133, 187, 204; Holdheim, *Verketzerung und Gewissensfreiheit,* passim; Ritter, *Samuel Holdheim,* 66, 76, 167; Jost, *Geschichte des Judenthums und seiner Sekten,* III, 352; Löw, *Gesammelte Schriften,* II, 206, 271, 455; Levin, *Reform des Judenthums,* 25, 56, 61; Philippson, *A. Z. d. J.,* XL (1876), 235.
[11] *Was hat Mohammed aus dem Judenthum aufgenommen?* Bonn, 1833.
[12] *Wissenschaftliche Zeitschrift für jüdische Theologie,* 6 vols., 1835-1848; *Jüdische Zeitschrift für Wissenschaft und Leben.* Breslau, 11 vols., 1862-1874.
[13] *Das Judenthum und seine Geschichte.* Breslau, 1865.
[14] Sadducäer und Pharisäer, *J. Z. W. L.,* II, 11-54.
[15] Geiger's thesis concerning the Pharisees has received recent endorsement from two non-Jewish scholars, namely, George Foot Moore, in his work *Judaism in the First Centuries of the Christian Era,* 2 vols., Cambridge, 1927, and R. Travers Herford, in his book *The Pharisees,* London, 1924.
[16] *Supra,* 26.
[17] *Supra,* 27.
[18] *A. Z. d. J.,* IX, 340.
[19] Vol. I, 2.
[20] *Ibid.,* I, 11.
[21] Hirsch remained faithful to this point of view; cf. the article, "Der Jude und seine Zeit," in his magazine, *Jeschurum,* I (1855), 14-25.
[22] *The Nineteen Letters of Ben Uziel* (Eng. tr.), 174. New York, 1899.

CHAPTER III

[1] The ceremony consequent upon the refusal to marry a deceased brother's childless widow in accordance with the Scriptural injunction, Deut. xxv. 5-11. Cf. "Levirate and Chalitza" in Mielziner's *Jewish Law of Marriage and Divorce,* 54-58. Cincinnati, 1884.
[2] The exact wording of this notice which appeared at the end of Mar.,

1838, was that the congregation desired a "theologian of comprehensive Biblical and Talmudical attainments, thorough scientific training and strict religiosity, who, besides fulfilling the functions of a *dayan*, is able to deliver instructive and edifying addresses every Sabbath in pure German"; eight rabbis applied for the position, and four others, Philippson, Holdheim, Herxheimer and Geiger, declared their willingness privately to accept the position.

³ Talm. Bab. *Aboda Zara*, 36 a, פשט איסורו בכל ישראל ;

אין גוזרין גזירה על הצבור אלא אם כן רוב הצבור יכולין לעמוד בה

Also *Baba Batra* 60 b. Cf. *supra*, 438, note 23.

⁴ *A. Z. d. J.*, II (1838), 113.

⁵ See his interesting account in a letter to his friends, M. A. Stern, published in *Nachgelassene Schriften*, V, 148, and J. Derenbourg, *A. Z. d. J.*, LX (1896), 257-8. (This interesting correspondence between Geiger and Derenbourg, extending over thirty years, was published by the former's son, Prof. Ludwig Geiger, twenty-two years after his father's death.)

⁶ *A. Z. d. J.*, IV, 66.

⁷ *Darstellung des Sachverhältnisses in seiner hiesigen Rabbinatsangelegenheit.* Breslau, 1842, 26.

⁸ Holdheim, *G. J. R. G. B.*, 63, note 6.

⁹ These incidents are given in detail in Geiger's history of the controversy, *Ansprache an meine Gemeinde* (Breslau, 1842), and in Schreiber's *Reformed Judaism and its Pioneers* (Spokane, 1892), 306ff.

¹⁰ "Ansprache an meine Gemeinde," *Nachgelassene Schriften*, II, 265; *W. Z. J. T.*, I, 256; cf. also his "Jüdische Geschichte von 1830 bis zur Gegenwart" (1849) in *Nachgelassene Schriften*, II, 265.

¹¹ Cf. Holdheim, *G. J. R. G. B.*, 173.

¹² *Darstellung des Sachverhältnisses*, etc. Appendix 1.

¹³ *Ibid.* Appendix 2.

¹⁴ *Rabbinische Gutachten über die Verträglichkeit der freien Forschung mit dem Rabbineramte.*

¹⁵ The response of Rabbi Fassel of Prossnitz, Moravia, was not included in these volumes for reasons stated by the governing board of the Breslau congregation in the preface to the second volume. The response was published in the *Literaturblatt des Orients*, Nos. 5-8, 1843.

¹⁶ *Theologische Gutachten über das Gebetbuch nach dem Gebrauche des neuen israelitischen Tempelvereins in Hamburg.* Hamburg, 1842.

¹⁷ *Supra*, 35.

¹⁸ *Rabbinische Gutachten über die Verträglichkeit u. s. w.*, I, 4.

¹⁹ *Ibid.*, I, 9.

²⁰ *Ibid.*, I, 12.

²¹ *Supra*, 32.

²² ראש אמונה. Prague, 1803; דבר בעתו. Vienna, 1820; עמוק השוה. Ofen, 1837; and ילד זקנים. Vienna, 1839.

²³ *Rabbinische Gutachten*, I, 18.

²⁴ *Ibid.*, I, 22.

²⁵ *Ibid.*, 23.

²⁶ *Ibid.*, 32.

²⁷ *Ueber die Autonomie der Rabbinen und das Prinzip der jüdischen Ehe.*

²⁸ *Supra*, 21.

²⁹ See the author's "Samuel Holdheim, Jewish Reformer," *1806-1861*, *Year Book C. C. A. R.* for 1906, 305-333; issued also as a separate publication and included in the Collection *Centenary Papers and Others*, 63-97. Cincinnati, 1919.

³⁰ *Rabbinische Gutachten*, I, 60.

³¹ *Ibid.*, I, 71. Holdheim's first publication dealing with the subject of reform in Judaism had been called forth by the Breslau affair. In the year 1840 he had published the pamphlet, *Der religiöse Fortschritt in deutschen*

Judenthume. Ein friedliches Wort in einer aufgeregten Zeit, in answer to the contention of a Dr. Lowisitz, who had argued that the culture of an age could not be considered a deciding factor in religious concerns in his pamphlet *Die Rabbinerwahl, zur Aufklärung der dabei vertretenen religiösen Interessen.* Breslau, 1840.

[32] A great rabbi, known as "The Light of the Exile," who lived from 960-1028; though born in France he settled in Mayence, where he founded a school; he was renowned as a Commentator of the Talmud, but he is best known for certain decrees which he issued, among others the one forbidding polygamy; see Graetz, *History of the Jews* (Eng. tr.). Philadelphia, 1894, III, 244.

[33] *Rabbinische Gutachten,* I, 86.

[34] *Ibid.,* I, 92.

[35] This rabbi was the central figure in one of the most unfortunate incidents of those stirring times in Jewish life. He became rabbi of the congregation of Lemberg, Galicia, in 1844; his reform tendencies and progressive views aroused great opposition among the orthodox party, and in Sept., 1848, he met his death, a victim of a fanatic who had poisoned his food. See his biography by his son, Jacob Kohn, in *Nachgelassene Schriften Abraham Kohn's mit einer Biographie desselben verfasst von seinem Sohne Jakob Kohn. Herausgegeben von Joseph Kobak.* Lemberg, 1856.

[36] *Rabbinische Gutachten,* I, 114.

[37] One of the standing charges of the opponents of reform was that the reformers were forming a new sect in Judaism, whereas the reformers claimed that they were simply applying the principle of tradition to the unusual circumstances in which the Jews were living in the new age. The difference between the rabbinical and the reform party in this matter may be put briefly thus, that the reformers made a distinction between *tradition* and *the traditions,* or between *tradition* and *traditionalism,* which the rabbinical party did not. *Supra,* 7.

[38] *Rabbinische Gutachten,* I, 115.

[39] The congregation celebrated the fiftieth anniversary of his service as rabbi Sept. 26, 1877. *A. Z. d. J.,* XLI (1877), 697.

[40] *Rabbinische Gutachten,* I, 121.

[41] A reform instituted by Hillel. It was found that the Mosaic command that all debts were to be canceled in the Sabbatical year interfered seriously with commercial activity; people were loth to lend money; therefore Hillel ordained that the creditor should make a deposition before a court which would empower him to collect his debt; or, in other words, that the Sabbatical year was not to cancel the debt. This institution was known as Prozbul (*Mish., Shebiith,* X, 3, 4).

[42] A reform of the patriarch Judah II; it is in connection with this permission that the famous expression is used that no law ought to continue in force that the people could not carry out (Talm. Bab. *Ab. Zara,* 36 a).

[43] *Rabbinische Gutachten,* I, 27.

[44] *Ibid.,* I, 131.

[45] *Ibid.,* I, 184.

[46] *Ibid.,* II, 10.

[47] *Ibid.,* II, 64.

[48] *Ibid.,* II, 83.

[49] *Nachgelassene Schriften,* V, 162.

[50] Ritter, *Die jüdische Reformgemeinde in Berlin,* 49. Berlin, 1902.

CHAPTER IV

[1] *Supra,* Chapter I.

[2] *Israelitische Annalen,* III, 353, 362.

³ Cf. Geiger's estimate of Mannheimer's work in his obituary article, *J. Z. W. L.*, III, 170.

⁴ *A. Z. d. J.*, I, 44, III, 637; *Isr. Ann.*, III, 14, 53.

⁵ *Ibid.*, I, 190; Löw, *Gesammelte Schriften*, II, 291.

⁶ *Isr. Ann.*, I, 213.

⁷ *Ibid.*. 228.

⁸ *A. Z. d. J.*, III, 394.

⁹ *Isr. Ann.*, I, 95.

¹⁰ *Ibid.*, 51.

¹¹ *Ibid.*. 14.

¹² *W. Z. J. T.*. I, 475

¹³ *Isr. Ann.*, I, 413, II. 127; Löw, *Ges. Schr.*, II. 295.

¹⁴ *Ibid.*, I, 142.

¹⁵ *W. Z. J. T.*, I, 465.

¹⁶ *A. Z. d. J.*, I, 63.

¹⁷ *Ibid.*, III, 26.

¹⁸ *Isr. Ann.*, II, 38.

¹⁹ *W. Z. J. T.*, I, 125.

²⁰ *Theologische Gutachten über das Gebetbuch nach dem Gebrauche des neuen israelitischen Tempelvereins zu Hamburg*, 71. Hamburg, 1842.

²¹ *A. Z. d. J.*, III, 34.

²² *Ibid.*, IV, 64.

²³ *Isr. Ann.*, II, 284, 290.

²⁴ *A. Z. d. J.*, IV, 21; *Isr. Ann.*, II, 11.

²⁵ In fact, two such seminaries were founded in Wilna and Zhitomir in 1848 and were controlled practically by the *maskilim*, the Russian counterparts to the German *meass'fim* (*Supra*, 6) of the eighteenth century. The rabbis who graduated from these seminaries were to influence the Russian Jews to accept modern ideas and to become more and more Russianized. The Jewish masses in Russia being ultra-orthodox, did not look favorably upon these seminaries nor upon their graduates, who, although, equipped with a good secular education, were rarely Talmudical adepts of the first rank. These seminaries existed about twenty-five years; they did not accomplish what was hoped by their founders. They did not displace the *yeshibot*. The conservatism of the Russian Jew was too strong. Cf. "The Jew in Russia" in the volume, *The Immigrant Jew in America*, 22. New York, 1906; Philipson, *Max Lilienthal, American Rabbi*, 38. New York, 1915.

²⁶ *A. Z. d. J.*, V, 20.

²⁷ *W. Z. J. T.*, I, 271.

²⁸ A series of letters, *d'un Israélite Français à ses coréligionnaires,* and signed Tsarphati; they appeared at irregular intervals, beginning in 1822, and continued for twenty years; they were concerned for the most part with urging reforms of various kinds, liturgic, ritualistic, and administrative, among the Jews of France, *Supra*, 30.

²⁹ "Conservons le Sabbat, fête de la création, changeons le jour; conservons l'alliance céleste, changeons le mode; émancipons la femme, elle fait part du genre humain. Conservons nos assemblées de prières, les magnifiques cantiques du Psalmiste, changeons l'idiome; introduisons successivement la prédication Protestante, l'orgue catholique, les accords des Meyerbeer, des Halévi."—*W. Z. J. T.*, IV, 259.

³⁰ *Theologische Gutachten über das Gebetbuch nach dem Gebrauche des neuen israelitischen Tempelvereins in Hamburg*, Introd. 10, 11.

³¹ In a letter to M. Veit, dated Dec. 11, 1841, Riesser deprecates the action of the orthodox party in calling in the aid of the government against the reformers; see Aus M. Veit's *Nachlass Mittheilungen von Ludwig Geiger; A. Z. d. J.*, LIX, 189. In a former letter he had denounced the unfortunate habit of the Jews to seek governmental interference in the management of their internal affairs. His own standpoint he expressed clearly

in the words, "Unser höchstes Prinzip muss immer das der Freiheit, der unabhängigen inneren Entwickelung sein," *ibid.*, 188.

[32] *Das neue Gebetbuch und seine Verketzerung; sine ira et cum studio.* Hamburg, 1841.

[33] *Stillstand und Fortschritt.* Hamburg, 1841.

[34] Dr. G. Salomon, the preacher of the congregation, also issued a history of the same several years later under the title *Kurzgefasste Geschichte des neuen israelitischen Tempels in Hamburg während der ersten 25 Jahren seines Bestehens.* Hamburg, 1844.

[35] See Geiger in letter of Feb. 9, 1842, to J. Derenbourg: *A. Z. d. J.,* LX (1896), 345.

[36] *Theologische Gutachten über das Gebetbuch nach dem Gebrauche des neuen israelitischen Tempelvereins in Hamburg.* Hamburg, 1842.

[37] *Ueber das Gebetbuch nach dem Gebrauche des neuen israelitischen Tempels zu Hamburg.* Hamburg, 1841.

[38] *Verketzerung und Gewissensfreiheit: ein zweites Votum.* Schwerin, 1842.

[39] *Jude und Nichtjude: eine Erwiderung auf die Schriften der Tripel-Allianz.* Amsterdam, 1842.

[40] *Supra,* 82.

[41] *Theologische Gutachten über das Gebetbuch nach dem Gebrauche des neuen israelitischen Tempelvereins in Hamburg,* 73ff.

[42] *Ibid.,* 94ff.

[43] *Orient,* 1842, Nos. 7, 8, 9.

[44] *Sendschreiben an Herrn Dr. Zacharias Frankel in Betreff seines im "Orient" mitgetheilten Gutachtens über das neue Gebetbuch der Tempelgemeinde in Hamburg.* Hamburg, 1842.

[45] "Erwiderung auf das von Herrn Dr. Salomon, Prediger am neuen israelitischen Tempel zu Hamburg, an mich gerichtete Sendschreiben." *Literaturblatt des Orients,* 1842, Nos. 23 and 24.

[46] Zangwill, *The Dreamers of the Ghetto,* 553. Philadelphia, 1898.

[47] *A. Z. d. J.* (1846), X, 100-102, where the rules governing the work of this commission are given; the most significant of these rules was the stipulation that the commission was to subject the contents of the prayer-book to a careful revision every five years so as to keep it abreast of the development of the time; to add new prayers, if necessary, to eliminate passages if this were found requisite. The purpose of this resolution was most laudable, viz., to make the prayer-book progressively expressive of the developing religious spirit through periodical revision. The resolution, however, remained a paper regulation, for the periodical revisions did not take place.

CHAPTER V

[1] Quoted in *Jewish Chronicle,* June 18, 1897, 17.

[2] Gaster, *History of the Ancient Synagogue of Spanish and Portuguese Jews,* 15. London, 1901.

[3] *Jewish Chronicle,* June 11, 1897, 12.

[4] This was clearly expressed as late as 1844 by Lord Chancellor Lyndhurst, who, in rendering a decision in a Jewish marriage case, said: "They [the Jews] are treated in these decisions as a distinct people, governed, as to this subject, by their own religious observances and institutions, among which marriage is included." *Voice of Jacob,* III, 128.

[5] Gaster, *History of the Ancient Synagogue of Spanish and Portuguese Jews,* 169.

[6] Picciotto, *Sketches of Anglo-Jewish History,* p. 302. London, 1875.

[7] *Ibid.*, 326.

[8] Jost, *Geschichte der Israeliten*, X, Part II, 69.

[9] H. Adler, "The Chief Rabbis of England," in *Papers read at the Anglo-Jewish Historical Exhibition*, 1887, 287. London, 1888.

[10] Picciotto, *Sketches of Anglo-Jewish History*, 371.

[11] Gaster, *History of the Ancient Synagogue of Spanish and Portuguese Jews*, 170.

[12] *Ibid.*, 17.

[13] For a description of the sorry state of public worship in England at this time see Prof. D. W. Marks' letter called forth by the death of his friend, Sir John Simon, one of the most active of the reformers of 1842. *Jewish Chronicle*, July 9, 1897, 7.

[14] P. xv.

[15] "The History of the Central Synagogue," by Michael Adler, *Jewish Chronicle*, Apr. 14, 1905, 16.

[16] Extract from minute-book of the New Synagogue, meeting of May 19, 1841, *Jewish Chronicle*, May 13, 1905, 28.

[17] *A. Z. d. J.*, V, 732.

[18] *Israelit des neunzehnten Jahrhunderts*, III, 167. Supplement to *Jewish Chronicle*, Jan. 29, 1892, 18.

[19] It is an interesting fact that the Bevis Marks congregation abolished in 1885 the announcement of the offerings because of the unseemly indecorum connected therewith. In 1904 the elders resolved to reintroduce these announcements on financial grounds; they held that the financial straits of the congregation were such that the money which members would be induced to offer if public announcement thereof were made at the services would aid materially in swelling a depleted treasury. The reactionary measure was carried by a majority of one, and called forth more than one strong protest. *Jewish Chronicle*, Feb. 19, 1904, p. 6, 26; Feb. 26, p. 6.

[20] See defense of the congregation's action in this matter of the second days of the festivals by B. E. (Benjamin Elkin), *Voice of Jacob*, IV (1844), 30-31; to this is appended an answer by the editor defending the traditional view; for a reply to this, see *ibid.*, 59; cf. also an anonymous pamphlet, "Holy Convocations, or Reasons for the Observance of the יום טוב שני." London, 1844.

[21] *Voice of Jacob*, I, 36, Nov. 26, 1841.

[22] Jost, *Geschichte des Judenthums und seiner Sekten*, III, 373; *Israelit des neunzehnten Jahrhunderts*, III, 57.

[23] The preacher's words on this all-important subject were: "We must, as our conviction urges us, solemnly deny that a belief in the divinity of the traditions written in the Mishnah and the Jerusalem and Babylonian Talmuds, is of equal obligation to the Israelite, with the faith in the divinity of the Law of Moses. We know that these books are human compositions; and though we are content to accept with reverence from our post-Biblical ancestors advice and instruction, we cannot unconditionally accept their laws. For Israelites there is but one immutable law, the sacred volume of the scriptures, commanded by God to be written down for the unerring guidance of his people until the end of time." The authority of the oral law was one of the chief points of difference between the traditionalists and the reformers. A pamphlet appeared taking the opposite view to that advocated by Mr. Marks; this pamphlet was entitled *Is there an Oral Law of Divine Origin and Therefore Binding upon the Jews?* by One of Themselves; see also article signed A. B. (Abraham Benisch) in *Voice of Jacob*, I, 18 (Mar. 18, 1842), entitled "In What Relation do those who deny the Oral Law stand to those who believe in it with respect to the keeping of the Festivals?" An answer to this appeared in pamphlet form shortly thereafter, entitled *Is the Oral Law of Divine Origin and therefore Binding upon the Jews? the advocacy of this Question Contested*, by a Member of the Community (John

Simon). Another pamphlet in defense of the reformers appeared in Oct.,
1842: *The Oral Law and Its Defenders*, A Review by a Scripturalist.
    [24] For a caustic criticism of this sermon see *Voice of Jacob*, I, 90, Mar.
4, 1842.
    [25] Two years later this rabbi preached a sermon (on Sabbath T'shubah,
1844) in which he deplored the secession of the members of the West London Synagogue from the mother congregation, as well as the causes that led
to it, and earnestly exhorted all parties to a conciliatory policy. *Voice of
Jacob*, IV, 39, 1844.
    [26] *Voice of Jacob*, I, 77, Feb. 4, 1842.
    [27] *A. Z. d. J.*, VI, 263.
    [28] On this point see *Voice of Jacob*, IV, 100, 111.
    [29] This refusal of the Elders to permit the burial of the members of the
congregation by the side of their beloved was a striking instance of religious
bigotry; no words are strong enough to condemn such acts that have been
performed so frequently in the name of religion among all sects. The new
congregation was compelled to secure a burial ground of its own. It was
two years and a half before it purchased its cemetery at Balls Pond. In the
interval Mrs. Horatio J. Montefiore, the wife of one of the organizers of
the new congregation, died. The application to the Elders of the Spanish
and Portuguese Synagogue to permit her burial in their cemetery was
refused. The new congregation entered immediately into an arrangement
with the Maiden Lane Synagogue whereby, upon payment of fifty pounds
per annum, they would be permitted to bury their dead in the cemetery of
that congregation and have their minister officiate at the funeral. This was
the only death in the congregation before the cemetery at Balls Pond was
acquired. *Voice of Jacob*, I, 101, Mar. 11, 1842.
    [30] For a full account of the successive steps taken in the matter, see
Picciotto, *Sketches of Anglo-Jewish History*, 383. The passing of the years
has witnessed the disappearance of most of the acrimony aroused in the formation period; for years the reform congregation has had representation in
the very Board of Deputies of British Jews which was so bitter in its opposition at the start. Strange to say, the reform congregation in 1903 was
almost as decided as the United Synagogue in the opposition to the Jewish
Religious Union. For opposition to Liberal Jewish Synagogue see p. 409ff.
    [31] See Supplement to *Jewish Chronicle*, Jan. 29, 1892, 19.
    [32] *Voice of Jacob*, I, 81ff.
    [33] *Ibid.*, IV, 164.
    [34] *Appeal of Congregation of the West London Synagogue of British
Jews, to their Brother Israelites Throughout the United Kingdom.* The correspondence that passed between Francis H. Goldsmid and Dr. Adler and the
deposition of the girl Johanna Engel, formed the appendix to the appeal.
Cf. Ludwig Philippson's opinion on the proceeding. *A. Z. d. J.*, X, 181-183.
    [35] *Voice of Jacob*, V, 59. This incident, together with the reform congre-
gation's "appeal," gave rise to a heated controversy between the two English
Jewish newspapers, *The Voice of Jacob* and *The Jewish Chronicle*, the
former supporting the chief rabbi, the latter the reformers.
    [36] *Voice of Jacob*, V, 183. Bearing closely upon this subject is the fol-
lowing official notice: The West London Synagogue of British Jews, situated in Burton St., Burton Crescent, in the parish and district of St. Pancras
in the county of Middlesex, being a building certified, according to law, as
a place of religious worship, was on the 4th day of December, 1846, duly
registered for solemnizing marriages therein pursuant to the Act of 6th and
7th Wm., Cap. 85. Witness my hand and seal this 5th day of December,
1846. (Signed) Joseph Ivimey, Superintendent Registrar. *Voice of Jacob*,
VI,, 52.
    [37] The Statutes of the United Kingdom and Ireland; 19 and 20 Vict.
1856, 674.

[38] The confirmation of two boys and two girls took place on New Year's Day, 1842. *Voice of Jacob*, I, 62.

[39] That the agitation aroused by the formation of the reform congregation was not without effect upon the congregations generally is apparent from the fact that in 1847 a pamphlet was issued, entitled *Laws and Regulations for all the Synagogues in the British Empire*. Although no reforms as such were enjoined, yet a number of paragraphs gave evidence of the change that had come upon the religious worship in Jewry. Thus the eighteenth paragraph prescribed decorum during the services, the thirty-first prohibited the sale of *mitzwot* within the synagogue, and the thirty-eighth made provision for the preaching of the sermon "on ordinary occasions immediately before תפלת מוסף and on ראש השנה before תקיעת שופר." *Voice of Jacob*, VI, 66-67. How little headway reform really made in "official English Judaism" grows apparent from the controversy between the chief rabbi and the Rev. Morris Joseph in 1893 on the subject of the retention of the petitions in the traditional liturgy for the reinstitution of the sacrificial worship in the temple at Jerusalem. The refusal of Mr. Joseph to recite these prayers led to his withdrawal from the clergy under the jurisdiction of the chief rabbi and his acceptance of the position of minister of the reform congregation.

[40] For the account of the foundation of the Liberal Jewish Synagogue in London, of which the Liverpool liberal congregation is an offshoot, see *infra*, 433.

CHAPTER VI

[1] *Frankfurter Verein der Reformfreunde.*

[2] See the author's *Old European Jewries*, 46-81. Philadelphia, 1894; *History of Jews in Frankfort* by A. Freimann and F. Kracauer, 30ff. Philadelphia, 1929.

[3] Graetz, *History of the Jews* (Eng. tr.), V, 529. Philadelphia, 1895.

[4] *W. Z. J. T.*, II, 148. For a full account of these services, see the centenary publication *Festschrift zur Jahrhundertfeier der Realschule der israelitischen Gemeinde (Philanthropin) zu Frankfurt am Main, 1804-1904*, 50-54. Frankfurt am Main, 1904. In 1813 the name *Philanthropin* was changed to *Real- und Volksschule der israelitischen Gemeinde*.

[5] *Supra*, 25.

[6] Jost, *Geschichte der Israeliten*, X, i, 100.

[7] xxxii. *Thesen über den Talmud* (Frankfurt, 1831) and the earlier portions of his chief work *Shulhan Aruk oder encyclopädische Darstellung des mosaischen Gesetzes*, four vols. Frankfurt, 1833-1840.

[8] A. Rebenstein, in Freund's *Zur Judenfrage in Deutschland*, II, 89. Berlin, 1844.

[9] *Supra*, 52.

[10] Cf. Holdheim, *Ceremonialgesetz im Gottesreich*, 49-50. Schwerin, 1845.

[11] See Holdheim's remarkable statement in Freund's *Zur Judenfrage in Deutschland*, II, 165-166, which is quoted below; also *ibid.*, 335.

[12] In his later writings Creizenach abandoned this position, which involved, besides the attempt to justify the reform movement by Talmudical authority, the effort to fit the Talmudical legislation to the needs of the new age, as the Talmud by means of its peculiar hermeneutics had done with the Biblical injunctions. He now advocated a return to pure Mosaism, thus disregarding the Talmudical period of Jewish development altogether; this was a serious misreading of the import of the idea of tradition, as shall appear.

[13] *W. Z. J. T.*, II, 149.

[14] Even Solomon Abraham Trier, the ultra-orthodox rabbi of Frankfort, acknowledged the necessity of sermons in the vernacular in a *derashah*

preached in Sept., 1832; because of his own inability to deliver such sermons he requested that young men who were capable of doing so apply to him in order that this need might be met. This concession on the part of Trier was admitted to be due to the attractiveness of the services in the Andachtssaal of the Philanthropin. See letter of Abraham Geiger to J. Derenbourg of date, Sept. 28, 1832, published in *A. Z. d. J.*, LX (1896), 61.

[15] Jost, *Geschichte der Israeliten*, X, part i, 101.

[16] *Israelit. Annalen*, I, 102. See also a correspondence between Senator Frederick Ihm, the referee for Jewish affairs, and the Directory of the Congregation, *ibid.*, 132-4.

[17] *I. N. J.*, II (1841), 82.

[18] Pp. 161-71.

[19] Jost, *Gesh. der Israeliten*, X, part iii, 212, note 3.

[20] *Offene Briefe über den Reformverein; I. N. J.*, vol. V, 1844, 171-175, 179-183, 187-191, 197-201, 205-209, 285-288, 293-297, 301-304; VI 1845, 41-43, 49-53, 57-59.

[21] *Ibid.*, V, 182.

[22] *Supra*, 115.

[23] "Professional theologians were excluded intentionally from the deliberations of the society."—Jost, *Gesh. der Isr.*, X, part iii, 213.

[24] Geiger, *Nachgelassene Schriften*, V, 169.

[25] M. Hess of Saxe-Weimar, editor of the *Israelit des neunzehnten Jahrhunderts*, which newspaper became, in a measure, the organ of the society, although Hess denied this through the declaration that he was not a member of the society nor a chronicler of its doings. *Orient*, No. 20, 1845.

[26] M. Isler, *Gabriel Riesser's Leben, nebst Mittheilungen aus seinen Schriften*, I, 359. Frankfort, 1867.

[27] *Supra*, 53, 81.

[28] *A. Z. d. J.*, VII (1843), no. 35.

[29] *Programm zu einer Erklärung deutscher Israeliten, Freunden religiöser Reform im Judenthume zur Beherzigung vorgelegt*, 1843.

[30] These documents were published in full in Freund's *Zur Judenfrage in Deutschland*, 1843, 257-65 and as the supplement to No. 44 of Vol. IV (1843) of the *Israelit des neunzehnten Jahrhunderts*.

[31] Except in the circumcision controversy in which Holdheim supported the position assumed by members of the society, *infra*.

[32] Isler, *Gabriel Riesser's Leben, nebst Mittheilungen aus seinen Briefen*, I, 358-9.

[33] The society itself answered its critics in an official document dated Dec., 1843, and signed by Dr. Neukirch in the name of the members of the society. The statements in the document are quite the same as those made by Stern, and given at length in the course of this article. See Freund's *Zur Judenfrage in Deutschland* (1844), 116-22; see also *A. Z. d. J.*, vol. VIII (1844), no. 1, p. 5; *Orient*, vol. V (1844), no. 6, p. 43.

[34] *A. Z. d. J.*, VII (1843), no. 33.

[35] "Der Frankfurter Reformverein vom Standpunkte des fortschreitenden Rabbinismus," *Literaturblatt des Orients*, 1843, nos. 46-8.

[36] *Ibid.*, 1844, nos. 1 and 2.

[37] *Ibid.*, 1843, no. 51.

[38] *A. Z. d. J.*, VIII (1844), No. 7.

[39] *Zeitschrift für die religiösen Interessen des Judenthums*, I (1844), 49-60.

[40] *Ibid.*, 60-72. Frankel opens his article by saying that the society "cannot be considered Jewish, and belongs to Judaism as little as to any other religion," and closes by declaring that "the reform society is the most unfortunate attempt that has ever been made. It has condemned itself and has been condemned by public opinion"; see also *ibid.*, 302, where he says "they were honest in their method, but their method was not that of Judaism."

⁴¹ *I. N. J.*, IV (1843), 183, 187, 191, 195, 203.
⁴² The open letters to Einhorn, Hirsch, and Mannheimer in Nos. 6-8 of vol. VI of the *Israelit des neunzehnten Jahrhunderts* consist for the most part of mere personalities, and therefore I dismiss them with this reference; they were the third series of open letters; the first two series to Stein and Gutmann contain the gist of the defense.
⁴³ *I. N. J.*, V (1844), 174. See also M. Creizenach, *Des frommen Israeliten Lehre und Leben, ibid.*, II, 21.
⁴⁴ *I. N. J.*, V (1844), 175.
⁴⁵ *Ibid.*, V (1844), 179.
⁴⁶ *Ibid.*, 180.
⁴⁷ *Ibid.*, 181.
⁴⁸ *Ibid.*, 188.
⁴⁹ *Ibid.*, 190.
⁵⁰ *Ibid.*, 190.
⁵¹ *Ibid.*, 197.
⁵² "Die Judenfrage," in *Deutsche Jahrbücher* for Nov., 1842; published separately, Brunswick, 1843. This anti-Semitic essay was one of the literary and journalistic sensations of that day, and elicited many replies from Jews; the claim of the enemies of the Reform Society that this essay gave the impulse to its formation rested without doubt upon the passage of the essay in which Bauer comments upon the statement of the advocates of the emancipation of the Jews that they desire to return to pure Mosaism; he declares this to be senseless, since Mosaism means sacrifice, priestly caste, and peculiar property legislation; its logical consequence is the Talmud; both Old Testament and Talmud are chimerical and unreal; emancipation will be impossible until the Jews cease to be Jews and become men,—in other words, "when they become in reality men who will not permit themselves to be separated from their fellow men by any barrier mistakenly considered essential."
⁵³ *I. N. J.*, V (1844), 198.
⁵⁴ *Ibid.*, 199.
⁵⁵ *Ibid.*, 200.
⁵⁶ *Ibid.*, 201.
⁵⁷ *Ibid.*, 209.
⁵⁸ *Ibid.*, 287.
⁵⁹ June 12-19, 1844.
⁶⁰ *I. N. J.*, V (1844), 287.
⁶¹ *Ibid.*, 290.
⁶² *Ibid.*, 294.
⁶³ *Ibid.*, 296.
⁶⁴ *Ibid.*, 297.
⁶⁵ "Es muss sich zeigen, ob das Positive des Judenthums in Geschichten oder in seiner Geschichte, in der Art, wie es geworden, oder in dem, was es geworden, besteht." *Ibid.*, 304.
⁶⁶ See A. Rebenstein's remarkable article "Unsere Gegenwart" in Freund's *Zur Judenfrage in Deutschland*, II, 13ff., 22ff. This and the article by Dr. S. Holdheim having the same title (*ibid.*, 149-71), are two most striking statements of the condition of religious affairs among the Jews of Germany at this stirring time, and of the true meaning and purpose of reform.
⁶⁷ See the letter of Dr. Theodor Creizenach, one of the founders of the society, written on Sept. 2, 1843, to Dr. Wilhelm Freund, the editor of the magazine *Zur Judenfrage in Deutschland*, and published in Vol. II of the same, 175-8; also the editorial article on the purpose of the society, in *I. N. J.*, VI (1845), 161.
⁶⁸ See five leading articles entitled "Der reine Mosaismus" (Pure Mosaism), in *I. N. J.*, II (1841), 1, 5, 9, 13, 17.
⁶⁹ Holdheim particularly gave expression to this thought. I reproduce several of his significant statements on the subject: "The present requires

a principle that shall enunciate clearly that a law, even though divine, is potent only so long as the conditions and circumstances of life, to meet which it was enacted, continue; when these change, however, the law also must be abrogated, even though it have God for its author. For God himself has shown indubitably that with the change of the circumstances and conditions of life for which he once gave those laws, the laws themselves cease to be operative, that they *shall* be observed no longer, because they *can* be observed no longer. . . . The present age and its guiding principle, as thus formulated, recognize the working of God in history; it believes truly and firmly in the providential guidance of the fortunes of mankind; it looks upon the deeds recorded in the history of mankind as the deeds of God, whereby he speaks as clearly as he ever did; a particular revelation of God to a single person is dispensable when God speaks to all and reveals his will to all" (Freund's *Zur Judenfrage in Deutschland,* II, 165f.). "True reform can rest only on the recognition of the truth that God commanded certain laws for certain times and certain conditions of life, and that it would be acting against the divine will to fulfill the law by a forced and casuistical interpretation of its meaning after the conditions have changed so essentially as to preclude the carrying-out of the law in its correct and original significance." *Ibid.* Salomon put this same idea in a most striking way at the Conference of Rabbis held at Brunswick in 1844, when he said, "The age also is a Bible through whose mouth God speaks to Israel" ("auch die Zeit sei eine Bibel, durch deren Mund Gott zu Israel spricht"), *Protokolle der ersten Rabbinerversammlung,* 91, Braunschweig, 1844; cf. also Geiger, in a communication to the Directory of the Breslau congregation, Mar. 19, 1846, "What the spirit of history wherein God reveals himself also, removes and has buried, no human skill can reawaken and reanimate." *Nachgelassene Schriften,* V, 190.

[70] This man was not a member of the Reform Society, but his action was in sympathy with the expressed views of the members of the society; therefore the society was made the target for the shafts of the opposition. It was not long before a second similar case of neglect to have the rite performed occurred, and this time the offending father was a member of the society. *I. N. J.,* V (1844), 24.

[71] At this time an anonymous publication appeared entitled, *Circumcision historically and dogmatically considered,* by Ben Amithai (*Ueber die Beschneidung in historischer und dogmatischer Beziehung*); this publication was looked upon generally as a pronouncement of the Reform Society; the author put the question, "Is circumcision an absolute condition of Judaism, so that an uncircumcised child cannot be considered a Jew, or is it not?" 5. He answered the question in the negative, and suggested another method of initiation into Judaism, viz., a solemn declaration by the father in an assembly of ten Israelites, that he desired to have the child received into the covenant made by God with Abraham and Moses.

[72] *I. N. J.,* V (1844), 69, 74, 84.

[73] *Supra,* 24.

[74] For an excellent account of the numerous attempts to enlist the aid of the government against the reformers see Jost, *Geschichte der Israeliten,* X, part iii, 225-34.

[75] *Rabbinische Gutachten über die Beschneidung, gesammelt und herausgegeben von Salomon Abraham Trier.* Frankfurt am Main, 1844.

[76] *Ibid.,* IX.

[77] *Ibid.,* XIII.

[78] *Ibid.,* VI.

[79] This response was published in *I. N. J.,* V, 121-5, 129-32, with an editorial footnote that it had been suppressed by the committee that had the publication of the responses in charge; see explanatory statement of the committee, *ibid.,* 176-7.

[80] The response has been included in the edition of his collected writings, see *Gesammelte Schriften von Dr. Zunz*, II, 191-203. Berlin, 1876.

[81] *Rabbinische Gutachten über die Beschneidung*, 4.

[82] *Ibid.*, 13.

[83] *Ibid.*, 14.

[84] *Ibid.*, 77.

[85] *Ibid.*, 99, 100.

[86] *Ibid.*, 101.

[87] *Ibid.*, 102.

[88] *Ibid.*, 26.

[89] *Ibid.*, 137.

[90] *Ibid.*, 140. See also his article, "Die Epoche des Maccabäer-Kampfes und die heutige Zeit—Eine Parallele," *Zeitschrift für die religiösen Interessen des Judenthums*, I, 117, 1844.

[91] See his letters of Aug. 25, 1843, and June 11, 1844, to M. A. Stern, *Nachgelassene Schriften*, V, 167ff., 173ff.

[92] Zunz had written in his response: "God forbid that we should tamper with this precept, which was in past times, and is still at the present day, reverenced as sacred by the whole Jewish people. Who will dare abrogate with impunity this holy rite?"

[93] *Nachgelassene Schriften*, V, 182-3.

[94] *Ueber die Beschneidung in religiös-dogmatischer Beziehung*, Schwerin and Berlin, 1844; cf. also his statement *G. J. R. G. B.*, 48. Berlin, 1857.

[95] The consideration of this third point was undoubtedly inspired by the utterances of Zacharias Frankel, the exponent of "positive-historical Judaism," in his magazine *Zeitschrift für die religiösen Interessen des Judenthums*, I, 6off. Frankel argued that if the father neglected to have his child circumcised the duty devolved upon the religious authoritative body. It is only through circumcision that the born Israelite receives the real sanctification. True, by the very fact of birth he is included in the congregation, but he does not become a full member thereof till he is circumcised. Therefore the act is to be considered partly in the light of a sacrament. In Judaism even more than in Christianity the sacramental reception of the child devolves upon the spiritual representatives of the community as a duty. For in Christianity the child is entirely without the fold until baptized, while in Judaism it is partly within owing to its birth. The religious authoritative body is not to punish the father, but to protect the child, and should call in the aid of the civil power, which is justified in interfering in such cases as threaten to disrupt Judaism.

[96] It will not be out of place to refer in this connection to a most interesting case that occurred a few years later. In 1847, a Mr. Hirsch, of Teterow, Mecklenburg-Schwerin, neglected to have his newly born son circumcised; he expressed the desire, however, to rear the child in the Jewish faith, and insisted that it be entered in the registry of Jewish births and receive its name in the synagogue in accordance with the custom then existing in Mecklenburg. The teacher, Salinger, who officiated in the community, did not know how to proceed in this exceptional case; he applied to the Jewish directorate for guidance; this in its turn referred the case to Dr. David Einhorn, the chief rabbi of the province, for decision. Einhorn authorized the teacher to name the child in the synagogue, and showed that even from the Talmudical standpoint the uncircumcised Jew is not to be excluded from the Jewish community if he has not willfully declared his purpose to cut himself loose; this is not the case in the present instance, for the father has declared expressly his desire to rear the child as a Jew, and certainly the innocent child is not to be excluded from the community for no fault of its own. He closes his letter of instructions in the following lofty strain: "May God bless the child, and adorn it with the virtues of an Israelite indeed, an Israelite of circumcised heart, and may all those who think that

the integrity of our divine religion, which our forefathers sealed with their noble blood a thousand times as a covenant between God and Israel and all mankind, is threatened by such occurrences, and are therefore sorely troubled, derive consolation from the thought that the divine by its very nature is imperishable, and that Judaism rests on the indestructible pillars of right, truth, and peace, which will not totter even though the earth wax old like a garment and the heavens vanish like smoke." The child was named in the synagogue on Sabbath Channukah. See *A. Z. d. J.*, 1849, 583; Einhorn, *Sinai*, II, 736-7. Baltimore, 1857.

[97] In his *Lehrbuch der mosaischen Religion,* published in 1826, Alexander Behr made the startling statement that circumcision was not a condition necessary for reception into the covenant of Israel, and asserted that its omission was somewhat like the neglect to eat unleavened bread during Passover. He denied all sacramental significance to circumcision. The amazing fact in connection with these statements is that the book was approved by Rabbi Abraham Bing of Würzburg and the rabbinate of Fürth, both ultra-orthodox. The words in the original are these: "Keineswegs ist die Beschneidung eine Bedingung zur Aufnahme in den Bund der Israeliten, deren Unterlassung wird vielmehr ungefähr dem Essen gesäuerten Brodes während der Osterzeit gleichgestellt, welche letzte Sünde sich von den deutschen Juden vielleicht die Hälfte zu Schulden kommen lässt, ohne dass unseres Wissens ein Rabbine es sich hätte beikommen lassen, sich darum zu kümmern. Hierin findet die unter christlichen Glaubensgenossen ziemlich verbreitete und von dem rabbinischen Juden weiter besseres Wissen ausgebreitete irrige Ansicht, als habe die Beschneidung bei den Juden, wie die Taufe bei den Christen, eine sacramentale Bedeutung, ihre Berechtigung und Würdigung. Dieser nicht einmal mosaische, sondern abrahamitische, ursprünglich ägyptische Gebrauch ist kein religiöser, sondern vielmehr ein blos nationaler, der wie die Opfer, die Vielweiberei und anders nach der Vertreibung der Juden aus Palästina und deren Ausbreitung im Occident hätte aufhören sollen, für diejenigen Juden, aber, welche nicht das gelobte Land, sondern das Land, in welchem sie geboren und erzogen, als ihr Vaterland betrachten, alle Haltbarkeit verloren und sich nur noch wie ein Krankheitstoff von Geschlecht zu Geschlecht fortgeerbt hat."

[98] In a letter to Wechsler in 1849 Geiger declares that some new form of initiation into Judaism must soon be found which should take the place of circumcision; his words are as follows: "Es muss nun ba'd eine Form gefunden werden, welche diese alte ersetzt; die Aussegnung der Wöchnerin dürfte nicht ganz genügen, die Anwesenheit des Kindes scheint gleichfall erforderlich, und der Anfang dazu könnte mit den Mädchen gemacht werden; dann würde allmählich, wie die Confirmation die Bar-Mizwah-Allfanzerei, so auch die neue Form die Beschneidung verdrängen." *Nachgelassene Schrift,* V, 202-3.

[99] Praised be Thou, O Lord our God, King of the Universe, who hast not made me a Gentile.

[100] Praised be Thou, O Lord our God, King of the Universe, who hast made me an Israelite.

[101] Praised be Thou, O Lord our God, King of the Universe, who hast not made me a woman.

[102] *Supra,* 101.

[103] *Supra,* 93.

[104] *Supra,* 35.

[105] Psalm, xcv., one of the introductory sections of the Sabbath eve service.

[106] *A. Z. d. J.,* IX, 709.

[107] See the next chapter.

[108] *Die Genossenschaft für Reform im Judenthume,* organized May 8, 1845. See Chapter VIII.

[109] *I. N. J.*, VI, 209-10.

[110] In addition to the articles and pamphlets referred to in the course of this chapter, the following may be mentioned as having been inspired by the Reform Society:—*Das moderne Judenthum, die Frankfurter Reformfreunde und die Neue Zeit*, von Albert Fränkel, Reutlingen, 1844. *Die Rabbinerversammlung und der Reformverein; letzte Auflösung der Judenfrage*, von Dr. W. B. Fränkel (an anti-Semitic screed by an apostate), Elberfeld, 1844. *An die israelitischen Reformfreunde in Frankfurt a. M.*, an anonymous poem by a Christian lady, *I. N. J.*, IV, 214. *Ueber den jüdischen Reformverein in Frankfurt*, von Prof. Dr. Nesselmann, *ibid.*, V, 32. *Zur Kritik der Beschneidungsfrage im Reformverein* von Dr. J. Bergson, *Literaturblatt des Israelit des neunzehnten Jahrhunderts*, 1847, nos. 44, 45, 46, 47.

CHAPTER VII

[1] "Die Rabbinerversammlung: Sendschreiben an einen befreundeten jüdischen Geistlichen," *W. Z. J. T.*, III, 313-32. See also his letter to Elias Grünebaum in *Nachgelassene Schriften*, V, 97.

[2] *W. Z. J. T.*, III, 321.

[3] *Ibid.*, 327.

[4] *Ibid.*, 331.

[5] *Jewish Encyclopedia*, art. "Rabbinical Conferences." The Bavarian District Assemblies held in 1835 were not rabbinical conferences in the strict sense, as laymen also participated in them. *Supra*, 37.

[6] For an account of this conference see a letter written by Geiger to Jacob Auerbach, *Nachgelassene Schriften*, V, 99; also his letters to J. Derenbourg of the dates Apr. 10, and Aug. 23, 1837, published in *A. Z. d. J.*, LX (1896), 188, 213.

[7] A letter written from Frankfort sets forth the hopes which this gathering had aroused in the hearts of the friends of progressive Judaism: see *W. Z. J. T.*, III, 476; see also Jost, *Geschichte des Judenthums und seiner Sekten*, III, 352.

[8] Holdheim, *Die erste Rabbinerversammlung und Herr Dr. Frankel*, 16, Schwerin, 1845. M. Simion, quoted in Holdheim, *Geschichte der Entstehung und Entwickelung der jüdischen Reformgemeinde in Berlin*, 38. Berlin, 1857.

[9] See the addresses of various communities to the Frankfort Conference, *Protokolle*, 243, 249-53, 260-6, 269.

[10] *A. Z. d. J.*, VIII (1844), 27. In a leading article that appeared several weeks later entitled "Annual Rabbinical Conferences" (*ibid.*, 117), Philippson states that the idea to issue a call for a conference was suggested to him in a letter that he had received from Dr. Max Lilienthal from Riga, Russia, on Nov. 26, 1843, wherein the writer requested him to call such a meeting; he had received also a communication from Rabbi Benedict Levi of Giessen, written on Jan. 2, 1844, containing an article advocating the organization of a rabbinical conference, and urging that he (Philippson) should take the initiative in the matter. *Ibid.*, 118. See Levi's own statement *Ein Stückchen Autobiographie, ibid.*, LXIII (1899), 175. An excellent survey of the conferences was given by Philippson in a series of sketches written on the fortieth anniversary of the Brunswick Conference; see *Geschichte der deutschen Rabbinerversammlungen und Synoden, ibid.*, XLVIII (1884), 229-31, 245-7, 261-4, 277-80, 293-5.

[11] *A. Z. d. J.*, VIII (1844), 337-9. *Nachgelassene Schriften*, I, 197-202.

[12] *Protokolle der ersten Rabbinerversammlung abgehalten in Braunschweig*, XIII. Braunschweig, 1844.

[13] *Ibid.*, XVI, 18.

[14] See also his *G. J. R. G. B.*, 113.

[15] *Protokolle,* 55; cf. also his statement, "Der Talmud spricht aus seinem Zeitbewusstsein und für dasselbe hatte er Recht; ich spreche aus einem höheren Bewusstsein meiner Zeit und für dasselbe habe ich Recht."— *Ceremonialgesetz im Gottesreich,* 50. Schwerin, 1845.

[16] *Protokolle,* 66.

[17] *Ibid.,* 16.

[18] *Ibid.,* 44.

[19] *Ibid.;* cf. also Holdheim, *G. J. R. G. B.,* 97.

[20] *Protokolle,* 91.

[21] *Supra,* 118.

[22] *Protokolle,* 48.

[23] *Ibid.,* 53.

[24] *Ibid.,* 54.

[25] *Ibid.,* 56.

[26] Author of the work *Die Religion des Geistes.*

[27] *Protokolle,* 66.

[28] Ever since Moses Mendelssohn in his *Jerusalem* claimed that Judaism has no dogmas this has been the subject of discussion. Geiger held that there are dogmas in Judaism, but no creed as a condition of salvation, *I. N. J.,* VII (1846), 222; twenty years later he wrote: "Est ist in Wahrheit zum Heile für das Judenthum, dass es in ihm nicht zur dogmatischen Fixirung irgend eines, und sei es auch des unzweifelhaftesten und des unzweifelsten Gedanken gekommen ist, zum wahren Heile des Judenthums, dass der einzelne Jude oder der jüdische Theologe nicht "seinen Glaubensbestand" an dem Glaubensbestande der Gesammtheit zu messen hat und danach seine Angehörigkeit zu beurtheilen ist, sondern dass lediglich der Massstab ist, inwiefern er sich selbst mit der Judenheit noch verbunden erachtet, und bei der Abweichung in wesentlichen Fragen von der herkömmlichen und noch geltenden Auffassung sich im innigen Zusammenhange mit dem in der Judenheit herrschenden Geiste weiss." *J. Z. W. L.,* VII, 9; see also *ibid.,* I, 279. Holdheim taught likewise that Judaism has dogmas but does not make their acceptance a *conditio sine qua non* of salvation as does Christianity; *G. J. R. G. B.,* 225ff. See the interesting debate on this subject by the members of the directorate of this congregation, *ibid.,* 229ff.; also Holdheim, *Haben die Juden Glaubensartikel oder nicht? A. Z. d. J.,* II (1838), nos. 4-9; and *Religionsprinzipien des reformierten Judenthums,* Berlin, 1847, "Die heilige Schrift hat sich nie in einem Bekenntnisse fixirt." Hess in a leading article in his *Israelit des neunzehnten Jahrhunderts* claimed that a creed is not objectionable if it be understood that the statement of creed is merely a consensus of opinion, and that it is left to each one to hold that conception of Judaism which appeals to his thought and conscience; in other words, a creed must not be made the measure of salvation, but is to be considered merely as a definition or declaration of principles, VI (1845), 330-1. S. Stern, the virtual founder of the Berlin Reform Congregation, contended that the "definite formulation of principles contradicts altogether the thought of development whereon reform builds"; quoted in Holdheim, *G. J. R. G. B.,* 229; see also his article *Die Aufgabe der jüdischen Gemeinde zu Berlin für die Gegenwart* (1844), in Freund's *Zur Judenfrage in Deutschland,* II, 359. For further discussion of this question see L. Löw, "Jüdische Dogmen," *Gesammelte Schriften,* I, 133-76, Szegedin, 1889; S. Schechter, "The Dogmas of Judaism," *J. Q. R.,* I, 48-61, 115-27; B. Felsenthal, "Gibt es Dogmen im Judenthume?" *Year Book C. C. A. R.,* VIII, 54ff.; M. L. Margolis, "The Theological Aspect of Reformed Judaism," *ibid.,* XIII, 192ff.; K. Kohler, *ibid.,* XV, 83ff.; F. Perles, *Bousset's Religion des Judenthums im neutestamentlichen Zeitalteter kritisch untersucht,* 112-116, Berlin, 1903; O. J. Simon, "Authority and Dogma in Judaism," *J. Q. R.,* V, 231-43; H. Hyamson, *ibid.,* 469-82; M. Güdemann, *Das Judenthum in seinem Grundzügen und nach seiner geschichtlichen Grundlagen dargestellt,* 67. Wien, 1892. *Ibid.,*

"Jüdische Apologetik," 184. Glogau, 1906; Leo Baeck, *M. G. W. J.* for 1926, p. 225; I. Scheftelowitz, *ibid.*, 433ff.

[29] See the author's "Tendencies of Thought in Modern Judaism," *New World*, IV, 610. Boston, 1895.

[30] *Infra*, Chap. XII.

[31] *I. N. J.*, VI (1845), 194-7.

[32] Appendix I to *Protokolle*, 94-8.

[33] *Ibid.*, 20.

[34] *Protokolle*, 73.

[35] *Ibid.*, 78, 79.

[36] *Ibid.*, 29.

[37] *Autonomie der Rabbinen*, 53, Schwerin, 1843; *Das Religiöse und Politische im Judenthume*, passim, Schwerin, 1845; cf. also Ritter, *Die jüdische Reformgemeinde zu Berlin*, 50, Berlin, 1902; Levin, *Die Reform des Judenthums*, 46-50, Berlin, 1895; the author's "Samuel Holdheim, Jewish Reformer," *Year Book C. C. A. R.*, XVI, 316-18.

[38] *Protokolle*, 27.

[39] *Supra*, 13, 14, 24, 31.

[40] *Protokolle*, 33-42.

[41] The praying shawl.

[42] The phylacteries.

[43] *A. Z. d. J.*, III (1839), 293; IV (1840), 123, 133, 158, 166, 174, 189, 307; *Israelitische Annalen*, II (1840), 243; *Zeitschrift für die religiösen Interessen des Judenthums*, I (1844), 301; *I. N. J.*, V (1844), 277, 327 (Holdheim); *ibid.*, 375 (Einhorn); *ibid.*, VI, 917 (Holdheim's answer to Einhorn); *A. Z. d. J.*, IX (1845), 194ff., 274ff., 289ff. (Einhorn's answer to Holdheim); *Die Reform des Judenthums* (a magazine which was edited by A. Adler and H. Wagner in the interest of the rabbinical conferences, and appeared only one year, 1846), 9, 17. See also Frankel's book, *Die Eidesleistung der Juden in theologischer und historischer Beziehung*, Dresden, 1847; Leopold Stein, *Der Eid more Judaico, wie solcher bei den Gerichten der freien Stadt Frankfurt noch in Uebung ist*, Frankfurt a. M., 1847; *ibid.*, *I. N. J.*, 73-6; D. Rothschild, *Der Eid der Juden*, Brilon, 1847; cf. also *A. Z. d. J.*, X (1846), 188-91, 206-7, 220-2, 248-9, 261-3, 616, 667; XIV, 137. For a historical sketch see *Zur Geschichte des Judeneides*, in L. Geiger's *Juden in Berlin*, 265-80, Berlin, 1871. The oath *more Judaico*, though abolished in lands where the Jew has received the rights of man, was still administered in Roumania as late as 1904; *Jewish Chronicle*, Aug. 19, 1904.

[44] *Israelitische Annalen*, II (1840), 57; *Die Reform des Judenthums*, 9.

[45] *Protokolle*, 41.

[46] This prayer, which is spoken at the opening of the service on the Eve of Atonement in congregations which use the traditional liturgy, is one of the favorite objects of attack of anti-Jewish writers; they declare that thereby the Jew absolves himself from all vows and promises that he might make during the coming year; however, Jewish authorities have always interpreted this to refer to such vows as the individual assumes voluntarily, and in which no other persons or interests are involved; in other words, "the formula has reference only to such vows in which the relation of the individual to his conscience or his Heavenly Father is involved." Still, because of the misinterpretation to which it was liable, it was important to eliminate it from the liturgy. As early as the fifteenth century Isaac ben Sheshet wrote to another rabbi to make the attempt to abolish the *Kol Nidre*, saying, that if he were to do this he would gain the praise of all wise men (*Resp.*, 394); quoted by Geiger in Freund's *Zur Judenfrage in Deutschland*, 3-4. See also Geiger, *Nachgelassene Schriften*, I, 134-6; *Revue des Etudes Juives*, XXXIX, 78; *Jewish Encyclopedia*, art. "Kol Nidre." Many congregations throughout Germany acted upon the recommendation of the Brunswick Conference and eliminated the *Kol Nidre* prayer from the service on

the following Day of Atonement. Leopold Stein, the poet among the reform rabbis, wrote a German hymn which was set to the traditional music of the *Kol Nidre*. In the interesting reminiscences of the nonagenarian, Rev. Prof. D. W. Marks, of London, he states that Stein told him that when he wished to abolish the *Kol Nidre*, his congregation was reluctant to dispense with the melody; he had therefore to promise that he would compose a poem which could be set to the same music. *Jewish Chronicle*, Jan. 11, 1907, 18.

[47] *Supra*, 131ff.
[48] *Protokolle*, 87-8.
[49] *Ibid.*, 89.
[50] *Ibid.*, 90.
[51] *Ibid.*, 91.
[52] David Cassel, *Woher und Wohin?* 12. Berlin, 1845.
[53] S. Stern, *Die gegenwärtige Bewegung im Judenthume*, 42. Berlin, 1845. A poem dedicated to the conference by a Christian admirer was republished many years later. *A. Z. d. J.*, LII (1888), 79.
[54] *A. Z. d. J.*, VIII (1844), 385.
[55] *Ibid.*, 387.
[56] "Die Rabbinerversammlung zu Braunschweig," *Zeitschrift für die religiösen Interessen des Judenthums*, I (1844), 289-308.
[57] "Die erste Rabbinerversammlung und Herr Dr. Frankel." Schwerin, 1845.
[58] "Die erste Rabbinerversammlung und ihre Gegner." Stuttgart, 1845.
[59] "Erwiderung auf Herrn Dr. Frankel's Angriff gegen die Rabbinerversammlung," *Orient*, V (1844), 378-82.
[60] Holdheim refers evidently to Frankel's article, "Ueber Reformen im Judenthume," *Zeitschrift für die religiösen Interessen des Judenthums*. I (1844), 1-27.
[61] Frankel answered Maier in an article entitled "Schreiben an den Herrn Kirchenrath Dr. Maier in Stuttgart," *Zeitschrift für die religiösen Interessen des Judenthums*, II (1845), 161-82.
[62] *Die Rabbinerversammlung und ihre Tendenz. Eine Beleuchtung für Freunde und Feinde*. Hamburg, 1845.
[63] What this true faith from the orthodox standpoint is conceived to be was stated most clearly in a remarkable manifesto issued shortly after this, viz. on Mar. 31, 1846, by S. Godscheaux, grand rabbi of Colmar, and L. M. Lambert, grand rabbi of Metz; this document was as follows: "it has become necessary that every Israelite be informed fully concerning the tactics of those who under the high-sounding names of reformers, and progressivists, preach atheism and irreligion, and who under the hypocritical pretence of making our religion more imposing and beautiful, really desire to sacrifice it to the advantages and indulgences of material life. Therefore we address ourselves anew to you, cherished brethren of Israel, and give you herewith a brief résumé of the fundamental principles of the Jewish religion as they are designated in the Talmud, and as our fathers have observed them:—

(*a*) The divine law is immutable and eternal like its Author; neither time nor conditions can change, much less abrogate it.

(*b*) The oral law is as truly the word of God as the written law.

(*c*) All institutions and regulations which were introduced into Judaism with the purpose of protecting the law are as unchangeable as the law itself.

(*d*) No assembly and be it of all the rabbis, yea be it of all Israel in conjunction with all the rabbis, has either the authority or the right to abrogate or to change the least portion of the law, whether oral or written, or the introduced institutions or regulations.

These are the principles of the true Israelitish belief in which our fathers lived, and for which they died; every reformatory attempt to change these constitutes rebellion against the religion binding upon all the children of Jacob, and leads to the way of destruction." *A. Z. d. J.*, X (1846), 290-1.

So also the constitution of the famous orthodox congregation of Frank-fort-on-the-Main, presided over for many years by Samson Raphael Hirsch, the greatest of the orthodox leaders of Germany in the nineteenth century, defines its standpoint as follows: "The old Jewish religious legislation which forms the fundamental statute of every Jewish community has given the Israelitish congregation also the fundamental rules for its religious guidance, and nothing could nor can obtain validity in it which is not in accord with this religious legislation as it has been handed down to us in Thora, Talmud, and the rabbinical codes of the *Shulchan Aruk.*"

[64] Other protests against the Brunswick Conference were issued by the rabbinate of Krakau, see *I. N. J.,* VI, 86; by Rabbi Nathan Marcus Adler of Hanover (later of London), and Hirsch Lehren of Amsterdam, *ibid.,* 30, and by D. Deutsch, rabbi in Sohrau, Upper Silesia אסיפה אסוף (Gathering of an Assembly) "oder Protestation gegen die Rabbinerversammlung," Bres-lau, 1846. This was a protest against both the Brunswick and Frankfort conferences. See also "Kritische Bemerkungen zu den Protokollen der ersten Rabbinerversammlung," *Literaturblatt des Orient,* 1845, nos. 48, 64, 80.

[65] *I. N. J.,* VI (1845), 128.

[66] *Ibid.,* 215.

[67] *Ibid.,* 222.

[68] *Ibid.,* 159.

[69] From an address signed by sixty Jews of Worms, *I. N. J.,* VI, 159. Mention must be made also of the pamphlet issued by Dr. A. Adler, entitled *Die sieben und siebzig sogenannten Rabbiner und die Rabbinerver-sammlung,* Mannheim, 1845; this in its turn called forth a defense of the signers of the protest from K . . . m (supposedly R. Kirchheim) in the form of an open letter, entitled "Offener Brief an A. Adler, Mitglied der Braunschweiger Rabbinerversammlung als Antwort auf sein Sendschreiben an die 77 sogenannten Rabbiner u. s. w." Bockenheim, 1845.

[70] Holdheim, *G. J. R. G. B.,* 25.

[71] *Die Versammlung der Rabbiner Deutschlands.* This was the official name adopted at Brunswick; see *Protokolle,* 87. This name was changed at Frankfort to *Die Versammlung deutscher Rabbiner* (Conference of German Rabbis).

[72] Geiger wrote a series of articles which appeared just before the con-vening of the conference in which he set forth what he thought the confer-ence should stand for and aim to accomplish; see "Einige Ansichten über die nächste Rabbinerversammlung," *A. Z. d. J.,* IX, 322ff., 340ff., 386ff., 398ff. The closing words of these articles express clearly the object of the conferences: "the only purpose that should be kept in mind is to strengthen the religious spirit of the present generation; all out-grown forms that have ceased to further the religious sentiment must either be abrogated or changed in accordance with the new life that the Jewish people are living now."

[73] For a fine statement of why the reform movement could be led suc-cessfully by men of this type only, cf. Holdheim, *G. J. R. G. B.,* 40. Berlin, 1857.

[74] *Protokolle und Aktenstücke der zweiten Rabbinerversammlung abge-halten in Frankfurt am Main, vom 15ten bis zum 28ten Juli, 1845,* 18. Frank-furt am Main, 1845.

[75] It is interesting to note that the first prayer-book that was constructed on the lines suggested in this report was Dr. David Einhorn's; the Hebrew portions in that prayer-book are the very ones suggested here. In that other prayer-book prepared by adherents of the reform movement, which is also the first to be issued by a body of rabbis and not by an individual, viz. The Union Prayer-Book, published by the Central Conference of American Rabbis, the same Hebrew scheme is followed.

[76] *Supra,* 156.

[77] After his break with the Rabbinical Conference Frankel attempted

to form a Conference of Theologians (*Theologenversammlung*) in accordance with these remarks; this conference of theologians was called for the fall of 1846 (Oct. 21), but the meeting never took place.

[78] For Geiger's views on this subject see also "Der Hamburger Tempelstreit" in *Nachgelassene Schriften*, I, 151, 153, 156; "Nothwendigkeit und Maass einer Reform des jüdischen Gottesdienstes" in *ibid.*, 212-14; also *A. Z. d. J.*, IX, 386, and *J. Z. W. L.*, VI, 5-8.

[79] Salomon had expressed himself similarly in his pamphlet, *Das neue Gebetbuch und seine Verketzerung*, 20ff. Hamburg, 1842.

[80] Maimonides, *Hil. Berakot*, I, 5; cf. Talmud *Jer. Berakot*, V, 9; VI, 10, etc.

[81] Holdheim expressed himself similarly in his response in the Geiger-Tiktin controversy; see *Rabbinische Gutachten über die Verträglichkeit der freien Forschung mit dem Rabbineramte*, 78-9; also *G. J. R. G. B.*, 16, 196-7.

[82] In these days of Zionistic agitation this contention of Geiger is of especial interest; a similar view in regard to the Hebrew was given expression to by Dr. Coblentz, rabbi in Bielefeld, in an article entitled "Zur Bekämpfung des unbewusst Nationalen im Gefühlsleben der deutschen Juden," *Populär-wissenschaftliche Monatsblätter zur Belehrung über das Judenthum für Gebildete aller Konfessionen*, XXV, 57-63, Frankfurt am Main, 1905; see also *Die Juden der Gegenwart*, 137, 267. Berlin, 1904.

[83] Philippson elaborated his views on the subject in a series of leading articles in his *A. Z. d. J.*, VIII, nos. 33, 43, 45, 52.

[84] Abraham Adler, the rabbi of Worms, was one of the keenest thinkers among the early reformers. He was a brother of Samuel Adler, rabbi of Alzey, later rabbi of Temple Emanuel, New York. With H. Wagner of Mannheim, Abraham Adler undertook, in 1846, the editing of a periodical in the interest of the rabbinical conferences entitled *Die Reform des Judenthums*. But one volume of this periodical appeared.

[85] The first public debate on this subject of reading from the Torah is very interesting in the light of what has taken place since. The question of reading from the Torah has been debated time and time again, and the religious leaders are still divided in opinion, as was the case at Frankfort; this became apparent once again in the year 1904, when the question was debated at the meeting of the Central Conference of American Rabbis at Louisville, Ky.; some desired a selection of passages for public reading, others advocated that everything in the Torah be read, some entered the lists for the triennial, others for the annual cycle. It is to be noted that the reading from the scroll is universal except in several radical reform congregations in the United States, one of which has removed the ark and scroll altogether.

[86] This point was constantly emphasized by Gabriel Riesser, the foremost champion of Jewish civil and political emancipation; he would not have religious reform required as a condition of citizenship. Cf. "David Honigmann's Aufzeichnungen aus seinen Studienjahren (1841-5)," *Jahrbuch für jüdische Geschichte und Literatur*, 1904, 141. In this the great religious reformers agreed with him, but they contended none the less that reform and nationalism were mutually exclusive terms; cf. Holdheim's statement, "only by the absolute separation of the political and religious elements in Judaism is a thoroughgoing reform possible." *Autonomie der Rabbinen*, Preface, VII.

[87] Einhorn embodied these views in his prayer-book עלת התמיד. For a clear exposition of the principles by which he was guided in this work see his statement "Die neue Gebetsordnung der Hai Sinai-Gemeinde zu Baltimore," *Sinai*, I, 97-100, 127-39. Baltimore, 1856.

[88] For an elaboration of Holdheim's views on this subject see his *Das Religiöse und Politische im Judenthum*, Schwerin, 1845; *Die Autonomie der Rabbinen*, 10, 20, Schwerin, 1843; he gave detailed expression to his ideas on the reform of the liturgy in a series of articles entitled "Ueber die

Prinzipien eines dem gegenwärtigen Religionsbewusstsein entsprechenden Cultus" which appeared in the *Literaturblatt des Israelit des neunzehnten Jahrhunderts*, 1846, 33, 42, 49, 53, 57, 61, 105, 109, 113, 117, 121, 125, 129, 133.

[89] Cf. his *Die Messiaslehre im Judenthum.* Leipzig, 1843.

[90] Stein changed his position on this subject radically during ensuing years. In his book *Die Schrift des Lebens*, published in 1872, he repudiated the belief in a personal Messiah. The people Israel is the Messiah, 319-36, notably 320 and 336.

[91] For his change of view on this subject also see *ibid.*, 318.

[92] The twenty-third day of Tishri; this holiday, which was celebrated on the day following the eight days of the Feast of Tabernacles, assumed a distinctive place in Jewish life. It was easily the most joyous of the festivals of the synagogue.

[93] The closing section of the Fifth Book of Moses.

[94] The opening section of the First Book of Moses.

[95] It is rather remarkable that this question should have occasioned no debate at the first public gathering in which it was broached. There has been no modern synagogal reform which has called forth more heated controversy than this of introducing the organ into the house of worship. Time and again it has been a bone of contention in congregations, and still to-day ranges Jews on opposite sides. The very first official expression we have on the question is the report of the committee submitted to this conference (*Protokolle*, 326-34) although there were individual expressions on this subject in the collection of opinions called forth by the reforms in the Hamburg temple in 1818, one of which was the introduction of the organ. The committee's report at the Frankfort Conference marshaled reasons in favor of the playing of the instrument. Sixty years later (1905) the question was still a living issue in Germany; the Cologne congregation was almost disrupted because of the resolution to introduce the organ. Four of the six members of the Berlin rabbinate in 1904 issued an opinion that the innovation was not against the principles of Judaism. (*Das Gutachten des Berliner Rabbinats über die Orgel, A. Z. d. J.*, LXVIII, 1904, 65; see also *ibid.*, 121, 349.) The celebrated Jewish scholar, A. Berliner, in that same year took a stand against the introduction of the organ; see his pamphlet *Zur Lehr und zur Wehr;* also the lengthy criticism of this pamphlet by Gustav Karpeles in defense of the organ, *A. Z. d. J.*, LXVIII (1904), 349-50; cf. also Geiger, *J. Z. W. L.*, I, 89-98; Philippson, *A. Z. d. J.*, XXV (1861), No. 48; Wiener, Wechsler, Adler, Kahn, Löw, Aub (all favorable), Landau (opposed), *ibid.* In Germany many conservative congregations have organs in their synagogues; in France it is universal; see program of central consistory of May, 1846, which ordered organs to be placed in the synagogues, *A. Z. d. J.*, X, 346. In England only the three so-called reform synagogues and the Liberal Jewish Synagogue have the organs, though at marriages the organ is used in orthodox synagogues. In the United States it is general, excepting in ultra-orthodox houses of worship.

[96] *Supra*, 154.

[97] Proceedings of the Berlin Reform Congregation of June 18, 1845, quoted by Holdheim, *G. J. R. G. B.*, 133.

[98] *Supra*, 156.

[99] This was republished in *A. Z. d. J.*, IX (1845), 174-76, and in the *I. N. J.*, VI (1845), 256; also in the proceedings of the Conference, *Protokolle und Aktenstücke d. zweiten R. V.*, 86.

[100] Published originally in *Frankfurter Journal;* also in *Protokolle*, 90.

[101] Republished *I. N. J.* (1845), 320.

[102] *Protokolle*, 235.

[103] *A. Z. d. J.*, IX (1845), 595.

[104] *Ibid.*, 624. *I. N. J.*, 331, 339. See, however, Philippson's explanation

of the incident, *A. Z. d. J.*, IX, 519. See also A. Adler "Beleuchtung der Gegenerklärung das Herrn Oberrabbiners, Dr. Z. Frankel, in No. 203 der Frankfurter Oberpostamtzeitung," *I. N. J.*, VI (1845), 313, 321.

[105] The bitterest denunciations and criticisms of the Frankfort Conference appeared in the columns of the *Orient;* as an example it suffices to refer to the קינה or Dirge in Hebrew by an anonymous poet wherein the rabbis assembled at Frankfort are called "destroyers and ruiners." As a further instance of the intensity of feeling aroused in the opposition by these conferences, the words of the editor of the English publication *The Voice of Jacob*, IV, 219, written after the adjournment of the Frankfort Conference, may be cited: "Had but a small section of the 116 rabbis who subscribed the Manifesto or protest (against the Brunswick Conference) condescended to assemble, out-reason and out-vote the 23 rabbis whose dicta they had at last occasion so solemnly to repudiate, there might have been less of heresy at this day raging among the people. That Manifesto has no doubt served as a standard round which to rally the faithful, together with those predisposed to condemn the heterodox party; but it may reasonably be doubted whether its dry denunciations have convinced one man of his errors or recovered one stray sheep to the fold. The right is with us; the truth is ours; and we thank God at last to see a growing disposition on the part of our proper leaders to rouse themselves from their lethargy, to buckle on their armor, and to do battle in a holy cause in which victory is assured."

[106] Geiger, "Vorträge über die Verhandlungen der Rabbinerversammlung," *I. N. J.*, VI, 345-7.

[107] The effect of this conference in awakening interest in Judaism among the indifferent was felt throughout Germany, *A. Z. d. J.*, X, 25.

[108] See Geiger *Vorläufiger Bericht über die Thätigkeit der dritten Versammlung deutscher Rabbiner.* Breslau, 1846.

[109] Geiger, *Die dritte Versammlung deutscher Rabbiner, ein Vorläufiges Wort zur Verständigung*, Breslau, 1846, 7.

"This question must be decided if Judaism is to exist on as a lasting influence and it will be decided if it is kept constantly on the tapis; it must be decided some one way or another by a ripe resolution of the community. One of the most essential institutions of Judaism is the day of consecration and rest, and with this Judaism itself must be rescued from the unspeakable confusion and haziness in whose maw the whole religious life is in danger of being swallowed; rescue from this confusion will ensue only when it is exposed vividly in its imperfection and emptiness."

[110] *Protokolle der ersten Rabbinerversammlung*, 37. *Supra*, 154.

[111] *Protokolle der zweiten Rabbinerversammlung*, 348-57.

[112] As will be seen later on, this constituted possibly the sharpest point of distinction in the views of the members of the conference, viz. whether the essential idea of the Sabbath is rest (*Ruhe*) or consecration (*Weihe*).

[113] No one was permitted to go further than two thousand cubits in one direction from his dwelling on the Sabbath; by the casuistical provision called *Erube T'chumin*, "combination of Sabbath-day journeys," this distance was extended two thousand cubits. By this provision some article could be placed on Friday at the Sabbath boundary, which was thus constituted a new dwelling point whence to measure a further two thousand cubits.

[114] According to the rabbinical law, nothing was permitted to be carried from one house to another on the Sabbath day; this prohibition, too, was evaded by a casuistical provision entitled *Erube Chatzerot*, "combination among inhabitants of courts." According to this the householders in a court or district were enabled to consider their habitations as a single dwelling, and thus carry things from house to house without breaking the Sabbath law. Both these provisions are instances of the accommodation of the rabbinical enactments to the needs of life, and are evidence of the extreme

lengths to which casuistry went for the ostensible preservation of the integrity of the rabbinical provisions.

[115] Eighty-four years have elapsed since the question of the collision between Sabbath observance and modern life was discussed for the first time in a public Jewish forum. The passing of time has more aggravated the problem. Sabbath desecration has become more and more flagrant among Jews, until now it is well-nigh universal wherever the medieval and ghetto conditions have disappeared. In the prayers offered in the synagogue God is thanked for the Sabbath, the day of rest, while in the marts of trade at that very hour the Jew is busy as on other days of the week, bartering and bargaining. The problem first discussed at Breslau is as far from being solved as ever, as appeared from occasional mention of the subject as recently as the year 1928 at the meeting of the World Union for Progressive Judaism at Berlin, unless the suggestion already made at that conference by Holdheim, that the Sabbath be transferred to the civil day of rest, be considered a satisfactory solution. An interesting parallel is afforded by comparing the first public debate on the Sabbath question at this Breslau Conference and public discussion of this same question many years later at the meeting of the Central Conference of American Rabbis at New Orleans in 1902, at Detroit in 1903, and at Cleveland in 1905. The same difficulties are presented; the same conflicting opinions are noted; here as there the majority cry, The Sabbath must be saved, but no efficient means for that salvation are offered; here as there a small minority declare that a transfer to Sunday will alone save the Sabbath institution for the Jew. Now as then it is evident that the weight of Jewish opinion inclines to the conviction that for the Jew there can be no Sabbath except the Saturday Sabbath, but again now as then it is just as evident that the collision between the actual conditions of life and Sabbath observance presents the greatest difficulty in Jewish practice and that after the lapse of all these years it is as far as ever, if not farther, from being settled.

[116] *Protokolle der dritten Versammlung deutscher Rabbiner*, 160; see also *Die dritte Rabbinerversammlung, ein Vorläufiges Wort zur Verständigung*, 4, "I am frank to confess that the results achieved by the Conference towards a solution of the Sabbath problem are small in comparison with the great collisions between Sabbath observance and life."

[117] *Protokolle*, 131. See also Stein, *ibid.*, 167. A. Adler, *ibid.*, 171. M. Levy, *ibid.*, 172.

[118] *Ibid.*, 111.

[119] *Ibid.*, 40.

[120] *Ibid.*, 51.

[121] *Ibid.*, 59. Holdheim argued that according to the Mosaic conception, rest is the fundamental idea of the Sabbath, but that in the development of Judaism consecration became the positive element of Sabbath observance and that at present this is the essential feature. See below.

[122] *Ibid.*, 83.

[123] *Ibid.*, 103.

[124] *Ibid.*, 143.

[125] *Ibid.*, 150.

[126] So also Samuel Hirsch, *I. N. J.*, VII, 266.

[127] *Protokolle*, 87.

[128] *Ibid.*, 77.

[129] *Ibid.*, 80.

[130] *Ibid.*, 97.

[131] *Ibid.*, 111.

[132] *Ibid.*, 145.

[133] *Ibid.*, 155.

[134] *Ibid.*, 118.

[135] *Ibid.*, 125.

[136] *Ibid.*, 59-73.
[137] *Ibid.*, 57.
[138] *Ibid.*, 87.
[139] *Ibid.*, 146.
[140] *Ibid.*, 130. Earlier in the debate A. Adler had hinted at this when he called the Sabbath a state institution (*Staatsinstitution*).
[141] *I. N. J.*, VII, 267-8.
[142] *Supra*, 203.
[143] *Protokolle*, 70-73.
[144] Holdheim touched this point in the open letters which he published on the work of the conference. His words are of interest. "The conference was convinced that the breach between religion and life could not be repaired by the resolutions adopted in the matter of Sabbath observance, and yet it had not the courage to even name the only possible extreme remedy, viz., the transfer to Sunday. They deceived themselves and others by the phrase that a proper celebration of the Sabbath would strengthen the religious sentiment once again and make the demands of life yield; they closed their eyes wilfully to the fact that existing conditions will not permit the re-institution of a proper celebration of the Sabbath, and therefore make the strengthening of the religious sentiment through this means impossible; this is possible of attainment only by a transfer of the celebration of the Sabbath." "Offene Briefe über die dritte Rabbinerversammlung," *I. N. J.*, VII, 364. For his further views on the subject see his *G. J. R. G. B.*, 49, 148, 183, 196, 204, 209.
[145] *Protokolle*, 94. In his first pamphlet on the work of the conference to which reference has been made several times, Geiger shows how impossible it was for the conference to make a pronouncement on the subject (*Die dritte Rabbinerversammlung, ein vorläufiges Wort zur Verständigung*, 8), but he declares that the institution of a supplemental service on Sunday is the prerogative of any congregation (9), and goes on to say: "I consider the need of the present [for a service on Sunday] as so important that it must be satisfied in spite of ulterior apprehensions of what may happen; but because of these apprehensions precautions should be taken when a service of this kind is instituted that will remove such apprehensions as far as possible." In later years he favored a service on Sunday once a month which would give a large portion of the congregation the opportunity to attend and at the same time not undermine the Sabbath. "Nothwendigkeit und Maass einer Reform des jüdischen Gottesdienstes," Breslau, 1861; republished in *Nachgelassene Schriften*, I, 226; see also his statement in *J. Z. W. L.*, I, 77-78.
[146] *Protokolle*, 82. See also *I. N. J.*, VII, 283, 330 note.
[147] *Ibid.*, 79.
[148] *Ibid.*, 115.
[149] *Ibid.*, 119.
[150] *Ibid.*, 125.
[151] *Ibid.*, 29-30.
[152] *Ibid.*, 149.
[153] *Ibid.* However, in discussing S. Adler's resolution (see below) he declared a service on Sunday to be an urgent need of the times (*Protok.*, 250); see also *A. Z. d. J.*, X, 502-3.
[154] An object of this resolution, aside from its main significance, was to encourage such reform organizations like the recently organized Berlin Reform Association. This association had attempted to come into close relations with the conference at the meeting in Frankfort the previous year. This year the Berlinese addressed a letter to the conference; after referring to the occurrence at the previous conference, the letter proceeded to set forth the work of both organizations; the writers claimed that both their association and the conference are at one in their campaign against petrified orthodoxy and in the attempt to express and promulgate the pure content of

Judaism. The letter was rather dictatorial in tone and aroused some resentment among the members of the conference. It was referred to a committee consisting of Stein, Einhorn, and S. Adler, with the instruction to prepare an answer. When this answer was submitted, it caused so much discussion and gave rise to such decided differences of view that the whole matter was dropped. (*Protokolle*, 278.)

[155] *Protokolle*, 249-50.

[156] Sunday services were introduced at this period by a number of congregations, notably the Berlin Reform Congregation, the full story whereof will form the subject of a subsequent chapter. In Königsberg a service on Sunday, in addition to the regular Sabbath service, was instituted May 30, 1847, by the rabbi J. L. Saalschütz; the orthodox party appealed to the government, calling attention to a ministerial rescript which forbade Jews to change their traditional mode of worship; the government accordingly ordered the cessation of services on Sunday (*A. Z. d. J.*, XI, 378, 428-9). The officers of the congregation succeeded in having this prohibition withdrawn, whereupon Sunday, June 13, was selected as the day for the introduction of these services; before this day arrived the government renewed its prohibition under threat of a heavy fine; after further negotiations the government finally gave its consent, and a regular Sunday service was instituted on August 1. A special ritual in German was composed for this service (*ibid.*, 448, 491, 523). In the sermon delivered on this occasion Dr. Saalschütz gave the history of the reform movement in the congregation and stated his reasons for favoring a service on Sunday (*ibid.*, 558-9).

Dr. S. Formstecher, of Offenbach, instituted a service on Sunday afternoon in 1847 (*ibid.*, 378, 428); his opponents petitioned the government to forbid his taking that step; the petition was rejected (*ibid.*, 504). The reform congregation of Pesth, Hungary, organized in August, 1848, held its services on Sunday.

Other interesting incidents indicate how widespread at this time was the desire for a religious service on the civil day of rest. In March, 1846, a number of members of the congregation of Brussels requested the introduction of a service on Sunday because they were unable to attend on Saturday and desired to go with their families to a religious service once a week (*ibid.*, X, 264-5). Fould, the Parisian banker, when a member of the Chamber of Deputies (1843), suggested the practicability of such a compromise (*Voice of Jacob*, III, 214). In 1845 a wealthy merchant of Frankfort-on-the-Main offered two thousand thalers toward the erection of a new synagogue on the condition that it be opened every fortnight for a religious service on Sunday, when the organ should be played and a sermon delivered (*Orient*, VI, 178). On December 8, 1850, a service on Sunday afternoon was instituted in Vienna for the benefit of the many apprentices whose occupations did not permit them to attend on Saturday (*A. Z. d. J.*, XIV, 712).

[157] *Year Book C. C. A. R.*, 1902. The Pittsburg Conference of 1885, however, had made a declaration permitting the conducting of services on Sunday; see Chap. XII.

[158] *Die dritte Versammlung deutschen Rabbiner, ein vorläufiges Wort zur Verständigung.*

[159] *Protokolle*, 190-93.

[160] *Ibid.*, 208-48.

[161] *Ibid.*, 33.

[162] *Ibid.*, 271-74, 291.

[163] *Ibid.*, 86.

[164] Dr. A. Arnhold, whose communication had caused the conference to take up the circumcision question, published a pamphlet on the subject after the adjournment of the conference, entitled *Die Beschneidung und ihre Reform mit besonderer Rücksicht auf die Verhandlungen der dritten Rabbinerversammlung*. Breslau, 1846.

[165] *Protokolle,* 279-90.
[166] *Protokolle der zweiten Rabbinerversammlung,* 189, 222.
[167] *Protokolle der dritten Rabbinerversammlung,* 9-11.
[168] These suggestions were embodied in a pamphlet which he had issued the preceding year entitled *Vorschläge zu einer zeitgemässen Reform der jüdischen Ehegesetze der nächaten Rabbinerversammlung zur Prüfung übergeben.* Schwerin, 1845.
[169] *Protokolle,* 298.
[170] מצוה שהזמן גרמה בה in contradiction of the Talmudical principle, which holds the opposite. *Talm. Bab. Quid.,* 29 b.
[171] *Protokolle,* 265.
[172] *Ibid.,* 265.
[173] *Ibid.,* 292.
[174] "The assembly shares the fate of all public bodies which follow expediency instead of principle; whilst it goes too far for the one, it does too little for the other." *Voice of Jacob,* VI, 11.
[175] Reprinted *A. Z. d. J.,* X, 505-8.
[176] In the same newspaper and reprinted *A. Z. d. J.,* X, 524.
[177] *Ibid.,* X, 527.
[178] See also *ibid.,* 528.
[179] Published first in *Frankfurter Journal* and reprinted *A. Z. d. J.,* X, 530-1.
[180] *Ibid.,* 573-74; see also a further article by Stein, "Die Rabbinerversammlung, ein Wort zur Verständigung an alle welche sich für dieselbe interessiren," *I. N. J.,* VII, 209; cf. also Geiger, *Nachgelassene Schriften,* V, 192.
[181] *Offene Briefe über die dritte Rabbinerversammlung, I. N. J.,* VII, 361-64, 369-72, 377-80. See also an anonymous article, "Ein Dialog über die dritte Rabbinerversammlung," *ibid.,* 289-92, 297-300.
[182] *Vorläufiger Bericht über die Thätigkeit der dritten Versammlung deutscher Rabbiner.* Breslau, 1844.
Die dritte Versammlung deutscher Rabbiner, ein vorläufiges Wort zur Verständigung. Breslau, 1846.
[183] *Sendschreiben an die löbliche Redaktion des Israelit des neunzehnten Jahrhunderts,* VII, 397.
[184] Geiger, *J. Z. W. L.,* VI, 170.
[185] *A. Z. d. J.,* XI, 608.
[186] *Ibid.,* XII, 470.
[187] *Protokolle der dritten Versammlung deutscher Rabbiner,* 266.
[188] *Ein vorläufiges Wort,* 12.

CHAPTER VIII

[1] Geiger, *Juden in Berlin,* 234.
[2] *Supra,* 25.
[3] See a communication from Cassel which states that Seligman Bär Bamberger, the renowned orthodox rabbi of Würzburg, thus expressed himself, *A. Z. d. J.,* X, 56.
[4] See the important compilation of the ordinances of the Prussian government touching the Jews, beginning with the famous *Judenreglement* of 1750, under the heading *Die kirchlichen Verhältnisse der Juden in Preussen* in Freund's *Zur Judenfrage in Deutschland* (Berlin, 1843), 117-24, 185-95; also *Ministerial Fragen das jüdische Kultus und Schulwesen betreffend, ibid.,* 196-212.
[5] For a description of this class as the most active enemies of reform

see the article "Welche sind die wirksamsten Feinde der Reform?" *A. Z. d. J.*, X (1846), 142.

[6] S. Stern, *Die Gegenwärtige Bewegung im Judenthum*, Berlin, 1845, 18, 35. An excellent delineation of religious conditions in Berlin Jewry at this time is given in David Honigmann's "Aufzeichnungen aus seinen Studentenjahren," 1841-5, published in *Jahrbuch für jüdische Geschichte und Literatur*, VII, 177. Berlin, 1904. Honigmann writes: "The religious conditions in the Berlin community might be said to have been rotten in many respects. While the obstinate strict conservative party offered the most stiff-necked resistance to even the most innocent innovation which was sought to be introduced in order to pay some slight tribute to esthetic and intellectual needs, on the other hand, all who had remained faithful to the spirit and essence of Judaism, and longed for an inner regeneration of its eternal ideas and their fusion with the higher religious consciousness of the present, found no true satisfaction in an external restoration of the ceremonial institutions, even though they were in modern garb."

[7] Jost, *Geschichte der Israeliten*, X, part 3, 189. Geiger, *Juden in Berlin*, 246-7.

[8] The negotiations with Frankel came to naught because the Dresden rabbi could not obtain from Eichhorn, the Minister of Public Worship, the assurance "that he should be recognized by the state as the chief rabbi of a religious community to whom the guidance of their spiritual affairs would be entrusted." The attitude of the Prussian state toward Judaism was that it was merely tolerated and its confessors had no ecclesiastical officials; the rabbis had no standing as spiritual chiefs, but simply as *Kausherwächter*, *supra*, 26. For the negotiations between Frankel and the officers of the Berlin congregation, see the interesting correspondence edited by S. Bernfeld in *Allegemeine Zeitung des Judenthums*, LXII (1898), 343-6, 356-8, 368-70, 389-91, 404, 437-9, 461-2, 486-8, 536-8, 569-70, 582-3, 595-7, 606-8.

[9] Jost, *Geschichte der Israeliten*, X, part 3, 188.

[10] *I. N. J.*, VI, 181.

[11] *Verein für die Wissenschaft des Judenthums*, *supra*, 26.

[12] *Statuten des Culturvereins*. Berlin, 1841. *Israelitische Annalen*, III (1841), 177, 179.

[13] *Was war, was ist, und was soll der Rabbiner sein? Ibid.*, 241.

[14] *Die Aufgabe des Judenthums und des Juden in der Gegenwart*.

[15] I. H. Ritter, *Die jüdische Reformgemeinde zu Berlin*, 50. Berlin, 1902.

[16] *Unsere Gegenwart* in Freund's *Zur Judenfrage in Deutschland*, II, 7-25, 65-102.

[17] *Die Aufgabe der jüdischen Gemeinde zu Berlin für die Gegenwart*, *ibid.*, 26-41, 123-36, 413-34.

[18] This brilliant writer is known also as Bernstein; he seems to have used both names indiscriminately. He wrote extensively in the Jewish press, edited for a short time a periodical, *Die Reform des Judenthums*, but is known chiefly in Jewish literature by his two famous ghetto novels, *Vögele der Maggid* and *Mendel Gibbor*. For a sympathetic estimate see David Honigmann, op. cit.

[19] Preface to the second edition of the lectures in book form. Berlin, 1853.

[20] The great stir caused by these lectures is commented on in the three Jewish journals of the time, the *Allgemeine Zeitung des Judenthums*, the *Orient*, and the *Israelit des neunzehnten Jahrhunderts*. For Holdheim's estimate of Stein's addresses and services see *Geschichte . . . der jüdischen Reformgemeinde in Berlin*, 58, 75-6, 116; cf. also Geiger, *Nachgelassene Schriften*, V, 178 (letter to David Honigmann of date Mar. 19, 1845), and Ritter *Die jüdische Reformgemeinde zu Berlin*, 51.

[21] *Die Aufgabe des Judenthums und des Juden in der Gegenwart*, second edition, 341-3. Berlin, 1853.

[22] *Die gegenwärtige Bewegung im Judenthume*, 11.

[23] *Ibid.*, 10.

[24] Holdheim, *G. J. R. G. B.*, 28.

[25] *A. Z. d. J.*, IX, 234-6, *I. N. J.*, VI, 129, 130. Holdheim, *G. J. R. G. B.*, 49-52. Levin, *Die Reform des Judenthums*, 34-39.

[26] *Supra*, 120. Ritter, *Die jüdische Reformgemeinde zu Berlin*, 54.

[27] The most bitter attack upon the "Aufruf" and the Berlin movement was made by David Cassel in his brochure, *"Woher und Wohin?"* Berlin, 1845. Otheranti-reform publications called forth by this appeal and the subsequent formation of the Berlin Reform Congregation were M. Kalisch, *Berlin's jüdische Reformation nach der Thronbesteigung Friedrich Wilhelm III und IV*, Berlin, 1846; Selig (later Paulus) Cassel, *Ansprache an die Gemeinde in Glogau* in *A. Z. d. J.*, IX, No. 26; S. Krüger, *Bedenken gegen die neusten Reform Bestrebungen im Judenthum;* J. Misses, *Beitrag zur Würdigung der Wirren im Judenthum*. Leipzig, 1845. Favorable to the reform movement were S. Stern, *"Die Aufgabe des Judenthums und des Juden in der Gegenwart,"* Berlin, 1845, which is really a commentary on the appeal by one of its chief framers. *Ibid., Die Religion des Judenthums*. Berlin, 1846. *Ibid., Was ist geschehen und was ist zu thun?* Berlin, 1847. *Noch ein Wort zur israelitischen Reformfrage—Eine Stimme aus dem Volke vielleicht auch eine Stimme in der Wüste*. Hamburg, 1845 (published anonymously, but its author was most likely E. Kley). J. L. Schwarz, *Was ist jüdische Religion? Ein Leitfaden für das Künftige Glaubens-bekenntniss der jüdischen Reformgemeinschaft*. Berlin, 1845. Cf. also *Die Verhältnisse der israelitischen Gemeinde zu Berlin, A. Z. d. J.*, IX (1845), nos. 42, 43, 44. See also "Zur neuesten Geschichte der jüdischen Gemeinde in Berlin" in *Literaturblatt des Orient*, 1845, 161, 180-94, 214, 236. *Israelit des neunzehnten Jahrhunderts*, VI, 165, 173, 180, 197, 204, 230, 288, 317, 325, 341, 349, 355, 367, 383, 399.

[28] See the article "Unsere Gegenwart" already referred to frequently; also *A. Z. d. J.*, IX, 375; and articles in the short-lived periodical, *Reform Zeitung, Organ für den Fortschrift im Judenthume*. Berlin, 1847.

[29] *Supra*, 117.

[30] *Supra*, 186.

[31] *Infra*, 245.

[32] One of the frequent charges advanced against reform was that it was a purely opportunist movement and that its object was to curry favor with the government by repudiating the traditional doctrines of the coming of the political leader (Messiah), the national restoration and the return to Palestine and thus gain civil emancipation. Even Gabriel Riesser entertained this suspicion in reference to some of the reformers of the day; see David Honigmann's "Aufzeichnungen aus seinen Studienjahren" (1841-5), *Jahrbuch für jüdische Geschichte und Literatur*, VII, 141. Berlin, 1904. This charge was unwarranted; certainly no one will deny now that Holdheim, Geiger, Einhorn, and the other leaders were sincere in their separation of the political and the religious elements in Judaism. For them the political phase had passed with the loss of national independence; for them, too, Judaism's Messianic mission was universal. This was the parting of the ways of the traditionalists and the reformers. It is more than likely that had civil emancipation not come, the reform movement would not have arisen; but in the spirit of freedom that had come into the world, the reformers recognized the working of God's providence, and in a line with the demand of that spirit reinterpreted Jewish doctrine, notably in regard to the significance of the political status of the Messianic question.

[33] On this point of the attitude of reform toward the ceremonial legislation, see Geiger, *W. Z. J. T.*, IV, 10. *Nachgelassene Schriften*, I, 15; Holdheim, *Das Ceremonialgesetz im Gottesreich*, Schwerin, 1845; "Ueber die das talmudische Judenthum durchdringende Ansicht von der absoluten Ewigkeit

des Ceremonialgesetzes, die höhere Anschauung der Propheten und das Reformprincip der positiven historischen Fortbildung," *I. N. J.*, VI (1845), 361-74, 368-74, 377-382, 401, 406. Holdheim's argument may be briefly stated thus: The validity of the ceremonial law existed in Israel only so long as the belief existed among the people that this ceremonial legislation was essential; when this belief ceased, the ceremonial legislation lost its validity; belief, then, is the chief thing, ceremonial secondary. See further Frank-furter, *Israelitische Annalen*, II (1840), 371; Einhorn, *Ausgewählte Pre-digten und Reden*, herausgegeben von Dr. K. Kohler, III. New York, 1881; Chorin, *Rabbinische Gutachten über die Verträglichkeit der freien Forschung mit dem Rabbineramte*, I, 18, Breslau, 1842; Abraham Kohn, *ibid.*, 104; Herxheimer, *ibid.*, 123; Samuel Hirsch in *Rabbinische Gutachten über die Beschneidung*, 53. Frankfurt a. M., 1844; K. Kohler, "History and Func-tions of Ceremonies in Judaism," *Year Book C. C. A. R.*, XVII, 205.

[34] H. G. Enelow, "The Synod in the Past and its Feasibility in the Present," *Year Book C. C. A. R.*, Vol. X (1900), 104-32.

[35] Holdheim, *G. J. R. G. B.*, 162.

[36] *Die gegenwärtige Bewegung im Judenthum; ihre Berechtigung und Bedeutung*, 44-5. See also Rebenstein's clear statement: "The synod shall restore Judaism to us in a form in which its eternal content is capable of living on in us. We wish to enter into relation with Judaism once again through living men, through a living institution, and be no longer fettered to dead letters and ther equally dead, closed interpretation." *A. Z. d. J.*, IX, 375.

[37] *Geschichte . . . der jüdischen Reformgemeinde in Berlin*, 40, 43, 117, 124, 131, 153, 161ff.; especially 119, 121.

[38] *Geschichte . . . der jüdischen Reformgemeinde in Berlin*, 220, note 3.

[39] Even the radical of radicals among the rabbis of that day, M. Hess, endorsed the synod idea in a leading article, "Die neuesten Reformbeweg-ungen," *I. N. J.*, VI (1845), 163; his words are "eine aus dem Volke her-vorgehende und seine intelligensten und gesinnungsedelsten Glieder zählende Versammlung, eine Synode ist am ersten geeignet, bei dem Werk der Re-form so wohl allen Gemeinsame festzustellen als die individuelle Glaubens-freiheit zu wahren."

[40] *A. Z. d. J.*, IX, 281.

[41] *Ibid.*, 297.

[42] *Ibid.*, 372.

[43] On the other hand, the address aroused the ire of the anti-reformers; thus the editor of the French newspaper, *L'Univers Israélit*, spoke of it as "a Jewish New Testament signed by 28 would-be evangelists."

[44] Holdheim, *Geschichte der Entstehung und Entwickelung der jüdischen Reformgemeinde in Berlin*, 107.

[45] The idea of holding a synod was not realized at this time. In Jan., 1846, the Berlin Reform Association issued a second appeal which urged strongly the convening of the synod. *A. Z. d. J.*, X, 117. *I. N. J.*, VII, 219, 220. A meeting of deputies to make preparations for the calling of a synod took place in Berlin, Apr. 14-16, 1846. This meeting was a dismal failure, only six delegates besides those from the Berlin society being present. A second gathering of deputies was called for Oct., 1847, but this proved no more successful. *A. Z. d. J.*, XI, 680. When the plan of holding the fourth rabbinical conference at Mannheim in 1847 was abandoned, the executive committee of the conference suggested that a synod be convened instead (*A. Z. d. J.*, XI, 470); but this call, too, resulted in no action. When a synod was convened finally in 1869 at Leipzig, and again at Augsburg in 1871, these were not synods for the especial discussion and determination of the principles and institutions of reform Judaism, as the Berlin reformers had purposed, but for the consideration of problems of all sorts affecting Jewry, although the spirit of reform permeated the gatherings, as is appar-

ent from the resolutions adopted, and notably from the remarkable addresses of the president, Prof. M. Lazarus; See Chapter XI.

⁴⁶ *I. N. J.,* VI, 181. Sachs preached so bitter a sermon against the Reform Society that fifty members of the congregation stepped into the ranks of the society. *A. Z. d. J.,* IX, 320. He permitted his feelings against the reform movement to carry him away to such an extent that he refused to receive several rabbis who had attended the Frankfort Conference and who called on him during their stay in Berlin.

⁴⁷ Stern, *Die gegenwärtige Bewegung im Judenthume,* 28.

⁴⁸ Holdheim, *G. J. R. G. B.,* 40, 112.

⁴⁹ Stern's lectures are an example of this; they were popular to the last degree, and served their purpose well, of arousing his hearers to action; but they fall far short of evincing a philosophical grasp of the subject—"The Mission of Judaism."

⁵⁰ *A. Z. d. J.,* X, 235; although twenty years later he wrote unfavorably of "das sektenartige Streben in das diese Gemeinde von ihrem ersten Auftreten sich verhärtete," *J. Z. W. L.,* III, 217.

⁵¹ *A. Z. d. J.,* X, No. 29; Frankel, *Zeitschrift für die Religiösen Interessen des Judenthums,* I, 95; Graetz, *Monatsschrift für die Geschichte und Wissenschaft des Judenthums,* 1869, 172.

⁵² *Protokolle der dritten Versammlung deutscher Rabbiner,* 13-15.

⁵³ *Ibid.,* 290.

⁵⁴ Levin, *Die Reform des Judenthums,* 43. Berlin, 1895.

⁵⁵ *Supra,* 166ff.

⁵⁶ "Their aim was the establishment of a German Jewish church for whose inner development no traditional laws should signify, but only the free creative religious consciousness of the present as it was now developing." Honigmann, op. cit., 179.

⁵⁷ Holdheim, *G. J. R. G. B.,* 143, 144, repeated approvingly by a later minister of the congregation, Dr. M. Levin, in his *Reform des Judenthums,* published on the fiftieth anniversary of the foundation of the congregation as a jubilee memoir, 94. Geiger, *Nachgelassene Schriften,* I, 228 (1861), concedes that the *shofar* might well be replaced by earnest, uplifting music, but advises that the old tones be retained to the exclusion, however, of too frequent blowing as had become customary in the New Year's service.

⁵⁸ In his prayer-book עלת תמיד; his classical rendering of the sublime prayer of the traditional liturgy אתה נגלית ends stirringly with the blowing of the *shofar.* In the Union Prayer-Book the traditional prayers זכרונות שופרות, and מלכיות are cast in modern garb, each prayer ending with the sounding of the *shofar;* the combined effect of prayer, blowing of the *shofar* and music is inspiring.

⁵⁹ The Emanuel congregation of New York contemplated instituting this reform in 1859. The advice of the rabbi, Dr. S. Adler, was sought. In his response he discussed the question thoroughly, both from the scientific and the practical standpoints. It was published under the caption *Das Entblösste Haupt* in Geiger's *Jüdische Zeitschrift für Wissenschaft und Leben,* III, 189-196; see also Geiger, *ibid.,* 141-3, where he quotes from medieval writers to the effect that the Jews of France worshiped with uncovered heads in the thirteenth century; see also Löw, *Eine Vorlesung über Barhäuptigkeit* in *Gesammelte Schriften,* II, 311-28. The first reformer to touch the subject was Aaron Chorin, of Arad, in 1826, in his *Iggeret Elassaf.* Holdheim wrote in reference to this custom that even "if Bible and Talmud had forbidden it expressly, they would simply have given expression to their Oriental point of view, and hence they would have commanded it for the Occidental Jews and have forbidden the opposite." Quoted in Levin, *Reform des Judenthums,* 95. Berlin, 1895. See also article, "Bareheadedness," in *Jewish Encyclopædia.* M. Hellwitz, presiding officer of the Jewish Con-

sistory of Westphalia, delivered an address in 1847 entitled *Das unbedeckte Haupt* (The Uncovered Head), wherein he advocated the adoption of this reform. One congregation, that of Soest, followed the suggestion, but permitted any individual member who had scruples in the matter to continue worshiping with covered head. Cf. also G. Deutsch, *Hüben und Drüben, A. Z. d. J.,* LXIV (1900), 427. See, too, *Year Book, C. C. A. R.* (1928), 589.

⁶⁰ The Liberal Jewish Synagogue of London permits the worshiper to follow his inclination in this matter; he who so wishes may worship with uncovered head and *vice versa.*

⁶¹ Other ordinances of the Mosaic legislation touching the priesthood persisted in the life of the Jewish communities without the synagogal service proper, *e.g.* the ransoming of the first born by the priest (פדין הבן), the prohibition to the priest to touch a dead body lest it make him unclean, the prohibition to marry a divorced woman, etc., etc. Through these things the descendants of the ancient priestly families continued to be considered a special order. The reform movement transferred definitely the idea of the priesthood from this special class to the whole people. Cf. on this subject Holdheim, *G. J. R. G. B.,* 42.

⁶² The congregation gave practical evidence of this interpretation of Israel's mission by discarding in 1847 the observance of Tisha b'ab, the annual fast day, commemorative of the destruction of Jerusalem; on the Sunday following Holdheim, in his sermon, declared that the destruction of Jerusalem was really the beginning of Israel's larger mission to the world and had therefore resulted in good. *A. Z. d. J.,* XI, 503.

⁶³ Cf. Geiger, *Nachgelassene Schriften,* I, 227.

⁶⁴ *Supra,* 219ff. Cf. also Geiger, *Die Stellung des weiblichen Geschlechts in dem Judenthume unserer Zeit, Wissenschaftliche Zeitschrift für jüdische Theologie,* III (1837), 1-14. As this was possibly the first note sounded for the religious emancipation of the Jewish woman, the closing words of the article may be reproduced: "Let there be from now on no distinction between duties for men and women, unless flowing from the natural laws governing the sexes; no assumption of the spiritual minority of woman, as though she were incapable of grasping the deep things in religion; no institution of the public service, either in form or content, which shuts the doors of the temple in the face of woman; no degradation of woman in the form of the marriage service, and no applying the fetters which may destroy woman's happiness. Then will also the Jewish girl and the Jewish woman, conscious of the significance of the faith, become fervently attached to it, and our whole religious life will profit from the beneficial influence which feminine hearts know how to bestow upon it." In 1846 the Israelitish Council of Schwerin issued a mandate which stated that women shall be considered on an equal religious footing with men, their admission to confirmation being tantamount to the declaration of their religious majority. *A. Z. d. J.,* XI, 28. In that same year Holdheim declared that woman was admissible to *minyan,* that is, that she could be counted as one of the ten whose presence was considered necessary before divine service could be begun. *Voice of Jacob,* VI, 123.

⁶⁵ Frankel, *Grundlinien des mosaisch talmudischen Eherechts,* XXIX; Perles, *Bousset's Religion des Judenthums im neutestamentliche Zeitalter kritisch untersucht,* 91; Abrahams, *Jewish Life in the Middle Ages,* 115. Philadelphia, 1896.

⁶⁶ The congregation *Anshe Emeth* of Albany, New York, under the leadership of Isaac M. Wise in 1851; see *Reminiscences of Isaac M. Wise,* edited by the author, 212. Cincinnati, 1901.

⁶⁷ The Jewish Religious Union of London, founded in 1902, gave as one of the reasons for its establishment the continued separation of the sexes in the synagogue with the implied inferiority of woman.

⁶⁸ *I. N. J.,* VI, 349.

⁶⁹ Levin, *Die Reform des Judenthums,* 95-6.

[70] The arguments pro and con on this vital question of the Sunday Sabbath as advanced at the meetings of this Berlin Reform Association are given at length in Holdheim's *G. J. R. G. B.*, 148-54, 180-84. They are not reproduced in this place because the subject has been treated in the chapter on the Breslau Conference, where the subject was discussed fully. *Supra,* 200ff.

[71] Mar., 1849.

[72] *Predigt bei der am 2 April stattgefundenen Einweihung des Gotteshauses der Genossenschaft für Reform im Judenthume.* Berlin, 1846.

[73] *A. Z. d. J.*, X, 233.

[74] *I. N. J.*, VII, 135-6.

[75] *Das neue Preussische Judengesetz gegeben den 23 Juli, 1847, publicirt den 5 Aug., 1847, nebst aller dazu gehörigen Ergänzungsgesetzen und einer Geschichte der Judengesetze in Preussen.* Berlin, 1847. For the edicts on the religious affairs of the Jews of Prussia up to 1843, see Freund's *Die kirchlichen Verhältnisse der Juden in Preussen* in *Zur Judenfrage in Deutschland*, I, 117-24, 185-95. Berlin, 1843.

[76] Stern, *Was ist geschehen und was ist zu thun?* 7.

[77] *A. Z. d. J.*, XIV, 299.

[78] Holdheim, *G. J. R. G. B.*, 229-30.

[79] See Paragraphs 2 of his *Religionsprincipien des reformirten Judenthums,* Berlin, 1847, reproduced in its entirety in Levin's *Die Reform des Judenthums,* 55-58.

[80] *Supra,* 149.

[81] For a full account of this whole proceeding see Holdheim's *G. J. R. G. B.*, 229-35.

[82] *A. Z. d. J.*, XIV, 223.

[82a] At present (1930) however, as has been the case for some time past, this congregation and two separatist ultra orthodox congregations, the Adath Israel of Berlin and the Adath Jeshurun of Frankfort on the Main, have been autonomous and are not subject to the jurisdiction of the chief congregation (Hauptgemeinde).

[83] *Unser Verhältniss zur Gesammtjudenheit* in *Die Reform des Judenthums,* 98-9.

[84] *Infra.,* 397.

[85] תורה ומצוה *Jüdische Glaubens und Sittemlehre;* this was used as the book of instruction in the school of the congregation until 1889, when it was superseded by the catechism prepared by I. H. Ritter, the successor of Holdheim in the rabbinical office.

[86] *A. Z. d. J.*, 1878, 292.

[87] Gebetbuch, *Verlag der jüdischen Reformgemeinde zu Berlin.*

[88] Geiger, *Juden in Berlin,* 204-5.

[89] This is discussed in detail *infra,* Chapter XIII.

[90] This has been strongly stated in a publication by Cæsar Seligman, rabbi in Frankfort-on-the-Main; see the introduction to his *Judenthum und moderne Weltanschauung.* Frankfort, 1905.

CHAPTER IX

[1] *Supra,* Chapter III.

[2] Republished *A. Z. d. J.*, IX (1845), 236-7; *I. N. J.*, VI, 131-2; see also Holdheim, *G. J. R. G. B.*, 131.

[3] Concerning this address to the Frankfort Conference, *supra,* 266.

[4] Note his definition of the rabbi's function in a congregation composed of many different elements, as was the case in the Breslau congregation— "Der Rabbiner welcher es mit der Gesammtgemeinde wohl meint, dem das

religiöse Leben aller am Herzen liegt wird innerhalb der schroffsten Gegensätze welche gegenwärtig in Leben und Wissenschaft sich geltend machen, vermittelund, belehrund, anregend auftreten, er wird über den Parteien sich zu erhalten bemüht sein und je schwieriger dies ihm in dem heftigen Drängen der Gegenwart ist mit um so grösserem Ernste muss er daran halten." *I. N. J.*, VI, 160.

[5] *Nachgelassene Schriften*, V, 117.

[6] Freund was one of the most prominent Jews in Germany at the time and a publicist of note; he edited the magazine *Zur Judenfrage in Deutschland*. This appeared during two years, 1843-44, and contains a number of notable articles by Freund, Rebenstein, Holdheim, S. Stern, and others. His antagonism to Geiger was most surprising, since the two men had been on an intimate footing, and besides Freund had been supposed to be in complete sympathy with the forward religious movement.

[7] *I. N. J.*, VII, 279.

[8] *Treuer Bericht über die letzten Ereignisse in der hiesigen jüdischen Gemeinde* (anonymous, but from Geiger's entourage). Breslau, 1846. Geiger, *Nachgelassene Schriften*, V, 117.

[9] *A. Z. d. J.*, X, 250.

[10] *Ibid.*, X, 235-37; *supra*, 471, note 45.

[11] *Fünf Sendschreiben der grossen Mehrzahl der Breslauer israelitischen Gemeinde an Herrn Dr. Geiger und an sich selbst.*

[12] *Vor neun Jahren und Heute. Ein Wort aus jener Zeit zur Verständigung für die Gegenwart.*

[13] An anonymous answer was published under the title *Addresse der Grossen Mehrzahl der Mitglieder der Breslauer israelitischen Gemeinde an Herrn Dr. Wilhelm Freund.* Breslau, 1846.

[14] *Die Breslauer Israeliten Gemeinde in ihrem Zerfalle und Verfalle. Eine Stimme aus der Gemeinde.*

[15] Fifteen years later, upon Holdheim's death, he again refused to accept the call of the Berlin Reform Congregation to become its rabbi for the same reason.

[16] *Grundzüge und Plan zu einen neuen Gebetbuche.*

CHAPTER X

[1] I. Einhorn, *Die Revolution und die Juden in Ungarn*, 44. Leipzig, 1851.

[2] *A. Z. d. J.*, 1879, 653.

[3] Einhorn, *Die Revolution und die Juden in Ungarn*, 48.

[4] *A. Z. d. J.*, VIII (1844), 583.

[5] *Ibid.*, 452. *Voice of Jacob*, III, 222.

[6] Many, if not the majority, of the 116 signers of the famous protest against the Brunswick Rabbinical Conference were Hungarian rabbis, *supra*, 160.

[7] This was one community in Hungary which was permeated with the reform spirit, due to the fact that it had been ministered to for so many years by Aaron Chorin, one of the most noted of the early reformers. Steinhardt was Chorin's successor.

[8] Einhorn, *Die Revolution und die Juden in Ungarn*, 48.

[9] *A. Z. d. J.*, VIII (1844), 468.

[10] Later he took the name of Eduard Horn, and attained great prominence as a publicist; he was exiled from his native land for his share in the revolution of 1848, but was permitted to return in 1867. He had a distinguished parliamentary career; in 1873 he was elected Secretary of State to the Ministry of Commerce. During the incumbency of that office, he died,

Nov. 3, 1875, at the age of fifty. His early religious activity was forcibly recalled when, as a member of the Hungarian national parliament, he introduced a bill to transfer the Jewish Sabbath from Saturday to Sunday. *A. Z. d. J.*, XXXVI (1872), 512.

[11] *Die Revolution und die Juden in Ungarn,* 55.

[12] *Zulässigkeit und Dringlichkeit der Synagogenreformen begutachtet von vorzüglichen in und ausländischen Rabbinen.* Vienna, 1845.

[13] *A. Z. d. J.,* XI (1847), 42.

[14] *Ibid.,* 694.

[15] *Zur Judenfrage in Ungarn.* Ofen, 1847.

[16] This opinion of Rabbi Schwab elicited answers from Holdheim, *Das Gutachten des Pesther Rabbinats über die Reformgenossenschaft daselbst* and from Ignatz Einhorn, *Einige Bemerkungen über das Gutachten des Herrn L. Schwab Rabbiner der israelitischen Gemeinde zu Pest.* Pesth, 1848.

[17] Such reforms as sermon in the vernacular, confirmation, choir with organ, had been introduced in Lugos. See *A. Z. d. J.,* XI (1847), 347. Moses Bruck, the preacher of this congregation, wrote several books on the ceremonial law. He and his whole congregation had to flee because of the atrocities of the Wallachians after the fall of the Hungarian Republic; he died at Szegedin in 1849 of the cholera.

[18] *I. N. J.,* 1848, 164-5.

[19] *Supra,* 255-7.

[20] *A. Z. d. J.,* XV (1851), 270.

[21] *Supra,* 255.

[22] Dr. David Einhorn's *Ausgewählte Predigten und Reden herausgegeben von Dr. K. Kohler,* 19-31. New York, 1881.

[23] For a description of this result of the Congress, cf. "Die Judenschaft in Ungarn," *A. Z. d. J.,* XXXVI (1872), 24. Cf. also the manifesto issued in 1880 by the rabbis of the orthodox party against the Buda-Pesth theological seminary, founded and sponsored by the "Congress" party. *Ibid.,* 1880, 374. As elsewhere the rigidly orthodox party looked upon modern education as neology; magyarization was confounded with reform. The *Yeshibah* at Pressburg continued along the traditional medieval lines. This *Yeshibah,* having received recognition as a public institution whose students were excused from military duty, the Minister of Public Worship startled the orthodox authorities when, in 1883, he issued an edict to the effect that all students (*bachurim*) who entered the Pressburg *yeshibah* must have passed successfully the examinations of the four lower classes of the gymnasium or the public school, and must be able to show a certificate from some public institution for "the public weal demands that the rabbis issuing from the *yeshibah* should possess a secular education, in addition to the requisite theological attainments, and should have a knowledge of the national language and attainments necessary for a beneficial career in our fatherland." *Ibid.,* XLVII, 1883, 404-5.

[24] Leopold Löw, "Frankfurt und Ofen-Pest" in *Gesammelte Schriften,* IV, 509.

[25] *A. Z. d. J.,* LIII (1889), 573-5. This manifesto of the orthodox rabbis caused the government to submit an inquiry to the secular heads of Hungarian Jewry. These, in a lengthy document of the date of Nov. 25, 1889, repudiated the contention of the orthodox rabbis that there were two wings of Jewish thought, although granting that there were different customs among various sections of Jews. They closed the communication thus: "Hence we request Your Excellency to refuse the request of the orthodox commission to recognize two wings of Jewish religious belief and to guarantee the uniform organization of Jewry by a decree as soon as possible." See *ibid.,* 789.

CHAPTER XI

[1] This has been stated frequently by leaders of orthodox Judaism. Samson Raphael Hirsch put it very tersely: "Das jüdische Gesetz ist vollkommen und alles an ihm ist fundamental:—man hat die Wahl sich voll und gang an ihm zu bekennen oder es zu leugnen" (*Jeschurun*, XV, 34). See also Friedländer, *The Jewish Religion,* 239, where, in proof of the contention that all commands are of equal weight, it is stated "The commandments 'Thou shalt love thy neighbor as thyself,' and 'a garment of divers kinds shall not come upon thee' stand side by side in the same paragraph"; see also *ibid.,* 235.

[2] M. Kalisch, *Das Verhältniss der jüdischen Gemeinden zu den Reformgenossenschaften nach den Kultusbestimmungen des Gesetzes vom 23 Juli, 1847,* 4. Berlin, 1848. This is the argument advanced by most anti-reformers who desire to maintain the status quo, but yet wish to vindicate to the individual the right of private judgment. Twenty years later a writer in the *Monatsschrift für Geschichte und Wissenschaft des Judenthums* (whose standpoint was just this of orthodoxy in practice and the greatest heterodoxy in theory) claims that Judaism is practice and not dogma; that a rabbi can entertain the freest opinions privately, but cannot carry these out in practice as a rabbi, because as such he is the representative of the congregation. XIX (1869), 328. This is in truth the position of modern German orthodoxy (1930), which blinks at the widest laxity in individual observances, but demands official conformity.

[3] *Supra,* 233.

[4] *Ibid.,* 373.

[5] See also *A. Z. d. J.,* XII (1848), 6.

[6] *Ibid.,* 470.

[7] *Ibid.,* 428.

[8] *Ibid.,* 601.

[9] *Ibid.,* 658, 675, 759.

[10] *Ibid.,* 469, 481.

[11] *Ibid.,* XIII (1849), 9. A few months later in the issue of June 11 (313-316), Philippson had a strong editorial entitled, "Die Synode und die Gegenwart," in which he set forth the absolute necessity of the synod which had to do for the present what the sanhedrin at Tiberias did for Judaism after the destruction of Jerusalem. A collection of opinions for and against the synod has been published by the Central Conference of American Rabbis, entitled "Views on the Synod," Baltimore, 1905. In this collection the opinions which are here referred to are quoted at length.

[12] See speech of Dr. A. M. Goldschmidt, rabbi of Leipzig, at the opening of Leipzig Synod. "*Verhandlungen der ersten israelitischen Synode zu Leipzig.*" Berlin, 1869.

[13] Several exceptions to this statement may be noted, but in lands outside of Germany; thus in 1850 a synod of Bohemian Jews convened upon the call of the government to work out a plan for congregational organization, *A. Z. d. J.,* XIV, 646, 679, 713, XV, 7. In 1856 a meeting of the grand rabbis of the different French consistories took place at Paris pursuant to a call issued by the grand rabbi of France, S. Ulmann. This meeting deliberated upon the necessity and advisability of introducing a number of reforms into the service; however, it was left to each grand rabbi to introduce the reforms or not, according to what seemed to him the needs of his consistory; see "The Jews of France," by S. Debre, *J. Q. R.,* III, 389ff.

[14] Thus a call was addressed on July 9, 1848, to the German rabbis by a Dr. Steinfeld to meet and advance the cause of reform. This, he claimed, should be done particularly in this time of freedom when liberty has been gained in all other fields. His call ended with these words: "Die Reform-

frage ist sehr drängend; sie ist unabweisbar; sie ist die höchste Nothwendigkeit; der ganze Bestand unserer Religion ist dabei interessirt und wir erblicken keine Zukunft für dieselbe, falls sie sich nicht aufrichtig und ganz der Reform sich in die Arme wirft," *A. Z. d. J.*, XII, 440. See also an article, "Die Reformfrage in diesen Tagen" (May 29, 1848), by Ludwig Philippson, in which he urges his coreligionists not to lose sight of the necessity of religious reforms because of the large political questions which were engaging the attention of all men. *Ibid.*

[15] *A. Z. d. J.*, XV (1851), 400, "Life has decided in favor of reform. Every Jewish house testifies to this; for here as everywhere it is the first step that counts. No matter what be the attitude of individuals and of separate congregations the reconciliation of the historical elements with the spirit of modernity will be accomplished."

[16] Geiger, *J. Z. W. L.*, I, 172-3. *Ibid.*, 251, *Alte Romantik neue Reaktim.*

[17] See Geiger, *J. Z. W. L.*, I, 251 (1862); II, 267; IV, 81-96. "Zur gegenwärtige Lage."

[18] *Was thut Noth? Ibid.*, III, 251-58.

[19] Geiger, *J. Z. W. L.*, VI, 169.

[20] This was urged because a number of prayer-books had been issued by individual rabbis (Geiger, Philippson, Stein, Aub and others). The divisions in the reform camp were emphasized by this tendency to produce individual prayer-books. The suggestion first made at the Cassel Conference to issue a union prayer-book for reform congregations did not bear fruit till 1894, when the Union Prayer-Book was issued by the Central Conference of American Rabbis.

[21] *A. Z. d. J.*, XXXII (1868), 691; the minutes of the conference were published as a supplement to No. IV of Vol. XXXIII (1869).

[22] Geiger, *Die Rabbinerversammlung in Cassel. Jüdische Zeitschrift für Wissenshaft und Leben*, VI, 241-47, where he discusses the character of the synod. This was to be deliberative and not authoritative; "die Macht der Ueberzeugung muss wirken, nicht die übertragene Gewalt."

[23] L. Philippson, *Geschichte der deutschen Rabbinerversammlungen und Synoden;* a series of articles written on the occasion of the fortieth anniversary of the Brunswick Conference. *A. Z. d. J.*, XLVIII (1884), 262.

[24] The synod was strongly urged by the rabbis because the resolutions of the rabbinical conferences had remained for the most part a dead letter. It was thought that the resolutions of a synod would be given heed to because the synod would be representative of all the elements in Jewry, rabbinical and lay, reform and orthodox. Cf. Philippson, *Die Synode, A. Z. d. J.*, LI (1887), 502.

[25] See *Jeshurun*, XIV (1868), 339-52, where S. R. Hirsch uses these words: "so hat die Reform einmal wiederum ihre völlige Impotenz, ihre völlige produktive Unfähigkeit erwiesen—sic hat ein schmähliches Fiasco gemacht." The bitterness of feeling of Neo-orthodoxy against reform appears also in several articles published about this time in the *Monatsschrift für Geschichte und Wissenschaft des Judenthums*, XIX, 81-88, 122-33. They were called forth by the jubilee celebration in the Hamburg Temple congregation in October, 1868, on the occasion of its fiftieth anniversary. The titles of the articles are sufficient indication of their contents, I, *Reform und Reformschwindel;* II, *Die Gebetmacherei.*

[26] Cf. *A. Z. d. J.*, XXXIII (1869), 61, 81, 101, 141. *Jewish Chronicle*, Jan., 1869; *Archives Israélites* (French), Feb. 1, 1869; *Educatore Israelitico* (Italian), Mar., 1869; *Occident* (American), Aug., 1868. Benoit Levy, in advocating the synod in *La Presse Israélite*, used the following passionate language. "See you not that nine-tenths of those who are *Bar Mitzwah* do not understand one word of the Bible? See you not that the young people do not come to the temple the whole year round? See you not that Hebrew and the Talmud have become the exclusive possession of the rabbis, and that if this

continues no one but they will be able either to understand or read Hebrew within the next twenty or thirty years? And do you not desire that efforts be made to ensure the education of the young, to shorten the prayers, and to change some ceremonies in order that as great a number as possible be attracted to the temple of our fathers?" On the other hand, the orthodox organs, notably the *Jeshurun*, were bitterly opposed to the synod because of the source whence the call emanated, viz. a rabbinical conference of a reform tendency. An article by Graetz entitled "Die Synode" (The Synod), in the *Monatsschrift für die Geschichte und Wissenschaft des Judenthums*, XIX (1869), 171-7, expressed the opinion of the orthodox. He claimed it to have been a mistake to have given the reform of the liturgy the first place among the proceedings of the projected synod. The object of the synod, said he, must be the healing of differences, restoration of unity, vivification of communal sentiment. "I cannot but feel that the synod will be a partisan reform synod," he continued, "despite the assurance of neutrality on the part of the promoters, and therefore it will not remove the split. The call for the synod should have come neither from Germany nor America, for there the differences between the parties are most pronounced, but from a country and from men who have the confidence of all Jews. The synod must avoid all words and resolutions that will contribute to any further disruption in Israel." Or, in other words, *Shulchan Aruk* Judaism or nothing. What was the need of a synod unless to interpret Judaism to meet the changed conditions? A modern synod must of necessity be a reform synod. The moment that there is an iota of change from any of the regulations laid down in the *Shulchan Aruk* reform begins; after that it is only a question of quantity.

[27] *Verhandlungen der ersten israelitischen Synode zu Leipzig*, 62. Berlin, 1869.

[28] *Ibid.*, 67-69.

[29] *Ibid.*, 203. This remark indicates the mistake so frequently made of confounding reform with negativism. True reform is positive. Of course it must first clear the ground of abuses that have grown up in the religious field, but it does not rest here; it has a positive interpretation of the religious content. Reform in Judaism rests as truly on a positive historical basis as does rabbinism; the accusation that it scouts tradition is unjust. True, it discredits certain traditions, but it builds upon the body of Jewish tradition as a developing force. In this sense the synod was of a reform tendency.

[30] *Ibid.*, 133.

[31] *Ibid.*, 101, 151. Joel, deep and brilliant scholar though he was, was an out-and-out representative of the Breslau school, which demands absolute fidelity to rabbinical tradition in practice, although conniving at the broadest freedom in thought. Thus a man may disbelieve in the restoration of sacrifices, but yet the prayers for this must be retained in the liturgy, because the tradition must not be tampered with. Shortly before the synod met a heated controversy had taken place between Joel and Geiger on this very question of the liturgy. Joel, in his *Zur Orientirung in der Cultusfrage* (1867), had broken a lance for the orthodox prayer-book, and had argued for the retention of the prayers for the restoration of sacrifices, the bodily resurrection and the personal Messiah. Geiger answered him in a lengthy critique "Etwas über Glauben und Beten, zu Schutz und Trutz," *Jüdische Zeitschrift für Wissenschaft und Leben*, VII, 1-59. Joel pleaded for unity in Israel even at the cost of individual conviction. Geiger contended for the right of progressive thought.

[32] Dr. A. Wiener, of Oppeln, handed in to the synod an elaborate dissertation on the dietary laws in reference to which, however, no action was taken. Twenty-six years later he published a work on this same subject which was undoubtedly the outcome of these early studies. This work is the best and most comprehensive study of the dietary laws from the historical, critical and reform standpoint that we have; it is entitled *Die jüdischen*

Speisegesetze nach ihren verschiedenen Gesichtspunkte zum ersten Male wissenschaftlich-methodisch geordnet und kritish untersucht. Breslau, 1895; see also C. G. Montefiore's review of the work, *J. Q. R.*, VIII, 392-413.

[33] *Verhandlungen*, 167.

[34] *Ibid.*, 212.

[35] *Verhandlungen der zweiten israelitischen Synode zu Augsburg*, 71.

[36] *Ibid.*, 134.

[37] See below where this interesting proposal is discussed at length.

[38] *Verhandlungen der zweiten israelitischen Synode*, 160. See also Dr. Nehemias Brüll's bold declaration, *ibid.*, 166.

[39] *Ibid.*, 181.

[40] *Ibid.*, 189.

[41] *Supra*, 155-6.

[42] *Verhandlungen der ersten israelitischen Synode*, 75.

[43] *Ibid.*, 78.

[44] *Ibid.*, 54.

[45] Lazarus' opening address at the Augsburg synod *Verhandlungen der zweiten israelitischen Synode*, 13, 14.

[46] *Verhandlungen der ersten israelitischen Synode, Anhang*, I, 218-39.

[47] *Ibid.*, 105, 106.

[48] *Ibid.*, statement, *ibid.*, 108.

[49] *Supra*, 288.

[50] *J. Z. W. L.*, VII, 161-67. *Verhandlungen der ersten Synode*, 256.

[51] *Ibid.*, 243-46.

[52] *Ibid.*, 114.

[53] *Ibid.*, 113.

[54] *Verhandlungen*, 116. Aub's remarks derive further interest from the fact that reference is made in them to a Union Prayer-Book, although disparagingly. The speaker claimed that there were so many differences, even among congregations that desired a reform of the old prayer-book, that it would be a long time ere they could even think of the proposition of producing one prayer-book for all. "As many cities, so many altars, gentlemen, and now we have even more altars than cities." This remark referred to the many individual prayer-books that had been prepared by individual rabbis or for individual congregations. This was not the case in Europe alone, but also in the United States. The manufacture of these individual prayer-books became the most notorious sign of the religious anarchy in modern Israel. The evil has been checked finally in the United States, by the appearance of the Union Prayer-Book, prepared by the Central Conference of American Rabbis, the nearest approach to a book of common prayer that the Jewish community has had since the prereform days; similarly the prayer-book published by the Union of Liberal Congregations in Germany in 1928 performs the function of a book of common prayer for these congregations. *Infra*.

[55] *Ibid.*, 145. A number of congregations had introduced the triennial cycle as recommended by the Frankfort Conference. In their name Geiger and others entered a protest against this resolution which had been adopted by a majority of one. The majority at a later session made declaration that their action was not to be understood as deprecating the triennial cycle, but that both customs are in accord with Jewish practice. *Ibid.*, 171, note.

[56] *Ibid.*, 126, 149.

[57] *Ibid.*, 153-4.

[58] *Ibid.*, 170.

[59] *Ibid.*, 163. Much disorder was caused by the repetition in *Shacharit* (the morning service) and *Mussaf* (the additional service) of the eighteen benedictions, notably by the so-called *lachash* or silent prayer which was never silent but a mumbling.

[60] *Ibid.*, 171-74, 186.

[61] On the three high feasts benedictions appropriate to the day were inserted in the *tefillah*.

[62] Ps. 113-18.

[63] *Verhandlungen*, 177.

[64] *Ibid.*, 178.

[65] The special prayer for rain.

[66] Supplications characterized by the formula Hoshana (חושע נא) "Save, we beseech Thee."

[67] The seventh day of the Feast of Tabernacles.

[68] *Verhandlungen*, 179.

[69] *Ibid.*, 179-80.

[70] The beautiful custom of holding a memorial service for the dead dates far back and was held on various holidays. At present, however, particularly in reform congregations, the custom is quite universal of holding this service on the Day of Atonement. See *Jewish Encyclopædia*, art. "Memorial Service."

[71] *Verhandlungen*, 180.

[72] The impressive portion of the afternoon service on the Day of Atonement beginning with *Alenu l'shabeach*.

[73] *Verhandlungen*, 181.

[74] The Sabbath before the Feast of Purim was known as Sabbath *Zakor*, taking its name from the pentateuchal section read on that day, Deut. xxv. 17-19; similarly Sabbath *Parah* took its name from the Pentateuchal section, Num. xix.

[75] *Verhandlungen*, 246-60.

[76] The high priest made it a festive occasion when, on the Day of Atonement, he entered the Holy of Holies in peace and came forth in peace without having suffered harm.

[77] *Ibid.*, 214.

[78] L. Philippson, *Zur Charakteristik der ersten jüdischen Synode*. Berlin, 1869.

[79] Geiger, *J. Z. W. L.*, VIII (1870), 81.

[80] Mention must be made in this connection of a transatlantic greeting to the synod at the opening session. Dr. Geiger read from a personal letter addressed to him by Rabbi Isaac M. Wise, of Cincinnati, in which the great American rabbi had written, "I intended to visit the synod, but I am unfortunately עבד עולם"; after describing the interest manifested in the synod in various parts of America, the communication closed with the words, "May God bless you."

[81] Lazarus in this address criticized sharply those who had failed to put in an appearance at this meeting. In 1887 he issued a volume of addresses and essays entitled *Treu und Frei*, in which this Augsburg address was included. Philippson, who had remained away from the Augsburg assembly, answered the criticism and made it the occasion for an estimate of the synods, explaining at the same time why they had failed. *A. Z. d. J.*, LI (1887), 501-3, 514-17.

[82] At about the same time A. Rebenstein urged the necessity of the reform of the marriage laws; see his article "Unsere Gegenwart" in Freund's *Zur Judenfrage in Deutschland*, II, 14-21.

[83] The rabbinical conference held in Philadelphia, U. S. A., in 1869 passed some resolutions on the subject; see below.

[84] Be thou sanctified to me by this ring according to the law of Moses and Israel.

[85] *Verhandlungen*, 41.

[86] Later this rabbi wrote on the subject of the reform of the marriage laws. *A. Z. d. J.* (1904), 426.

[87] *Ibid.*, 68.

[88] From the seventeenth of Tammuz, the day on which the first breach

was made in the walls of Jerusalem by the Romans, to the ninth of Ab, the day of the destruction of the city.

[89] Cf. Landsberger "Ueber Eheschliessungen zwischen Pesach und Shabuoth" in Geiger's *Jüdische Zeitschrift für Wissenschaft und Leben*, VII (1869), 81-96.

[90] See Einhorn's "Morning Service for the Anniversary of the Destruction of Jerusalem" in his prayer-book (Eng. tr.), 319-39, notably the lofty prayer, 330-33.

[91] Mielziner, *The Jewish Law of Marriage and Divorce*, 112-14. Cincinnati, 1884.

[92] *Verhandlungen*, 128-35, 138-55.

[93] *Ibid.*, 110-14, 157, 158.

[94] *Ibid.*, 109. Lehmann, who had been one of the most active members of the Leipzig Synod, and who was one of the clearest thinkers among the Jews of Germany among the advocates of progress in Judaism, published just before the convening of the Augsburg Synod a pamphlet entitled *Zur Synode* (Breslau, 1871), in which he discussed the various subjects to be brought before the forthcoming synod and called upon the congregations to participate actively in the gathering by sending delegates. Fifteen years later he published his *Die Juden, Einst und Jetzt* (Dresden and Leipzig, 1886), in which he urged strongly many religious reforms.

[95] *Ibid.*, 174-204.

[96] *Ibid.*, 205-10. The same specific question had been discussed at length at Breslau and decided in the same manner.

[97] *Supra*, 303-4.

[98] *Verhandlungen*, 225-33.

[99] *A. Z. d. J.*, XXXV (1871), 780-1.

[100] In 1891 Emil Lehmann, of Dresden, published a series of articles entitled "Letters to a Friend." In the third of this series he urged the convening of a third synod to consider the many vexing problems, religious and other, of German Jewry. He claimed that not only the internal confusion but also the external situation caused by the attacks of anti-Semitism demanded urgently the full and wise consideration of the best minds among the Jews in convention assembled. *A. Z. d. J.*, LV (1891), 159.

[101] See the pamphlet *Views on the Synod*, a compilation of opinions on the synod pro and con compiled by a committee of the conference. At the Indianapolis Conference in July, 1906, a majority declared against the advisability of the formation of a synod.

[102] From Majority report of the Committee at Louisville Meeting of Central Conference of American Rabbis, *Year Book* No. XIV, 147.

CHAPTER XII

[1] In observance of the one hundredth anniversary of the establishment of this first American Jewish reform congregation a symposium on the general theme, "A Revaluation of Reform Judaism," was conducted at the session of the Central Conference of American Rabbis held at Cedar Point, Ohio, in June, 1924. *Year Book C. C. A. R.*, XXXIV, 222ff.

[2] B. A. Elzas, "The first Confirmation ceremony in the American Synagogue," *Jewish Tribune*, Portland, Oregon, May 18, 1906, p. 17. *Ibid.* "New Material on the First Reform Movement in America," in Literary Supplement to the *American Hebrew*, New York, Dec. 7, 1906.

[3] A. J. Moses, "The Origin of Jewish Reform in America," *American Hebrew* for Jan. 29, 1886.

[4] B. A. Elzas, *The Jews of South Carolina*, 147-65. Philadelphia, 1905.

[5] M. Mayer, "Geschichte des religiösen Umschwunges unter den Israeliten Nord-Amerikas," *Sinai*, vol. I, 105. Baltimore, 1856.

[6] *Sinai*, vol. I, 172.

[7] *The Occident*, X, 226. Elzas, *The Jews of South Carolina*, 210.

[8] At one time, however, many of the foremost leaders in American Jewry, recognizing the evils of individualistic disorganization, urged the necessity of the formation of a central representative organization or assembly; see *supra, 328.*

[9] For a vivid description of conditions in American Jewish congregations before the year 1848 see *Reminiscences* by Isaac M. Wise, 71ff. Cincinnati, 1901.

[10] Cf. Voorsanger, *The Chronicles of Emanuel*, 60-94. San Francisco, 1900.

[11] Myer Stern, *History of Temple Emanuel* of New York, 14. New York, 1895.

[12] *Sinai*, vol. I, 201.

[13] *Reminiscences*, by Isaac M. Wise, 149, 155ff.

[14] Philipson, *The Oldest Jewish Congregation in the West*. Cincinnati, 1924.

[15] *The History of K. K. Bene Yeshurun from the date of its Organization*. Cincinnati, 1892.

[16] "Outlines of the History of the Reform Congregation Keneseth Israel," 5, in *Year Book of Reform Congregation Keneseth Israel* for 1890-91.

[17] *Sinai*, vol. IV, 154.

[18] *Ibid.*, vol. VI, 162.

[19] Philipson, *Max Lilienthal, American Rabbi*. Cincinnati, 1915.

[20] *The Asmonean*, vol. X (1854), 85.

[21] *Reminiscences*, by Isaac M. Wise, edited by David Philipson. Cincinnati, 1901. *Isaac M. Wise*, Max B. May. Cincinnati, 1916.

[22] *The Israelite*, vol. I (1854), 20.

[23] *Antrittspredigt gehalten im Tempel des Har Sinai Vereins*, von Dr. David Einhorn, 6, 8. Baltimore, 1855.

[24] *Ibid.*, 9, 10.

[25] *Sinai*, II, 534.

[26] *Supra*, 337.

[27] Appendix to *Kol Kore Bamidbar: Ueber jüdische Reform*, by B. Felsenthal, 37. Chicago, 1859.

[28] *Kol Kore Bamidbar*, 1.

[29] *Ibid.*, 11.

[30] *Ibid.*, 12.

[31] *Ibid.*, 17.

[32] Leipzig, 1842.

[33] *Ibid.*, 1843.

[34] *Ibid.*, 1843.

[35] Trier, 1854.

[36] Leipzig, 1844, 67-69.

[37] *Protokolle der Rabinner Conferenz abgehalten zu Philadelphia*, 86-7. New York, 1870.

[38] The pronouncements of the conference on the subject of marriage were in the reform spirit. They declared: (1) The bride shall no longer be a passive party to the marriage ceremony, but a mutual consecration by both bridegroom and bride shall take place by their speaking the same formula of marriage and by the exchange of rings. (Cf. *Supra*, 309.) (2) The following is the formula of marriage: "Be consecrated to me as wife (as husband) according to the law of God." (3) For the traditional benedictions ברכת אירוסין there shall be substituted such a benediction as sets forth the full moral grandeur of marriage, emphasizes the Biblical idea of the union of husband and wife into one personality (והיו לבשר אחד), and designates

purity in wedlock as a divine command. (4) Polygamy contradicts the idea
of marriage. The marriage of a married man to another woman is as little
possible as the marriage of a married woman to another man, and must be
considered null and void. (5) The priestly marriage laws which presupposed
the greater holiness of the Aaronides have lost all significance since the
destruction of the Temple and the disappearance of the old sacrificial cult,
and therefore hold no longer.

The conference made also a definite declaration concerning the *chalitzah*
ceremony. "The command to marry the brother-in-law and in case of his
refusal to take off the shoe, etc., has lost for us all sense, all importance and
all binding force." On the subject of divorce the conference passed the following resolutions: (1) From the Mosaic and rabbinical standpoint divorce
is a purely civil act, which never received religious consecration; it is therefore valid only when it proceeds from the civil court. The so-called ritual
Get is invalid in all cases. (2) A divorce given by the civil court is valid
in the eyes of Judaism if it appears from the judicial documents that both
parties have consented to the divorce; but when the court has decreed a
divorce against the wish of one or other of the couple, Judaism on its part
can consider the divorce valid only when the judicial reasons for granting
the divorce have been investigated and found of sufficient weight. It is
recommended that before deciding the rabbi obtain the opinion of experts.
(3) The decision of the question as to whether, in doubtful cases, the husband or wife is to be declared dead after lengthy disappearance is to be left
to the law of the land. Cf. *Supra*, 315.

[39] Authentic Report of the Proceedings of the Rabbinical Conference
held at Pittsburg, Nov. 16, 17, 18, 1885, *Jewish Reformer* for Jan. 15,
1886, 4.

[40] The conservative party roused to action by what they held to be the
destructive tendency of the Pittsburgh Conference founded the Jewish Theological Seminary of New York for the training of rabbis for conservative
congregations. The first president of the seminary was the Rev. Sabato
Morais of Philadelphia.

[41] Cf. the presidential address at the Atlantic City Conference of 1898,
Year Book for 1898, 12.

[42] *Year Book C. C. A. R.*, XXXIX (1929), 536-51.

[43] *Ibid.* (1899), 28.

[44] *Judaism at the World's Parliament of Religions.* Cincinnati, 1894.

[45] *Infra.*, 372-3.

[46] *Year Book*, I, 31, 80-125.

[47] *Ibid.*, VI, 63.

[48] *Ibid.*, VII, 16, 17.

[49] *Ibid.*, 10.

[50] *Ibid.*, IX, 12.

[51] *Ibid.*, XLI.

[52] *Year Book C. C. A. R.*, XXVIII, 133-34.

[53] *Ibid.*, XXX, 140-41.

[54] See Philipson, "The Reform Prayer-Book," *Journal of Jewish Lore
and Philosophy*, Vol. I, 69-82, 211-23. Cincinnati, 1922.

[55] *Supra*, passim.

[56] B. A. Elzas, "The First American Jewish Reform Prayer-Book," *The
Jewish Voice*, St. Louis, Mo., May 21, 1909.

[57] *Sinai*, vol. I, 91-100, 129-39.

[58] *Year Book*, V, 32.

[59] *Ibid.*, XXIV, 127.

[60] *Ibid.*, XXVIII, 66.

[61] *Protokolle*, 39, 41.

[62] 1879, No. 12.

[63] רק חזק ואמץ. Extracts from *Proceedings of Chicago Sinai Congre-*

gation at its annual meeting, Mar. 26, 1885, and special meeting, Apr. 9, 1885, 4.

[64] Authentic Report, etc., *Jewish Reformer*, Jan. 22, 1886, 4.

[65] These responses, together with other papers on the *Milath Gerim* question, were published in the *Year Book of the Central Conference* for 1891-92, 66-128.

[66] *Ibid.,* 24.

[67] *Ibid.,* for 1892-93, 15-19, 33-37.

[68] *Year Book C. C. A. R.,* XX, 106.

[69] *Judaism—A Manual for the Instruction of Proselytes,* 43. Cincinnati, 1928.

[70] *Supra,* 195ff.

[71] Cf. the words of Dr. K. Kohler: "Late Friday evening services are altogether an innovation—an innovation of a dubious character, in so far as they make those who attend them feel that they have done their duty toward the Sabbath." *Year Book C. C. A. R.,* XVI, 62.

[72] At the Brunswick Rabbinical Conference in 1844. *Supra,* 154-5.

[73] *Year Book C. C. A. R.,* XIII, 103-22.

[74] *Ibid.,* 77.

[75] *Ibid.,* XIV, 119.

[76] *Ibid.,* XVII, 87-113. The conclusions reached by the committee as a result of its investigations are as follows: (1) The Sunday service is found to be helpful to the maintenance and cultivation of the religious spirit among the people, particularly the men and the young people. (2) In view of the non-attendance of the people in general on Saturday, the Sunday service affords a weekly opportunity for worship, apart altogether from the question of Sabbath observance. (3) The Sunday service brings the congregation, especially the male portion thereof, under the more direct and more constant influence of the pulpit, which often leads to a more energetic communal and congregational activity. (4) The Sunday service, in almost every instance, is attended by a considerable number of non-Jews, who in that way are given enlightenment on Jews and Judaism, and are afforded an opportunity for possessing themselves of our conception of religion.

[77] There has been a vast change in the position of woman in the synagogue, owing to the influence of the reform movement. In 1852, at the dedication of the Bene Israel synagogue in Cincinnati, the question of permitting women to participate in the choir aroused much discussion, the opposition holding that woman, according to Jewish custom, could have no voice in the public services; the matter was decided in the affirmative only after great efforts had been put forth by the liberal wing. Nowhere was the Orientalism of the synagogue more pronounced than in the inferior position assigned to woman in the public religious life. It is a far cry from that discussion in 1852 to the action of a number of congregations admitting woman to full membership with the same privileges and prerogatives as the men. At the convention of the Union of American Conregations held at Baltimore in 1891, the delegation of the Berith Kodesh congregation of Rochester, N. Y., counted a woman as one of its number. The Council of Jewish Women, organized in 1893, and the National Federation of Temple Sisterhoods organized in 1913 with their numerous branches throughout the country, offer striking testimony of the active rôle that woman is now playing in the public religious life of the Jews of this country.

[78] This was first done in Albany in 1851; *Reminiscences,* by Isaac M. Wise, 212.

[79] See the author's "Confirmation in the Synagogue," in the *Year Book C. C. A. R.,* I, 43-58.

[80] *Jewish Daily Bulletin,* July, 6, 1927.

[81] Address by Rabbi Israel Goldstein on "The Rabbinical Assembly—An Appraisal," *Jewish Daily Bulletin,* July 17, 1927.

[82] *American Israelite,* Apr. 5 and 12, 1929.
[83] Editorial in *S. A. J. Review,* Dec., 1927.

CHAPTER XIII

[1] On the twenty-fifth anniversary of the convening of the Leipzig Synod, Dr. Heinrich Meyer Cohn, in an article entitled "Vor fünf und zwanzig Jahren," claimed that the reason why the synods had exerted so little influence lay in the fact that they had concerned themselves only with the reforms of a few externals, instead of attempting a reinterpretation of the whole content of the religion; see *A. Z. d. J.,* LVIII (1894), 338-40. These strictures were answered by Dr. A. Wiener, of Oppeln, a participant in both synods. *Ibid.,* 559-61, 570-71.
[2] *Ibid.,* XXXVI (1872), 314.
[3] Lazarus, the foremost philosophical thinker among German Jews, was among the most ardent of reformers; he recognized fully the sorry state of Judaism in Germany, with its contradictions between theory and practice. Time and again he gave utterance to weighty words calling attention to the perilous position of the faith; never did he express this more clearly than in an address delivered on the centenary of the death of Moses Mendelssohn, entitled "Moses Mendelssohn in seinem Verhältniss zu Juden und Judenthum." His words on that occasion were: "The decay of a religion, as well as of every spiritual society, must ensue if a large, yea, a very large portion of its confessors, no longer observe hundreds upon hundreds of its injunctions, no longer recognize their validity in their hearts, but nevertheless permit them to stand as injunctions of the faith. Several attempts at reform were made in rabbinical conferences and synods, but these remained without successors for reasons with whose discussion we are not concerned here. The only final true and real reason why we refrain from constant work at this reform is laziness. . . . A religion whose teachers and leaders lack the courage to propose to themselves the question, What is in fact our law, what is it still capable of being?—such a religion is in the greatest danger. We are letting it go." See *Deutsche Revue,* 1886, 215-28.
[4] *A. Z. d. J.,* XXXVII (1873), 738.
[4a] *Supra,* 256.
[5] The course of events in Frankfort-on-the-Main following the passing of this law is instructive. Samson Raphael Hirsch had formed the *Israelitische Genossenschaft* in 1866. He and his congeners, much as they affected to be strictly orthodox, were far removed from the traditional standpoint, for they had assimilated themselves to the culture of their surroundings; Jews had outgrown the religious standpoint of rabbinism just as they had passed beyond its cultural phase. To attempt a union of the two was artificial, unnatural, and romantic. This, however, was the course of Hirsch. After the Law of Withdrawal was passed, the main congregation of Frankfort, in order to prevent the orthodox members from seceding, offered to provide for all the ritual needs of the orthodox and to arrange for a service that would meet their desires, *i.e.* to construct a synagogue in which the service would be conducted altogether along traditional lines. Hirsch declared that the orthodox who would take advantage of this offer and not join his congregation were guilty of treason to Judaism. The congregation appealed to that pillar of orthodoxy, S. B. Bamberger, of Würzburg, who decided for the congregation and against Hirsch. The latter now issued an "Open Letter to District Rabbi S. B. Bamberger in Würzburg," in which he accused Bamberger of inconsistency, inasmuch as on Jan. 21, 1872, he had said that a Jew who did not believe in a personal Messiah, the descendant of David, the restoration of the Jewish people to Palestine, and the reinsti-

tution of the sacrifices, is a renegade. Since the Frankfort congregation had repudiated these doctrines, no true orthodox Jew, even according to Bamberger, could remain within its fold. This called forth a pamphlet, *Open Reply by X,* in which the writer contends that Hirsch, in fomenting strife and inducing men to leave the congregation acts against the spirit of Talmud and Shulchan Aruk; Hirsch himself would be severely condemned by orthodox rabbis of Hungary, Galicia, etc., for permitting marriages to take place in his synagogue, for delivering German sermons and similar departures from traditional custom. Bamberger, too, censured Hirsch in an "Open Reply" in which he defended his course. S. Süskind, rabbi of Wiesbaden, also took a hand in this controversy. He subjected to a critical review the statutes of Hirsch's congregation, notably the clause that declared the Talmud and Shulchan Aruk the fundamental law of the congregation. See *Die Statuten der israelitischen Religionsgenossenschaft zu Frankfurt a. M.,* Beleuchtet von S. Süskind, Rabbiner zu Wiesbaden. Wiesbaden, 1876. This attack called forth several answers, notably *Die Angriffe des Herrn Rabbiner Süskind zu Wiesbaden gegen die Statuten der israelitischen Religionsgenossenschaft zu Frankfurt a. M.,* Beleuchtet von S. Frankfurt am Main, 1876; and *Heimleuchtung des Herrn Rabbiner Süskind* von einen Paganus Frankfurt a. M., 1876.

[6] N. Samter, *Judentaufen im 19 Jahrhunderts,* 145ff. Berlin, 1906.

[7] *Verhandlungen und Beschlüsse der Rabbinerversammlung zu Berlin am 4 und 5 June, 1884,* 17-18. Berlin, 1885.

[8] In 1876 Ludwig Philippson described this condition as "the peculiar phenomenon that men who long ago have rejected all Jewish commands in their own lives, enter the lists for every Piut and Nigun, and rave frantically against the least reform in the service." *A. Z. d. J.,* XL (1876), 379.

[9] Die Berliner Neu-orthodoxie die mit dem Schinkenstullen in der Hand für den *Shulchan Aruk* schwärmen, *ibid.,* LXII (1898), 532.

[10] Gustav Karpeles in review of I. H. Ritter's posthumous book, *Die jüdische Reformgemeinde zu Berlin, ibid.,* LXVI (1902), 288; compare a similar description of conditions in Prague, which applied to all the larger communities in Germany, Austria, France, England, and Italy—"the congregation passes as conservative; the banner must cover everything, the institutions must remain unchanged even though the form is emptied of all significance." *Ibid.,* LIX (1895), 209.

[11] This statement was not exact as such a service was conducted in the Berlin reform temple. The meaning was, of course, that none of the synagogues of the main congregation (*Hauptgemeinde*), of which there were five, met the needs here expressed.

[12] Julius Plotke "Sabbathfeier am Sonntag" (in opposition), *A. Z. d. J.,* 1897, 148-9; Levinstein replied to this, *ibid.,* 184-6. Benas Levy suggested the holding of a trial service on Sunday in one Berlinese synagogue to determine whether this was really desired. *Ibid.,* 186; Emil Breslauer opposed Sunday service in his article "Sonntaggottesdienst." *Ibid.,* 452.

[13] *A. Z. d. J.,* LXII (1898), 86.

[14] Previous to this election two additional articles appeared in the columns of the *A. Z. d. J.,* LXII (1898), 531 and 541, entitled "Unsere Orthodoxie," that set forth vividly religious conditions among the Jews of the German capital. In these articles the editor, Gustav Karpeles, strongly arraigned the orthodox, who, while aiming to keep the congregation officially "pious" (*fromm*), themselves disregard every law of the *Schulchan Aruk* in their private lives. He pleads for the election of liberal representatives who will make provision also for the thousands of Berlinese Jews who desire more German in the service and a supplemental service on Sunday. Only thus can the indifference be overcome and the conversions to Christianity be stayed. "To be a Jew means to favor progress without disregarding the old. The inner life-force of Judaism has always consisted in building further

on existing foundations. We do not wish to be *Shulchan Aruk* mummies. Let every Jew be pious according to his own interpretation; but no one can presume to pose as dictator over the consciences of others. In the congregation of Berlin there must be room for every tendency in Judaism, but never for zealotry and heresy-hunting."

[15] At this time, too, Levinstein appeared in the arena with another pamphlet urging the election of representatives who would introduce a service on Sunday. See his *Die Repräsentanten Wahlen, Förderung des Sonntaggottesdienstes*, Berlin, 1901. This was answered in a pamphlet issued by the Union of Synagogue societies of Berlin and its suburbs, *Erwiederung an Herrn Gustav Levinstein auf seine neueste Schrift die Repräsentanten Wahlen*, etc.; see also the pamphlet *Der Liberalismus macht selig und der Sonntaggottesdienst mach liberal, Ein Wort zur Verständigung an Herrn Gustav Levinstein von Dr. Heinrich Loewe*. Berlin, 1901.

[16] This, too, despite the fact that four of the six rabbis of the community had submitted opinions in favor of the organ, viz. Maybaum, Rosenzweig, Stier and Blumenthal; of the two others, one, Weisse, opposed the organ on the ground of policy, the other, Eschelbacher, for religious reasons.

[17] This society issued publications from time to time entitled *Mittheilungen des Liberalen Vereins*, etc.

[18] In 1888 a children's Sabbath afternoon service was instituted in Berlin in a number of synagogues. This service followed the general lines of the *mincha* (afternoon) service except that the prayers צדק צדקתך, ואני תפלתי and ובא לציון were omitted and that only the second section of the עלינו prayer was used and this in German to the words ונאמר והיה which closing words were read in Hebrew; a German sermon was preached; the service lasted forty-five or fifty minutes. In 1900 Dr. Eschelbacher, of a decidedly conservative bent, was elected one of the rabbis of the community; he refused to participate in or to preach at this children's service because of the departure from the traditional ritual by the omission of the above-mentioned portions. The conservative majority of the representatives at the meeting of Mar. 23, 1902, resolved to abolish the changes that had been made and to have the traditional *mincha* service entirely in Hebrew. Ludwig Geiger protested strongly, but to no avail. *A. Z. d. J.*, LXVI (1902), 148-50.

[19] After the death of Moritz Lazarus, in 1903, a number of his aphorisms on Judaism were published; although published well nigh thirty years ago, several of these still reflect the German Jewish religious situation so clearly that one or two may well be quoted here. "The retention of the old because it is old—the denial of progress in development, the assertion that everything has been known, and better known at that, may signify a virtue of modesty for the individual; for the community it is a lie." "From now on we should confess only that which we consider true to-day in accordance with our religious knowledge and consciousness, that which we recognize as agreeing with the spirit of Judaism—hence we should draw our conclusions for the salvation and preservation of our coreligionists, not from a written codex, but from the knowledge of the entire content of Judaism and from a firm inner conviction.

[20] *A. Z. d. J.*, LVII (1893), 361.

[21] *Ibid.*, Supplement to Sept. 6, 1895, 3.

[22] Seligman is one of the most progressive rabbis of Germany. A course of addresses delivered by him at that time evidenced a splendid grasp of the problems with which Judaism has to grapple in Germany still today; these were published under the title *Judenthum und Moderne Weltanschauung*. Frankfort-on-the-Main, 1905. In his preface he discloses a clear comprehension of the changed course which modern views and conditions force upon the Jewish thinker who is awake to the signs of the time.

[23] The three weeks between the seventeenth of Tammuz, the day when the final onslaught of the Romans on Jerusalem began, and the ninth of Ab,

the day of the destruction of the City and the Temple, were observed as days of mourning by the Jews. Similar resolutions were passed at the Augsburg Synod. *Supra,* 311-12.

[24] *A. Z. d. J.,* XLVII, 106. *Ibid.,* 439. For opinions con, *ibid.,* XXXVIII, 225-6 (Philippson), LVIII, 376-8, 392-3 (Stössel); pro, XLIX, 564 (Wiener), LIV, Supplement to Apr. 11, p. 3. (Zadoe Kahn); for regulations in various German communities concerning funeral services at cremations, *ibid.,* LXVII, 289-90. The Central Conference of American Rabbis delivered an opinion at its meeting in New York, 1892, that cremation is not anti-Jewish or irreligious. II (1892). *Year Book,* 1892, 41.

[25] *A. Z. d. J.,* LXIII, 318-20.

[26] According to the law in Deut. xxv. 3-10, a brother was compelled to marry his deceased brother's childless widow. The brother was called *yibum.* If he refused, the widow performed the act of *chalitzah* as there described. In modern days this practice has died out among reformers; even among the strictly orthodox the *yibum* usually permits the widow to perform this act, thus satisfying the law and evading the duty laid upon him.

[27] Life, then, is the great reformer. The religious anarchy prevalent among Jews due to disregard of the traditions and the absence of any official representative body to formulate a new *vade mecum* of Jewish practice and observance is strongly evidenced whenever any point of practice or observance is discussed. There is no recognized authority thus far in modern Jewish life. The Augsburg Synod had declared *chalitzah* of no significance, and had also resolved that marriages could be performed between Passover and the Feast of Weeks and during the three weeks preceding the month of Ab, but this conference of liberal rabbis seemed to be absolutely unconscious of this, so little impression did these synods leave and so little authority did they have.

[28] "In our day it is no longer a question of obeying this law or that, of observing this ceremony or that, but the welfare of the religion itself is in the balance." These words of a Jewish preacher were quoted with impressive sanction by a writer, Dr. Bernhard Weiss, who diagnosed skillfully the attitude of the young men toward Judaism; see "Jugend und Judenthum," *A. Z. d. J.,* LXVIII (1904), 448.

[29] At this meeting of the Society of Liberal Rabbis held on Jan. 2, 1907, a committee was appointed to prepare a revised code of the marriage laws which is to declare formally that the prohibitions of certain marriages for the priests are no longer valid. What a tragi-comedy! With vital issues pressing for solution on every side a committee was appointed to make declaration about the prohibited marriages of the priestly caste, a meaningless survival of the outgrown sacrificial stage of the religion and *voila tout!*

[30] Cæsar Seligman, *Judenthum und Moderne Wiltanschauung,* preface. Frankfurt am Main, 1905.

[31] "Richtlinien zu einem Program für das Liberale Judenthum" in Seligman, *Geschichte der jüdischen Reform Bewegung,* Frankfurt am Main, 1922.

[32] *Die Geschichte des Jüdisch-liberalen Jugendverein zu Breslau von Fritz Stoffen, Jüdisch Liberaler Jugendverein Abraham Geiger Breslau Festschrift zum 10 Jahrg.* (1923), 19-26.

[33] *Supra,* 257.

[34] תפלות לכל השנה *Gebetbuch für das ganze Jahr bearbeitet im Auftrag des liberaler Kultus Ausschusses des preussischen Landesverbandes jüdischer Gemeinden,* Frankfort am Main, 1929.

[35] See the reference to the American achievement in the preface to the recently published German Union Prayer-book, p. xiii.

[36] *American Hebrew,* New York, Sept., 6, 1930, p. 546.

[37] Order of Prayer as used at the Sabbath afternoon services at Hampstead, with an English paraphrase of the Hebrew Text, arranged and written by the Rev. Morris Joseph, 5650-1890.

[38] Shortly after this the ministry of the Hampstead Synagogue, then just completed, was offered Mr. Joseph. He was inhibited, however, by the Chief Rabbi, because, among other things, he objected to praying for the reinstitution of the sacrificial worship. In 1893 Mr. Joseph was elected minister of the West London Synagogue of British Jews.

[39] The Ideal in Judaism and Other Sermons, by the Rev. Morris Joseph, preached during 1890-91-92. London, 1893.

[40] See sermon Jewish Chronicle, 1899, June 23, p. 20. See also the interesting communications on this subject of Sunday services by L. G. Greenberg, C. G. Montefiore and O. J. Simon (all in favor), ibid., June 30, 1899, 8-9, and by Samuel Montagu, K. M. (Lady Magnus), and F. D. Mocatta (all against), ibid., July 7, p. 8, and July 14, p. 9; also a letter from F. H. Harvey Samuel (in favor), ibid.

[41] Jewish Chronicle, July 28, 1899, 8-9.

[42] Mr. Simon summarized his opinions on this subject in the Jewish Quarterly Review, IX, 177-84 (Jan., 1897); see the interesting symposium called forth by his views, ibid., 184-223; Mr. Simon replied to his critics, ibid., 403-28. See also his article, "The Unity of the Religious Idea," Fortnightly Review, Apr., 1889.

[43] Jewish Chronicle, Jan. 29, 1897, 3-4. An amusing incident in connection with this expression of views on missionary Judaism was the reception of a dispatch by the chief rabbi from St. Petersburg to this effect, "Anti-Semitic press spreads the information that Mr. Simon, of London, contemplates the formation of a Missionary Society for the purpose of converting members of other creeds to Judaism. Explanation needful." (See Jewish Chronicle, Jan. 29, 1897, 12.) Everything is grist for the anti-Semitic mill, even the most improbable schemes of visionary idealists.

[44] Jewish Chronicle, Oct. 20, 1899.

[45] At the general meeting of the members of the Jewish Religious Union held Oct. 22, 1903, at the beginning of the second year's work, the president, Mr. C. G. Montefiore, in his address, stated the reasons that had led him and his confrères to organize the Union. He said that the Union had been founded by various men and women of the Jewish faith by no means all holding identical views of Judaism, but agreeing to see facts as they were, and not to misinterpret these facts. They were agreed also that the facts, though sad in some respects and regrettable, were not so black as to justify despair; and the people who had founded the Union were agreed that it was not wrong, but right, to try and find a remedy for the sad state of things that they saw around them. They saw that a great many persons in the East and West of London were drifting away from Judaism, were becoming Jews only in name—nominal Jews, so-called. Often they drifted away from religion altogether, but at any rate the desertions from Judaism and religion were sufficiently sad and agitating to anyone who wished to consider the future of Judaism. They did not think it was right to shut their eyes to these facts and refuse to see them and deal with them. They also decided not to accept them as irremediable. They did not think these facts were due to mere apathy, indifference, and decay of all kinds of religious sentiments. No doubt these causes were part causes, but they felt that these were not the only causes. They had felt that they were due to a lack of sympathy for the existing embodiment of Judaism. While large numbers felt sympathy for and satisfaction with the religious services of the synagogue, they could not blind themselves to the fact that there were many persons who did not find that satisfaction and did not feel this sympathy. It was a mistaken policy that nothing should be done for these persons. Jewish Chronicle, Oct. 30, 1903, 15.

[46] See report of the secretary, A. Lindo Henry, at meeting of Oct. 20, 1903; *Jewish Chronicle*, Oct. 30, 1903, 15.

[47] *Jewish Addresses delivered at the services of the Jewish Religious Union during the first session, 1902-3*, 1-15. London, 1904.

[48] *Jewish Chronicle*, Oct. 24, 1902, 11.

[49] A flood of communications in criticism of the Union deluged the columns of the Jewish press; see particularly the letter of M. Hymanson, *Jewish Chronicle*, Jan. 23, 1903, 6, and of בן יצחק, *ibid.*, Jan. 30, 8.

[50] See Sermon *Jewish Chronicle*, Dec. 12, 1902, 8.

[51] *Jewish Chronicle*, Jan. 9, 1903, 11-12.

[52] *Ibid.*, Apr. 24, 1903, 19.

[53] *Ibid.*, 20.

[54] *Ibid.*, Apr. 3, 1903, 12.

[55] *Liberal Judaism*, by Claude G. Montefiore. London, 1903.

[56] *Jewish Addresses delivered at the services of the Jewish Religious Union during the First Session, 1902-3.* London and Edinburgh, 1904.

[57] *A Selection of Prayers, Psalms and other Scriptural Passages and Hymns for use at the services of the Jewish Religious Union.* London, 5664-1903.

[58] *The Jewish Religious Union and Its Beginnings*, 5.

[59] *Ibid.*, 15.

[60] *Ibid.*

[61] *Supra*, 75ff., 100ff., 251, 257ff., 478, n. 20; 480, n. 50; 358, 367; see also Philipson "The Jewish Reform Prayer-Book," *Journal for Jew. Law and Philosophy*, I, 69ff., 261ff.

[62] *Supra*, 415.

[63] "Jews in France," by S. Debre, *Jewish Quarterly Review*, III, 417ff.

[64] *A. Z. d. J.*, 1884, 769.

[65] *Ibid.*, 1896, May 22, Supplement, 4.

[66] *Jewish Chronicle*, Oct. 22, 1903, 20.

[67] In his book *Une Religion Rationalle et Laïque, La Religion du XXe Siècle.* Dijon, 1904. Germain Levi gave expression to his liberal standpoint.

[68] According to a news item which appeared in Jan., 1930, the assimilationists of Warsaw were planning the formation of reform congregations and were sending a delegate to confer with liberal Jewish leaders in that city. See *Jewish Daily Bulletin* for Jan. 15, 1930.

[69] *Supra*, Chapter VIII.

[70] The Haskalah movement in Russia in the nineteenth century, although similar to the Meass'fim movement in Germany in the eighteenth century, in that it familiarized the Jews with modern culture and literature, yet did not develop into an organized effort for religious reform, as proved the case in Germany.

[71] Ps. xliii. 3.

INDEX

Aaronic priesthood, Reform Judaism's interpretation of, 6, 248, 354-5.

Abarbanel, 148.

Abrahams, Israel, 404, 410, 415-7, 421-2.

Adler, Abraham, 41, 143, 154, 163, 184, 193, 194, 196, 223, 242, 244; on Sabbath observance, 154, 155; on Messianic question, 177; on abolition of *aufrufen*, 182; on equality of woman with man, 182; on Sabbath question, 203.

Adler, L., 61, 133, 287, 288, 291, 301, 308, 323.

Adler, Nathan Marcus, 105, 133; on circumcision, 134; protest against Brunswick Conference, 161.

Adler, Samuel, 41, 143, 155, 163, 184, 193, 196, 199, 215, 216, 223, 340, 348; on reform, 147; on intermarriage, 150; on prayer, 167; on vernacular as language of prayer, 167; on position of woman, 184; on Sabbath question, 202; on Sunday service, 211; freedom is the Messiah, 349.

Akiba, Rabbi, 99, 312.

Albany, New York, reform in, 335, 336.

Alexius, Frederick Christian, Duke of Anhalt, 76.

Angelology, in Judaism, of Persian origin, 1.

Anti-Semitism, German rabbis on, 384-6.

Arad, Hungary, reform in, 276ff.

Arnhold, A., on circumcision, 216.

Aron, Arnaud, 79.

Astruc, E. A., 291, 301; on unity in Judaism, 293.

Aub, H., 133.

Aub, Joseph, 41, 61, 71, 82, 141, 287, 289, 291, 295, 305, 308; on creed, 302; on tisha beah, 312-13; on progress in religion, 315.

Auerbach, B. H., 133, 161.

Auerbach, Isaac, 23.

Auerbach, Jacob, 163, 186, 193, 194, 308; on significance of Hebrew, 170; on Hebrew in service, 171; on Messianic question, 177; on Sabbath question, 201, 206-7.

Auerbach, J. L., 34, 82, 227.

Augsburg Synod, 307ff; on marriage reforms, 309ff.; on Sabbath observance, 318ff.; on circumcision, 320; on proselyte bath, 320-1; on celebration of channukah, 321-2.

Babylon, influence on Judaism, 1.

Bach, Gaston, 424.

Bachya, ibn Paquda, 72.

Baeck, Leo, 397, 400, 429, 432, n. 28, 459.

Balfour, Arthur J., 362.

Ballagi, Prof., 270.

Baltz, Fr., Th., 183.

Bamberger, J., 133, 161.

Bamberger, S. B., 133; protests against Brunswick Conference, 161.

Bameh madliqin, abolition of, 36.

Bar Mitzwah, ceremony, reform of, 377, 393.

Barnet, A. L., 102.

Bauer, Bruno, 126.

Bauer, Marcus, 270.

Bavaria, reform in, 76-7.

Beer, Jacob Herz, 23, 27, 30, 227.

Bendavid, Lazarus, 12.

Bene Israel congregation, Cincinnati, 336.

Benet, Mordecai, condemns reform movement, 33.

Bene Yeshurum congregation, Cincinnati, 336.

Ben Israel, 143, 193, 287.

Bergman, L., 432.

Berkowitz, H., 371.

Berlin, Early Reforms in, 21ff.

Berlin *Jüdische Gemeinde*, 399.

Berlin Reform Congregation, 225ff.; address to the Frankfort Conference, 186-7; address to the Breslau Conference, 243-4; appeal to the Jews of Germany, 230ff; call for